Altruism & Altruistic Love

Altruism & Altruistic Love

Science, Philosophy, & Religion in Dialogue

Edited by

STEPHEN G. POST
LYNN G. UNDERWOOD
JEFFREY P. SCHLOSS
WILLIAM B. HURLBUT

OXFORD
UNIVERSITY PRESS

2002

OXFORD
UNIVERSITY PRESS

Oxford   New York
Athens   Auckland   Bangkok   Bogotá   Buenos Aires   Cape Town
Chennai   Dar es Salaam   Delhi   Florence   Hong Kong   Istanbul   Karachi
Kolkata   Kuala Lumpur   Madrid   Melbourne   Mexico City   Mumbai   Nairobi
Paris   São Paulo   Shanghai   Singapore   Taipei   Tokyo   Toronto   Warsaw

and associated companies in
Berlin   Ibadan

Library of Congress Cataloging-in-Publication Data
Altruism and altruistic love : science, philosophy, and religion in dialogue /
edited by Stephen G. Post . . . [et al.].
     p.   cm.
Includes bibliographical references.
ISBN 0-19-514358-2
1. Altruism.
I. Post, Stephen Garrard, 1951–.
BJ1474 .A472   2001
171'.8—dc21   00-068140

9 8 7 6 5 4 3 2 1

Printed in the United States of America
on acid-free paper

PREFACE

Robert Frost once wrote, "Something there is that doesn't love a wall." We would like to thank the John Templeton Foundation for the courage and vision to engage such a wide group of scholars from various disciplines on the topics of altruism, love, empathy, and compassion in a dialogue that overcomes walls of division. Its financial support made possible an initial conference, titled "Empathy, Altruism and Agape: Perspectives on Love in Science and Religion," in October 1999. The task of chapter preparation and editing took place over the course of the following year, involving further efforts at integration of the sciences and humanities. This further evolution was also made possible with support from the foundation. Abundant gratitude goes to Sir John Templeton for his belief that love and altruism are at the core of "ultimate reality" and human nature and for his willingness to commit funds to allow the scholarly community to explore the scientific, psychological, and theological dimensions of love. His enthusiasm encouraged Dr. John M. Templeton Jr. and Charles L. Harper Jr. to build on this core belief by proposing the project that gave rise to this book. Judith Marchand, Allyson McHugh, and the entire foundation staff are also commended for facilitating the work so positively. The challenge presented by the John Templeton Foundation has planted the seeds for subsequent research and scholarship at this union of disciplines.

We thank the Fetzer Institute for its support and commitment to this project and to the fields of study touched by this book and the late John Fetzer for his willingness to initiate a nonprofit foundation that has the bold intention to be based on unconditional love. Fetzer's public financial commitment to pursue this area of study provides an opportunity to bridge various perspectives and to build a deeper

understanding of these complex topics with research that can be effectively translated into action.

Thanks also to Greg Fricchione, Lawrence Sullivan, and David G. Myers and
again to Charles L. Harper Jr. for joining our extended planning committee as it
sought to identify scholars who could best contribute to the project. We are also
deeply appreciative of those practitioners of altruism and altruistic love who contributed to the initial conference, thereby providing scholars with a sense of lived
altruism. These practioners include Dame Cicely Saunders, originator of the modern hospice movement; Reverend Eugene Rivers of Ella J. Baker House in Boston;
and Joan Eads, zone coordinator of L'Arche USA.

This project was supported, in part, by grants to Jeffrey Schloss from Westmont College and the Discovery Institute that allowed him to devote his energy
and talents to it.

Finally, thanks to the Center for Biomedical Ethics of the School of Medicine
at Case Western Reserve University for providing necessary materials and allowing
time for the overall facilitation of the editorial endeavor by Stephen G. Post, and to
the Institute for Research on Unlimited Love, of which Post is president.

Cleveland	S. G. P.
Kalamazoo	L. G. U.
Santa Barbara	J. P. S.
Palo Alto	W. B. H.
November 2001	

CONTENTS

CONTRIBUTORS

C. DANIEL BATSON is a social psychologist and professor of psychology at the University of Kansas. He has conducted a number of experiments on empathy and altruism (some funded by the National Science Foundation), is the author of *The Altruism Question: Toward a Social-Psychological Answer* (1991), and is coauthor (with Patricia Schoenrade and Larry Ventis) of *Religion and the Individual: A Social-Psychological Perspective* (Oxford University Press, 1993).

DON S. BROWNING is Alexander Campbell Professor of Religious Ethics and the Social Sciences at the University of Chicago Divinity School. He is the principal investigator of the Religion, Culture, and Family Project, financed by a grant from the Lilly Endowment, that resulted in the publication of an 11-book series on various topics pertaining to the contemporary debate on the family. His writings on psychology, Christianity, and images of human fulfillment span four decades.

ANTONIO R. DAMASIO is Van Allen Distinguished Professor and head of the Department of Neurology at the University of Iowa and adjunct professor at the Salk Institute in La Jolla, California.

Damasio's work has focused on elucidating critical problems in the fundamental neuroscience of mind and behavior at the level of large-scale systems in humans, although his investigations have also encompassed Parkinsonism and Alzheimer's disease. His contributions have had a major influence on our understanding of the neural basis of decision making, emotion, language, and memory.

Antonio Damasio's book *Descartes' Error: Emotion, Reason, and the Human Brain* (1994) has been published in more than 20 countries. His new book is *The Feeling of What Happens: Body, Emotion, and the Making of Consciousness* (1999).

HANNA DAMASIO is Distinguished University of Iowa Professor of Neurology and director of the Laboratory of Human Neuroanatomy and Neuroimaging at the University of Iowa College of Medicine, and adjunct professor at the Salk Institute for Biological Studies.

The book she authored on her early lesion analysis techniques (*Lesion Analysis in Neuropsychology*, published by Oxford University Press) was named "outstanding book" in bio- and medical sciences by the Association of American Publishers (1989), has been translated into Japanese, and is used worldwide. Her book *Human Brain Anatomy in Computerized Images* (Oxford University Press, 1995) is the first brain atlas entirely based on computer reconstructions of living human brains. In 1992 she shared the Pessoa Prize with Antonio Damasio. In 1995 she was elected to the American Neurological Association and became a Grand Official of the Order of Santiago da Espada (a Portuguese merit order that distinguishes achievements in the sciences). In 1997 she was elected a fellow of the American Academy of Arts and Sciences.

FRANS B. M. DE WAAL was trained as a zoologist and ethologist in the European tradition at three Dutch universities (Nijmegen, Groningen, Utrecht), resulting in a Ph.D. in biology from the University of Utrecht, in 1977. His dissertation research concerned aggressive behavior and alliance formation in macaques. In 1975, a 6-year project was initiated on the world's largest captive colony of chimpanzees at the Arnhem Zoo. Apart from a large number of scientific papers, this work found its way to the general public in the book *Chimpanzee Politics* (1982). In 1981, de Waal accepted a research position at the Wisconsin Regional Primate Research Center in Madison, Wisconsin. There he began both observational and experimental studies of reconciliation behavior in monkeys. He received the *Los Angeles Times* Book Award for *Peacemaking among Primates* (1989), a popularized account of 15 years of research on conflict resolution in nonhuman primates. Since the mid-1980s, de Waal also worked with chimpanzees at the Yerkes Regional Primate Research Center and with their close relatives, bonobos, at the San Diego Zoo. In 1991, de Waal accepted a joint position in the Psychology Department of Emory University and at the Yerkes Regional Primate Research Center, both in Atlanta. His current interests include food sharing, social reciprocity, and conflict resolution in primates, as well as the origins of morality and justice in human society. His most recent books, *Good Natured* (1996) and *Bonobo: The Forgotten Ape* (1997), discuss the evolutionary origin of human morality and the implications of what we know about bonobos for models of human social evolution.

GREGORY L. FRICCHIONE is a physician and associate professor of psychiatry at the Harvard Medical School. He is also Director of Mental Health at the Carter Center. His clinical work has been instrumental in establishing the use of lorazepam as a first-line treatment for the catatonic syndrome. His research in neuroimmunology and neuropsychiatry has focused on macrophage-endothelial cell interaction, with resulting publications in the *Journal of Immunology, Immunology Today, Endocrinology,* the *American Journal of Hematology,* and in various neurology and psychiatry journals. Recently, he has been studying the important role brain evolution may play in the human spiritual imperative. He is a codirector of the Harvard Medical School course on spirituality and medicine.

RUBEN L. F. HABITO is professor of world religions and spirituality at Perkins School of Theology, Southern Methodist University. He has served as resident Zen teacher at the Maria Kannon Zen Center, based in Dallas, Texas, since 1990, and has also been active in the promotion of interreligious dialogue among practitioners, as well as academics. Among his publications, *Total Liberation: Zen Spirituality and the Social Dimension* (1989) and *Healing Breath: Zen Spirituality for a Wounded Earth* (1993) specifically address the question of the cultivation of wisdom that flows into a compassion, which in turn grounds engagement in socioecological transformation.

WILLIAM B. HURLBUT is a physician and lecturer in the Program in Human Biology at Stanford University, teaching courses in biomedical ethics. His main areas of interest involve the ethical issues associated with advancing technology and the integration of philosophy of biology with Christian theology. He has cotaught courses with Luca Cavalli-Sforza, director of the Human Genome Diversity Project, and with Nobel Laureate Baruch Blumberg. Currently, he teaches upper-division courses that include "Adam 2000: Images of Human Life in the Age of Biomedical Technology" and "Ethical Issues in the Neurosciences." He has consulted with the Center for Security and International Cooperation on a project formulating policy on chemical and biological warfare and with the National Aeronautics and Space Administration (NASA) on projects in astrobiology.

THOMAS R. INSEL, neuroscientist and psychiatrist, is presently director of the Yerkes Regional Primate Research Center, professor of psychiatry at Emory University School of Medicine, and adjunct professor of psychology at Emory University College of Arts and Sciences. As director of the center, he is responsible for leadership of a $16 million research institute with 140 scientists involved in primate studies of infectious diseases, reproductive physiology, cardiovascular function, neurology, vision, communication, and the biological bases of behavior. As professor of psychiatry, Insel leads a research team focused on the neurobiology of complex social behaviors, including parental care, pair bonding, and aggression. After completing his postgraduate training, Insel joined the intramural program of the National Institute of Mental Health (NIMH), where he remained for the subsequent 15 years. At the NIMH, he had two quite independent research careers. From 1979 until 1984, he initiated and developed the first program for the study of adults with obsessive-compulsive disorder in the United States. He was the first U.S. investigator to demonstrate the unique antiobsessional properties of serotonin uptake inhibiting drugs and the first to suggest a serotonin hypothesis of obsessive-compulsive pathophysiology. This work, which was recognized with the

A. E. Bennett Award from the Society for Biological Psychiatry in 1986, established the concept of antiobsessional drugs as a new research area for neuropharmacology. He received the Outstanding Service Medal from the U.S. Public Health Service (1993) and the Distinguished Alumnus Award from Boston University School of Medicine (1997) and was asked to give several distinguished lectures in this country and abroad. Insel joined the faculty of the Emory University School of Medicine and the Yerkes Regional Primate Research Center in 1994.

JEROME KAGAN is Starch Professor of Psychology at Harvard University and codirector of the Mind-Brain-Behavior Initiative at Harvard. His research has addressed cognitive and emotional development in children, with a special concern for the role of temperament in personality and in understanding of the moral emotions. His most recent book, *Three Seductive Ideas* (1998), devotes a chapter to the unique moral competences of humans and their relation to empathy and altruism.

MELVIN KONNER is Samuel Candler Dobbs Professor of Anthropology and associate professor of psychiatry and neurology at Emory University. He has held NIMH and NSF research grants and has been a fellow of the Center for Advanced Study in the Behavioral Sciences, the John Simon Guggenheim Memorial Foundation, the Social Science Research Council, and the Foundations Fund for Research in Psychiatry.

KRISTEN RENWICK MONROE is professor of politics and associate director of the Program in Political Psychology at the University of California at Irvine. She has taught at Princeton University, New York University, the State University of New York at Stony Brook, and the University of British Columbia. Monroe's most recent book is *The Heart of Altruism* (1996), which was awarded the 1997 Best Book Award by the American Political Science Association Section in Political Psychology and nominated for the Pulitzer Prize. She is the editor of several books, including *Contemporary Empirical Political Theory* (1997) and *The Economic Approach to Politics: A Reassessment of the Theory of Rational Action* (1991), and the author of *Presidential Popularity and the Economy* (1984).

SAMUEL P. OLINER is professor of sociology at Humboldt State University and the founder and general director of the Altruistic Personality and Prosocial Behavior Institute, as well as founding editor of the *Humboldt Journal of Social Relations*. His books include *Toward a Caring Society: Ideas into Action* (coauthored with Pearl M. Oliner, 1995); *Embracing the Other: Philosophical, Psychological, Historical Perspectives on Altruism* (coedited with Pearl M. Oliner, Lawrence Baron, Lawrence A. Blum, Dennis L. Krebs, and M. Zuzanna Smolenska, 1992); and *The Altruistic Personality: Rescuers of Jews in Nazi Europe* (coauthored with Pearl M. Oliner, 1988).

STEPHEN J. POPE is associate professor of social ethics and chairperson of the theology department at Boston College in Chestnut Hill, Massachusetts. He is the author of *The Evolution of Altruism and the Ordering of Love* (1994).

STEPHEN G. POST is professor and Associate Director for Educational Programs, Center for Biomedical Ethics, School of Medicine, Case Western Reserve University. He also serves as a Senior Research Scholar in the Becket Institute at St. Hugh's College, Oxford University. In 1995, Post completed his work as associate editor of the five-volume *Encyclopedia of Bioethics* with support from the National Science Foundation and the National Endowment for the Humanities. He is the author of six books, including *The Moral Challenge of Alzheimer Disease* (2nd ed., 2000). Post is also the author of numerous articles and books on the concept of love in Western religious thought; his articles have appeared in venues such as the *Journal of Religion*, the *Journal of the American Academy of Religion*, and the *Journal of the American Medical Association*. Post serves as president of the Institute for Research on Unlimited Love.

STEPHANIE D. PRESTON is a doctoral student in behavioral neuroscience in the department of psychology at the University of California, Berkeley. She works closely with Frans B. M. de Waal and is collaborating with him in a series of research projects and publications.

MICHAEL RUSE is Lucyle T. Werkmeister Professor of Philosophy at Florida State University. He is the author of a number of books, most recently *Can a Darwinian Be a Christian: The Relationship between Science and Religion* (2001). A Templeton Book Award winner, he is a former Guggenheim Fellow, a Killam Fellow, and a fellow of the Royal Society of Canada.

JEFFREY P. SCHLOSS received his undergraduate training in philosophy at University of the Pacific and in biology at Wheaton College. He pursued postbaccalaureate training in ecology and evolutionary biology at University of Virginia, University of Michigan, and Washington University, where he received a Ph.D. in 1983. He has taught at the University of Michigan, Wheaton College, Jaguar Creek Rainforest Research Station, and Westmont College, where he is currently professor of biology. He also serves as Director of Biological Programs for the Christian Environmental Association and science consultant for the Christian College Coalition Faculty Development Program in Faith and Learning. He has been a Danforth Fellow, an American Association for the Advancement of Science (AAAS) Fellow in Science Communication, and a fellow of the Discovery Institute. His dual research interests include ecophysiological adaptions of poikilohydric plants to forest microclimate and sociobiological theories of human altruism and religious faith.

ELLIOTT SOBER is Hans Reichenbach Professor and Henry Vilas Research Professor of Philosophy at the University of Wisconsin, Madison, where he has taught since 1974. Sober's research is mainly in the philosophy of science, particularly in philosophy of evolutionary biology. His books include *The Nature of Selection: Evolutionary Theory in Philosophical Focus* (1984), *Reconstructing the Past: Parsimony, Evolution, and Inference* (1988), *Philosophy of Biology* (1993), *From a Biological Point of View* (1995), and, most recently, *Unto Others: The Evolution and Psychology of Unselfish Behavior* (1998), coauthored with David Sloan Wilson. Sober is currently doing research on the conflict between evolutionism and creationism, on the concept of scientific testability, and on methodological questions concerning how we go about attributing mental states to nonhuman organisms.

LYNN G. UNDERWOOD is vice president of the Fetzer Institute, a nonprofit private foundation, at which she develops collaborative research projects with other organizations and does program planning, review, and evaluation. She coedited *Measuring Stress*, a text intended as a tool to help in study designs examining the interface between stress and health, published by Oxford University Press. She has led the development and cosponsorship of various workshops with the National Institutes of Health, including one on the biobehavioral aspects of pain with 10 NIH Institutes and one on spirituality and aging with the National Institute on Aging. She also develops Fetzer-sponsored research funding initiatives. Current research interests include the role of various dimensions of religiousness and spirituality in living with disability.

DAVID SLOAN WILSON is an evolutionary biologist who studies a broad range of subjects relevant to humans, in addition to nonhuman species. He is best known for his work on multilevel selection theory, in which altruism and other prosocial behaviors evolve by benefiting whole groups, despite being selectively disadvantageous within groups. He has published in philosophy, psychology, and anthropology journals, in addition to his mainstream biological research. With philosopher Elliott Sober, he is author of *Unto Others: The Evolution and Psychology of Unselfish Behavior* (1998).

EDITH WYSCHOGROD is J. Newton Rayzor Professor of Philosophy and Religious Thought at Rice University. Her field of specialization is continental philosophy of religion and ethics. She has been a Guggenheim Fellow (1995–1996), president of the American Academy of Religion (1992–1993), and a fellow of the National Humanities Center (1981–1982). Her books include *An Ethics of Remembering: History, Heterology, and the Nameless Others* (1998), *Saints and Postmodernism: Revisioning Moral Philosophy* (1990), *Spirit in Ashes: Hegel, Heidegger, and Man-Made Mass Death* (1985), and *Emmanuel Levinas: The Problem of Ethical Metaphysics*, to be reissued in 2000. She is currently coediting a volume on contemporary ethical problems such as responsibility in a technological age, globalization, economy, and moral identity from the perspective of continental thought.

The annotated bibliography was prepared by MICHAEL E. McCULLOUGH, Ph.D., associate professor of psychology at Southern Methodist University, and SHELLEY DEAN KILPATRICK, Ph.D., Department of Pediatrics, UCLA.

Altruism & Altruistic Love

General Introduction

STEPHEN G. POST, LYNN G. UNDERWOOD,
JEFFREY P. SCHLOSS, & WILLIAM B. HURLBUT

In the context of human behavior, altruism, from the Latin root *alter* (meaning "other"), concerns the place of the other in moral experience, especially when the other is in need. An altruist intends and acts for the other's sake as an end in itself rather than as a means to public recognition or internal well-being, although such benefits to self need not be resisted. In altruism, solipsism, the view that the self is all that exists or can be known (*solus*, meaning "alone," and *ipse*, meaning "self") is transcended: Self no longer perceives self as the only center of worth and no longer perceives worth in others only to the extent that they contribute to egoistic interests. In essence, as one is altruistic, one realizes the independence of others from his or her use and senses that his or her claims to ontological centrality are illusory.

Altruism, especially when it extends beyond biological relations (kin altruism) and beyond "tit-for-tat" calculations grounded in self-interest (reciprocal altruism), is widely lauded and is commonly considered a foundation of moral life, although it need not imply the total eclipse of self-concern or a quest for self-immolation. In its fullest expression, which may include significant self-sacrifice in the aid of strangers or even enemies, altruism is a source of perennial fascination across cultures. Regardless of its duration, intensity, emotional engagement, sacrifice, and extensivity, the common feature of altruism is affirmation of and care for "the other as other" (a phrase that seems ubiquitous in contemporary moral philosophy of "alterity," especially in the context of phenomenology).

We use both "altruism" and "altruistic love" in the book title. Biologists use altruism to refer to actions that benefit the reproductive success of others at expense to the self, making no reference to motivation or conscious intentions. Social scientists often focus on psychological altruism in efforts to measure the extent to which altruistic acts are genuine. In human beings, and perhaps in some other highly developed species, the possibility of motivational or psychological altruism seems significant. Human altruism can be minimalist and for the most part emotionally uninvolved, such as the everyday respect for others that is expressed in etiquette and adherence to the minimal principle of nonmaleficence. It can become fuller or more idealistic in its expression, as in the case of efforts to actively assist others in genuine need.

What is at the very core of human altruistic love, which is altruism grounded in deep empathic affirmation? Phenomenologist Jules Toner defined love as "affirmative affection" (1968). We all know what it feels like to be valued in this way, and we remember loving persons who conveyed this affective affirmation through tone of voice, facial expression, a hand on the shoulder in time of grief, and a desire to be with us. This affection is affirming, which is to say that the agent of affirmation sees preciousness in us as we are. Altruistic love, which is uniquely human however much certain of its building blocks might be found in nonhuman species, is an intentional affirmation of our very being grounded in biologically given emotional capacities that are elevated by world view (including principles, symbol, and myth) and imitation into the sphere of consistency and abiding loyalty. As such, altruistic love is the most complex and interesting expression of human altruism.

Altruistic love is very closely linked to care (*cura*), which is love in response to the other in need. Care is the form love takes when it is attentive to the other in need. Love implies benevolence, care, compassion, and action. Compassion, for example, is the form love takes in response to suffering; it is a readiness to enter into the other's suffering. Justice is the concern of love and care because no individual agent can attend to the needs of all and eventually must give attention to the underlying social and economic inequalities that give rise to need. But the essential core of love exists prior to these expressions of love. In the words of Irving Singer, "To love another person is to treat him with great regard, to confer a new and personal value upon him" (1985, p. 11). Yet those who claim to be persons of altruistic love and who fail to act on behalf of others insofar as they are able manifest an obvious contradiction, for love implies action.

Altruistic love is a human ideal across most, if not all, religions. One can argue about the extent to which religions succeed or fail in teaching and implementing a love idealism that goes beyond insular "tribal" interests. This is in part a matter for empirical investigation, although at face value it appears that esteemed religious altruists have accomplished much for all humanity. Desmond Tutu and Abraham Joshua Heschel, prophets of justice; Gandhi and Martin Luther King Jr., nonviolent liberators; Bonhoeffer, opponent of Hitler; Dorothy Day, feeder of hungry laborers; Eugene Rivers, bringer of peace to inner cities; Dame Cicely Saunders, giver of new hope to the dying; Jean Vanier, founder of l'Arche; Dag Hammarskjöld, seeker of peace in the Congo; and the Dalai Lama of Tibetan Buddhism—these are only a few examples of modern leaders whose deep religious convictions about love and justice shaped their contributions to public life, political change, and human progress.

There is no doubt that numerous entirely secular individuals have achieved high levels of other-regard, and some authors in this book (for example, Monroe) do not see religion as a crucial element in the formation of altruistic personalities. Yet history is also filled with the accomplishments of those who perceived a relationship with a Supreme Being or Divine Love and who interpreted their altruism as a direct consequence of this perception. These figures are spiritual cosmopolitans absorbed in other-regarding service. We are sometimes too exclusively interested in what they do rather than in why they do it, because, as Martin Luther King Jr. often commented, the "what" depends on the "why." They do just "happen" to be deeply spiritual persons. The more we can understand about them, scientifically and otherwise, the better. We do not suggest that altruistic love in its embrace of all humanity absolutely requires a spiritual and religious foundation; yet we cannot ignore the narrative of human history and experience indicating that this foundation is quite often present, even in modernity. For some, this may suggest that altruistic love is a cosmic force of some type in which human beings are able to participate, for example, through "grace." We are interested in knowing more about "the inspired apostles of love . . . the great moral teachers of humanity . . . founders of all genuine religions . . . the true sages, seers, and prophets of practically all countries, cultures, and periods" (Sorokin, 1954, p. 485).

Where, however, does science come into view with regard to the study of human altruism and to its most intensive and extensive expression in love for humanity? How does the scientific study of altruistic actions in nonhuman species pertain to human altruism, if at all? How can we better understand human altruistic motivations and actions with a focus on all that these involve evolutionarily, genetically, developmentally, neurologically, emotionally, and conceptually? It is in the context of the dialogue between science, philosophy, and spiritual traditions that this book addresses various views of the roles of altruism and egoism.

It must be stated from the outset that there has been a theoretical trend in social scientific research, as well as in evolutionary biology, that generates cause for honest doubt about the very possibility of human altruism in any form. There may be some possible element of credibility enhancement in this hermeneutics of doubt. As Robert H. Frank writes, "The flint-eyed researcher fears no greater humiliation than to have called some action altruistic, only to have a more sophisticated colleague later demonstrate that it was self-serving" (1988, p. 21). Yet there is a body of coherent theory and data that casts some doubt on altruistic motivations, and this demands serious and balanced attention. The authors in this book take disparate positions, and we have not attempted to create any false impressions of unity.

The hermeneutics of doubt is grounded in the difficulty of proving, once and for all, the existence of psychologically altruistic motivations; such doubt is sometimes a matter of implication, as is the case when all living creatures are understood as conduits for the transmission of "selfish genes." (There are also those, known in moral philosophy as ethical egoists, who believe that even if genuine human altruistic motivations and acts are possible, they should be forbidden in order to encourage others to stand on their own two feet). Yet the attribution of "selfishness" to genes—a questionable importation of moral language into the domain of DNA—is compatible with authentic altruism on the part of the individual. As Matt Ridley puts it, "Selfish genes sometimes use selfless individuals to achieve their ends" (1996, p. 20).

One might ask whether the burden of proof should be placed on those who believe that human nature contains altruistic capacities alongside egoistic ones or on those who believe that genuinely altruistic capacities do not exist. Our intent in this book is to grapple honestly with current scientific questions about the existence of genuine altruism and to explore the nature of human other-regarding motives and acts.

This book brings together the work of leading biologists, social scientists, philosophers, and religion scholars. Although many philosophers and theologians have waxed eloquent about other-regarding motivations and acts, often with impressive grounding in the history of ideas, intellectual and practical progress now rests in the dialogue with scientific knowledge. On the other hand, many scientists have furthered our understanding of the phenomenon of altruism without nuanced interpretation of the human experience. Our purpose in publishing this volume is to enhance the dialogue on altruism across fields and disciplines in order to make progress in understanding and perhaps eventually in practice. We take to heart Irving Singer's recommendation in the conclusions to his monumental study of the history of the idea of love; that is, "the most promising opportunity for us in the twentieth century is to be found in a synthesis of scientific and humanistic approaches to human affect" (1987, p. 345). Singer adds that although evolutionary biologists define altruism in a way that "does not necessarily imply sentiments of benevolence or love" (1987, p. 358), their work does provide a heuristic key into altruism and altruistic love. Similarly, Singer finds value in a closer examination of how altruism and altruistic love are related to developmental stages in the human. Our book is consistent with Singer's signposts for the future, although we have added the study of the neurology of emotion to the mix.

On the Matter of Altruistic Extensivity

The neo-Darwinian emergence in evolutionary biology of kin altruism and reciprocal altruism must be viewed favorably as an antidote to the old social Darwinian paradigm of the ruthless survival of the fittest. The selfish-gene paradigm allows for a great deal of altruism toward those recognized as carrying a significant portion of one's own genes, and the tit-for-tat model of reciprocal altruism allows for the emergence of a great many social sentiments in human and some nonhuman animals—including cooperation, sympathy, kindness, and trust. Yet the scope of altruism is limited by a set of underlying reproductive and self-interested priorities. A perennial ethical and spiritual challenge in human society is how to broaden the scope of altruism to the extent that all human beings, simply as human existents, are equally regarded (Outka, 1972).

One of the twentieth century's pioneer social scientists of altruism was Pitrim A. Sorokin, whose work, *The Ways and Power of Love* (1954), represents the initial attempt to contextualize concepts of human and divine love within the scientific literature on altruism and egoism. During the 1940s and 1950s, Sorokin directed the Harvard Research Center in Creative Altruism, which attracted the attention of eminent scholars and practitioners of altruism and altruistic love, both secular and religious, from around the world. He studied the creative energy of altruistic love and the techniques of altruistic transformation embedded in cultural and religious rights of passage. Sorokin first used the term *altruistic love* to describe this particular form of human altruistic behavior, and we therefore are compelled to give him some attention here. Sorokin also coined the term *extensivity* in the field of altruistic studies and related it to "intensity" of altruism or "love."

Sorokin developed an ideal typology of altruism based on large-scale interview and questionnaire studies. He described a set of persons whose love is "very intense toward a small in-group (their family, their friends, their clique or sect or faction), but whose love for anybody beyond this little universe is nonexistent. The extensity of their love is thus very low" (1954, p. 19). Sorokin collected 1,000 cases of "American Good Neighbors" and analyzed them along the axes of extensity, intensity, duration, motivational purity, and overt action. Among his many useful conclusions, Sorokin defined the key problematic in altruism as "the tragedy of tribal altruism," or the blunt fact that "in-group altruism" inevitably means "out-group egoism" (p. 459). It was in fact Sorokin who coined the now commonly used term *in-group altruism*.

Sorokin stressed the need to move from tribal egoism to universal altruism and considered in-group altruism, no matter how genuine, as the most serious of continuing human problems. He described the social dynamics of the common in-group persecution of those persons who are able to achieve degrees of extensivity beyond group insularity, and he attempted to study those persons in depth in order to better understand the roots of their exemplary lives. His words are impassioned: "An exclusive tribal solidarity—known also as tribal patriotism, tribal loyalty, and tribal altruism—has mercilessly set man against man, and group against group. It has killed more human beings and destroyed more cities and villages than all the epidemics, hurricanes, storms, floods, earthquakes, and volcanic eruptions taken together. It has brought upon mankind more suffering than any other catastrophe" (1954, p. 461).

In other words, as contemporary evolutionary psychologists argue, the human propensity to aid and cooperate with others evolved in the context of intergroup conflict, and thus the complement of prosocial capacities is the tendency to form exclusionary alliances. The aggressive aspects of human nature had already been highlighted by presociobiological ethologists such as Konrad Lorenz. The most significant moral, scientific, and religious challenge that we face as a species is the overcoming of intergroup conflict. Sorokin suggested that human beings should turn their hate and aggression against disease, starvation, poverty, and other assaults on human well-being. If the inevitable correlate of altruism is aggression, then is the capacity for empathy potent enough to overcome the in-group/out-group barrier and to inhibit aggressive tendencies because of

the distress that the empathic observer feels in response to the noxious consequences of aggression (Feshbach & Feshbach, 1986)? Can the symbols that live in
us and in which we live bring us to full equality regarding altruism? Is empathy so
thoroughly the product of in-group evolution that in-group insularity is ineradicable? The question here is not just whether empathy can be extended, that is, if it
is heavily or entirely constrained by in-group evolutionary origins. The further
question is how empathy, which by its very nature is ethically neutral, can be used
as a tool for nurture rather than for exploitative control. Even within groups, as
Joseph Conrad vividly depicts in his novels and as Hitler understood to his political advantage, the ability to sense what others are feeling can be used either to provide sensitive care or to manipulate, even cruelly dominate. Evolutionary debates
over the very origin and significance of empathy—not just its group domain but
its biological function—are crucial, well grounded, and not yet resolved.

The theme of in-group altruism and out-group aggression is central to another significant work on the science of altruism, Elliott Sober's and David Sloan
Wilson's *Unto Others: The Evolution and Psychology of Unselfish Behavior* (1998).
This work is provocative in its critique of both social scientific and evolutionary
biological assumptions that too easily disparage the human capacity for altruism,
with regard to both motivation and action. Yet this work is highly debated by
many of the primary contemporary architects of evolutionary theory. Sober and
Wilson argue that unless the human capacity for altruism is in fact a reality by scientific analysis, there is a certain futility in recommending it, for otherwise in the
final assessment one is only toying with an exalted illusion.

The dominant theory of evolutionary biology looks at acts that increase the
fitness (survival and reproduction) of others at expense to the individual. In this
biological sense, altruism does not imply any conscious benevolence. The conclusion offered by many sociobiologists is that such altruistic acts are all a matter of
either inclusive fitness, such that one's own genes are passed on through relatives
who also possess said genes, or of reciprocal altruism, from which the self derives
compensatory reproductive benefits. Robert Trivers, George Williams, and John
Maynard Smith are all associated with this perspective. Sober and Wilson, however, take a different view. They argue for a form of group altruism in which acts
on behalf of other members of the group go beyond kin interests and reciprocity
to the group as a whole. The survival of a group against competitors would make
forms of altruism beyond individual reproductive and survival interests evolutionarily plausible. Sober and Wilson thus argue for "genuinely altruistic traits"
(p. 6). They conclude that "Altruism can be removed from the endangered species
list in both biology and the social sciences" (p. 337). The reader should keep this
debate and its consequences in mind throughout this book and will find that our
authors take different views as they wrestle with it. Group selection remains controversial but has significant defenders beyond Sober and Wilson (Boehm, 1999).

If group selection theory is valid, the problem of aggressive acts against or indifference to outsiders becomes even more significant. As Sober and Wilson put it,

> In any event, it is worth saying here that our goal in this book is not to paint a rosy pic-
> ture of universal benevolence. Group selection does provide a setting in which help-

ing behavior directed at members of one's own group can evolve; however, it equally provides a context in which hurting individuals in other groups can be selectively advantageous. Group selection favors within-group niceness *and* between-group nastiness. (p. 9)

This is important because, if altruism evolves within groups that compete with other groups, aggressive behavior toward outsiders, which is fully substantiated historically and anthropologically, may be difficult to overcome.

We leave further details of the scientific discussion to the specific sections of our book, although the reader by now has a sense of our broad terrain. Intellectuals have long taken sides in the egoism-altruism debate, although in different language games. In the Age of Enlightenment, philosophers contrasted benevolence and sympathy with love of self; theologians contrasted disinterested beneficence and charity with selfishness. Medieval thinkers contrasted *amor concupiscentiae* (self-love) with *castus amor* ("pure" love). Contemporary Protestant thought contrasts *eros* with *agape*, whereas psychologists speak of narcissism and its alternatives. Sociologist Auguste Comte (1798–1857) coined the terms *altruism* and *egoism*, by which he meant an unselfish desire to live for others in contrast to the impulse to benefit and gratify the self. The extensive study of altruism and egoism in the sciences has yet to adequately inform reflection in the humanities, which have generally tended to ignore scientific data in discussing such phenomena as compassion, kindness, and love. Similarly, the sciences have much to benefit from the insights of the humanities into aspects of the phenomena that are possibly beyond the reach of science and yet crucial to the overall human and cultural context.

Our task is to better understand the emergence of the capacities for altruistic actions and for empathic affect and how these contributed to a larger capacity for love. Setting aside all dualism and reductionism, our task is to better understand this transposition and genesis from above, within, and below. We have no interest in Platonic or Cartesian views of the self that bifurcate body and mind/soul, thereby relegating the scientific study of the neurological, biological, and evolutionary features of human altruism and altruistic love to irrelevancy.

Organization of the Book

We begin this book with a section on the definition of altruism and altruistic love as these are considered in the sciences and humanities. Part of the difficulty in engaging in significant dialogue across fields is that different disciplines mean different things by the same word. All fields of study can make greater progress in knowledge by conversation across boundaries, although this requires as much conceptual clarity as possible. Some attention in this section is also given to the phenomenology of human altruism and altruistic love. We begin with attention to human experience, bracketing out all heuristic filters, scientific and otherwise, that might be reductionistic.

The second section takes up the social scientific research into the question of the reality and nature of altruism and altruistic love, considered both quantitatively and qualitatively. Social scientists have addressed altruism in a variety of contexts. Those most relevant to this book address underlying motivations rather than merely helping actions. This section highlights the disagreement in social science over the authenticity of other-regarding motivation. The social scientific approaches represented here examine rescue behavior that may place the agent at risk. But there is also investigation of daily acts of love, care, and kindness, which value the other and seem motivated primarily by desire for the good of the other.

The third section of this book takes up the powerful debates within evolutionary biology and evolutionary psychology regarding altruism. To what extent are all forms of altruism determined and limited in scope by selfish genes, as some evolutionary biologists would suggest? Is group altruism scientifically valid? If so, what are the implications of this for human altruism? Can human altruism ever extend beyond in-groups to out-groups and even to the religious and philosophical moral ideal of all humanity being equally considered? What scientific explanations are there for genuinely counterreproductive altruistic behavior in various nonhuman species, and what do these explanations imply for human beings? Are human acts of radical self-sacrifice for the good of others contrary or consistent with nature and human nature as understood by evolutionary paradigms? How do data from the biological sciences compare with those from the social sciences regarding the existence of altruistic love at various levels of inclusivity?

The fourth section considers the emotional aspects of altruistic love, focusing on the role of empathy in both humans and nonhumans. A substance dualist view of the moral agent has historically focused entirely on properties of disembodied mind or soul, dismissing the biology and evolution of empathy and other affective states that contribute to love. How can empathy be better understood in its biological context? How does variation in neurobiological capacity for empathy affect cognitive functioning and the ability to act in a loving manner? Why are some persons more or less empathic than others? What biological processes are at work that encourage or inhibit the expression of altruistic love? How strong an influence on behavior is empathy, how much is it used for loving purposes, and is it a necessary feature of love in humans? What are the biological processes of attachment and bonding that pertain to empathy? What are the discontinuities between human and nonhuman capacities that allow for the emergence of a regard for the other as other? Do humans really have the capacity to practice altruistic love, and how do culture and symbol influence this capacity? What are the implications of altruistic love for a larger view of nature, human nature, and the universe?

The fifth section takes up altruistic love in its religious contexts but with an eye toward emerging areas for future study. Attentive to the best science and to religion pluralistically considered, this volume attempts to establish a framework for dialogue that will hopefully shape the discussion of altruistic love for some time to come.

In summary, these are some of the central questions that are at least raised, if not fully resolved, in this volume. We hope the volume can serve as a springboard for research into the following questions:

- What are the evolutionary origins and neurological substrates for altruistic behavior?
- What developmental processes foster or hinder altruistic attitudes and behavior in various stages of life from early childhood onward?
- To what extent do human individuals and societies manifest behavior that is motivationally or consequentially altruistic? What psychological, social, and cultural factors influence altruism and caring?
- Do spiritual and religious experiences, beliefs, and practices influence altruism?
- How does the giving and receiving of altruistic love interact with personal well-being and health?
- How can researchers from various disciplines collaborate to enhance this field of study?
- Overall, is it possible to gain new insights that can be utilized to help people and their communities to better appreciate the significance and importance of love and to benefit from its expression as a lived reality?

Finally, let us make a concluding comment about the science-religion dialogue over evolution and altruism. It is interesting to note that all the axes of theoretical tension described in the introduction—freedom versus determinism, individual versus group functionalism, material versus ideational agency, and the essential selfishness versus the loving competence of human nature—were philosophical and theological controversies centuries before evolutionary theory entered the fray. Although it is tempting to ascribe disagreement between scientific and theological perspectives on these issues to disciplinary conflict, it may reflect more the inherent and abiding ambiguities of human nature itself. The various disciplines are engaging common poles of human experience, though with different methods and metaphors . . . the very thing that may provoke mutual refinement.

REFERENCES

Boehm, C. (1999). *Hierarchy in the forest: The evolution of egalitarian behavior.* Cambridge: Harvard University Press.

Feshbach, S. F., & Feshbach, N. D. (1986). Aggression and altruism: A personality perspective. In C. Zahn-Waxler, E. M. Cummings, & R. Iannotti (Eds.), *Altruism and aggression: Biological and social origins* (pp. 189–217). Cambridge: Cambridge University Press.

Frank, R. H. (1988). *Passions within reason: The strategic role of the emotions.* New York: W. W. Norton.

Outka, G. (1972). *Agape: An ethical analysis.* New Haven, CT: Yale University Press.

Ridley, M. (1996). *The origins of virtue: Human instincts and the evolution of cooperation.* London: Penguin.

Singer, I. (1984). *The nature of love. Vol. 1: Plato to Luther.* 2d ed. Chicago: University of Chicago Press.

Singer, I. (1987). *The nature of love. Vol. 3: The Modern World.* Chicago: University of Chicago Press.

Sober, E., & Wilson, D. S. (1998). *Unto others: The evolution and psychology of unselfish behavior.* Cambridge: Harvard University Press.

Sorokin, P. A. (1954). *The ways and power of love: Types, factors, and techniques of moral transformation.* Boston: Beacon Press.

Toner, J. (1968). *The experience of love.* Washington: Corpus Books.

Part I

DEFINITIONS

Introduction to Part I

STEPHEN G. POST

Academic disciplines tend to erect walls of separation, developing independent language games and definitions of terms, and sometimes even contending for supremacy in the world of thought. But progress in altruism and altruistic love is too important to humanity to be slowed by separatism. Nevertheless, disciplines must have their unique methodologies and heuristic keys. So what is needed is a new field of altruistic studies, one in which the walls of separation between disciplines are replaced by low, neighborly fences that encourage conversation, respect, and collaboration. As Robert Frost wrote, "Something there is that doesn't love a wall."

A certain acrimony has surrounded the study of altruism, often prompted by the arrogant assumption that a single discipline could provide the one and only hermeneutic. Altruism and altruistic love, however, are sufficiently complex so that, above all, humility is needed. It is unlikely that either of these phenomena will ever be fully understood by the life sciences, the social sciences, or the humanities, even if they are in creative conversation rather than walled off from one another.

In this section, the authors have been asked to do their best to clarify what they mean by altruism and altruistic love. Elliott Sober, a philosopher of science whose focus is on evolutionary biology, provides "The ABCs of Altruism," defining altruistic behavior as enhancing "the fitness of someone else (the 'recipient') at some cost in fitness to the donor." The honeybee, for example, to benefit the group,

15

disembowels itself when stinging an intruder. A mindless organism can, in this sense, be an altruist. Sober then turns to definitions of psychological altruism, psychological egoism, and psychological hedonism, a subset of egoism. Here he moves to the human domain of motive and intentionality. His position is pluralistic in the sense that he recognizes that whatever egoistic inclinations humans have, there are altruistic ones as well. Sober realizes that this is difficult to prove once and for all, because it is always possible to assert that even the most altruistic act is driven by a desire to avoid guilt or to feel good about oneself. Sober ends his chapter with the suspicion that the popularity of a purely egoistic image of the human self is shaped by a culture of individualism and competition.

Edith Wyschogrod, an eminent phenomenologist and moral philosopher, provides a broad definition of human altruism as "an action favoring other individuals at the expense of the altruist." All moral experience, she argues, begins in discovering the other "as an ethical datum that makes a claim upon the self to engage in other-regarding acts." She devotes attention to the problem of genetic reductionism, that is, interpreting human behavior in purely genetic terms. These are terms that she brilliantly associates with the Pythagorean tradition. In her discourse on discovering the other as other ("alterity"), she directly challenges the idea that ethical life is possible from the vantage point of self-interest, no matter how enlightened to long-term perspectives. Wyschogrod's "Pythagorean Bodies and the Body of Altruism" provides a highly original and rigorous phenomenological analysis of altruism. The reader benefits not only from her ideas but also from the exercise of reading an important genre of philosophy.

Jerome Kagan, a leading psychologist of human development, defines altruism as the "helping agent's awareness of the need of another and the intention to be of assistance." Intentionality, rather than actual outcomes, is central to this definition. Kagan, in his "Morality, Altruism, and Love," is particularly critical of evolutionary biology, which he believes provides ideological support for a culture of narcissism. He is also highly critical of those who extrapolate from nonhuman animal models to human behavior. The human being is, Kagan asserts, utterly unique, emergent from evolution with the gift of a moral sense that includes a propensity to care for the other, although this propensity can be culturally undermined to degrees.

I have reserved my own chapter in this section, "Altruism and Altruistic Love: The Tradition of Agape," for an attempt at bringing together the different disciplinary languages of altruism in a manner that takes all the relevant disciplines seriously and points toward the meaning of the phenomenon of altruistic love as the epitome of altruistic intent and behavior in humans. As is the case in Wyschogrod's chapter, this chapter also engages the dialogue between the sciences, philosophy, and religion.

Across all these chapters, the authors share a common conclusion that altruistic motivations and actions are humanly possible. Although it remains true that altruistic motivations are hard to prove absolutely, on which side of the altruism-egoism debate should the burden of proof be placed?

1

The ABCs of Altruism

ELLIOTT SOBER

In this chapter, I provide a conceptual map of some of the main questions that have been posed about altruism. What biologists mean by the term *altruism* is not at all the same as what psychologists and ordinary people mean by the term. After explaining the difference between evolutionary and psychological altruism and how the latter is related to the concept of love, I focus on the evolutionary concept and describe how it is possible for the competitive process of natural selection to lead to the evolution of altruistic traits. Then I turn to the psychological concept and describe how it is related to, though different from, the concept of morality.

Evolutionary Altruism

A trait is said to be evolutionarily altruistic by virtue of the effects it has on *fitness*. An organism's fitness is its ability to be reproductively successful; an organism's survival is relevant to its fitness only to the extent that survival promotes reproductive success. An altruistic behavior is one that enhances the fitness of someone else (the "recipient") at some cost in fitness to the donor. Thus a mindless organism can be an evolutionary altruist. Darwin thought that the barbed stinger of the honeybee is an altruistic trait—the bee disembowels itself when it stings an intruder to the nest; the stinger keeps pumping venom even after the bee has perished, thus conferring a benefit on the group.

The puzzle about evolutionary altruism is that it appears to be a trait that natural selection will stamp out, not promote. If altruists and selfish individuals live in the same group, altruists will donate fitness benefits to others, whereas selfish individuals will not. Altruists may receive benefits from the donations of other altruists, but so too may selfish individuals be on the receiving end. Altruists thus create a "public good" (a term from economics) at a cost to themselves; this good benefits both altruists and selfish individuals alike. It follows that altruists will be less fit than selfish individuals in the same group. Natural selection is a process that causes fitter traits to increase in frequency and less fit traits to decline. How, then, can natural selection explain the existence of evolutionary altruism?

Darwin's answer was the hypothesis of *group selection.* Although altruists are less fit than selfish individuals in the same group, groups of altruists will be fitter than groups of selfish individuals. Hives that contain bees with stingers will be more successful than hives whose bees lack stingers. Altruistic traits evolve because they benefit the group and in spite of the fact that they are deleterious for the individuals that have them.

Darwin was a "pluralist" about natural selection; he held that some traits evolve because they are good for the individual, whereas others evolve because they are good for the group. This pluralism became a standard part of the evolutionary biology practiced during the decades in which the Modern Synthesis was created (1930–1960). The idea of group adaptation was often applied uncritically during this period, but the same can be said of the idea of individual adaptation. This situation changed in the 1960s, when group selection was vigorously attacked. Its exile from the subject was hailed as one of twentieth-century biology's major advances. Since then, the hypothesis of group selection has been making a comeback; many biologists now think that group selection is theoretically well grounded and empirically well supported as the explanation of some (but by no means all) traits, whereas many others continue to reject it. The dust has not yet settled, but my impression is that *multilevel selection theory*—the idea that selection processes can and do occur at all levels of the biological hierarchy—is on its way to becoming a standard feature of evolutionary thinking (Sober and Wilson, 1998).

Psychological Altruism

In contrast with the concept of evolutionary altruism, psychological altruism is a property that applies only to individuals who have minds. A honeybee may be an evolutionary altruist, but it presumably is not a psychological altruist. And if, out of the goodness of my heart, I encourage you not to have children, my behavior may be an instance of psychological altruism, but it is not evolutionarily altruistic (assuming that my action does not enhance your fitness).

Although the concept of psychological altruism gets applied to people and to actions, the best place to begin is to think of psychological altruism as a property of motives or desires or preferences. Eve's desire that Adam have the apple is *other-directed*; the proposition that she wants to come true (*that Adam has the apple*) mentions another person but not Eve herself. In contrast, Adam's desire that he have the apple is *self-directed*. In addition to purely self-directed and purely other-directed desires, there are *mixed* desires, wherein people desire that they and specific others be related in a certain way; had Eve wanted to share the apple with Adam, her desire would have been mixed.

An altruistic desire is an other-directed desire in which what one wants is that another person do well. This may involve your wanting the other person to have what he or she wants, or it may involve wanting the other person to have what you think would be good for him or her.

Well-wishing can be nonpaternalistic or paternalistic. Altruistic desires, understood in this way, obviously exist. The controversy about psychological altruism concerns whether these desires are *ultimate* or merely *instrumental*. When we wish others well, do we ever have this as an end in itself, or do we care about others only because we think that how they do will affect our own welfare? The theory known as *psychological egoism* maintains that all ultimate motives are self-directed. When Eve wants Adam to have the apple, she has this other-directed desire only because she thinks that his having the apple will provide her with a benefit.

Psychological hedonism is one variety of egoistic theory. Hedonism claims that the only ultimate motives that people have are the attainment of pleasure and the avoidance of pain. The only things we care about as ends in themselves are states of our own consciousness. This special form of egoism is the hardest one to refute. It is easy enough to see from human behavior that people don't always try to maximize their access to consumer goods. However, even when someone chooses a job with a lower salary over a job that pays more, the hedonist can say that this choice was motivated by the desire to feel good and to avoid feeling bad. Indeed, hedonists think they can explain the most harrowing acts of self-sacrifice—for example, the soldier in a foxhole who throws himself on a live grenade to save the lives of his comrades. The soldier supposedly does this because he'd sooner not exist at all than live with the knowledge that he had allowed his friends to perish. This hedonistic explanation may sound strained; why not say instead that the soldier cared more about his friends than he did about his own survival? But that the explanation sounds strained does not mean that it must be false.

Because hedonism is difficult to refute, egoism is also difficult to refute. However, that does not mean it is true. Human behavior also is consistent with the view called *motivational pluralism*; this is the claim that people have both self-directed and other-directed ultimate aims.

This theory does not assert that there are human actions that are driven by purely other-directed ultimate desires. Perhaps one consideration that lurks behind everything we do is a concern for self. What pluralism asserts is that some of our ultimate desires are other-directed. Because actions may be caused by several desires acting at once, pluralism is best understood as a claim about the character of our desires, not about the purity of our actions.

It is an interesting fact about our culture that so many people are certain that egoism is true and that so many others are certain that it is false. A Martian anthropologist might find this surprising, in view of the fact that the behavior we observe in everyday life seems to be consistent with both egoism and pluralism. Our convictions evidently have outrun the evidence we have at hand. Is the popularity of egoism due to the fact that we live in a culture that emphasizes individuality and economic competition? Is the popularity of pluralism due to the fact that people find it comforting to think that benevolence is an irreducible part of human nature? These questions are as fascinating as they are difficult to answer.

Altruistic Love

Love is an emotion, so it, like psychological altruism, belongs to the realm of the mental. The honeybee is not a psychological altruist, nor can it be said to sacrifice its life out of love for its nestmates. Love comes in many varieties; it can be sexual or platonic, and it can be self-centered or altruistic. Altruistic love, of course, entails an altruistic motive or desire or preference on the part of the lover. However, the converse does not hold; the existence of an altruistic desire does not entail the presence of love. When I read about the disasters that happen to strangers far away, I find myself wanting them to be better off. I wish them well, but I do not find in my heart the emotion of love. In fact, I don't detect in myself any emotion at all as I casually peruse the morning newspaper. Perhaps this introspective impression is not correct, but it seems perfectly possible to have an unemotional altruistic desire.

What, then, is the extra ingredient that turns an altruistic desire into altruistic love? This is an instance of a larger question. What is an emotion, and how does it differ from a mere desire? When I nearly have an automobile accident while driving my car, I experience fear. I believe that I am in danger, and I want to be safe. But fear is something more than this belief and this desire. It is a feeling. But what *is* a feeling, and what distinguishes one feeling from another? This is a difficult question; indeed, it isn't even clear what the appropriate vocabulary is in which one should attempt to construct an answer. So let us focus, more modestly, on psychological altruism. Altruistic motivation is part, if not the whole, of altruistic love. We know well enough what psychological altruism is and how it differs from evolutionary altruism.

The Prisoners' Dilemma: Rational Deliberation

Game theory was first invented in mathematical economics (Von Neumann & Morgenstern, 1944). Only later was it brought within evolutionary theory (Maynard Smith, 1982). Perhaps the most famous game analyzed in game theory is the *prisoners' dilemma*. After explaining how this game works when it is formulated as a problem about individual decision making, I show how the problem was reformulated in evolutionary game theory. The solution that is correct in the one context differs from the solution that makes sense in the other (Skyrms, 1994). Understanding this is the key to seeing what it takes for altruism to evolve.

Suppose that the police arrest you and your accomplice in crime. They take you into separate rooms and interrogate you separately. If both of you remain silent, they will have very little evidence against you, and so you can anticipate being put in jail for only a short period of time, say 3 months. However, the police tell you that if you provide them with full information and your accomplice remains silent, they'll let you go free (0 months in jail). They also say that if your accomplice tells all, but you remain silent, you'll go to jail for 9 months. And if both of you spill the beans, you'll each go to jail for 6 months. What should you do? You have two choices (confess or remain silent), and there are four possible situations you might be in, depending on what you and your accomplice do:

		The other person	
		remains silent	confesses
You	remain silent	−3 months	−9 months
	confess	0 months	−6 months

I use negative numbers to represent the payoffs you would receive in different circumstances because I want bigger numbers to represent better outcomes—you would rather have 0 months in jail than 3, and you would rather have 6 months in jail than 9.

Given these payoffs, you decide to confess—this action is said to "dominate" the other, meaning that it is the better action, no matter what the other person does. Your accomplice is in exactly the same position, so he decides to do the same thing. Thus, when both players are rational, both end up in jail for 6 months. If both had behaved irrationally and chosen to remain silent, each would have been better off, because then each would have gone to jail for only 3 months. In this case, universal rationality leads to a worse outcome than universal irrationality. In many situations in real life, we think that being rational helps us obtain better outcomes. The prisoners' dilemma seems paradoxical because it shows how this connection between rationality and doing well is not inevitable.

After the prisoners' dilemma was invented at the RAND Corporation in 1950,[1] it was used to model a number of real-world social dilemmas. One of them was the question of whether the United States should continue to stockpile nuclear weapons in its cold war arms race with the Soviet Union. Because the model builders were giving advice to the U.S. government, I represent the payoffs that the United States would receive in four circumstances:

		USSR	
		disarms	arms
U.S.	disarms	Second Best	Fourth Best
	arms	Best	Third Best

The best outcome for the United States would be for it to arm itself and for the USSR not to; although armaments cost money, this cost would be more than compensated for by the power the United States would obtain. The worst outcome for the United States would be for the United States to disarm and for the USSR not to, because then the USSR would have power over the United States. The second and third best outcomes are ones in which the United States and the

USSR do the same thing. It would be better for the United States if both sides disarmed than if neither did; this would save money and also reduce the chance of a devastating nuclear war. Given these payoffs, the United States should arm itself; the USSR, faced with the same problem, should do the same thing. It would have been better for both if both had disarmed, but this is not what rational deliberation dictates.

The prisoners' dilemma also had an impact on the budding environmentalist movement. Garrett Hardin (1968), in his influential paper "The Tragedy of the Commons," describes a hypothetical community of farmers who use a shared parcel of land ("the commons") for grazing. Each farmer can either put the maximum number of animals out to graze on this commons or put some lesser number there. Each farmer gets a higher income by using the commons to the utmost; however, when all the farmers do this, they overexploit the commons and ruin it. For Hardin, the prisoners' dilemma distills the essence of how free-market capitalism can destroy the environment and make everyone worse off.

With these three examples in mind, let's extract the abstract structure of the prisoners' dilemma game. Remaining silent in the first game is an instance of "cooperating" with your accomplice. Disarming is an instance of "cooperating" with the Soviet Union in the second game. And restraining your use of the commons is a case of "cooperating" with the other farmers in the third. Similarly, confessing to the police is an instance of "defecting" against your accomplice in the first game, arming is a case of "defecting" against the Soviet Union in the second, and using the commons to the maximum is an instance of "defecting" in the third. The terms *cooperate* and *defect* became standard in the game theory literature. They mean exactly the same thing as *altruism* and *selfishness* do in evolutionary game theory. The abstract structure of the payoffs you receive in a prisoners' dilemma, then, is as follows:

		The other person behaves	
		altruistically	*selfishly*
You behave	*altruistically*	$x - c + b$	$x - c$
	selfishly	$x + b$	x

When you and the other person behave selfishly, no benefits are donated, and none are received; call the payoff that you receive in this circumstance "x." If you behave altruistically and the other person is selfish, you donate a benefit that costs you c to produce, and you receive nothing in return. So your payoff is $(x - c)$. If you behave selfishly and the other person behaves altruistically, you receive a benefit, but you don't pay the cost of producing a donation, so your payoff is $(x + b)$. Finally, if you and the other person both behave altruistically, each of you pays the cost of donation, but each of you also receives a donation from the other person; in this case your payoff is $(x - c + b)$. As mentioned earlier, a dominance argument entails that you should be selfish. The same argument leads the other person to choose the same action. If both players behave selfishly, both do worse than they would have if both had behaved altruistically; notice that $x - c + b > x$, if $b > c$.

Payoffs are supposed to reflect your "utilities." What are these? As the examples illustrate, they could be avoiding jail, attaining power and safety, taking in dollars, or anything, as long as the actors prefer more of the quantity over less. Well, *almost* anything. Suppose you are in the original prisoners' dilemma situation and that you care about what happens both to you *and* to your accomplice; you care about these equally. Then your utilities will be as follows:

		The other person	
		remains silent	confesses
You	remain silent	−3−3 = −6 months	−9−0 = −9 months
	confess	0−9 = −9 months	−6−6 = −12 months

Now a dominance argument tells you to remain silent. If your partner is similarly motivated, both of you will choose to remain silent, and so you will each go to jail for only 3 months. This is *not* a prisoners' dilemma in the sense in which that term that has become canonical in game theory, because rational deliberation does not lead both parties to a solution that is worse than the one they would have obtained if both had been irrational. Yet the payoffs illustrated describe the situation that the prisoners would face if their utilities were as described.

This tells us something about what "utility" means in the prisoners' dilemma game. The assumption is that a person's utilities do not reflect any concern for what happens to the other player. It is not that game theory cannot handle utilities that reflect self-interest and benevolence simultaneously; after all, the previous table represents people who care about self and other in equal measure. Rather, my point is that this notion of utility is banished from formulations of the prisoners' dilemma.

In fact, the limitation on what utility means in the prisoners' dilemma is even more severe. Suppose you are a psychological egoist of the hedonistic variety. All you care about ultimately is experiencing pleasure and avoiding pain. You are being interrogated by the police, and you recognize that your pleasure and pain will be affected in two ways by what transpires. First, going to jail will cause you pain. But suppose you will find it equally painful to know that your accomplice is in jail (if he serves *n* months in jail, this will cause you as much pain as would be delivered by your spending *n* months in jail yourself). In this case, just as in the case of genuine benevolence, you will choose to remain silent. If your utilities are as described, then you are not in a prisoners' dilemma, properly so called. Utility in the prisoners' dilemma has to be "crassly egoistic," not just egoistic.

The Prisoners' Dilemma: Evolutionary Game Theory

Although rationality leads to universal selfishness when the prisoners' dilemma is formulated as a problem about rational deliberation, it turns out that natural selection does not inevitably lead to universal selfishness when the game is transposed to an evolutionary context. Instead of having two players choose how they will behave, we imagine that there are two types of organism, selfish and altruistic. Here selfishness and altruism are defined in terms of their fitness effects, not psychologically. A large number of organisms divide into pairs, and the individuals in a pair interact with each other. The payoffs they receive are in the currency of reproductive success; those who receive higher payoffs have more babies. Individuals are assumed to reproduce asexually; it also is assumed that offspring exactly resemble their parents. The next generation therefore may display a mix of altruists and selfish individuals different from the mix found in the previous generation. The members of this new generation then form up into pairs and play the game again. They produce the third generation, and so on.

When this process takes place over many generations, what ultimately happens to the frequencies of altruism and selfishness? That depends on how pairs are formed. If individuals pair at random, then selfish individuals will be fitter than altruists, and so altruism will decline in frequency and go extinct. However, if like always pairs with like, then altruists interact exclusively with each other and thus obtain a payoff of $(x - c + b)$, whereas selfish individuals interact exclusively with each other and thus obtain a payoff of x. If $b > c$, altruists will be fitter than selfish individuals, and so altruism will increase in frequency. I have just described two extreme cases—in which individuals associate randomly and in which like always pairs with like; in between these two extremes are different degrees of positive association. The crucial factor for altruism to evolve is that there be some tendency for like to associate with like—how strong this tendency needs to be if altruism is to evolve depends on the values of the costs and benefits involved.[2]

Cultural and Genetic Evolution

Although biologists modeling the evolution of altruism usually assume that different phenotypes correspond to different genes, this assumption is not needed in an evolutionary model. If parents transmit their traits to their offspring by teaching, altruism can evolve by cultural evolution. Evolution by natural selection requires a mechanism of inheritance, but the core idea here is just that offspring resemble their parents. The idea that learning and culture also can provide a mechanism of inheritance is worth bearing in mind when one considers Darwin's hypothesis about how human morality evolved:

> It must not be forgotten that although a high standard of morality gives but a slight or no advantage to each individual man and his children over the other men of the same tribe, yet that an increase in the number of well-endowed men and advancement in the standard of morality will certainly give an immense advantage to one tribe over another. There can be no doubt that a tribe including many members who, from possessing in a high degree the spirit of patriotism, fidelity, obedience, courage, and sympathy, were always ready to aid one another, and to sacrifice themselves for the common good, would be victorious over most other tribes; and this would be natural selection. At all times throughout the world tribes have supplanted other tribes; and as morality is one important element in their success, the standard of morality and the number of well-endowed men will thus everywhere tend to rise and increase. (Darwin, 1871, p. 166)

As Darwin notes, human history is filled with cases of group competition. To think of this history within an evolutionary framework, one need not assume that these cultural differences between groups are due to the fact that people in different cultures have different genes. Even if cultural groups were genetically identical, they still could differ in their phenotypes and still could faithfully transmit those phenotypes across the generations. Even if the evolution of altruism in social insects turns out to be an exclusively genetic process, the evolution of altruism within human beings needs to be understood from the dual perspective of genetic and cultural change.

In fact, there are two ways in which cultural evolution can depart from the usual pattern of genetic evolution. To see what these are, consider the following three types of selection process (Sober, 1993):

	Mechanisms of heredity	Definitions of fitness
I	genes	having babies
II	learning	having babies
III	learning	having imitators

In Type I processes, genes provide the mechanism of inheritance, and fitness is measured in terms of biological reproduction. The process of cultural group selection (Boyd & Richerson, 1985) that I just described is of Type II. Learned traits, no less than traits that are genetically transmitted, can affect the survivorship of individual people and how reproductively successful they are. In Type III processes, ideas are transmitted by learning, and they succeed and fail for reasons that have nothing to do with their impact on the reproductive success of the individuals who accept them. Here we are recognizing the possibility to which Dawkins (1976) gave the name "meme." An example of this type of process is provided by the drastic reduction in family size that took place at the end of the nineteenth century in Europe. The "demographic transition," as it is called, apparently involved a trait with lower biological fitness replacing a trait with higher biological fitness. Having smaller family size was an attractive idea in spite of its Darwinian disutility. The trait had high cultural fitness, and a Type III process led to its spread. In saying this, I am not explaining *why* reduction in family size was suddenly an idea whose time had come. Rather, I am simply noting that the process spread by a Type III process. It is important to recognize that moralities can change for the same reason. In saying that moralities evolve by a selection process, we are not limiting ourselves to models of the first two types.

Altruism and Morality

Altruism, whether evolutionary or psychological, frequently strikes people as a good thing. Because of this, altruism's dark side needs to be held clearly in view if we are to understand the moral dimensions of altruism and also its evolutionary and psychological character.

The process of group selection does not eliminate competition from the evolutionary process but merely transposes it up one level. In group selection, groups compete with other groups, just as in individual selection, individuals in a group compete with each other. In *The Origin*, Darwin (1859) says that he uses the term *struggle for existence* to encompass two different types of situations. Two dogs may fight with each other over a bone, but two plants may each struggle against the drought. Individual selection will favor the stronger dog in the first case, but it also will favor the stronger plant in the second. Natural selection does not have to involve individuals actively interfering with each other. In the case of the dogs, one of them gets the bone only if the other does not; but in the case of the plants, how well one plant stands up to the sun does not affect how well the other does.[3] Applied to the case of group selection, Darwin's point means that group selection can be a process in which groups actively interfere with each other, but it also can be a process in which groups respond with varying degrees of success to a common environmental problem.

What does this tell us about the evolution of altruism? An individual who is an evolutionary altruist benefits the group at cost to the self. Altruists might donate food to members of their own group, or they might burn the crops of other groups. Either way, they help their own group to do better in the struggle with other groups. Group selection can promote within-group niceness, but it also can promote between-group nastiness. It is an obvious fact about nature that the process of individual selection has left plenty of room for individuals to be nasty to each other. We should expect no less of group selection—it can lead groups to be nasty to each other. Group selection doesn't always lead the lion to lay down with the lamb; it can lead lions to cooperate with each other to bring down lambs.

There is a similar dark side to psychological altruism. How can a noninstrumental concern for the welfare of others be morally bad? The easiest way to see this is to realize that being nice to someone can involve being nasty to third parties. If Alan cheats Beth at cards because he wants to give the money to Carol, we may decide that his dishonesty was altruistically motivated *and* morally wrong. A macabre illustration of this point may be found in the training that Nazi concentration camp guards and physicians received. They were told that the revulsion they might experience in carrying out the Nazi genocide was a cost they should be willing to pay for the good of the German people (Lifton, 1986). Altruistic motivation can underwrite evil (Sober and Wilson, 1998).

There is another sort of separation that we need to recognize between altruism and morality. Altruistic ultimate desires, if they exist, involve a concern that this or that individual do well. Perhaps a parent wants her children to do well for reasons that go beyond her belief that this will redound to her benefit. Indeed, this desire may be a cognitive state that some of our primate relatives occupy. The point I am emphasizing is that altruistic concern for specific others is not the same as the acceptance of a general moral principle. If I want my children to prosper, it is a separate question from whether I think that all children should be nurtured by their parents. Moral principles are general and impersonal in what they say. They do not mention self or specific others but describe what anyone in a generally characterized situation is permitted or obliged to do. Even if altruistic desires existed before modern humans evolved, I suspect that abstract moral principles are a uniquely human achievement.

Most of us recognize this distinction between the specific desires we have and the general moral principles we accept when we compare catastrophes that happen to those who are near and dear with similar catastrophes that happen far away to people we do not know. Our moral principles tell us that the two catastrophes are equally bad if they caused the same amount of suffering and devastation and death. However, most of us care about the one more strongly than we care about the other. Even if we are not wholly indifferent to the distant event, our desire that the victims receive help is weaker in this case than it is in the one that happens closer to home. Our desires—including our altruistic desires—sometimes reflect differences that our moral principles tell us are irrelevant.

This division between altruistic desires and moral principles recurs when we consider the concept of love. We do sometimes speak of generalized love—love for humanity or love of all living things—but love is perhaps most familiar when it is focused on particular individuals. Most of us have loving relationships with only a small circle of individuals; and even within that circle, our love of some individuals is more intense than our love of others. We recognize the possibility that this circle might be expanded and that the love we feel for those within the circle might be made more intense. But what is far more difficult to contemplate is the idea that we might simultaneously greatly expand the circle *and* love all the individuals in it equally. A perspectival painting can be enlarged to encompass more of the landscape, but it still remains perspectival. Perhaps love, like altruistic desire, obeys a different logic from that of our ethical principles.

If general ethical principles and specific altruistic desires are distinct in the way I have suggested, why do human beings have them both? Or, to give this question a temporal dimension, if specific altruistic desires were part of the human phenotype before general ethical principles came along, why did the latter become part of that phenotype? One possible explanation is the social function that moral principles serve. Moral principles are devices for encouraging group-beneficial desires and behaviors. Human beings evolved in a social environment; the desires we have are influenced by that social environment. The morality espoused and enforced by our elders is a powerful influence on the type of person we grow up to be. Moralities will evolve by group selection when they influence the behaviors of individuals and vary with respect to how much they promote the group-beneficial character of those behaviors. As noted before, it doesn't matter whether moralities are transmitted genetically or culturally for this process to go forward.

The idea just described is that human moralities have fitness consequences, just like the barbed stinger of the honeybee. This can be true even if moralities are transmitted by learning and barbed stingers by genes. However, as the previous discussion of three types of selection process suggests, we need to remember that moralities can change for purely cultural reasons that have nothing to do either with genetic transmission or with the effect of moral beliefs on having babies. The morality accepted within a group (or the mix of moralities that are accepted) can affect the survivorship and reproductive success of individuals, but ideas have a way of jumping from head to head for reasons that are orthogonal with the goal of having babies. A morality has biological effects, but it also has cultural meanings that can lead it to wax or wane. The phenomenon of human morality needs to be analyzed from both angles.

NOTES

1. The abstract structure of the prisoners' dilemma game was first described by Merrill Flood and Melvin Dresher; Albert Tucker (also at RAND) invented the prisoners' story to illustrate the game and thus gave the game its name (Poundstone, 1992).

2. This is true in the "one-shot" prisoners' dilemma, in which players interact with each other only once. However, the question is more subtle for the "iterated" prisoners' dilemma, in which players in a pair interact repeatedly, each time producing an altruistic or a selfish behavior. As Axelrod's (1984) simulations show, cooperative strategies (such as tit-for-tat) can evolve even when pairs are formed at random. However, when this is true, there still is a correlation between the *behaviors* produced by individuals, even though the *strategies* used by the two players are uncorrelated. For an example of what this means, see the discussion in Sober (1993, pp. 115–117).

3. The dogs are playing a "zero-sum game," whereas the plants are not (Sober, 1984, p. 17).

REFERENCES

Axelrod, R. (1984). *The evolution of cooperation.* New York: Basic Books.
Boyd, R., & Richerson, P. (1985). *Culture and the evolutionary process.* Chicago: University of Chicago Press.
Darwin, C. (1859). *On the origin of species.* London: John Murray.
Darwin, C. (1871). *The descent of man and selection in connection with sex.* London: John Murray.
Dawkins, R. (1976). *The selfish gene.* Oxford: Oxford University Press.
Hardin, G. (1968). The tragedy of the commons. *Science, 162,* 1243–1248.
Lifton, R. (1986). *The Nazi doctors: Medical killing and the psychology of genocide.* New York: Basic Books.
Maynard Smith, J. (1982). *Evolution and the theory of games.* Cambridge: Cambridge University Press.
Poundstone, W. (1992). *Prisoner's dilemma: John von Neumann, game theory, and the puzzle about the bomb.* New York: Doubleday.
Skyrms, B. (1994). Darwin meets the logic of decision: Correlation in evolutionary game theory. *Philosophy of Science, 61,* 503–528.
Sober, E. (1984). *The nature of selection: Evolutionary theory in philosophical focus.* Cambridge: MIT Press.
Sober, E. (1993). *Philosophy of biology.* Boulder, CO: Westview Press.
Sober, E., & Wilson, D. (1998). *Unto others: The evolution and psychology of unselfish behavior.* Cambridge: Harvard University Press.
Von Neumann, J., & Morgenstern, O. (1944). *The theory of games in economic behavior.* New York: Wiley.

2

Pythagorean Bodies and the Body of Altruism

EDITH WYSCHOGROD

Altruistic behavior may be minimally defined as action favoring other individuals at the expense of the altruist. For the evolutionary biologist, the cost and benefit of such behavior may be seen in terms of its usefulness to the survival of the individual or, alternatively, in light of its reproductive success. These claims can themselves be seen as undermining the view that genetically programed altruistic behavior is genuinely other-regarding, as these goals are compatible with the action of selfish genes. Moreover, if altruistic behavior is genetically programmed, whether other-regarding or selfish, it is defined nonsubjectively. It can be argued, alternatively, that altruism is best understood by inquiring into the subjective motivations and psychological capacities for acts of self-sacrificial giving. Aspects of both positions are taken up in a variety of contexts in Parts II and III of this volume.

I proceed otherwise than by examining the dichotomies of cultural-versus-genetic or subjective-versus-objective interpretation by proposing a third alternative, that of ethical meaning that arises in the encounter with another human being. I maintain that altruism is contingent on relating to the other not as a content of one's own consciousness—as a perception of or an emotional response to the other—but rather as an ethical datum that makes a claim on the self to engage in other-regarding acts. In this view, the other is not apprehended first through empathy or sympathy (whether genetically or culturally programmed) in that both of these affects require envisaging the other as another "me" and begin from my standpoint: "How would it be for me if I were the other?" This is not to say that empathy and sympathy are not desirable but rather that they presuppose a prior and irreducible relation to the other.

As defined by common sense, altruism may be seen as endorsing actions that exceed the limits of what is taken to be one's duty, whether by the control of contrary inclinations and interests or without effort (Urmson, 1958). Thus actions having the effect but not the purpose of aiding a recipient at the expense of an agent may count as altruistic. However, I hew to the view that full-fledged altruism exceeds what can be termed magnanimity or generosity and that authentic altruism is radical other-regarding behavior or alterity-altruism, a term I use to describe unreservedly placing one's bodily self and material goods at the disposal of another or others. Egocentric propensities are shed in the interest of ameliorating the suffering of the other even before one calculates the other's needs, in that calculation follows from the prior encounter with the other.

Important to my argument is the claim that differing conceptions of altruism presuppose differing accounts of the body but that any single account may cut across the lines of genetic, sociobiological, psychological, and theological interpretations. I shall not engage the question of whether the fine-tuning of the evolutionary process that allowed altruistic behavior to emerge implies that the process is the result of deliberate design (Polkinghorne, 1996), although the issue remains one of compelling interest. I hope rather to show that the comprehension of the body in terms of its genetic code may be compatible with at least one theological depiction of the body after death but that this view is incompatible with an understanding of the body required by alterity-altruism.

I consider first the conception of corporeality that is presupposed in the assertion that altruism may be, wholly or in part, genetically programmed. In this account, the body is an intricate system of coded information that governs its form, capacities, and behaviors as they are determined by the biochemical molecules that are its genetic building blocks. The body of everyday experience that can touch or be touched, the body as a haptic field, is dematerialized, dissolved into inheritable codes amenable to computational modeling. Because the pre-Socratic philosopher Pythagoras, who believed that numbers are the elements of all things, prefigured this interpretation of the body, I shall henceforth refer to the body thus understood as the Pythagorean body. It is not my aim to contest the demonstrable utility of genetically coded information in the context of evolutionary biology but rather to show that the Pythagorean body differs from the sensate body that feels pain and suffering and that is required by alterity-altruism. As Holmes Rolston III has pointed out in one of his Gifford Lectures, "Genes are no more capable of sharing than of being selfish . . . where 'sharing' and 'selfish' have their deliberated, moral meaning" (1999, p. 49). To attribute either altruism or selfishness to genes is to see them as moral agents rather than transmitters of information.

Although theologian John Milbank (1990) does not consider altruism in the context of genetic programming, he has challenged both the intelligibility and the desirability of radically self-sacrificial altruism grounded in otherness, contending that otherness is a vacuous concept and is, in effect, incoherent. Milbank's principal charge against radical altruism is that it is contingent on the vulnerability of the other, which, in turn, depends on the fact that she or he will die. Thus alterity-altruism cannot be realized, because the mortality of agent and recipient cuts off continuous and ongoing beneficence to the other. Instead, Milbank insists, ethics calls for a resurrection body that allows for individual continuity and a joyful communion with others.

I hope to show that alterity-altruism can escape Milbank's objections largely because those objections rest on a misinterpretation of the body as understood in alterity-altruism. Moreover, I support the (perhaps surprising) claim that the body of evolutionary biology and Milbank's account of the resurrection body are strongly linked in that each substitutes a version of the Pythagorean body for the body as a sentient field that can experience pain and suffering. Although useful in the context of evolutionary biology, I hope to pinpoint difficulties inherent in the theological application of this view.

Pythagorean Bodies: The Individual as Code

As a starting point for understanding the Pythagorean body, it may be useful to consider a standard formulation of altruism and egoism as seen by evolutionary biology, that is, in terms of their potential for the enhancement of fitness and their capacity for replication. Wim J. van der Steen writes: "The terms altruism and egoism . . . are related to fitness in terms of reproductive interests. A behavior is altruistic if it increases the fitness of the recipient and decreases the fitness of the organism exhibiting the behavior. The terms egoism and selfishness represent the converse relationship" (1999, p. 12). The reduction of fitness to the capacity for self-replication is seen as intrinsic to the Pythagorean body that I describe.

By interpreting the body as serving reproductive interests, evolutionary biology redesigns the body of ordinary experience into the body as coded information. What is envisaged is not merely that the body in the everyday sense is subject to genetic programming but, more radically, that the relation between the form of the organism, the phenomenological body, can be severed from what counts as the individual biological entity that is both the agent and recipient of altruistic activity. Evolutionary biologists will no doubt recognize the position of Richard Dawkins, who famously refers to the selfishness of genes and who offers no disclaimer to the assertion he cites of D'Arcy Thompson to the effect that "any animal form can be transformed into a related form by a mathematical transformation although . . . the translation may not be a simple one" (Dawkins, 1982, p. 2). Dawkins maintains that, in his account of this avowedly radical stance (now only somewhat modified), he is "not trying to convince anyone of the truth of any factual proposition [but rather opening] a way of looking at new facts and ideas, and a way of asking new questions about them" (1982, p. 1). The gene's-eye view of evolution sees evolution as taking place not on behalf of the organism as the indivisible unit of biological individuality but rather in the interest of the gene, "that little bit of chromosome that lasts for many generations" (Dawkins, 1976, p. 33), so that modes of inheritance heretofore ascribed to organisms are now attributed to genes.

An organism has manifest characteristics that are the result of the interaction of genetic makeup and environment, characteristics known as its phenotype. What is perceived as radical in Dawkins's description of the phenotype is his expansion of standard accounts to include not only the organism's perceptible attributes but also the outcome of gene activity that lies outside the bodies in which the genes are lodged (1982). Thus an individual entity made up of genes is extended beyond the organism (whether unicellular or complex) that the genes inhabit so as to constitute a new individual.

To make sense of this contention, it is crucial to see the centrality of replication in Dawkins's account of the gene's operations: It is in the interest of reproducing itself, the gene, rather than the phenotype, that natural selection takes place. For Dawkins a replicator is anything of which copies can be made. Information bearing DNA molecules, gene strings, are replicators, active when their effects lead to their being copied, passive when they die out. For Dawkins, the gene is the "unit of heredity" that is retained in the evolutionary process. Only those likely to be copied survive, whereas passive replicators become extinct (Dawkins, 1982). This account is complicit with Dawkins's famous claim that "the predominant quality in a successful gene is ruthless selfishness . . . which will give rise to selfishness in individual behavior" (Dawkins, 1976, p. 2). A gene can achieve its goals through self-sacrificial acts on the part of individual animals, but such putatively altruistic acts are undertaken in the interest of gene replication.

What remains clear is that although the phenotype continues to be "the all important instrument of preservation; it is not that which is preserved" (Dawkins, 1976, p. 114) or, as Dawkins also avers more graphically, "a body is the gene's way of preserving the genes unaltered" (1976, p. 22). He disclaims the view that gene selfishness is the way things ought to be and concedes that environmental factors play a role in determining altruistic behavior. Despite these caveats, the hegemony of the gene in his account does not support his assertion that gene determinism can be avoided. Although E. O. Wilson takes a more benevolent view of the direction of evolution, he nevertheless argues that genes predispose people toward cooperative behavior. He writes: "Such a process repeated through thousands of generations inevitably gave birth to the moral sentiments. . . . These instincts are vividly experienced by every person variously as conscience, self-respect, remorse, empathy, shame, humility, and moral outrage" (Wilson, 1998, p. 253).

Many evolutionary biologists and psychologists, in conformity with Dawkins's general view, argue that even complex human behaviors that involve cooperation are undertaken in the interest of survival and are genetically anchored. In an oft-cited example, I. M. Cosmides and J. Tooby, invoking both computational and genetic models, are reported to appeal to the famous prisoners' dilemma, a situation invented by game theorists in which alternatives for gaining freedom are based on the willingness of a pair of prisoners to incriminate one another. One prisoner is offered freedom on the condition that he or she confess and the other prisoner does not. If one confesses, the nonconfessing prisoner receives a heavy sentence; if both confess, they receive moderate sentences; and if neither confesses, sentences will be light. It is obviously in the interest of both not to confess (van der Steen, 1999; Langton, 1996, pp. 82–85). It is concluded on the basis of experiment that cooperation becomes feasible when rules of detecting cheating are learned over a series of tries. Acquired in the interest of self-preservation, genetically anchored rules of prudence determine the outcome (Wyschogrod, 1990).[1]

What is important is not only the claim that self-preservation may be behind cooperation but also that if Dawkins's version of neo-Darwinism is to be believed, the purpose of replication is neither the perpetuation of the species nor of the individual organism as the unit of natural selection but rather the conservation of the active germ replicator. To be sure, difference does not disappear, because each gene is defined in relation to alternative forms of the gene (the alleles), but the gene remains the unit of selection. The germ-line replicator is for Dawkins the "ancestor of an indefinitely long line of descendents" (1982, p. 83). Science fiction aficionados are likely to recognize that replicants serve to expand power either through deception, a technique not foreign to intruder genes, or by virtue of a sheer increase in the number of copies. Although some germ lines may die out, "any germ line replicator is potentially immortal" (Dawkins, 1982, p. 83). Crucial for the understanding of the Pythagorean body in the context of evolutionary biology is the claim that a gene line has no rigid boundaries, that it is potentially immortal, and that the purpose of natural selection is preservation of the gene line.

Whose Life Is It Anyway? Artificial Life

The interpretation of the body as code lends itself readily to the modeling of artificial life, life that is humanly contrived, through the use of computational prototypes, thus further attesting the pervasiveness of Pythagorean design. In turning to computational paradigms for understanding biological life, Christopher Langton asserts that life is not a property of matter but rather of its organization, for which computational models are eminently suited, so that now research can be directed away from "the mechanics of life to the logic of life" (1996, p. 47). It could be argued that the creation of artificial life would be served most effectively by relying on the organic chemicals of carbon-chain chemistry. Apart from the practical difficulties inherent in this effort, Langton contends that more can be learned from the "creation of life *in silico*" in that it opens up the "space of *possible* life" (1996, p. 50).

In essence, what is being sought is the generating of behavior through the creation of computational automata. The effort to create robotic forms through the use of available technologies has a long history, including the development of such humanoid replicas as clockwork automata (Beaune, 1990). By contrast, present models see the genotype as "a bag of instructions" that specifies behaviors or modifies structures that are activated through them. It can be concluded that now the human agent steps out of the picture as breeder and allows the computer to engage in the process of natural selection (Langton, 1996).

In one well-known simulation system, the Tierra, even the earlier proxies for the human agent, the algorithmic breeding agents, are eliminated. The computer programs themselves compete for CPU (computer processing unit) time and memory space. Programs piggyback on themselves: To be reproduced they simply require the act of self-reproduction. Langton maintains, "The programs reproduce themselves and the ones that are better at this task take over the population" (1996, p. 88). In a recent popular account of the work of Alexander Rich and his associates, it has been reported that actual DNA too can overwrite itself as it is being read in accordance with the direction of curvature of its shape (Hilts, 1999, p. 12).

Thomas S. Ray, the developer of Tierra, contends, "There is no connection between the Tierran world and the real physical world. I have created a virtual universe that is self-contained" (Ray, 1996, p. 12). It may be argued that computers can only do what their programs enable them to do but cannot generate mutations or novel animal behavior. However, it is now claimed that, if sufficiently powerful, computers are unpredictable. Langton writes, "It is impossible to determine any non-trivial property of the future behavior of a sufficiently powerful computer from a mere inspection of its program and its initial state. The only way to determine phenotype changes is to run the program" (1996, p. 58).

The Body of Altruism

For the alterity-altruist, the body of the other as other is not the body understood as the coded information that governs its form and behaviors, nor even as the body as given in ordinary experience. The alterity-altruist does not deny that, in our everyday relations with others, we see the body as an ensemble of characteristics—tall or short, agile or awkward—but first and foremost, the body is seen as sentient, capable of suffering. As such, the vulnerable body of the other imposes on the self an obligation to use its body and extended powers—its goods, skills, and institutional resources—to relieve the distress of the other. I call this sentient body, as both agent and recipient of altruistic acts, the "lived body," an expression coined by Edmund Husserl (1970, pp. 16–17), originator of the phenomenological approach to philosophy, and later adopted by Maurice Merleau-Ponty (1962).[2]

For the alterity-altruist, the suffering of the other is seen as always ahead of efforts to ameliorate it, and thus it provides a spur for ongoing altruistic action. Alterity-altruism is intrinsically excessive and reflects a willingness to expend more, up to and including the body of the altruist (Wyschogrod, 1990). Not everyone sees the body of the other as issuing an imperative to sacrifice the self in the other's interest, in that such imperatives may be obscured by the social and cultural self-presentation of the other or by the ingrained egoism of the observer. Nor do all who grasp the other as issuing imperatives respond. I argue, however, that without denying the context-laden situations in which others are seen, the body of the other in its primordiality is apprehended as mandating other-regarding behavior and is the precondition for less self-sacrificing modes of right conduct, such as those deemed obligatory by theories of virtue or utility.

By contrast, the Pythagorean body can be viewed as an etiolation, a thinning out to the vanishing point of the body's materiality so that nothing is left of the lived body but the abstractness of code. It could be argued that the concept of the lived body was not developed by phenomenological philosophers as a response to the view of the body as code but rather of the body as a physical object, similar to other objects, as envisaged by philosophies influenced by early modern science. To perceive the body as object is, for Husserl, Merleau-Ponty, and other phenome-nologists, a misreading of self-world transactions, a construing of the body in terms of matter, motion, and force, when, in their view, one's body is not an object among others but the subject of experience. As William James put the matter ear-lier: "The body is the storm center, the origin of coordinates, the constant place of stress" (1912/1976, p. 86).

It could be maintained that the body as ruled by the physical laws of early modern science is, at least in part, accessible to sensory experience and thus open to phenomenological recasting, whereas the Pythagorean body lies outside the range of everyday perceptual experience. It can be argued in response that the acu-ity of the description of the lived body is not contingent on the philosophical claims to which it is a response, whether they are the claims of early modern sci-ence or of computational modeling, but rather on its usefulness in describing the body's engagement in the world. What is missing in Merleau-Ponty's account of the body (and those of other phenomenologists) is the claim that the body as sen-sate is always (and already) an ethical body. Thus, although their work serves as an entering wedge for seeing the body otherwise than as Pythagorean, the full range of meanings of the body as sensate and, as such, of the suffering body as a source of ethical meaning has not yet been grasped.

In sum, the utility of the Pythagorean modeling of the body as relevant to the understanding of animal life is not here called into question. Computational ex-plorations of the mechanisms of the selection of traits may have significant conse-quences for the further discernment of genetic processes and their implications for medicine, ecobiology, and the like. I claim that even if Pythagorean bodies ex-hibit behaviors that appear to have ethical import—egoistic or altruistic—as in-sensate, such bodies cannot generate or express ethical meaning. In addition, when the other is seen as a vulnerable corporeal subject, there is no reason to fall back on consciousness as the ghost in a machinelike body as the default position, as it were, to explain altruistic conduct. At the same time, there is no need to adopt the view that altruistic motives are identical with the brain states that accompany them. Radical altruism requires a body-subject that exists as the indissoluble unity of consciousness and the sensate.

Milbank's Objections

In posing the sensate body as the mode of corporeality to be linked with alterity-altruism, I have argued that a body that is subject to pain and suffering is appre-hended as demanding other-regarding behavior. Some cogent criticisms of radical altruism that depend on experiencing the other as an ethical datum must be ad-dressed if the position is to be sustained. John Milbank mounts a theological argu-ment against radical altruism, asserting that it is not the body of the other as other but the resurrection body that is the true ground of ethics.[3] I hope to show that, although Milbank might be expected to base his position on premises radically opposed to those of evolutionary biologists such as Dawkins, to the contrary, self-preservation and survival are at the heart of his account, and these goals are linked to the Pythagorean body.

By Milbank's account (1999), recent tendencies to base altruism on the apprehension of the other are incoherent. Instead he espouses the view that reciprocal gift-giving as communal exchange is preferable to radical altruism and that this ideal can be fully realized only in an afterlife. Milbank contends that for alterity-altruists "the highest ethical gesture is a sacrificial self-offering which expects no benefit in return," a gift of self with no expectation of reciprocity (1990, p. 33). He concedes that for alterity-altruism as represented in the thought of Emmanuel Levinas (1969), any attempt to grasp the other through cognitive acts or acts of empathy or sympathy reduces the other to the measure of one's own consciousness and thus renders radical alterity self-refuting. In response, Milbank notes that phenomenologists acknowledge that not only the other but also many phenomena are apprehended in a partial manner, that is, their depths and even their surfaces withhold themselves from perceptual grasp. For example: "We never feel our words exactly capture a rainbow" (Milbank, 1999, p. 34). Thus we may appropriate phenomena cognitively and emotionally while acknowledging that these phenomena may be attended by an aura of mystery. In sum, Milbank contends, phenomenologists recognize that, when consciousness intends or aims at its objects, the meaning-possibilities of phenomena are preset but that those phenomena may nevertheless not reveal themselves fully.

The alterity-altruist may reply that some entities manifest themselves in multiple ways. For Levinas, the human face can be given as a visual form but may also reveal itself more primordially as an enigma that is given as always (and already) having ethical meaning. For Levinas, the body of the other is first apprehended as opaque, as resistant to manipulation or possession, in contrast to the incompleteness that surrounds phenomena. Ethical meaning is not apprehended as incomplete but rather gives itself not as a visible form but as a demand that no violence be committed against the other (Levinas, 1982). There is no translation rule that would convert this imperative into a missing part of an "is." (It could be argued somewhat analogously that an ecobiologist might say that nature can be seen as corporeal and vulnerable and as issuing an imperative to do no harm to the ecosystem, even if the system can also be seen alternatively as the complex subject of scientific inquiry.) In sum, Milbank fails to distinguish the givenness of the other as enigmatic from the incomplete mode of givenness of certain phenomena.

Milbank's effort to show that alterity-altruism is incoherent reflects another, quite different, misunderstanding of otherness. He contends that altruism based on otherness provides the altruist with the satisfaction of helping others and is thus not entirely self-sacrificial. Radical altruism terminates in egoism because knowing oneself as giver is already a source of self-satisfaction. Such gratification, he continues, is unavoidable, for even if one-way giving remains an unfulfillable aspiration whose consummation is precluded by my death, I can still imagine the other's future receipt of the gift with pleasure. But Milbank fails to acknowledge a crucial condition of alterity-altruism: As altruist, one experiences oneself as the recipient of an imperative, so that one signs on, as it were, before one can identify oneself as a giver. One is committed to obedience prior to understanding why or how the imperative is to be implemented. The view of the alterity-altruist can be seen as psychologically plausible in the light of what is known as the James-Lange theory of emotion, according to which behavior may precede the emotion believed to cause it.

Milbank again misses the point when he recasts alterity-altruists as, in effect, creating a system of replicants. The other who is not grasped in some way perceptually and cognitively, he insists, is an empty abstraction, so that, in the absence of differentia, every other is the equivalent of every other other. Milbank here affixes a verbal or terminological, rather than an existential or lived, meaning to the word *other*. In Milbank's restrictive reading, *other* means just another like this one or, more simply, just one more. But the *other* of the alterity-altruist refers to an embodied being who is already an individual. In conformity with Aristotle's dictum that matter individuates, for the alterity-altruist imperatives apply to singular bodies.

Linked to Milbank's contention that the other is a meaningless term is his claim that otherness entails homogeneity, the likeness of each other to all others, so that one responds to all others who enter one's purview in the same way. Thus Milbank contends that there can be no grounds for discriminating between worthy and unworthy others, between sham and genuine suffering. What is intended by alterity-altruists, however, is that an individual other in her or his fleshly comportment is a precondition for ethics and that this precondition does not yet require determining what specific action is to be taken. Far from precluding the need for the creation of laws and normative institutions for the resolution of moral dilemmas, the development of legal and social structures is crucial but remains contingent on a prior condition, the breaking in of the other in her or his fleshly specificity into one's self-satisfaction. It is in the light of this breaking in that a social space for normative reflection and action is opened.

Death and the Resurrected Body

The most important part of Milbank's argument is the claim that alterity-altruism is death driven, that the other's vulnerability is premised on the fact that he or she will at some point die: Vulnerability is contingent on mortality. It could be said in reply that ethics is grounded in the suffering body and not in the body as mortal. Although alterity-altruists might refrain from endorsing this claim, it could be argued further, as Stoicism maintains, that death provides relief from suffering and, in that regard, constitutes a benefit.

Milbank's criticisms of an ethics of alterity that I have thus far considered presuppose that alterity-altruists espouse an abstract conception of otherness that is both contentless and nonmaterial. Thus he attributes to the alterity-altruist's view of the other one of the principal characteristics of the Pythagorean body, its nonmateriality and abstractness. But, in fact, it is Milbank's own view of the body that approximates features of the Pythagorean body that I attributed earlier to many evolutionary biologists.

Recall that Milbank alleges that alterity-altruists are death driven. By making death the ultimate source of altruism and altruism the source of ethics, alterity-altruists, he contends, are compelled to dissociate a belief in immortality and resurrection from what they hold to be good. Milbank argues that a network of complex reciprocal acts of giving that would result in joyful communion and the happiness of each is preferable to self-sacrificing altruism. His insistence that an afterlife is needed to ensure this outcome is remarkably reminiscent of Immanuel Kant's argument for immortality. According to Kant (1790/1951, p. 294), if one has lived in conformity with the moral law, one deserves to be happy, but because happiness cannot be achieved within the compass of the present life, it can only be attained in a postmortem existence. For Milbank, what he calls an "eschatological banquet" is impossible in this life. What is more, only an afterlife can provide the time to redress the grievances of those whom one has injured (Milbank, 1999). None but an infinitely extending community of those possessing a resurrection body can hope to fulfill these conditions. I shall not enter into the conception of punishment, neglected by Milbank, that is often a corollary of this view and that precludes anticipating bliss for everyone; I turn instead to some implications of Milbank's account of resurrection.

For Milbank, to be resurrected is to be in some fashion continuous with the being one is when alive and also to be bodily incorporated into the divine life. We may presume that this replica of oneself is one in which the dross of immorality is refined away and only those qualities that can contribute to a social whole powered by love are selected for everlasting life. However far removed it may seem to be from the premises of evolutionary biology, is this claim not in an important respect a variant of Dawkins's definition of the germ-line as "that part of bodies that is potentially immortal in the form of reproductive copies" (1982, p. 83)? The resurrection body as Milbank construes it is not a replica of the phenomenological body but an altered body, a mutation that demands self-preservation in the interest of perpetuating its own joy and the joy of others. But, it must be asked, is such a resurrection body an ethical body if no thought is given to the living? Moreover, if the one who is resurrected remains attentive to the suffering of those left behind, how joyful and, more to the point, how moral would such an eschatological banquet be?

NOTES

1. This argument is summarized in the larger context of distinguishing prudential motives from altruistic motives that may determine the actions of saints.

2. Phenomenological philosophy, a school of thought that began by stressing the active role of consciousness, was at first identified with idealism but later focused on descriptions of the concrete world. However, neither thinker posits the absolute alterity of the other person. For Husserl, the other is apprehended through empathy and thus as another "me." Although Merleau-Ponty thought of the body as a vehicle of meaning, he saw meaning as arising in acts of reciprocal comprehension rather than in the apprehension of the otherness of the other person.

3. Milbank disputes the view that theology can adapt the methods of the social or natural sciences to its efforts at self-legitimation. His position, often referred to as radical or-

thodoxy, uses postmodern strategies to restore the possibility of theology's positioning itself as a master discourse.

REFERENCES

Beaune, J. C. (1990). The classical age of automata: An impressionistic survey from the sixteenth to the nineteenth century (I. Patterson, Trans.). In M. Feher, R. Nadoff, & N. Tazzi (Eds.), *Fragments of a human body* (Pt. 1). New York: Zone Books.

Boden, M. A. (Ed.). (1996). *The philosophy of artificial life.* New York: Oxford University Press.

Dawkins, R. (1976). *The selfish gene.* Oxford: Oxford University Press.

Dawkins, R.(1982). *The extended phenotype: The gene as the unit of selection.* Oxford: Freeman.

Feher, M., Nadoff, R., & Tazzi, N. (Eds.). (1990). *Fragments of a human body* (Pt. 1). New York: Zone Books.

Hilts, P. J. (1999, June 29). Left-handed NA is no fluke, study says. *New York Times*, p. F12.

Husserl, E. (1970). *The crisis of European sciences and transcendental phenomenology* (D. Carr, Trans.). Evanston, IL: Northwestern University Press.

James, W. (1976). *Essays in radical empiricism.* Cambridge: Harvard University Press. (Original work published 1912)

Kant, I. (1951). *Critique of judgment* (J. H. Bernard, Trans.) New York: Haffner Press. (Original work published 1790)

Langton, C. G. (1996).Artificial life. In M. A. Boden (Ed.), *The philosophy of artificial life* (pp. 39–108). New York: Oxford University Press.

Levinas, E. (1969). *Totality and infinity* (A. Lingis, Trans.). The Hague: Martinus Nijhoff.

Merleau-Ponty, M. (1962). *Phenomenology of perception* (C. Smith, Trans.) London: Routledge and Kegan Paul.

Milbank, J. (1990). *Theology and social theory: Beyond secular reason.* Oxford: Blackwell.

Milbank, J. (1999).The ethics of self-sacrifice. *First Things, 91,* 33–38.

Polkinghorne, J. (1996). *Beyond science: The wider human context.* Cambridge: Cambridge University Press.

Ray, T. S. (1996). An approach to the synthesis of life. In M. A. Boden (Ed.), *The philosophy of artificial life* (pp. 111–145). New York: Oxford University Press.

Rolston, H., III (1999). *Genes, genesis and God: Values and their origins in natural and human history.* Gifford Lecture, University of Edinburgh, 1997–1998. Cambridge: Cambridge University Press.

Urmson, J. O. (1958). Saints and heroes. In A. I. Melden (Ed.), *Essays in moral philosophy* (pp. 198–216). Seattle: University of Washington Press.

van der Steen, W. J. (1999). Evolution and altruism. *Journal of Value Inquiry, 33*(1), 11–29.

Wilson, E. O. (1998). *Consilience: The unity of knowledge.* New York: Knopf.

Wyschogrod, E. (1990). *Saints and postmodernism: Revisioning moral philosophy.* Chicago: University of Chicago Press.

3

Morality, Altruism, and Love

JEROME KAGAN

Humans have the capacity to judge others as good, to feel empathic with their needs and states, and to act in ways that benefit them. Agents who exploit these competences experience a feeling of self-enhancement. This emotionally toned reciprocal relation between persons is probably unique to our species and a necessary requirement for a civil society. I begin with a description of actual psychological phenomena, rather than definitions of the familiar words *moral, altruistic,* and *love,* because each of these words has multiple meanings. That is, each is linked to semantic networks that vary in their sense and referential meaning; therefore, the meanings of the three concepts in the title of this chapter depend on the specific network activated. The word *wolf* provides an example. The semantic network dominated by the concepts *carnivore, wild,* and *dangerous* generates a meaning different from the one dominated by the concepts *vertebrate, mammal,* and *evolution* (remember, the wolf is the phylogenetic origin of the gentle beagle). The network for altruism that contains representations of bees, ants, and porpoises generates a meaning that is distinct from the one that features representations of nurses, teachers, and motorists helping strangers fix flat tires. Even though a porpoise and a stranded motorist are helped by the action of a conspecific, only in the latter case did the helping agent infer the need of the other. But that feature awards a special meaning to the term *altruism*. Because almost every behavior—animal or human —has more than one set of causal conditions, it is usually not possible to infer the state of the organism from observed actions.

Further, every network of representations can emphasize either features shared with other objects and events, on the one hand, or features that render the referent distinctive, on the other. The network for *wolf* that emphasizes fur, four limbs, and internal digestive organs refers to features shared with other mammals. By contrast, the network dominated by the features hunting in a pack, howling at night, and killing sheep distinguishes wolves from most mammals. Analogously, the network for altruism that emphasizes an animal who benefits from the behavior of another refers to features shared with many animals. But the representation of a person stopping on a highway to help a stranger refers to a distinctively human feature.

The present discussion of morality, altruism, and love awards salience to those meaning networks that refer to distinctively human features, rather than those shared with other primates, because I believe that the automatic tendency to infer the thoughts and feelings of others, the continual concern with the evaluation of good and bad events, and the capacity for shame, guilt, and pride are uniquely human competences.

Morality

Humans act in order to experience two distinctly different psychological states. One is a feeling that originates in changes in one or more of the sensory modalities; for example, an increase in excitation, as in sweet tastes and soft touches, or a decrease in excitation, as in pain. This motive for sensory pleasure is present in all sensate animals.

The second desired state, unique to humans, has its origin in thought rather than in sensation and involves a relation between representations of ethical standards and a particular action, feeling, or thought. This relation assumes two forms. On the one hand, individuals wish to avoid situations in which there is an inconsistency between their standards and their actions or intentions because such inconsistencies create the unpleasant states of uncertainty, shame, guilt, or anxiety. On the other hand, individuals try to act in ways that create consonance between their representations of an ideal state of affairs and a particular behavior, thought, or feeling (Kagan, 1998). When consonance occurs, the person experiences momentarily a feeling that one might call enhanced virtue. Although the desires to avoid the dissonance that follows violation of standards and to attain the consonance that follows the meeting of standards lead to different behaviors and feelings, both states depend on a cognitive evaluation of the relation between an idea and some response.

Economists ignore the distinction between a state of sensory pleasure and states of dissonance or consonance with a standard because these phenomena resist exact quantification. Economists simply declare that all economic decisions are based on the desire to maximize satisfaction and leave to their readers the task of detecting the precise meaning of satisfaction.

Primatologists select different features as referents for morality. Frans de Waal (1996), for example, nominated responses such as food sharing, grooming, and other acts that benefit a conspecific as signs of morality. He could not select an appreciation of the concepts of good and bad, capacity for guilt, or a rationally derived conclusion that an action was in the best interest of self or society because he cannot know the animal's internal state. However, food sharing and grooming can be the product of instrumental learning; hence, their display does not require the assumption that the helping animal is aware of the state of the conspecific it is aiding. Animals often share food in order to avoid attack for failing to do so. Humans share resources, often with strangers, in order to avoid a state of guilt. The motive to avoid attack and the desire to avoid guilt are psychologically different aversions.

I do not suggest that the human moral sense is completely discontinuous with all primate dispositions. It is likely that the infant's ability to feel sensory discomfort and comfort, along with the young child's sensitivity to adult behaviors that signify desired and undesired behaviors, are derivatives of similar primate competences. Monkeys and apes have a keen sensitivity to the facial expressions, vocal signals, and postures of others. But five novel abilities were added when Homo sapiens appeared in Africa about 150,000 years ago:

1. The ability and habitual tendency to infer the thoughts and feelings of others
2. Self-awareness
3. Application of the categories "good" and "bad" to objects, events, and self
4. Reflection on past actions
5. The ability to decide that a particular action could have been suppressed

The combination of these five features created a novel, biologically prepared competence that begins its growth by the second birthday and is usually mature by the beginning of the third decade. The first signs of a moral sense can be observed in any setting with children. A 2-year-old who looks warily toward a parent after spilling food on her clothes announces, in face and posture, that she knows she has committed an act that violates what is proper. But in order to infer the more inclusive category of "bad acts," children have to discover connections among three different events: their actions, the outcomes of those actions, and, especially, the adult's subsequent reactions to the child. Creation of this category is delayed because the ability to make categorical inferences based on a temporal sequence of events is fragile in the 1st year. The infant mind is not biologically ready to discover the concept "punishable behavior." The mind of the 3-year-old is ready to make that discovery.

However, acquisition of this concept cannot explain why children impose a "good/bad" label on punished actions—usually aggression toward another, property destruction, disobedience, and failure to keep the body clean. One argument begins with the reasonable assumption that the infants' regular experiences with sensory states of pleasure and discomfort create two distinct schematic categories for feeling states that, at this early age, are free of symbolism. As a result, an experience that generates one or the other of these states will be assimilated to one of these categories. The second assumption is that discrepant events that cannot be assimilated immediately generate a state of uncertainty (Kagan, 1984). If the young child does not understand why an adult disapproved of or punished an action, he or she feels uncertain, and this feeling will be assimilated to the schematic category for discomfort. Children become both linguistically compe-tent and aware of their feeling states during the second year. Therefore, when a state of uncertainty following punishment for violation of a sanctioned behavior pierces consciousness, the child is motivated to categorize it symbolically.

The symbolic category applied is likely to be close in sense meaning to the adult understanding of the word *bad* because adults have used that label to name unpleasant events. Initially, actions are the only members of the category; but, by 4 or 5 years of age, objects, feelings, thoughts, and the self have become exemplars. When that growth in cognitive talent has occurred, individuals try continually to find, or to produce, evidence, usually through their actions, that affirms the self's membership in the category "good" and to try to avoid any information that im-plies the self is "bad." Each affirmation produces a state of "enhanced virtue."

The ability to empathize with the distress of another, a second independent human competence that has obvious relevance for morality, also emerges by the second birthday (Zahn-Waxler, Cole, & Barrett, 1991). Two- to 3-year-olds are able to infer the feelings of another and to show signs of tension if another person is in distress. Some may offer penance if they believe they caused the distress.

Although 3-year-olds are aware that objects, acts, and self can be good or bad, they remain protected from the feeling of guilt that follows the recognition that they could have suppressed an act that violated a personal standard. The 3-year-old knows that breaking a glass is wrong but has no conception that the behavior that broke the glass could have been avoided. The experience of guilt requires the advances in cognitive ability, usually between 5 and 7 years of age, that allow the child to rerun the behavioral sequence mentally and decide whether the action could have been suppressed. If she believes the action could have been avoided, she is responsible and, therefore, is likely to experience guilt. Thus the capacities to apply good and bad to events, objects, and self, to feel guilt and empathy, and to be aware of self as an object motivate humans to spend much of their waking days af-firming the virtue of the self and avoiding any signs of its compromise. As we shall see, this imperative makes a contribution to altruism and love.

The positing of a biological foundation for human morality does not mean that the details of one particular ethical system are more natural or more adaptive than another. Humans inherit an ability to acquire language, but no one language is more natural or adaptive than another. A concern with good and bad is an easy classification for children to learn because of the structure of the human brain. But the bases for many of the specific actions, feelings, and thoughts that are cate-gorized as good or bad lie in the local culture, beyond the genome's reach.

Altruism

My discussion of altruism focuses on the network that emphasizes the helping agent's awareness of the need of another and the intention to be of assistance rather than the network favored by behavioral biologists that refers only to behav-iors of an agent that benefit another. Biologists are unable to theorize about the intentions of bees, mice, or monkeys; hence they categorize as altruistic any behavior that benefits another. But that decision awards a special, albeit legitimate, meaning to the term *altruism*. If someone puts an old television set in the garbage and a poor passerby takes the set home for personal use, the former has not committed an altruistic act, even though the latter individual benefited. Indeed, even if an action did not help another, the agent could be viewed as altruistic. An adult who jumps in a cold lake to save a child but, because of incompetence, drowns both of them has committed an altruistic act because the adult's intention was benevolent. Many parents who have altruistic motives toward their children behave in ways that do not benefit the child. But the central semantic feature of the network for human altruism is not the outcome of an action but a behavior that was preceded by an intention to help someone perceived to be in need.

Even though action motivated by the awareness of need in a person is the primary feature of human altruism, there are, nonetheless, at least three different bases for behaviors that do help another. One motive serves the moral sense. The helping agent acts in accord with a personal ethical standard to aid those in distress in order to experience a feeling of enhanced virtue or to avoid a feeling of compromised virtue because the agent was able, but failed, to help the other.

Second, love for another can also motivate altruistic acts. That is, the helping agent aids the beloved either because of gratitude for the pleasures the latter has supplied or to attain the vicarious emotion that follows enhancing the state of a person with whom one is identified. The helping agent experiences vicariously the pleasure he or she assumes the love object is experiencing. This state can be distinguished, at least subjectively, from the feeling of enhanced virtue.

A third basis for behavior that helps others is most different from the first two. Some individuals will aid another in order to create a state of indebtedness in the latter; in some cases the agent intends to exploit that indebtedness at a later time. Thus public acts that appear to an observer to be equally altruistic can serve different intentions. A visit to a relative in a hospital, for example, can be motivated by any of these three bases for altruism.

Love

The concept of love, which biologists do not ascribe to animals, refers to an emotional state rather than to an intention, action, or moral judgment (Singer, 1984). However, like the concepts moral and altruistic, love, too, is part of different meaning networks. Two networks are applied frequently, the other two less often.

The network most often activated by contemporary Europeans and Americans makes sexual attraction to and arousal by another person the primary feature—this is the love of popular songs and paperback novels. However, most languages contain other words for this sensory state, which St. Augustine called *cupiditas*, when it occurs without reference to other psychological features of the beloved, especially features that the lover regards as good and would like to possess. If respected novelists are a source of clues to the qualities that, with sexual arousal, generate love, then loyalty, strength, special talents, wisdom, maturity, gentleness, empathy, nurturance, wealth, power, and status, along with physical attractiveness, appear to be the primary features that create the state that St. Augustine called *caritas*.

In Bernhard Schlink's 1997 novel *The Reader*, a 15-year-old boy falls in love with an illiterate older woman because she treats him as an adult in their regular sexual encounters. The adolescent's participation in a mature sexual relationship permitted him to feel the enhanced status of an adult. Individuals fall in love with different beloveds because they value different qualities. Some value attractiveness, others intellect, gentleness, wealth, power, or a particular talent. Each hierarchy of preference renders the agent maximally receptive to loving a particular class of individuals. Knights were more enhanced by romantic relations with a woman of nobility than with an equally beautiful peasant woman they had bedded.

A second meaning network for love refers to feelings toward a person who is a source of pleasures that are not obviously sexual. The child says and may believe that he loves his mother because she provides sensory gratifications and protections from the unpleasant uncertainties of harm, distress, and abandonment. Current psychological theory calls this relation attachment. Freud's desire for theoretical parsimony motivated him to declare that this state was libidinal.

A third, less often exploited network refers to feelings toward others who possess qualities that the lover wishes to command, even though the target is a source of neither sensory pleasure nor sexual arousal. If the lover enjoys an affectively close relationship with the admired target, the former will feel enhanced by the relationship. This meaning of love, which we alluded to in the section on altruism, has an ethical component, for the beloved possesses qualities that the agent regards as good.

A similar mechanism applies when individuals say they love a particular object or place. A person who owns one of only 20 eighteenth-century porcelain clocks made by a renowned craftsman is enhanced by its presence in the living room. Others are enhanced by a weekend home on a high mountain because of the knowledge that the aesthetic arrangement of ridge and valley is rare and difficult to attain and, therefore, that only a few can enjoy the privilege of possession. Agents are enhanced by these impersonal targets because they match private standards for the ideal exemplar of that category; hence possession of the object adds to the individual's feeling of virtue. This state is different from the sensory pleasures of a deep sleep after fatigue, of cool water when thirsty, or of a warm fire when cold. These events bring sensory pleasure, but few individuals fall in love with beds, water, or fire because these objects are easy to obtain and the features that permit the sensory pleasure are inherent in their structure.

The Notion of the Ideal

It is not clear how individuals acquire representations of ideal persons, objects, or places that can become love objects. At least two independent processes seem relevant. First, the child learns from the local culture the qualities that are desirable to obtain by noting which characteristics are praised, as well as inferring those qualities that are the opposite of those that are criticized.

A second contribution to the construction of the ideal relies on appreciating the difficulty of attaining a desired quality. Mathematicians claim that the difficulty of apprehending a new solution is a critical feature of proofs that are deemed beautiful. The 10-year-old has learned that receiving a grade of 100 on every school quiz is praiseworthy but difficult. The adolescent knows that continued poise with strangers, serving tennis aces, and refusing a temptation when there is an unpleasant obligation to perform are admired but difficult. Thus individuals who possess, or are believed to possess, desirable qualities that are difficult to acquire are admired and can become potential beloveds.

There is probably a biological contribution to a small number of idealized qualities. Infants prefer sweet tastes to sour ones, consonant chords to dissonant ones, circular patterns to linear designs, symmetry to asymmetry, and red to blue (Fantz, 1963; Haith, 1980; Zentner & Kagan, 1996). The attraction to particular physical features in humans must be based partly on a biological preference for relatively symmetrical, unblemished faces and particular body proportions. Local mores are always relevant, however; the seventeenth-century Dutch liked chubbier women than did the twentieth-century Dutch.

Biological processes probably influence preferences for certain human movements and render as ideal the individuals who display them. A point in any athletic contest can be gained with or without beauty of action. The movements of such athletes as Michael Jordan and Pete Sampras come close to that ideal.

Thus biology and experience are interlaced in the creation of representations of perfection in human traits and activities. These representations lie waiting for encounters with persons who possess the ideal features. The person who supplies the match becomes an admired target. Should the target and admiring agent develop an emotionally close relationship, the probability of the latter loving the former is increased.

Reflection on the historical changes in the referents for the family of feelings called love, contrasted to those of lust, suggest that humans cannot help but establish notions of ideal states that are difficult to attain, whether a feeling of spiritual merger with God, a totally gratifying relation with another person, or simply being in a state of passion in relation to some person, object, or activity. Sadly, when the desired object or state is gained, many individuals are likely to select another. The enemy of every ideal is its attainment.

A Modern Crisis

When a society's self-appointed commentators become concerned with a particular theme, it is usually because a large number of citizens have detected a discrepancy between current societal conditions and a representation of a past ideal. The convening of the conference from which this volume arose, which probably would not have occurred 40 years ago, implies that morality, altruism, and love have become more insistent nodes of uncertainty. A large number of Americans have detected a discrepancy between the current features of these concepts and those in the semantic networks they learned as adolescents. Similar discrepancies have occurred in the past; sixteenth-century scholars also complained that humans were excessively selfish and narcissistic.

A popular diagnosis of America's current state is that a combination of changes in family practices, social structure, media content, and institutional mores have made actualization of the self the only important ethical imperative, rather than one among several ideals. The socialization of middle-class children toward perfection of the self, usually through personal achievement, has been accompanied, not surprisingly, by increased suspicion of the motives of others. If everyone acts primarily out of self-interest, it would seem adaptive for all to adopt the same strategy. This seemingly rational conclusion, although it is fundamentally an ethical idea, is conducive to neither altruism nor love. A line in a Judy Collins song of the 1960s complained: "This is a bad time for lovers, everyone wants to be free." Perhaps that is why there is nostalgia for movies such as those based on Jane Austen's novels, in which both men and women were enhanced by their love relation with a partner.

Altruism and love may have become less frequent states in American society than they were 100 years earlier because the current generation of young adults was socialized to treat the self as the most significant object to enhance. The current ethical imperative demands that each person devote most of their energy to acquiring characteristics that add to the self's accomplishments, beauty, power, or wealth. Although enhancement of virtue can be achieved through loving another who possesses ideal qualities, those who are continually enhancing the self through personal perfection may have a less pressing need to be in a love relation.

In addition, the continuing dilution of shame over violating community norms, due partly to a lack of consensus on ethical values, leaves many adults with a weaker motive to affirm the self's virtue. That is, the praiseworthy standard to be tolerant of the values of all groups compromises the emotional power of any particular standard, leaving many without a pressing need to be loyal to local norms in order to gain a sense of virtue. Increased tolerance for the ethics of others and singular devotion to self-actualization, both of which are celebrated American values, appear to have exacted the price of making it harder to love another.

As contemporary women gain education and vocational goals, their need for enhancement by accomplished, talented men becomes weaker. The intensity of sexual arousal and the pleasures of erotic gratification have not changed, but the component of love that involves a feeling of enhanced virtue because of the relation may have been diluted. I am not certain, however, that most Americans would want to exchange the gain in tolerance and women's empowerment for the earlier emulation of intense loyal romantic love.

The Use of Money

Many industrialized states are pursuing the historically rare and difficult goal of attempting to make the symbolic signs of virtue attainable by the largest number of citizens. Although the specific qualities that signify virtue vary with culture and history, nonetheless, family pedigree, property, education, and particular skills, along with honesty, loyalty, courage, and charitable impulses, have been treated most of the time as symbolic of virtue. Although pedigree cannot be changed, the acquisition of wealth, education, skill, and character habits are potentially attainable by many, given the proper decisions by families, schools, and governments. However, the need to reduce racial and class tension in modern America, especially since the 1960s, mandated that neither family pedigree, religion, race, nor educational attainment be regarded as primary symbols of a person's worth. As a result, it was necessary that wealth ascend in importance.

Critics of American society, domestic and foreign, criticize America's excessive concern with money. Although this motive was also present in colonial times, it has now become an obsession. However, this preoccupation with the material is understandable if we acknowledge the community's commitment, over the past 30 years, to awarding more dignity to members of economically disadvantaged ethnic minorities. When Americans realized that public schools were failing the children of the poor, the earlier optimistic premise that attainment of an education and, as a result, upward mobility were possible for all with talent and motivation lost some of its validity. Hence many citizens were reluctant to use academic failure as a sign of an ethical flaw. If outstanding academic achievement was restricted too often to children born to parents living in clean, quiet, middle-class suburbs, it was not fair to blame poor children for events beyond their control.

The replacement of traditional symbols of virtue with the acquisition of wealth has allowed many more to harbor the belief, some might say the illusion, that this concrete sign of worth is attainable. This change in the ethical evaluation of money has had benevolent consequences. America is more tolerant of the values of ethnic minorities now than it was earlier in the century, and the burning of our cities has become a less common occurrence. Perhaps the celebration of wealth is the price America has to pay to enjoy a reduction in social tension. There are no free lunches.

The Influence of Evolutionary Biology

The premises of evolutionary biology, which imply that looking out for the self first is also characteristic of animals acting to maximize fitness in the service of fecundity (Wilson, 1975), have contributed to the resurgent narcissism. The belief that anger, self-interest, and competitiveness should not be suppressed because they are natural components of our evolutionary heritage has advantages in a society in which a large number of strangers must compete for a small number of positions of dignity, status, and economic security. Under these conditions it is adaptive to be self-interested and disadvantageous to be too cooperative, too loyal, too altruistic, or too reluctant to protest unjust advantage taken by another. But rather than acknowledge that the structure of our society has forced each of us to adopt self-interest as the first rule, many Americans find it more attractive to believe that this mood is an inevitable remnant of our animal heritage and, therefore, one we must learn to accept.

However, anyone with a modest knowledge of animal behavior and only minimal inferential skill could find examples of animal behavior to support almost any ethical message desired. Those who wish to sanctify the institution of marriage can point to the pair bonding of gibbons; those who think infidelity is more natural can point to chimpanzees. If one believes that people are naturally sociable, point to baboons; if one thinks they are solitary, point to orangutans. If one is certain males should dominate females, point to macaques; if one holds the opposite belief, point to bonobo chimps. Nature has enough diversity to fit almost any ethical taste. I believe it is an error to assume that any human ethic is a clear derivative of some particular class of animal behavior. The concern with right and wrong, the control of guilt, and the desire to feel virtuous are, like the appearance of milk in mammalian mothers, a unique event that is discontinuous with what came before. The continual desire to enhance the virtue of the self is a novel feature of our species. Although it has a firm foundation in the human genome, it is not an obvious derivative of the characteristics of apes and monkeys.

Humans are selfish and generous, aloof and empathic, hateful and loving, dishonest and honest, disloyal and loyal, cruel and kind, arrogant and humble; but many feel a little guilty over an excessive display of the first member of those pairs. The resulting dysphoria is unique to humans, and they are eager to have it ameliorated. Confession or psychotherapy are effective for some, especially if the priest or therapist is respected. I suspect that some people feel better when they learn that their less social urges are natural consequences of their phylogenetic history. The current high status of the biological sciences has made it possible for students of evolution to serve as therapists to the community.

Summary

The evolution of the human brain was accompanied by a preoccupation with good and bad, the ability to infer the feelings and thoughts of others, and a desire to enhance the self's virtue and to avoid experiences that might compromise the evaluation of virtue. These competencies are a component of some forms of altruism and of some love relationships. The current concern with perfecting the self and the increased tolerance for the ethical values of all groups have weakened the motive for altruism and love as attractive strategies to enhance the feeling of virtue that requires continuous affirmation. Some narcissism is probably necessary for hope, joy, and love, but an excessive level, like too much steak, sun, and strawberry shortcake, is malevolent. Montaigne's warning, "Moderation, above all," is a useful maxim to rehearse.

REFERENCES

de Waal, F. B. M. (1996). *Good natured*. Cambridge: Harvard University Press.
Fantz, R. L. (1963). Pattern vision in newborn infants. *Science, 140,* 296–297.

Haith, M. M. (1980). *Rules that babies look by*. Hillsdale, NJ: Erlbaum.

Kagan, J. (1984). *The nature of the child*. New York: Basic Books.

Kagan, J. (1998). *Three seductive ideas*. Cambridge: Harvard University Press.

Schlink, B. (1997). *The reader*. New York: Pantheon.

Singer, I. (1984). *The nature of love*. Vol. 2. Chicago: University of Chicago Press.

Wilson, E. O. (1975). *Sociobiology*. Cambridge: Harvard University Press.

Zahn-Waxler, C., Cole, P. M., & Barrett, K. C. (1991). Guilt and empathy. In J. Garber and K. A. Dodge (Eds.), *The development of emotion regulation and disregulation* (pp. 243–272). Cambridge: Cambridge University Press.

Zentner, M. R., & Kagan, J. (1996). Perception of music by infants. *Nature, 383,* 29.

4

The Tradition of Agape

STEPHEN G. POST

Altruism (*altrui*, "somebody else") is a broad classification for other-regarding actions. In the introduction to this book, the highest human expression of altruism, altruistic love, was briefly presented phenomenologically as involving both a judgment of worth and a related "affirmative affection." Altruistic love, which is uniquely human, is an intentional affirmation of the other, grounded in biologically given emotional capacities that are elevated by worldview (including principles, symbol, and myth) and imitation into the sphere of consistency and abiding loyalty. As such, altruistic love is the epitome of human altruism, which can take various forms, from respect to distributive justice. Altruistic love is closely linked to care, which is love in response to the other in need. It is closely linked to compassion, which is love in response to the other in suffering; to sympathy, which is love in response to the other who suffers unfairly; to beneficence, which is love acting for the well-being of the other; to companionship, which is love attentively present with the other in ordinary moments. Altruistic love is also linked to justice because the altruistic moral agent can respond in care only to a limited and proximate number of persons; the agent must therefore consider those larger social patterns of social and distributive injustice that deny all persons the goods necessary for essential well-being (Churchill, 1987). Hence the notion of "the love that does justice," associated with thinkers such as Reinhold Niebuhr and Martin Luther King Jr.

51

Altruistic love does not eclipse care of the self (to be loosely distinguished from self-indulgence), for without this the agent would eventually become unable to perform altruistic acts. Altruistic love does not demand self-immolation, although it can require significant self-sacrifice and even great risk when necessary. The core definition of altruistic love, however, is not sacrifice but rather an affective, affirming participation in the being of the other (Vacek, 1994). Love is first a response to the "present actuality" of another as he or she is in irrevocable worth, and it is secondarily the eudaemonistic encouragement toward fullness of being.

Altruistic love implies acts on behalf of the other, but beneficent acts can flow from a variety of motivations, such as duty, social conformism, or self-interest or from a disposition in which affective engagement does not rise to the level of love. Rescue behavior, for example, can be quite automatic and genetically determined to some extent, while lacking the affective feature of love. A Navy lieutenant, for example, although hampered by heavy winter clothing, "dove into the water, rescued the injured man before he could go down the second time and supported him against a strong tidal current until, with the aid of a line, he was brought alongside a lighter. But for his prompt and valiant action, performed at great risk to his own life, another man would undoubtedly have drowned." There are no obvious empathic considerations in this event, although there is in all probability a sense of duty and possibly a broader sense of moral imperative. In contrast, there are many rescue behaviors that do have a deeply affective and personal basis, from the desperate effort of a parent to save a child to messianic death on the cross as interpreted by Christian tradition.

As existential phenomenology underscores, altruistic love can be identified in part because it elicits a sense of joy in the other, who feels inwardly "a home in which it is safe to play" (Sadler, 1969, p. 212). In essence, "phenomenological investigations indicate that the playground of freedom is love" (Sadler, 1969, p. 219). The other who receives affective affirmation and all its sequelae, such as compassion and care, will sense a freedom from anxiety, that is, a certain safe haven in love in which the stresses of devaluation and isolation are removed. Scientific research supports these observations. For example, receiving love (defined as affective affirmation and absence of social isolation) was the most significant correlate of self-esteem in a sample of patients with multiple sclerosis (Walsh & Walsh, 1989). In a remarkable study, participants who merely watched a documentary film about the work of Mother Teresa of Calcutta showed a rise in the concentration of salivary immunoglobulin A (S-IgA), a marker of immune function; moreover, S-IgA levels remained high an hour after the film ended only in those participants who were asked to recall times in their lives when they felt most loved or loving (McClelland, 1986). Considerable work could be done on the physiological measures of giving and receiving altruistic love (Levin, 2000). It seems plausible to hypothesize that, emotionally and physiologically, human beings need altruistic love. Attachment theory suggests that the general need for love may derive from infant experience, as Jaak Panksepp discusses in his endocrinological study of the emergence of caring emotions on the mother-offspring axis of primates (1998). The work of Thomas R. Insel (1997) and C. Sue Carter (1998) further defines the endocrinology of maternal affection, focusing on oxytocin, which can convert a rat with no interest in offspring into a devoted and effective mother. Vasopressin is also involved (Insel, 1997). In humans, prolonged dependent infancy required a lengthened period of maternal altruism, for these two factors must obviously be kept in evolutionary balance. The evolution of altruism across species is linked to the preservation of offspring, and the most hard-core manifestation of this is the occurrence of maternal altruism. The human infant requires tremendous love, and this need does not disappear over the course of the life span; however, it is modified.

People tend to remember well over the years those from whom they receive warm, generous love; conversely, people also remember those who have shamed and humiliated them. The opposite of love can be observed in episodes of malignant social psychology, which include intimidation, stigmatization, invalidation, objectification, mockery, disparagement, and all those elements of human experience that convey to others that their very existence rests on a mistake (Kitwood, 1997). An opposite of love is cruelty, as the opposite of being is nonbeing (you are outside of my status hierarchy, my coalition, and therefore you do not and will not exist).

This memory of being loved seems important even to those whose cognitive capacities are either undeveloped or diminished. Jean Vanier, founder of l'Arche, an international movement of communities for people with intellectual disabilities, includes as the first feature of love, in the context of persons with retardation, the revelation of worth or value: "To reveal someone's beauty is to reveal their value by giving them time, attention, and tenderness" (1998, p. 22). Understanding, communication, and the celebration of the other's life in a personal manner convey a liberating and an empowering sense of worth. Tom Kitwood, in defining love within the context of dementia care, includes comfort in the original sense of tenderness, closeness, the calming of anxiety, and bonding (1997). People with severe dementia generally respond better to a caregiver whose affect is affirming in tone (Post, 2000).

Human Altruism: Discovery of the Other as Other

Altruism, even without the emotionally intense features that are associated with love, concerns the role of the other in moral experience. By the strictest definition, the altruist is someone who does something for the other and for the other's sake, rather than as a means to self-promotion or internal well-being—for example, the feeling of inner satisfaction. A more balanced definition would indicate that a sense of internal well-being as an indirect side effect of altruistic behavior does not imply that the agent's psychological motive is somehow impure and egoistic. By this definition, psychological altruism is more or less an established fact from the social scientific perspectives (Batson, 1991; Sober & Wilson, 1998). Many philosophers have argued for the reality of altruism, even if mixed with some subordinated egoistic desires to get what the self wants or needs, so long as the controlling aim is to give to the other what he or she may want or need (Hazo, 1967). Psychological altruism exists when the agent seeks to promote the well-being of the other "at least primarily for the other person's sake" (Hazo, 1967, p. 18). However, if altruistic acts are purely tactical, then there is no genuine psychological altruism present, and the action is primarily egoistic. In cases in which altruistic desires are primary, the agent might on some level seek satisfaction in a caring act well done or in his or her moral improvement, and the agent might have some subordinated hope for mutuality or recognition.

In the broadest terms, the altruist no longer sees the self as the only center of value but discovers the other as other (Levinas, 1969; Ogletree, 1985; Wyshogrod, 1990) rather than as an entity in orbit around the self in its egoism. Claims of the self to ontological centrality are set aside. As Ogletree writes:

> Apart from the "other" and the claims which she or he can make upon me, "Morality"—if one can call it that—is but the shrewd management of life's exigencies in light of my more or less arbitrary personal preferences. Whether it be refined and subtle and sophisticated, or careless and thoughtless and unreflective, such morality finally boils down to egoism, the assessment and utilization of all aspects of the world in terms of my own purposes. (1985, p. 35)

The contractarian theory of ethics, associated with John Rawls (1971) and the tradition of Thomas Hobbes, is dismissed here as pseudoethics because it only builds on the strategic self-interest of egoists attempting to maximize their future prospects. Some evolutionary biologists have endorsed this contractarian model of ethics, although the recent resurgence of group selection theory may imperil their analysis (Alexander, 1987). It is far from obvious that evolutionary biology and psychology require this too easy capitulation to enlightened egoism.

Altruism is virtue to all but the ethical egoist, who holds the view that even if psychological altruism exists it should never be implemented, for it only encourages dependence and weakness in the recipient. The ethical critique of egoism is most clearly associated with Emmanuel Levinas (1969). In contrast to Sartre, who viewed the decentering of the self through the presence of the other as a threat to personal integrity ("the look"), Levinas views this decentering as a call to moral life, which begins precisely when the egoism of the self has been called into question quite literally by the face of the other. The other's expression summons me to take another center of meaning into my world.

Yet it is precisely the authenticity of this discovery of the other as other that some social scientists and evolutionary biologists doubt. Their facile assertions of universal egoism in the context of kin selection and reciprocal altruism or of psychological egoism in the social sciences undermine our ideals with regard to the moral summons of the other into any form of altruism, let alone altruistic love. Yet as other sections of this book point out, these assertions are themselves under vigorous attack and are not holding up too well.

This discovery of the other as other is often the subject of novels and plays that capture the moral transformation of the cold uncaring egoist into an empathic other-regarding presence. In many cases, these scenarios involve persons whose transformation is grounded in their having been diagnosed with a life-threatening illness that highlights the shallow nature of their egoistic pursuits and leads to an emotional and conceptual migration toward the ontological reality of the other. There is an affective aspect of other-regard in all its forms. Augustine, Thomas Aquinas, Adam Smith, David Hume, and others rightly emphasized that the moral life and inclination is to a significant degree a matter of an underlying affective attunement to the other.

This biological-affective approach to ethics as recognition of the other as other had its firmest roots in the Scottish Enlightenment's urge to find a constant force in human nature akin to gravity in the universe. In other words, there must be a force in human experience that creates a pull between persons as gravity does between planets. Such a force could not possibly be reason alone, although reason has an instrumental role in clarifying the facts of any given case in order to discern the fittingness of sympathy. The Scottish moralists recognized that only such an affective power could lead to helping actions. Sympathy (the word *empathy* not yet having been coined) was the glue tying together the social and moral world, without which there would be no connections between persons, as there would be none between planets in a universe without gravity. One can thus speak of the natural law of empathy and/or sympathy. As for a formal distinction, I define empathy as the ability to feel the emotional state of another and sympathy as a narrower sort of empathy in the context of another's need or suffering.

But for all the wonders of empathy, how strong a force is it? The study of empathy in nonhuman animals, especially ones with whom we share much genetically, should be welcome even as the distinctive features of the human are asserted. Human empathy is mediated by the moral imagination and culture. If I hear a folk singer in the train station playing an old tune about how behind every hobo there was once a young person full of dreams, I may pause for an empathic interlude on my way to the airport. Some persons might even volunteer for service in a homeless shelter. Empathy is a force, but it can be exceedingly weak or exceedingly strong. The elevation of empathic capacities into a reliable affirmation of the other requires a conceptual act of valuation—that all human lives have equal worth. A diminution of empathy seems to occur when human development is skewed early on. The child is the confluence of two beings, and of all the human affections, those of mothers and fathers seem to be the most natural and instinctive. The omission of parental love adversely affects the emergence of love in the child, who, not having received love, is therefore unable to give it.

Altruism and altruistic love require more than affective underpinnings. Philosopher Charles Taylor, in a sweeping study of the history of ideas that shapes modern Western identity, finds that underlying our Enlightenment and secular theories of universal respect for persons and our assumptions about far-reaching obligations of justice and benevolence is "the strong sense that human beings are eminently *worth* helping or treating with justice, a sense of their dignity or value. Here we have come into contact with the moral sources which originally underpin these standards" (Taylor, 1989, p. 515). Taylor asks "whether we are not living beyond our moral means in continuing allegiance to our standards of justice and benevolence. Do we have ways of seeing-good which are still credible to us, which are powerful enough to sustain these standards?" (1989, p. 517). Rather boldly, he asks if the "naturalist seeing-good" is "fundamentally parasitic" on the original model of agape. And further, "How well could it survive the demise of the religion it strives to abolish?"(1989, p. 517). Here is the underpinning of "seeing-good":

> The original Christian notion of *agape* is of a love that God has for humans which is connected with their goodness as creatures (though we don't have to decide whether they are loved because good or good because loved). Human beings participate through grace in this love. There is a divine affirmation of the creature, which is captured in the repeated phrase in Genesis I about each stage of creation, "and God saw that it was good." *Agape* is inseparable from such a "seeing-good." (1989, p. 516)

This underpinning exists in all the great world religious traditions in one form or another. Its Christian expression is grounded in Judaism's Leviticus 19:18: "You shall love your neighbor as yourself," expanded broadly to strangers, for "you were strangers in the land of Egypt" (Lev. 19:34). Taylor's comments press me toward a consideration of the religious features of altruism and altruistic love.

Altruism, Altruistic Love, and Agape

Altruism is other-regarding, either with regard to actions or motivations; *altruistic love* adds the feature of deep affirmative affect to altruism; *agape* is altruistic love universalized to all humanity as informed by theistic commitments.

Agape is the Greek word appropriated by the writers of the New Testament to present a form of unlimited altruistic love that has its rough equivalents in Judaism, Buddhism, and other great religious traditions. Agape love is other-regarding love as defined previously but elevated by an overwhelming sense of equal regard derived from a spiritual belief in the love of the Supreme Being for all humanity. Agape, when manifest, expands the scope of love to the enemy (although what action this implies, especially when the lives of innocent others are imperiled, is an exceedingly complex matter), makes all strangers into neighbors, and extends affective presence and care to persons with severe derangement, dementia, or retardation.

Some "agapists" have written of agape as a matter of rather mechanical impersonal bestowal on those who have no desirable attributes and are devoid of value. This position is both arrogant and blind. A countervailing personalist view of agape is that in every human person there is an intrinsic and unique worth that love insists on discovering even when it has been obscured by abuse, hatred, or illness. On the most fundamental level of consent to being, "all that is is good." Agape, like all other-regarding love, takes a personal interest in the particular features of the neediest person. Even on the receiving end at the soup line or in the homeless shelter, one would expect personalism. Agape is a form of love, and therefore it is "I-Thou" rather than "I-It."

Gene Outka writes of the core of agape as love of neighbor, meaning "(1) he is valued as, or in that he is, a person qua human existent and not because he is such-and-such a kind of person distinguishing him from others; and (2) a basic equality obtains whereby one neighbor's well-being is as valuable as another's" (Outka, 1972, p. 12). This is both an equality of existence and between existents that, Outka argues, is both irrevocable and unalterable. But as Vincent Brummer argues, God's love is based on "appreciation of the individuality of each neighbor as a person." Although we are all in one sense equal, we are also different, unique, and irreplaceable. Thus, argues Brummer, divine love is not impartial, but universally partial. It is, then, a ubiquity of special relational love based on unique worths (Brummer, 1993, p. 212).

Agape love will leap over in-group barriers when the sense of belonging to all humanity as one family of the Supreme Being arises from deep within. Virtually all major religions at some point speak of core elements of religious experience that reveal a true self, freed from illusion, that is also the universally affirming self. Such generous devotion to others seems to come from above: "As the Father has loved me, so have I loved you" (John 15:9) and, equally, from imitation.

The power of this spiritual form of altruistic love is something that most of us find fascinating. Gandhi so identified with the oppressed that he took on himself their burdens, and by prayer, brilliant social organization, and nonviolent methods of resistance he set the people of India free first spiritually and then politically. Gandhi's teachings on nonviolence were an expression of what he termed the universal "law of love," which he felt lies within human nature but which can only be fully realized by those who "possess a living faith in the God of Love" (Gandhi, 1970, p. 63). He equated the law of love with the laws of gravitation and energy lying at the very heart of the universe. Pitirim A. Sorokin noted that the great sages of love, known across cultures as saints, seem to embody an attractive force of love that they have discovered as objectively existing in the universe and that is associated with a Supreme Being or "Supraconsciousness" (1954).

Something is at work in love for all humanity that has connections with spirituality. It may be worth recalling something so widely influential as the medieval Oath of Maimonides:

> The eternal providence has appointed me to watch over the life and health of Thy creatures. May the love for my art actuate me at all times; may neither avarice nor miserliness, nor thirst for glory or for a great reputation engage my mind; for the enemies of truth and philanthropy could easily deceive me and make me forgetful of my lofty aim of doing good to Thy children. May I never see in the patient anything but a fellow creature in pain.

These are the words of a Jewish physician in Egypt who treated people of all races and creeds in Cairo and Fostat for reasons of Torah universalism. He wrote in his journal:

> I dismount from my animal, wash my hands, go forth to my patients and entreat them to bear with me while I partake of some light refreshment, the only meal I eat in 24 hours. Then I go to my patients and write prescription and directions for their ailments. Patients go in and out until nightfall, and sometimes even, as the Torah is my

faith, until two hours or more into the night. I converse with them and prescribe for them even while lying down in sheer fatigue. When night [falls,] I am so exhausted that I can hardly speak. (Maimonides, 1917, p. 261)

In the writings of Maimonides, the extension of kin language prevails. The language of sibling relationships under a common parental God is almost ubiquitous in the monotheistic religions and in the exhortations of agapic practitioners.

The genius of this agape love is its family design. Humanity is understood as responding to God in filial love and to one another as universal brothers and sisters. Local boundaries of blood relationship are transcended in the discovery of larger spiritual relationships binding all persons together in one family. The family spirit is made inclusive. Catherine A. Salmon has studied the way in which kin terms such as "brothers" and "sisters" and "motherland" are frequently used in political speeches (Salmon, 1998). The same usage occurs in religious speech in the effort to encourage universal commitments. The use of such language in evoking loyalty to wider causes has been studied and is predictable rhetoric from the perspective of evolutionary psychology (Salmon, 1998).

Agape must be contrasted with romantic love without denying it. Jose Ortega y Gasset described romantic love as focusing attention on a single other and tending to blot out the remainder of the universe, "like a rooster before a hypnotic white line" (1983, p. 15). It is helpful to distinguish agape, however, as based on an appreciation of the unique value of another against a background of equal regard and attentiveness to the full field of such value. Similarly, agape love must be contrasted with friendship love without denying it. As the Shakespeare of the Anglican divines, Jeremy Taylor, wrote: "When friendships were the noblest things in the world, charity was little" (as cited in Meilaender, 1981, p. 1). Agape displaced philia, for the latter is preferential. The preferential love at the core of Greek and Roman moral thought can be retained, as it seems a permanent feature of human nature; but it must be undergirded by a love for all humanity lest it become insular and finally cruel to outsiders.

Beliefs and actions are important, but we must first of all feel in the right way. Hence the Pauline words: "If I give everything I have to feed the poor . . . but have not love, I gain nothing" (1 Cor. 13:2–3). We have to "get a feel for the preciousness of all human beings," argues Vacek (1994, p. 8), and develop this set of affections through the contemplation of narratives and through rights of passage that lead us to see worth. One thinks of holding the hand of the person with severe retardation or kissing the person with advanced Alzheimer's disease.

I view agape as natural altruistic love universalized, and therefore I qualify as a Christian humanist rather than as a Calvinist who sees ethics entirely in terms of that which is opposed to human nature. I am generally skeptical of theologians who have ignored the biological and anthropological underpinnings of agape love because they have radically separated natural love from agape, usually arguing that no such love exists in human nature. Contrary to Thomas Henry Huxley's famous assertion that ethical progress depends on combating the "cosmic process" of evolution, which such theologians celebrate, can we rather argue that human nature is biologically fine-tuned through evolution to take the leap into universality? Can we say that agape has its origins in the deepest foundations of the universe and that all the building blocks for this leap in human love suggest a telos? This is a leap, however, that does not diminish the moral significance of familial love or friendship but rather builds on them as stepping stones to things wider. In other words, agape forces us to honestly confront the ordering of our love and care with respect to both the nearest (those persons such as children and parents) and the very neediest on the face of the earth.

Extensivity and the Possibility of Unlimited Agapic Love: Is It Illusion?

Altruistic love in humans is expected and nearly ubiquitous on the parent-child axis. In general, we feel no need to offer an apologetics for our sense of special obligation to relatives, although this sense ought not to obscure obligations to the neediest. Human beings are heavily affected by genes, as well as by culture, no matter how free and autonomous they perceive themselves. They are typically good kin altruists.

Altruism in the biological use of the term does not imply any conscious benevolence on the part of the performer. It is a behavior that decreases the chances of reproduction or survival of the performer while increasing these chances for another member of the same species. "Inclusive fitness" or "kin selection" extends genetic fitness from individual reproductive success to the broader context that includes the fitness of relatives. The individual's altruistic actions on behalf of the reproductive success of his or her relatives who are likely to share identical genes are advantageous, "from the gene's point of view" (Dawkins, 1989). Altruistic acts to benefit individuals with the greatest degree of relatedness make sense in terms of gene dissemination so long as the cost to the altruist is outweighed by the relatives' gain.

Kinship bonds are an obviously central part of the human social dynamic. Altruistic love in humans is understandable as capacities evolved in the context of kin altruism. As Robert Wright comments, kin altruism would lead to capacities to recognize children and siblings and defend them, "genes, in other words, leading to sympathy, empathy, compassion: genes for love" (Wright, 1994, p. 158). Evolution favors a powerful and narrowly directed altruism, rather than a weak and diffuse form. So, "brotherly love in the literal sense comes at the expense of brotherly love in the biblical sense; the more precisely we bestow unconditional kindness on relatives, the less of it is left over for others"(Wright, 1994, p. 160).

Evolutionary biology also examines the evolution of reciprocal altruism or cooperation between unrelated individuals. There is no need for me to enter into the discussion of game theory and other models of reciprocal altruism. The evidence indicates that many species are excellent scorekeepers, able to identify non-reciprocators, or "cheaters," and to purge them from various coalitions when their time of need arrives. In sum, conditional altruism benefits the individual's survival interests and indirectly the interests of kin. Altruism in this "tit for tat" mode is shaped by and limited by the contours of individual self-interest. Any forgiveness of cheaters is strictly conditional on their not cheating again. Some biologists refer to reciprocal altruism as "soft core" in comparison with "hard core" kin altruism, which is not conditioned by "tit for tat."

If human beings are rather heavily biased toward kin (relatively unconditional) and reciprocal (highly conditional) altruism, what are the implications of this for the universal and unconditional love of neighbor who is both everyone and anyone? Is such lofty idealism so antithetical to the grain of evolved human nature that we must dismiss it as illusory and self-deceptive, perhaps allowing certain individuals to gain social prestige? However much religions and their historically related moral philosophical developments refer to universality of moral standing, none have ever achieved a real world of universal concord and unlimited love.

There actually is important evidence that altruism evolves toward the well-being of the population group as a whole in its competition with other groups (Sober & Wilson, 1998). This group altruism is distinct from both kin and reciprocal altruism. This allows for some greater optimism about underlying human propensities. Yet this leaves us with the stark reality of in-group altruism and out-group aggression. A certain xenophobia has plagued human history, which has been riddled by racism, war, tribalism, and genocide. Darwinians see these tendencies as deeply rooted in evolved human nature (Crook, 1994; Jolly, 1999).

Theologian Reinhold Niebuhr died before the advent of contemporary neo-Darwinism. Much of what he wrote, however, accords with this science. For example, "Only a mutual love, in which the concern of one person for the interests of another prompts and elicits a reciprocal affection, are the social demands of historical existence satisfied" (1941, p. 69). Further, "the sacrifice of the self for others is therefore a violation of natural standards of morals, as limited by historical existence" (Niebuhr, 1941, p. 69). Niebuhr understood that reciprocal patterns cannot be strictly dominated by a calculating tit-for-tat, for then they are hampered by fear. Reciprocal relations would be difficult to initiate or sustain without some nonreciprocal features within the broader context of reciprocity. Evolutionary biologists make room for similar features.

Niebuhr was also well aware of the power of consanguinity. He often commented on the strength of love within the sphere of family relations and its dramatic diminution in larger contexts beyond kinship. Love within the bounds of consanguinity and reciprocal relations is the human norm, however much the New Testament espouses an utterly nonprudential love universalism. Niebuhr felt that such universalism provided the ultimate ethical norm and that it has a corrective relevance to human natural propensities but that its realization remains an "impossible possibility."

It seems that the unlimited agape love that Niebuhr understood as the highest norm despite the impossibility of its full human realization is fundamentally resonant with the "hard core" of kin altruism, particularly in the love of parents toward children. In the Christian tradition, agape is modeled after kin altruism writ large to all humanity. Erich Fromm remains relevant in emphasizing the uniquely deep features of parental love, especially when the infant is loved unconditionally: "I am loved because I am" (Fromm, 1956, p. 39). Further, "there is nothing I have to do in order to be loved—mother's love is unconditional, it need not be acquired, it need not be deserved" (1956, p. 39). We are saved from the anxiety of separation from "intra-uterine existence" (1956, p. 38). Such love is "partly rooted in an instinctive equipment to be found in animals as well as in the human female" (1956, p. 50). Men are also fully capable of parental love, perhaps with a somewhat different feeling tone.

The extensivity of altruistic love is typically limited. Love within the sphere of the near and dear is more or less natural and universal, and "tit for tat" coalition building ("one good turn deserves another") is also ubiquitous. Group altruism, if it exists, does not explain the capacity to love the outsider. But the astounding and perhaps unique feature of human love is that it very often is remarkably extensive, particularly among the saints of all traditions, suggesting something akin to a phase change. Neuropsychologist Malcolm Jeeves discusses this notion of "emergence" in terms of a flame that becomes possible when a richer mixture of gas molecules reaches the point of flammability. He writes of advanced levels of "complexity" in organization: "Complete continuity of biological development, phylogenetically and ontogenetically, does not rule out the possibility of a radical change in cognitive/spiritual capacities at some point along a process of continuity at the physical level"(Jeeves, 1998, p. 87). Here I think the contribution of Jerome Kagan on the remarkable discontinuities between human and nonhuman capacity is highly significant (Chapter 3, this volume).

Holmes Rolston suggests that in human evolution there is "a critical new turning point"(1999, p. 259). The capacity for altruistic acts and for empathy are transposed into the new and higher key of human love, and the ideal of altruistic love is both established and practiced. This transposition to the key of altruistic love has to do with the evolution of the brain and the "prehistory of the mind," as Steven Mithen puts it (1996). It has to do with the quest for logical consistency and for the discovery of an inner self through world religions that is affectively attuned to the goodness of us all. It has to do with an imagination that can see behind the homeless beggar a young woman who once had wonderful dreams. In the words of George Herbert Meade, the emphases on helping and assisting the stranger in the "universal religions" illustrate "the tendency of religion to complete itself, to complete the community which previously existed in an abstract form" (Meade, 1934, p. 306).

Rolston allows that group survival and pseudoaltruism "has a certain plausibility dealing with tribal religions," but the theory "is powerless to explain the universalism in the major world faiths" (Rolston, 1999, p. 329). As Rolston writes,

If the function of religion is to provide fervent loyalty for a tribal group, urging one's religion on aliens is exactly the wrong behavior. Missionary activity is helping to ensure the replication of genes unlike one's own. If one has a religion that serves his genes, holds his society together well, and produces numerous offspring, then the last thing he wants to do is share his religion with others. . . . Proselytizing those foreign genes is the worst religious mistake you can make from a genetic viewpoint, and yet it has been the secret of success of all the world's great religions: evangelicalism in Christianity or the bodhisattva's vow in Buddhism. (1999, p. 330)

In other words, "the one thing impossible is a xenophobic altruism" (Rolston, 1999, p. 331). Rolston points out, in a discussion of "testing religions cognitively," that although there are about 100,000 religions in the world, "the religions that have spread worldwide, that persist and develop over the centuries, are quite few: about ten religions form the chapters in the typical world religion textbook" (1999, p. 334). The test for staying power on this level is the capacity for universalism, for the love of "all humanity."

Talcott Parsons summarized the conclusions of Max Weber: "Religion is as much a human universal as language or an incest taboo, which is to say a kinship system" (1963, p. xxviii). What do I mean by religion? It is sometimes said that because religions vary so much, there is no adequate single definition. Yet it is, I think, still possible to offer a loose general definition as follows: Religion is the feeling that our human presence is not the greatest presence, that behind the phenomenal world is something more and greater than ourselves. Thus I would not object to the words of Rolston that religion has to do with a claimed "Presence immanent and transcendent, stirring in the Earth history" (1999, p. 334), a claim "generated confronting nature" that asks "Why is there something rather than nothing? Why is there something of a kind that spins this surprising kind of universe?" (1999, p. 295). And, especially, how is it that the earth is so fine-tuned as to allow for the generation of life?

The modest claims of religious naturalism based on science are very significant rational underpinnings for a new appreciation of religious beliefs, practices, and actions, as an enormous amount of serious writing since the early 1990s suggests. The modern effort to take science seriously as a natural theological perspective has roots that reach back to earlier decades in writings that are often well worth reviewing. If significant scientists conclude that the laws and constants that underlie our universe are the only ones that could have given rise to a world hospitable to the evolution of intelligent life, then it is improbable that such a particular combination of forces and laws could be arbitrary. Under conditions of such fine-tuning, the occurrence of intelligent life that has perennially manifested religious consciousness, belief, and behavior begins to seem purposeful. It is reasonable to view the emergence of life as within the nature of things, as the accident waiting to happen, as an inevitable contingency due to the fabric of the universe and of the earth; it is also reasonable to posit a Supreme Being who generates such astounding potentialities. Is that Supreme Being itself absolute unlimited agapic love, in which we participate?

Our task is to better understand the emergence of the capacities for altruistic actions and for empathic affect and how these contributed to a larger capacity for love that is both human and divine. Setting aside all dualism and reductionism, our task is to better understand this transposition and genesis from above, within, and below.

Much can be learned from the great exemplars of altruistic love for all humanity. All of these figures act in profound love because they feel that their work in society (*polis*) is in concert with the nature of unlimited love at the heart of the anthropic universe (*cosmos*). They are then spiritual cosmopolitans absorbed in other-regarding service. We are sometimes too exclusively interested in what they do rather than in why they do it, because the "what" depends on the "why." Their acts emerge from an empowering form of love. They do just "happen" to be deeply spiritual persons. The more we can understand about them, scientifically and otherwise, the more effectively we can educate and encourage future generations to emulate them. It may be that the most exemplary altruism is often associated with the agent's personal experience of the utter enormity of the Transcendent, including a sense of overwhelming awe. Overawed, the deeply humbled self is transformed through something like an ego-death to a new self of profound humility, empathy, and regard for all human and other life. This phenomenon can be studied across cultures and time.

REFERENCES

Alexander, R. D. (1987). *The biology of moral systems*. New York: Aldine de Gruyter.

Batson, D. (1991). *The altruism question: Toward a social-psychological answer*. Hillsdale, NJ: Erlbaum.

Brummer, V. (1993). *The model of love: A study in philosophical theology*. Cambridge: Cambridge University Press.

Carter, C. S. (1998). Neuroendocrine perspectives on social attachment and love. *Psychoneuroendocrinology, 23*, 779–818.

Churchill, L. R. (1987). *Rationing health care in America: Perceptions and principles of justice*. Notre Dame, IN: University of Notre Dame Press.

Crook, P. (1994). *Darwinism, war and history: The debate over the biology of war from "The Origin of Species" to the First World War*. Cambridge: Cambridge University Press.

Dawkins, R. (1989). *The selfish gene*. 2d ed. Oxford: Oxford University Press.

Fromm, E. (1956). *The art of loving: An enquiry into the nature of love*. New York: Harper & Row.

Hazo, R. (1976). *The idea of love*. New York: Praeger.

Gandhi, M. K. (1957). *The law of love*. Bombay: Bharatiya Vidya Bhavan.

Insel, T. R. (1997). A neurobiological basis of social attachment. *American Journal of Psychiatry, 16*, 726–735.

Jeeves, M. (1998). Brain, mind, and behavior. In W. S. Brown, N. M. Murphy, & H. N. Malony (Eds.), *Whatever happened to the soul? Scientific and theological portraits of human nature* (pp. 73–98). Minneapolis: Fortress Press.

Jolly, A. (1999). *Lucy's legacy: Sex and intelligence in human evolution*. Cambridge: Harvard University Press.

Kitwood, T. (1997). *Dementia reconsidered: The person comes first*. Buckingham, England: Open University Press.

Levin, J. (2000). A prolegomenon to an epidemiology of love: Theory, measurement, and health outcomes. *Journal of Social and Clinical Psychology, 19*, 117–136.

Levinas, I. (1969). *Totality and infinity: An essay on exteriority* (A. Lingis, Trans.). Pittsburgh: Duquesne University Press.

McClelland, D. C. (1986). Some reflections on the two psychologies of love. *Journal of Personality, 54*, 334–353.

Maimonides. (1917 [original date unknown]). Prayer of Moses Maimonides. *Bulletin of the Johns Hopkins University Hospital, 28*, 260–261.

Meade, G. H. (1934). *Mind, self and society from the standpoint of a social behaviorist*. Chicago: University of Chicago Press, 1934.

Meilaender, G. C. (1981). *Friendship: A study in theological ethics.* Notre Dame, IN: University of Notre Dame Press.

Mithen, S. (1996). *The prehistory of the mind: A search for the origins of art, religion, and science.* London: Phoenix.

Niebuhr, R. (1941). *The nature and destiny of man: A Christian interpretation.* Vol. 2. New York: Scribner's.

Ogletree, T. W. (1985). *Hospitality to the stranger: Dimensions of moral understanding.* Philadelphia: Fortress Press.

Ortega y Gasset, J. (1983). On love: Aspects of a single theme. In D. L. Norton & M. F. Kille (Eds.), *Philosophies of love* (pp. 15–20). Totowa, NJ: Helix Books. (Original work published 1957)

Outka, G. (1972). *Agape: An ethical analysis.* New Haven, CT: Yale University Press.

Panksepp, J. (1998). *Affective neuroscience: The foundations of human and animal emotions.* Oxford: Oxford University Press.

Parsons, T. (1963). Preface to M. Weber, *The sociology of religion.* Boston: Beacon Press.

Post, S. G. (2000). *The moral challenge of Alzheimer disease.* 2d ed. Baltimore: Johns Hopkins University Press.

Rawls, J. (1971). *A theory of justice.* Cambridge: Harvard University Press.

Rolston, H. (1999). *Genes, genesis and God: Values and their origins in natural and human history.* Cambridge: Cambridge University Press.

Sadler, W. A. (1969). *Existence and love: A new approach to existential phenomenology.* New York: Scribners.

Salmon, C. A. (1998). The evocative nature of kin terminology in political rhetoric. *Politics and the Life Sciences, 17,* 51–57.

Sober, E., & Wilson, D. S. (1998). *Unto others: The evolution and psychology of unselfish behavior.* Cambridge: Harvard University Press.

Sorokin, P. A. (1954). *The ways and power of love: Types, factors, and techniques of moral transformation.* Boston: Beacon Press.

Taylor, C. (1989). *Sources of the self: The making of modern identity.* Cambridge: Harvard University Press.

Vacek, E. C. (1994). *Love, human and divine: The heart of Christian ethics.* Washington: Georgetown University Press.

Vanier, J. (1998). *Becoming human.* New York: Paulist Press.

Walsh, A., & Walsh, P. A. (1989). Love, self-esteem, and multiple sclerosis. *Social Science and Medicine, 29,* 793–798.

Wright, R. (1994). *The moral animal: Why we are the way we are.* London: Abacus.

Wyschogrod, E. (1990). *Saints and postmodernism: Revising moral philosophy.* Chicago: University of Chicago Press.

Conclusion to Part I

STEPHEN G. POST

The various definitions put forward in the chapters of this section resist summary. Other chapters in this book are also heavily definitional at points (see especially Underwood, Chapter 5; Batson, Chapter 6; Ruse, Chapter 9; Pope, Chapter 10; Wilson and Sober, Chapter 11; Schloss, Chapter 13; and Browning, Chapter 19). The reader who struggles with the meanings of *altruism* across the sciences and humanities will go through a certain seasoning process while reading this book in its entirely.

It is no easy task to keep matters straight, especially when the history of ideas at the broad interface of altruism and egoism is so vast. Batson (Chapter 6), for example, often draws from the tradition of eighteenth-century British Moralists and builds on the distinction between benevolence and self-love that framed the thought of Bishop Butler and others as he further elaborates the modern sociological concepts of altruism and egoism associated with Comte. Others, such as Browning (Chapter 19), draw on classical Protestant distinctions between eros and agape, although agape is a term that precedes Christianity in Roman antiquity and that has its rough equivalents in a number of world religious traditions that at least espouse the ideal of "unlimited love for every human being without exception" (Templeton, 1999, p. 1). Things become even more complicated when a notion of moral condemnation, such as "selfishness," is applied to genes.

In addition to working with the matter of definition, the reader will also want to bear in mind the insight of Jerome Kagan (Chapter 3). The human person is extraordinarily complex. Evolved genetically based human tendencies are by no means determinative of human behavior. Human beings certainly live under genetic influences, but many of these influences are akin to rather vague susceptibilities that may or may not manifest in actual behavior and that may or may not contribute to human flourishing. As Malcolm Jeeves has written, "Complete continuity of biological development, phylogenetically and ontogenetically, does not rule out the possibility of a radical change in cognitive/spiritual capacities at some point along a process of continuity at the physical level" (1998, p. 87). The same material "stuff" of the brain that is common to humans and primates, for example, can reach a level of structural complexity in the human such that a "phase change" occurs, giving rise to new properties of mind, consciousness, and self-determination. In Chapter 17 of this book, Preston and de Waal emphasize continuities between humans and nonhuman primates with regard to empathy, for example. Exactly where continuities end and discontinuities begin is difficult to discern.

REFERENCES

Jeeves, M. (1998). Brain, mind, and behavior. In W. S. Brown, N. Murphy, & H. N. Malony (Eds.), *Whatever happened to the soul? Scientific and theological portraits of human nature* (pp. 73–98). Minneapolis: Fortress Press.
Templeton, J. (1999). *Agape love: A tradition found in eight world religions.* Philadelphia: Templeton Foundation Press.

Part II

HUMAN MOTIVATION AND ACTION

Introduction to Part II

LYNN G. UNDERWOOD

This section takes up some of the social scientific research into the nature and reality of altruistic acts, altruistic love, and compassionate love. The studies examine rescue behavior that places the agent at risk, as well as daily acts of love, care, and kindness which seem to be based on valuing the other and to be primarily motivated by desire for the good of the other. The studies in this section address underlying motivations, as well as observable actions. They also highlight the disagreement in social science over the authenticity of other-regarding motivation.

Social science research into these questions has proceeded both quantitatively and qualitatively. Using a variety of social scientific methodologies, the authors in this section illuminate our understanding of altruistic actions and compassionate love from a variety of perspectives. The effort to study and understand human motivation and action presents well-known difficulties that are not present in the study of many other aspects of nature. In the future, nonlinear dynamics and complexity theory may give us additional ways of examining complex systems such as human motivations and behavior. Developments in self-report methodologies will further this work. Nevertheless, the methodologies and tools that are currently available to study the topic are various and often sophisticated and can provide us with answers to many questions.

The field is extremely complex. Thus, as indicated in the definitional analyses in Part I of the book, we are addressing a *set* of concepts in this book. Envisioning how research results might be used can help focus the conceptual issues. If we can understand the various factors that promote the inner growth and outer behaviors that constitute valuing the other for his or her own sake, we might be able to develop ways to encourage such growth and behavior in ourselves and others. We can begin by considering the kinds of attitudes and behaviors that others have toward us that make us feel valued, loved, cared about, and cared for. The full expression of inspired compassionate love would have the ideal impact on us. But even less significant altruistic acts are of basic value.

Words and actions that are centered on the good of the other are the end result of a process. The process begins with a baseline of human biology—emotions, cognitive processes, and physical predispositions, influenced by genetics and environment. In addition, particular situations provoke thoughts and feelings. The baseline is influenced by the environment, the culture, and the social and familial setting. From these baseline conditions, this substrate, the individual can choose to act for the benefit of the other, to give of the self for the other. Scientifically studying this process is difficult. The motivations involved are crucial, of course, but hard to observe or measure. The subtle sifting of other-regarding motives from those that are primarily selfish is not easy. The resulting behaviors flowing from these motives can frequently be measured. But there are difficulties at this stage as well, particularly because actions often flow from a combination of altruistic and nonaltruistic motivations and from frequently inaccurate understandings of the needs of the other. The authors in this section have tackled this complex process in a variety of ways.

In Chapter 5 I focus on the *subjective* aspects of compassionate love and the decision-making processes involved. I lay out a model of the process of expressing compassionate love (altruistic love) that can help with the scientific exploration of the topic. The model includes the baseline conditions that are highlighted by Insel (Chapter 14), Damasio (Chapter 15), and Kagan (Chapter 3). I then summarize two studies that use questions that can begin to quantify this subjective aspect. The chapter also presents a qualitative study that looks at a variety of issues, including some of the obstacles to expressing compassionate love, the psychological mechanics involved in expressing compassionate love, and the kinds of things that facilitate such expression. The study places emphasis on examining potential transforming effects of compassionate behavior on the altruistic person and examines in their complexity the motivational issues that are considered crucial to the study of this topic. The particular approach to qualitative methodology of this study may yield insights for future research.

The assumption of much scientific research has been that all behavior is selfish. Daniel Batson's work, described in Chapter 6, challenges this fundamental assumption. His findings are based on many years of methodologically careful experimentation in the area of social psychology. His "empathy-altruism" hypothesis is that other-oriented emotional response congruent with the perceived welfare of another individual evokes a motivational state with the ultimate goal of increasing the other's welfare. This definition fits well with the definition of compassionate love I use in Chapter 5. However, his more narrow definition is particularly useful for the types of experimental models he has developed. Both Batson and I aim to reveal underlying motivation that may not always be explicit. Batson, in more than 25 experiments, has slowly worked to distinguish self-directed primary motives from truly altruistic motives. Batson considers three classes of egoistic explanation: (1) reward seeking, including material, social, and self-rewards; (2) punishment avoidance, including material, social, and self-punishments; and (3) aversive arousal reduction, reducing the arousal produced by witnessing another in need. The results presented here make a very strong case that one can find and construct situations in which these explanations do not fully explain action, leaving us with the conclusion that truly other-directed motivations are valid.

Kristen Monroe, in Chapter 7, challenges the way we think about altruistic behavior. Unlike some, she defines altruism in terms of *actions* rather than *motives*, though she includes the goal of the action as part of her definition of altruism. Coming from the perspective of political science while drawing from other disciplines, she sees how we view the other, especially the notion of "shared humanity," as critical to whether we are inclined to be altruistic. Much of her work draws on examinations of acts of dramatic altruism, including the behavior of rescuers of Jews in World War II, Carnegie Medal winners, and philanthropists. Critical to her approach are the ideas that our perception of self in relation to others strongly affects our decision to be altruistic and that our sense of identity constrains our choices. She maps a set of potentially fruitful areas for future research on this topic. She challenges the typical rationalist, selfish view of the human being, giving an alternative explanation of behavior. Monroe also argues for more empirically based theories of ethical behavior.

Samuel Oliner (Chapter 8) analyzes the altruistic behaviors of two groups, rescuers of Jews during World War II and volunteers working with the dying today. He gives insights into the motivations, personalities, and backgrounds of those who behave altruistically. Particularly valuable in this chapter are the quotations drawn from his interviews with those who have been altruistic. They enable us to catch a glimpse of the "real thing." He and Pearl Oliner have been pioneers in this field of study and have accumulated a vast amount of material over the years that is valuable for identifying differences between those who chose to be rescuers and those who chose not to be. Religious, family, and social backgrounds are explored and likely positive and negative influences identified. Oliner also presents some theories as to the basis of altruistic behavior.

To wrap up this introduction, I turn to a quotation from Jean Vanier, in his book *Becoming Human*, which reminds us of the value of much of the work in this section and sets the tone for our investigations into the modes and motivations of compassionate love and altruism:

> Evolution of thought can mean searching and grasping in the dark, sometimes in anguish, rethinking answers, formulating them in new words and new ways. Philosophy, anthropology, theology, and those sciences that tell us what it means to be human can be dangerous if they are considered ideologies that dictate reality; instead they need to be understood as the means by which we humbly listen to and marvel at reality. (1998, p. 16)

REFERENCE

Vanier, Jean. (1998). *Becoming human.* Mahwah, NJ: Paulist Press.

5

The Human Experience of Compassionate Love

Conceptual Mapping and Data from
Selected Studies

LYNN G. UNDERWOOD

In order to do adequate research on compassionate love, it is important to clearly articulate the various essential components, the conditions that might foster and those that might impede its expression, and to develop methodologies for assessment. In this way we might develop ways to encourage and foster this quality appropriately in people's lives. This chapter emphasizes the subjective experience of the person attempting to express compassionate love.

There is something essentially ineffable and powerful in the reality which the words *agape, compassion, unconditional love,* and *self-giving love* attempt to describe. The word *altruism* is nested within them, but these other words capture an investment of self deeper than *altruism* suggests, a dimension that cannot be fully assessed through external evaluations of actions. In the following, I use the words *compassionate love* to represent that richer concept. *Altruistic love* begins to reflect these ideas as well. I describe later why I chose *compassionate love* as the most representative and acceptable phrase to describe this concept.

Background

Key Features

Identifying some of the key aspects of compassionate love as it is viewed in this chapter helps to pin down the term for use here. The definitive features draw extensively on the research results discussed later in this chapter but also on the writings of others in psychology, sociology, ethics, and theology.

FREE CHOICE FOR THE OTHER   "Compassion is a manifestation of love. And love, whatever else it may be, is something that involves choices. Love is the one true source of freedom in the midst of the suffering human finitude entails. Choosing between options is a condition of freedom in finitude" (Sulmasy, 1997). Our freedom is often constrained, but within those constraints we exercise choice.

COGNITIVE UNDERSTANDING OF THE SITUATION   Cognitive understanding includes evaluations of contexts and meaning in religious and nonreligious frameworks. Ethical judgments and issues of justice can enter in here, as can knowledge of the details of culture and individual differences. Intellectual understanding of another's situation helps one to act effectively for him or her.

UNDERSTANDING OF SELF   This includes knowing our agendas and ourselves adequately so that we can choose as freely as possible, in order to strengthen and to give life to the other. Sir William Osler, the famed professor of medicine, said, in 1905, "at the outset appreciate clearly the aims and objects that each one of you should have in view—a knowledge of disease and its cure, and a knowledge of yourself." It is similar in all areas in which we express fully compassionate love for the other.

TO VALUE THE OTHER AT A FUNDAMENTAL LEVEL   In a lecture given by Immanuel Jokobovits (at that time Chief Rabbi of the British Commonwealth) at the medical school at which I was working in the 1980s on ethics in medicine, the element that was most striking was the speaker's emphasis on the infinite value of each human being and on the importance of taking this as a starting point for action. "The humble beauties of human nature leapt out" was a phrase used by Evelyn Underhill (1976) to describe that which we often miss in the other.

OPENNESS AND RECEPTIVITY   Openness and receptivity can include the awareness of being part of something important beyond oneself and the freedom to let oneself be open. The role of divine inspiration could also be included here. This attitude also allows one to see opportunities for the expression of compassionate love in specific situations (Nouwen, 1972).

RESPONSE OF THE HEART   The emotional part of the brain is essential to much of good decision making (Damasio, 1994), and this extends to decision making in the area of compassion. Emotional understanding plays a role in fully grasping the situation in order to choose the appropriate action. Analysis of children's prosocial behaviors links to this component as early as age 2 (Zahn-Wexler, 1979). We can listen with the heart to balance mercy and justice.

Limitations of Freedom

Freedom is required to fully express compassionate love, yet each person's freedom is limited in a variety of ways. There are *physical limitations,* such as disability or material resource limits. Hormonal and biological factors can also limit freedom (see Insel, Chapter 14, this volume). *Social structures and environment* can create undue pressures for self-protection or can obstruct altruistic behaviors through resource restrictions. Social support from others can increase ability to give. There are *emotional limitations.* People have varying degrees of baseline empathic ability, emotional stability, and extroversion (see Damasio, Chapter 15, and Kagan, Chapter 3, this volume). *Cognitive factors,* such as contexts for meaning, religious and nonreligious frameworks of values, priority structures, and intellectual capacities to understand needs in a situation, influence the starting conditions for the expression of love (see Browning, Chapter 19, Pope, Chapter 10, and Habito, Chapter 21, this volume). Much of the work represented in other chapters of this volume articulates various aspects of the substrate that affect the capacity of a person to express compassionate love in particular situations. Genetic factors, neural structure, cultural and religious cognitive frameworks, and social settings can all limit our freedom.

MOTIVES THAT DETRACT FROM COMPASSIONATE LOVE   There are motives that detract from the quality of altruistic, compassionate love in words or actions. Some of these more negative motives are frequently present in our acts of love, but as these factors dominate, the quality of compassionate love, other-regarding love, in the act decreases. These include factors such as:

- need for reciprocal love and affection
- need to be accepted by others or by God
- need to belong
- guilt
- fear
- seeing the other as an extension or reflection of oneself (ego)
- pleasure in looking well in the eyes of others
- control of the other through their indebtedness
- desire to exercise power over others
- desire to reinforce positive image of self and feelings of superiority
- desire to avoid confrontation

It is assumed in this chapter that the motives for compassionate actions and words are important. This is not to say that altruistic actions without other-regarding motives are not of value, but that they are somehow qualitatively different.

The motives just mentioned and others have been articulated well by a variety of authors. C. S. Lewis (Lewis, 1960/1991) describes "need loves" as a baseline of different feelings on which more "other-regarding" love is built but that can also detract from the full expression of compassionate love. As Vanier writes, "We set out on the road to freedom when we begin to put justice, heartfelt relationships, and the service of others and of truth over and above our own needs for love and success or our fears of failure and of relationships" (1998, p. 115). Thomas Merton often argued that as we enhance our inner capacity for wholeness and freedom, we strengthen our outer capacity to love and serve. If this inner freedom is lacking, all our efforts to help others or the world will be marred by what he called "the contagion" of our own ego-centered attachments and illusions. Van Kaam writes of "developing an ability to respond fully, not just react, which can contribute to the growth of inner holiness, because it is not easily poisoned by the heady wine of successful behavior which makes me look well in the eyes of those around me" (1964, p. 101).

ADDITIONAL ISSUES   Any research or investigation into factors that might encourage the expression of compassionate love needs to address some additional questions: Where are the boundaries between self and other (how do we define self—the issue of true self vs. masks or inaccurate understandings of self)? Where does compassion for self come in? How do we effectively balance mercy and justice as we try to express loving compassion? Another important issue is that of creating spaces for compassionate behavior from others, being open to receiving the generosity of others, and creating opportunities and settings in which expression of compassionate love in others is encouraged.

A Basic Model

The various elements in this model can be represented in Figure 5.1. On the left-hand side of the diagram is the individual, nested in his social and physical environment. This is where the "limitations of freedom" discussed previously fit in, including physical, social, emotional, and cognitive limitations. In this substrate there are also characteristics that encourage the expression of compassionate love in people. For example, preliminary results from a study in Lithuania, supported by the Fetzer Institute, which is looking at health outcomes, also examines what enables people to make positive moral choices in difficult circumstances. Factors important in encouraging compassionate choices in people in that population included experience of suffering by the giver, older age, family and peer environments, and the role of the media (P. Kaufmann, personal communication, September 1999). Being loved by others and by the divine can also foster and empower one's capacity to express love to others.

The person expresses himself or herself in actions and expressions (far right side of Figure 5.1). In the middle are motivations and discernment, the internal processes involved in making decisions concerning actions. Compassionate love fully expressed, shown by the arrow curving up, indicates flow resulting from a

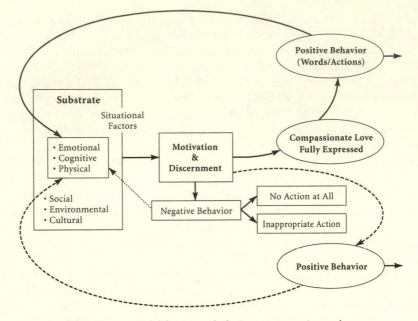

Figure 5.1.   Model for research design—compassionate love

balance of appropriate motives and wisdom. These behaviors and words display varying degrees of emotional expression and can lead to varying perceptions by others. They can lead to concrete changes in the individual and the environment. Compassion can also be expressed by making space for others to give. Allowing others to give is frequently an undervalued way of being compassionate, but it can liberate compassion in the world very effectively and counterbalance feelings of indebtedness and powerlessness in the person helped. In an article on agape in a clinical setting, Alan Mermann, a physician at Yale, emphasized the importance of creating spaces for the other to give and emphasized that being open to receiving does not diminish our gift of self (Mermann, 1993). An additional element emphasized in this model is that compassionate love, when driven by positive motivation and appropriate discernment, can have positive effects on the development of the person, contributing to moral and spiritual growth and additional insight and wisdom. Mermann also expressed well the dynamics of how love expressed in this way can "form and mold our psyches": that by expressing agape we can actually encourage humility, appreciate the hollowness of praise, and obtain a more realistic perspective on life and self.

But when the motives for self outweigh those for other, or when there is an inappropriate action given the various factors to be considered, another set of circumstances results (see the downward-curving arrows in Figure 5.1). On the one hand, this situation can lead to no action or to action that is inappropriate for the circumstances, resulting in negative or neutral effects on the person. On the other hand, it can result in positive action, someone doing good things for the wrong reason. Major ill effects of this kind of action are often on the person acting. The details depend on the particular mixture of motives. An example would be some-one doing a positive act from a motive of self-aggrandizement or in order to be loved in return. This kind of action can lead to positive feedback for the selfish motive, encouraging more of such behavior. Inner discernment could alert the person to the negative motive, however, and guide future motivation of behavior. Alternatively, inappropriate discernment could lead to inadequate care of self, in-adequate balance of needs of self and other, and this could lead to exhaustion and burnout (Carmel & Glick, 1996).

This process of action, internal feedback, inner correction, and action is im-portant to the process of expressing love and of growing in the capacity to love. We are not always able to articulate this process because much of it happens implicitly. This process, acknowledged or not, makes up much of compassionate love, from the inside-out perspective.

Empirical Studies

To illuminate this model from the perspective of the subjective experience of the person attempting to express compassionate love is challenging, particularly to do so as a scientist attempting to investigate this territory scientifically. I present some results from studies currently in various stages of completion that can help us see how individuals map this territory in daily life. The studies focus on the subjective experience, the view from the inside out. The following studies build on self-report methodologies of varying types. Despite their limitations, self-reports can give subtle illumination of motivations and other internal conditions that are key to the expression or inhibition of compassionate love. These reports give this illu-mination in ways that can contribute substantially to our understanding. As indi-cators of the inner experience during the giving of compassionate love, these re-ports help us assess what is happening.

Self-reports are limited in a variety of ways and should not be relied on alone to determine whether a person is feeling and expressing compassionate love. It is also necessary to assess the objective features of words and actions designed to be compassionate. Such features would include perceptions by others, especially the recipients, as well as other outcomes of such expressions—both effects on the in-tended recipient and internal effects on the person giving, such as spiritual and moral growth. Biological measures, such as neural imaging and heart rate vari-ability, could also be helpful. Acknowledging their limitations, self-reports can give subtle illumination of motivations and other internal conditions that are key to the expression or inhibition of compassionate love in ways that can contribute substantially to understanding.

Spiritual Contributions to Quality of Life: WHO

In a project with the World Health Organization (WHO; Lofty, 1998), a group of people from various cultures and from the major traditions (Buddhist, Hindu, Muslim, Christian, Jewish, indigenous, agnostic, atheist) gathered to develop an instrument to measure spiritual contributions to quality of life. Work in focus groups in various countries is following this initial work. The working group determined that one of the important features of quality of life across all traditions was giving other-centered love and compassion, and they identified questions that might draw out the degree and importance of this in people's lives. In subsequent interviews, the mean importance rating of the relative contributions of the degree and importance of self-giving love and compassion to quality of life was 3.88. (The importance items that were given to focus groups were rated on a five-point Likert scale, ranging from 1, *not important,* to 5, *extremely important.*) This factor was well endorsed by both religious and nonreligious groups.

Some of the questions which addressed the giving of other-centered love and compassion included:

- How much do you find that putting others' needs before your own desires gives you happiness?
- To what extent do you take pleasure in the success of others?
- To what extent does feeling caring and compassion toward others without expecting or hoping for anything in return enhance your quality of life and well-being?
- To what extent do you feel good when you help others?
- How much does sacrificing your own interests for those of others improve the quality of your life?

Testing in eighteen individual countries across religious traditions is the next stage in identifying the best questions to elicit the qualities of loving-kindness, selflessness, and acceptance of others as contributors to quality of life. These and other questions are undergoing focus group evaluation. Translation and back-translation issues are of crucial importance for this instrument, as it is designed to be used in many languages and with many religious and ethnic groups.

The importance of an emotional component varied across religious groups. One of the reasons I chose *compassionate love* as the phrase to use in this chapter had to do with work from the contemplative interviews that I discuss later, together with discussions in Geneva with members of the working group across religious traditions. For many, *love* was too inclusive of a variety of other concepts, such as romance, but *compassion* alone left out some of the emotional and transcendent components which the word *love* brings in. *It points up the importance of picking a number of features and focusing on those features, which make up the key concept, and not putting too much weight on a single word or phrase.* A paragraph describing these features was designed to help the focus groups come to some clarity about the basic concept.

Other factors on the quality-of-life survey may be relevant to the present work. There was a factor that addressed Acceptance of Others, which is taken to play a role in one's capacity to value the other. (This was given an importance rating of 3.85.) In some of the preliminary results from the focus groups, not surprisingly, receiving love and acceptance from others may also significantly contribute to quality of life.

One of the important preliminary findings of this project is that qualities that are not obviously oriented toward self-interest can be important in improving satisfaction with life for people in their everyday lives throughout the world. Quality of life is not only determined by physical health, mental health, and economic status but also by some other-oriented features. Giving of self for the other has been rated as important to the quality of one's life, in a variety of settings and cultural contexts, to people throughout the world. Specific questions that draw out this feature most effectively, as identified in this project cross-culturally, will help future work in this area.

Daily Spiritual Experience Scale

In another set of studies, the object was to assess daily spiritual experiences (DSE), the day-to-day inner experiences that accompany ordinary spiritual life, to see how they relate to physical and mental health outcomes. The Fetzer Institute formed a working group with the National Institute on Aging to develop a multidomain measure of religiousness/spirituality for use in health studies. In the context of this project I developed a 16-item scale of daily spiritual experiences (Underwood, 1999).

This scale included the item "I feel a selfless caring for others," designed to measure feelings of compassion. In a U.S. study that made use of this scale, the average score was "most days." Thirteen percent responded, "many times a day," whereas 15% said "never or almost never" or "once in a while" (Figure 5.2). This item shows significant variation across the sample. People do not just automatically give a positive response, and some people rarely experience this feeling. Structured interviews across varied socioeconomic and cultural groups, to assess the construct validity of this item, confirmed that it accesses some of the experience of giving compassionate love. The general interpretation of the item in these interviews confirmed that although the word *selfless* was used, the meaning conveyed was that of a primary other-centeredness rather than of a total abnegation of self. Using *selfless* as an adjective enables this item to measure a type of caring that has giving to the other, rather than total denial of self, as its primary motivation.

In developing quantitative self-report measures of subjective experience, wording of questions and their context is particularly important. The qualitative studies that preceded the development of this instrument revealed that the statement "I give to others without expecting anything in return" (which was not included in the final scale) hinted at a mildly cynical approach or a martyred begrudging for many respondents. It is crucial to do initial evaluations of the wording of self-report measures to confirm that the concept that the investigator is trying to find out about is very close to what the participants are actually hearing in the question and responding to.

One other question on the DSE scale that related to our current topic was "I accept others even when they do things I think are wrong." This item was designed to measure the concept of mercy, an attitude toward the other that might facilitate a full expression of compassion. The responses on this item ranged from 20%

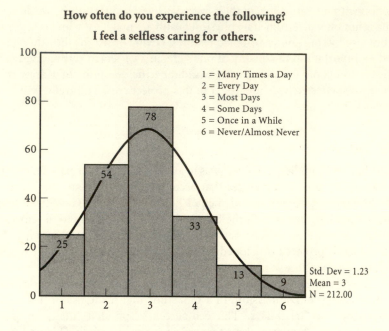

How often do you experience the following?
I feel a selfless caring for others.

1 = Many Times a Day
2 = Every Day
3 = Most Days
4 = Some Days
5 = Once in a While
6 = Never/Almost Never

Std. Dev = 1.23
Mean = 3
N = 212.00

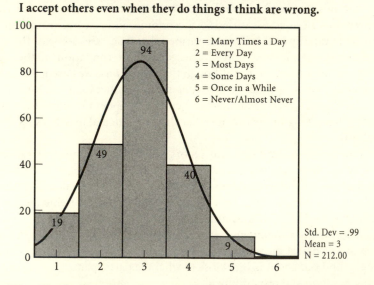

How often do you experience the following?
I accept others even when they do things I think are wrong.

1 = Many Times a Day
2 = Every Day
3 = Most Days
4 = Some Days
5 = Once in a While
6 = Never/Almost Never

Std. Dev = .99
Mean = 3
N = 212.00

Figure 5.2. Distribution of questions assessing the experience of compassion and mercy

reporting experiencing this feeling "many times a day" to 10% reporting this feeling "never," "almost never," or "once in a while" (Table 5.1). Although the 16-item DSE overall psychometrically identifies a single factor in previous work, when correlated with different types of empathy, higher scores on the two questions isolated here were correlated differentially with a number of variables. Those who scored higher on the two compassion and mercy questions also scored higher on Emotional Empathy and Perspective Taking, the more positively oriented kinds of empathy. Their responses were also correlated with greater other-forgiveness (Table 5.1; Zechmeister, 1999). In a study of test-retest reliability, scores on these items stayed consistent over a 2-week period, indicating that this is a relatively stable element in the short term. Long-term follow-up remains to be done. These items have been embedded in a large longitudinal study of health of women and in a study of the daily experience of pain. It will be interesting to note the future correlations of these items with healthy behaviors and outcomes.

An important issue in addressing self-reports of these experiences is the degree to which respondents are aware of their own motives and feelings and how critical an eye is applied to the assessment of their internal states. These considerations limit the conclusions one can make based on such assessments. Nevertheless, quantitative assessments such as these can provide useful information.

Table 5.1. Correlations between DSE Scores and Trait Measures

Trait Measure	Compassion/Mercy Items	Total DSE (16 items)
Positive Affect[a]	−.08	−.29**
Negative Affect[a]	.08	.16
Trait Anger[b]	.07	.06
Fantasy[c]	−.11	.03
Emotional Empathy[c]	−.11	.03
Perspective Taking[c]	−.38**	−.27**
Personal Distress[c]	.01	.06
Total Empathy[c]	−.34**	−.13
Forgive Self[d]	−.01	−.14
Forgive Other[d]	−.32**	−.12
Total Forgive[d]	−.21*	−.17

Source: Adapted from Zechmeister (1999).

*Correlation is significant at the 0.05 level (2-tailed).

**Correlation is significant at the 0.01 level (2-tailed).

[a]Positive and Negative Affect were assessed using Watson and Clark's Positive and Negative Affect Scale (PANAS). For this sample, Cronbach's alpha for the 10-item Positive Affect scale was .79, and .86 for the 10-item Negative Affect Scale.

[b]Trait Anger was assessed using Spielberger's 10-item measure. Cronbach's alpha for this sample was .87.

[c]The four types of empathy were assessed using the Davis Interpersonal Reactivity Index (IRI); Total Empathy is the sum of each 7-item subscale. Cronbach's alphas for the scales were as follows: Fantasy = .74; Emotional Empathy = .81; Perspective Taking = .77; Personal Distress = .73; Total Empathy = .81.

[d]Self-forgiveness and Other-forgiveness are two 5-item measures that assess dispositional tendencies to forgive developed by Zechmeister (1999); Total Forgive is the sum of these two subscales. Cronbach's alpha for each was .74, .69, and .71, respectively.

Contemplative Study

Contemplative traditions have developed methods to help people in their religious development and discernment, methods that can aid in exploring and defining motives and thus help in discerning loving, compassionate action. By giving insight into the processes involved in expressing compassionate love, the contemplative tradition can increase for the individual the quality of awareness of motives. It can enable one to sift through motives and more effectively choose actions. It can also illuminate the motives and sources of compassion that are most likely to lead to personal and spiritual growth. Besides leading to more loving, compassionate behavior, insights from this approach can inspire further experimental and observational studies and development of better self-report measures.

As the basic model (Figure 5.1) indicates, motives and discernment can be crucial to whether the act has power in the world and whether it transforms and builds up the person who does it. In addition to motivational issues, we traverse other complex inner terrain as we make choices to speak and act with compassionate love in particular situations. Figure 5.3 elaborates on this process. Even assuming the situation is driven by the motivation of good for the other, we still have a variety of other issues. There is a general attitude of heart with which life is approached, and each situation is addressed in that context. In addition, various issues need to be balanced. One needs to balance the interests and claims of the self versus those of others. The claims of justice need to be qualified by mercy. Related to "self versus others" but not exactly the same is the issue of receiving versus giving. We need to balance giving to others with an openness to receive, thus enabling the other to give. Appropriate tradeoffs between long-term and short-term benefits must be made. Likewise, a balance must be found between those we are close to and strangers.

To explore some of this subjective complexity effectively, I chose to supplement the typical self-report methodology with an approach articulated by Han de Wit (1991). De Wit describes compassion as "contemplative action" and thinks that it has experiential value on the spiritual journey, that it awakens a particular experience of reality, one that is characterized by the fruits of mercy and insight. According to many religious traditions, human beings possess a mental discernment (discriminating awareness) that allows them to clarify their experience, a capacity to distinguish between illusion and reality, self-deception and truth. It is his conclusion that, as a rule, this discriminating awareness does not function adequately but that it can be cultivated and trained in such a way that we are able to view our own mental domain clearly and to recognize our own mental patterns. On the basis of this, we can also learn to identify the causal connections between what we think, say, and do. Internally we go through a process of weighing our motives consciously and intuitively assessing the situation, drawing on empathy and notions of justice and fairness and determining the appropriate action. That action in turn shapes our own moral and spiritual development, as well as, it is hoped, having good effects on the world around us. De Wit talks about people who have developed a particularly acute sense of this process and who devote a good portion of their lives to the inner cultivation of spiritual life that predisposes to

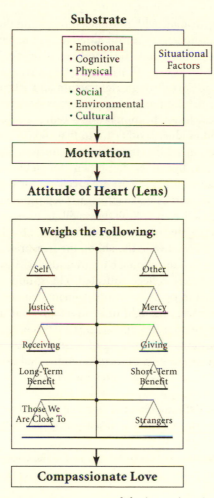

Figure 5.3. Complementary ways to approach loving action: Attitude of heart and conscious decisions

mercy and insight, to contemplative action, and to compassion. These people include in particular monastics from Buddhist and Christian traditions, as well as those from a variety of other traditions, such as Sufi Muslims. But his analysis also applies to those who have been inspired by these approaches in their individual religious and spiritual lives and who cultivate these approaches in other ways.

This analysis of contemplative psychology formed the inspiration for a series of structured interviews with Trappist monks. Trappist monks are Christians who follow the Benedictine Rule. Their order has been ongoing since the Middle Ages. They are moderately isolated in a path that aims to integrate the life of the spirit with their daily work lives. The monks I interviewed run a mail-order food business in the abbey to support themselves, but their primary daily structure centers around six set times of community prayer, chanting psalms, and reading Scripture. Time is also set aside during the day for silent meditative prayer. This abbey has had ongoing dialogue with Buddhist monks, and they have found common ground in their approaches, despite differences in beliefs. Silence is an important part of life in the monastery, and meals are taken in silence.

The teachings the monks draw from emphasize issues such as how to discern right motive and how to sort through right action and attitude. They point out pitfalls to be aware of, such as those discussed earlier relating to motives that detract from compassionate love. The monks also accept the core value of expressing compassionate love and hold each other up to that standard within the community more than many groups do, so the refining element of community also plays a part. For some people, the inner equipment for detecting motives and the process they go through in discernment are excellent; for others, these skills are rusty or minimal. The monastics make efforts to keep the detection equipment in good shape, and they practice and refine their skills in using it.

My initial studies consisted of structured, in-depth interviews with 13 monastics. Among those interviewed were the abbot, the treasurer, a cook, and a tailor. Ages ranged from 35 to 75. Educational backgrounds varied, although the majority of those interviewed were college educated. This group was selected not because they were assumed to be more compassionate than an average population sample but because they were thought to be more aware of the process one goes through as compassionate decisions and actions are taken.

The following questions give an idea of some of what was included in the structured interview. It was framed to focus on individual experience rather than to lead to intellectual assessment or abstract answers:

- What are the key defining features/essential components of compassionate love, agape, unconditional love, and self-giving love? What is the best phrase to describe this concept?
- Describe the internal process by which you make choices when confronted with a daily event calling for decision between self and other and calling for words or actions.
- Describe the internal process by which you make choices when confronted with a daily event calling for a decision between balancing mercy and justice.
- What motives detract from the expression of compassionate love?
- How do you envision self and other when in the process of daily interactions? Do self and other always feel distinct?
- What role does empathy, mentally identifying with the other, play in compassionate love? Is it necessary?
- What practices help you to more appropriately express compassionate love in your life?

One of the key findings was the degree of individual difference. The language used and approaches taken varied enormously, a particularly interesting result given the selection bias of the sample in terms of common belief system, common environment, and common lifestyle. Each person, although valuing compassionate love highly, had his own unique approach to the incorporation of compassionate love into daily life.

KEY DEFINING FEATURES   There were, however, some common factors. Central features of compassionate love that they cited included humility, trust, respect, unselfishness, receptivity, openness, and detachment. A few of the other main features that were mentioned as essential features of compassionate love were as follows: "To set aside one's own agenda for the sake of, to strengthen, or to give life to the other." "To experience, be present, to the situation of the other." "To have a mature view of reality." "To accept self in order to accept others." "To really listen to the other." "To deny self for something greater." "To suffer with another." "To help another become fully themselves." Each of these features merits further exploration than space allows here. One interesting fact to note is the practical concreteness of the features and the relative absence of obvious religion-specific language.

APPROACHES TO CHOICE AND ACTION   Two basic approaches emerged for balancing issues and sifting motives as decisions were made about how best to express compassionate love in situations. Some monks were more analytical, using a decision-making process relevant to specific situations. Others were more intuitive, depending on a "way of life" or a "lens" on which to base individual decisions. These approaches are both captured to some extent in Figure 5.3. Although some monks were more analytic and some more intuitive, most used a combination of the two approaches.

Descriptions of the way-of-life lens included the following: valuing the other, feeling of willingness, no awareness of the details of whether one was acting compassionately or not until afterward, "not depending on others for identity." A number of the monks said things such as "compassion is a way of life." There were specific basic underlying attitudes that shaped compassionate decisions. For example, if one depended on others for identity, then it was harder to be freely compassionate.

On the other hand, the following responses describe the approach of those taking the more analytical approach. There was much overlap among the individuals but also distinctive styles and tools that reflected many individual characters. "I ask in each decision situation, how much of me is in this? If there is too much of me, then how can I shift toward the other?" "I quiet myself down, to get myself out of the way." It was considered important to let go of "grasping" feelings. One monk said that it was important to make sure that what others would say was not driving his actions. The following quote is particularly illuminating with respect to process: "In some cases the natural pull is easier than in others. So in some cases the pull of nature can facilitate compassion. But sometimes it doesn't. So one's actions cannot be determined by natural pulls."

It was pointed out that ultraconscientiousness can be a danger—the motivation of claiming the "higher moral ground" is not a solid foundation for expressions of compassionate love. One monk described the process of weighing values, noting that he gave some weight to his own needs but gave them less weight than he gave to the needs of others. The importance of clear perception and also of utilizing intuition was expressed. Another monk described how, early on in his time in the monastery, he made a decision to do good because it was good, not for the approval of others; to correct for his own inclinations, he made sure that he spent a lot of effort doing good that was unseen.

SELF AND OTHER   Following are some reflections on how people view self and other in the process of daily interactions. The majority, seven of those interviewed, saw self and other as distinct. For these, although there was a link between self and the other, the distinction was also there. On the other hand, some articulated it as a blurred distinction. One comment in this regard was, "the distinction dissolves when in a compassionate moment." Those who found the distinction blurred also talked about levels of engagement: "we unite at a deeper level of the self" or "we are all one at a deep level." One raised the point that when we can help others we might actually hurt the self, and the realization of that distinguishes self and other; but the act is carried out nevertheless. In the answers to the questions on empathy, it emerged that although most felt it was important or helpful to be able to identify with the other, only two felt it was essential to do so in order to express compassionate love. Because the substrate components of capacity for empathy and empathic accuracy can vary across individuals, this finding suggests that those who may not be empathically gifted still have the opportunity to express compassionate love.

PRACTICES   Another important purpose of these interviews was to try to find out which practices might encourage and sustain the expression of compassionate love. Here was a crucial question, as one of the main goals of this research is to look at how one might encourage compassionate love to be more fully expressed. In the interviews, individual practices and practices within the community were both emphasized as being helpful.

As an individual, it was considered important to develop a strong identity and awareness of who one is, an identity that does not depend on other people. Spending quiet time and time alone was one way to foster that identity and awareness and was felt to support the compassionate life generally. This practice helps one to be able to be at ease with oneself. Prayer was frequently cited as a key element that supported compassionate love—connecting with a common "ground of being" was how one monk expressed it. Spiritual reading was important to ground oneself in writings of wisdom. The doing of compassionate things in and of itself can encourage one to do more.

Community and relationships are seen as important, too. It is helpful to live in a community that supports the value of love, as well as the value of cultivating awareness of motives, and that encourages both. The critique of an aware community is very helpful, too. In the monastic community, for example, "do-gooders bug people." This attitude helps to keep people from falling into inappropriate motives for helping others. Living a generally unselfish lifestyle helps one to make particular unselfish decisions. Also, to live a life balanced between respect for self and respect for others can support the expression of compassion. Listening to others was considered a key feature for the majority of monks—to know when an action would be really compassionate, to understand the pain and the needs of another, and to value others as they are. Learning about people and how the world functions was important in making correct decisions. It was mentioned that it was easier in the monastery to avoid aggression and violence, and this was helpful in creating an atmosphere conducive to compassion.

To reflect fully on the results of these interviews would take us beyond the length of this chapter, but a few comments are possible. It was obvious that the integration of feelings and cognitions was crucial to making free choice for the other, as was an understanding of self and the situation. Openness and receptivity were important, and the need to really listen—to people and to life—came up time and again. A balanced view of the importance of self and other was also important. A spiritually grounded perspective on oneself and one's identity can counterbalance tendencies to define oneself and others in terms of what one has or how one fits functionally in the world, a perspective that may have important implications for appropriate expression of compassionate love (Underwood, 1995). The levels of individual differences give insight into the many strategies and attitudes that people can use to express compassionate love fully in their lives.

The degree of self-awareness of internal processes that arises from a contemplative lifestyle can provide a magnifying lens for examining the process of expressing compassionate love. Results of structured interviews with monastics have explored the usefulness of this method. Insights from this approach can inspire further experimental and observational studies and can lead both to better self-reports and to more loving, compassionate behavior.

The quality of compassionate love that is present in an act has to do with the motives and ways of expression. Actions that flow from those motives and ways of expression feed back into the spiritual and moral life of the person. The motives affect whether and how the action contributes to the person's growth and the contribution it can make to the flourishing of others.

Conclusions

One major goal of research on compassionate love is ultimately to give additional insight into how compassionate love might be fostered in individuals and societies. In order to do this well, it is important to understand the key features of compassionate love, the substrate of conditions that influence freedom of expression, and the motives that detract from the quality of loving compassion. Clarification of additional issues, such as the concept of self and its boundaries, and balancing of priorities are important for the effectiveness of such a model. Various methods, such as external assessment of outcomes, self-report, and experimental models, can all support our understanding of the topic. Scientific research methods in this area can benefit from methods that utilize tools for clear discernment and awareness of internal processes.

REFERENCES

Carmel, S., & Glick, S. (1996). Compassionate-empathic physicians. *Social Science and Medicine, 43*(8), 1253–1261.

Damasio, A. R. (1994). *Descartes' error.* New York: Putnam.

de Wit, H. F. (1991). *Contemplative psychology.* Pittsburgh: Duquesne University Press.

Lewis, C. S. (1991). *The four loves.* Orlando: Harcourt Brace. (Original work published 1960)

Lofty, M. (1998). WHO and spirituality, religiousness, and personal beliefs (SRPB): Report on WHO consultation, June 22–24, 1998. Unpublished report. Washington: World Health Organization, Division of Mental Health and Prevention of Substance Abuse.

Mermann, A. C. (1993). Love in the clinical setting. *Humane Medicine, 9*(4), 268–273.

Nouwen, H. J. M. (1972). *With open hands.* Notre Dame, IN: Ave Maria Press.

Sulmasy, D. P. (1997). *The healer's calling.* Mahwah, NJ: Paulist Press.

Underhill, E. (1976). In L. Barkway & L. Menzies (Eds.), *An anthology of the love of God.* London: Mowbray.

Underwood, L. G. (1995). A working model of health: Spirituality and religiousness as resources: Applications for persons with disability. *Journal of Religion, Disability and Health, 3*(3), 51–71.

Underwood, L. G. (1999). Daily Spiritual Experience. In *Fetzer NIA Multidimensional Measurement of Religiousness/Spirituality for use in health research* (pp. 11–17). Kalamazoo, MI: Fetzer Institute.

Vanier, J. (1998). *Becoming human.* Mahwah, NJ: Paulist Press.

van Kaam, A. (1964). *Religion and personality.* Englewood Cliffs, NJ: Prentice-Hall.

Zahn-Wexler, C., & Redke-Yarrow, M. (1979). Child rearing and children's prosocial initiations toward victims of distress. *Child Development, 50,* 319–330.

Zechmeister, J. S. (1999). Daily Spiritual Experience: Descriptive statistics for each item. Unpublished manuscript.

6

Addressing the Altruism Question Experimentally

C. DANIEL BATSON

We humans can and do act to benefit others. We stay up all night to comfort a friend who has just suffered a broken relationship. We send money to rescue famine victims halfway around the world, or to save whales, or to support public TV. We spend millions of hours per week helping as volunteers in hospitals, nursing homes, AIDS hospices, fire departments, rescue squads, shelters, halfway houses, peer counseling programs, and the like. What motivates us to help others in these ways?

The most common answer in Western thought is that we benefit others to benefit ourselves. Everything we do, no matter how noble and seemingly self-sacrificial, is really directed toward the ultimate goal of self-benefit. We gain gratitude, admiration, and a good feeling about ourselves; we avoid guilt; we put ourselves in line for help should we need it. The list of self-benefits is long. This view is called universal egoism. Yet is it true that other people, however dear, are simply complex objects in our environment—important sources of stimulation and gratification, of facilitation and inhibition—as we each pursue self-interest? Or can we care for others, too? If so, for whom: for immediate family, for friends, for nation, for all humanity? Answers to these questions would tell us something about how interconnected we humans really are, about how truly social we are. Behind the question of motives for helping is, then, an even more fundamental question of human nature, the question of whether altruism is within the human repertoire. This is the altruism question.

Defining Altruism and Egoism

If we are to make any headway in answering the altruism question, then we must first clearly specify the difference between altruism and egoism and do so in a way that takes into account the subtle forms of self-benefit just noted. We must adopt definitions that do not distort or oversimplify the egoism-altruism debate. We can best do this, I think, by following the lead of Auguste Comte (1798–1857), who is credited with coining the term *altruism*. Before Comte, the question of why we help others was discussed under a variety of headings, including benevolence, charity, compassion, friendship, and love. Comte's differentiation between altruism and egoism brought the question into sharper focus.

Comte (1851/1875) considered altruism and egoism to be two distinct motives within the individual. He did not deny the existence of self-serving motives, even for helping; the impulse to seek self-benefit and self-gratification he called *egoism*. But Comte believed that some social behavior was an expression of an unselfish desire to "live for others" (p. 556). It was this second type of motivation to benefit others that he called *altruism*.

One popular rejoinder to Comte's proposal of altruism, made by philosophers of his day, went as follows: Even if it were possible for a person to be motivated to increase another's welfare, such a person would be pleased by attaining this desired goal, so even this apparent altruism would actually be a product of egoism. This argument, based on the general principle of *psychological hedonism*, has been shown to be flawed by later philosophers, who have pointed out that it involves confusion between two different forms of hedonism. The strong form of psychological hedonism asserts that attainment of personal pleasure is always the goal of human action; the weak form asserts only that goal attainment always brings pleasure. The weak form is not inconsistent with the possibility that the ultimate goal of some action is to benefit another rather than to benefit oneself, because the pleasure obtained can be a consequence of reaching the goal without being the goal itself. The strong form of psychological hedonism is inconsistent with the possibility of altruism, but to affirm this form is simply to assert universal egoism; as such, it is an affirmation about matters of fact that may or may not be true. (MacIntyre, 1967, reviews these philosophical arguments.)

Comte coined the term *altruism* in juxtaposition to egoism over a century ago, and, understandably, his concept is dated. It is an odd alloy of phrenology, conditioning principles, assumptions about emotional contagion, and utopian moralizing. Fortunately, I believe that his concept can be recast and expressed more usefully, without changing its basic meaning, by employing a more modern view of motives as goal-directed forces within the individual.

Employing this view of motivation, I suggest the following definitions: Altruism is a motivational state with the ultimate goal of increasing another's welfare. Egoism is a motivational state with the ultimate goal of increasing one's own welfare. Altruism and egoism, thus defined, have much in common. Each refers to goal-directed motivation; each is concerned with the ultimate goal of this motivation; and for each, the ultimate goal is to increase someone's welfare. These common features provide the context for highlighting the crucial difference: Whose welfare is the ultimate goal—another person's or one's own? These definitions are, I believe, true to the egoism-altruism debate in Western thought.

The Research Problem

Given these definitions, helping another person—even at great cost to oneself—may be altruistically motivated, egoistically motivated, both, or neither. To ascertain that some act was beneficial to another and was intended (i.e., was helpful) does not in itself say anything about the nature of the underlying motivation. In order to know whether a given motive for helping is altruistic or egoistic, we must determine whether benefit to the other is (1) an ultimate goal, and any self-benefits are unintended consequences (altruism); or (2) an instrumental means to reach the ultimate goal of benefiting oneself (egoism). The formal structure of the research problem is sketched in Table 6.1.

If helping benefits both the person in need and the helper, as it often does, how are we to know which is the ultimate goal? This puzzle has led many scientists to give up on the altruism question, concluding that it cannot be answered empirically. I think this surrender is premature. I think we can empirically ascertain people's ultimate goals; indeed, we do it all the time. We do it when we infer whether a student is really interested or only seeking a better grade (What happens to the student's interest after the grades are turned in?), why a friend chose one job over another, and whether politicians mean what they say or are only after votes. We also do it when someone does us a favor or is kind.

Three principles are important when attempting to discern a person's ultimate goal. First and most obviously, we do not observe another person's goals or intentions directly; we infer them from the person's behavior. Second, if we observe only a single behavior that has two potential ultimate goals, the true ultimate goal cannot be discerned. It is like having one equation with two unknowns; a clear answer is impossible. Third, we can begin to draw reasonable inferences about the ultimate goal if we can observe this person's behavior in different situations that involve a change in the relationship between the two potential ultimate goals. The behavior should always be directed toward the true ultimate goal.

Table 6.1   Formal Structure of the Altruism Question

	Outcomes of helping	
Nature of the motive to help	Relieving the other's suffering	Receiving self-benefits
Altruistic	Ultimate goal	Unintended consequence
Egoistic	Instrumental goal	Ultimate goal

Note: Adapted from Batson (1990).

Adopting these principles, two steps are necessary to infer the nature of a person's motivation from his or her behavior. First, we must conduct a conceptual analysis of the various potential ultimate goals for the person's action. Unless we have some idea that a given goal might be the person's aim, there is little likelihood of concluding that it is. Second, we need to observe the person's behavior in systematically varying circumstances. Specifically, the circumstances need to vary in a way that disentangles the relationship between potential ultimate goals, making it possible for the person to obtain one goal without obtaining the other. The person's behavioral choices in these situations should prove diagnostic, telling us which of the goals is ultimate, because the behavior should always be directed toward the ultimate goal. These two steps provide an empirical basis for inferring the nature of a person's motivation.

Over the past 20 years, other social psychologists and I have used this two-step logic to address the question of the existence of altruism in humans. First, we have developed a conceptual analysis that identifies (1) three general classes of egoistic motives for helping and (2) one likely source of altruistic motivation. Second, we have conducted laboratory experiments in which we have systematically varied circumstances in an attempt to disentangle the altruistic ultimate goal (benefiting the other) from one or more possible egoistic ultimate goals (benefiting the self).

The Empathy-Altruism Hypothesis and Its Egoistic Alternatives

The three general classes of egoistic motives for helping that we have considered are: (1) reward seeking—including material, social, and self-rewards; (2) punishment avoidance—including material, social, and self-punishments; and (3) aversive-arousal reduction—reducing the arousal produced by witnessing another in need. The likely source of altruistic motivation that we have considered is empathy. By *empathy* I mean *an other-oriented emotional response congruent with the perceived welfare of another.* If the other is perceived to be in need, then empathic emotions include feelings of sympathy, compassion, tenderness, and the like. This emotional reaction has been named as a source—if not *the* source—of altruism by Thomas Aquinas, David Hume, Adam Smith, Charles Darwin, Herbert Spencer, William McDougall, and several contemporary psychologists. (The empathic emotion described here should not be confused with the cognitive ability to correctly perceive another person's internal state, sometimes called "empathic accuracy"—e.g., Ickes, 1993—which is neither sufficient nor even necessary to produce empathic emotion.)

I call the proposal that feeling empathy for a person in need evokes altruistic motivation to relieve that need the *empathy-altruism hypothesis.* This hypothesis claims that empathy evokes motivation directed toward the ultimate goal of reducing the needy person's suffering; the more empathy felt for a person in need, the more altruistic motivation to have that need reduced. The empathy-altruism hypothesis does not deny that reaching the hypothesized altruistic goal is likely to enable the helper to gain rewards, avoid punishments, and reduce aversive arousal. It claims that these benefits to self are not the ultimate goal of empathy-induced helping; they are unintended consequences.

Considerable evidence supports the idea that feeling empathy for a person in need leads to increased helping of that person (Coke, Batson, & McDavis, 1978; Dovidio, Allen, & Schroeder, 1990; Krebs, 1975; see Batson, 1991, and Eisenberg & Miller, 1987, for reviews). To observe an empathy-helping relationship, however, tells us nothing about the nature of the motivation that underlies this relationship. Increasing the other person's welfare could be (1) an ultimate goal, producing self-benefits as unintended consequences; (2) an instrumental goal on the way to the ultimate goal of gaining one or more self-benefits; or (3) both. That is, the motivation could be altruistic, egoistic, or both (see Table 6.1).

The Virtue of Experiments

I believe that experimental methods are ideal for teasing these possibilities apart. An experiment can be described as a causal caricature. A caricature is an artificial, usually simplified, reconstruction of some natural phenomenon; it selectively emphasizes essential components. A caricature is not a mirror of reality; it is an intentional distortion. Yet, if well done, it may reveal reality better than a mirror because the essential components stand out.

The experimental caricature is created with a specific purpose in mind—testing one or more causal hypotheses. Virtually all scientific hypotheses are causal; they have an underlying "if . . . , then . . ." form. An experiment allows one to test for the existence of this causal relationship by varying (manipulating) selected "if" dimensions (independent variables) and observing the effect on selected "then" dimensions (dependent variables). Nonessential factors are excluded by one of two techniques. They may be eliminated by control of the environment (as in a laboratory), or they may be neutralized by random assignment of the entities being studied to independent variable conditions. Within the limits of chance, random assignment allows us to create identical groups out of different individual entities, in turn allowing us to place the same entities (aggregated) in different circumstances.

The resulting caricature provides a situation in which, except for chance variation, the only differences between the entities in different experimental conditions are the differences created by manipulation of the independent variable(s). Under these circumstances, if one or more independent variables correlate with one or more dependent variables, then one can infer with confidence that the independent variables caused changes in the dependent variables. This clarity of inference makes experiments ideal for testing a causal hypothesis. The hypothesis suggests which variables should be included in the experimental caricature and what the causal relationship between these variables should be. A good experiment, in turn, can give the hypothesis an unequivocal opportunity to show itself wrong—when the predicted causal relationships fail to appear.

Experimental Designs to Test the Empathy-Altruism Hypothesis against the Egoistic Alternatives

If we are to employ the experimental method to test the empathy-altruism hypothesis against one or more of the egoistic alternatives, then we need to provide research participants with an opportunity to help a person in distress. We also need to manipulate not only the level of empathy felt for that person but also a cross-cutting variable that changes the relationship between two potential ultimate goals: (1) increasing the other's welfare (altruism) and (2) increasing one's own welfare in some way (egoism). Table 6.2 presents a taxonomy of cross-cutting variables that achieve this end for one or more of the egoistic alternatives to the empathy-altruism hypothesis. These variables do not change the goal(s); they change the attractiveness or availability of different behavioral routes to the goal(s). As a result, each variable listed in Table 6.2 allows us to make different empirical predictions for the empathy-altruism hypothesis and at least one of the egoistic alternatives. By setting up experiments that include these cross-cutting variables, we can test the competing predictions and thereby assess the validity of the different hypotheses.

AVERSIVE AROUSAL REDUCTION   The most frequently proposed egoistic explanation of the empathy-helping relationship is aversive arousal reduction. This explanation claims that feeling empathy for someone who is suffering is unpleasant and that empathically aroused individuals help in order to benefit themselves by

Table 6.2   Variables That Can Differentiate Altruistic and Egoistic Motives for Helping

| | | Egoistic motive | | |
Variable	Altruistic motive	Arousal-reducing	Punishment-avoiding	Reward-seeking
1. Viability of escape: Can the goal be reached by escape without helping?	Escape not viable	Escape viable (from victim's distress)	Escape viable (from own shame, guilt)	Escape not viable
2. Necessity of one's help being effective: Must one's help be effective to reach the goal?	Necessary	Necessary	Not necessary (if ineffectiveness justified)	Not necessary (if ineffectiveness justified)
3. Acceptable helpers: Whose help can attain the goal?	Oneself; others	Oneself; others	Oneself; others	Only oneself
4. Need for rewards of helping: What is the effect of increased need for the rewards of helping?	No effect	No effect	No effect	Increased motivation
5. Salient cognitions: What cognitions are salient when deciding whether to help?	Victim's welfare; costs of helping	Aversive arousal; costs of helping	Anticipated punishments; costs of helping	Anticipated rewards; costs of helping

Note: Adapted from Batson (1987).

eliminating their empathic feelings. Benefiting the victim is simply a means to this self-serving end.

Two variables in Table 6.2 produce different empirical predictions for the aversive arousal reduction explanation and the empathy-altruism hypothesis: viability of escape and salient cognitions. Specifying cognitions clearly relevant to aversive arousal reduction is difficult, so research has focused on the escape variable. The aversive arousal reduction explanation predicts that if helping is at least moderately costly and if empathically aroused individuals can easily escape continued exposure to the person's suffering, then they will escape instead of helping. They will do this because either helping or escaping can enable them to reduce aversive empathic arousal: Helping removes the source of the aversive arousal; escaping removes contact with the source. In contrast, the empathy-altruism hypothesis predicts no reduction of empathically aroused helping when escape is made easy because escaping brings one no nearer the altruistic goal of relieving the victim's suffering; only helping (or someone else helping) does that.

We can, then, experimentally test the relative merits of these two hypotheses by presenting some empathically aroused individuals with an opportunity to help in a situation in which escape from continued exposure to the target person's suffering is easy and others with the same opportunity in a situation in which escape is difficult. The aversive arousal reduction explanation predicts less helping in the former situation than the latter; the empathy-altruism hypothesis does not.

EMPATHY-SPECIFIC PUNISHMENT   A second egoistic explanation claims that people learn through socialization that they have an obligation to help, and so additional shame and guilt for failure to help are attendant on feeling empathy for someone in need. As a result, when people feel empathy, they are faced with impending social or self-censure beyond any general punishment associated with not helping. They say to themselves, "What will others think—or what will I think of myself—if I don't help when I feel like this?" and then they help out of an egoistic desire to avoid these empathy-specific punishments. Table 6.2 lists three variables that produce different behavioral predictions for this empathy-specific punishment explanation and for the empathy-altruism hypothesis.

First, the empathy-specific punishment explanation can be tested by varying a second form of escape—escape from shame and guilt for not helping. This explanation predicts that any circumstance that enables the empathically aroused individual to escape from the anticipated social and self-censure for a failure to help should reduce the rate of helping; the empathy-altruism hypothesis predicts no reduction. To compare these predictions, one might make any anticipated punishment associated with empathy easier to escape by making helping decisions anonymous or by providing potential helpers with a face-saving excuse for not helping. Anonymity should reduce the threat of social censure; a face-saving excuse should reduce the threat of self-censure and guilt.

Second, consider the effect of providing empathically aroused individuals with information about the effectiveness of their helping. Because those who sincerely try to help are exempt from censure and blame even if their efforts fail (after all, "it's the thought that counts"), the empathy-specific punishment explanation predicts that the empathically aroused individual should not be especially concerned if a sincere attempt to help does not succeed. But the empathy-altruism hypothesis predicts that an unsuccessful attempt to help, even if sincere, will be disappointing.

Third, when deciding whether to help, the empathy-specific punishment explanation predicts that empathically aroused helpers will be thinking about the punishments for not helping (e.g., guilt, shame) because avoiding these punishments is the ultimate goal. The empathy-altruism hypothesis predicts that they will be thinking about the needy other's welfare because the other's welfare is the ultimate goal. To ask empathically aroused helpers to tell us their goal-relevant thoughts is, of course, problematic; it assumes that they know and will report these thoughts. Fortunately, Stroop (1938) has provided a less reactive means of determining what people are thinking; it involves having them name as quickly as possible the color of ink in which words or other visual stimuli related to their thoughts appear. As Geller and Shaver (1976) observed concerning the Stroop procedure: "In general, it appears that latency of color naming for a particular word will increase whenever a subject has been thinking about something related to that word" (p. 101). Employing a Stroop procedure, it should be possible to assess the goal or goals associated with the empathy-helping relationship by examining the association between empathy-induced helping and color-naming latency for words related to different possible goals for helping (for the goal of punishment avoidance, words such as *guilt, shame, duty,* and *should*).

EMPATHY-SPECIFIC REWARD   The third major egoistic explanation claims that people learn through socialization that special rewards in the form of praise, honor, and pride are attendant on helping a person for whom they feel empathy. As a result, when people feel empathy, they think of these rewards and help out of an egoistic desire to gain them. Table 6.2 lists four variables that produce different behavioral predictions for this empathy-specific reward explanation and for the empathy-altruism hypothesis.

Two of these variables are ones already discussed: effectiveness of helping and salient cognitions. Paralleling the methods just proposed for testing the empathy-specific punishment explanation, each of these variables could be used to test the empathy-specific reward explanation. Concerning effectiveness, as is true for avoiding punishments, one's help need not be effective to gain rewards. The rewards for helping are available to those who sincerely try to help even if their efforts fail, so the empathy-specific reward explanation predicts that the empathically aroused individual should not be especially concerned if a sincere attempt to help does not succeed. Concerning salient cognitions, the empathy-specific reward explanation predicts that empathically aroused helpers will be thinking about the rewards of helping (e.g., praise, pride) because getting these rewards is their ultimate goal. Once again, a Stroop task could be used to assess the salience of thoughts about rewards.

Third, only one's own helping makes one eligible for the rewards of helping; someone else's helping does not. Therefore, the empathy-specific reward explanation predicts that, when helping involves negligible costs to self, empathically aroused individuals should be more pleased if the suffering person's need is removed as a result of their own action than as a result of someone else's action. If someone else helps, the rewards are lost. But if empathically aroused individuals are altruistically motivated to have the person's need relieved, then either their own or someone else's helping will suffice. The empathy-altruism hypothesis predicts equal pleasure, regardless of whose action relieves the person's suffering.

To test these competing predictions, one could measure the mood of empathically aroused individuals after they learn that someone else, or fate, has beaten them to the punch and relieved the victim's distress. If these individuals are seeking rewards for helping, their mood should not be enhanced by this information; it might even grow worse. If these individuals are altruistically motivated, they should be pleased.

Finally, the empathy-specific reward explanation predicts that introducing any factor that increases or decreases the empathically aroused individual's need for the rewards sought when feeling empathy will increase or decrease the rate of helping accordingly; the empathy-altruism hypothesis predicts no effect for such factors. To compare these predictions, some need-increasing factor, such as a threat to one's self-concept as an empathic person (Steele, 1975), might be introduced and the effect on the empathy-helping relationship assessed. Alternatively, empathically aroused individuals might be led either to anticipate or not to anticipate a rewarding experience even if they decide not to help. Anticipating such an experience should reduce helping if these individuals are helping because they have a special need for the resulting rewards; it should have no effect if they are helping out of an altruistic desire to benefit the person in need.

SEQUENTIAL TESTING   Not surprisingly, no single one of the proposed cross-cutting variables listed in Table 6.2 allows a clear test of the empathy-altruism hypothesis against all three egoistic alternatives. Therefore, it is necessary either to conduct an experiment in which several cross-cutting variables are manipulated at once—which seems unwieldy and unwise—or to conduct a series of experiments in which the egoistic alternatives are tested one after another. Following the latter strategy, care must be taken when moving from testing one egoistic alternative to testing another; the experimental situations must remain comparable so that cumulative comparisons can be made. The best way to maintain comparability is to use the same need situations, the same techniques for manipulating empathy, and the same dependent measures across experiments, changing only the cross-cutting variables.

Results

More than 25 experiments have now been conducted in which one or more of the cross-cutting variables in Table 6.2 have been manipulated and in which empathy for a person in need has been either manipulated, measured, or both (see Batson, 1991, for a review of more than 20 of them). Cumulatively, these experiments have used each of the cross-cutting variables and have tested all but one of the differential predictions in Table 6.2. For reasons noted earlier, there has been no attempt to assess the salience of cognitions associated with aversive arousal reduction.

With remarkable consistency, results of these experiments have shown patterns as predicted by the empathy-altruism hypothesis. Results have failed to support any of the egoistic alternatives. To the best of my knowledge, there is at present no plausible egoistic explanation of the cumulative evidence from these experiments. The evidence has led me to conclude—tentatively—that the empathy-altruism hypothesis is true. Empathic emotion does, it seems, evoke altruistic motivation in humans.

Current and Future Experimental Research

The discovery of experimental support for the empathy-altruism hypothesis is not an end but a beginning of further research. Experimental work based on the empathy-altruism hypothesis is currently under way in five different areas.

Practical Implications of the Empathy-Altruism Hypothesis

One implication of the empathy-altruism hypothesis is that people may at times be motivated to suppress or avoid empathic feelings in order to avoid altruistic motivation. Empathy avoidance may be a factor, possibly a central one, in the experience of burnout among caseworkers in the helping professions. Aware of the extreme effort involved in helping their clients or of the impossibility of helping effectively, these caseworkers—as well as nurses caring for terminal patients and even pedestrians confronted by the homeless—may try to avoid feeling empathy in order to avoid the resulting altruistic motivation. Experiments have shown evidence of such empathy avoidance. There seems to be, then, egoistic motivation to avoid altruistic motivation.

More positively, experiments have tested the possibility that empathy-induced altruism can be used to improve attitudes toward stigmatized out-groups. Thus far, results look quite encouraging. Inducing empathy has improved attitudes toward racial minorities, people with AIDS, the homeless, and even convicted murderers. Empathy-induced altruism has also been found to increase cooperation in a competitive situation—even when one knows that the person for whom one feels empathy has acted competitively.

Other Sources of Altruism

Research has also begun to explore possible sources of altruistic motivation other than empathic emotion. Several have been proposed, including an "altruistic personality" (Oliner & Oliner, 1988), principled moral reasoning (Kohlberg, 1976), internalized prosocial values (Staub, 1974), and devout, intrinsic religion (Allport, 1966). There is some evidence that each of these potential sources is associated with increased motivation to help, but as yet, it is not clear that these motivations are altruistic. They may be, or they may be an instrumental means to the egoistic ultimate goals of (1) maintaining one's positive self-concept or (2) avoiding guilt.

Experimental methods like those used to test the empathy-altruism hypothesis hold promise of clarifying matters.

Experiments have already helped clarify the nature of the motivation to help associated with different ways of being religious. Batson, Schoenrade, and Ventis (1993) summarize research on the association of different dimensions of individual religion with compassion and caring for others in need, the sort of caring exemplified by the Good Samaritan. The research indicates, first, that general religious activity and interest are associated with more stringent moral standards and with seeing oneself and being seen by others as more concerned for the welfare of people in need. But when confronted with someone in need, individuals who are more religious are not any more helpful than those who are less religious unless self-presentation concerns have been aroused.

Focusing more specifically on different ways of being religious, research indicates that devout, intrinsic religion is associated with reporting that one is helpful and concerned for others, and it is associated with increased helping in response to direct, low-cost requests. But the helping behavior associated with this dimension often is not responsive to the expressed needs of the person seeking help (Batson & Gray, 1981; Darley & Batson, 1973). It does not seem to be motivated by concern for the needy person's welfare but by self-concern to show oneself to be a good, kind, caring person (Batson et al., 1989). In contrast, a second way of being religious, as an open-ended quest, is not associated with reports of helpfulness or with increased amounts of helpfulness, but it is associated with helping that seems responsive to the expressed needs of the person seeking help. Whether this helping is motivated by an altruistic concern for those in need is not as yet clear.

Beyond Egoism and Altruism: Other Prosocial Motives

Thinking more broadly, beyond the egoism-altruism debate that has been a focus of attention and contention for the past two decades, might there be other forms of prosocial motivation, forms in which the ultimate goal is neither to benefit self nor to benefit another individual? Two seem especially worthy of consideration.

COLLECTIVISM Collectivism is motivation to benefit a particular group as a whole. The ultimate goal is not one's own welfare or the welfare of specific others; the ultimate goal is the welfare of the group. Robyn Dawes and his colleagues put it succinctly: "Not me or thee but we" (Dawes, van de Kragt, & Orbell, 1988). They suggested that collectivist motivation is a product of group identity (Tajfel, 1981; Turner, 1987).

As with altruism, what looks like collectivism may actually be a subtle form of egoism. Perhaps attention to group welfare is simply an expression of enlightened self-interest. Dawes and his colleagues (Dawes, van de Kragt, & Orbell, 1990) have conducted some research to address this question of the underlying motivation, but more is needed.

PRINCIPLISM Not only have most moral philosophers argued for the importance of a prosocial motive other than egoism, but most since Kant have also shunned altruism and collectivism. They reject appeals to altruism, especially empathy-induced altruism, because feelings of empathy, sympathy, and compassion are too fickle and too circumscribed. Empathy is not felt for everyone in need, at least not to the same degree. They reject appeals to collectivism because group interest is bounded by the limits of the group; it not only permits but may even also encourage harm to those outside the group. Given these problems with altruism and collectivism, moral philosophers have typically advocated prosocial motivation with an ultimate goal of upholding a universal and impartial moral principle, such as justice (Rawls, 1971). To have another "ism," I call this moral motivation *principlism*.

Is acting with an ultimate goal of upholding a moral principle really possible? When Kant (1785/1898) briefly shifted from his analysis of what ought to be to what is, he was ready to admit that the concern we show for others that appears to be prompted by duty to principle may actually be prompted by self-love. The goal of upholding a moral principle may be only an instrumental goal pursued as a means to reach the ultimate goal of self-benefit. If this is true, then principle-based motivation is actually egoistic. Once again, we need to know the nature of a prosocial motive. And once again, experimental designs similar to those used to test the empathy-altruism hypothesis are helping us find out.

Conflict among Prosocial Motives

Different forms of prosocial motivation are usually assumed to be mutually supportive and cooperative. Indeed, altruism, collectivism, and principlism are often confused or equated. If, however, these motives involve different ultimate goals, they may at times conflict rather than cooperate. For example, concern for the welfare of a specific person or persons (altruism) may conflict not only with self-interest but also with concern for the welfare of the group as a whole (collectivism) or concern with upholding a moral principle (principlism). Experimental evidence of such conflicts has begun to appear (Batson et al., 1999; Batson, Batson, et al., 1995; Batson, Klein, et al., 1995).

The Self-Other Relationship

To entertain the possibility of distinct prosocial motives (egoism, altruism, collectivism, and principlism) with distinct ultimate goals begs for a better understanding of cognitive representation of the self-other relationship. Several representations have been proposed. Concern for another's welfare may be a product of (1) a sense of "we"-ness based on cognitive unit formation or identification with the other's situation; (2) the self expanding to incorporate the other; (3) the self-other distinction remaining, with one distinct person caring for another; (4) the self being redefined at the group level, at which "me" and "thee" become interchangeable parts of a self that is "we"; or (5) the self dissolving in devotion to something outside itself, whether another person, a group, or a principle.

Most of these proposals seem plausible; some even seem profound. Yet not all can be true, at least not at the same time. Experimental research has begun to shed light on this complex problem.

Limitations of Experimental Research

As with any research, there are limitations to the experiments I have mentioned. Let me briefly discuss four.

The Open-Set Problem

There is a logical limit to the experimental tests of the empathy-altruism hypothesis. The various self-benefits of helping necessarily follow the attempt to benefit the person in need. Because of this asymmetry, experimental tests have focused on the three proposed egoistic alternatives. Only if results fail to show the pattern predicted by any of these alternatives and instead show the pattern consistently predicted by the empathy-altruism hypothesis can we conclude that the latter hypothesis is valid. Even then, we can accept the empathy-altruism hypothesis as valid only so long as no new plausible egoistic explanation can be proposed that accounts for the existing evidence. That is why my conclusion that empathic emotion evokes altruistic motivation remains tentative.

Of course, this open-set problem is not unique to experimental tests of the empathy-altruism hypothesis. Any time a plausible alternative explanation can be offered for data thought to support some hypothesis, the validity of that hypothesis is cast in doubt. In itself, this is not a basis for pessimism. It is not enough simply to say that another version of egoism *can* be invented; it is necessary to actually invent one, one that can explain all relevant existing data. To propose an egoistic explanation for one set of results when that explanation is clearly contradicted by another set will not do.

The data supporting the empathy-altruism hypothesis are extensive, diverse, and interconnected. I know of no plausible egoistic explanation for these data. If, however, someone can come up with such an explanation, then we need to design new experiments to test it. The case is never fully closed.

Undergraduate Samples

The experiments discussed are limited in the population sampled. Participants in almost all have been undergraduate students in introductory psychology courses at universities in the United States. It would certainly be good to conduct conceptual replications of these experiments with different populations.

At the same time, I do not think the narrowness of the population sampled undercuts the basic importance of this research for two reasons. First, were it true that empathy induces altruism only among undergraduate students in the United States, that fact would still sound a death knell for universal egoism. Second, I know of no good reason to think that, if empathy induces altruism among undergraduate students in the United States, it does so only there. The frequency of occurrence and the strength of empathy may, and likely does, vary across age, gender, socioeconomic class, and culture. The conditions that evoke empathy are also likely to vary, as are the behavioral manifestations of an altruistic motive. But none of these are what the experiments were designed to test. They were designed to test the empathy-altruism hypothesis, the claim that empathic emotion evokes altruistic motivation. Is there reason to think that if and when empathy is experienced it produces altruistic motivation only in the narrow population tested? It seems most unlikely that our luck in selecting a research population was that good.

Rather than assessing generality by conducting experiment after experiment with samples from population after population, I would recommend that our tests of generality be theory driven. Is there a theoretical basis to suspect that a given population might be unable to experience empathy or that for them empathy might fail to evoke altruistic motivation (e.g., sociopaths or patients with ventro-medial prefrontal lesions)? If so, we should test to see. This theory-driven strategy encourages audacious leaps of generalization. Are, for example, chimpanzees capable of experiencing empathic feelings? If so, do these feelings evoke altruistic motivation in them as well? There are theoretical reasons for thinking empathy-induced altruism might be part of chimpanzee nature; there are also theoretical reasons for thinking it might not. Experiments might help answer these important questions.

Inappropriate Experiments

I believe that laboratory experiments are ideal for addressing the issue of underlying motivation that lies at the heart of the altruism question. In an experiment one can introduce the necessary variation to disentangle potential ultimate goals. But laboratory experiments are certainly not ideal for addressing many other interesting and important questions about empathy, altruism, helping, and, more generally, about human goodness. Let me mention three examples.

First, the contrived nature of experiments, which is their major virtue, renders them useless for assessing the natural frequency of phenomena such as volunteerism, contributions to charities, and so on. Survey research or some less obtrusive observational technique is far better. Second, interviews and analyses of life histories are far better if one wants to understand the character of someone like Raoul Wallenberg or Mother Teresa. Comparison of groups of individuals randomly assigned to experimental conditions, which allows for clear causal inference, renders experiments insensitive to extreme or unusual cases; these cases become error variance. Third, longitudinal studies, not experiments, are needed to trace the etiology of empathic responding, moral reasoning, and moral behavior.

My reason for calling attention to the important role that experimental research can and should play in furthering our understanding of altruism—its nature, antecedents, and consequences—is not to suggest that all or even most research on empathy and altruism should be experimental. Rather, it is to suggest that research methods need to be carefully matched to the questions being addressed. To attempt to determine whether the motivation to help evoked by empathy is altruistic or egoistic using surveys, questionnaires, interviews, or longitudinal studies is, I think, doomed to failure. Of the research methods I know, only experimentation is up to this task. But this is not the only important task.

Ethical Issues

Finally, the experiments I have discussed raise thorny ethical issues. These issues are rooted in mire produced by two facts. First, researchers and scholars are not the only ones who care about empathy and altruism. Most research participants see themselves as good, kind, caring people, and they want to be seen that way by others. Second, research on empathy and altruism focuses on relatively hot, active processes—the interplay of values, emotions, motives, and behavior. These processes may not be accessible to cool introspection.

To reap a fruitful harvest from the mire that these two features create, one must avoid the pitfalls of demand characteristics, evaluation apprehension, social desirability, self-presentation, and reactive measures. Consequently, most of the experiments I have mentioned employ high-impact deception procedures of the sort made famous—some would say infamous—in the social psychology of the 1960s (e.g., Milgram, 1963). More ethically palatable procedures, such as presenting research participants with descriptions of hypothetical situations and asking them to report what they would do, are of limited use when trying to determine the nature of prosocial motives. So are retrospective accounts of why one acted as one did. Commitment to actual behavior—if not the behavior itself—is almost always required. This means one must either (1) create or intrude into situations in which people are actually suffering or (2) successfully deceive participants into believing that someone is suffering and deceive them about the true purpose of the research until their participation is complete. Neither option is ideal, but I much prefer the second. Obviously, when conducting such research, one incurs special responsibility to protect the welfare and dignity of participants.

Some universities no longer allow the use of high-impact deceptions of the kind needed to address fundamental questions concerning empathy and altruism. It is ironic that research on prosocial, ethical behavior has been one of the areas to suffer most from restrictions imposed in response to concerns about research ethics.

Few would disagree that society could benefit from increased sensitivity to and concern for others. Crimes of rage, drive-by shootings, child and spouse abuse, neglect of the homeless, the plight of people with AIDS, the growing disparity between rich and poor (and smug callousness toward the latter) provide all-too-frequent reminders of a crying need. Given the societal importance of understanding when and why people care for others, given the apparent necessity of using high-impact deception research to provide this understanding, and given the dangers of obtaining misleading information using other methods, it is not allowance of high-impact deception research—but rather a blanket prohibition of it—that I find unethical.

Summary and Conclusion

Why do people help others, even at considerable cost to themselves? What does this behavior tell us about the human capacity to care, about the degree of interconnectedness among us, about how social we humans really are? These classic philosophical questions have resurfaced in social psychology in the past several decades. Experimental research has tested the claim that empathic emotion evokes altruistic motivation—motivation with the ultimate goal of increasing another's welfare. Results of the more than 25 experiments designed to test this empathy-altruism hypothesis against various egoistic alternatives have proved remarkably supportive of it, leading to the tentative conclusion that feeling empathy for a person in need does indeed evoke altruistic motivation to help that person.

To have experimental evidence that empathic emotion evokes altruistic motivation in humans is a substantial gain. It provides a scientific answer to a philosophical question that has been around for centuries. It also points to important resources that we can and should tap in trying to build a more caring, humane society. At the same time, this new knowledge confronts us with a number of pressing additional research questions about (1) practical implications of the empathy-altruism hypothesis, (2) possible sources of altruistic motivation other than empathy, (3) possible prosocial motives other than altruism, (4) how one might orchestrate prosocial motives so that they cooperate rather than compete within the life of the individual, and (5) cognitive representation of the self-other relationship. A lot may depend on our ability to answer these research questions accurately in the years to come. And if we want accurate answers, experiments need to play a central role in our research plans.

REFERENCES

Allport, G. W. (1966). Religious context of prejudice. *Journal for the Scientific Study of Religion, 5,* 447–457.

Batson, C. D. (1987). Prosocial motivation: Is it ever truly altruistic? In L. Berkowitz (Ed.), *Advances in experimental social psychology* (Vol. 20, pp. 65–122). New York: Academic Press.

Batson, C. D. (1990). How social an animal? The human capacity for caring. *American Psychologist, 45,* 336–346.

Batson, C. D. (1991). *The altruism question: Toward a social-psychological answer.* Hillsdale, NJ: Erlbaum Associates.

Batson, C. D., Ahmad, N., Yin, J., Bedell, S. J., Johnson, J. W., Templin, C. M., & Whiteside, A. (1999). Two threats to the common good: Self-interested egoism and empathy-induced altruism. *Personality and Social Psychology Bulletin, 25,* 3–16.

Batson, C. D., Batson, J. G., Todd, R. M., Brummett, B. H., Shaw, L. L., & Aldeguer, C. M. R. (1995). Empathy and the collective good: Caring for one of the others in a social dilemma. *Journal of Personality and Social Psychology, 68,* 619–631.

Batson, C. D., & Gray, R. A. (1981). Religious orientation and helping behavior: Responding to one's own or to the victim's needs? *Journal of Personality and Social Psychology, 40,* 511–520.

Batson, C. D., Klein, T. R., Highberger, L., & Shaw, L. L. (1995). Immorality from empathy-induced altruism: When compassion and justice conflict. *Journal of Personality and Social Psychology, 68,* 1042–1054.

Batson, C. D., Oleson, K. C., Weeks, J. L., Healy, S. P., Reeves, P. J., Jennings, P., & Brown, T. (1989). Religious prosocial motivation: Is it altruistic or egoistic? *Journal of Personality and Social Psychology, 57,* 873–884.

Batson, C. D., Schoenrade, P., & Ventis, W. L. (1993). *Religion and the individual: A social-psychological perspective.* New York: Oxford University Press.

Coke, J. S., Batson, C. D., & McDavis, K. (1978). Empathic mediation of helping: A two-stage model. *Journal of Personality and Social Psychology, 36*:752–766.

Comte, I. A. (1875). *System of positive polity.* Vol. 1. London: Longmans, Green & Co. (Original work published 1851)

Darley, J. M., & Batson, C. D. (1973). From Jerusalem to Jericho: A study of situational and dispositional variables in helping behavior. *Journal of Personality and Social Psychology, 27,* 100–108.

Dawes, R., van de Kragt, A. J. C., & Orbell, J. M. (1988). Not me or thee but we: The importance of group identity in eliciting cooperation in dilemma situations: Experimental manipulations. *Acta Psychologica, 68,* 83–97.

Dawes, R., van de Kragt, A. J. C., & Orbell, J. M. (1990). Cooperation for the benefit of us—not me, or my conscience. In J. J. Mansbridge (Ed.), *Beyond self-interest* (pp. 97–110). Chicago: University of Chicago Press.

Dovidio, J. F., Allen, J. L., & Schroeder, D. A. (1990). The specificity of empathy-induced helping: Evidence for altruistic motivation. *Journal of Personality and Social Psychology, 59,* 249–260.

Eisenberg, N., & Miller, P. (1987). Empathy and prosocial behavior. *Psychological Bulletin, 101,* 91–119.

Geller, V., & Shaver, P. (1976). Cognitive consequences of self-awareness. *Journal of Experimental Social Psychology, 12,* 99–108.

Ickes, W. (1993). Empathic accuracy. *Journal of Personality, 61,* 587–610.

Kant, I. (1898). *Kant's Critique of Practical Reason and other works on the theory of ethics.* 4th ed. (T. K. Abbott, Trans.) New York: Longmans, Green & Co. (Original work published 1785)

Kohlberg, L. (1976). Moral stages and moralization: The cognitive-developmental approach. In T. Lickona (Ed.), *Moral development and behavior: Theory, research, and social issues* (pp. 31–53). New York: Holt, Rinehart, & Winston.

Krebs, D. L. (1975). Empathy and altruism. *Journal of Personality and Social Psychology, 32,* 1134–1146.

MacIntyre, A. (1967). Egoism and altruism. In P. Edwards (Ed.), *The encyclopedia of philosophy* (Vol. 2, pp. 462–466). New York: Macmillan.

Milgram, S. (1963). Behavioral study of obedience. *Journal of Abnormal and Social Psychology, 67,* 371–378.

Oliner, S. P., & Oliner, P. M. (1988). *The altruistic personality: Rescuers of Jews in Nazi Europe.* New York: Free Press.

Rawls, J. (1971). *A theory of justice.* Cambridge: Harvard University Press.

Staub, E. (1974). Helping a person in distress: Social, personality, and stimulus determinants. In L. Berkowitz (Ed.), *Advances in experimental social psychology* (Vol. 7, pp. 293–341). New York: Academic Press.

Steele, C. M. (1975). Name calling and compliance. *Journal of Personality and Social Psychology, 31,* 361–369.

Stroop, J. R. (1938). Factors affecting speed in serial verbal reactions. *Psychological Monographs, 50,* 38–48.

Tajfel, H. (1981). *Human groups and social categories: Studies in social psychology.* Cambridge: Cambridge University Press.

Turner, J. C. (1987). *Rediscovering the social group: A self-categorization theory.* London: Basil Blackwell.

7

Explicating Altruism

KRISTEN RENWICK MONROE

What do we know about empathy, altruism, and agape, and what are the most promising avenues for future research? This chapter discusses the two fundamental questions addressed in this volume by focusing on the social scientific research into the nature of altruistic love.

In the first section, I discuss altruism as conceptualized by social scientists and summarize my own empirical research, based on narrative interviews with philanthropists, recipients of the Carnegie Hero Commission Award, and rescuers of Jews during World War II. In the second section, I address future research on altruism by responding in general terms to the questions posed by the editors of this volume. The final section becomes more specific, outlining two particular projects that I believe might enrich future research. One argues for a paradigm shift within social science, away from reliance on theories that privilege self-interest over human needs for sociability and toward theories that more accurately capture the full range of the human psyche. The other argues for developing more empirically based theories of ethical behavior and suggests the beginning of such a theory, one that roots universal moral behavior not in religion or reason but in identity and a sense of self.

Conceptualizing and Measuring Altruism

I begin with a caution concerning conceptualization and methodology, a caution that may be of particular relevance in a volume that speaks to a broad audience.

Empathy, altruism, and agape are not the same phenomenon. Their causes thus may differ. Furthermore, our empirical research frequently operationalizes and measures them differently. Therefore, we must not waste time disagreeing over what causes empathy, altruism, and agape without first making sure that when we speak of empathy, altruism, and agape, we refer to the same thing or at least make explicit how we differ in our conceptualizations of these phenomena. My research has been on altruism, and I restrict my comments to that phenomenon, although I do discuss empathy later in this chapter.

What do we mean by altruism, a term not in existence until Auguste Comte introduced it in the 1830s? Traditionally, altruism refers to action intended to benefit another, even when such action risks possible sacrifice to the well-being of the actor. This conceptualization entails several critical points: (1) Altruism must involve action. Good intentions or well-meaning thoughts are not enough. (2) The action must have a goal, although the goal may be either conscious or reflexive. (3) The goal must be designed to help another. If another person's welfare is an unintended or secondary consequence of behavior motivated primarily to further one's own welfare, the act is not altruistic. (4) Consequences are less important than intentions. (5) Altruism sets no conditions. The purpose of the altruistic act is helping another; there is no anticipation or expectation of reward for the altruist. In addition to these five points, conceptualizations of altruism often contain a sixth: (6) Altruism must carry the risk of diminution of the actor's well-being. Acts that improve both the actor's and another's welfare are usually considered collective action. This aspect is more widely debated in social science, however, and is not always considered critical.

There are, of course, many different variants on this basic conceptualization, and some of the failure to focus on critical conceptual distinctions may explain why there are so many contradictory findings concerning altruism. A further, closely related problem concerns different ways of operationalizing altruism.[1] A study that draws conclusions about altruism based on how two-year-olds share toys speaks only tangentially to a study of altruism as conceptualized and operationalized by cooperation among ants or the allocation of family resources among charities and kin. Furthermore, altruism in the laboratory may differ in significant ways from altruism in what we often call the real world. We should be careful that critical conceptual and methodological distinctions do not engender substantive misunderstanding over the nature and causes of altruism.

This confusion is perhaps understandable, as we often find it useful for analytical purposes to make altruism a bifurcated phenomenon, dividing the world into altruists and nonaltruists. But the potential for altruism exists in all people. Indeed, many of us perform occasional acts of genuine altruism, and all but the most misanthropic engage in limited and sporadic volunteer activities or charitable giving. We engage in altruistic-like behavior, in other words, without being full-fledged altruists. In our scholarly discussions of altruism, then, we must take care to distinguish between altruism and closely related prosocial acts, such as giving, sharing, cooperating, and deep, generous love that might be other-regarding without fulfilling the five (or six) critical components listed previously as central to altruism. Nor should we confuse these diverse phenomena in our empirical work. We must recognize the subtle differences in behavior that emerge as we move along a conceptual continuum from pure self-interest to pure altruism. Works that dichotomize altruism, focusing complex acts into only the bifurcated categories of altruism and egoism, will miss much of the subtlety of the phenomenon.

Substantive Findings to Date

Given these caveats, what can I tell you about altruism, based on my own empirical research?[2] My work consisted of in-depth interviews with individuals in three categories: philanthropists, recipients of the Carnegie Hero Commission Award, and rescuers of Jews in Nazi Europe during World War II. All these individuals, 25 of whom were interviewed between 1988 and 1994, met the conditions for altruism described previously.[3] In terms of sociocultural predictors, my prior analysis suggests that none of the traditionally offered correlates of altruism consistently and systematically explains altruism or behavior by altruists. Indeed, altruists look much like other human beings in their educational, religious, and socioeconomic characteristics. On these dimensions, the backgrounds and early childhood experiences of altruists reflect those of the rest of humanity: They are complex and varied.

What about the different theories used to explain altruism? I found that analyses that remain set within the paradigmatic confines of self-interest can produce only limited explanations of altruism. Such paradigms are the norm in social science, with the possible exception of psychology. Reciprocity, clusters of altruists, and group or kin selection—all typical explanations from evolutionary biology and economics—have no predictive power for altruists, nor does the cost-benefit calculus or the psychic gratification hypothesis of economics. The economists' idea that people care first for their individual and family needs and only then give to others or that they allocate some division of resources between themselves and others does have a limited explanatory power for charitable giving by traditional rational actors, such as the entrepreneurs I interviewed as a control group; but this influence decreases as we consider individuals who approach the pure altruism end of our conceptual continuum, as judged by the consistency of their altruistic actions over the course of their lifetimes and as judged by the extent to which their altruism threatened their own lives and the lives of their loved ones, as it did for rescuers of Jews. Biological explanations stressing birth order and psychological emphasis on stable family relations fail, but establishing personal ties with the recipient does seem to predict charitable activities by the entrepreneur and, to a lesser extent, the philanthropist. I discounted social psychological theories stressing the importance of self-reinforcement, role models, or social learning because these factors work no better in predicting behavior by altruists than they do for typical rational actors. These traditional explanations, then, offer limited explanations for altruistic-like acts by rational actors but fail to explain altruism itself.[4]

What Does Cause Altruism? Perceptions of a Shared Humanity

The essential failure of both traditional sociocultural correlates and these more elaborate social science theories to provide adequate explanations for altruism leaves us in a quandary: What is the critical component that does account for altruism? How can we best explain behavioral differences between altruists and the self-interested individuals who exist at the heart of disciplines as disparate as evolutionary biology, psychology, and economics and rational choice theory? I found a psychological explanation, centering on cognitive frameworks and perceptions, most useful. I argue that what I call the altruistic perspective provides the critical component, particularly the altruist's perception of himself or herself in relation to others. All the altruists I interviewed saw themselves as individuals strongly linked to others through a shared humanity. Their cognitive-perceptual frameworks differed consistently and significantly from those of traditional rational actors in this one regard. Furthermore, two important and striking behavior patterns flowed naturally from this perspective. These concerned spontaneity and choice.

SPONTANEOUS ACTS   Surprisingly, altruistic behavior does not correspond to the accepted wisdom in Western ethics in which ethics are a function of agonistic choice.[5] Nor did altruism appear to arise from the dominance of reason over the baser passions.[6] Many rescuers of Jews, for example, endured long time periods of difficult and dangerous living situations, including torture and time in prison or concentration camps; despite this, however, their decisions to risk their lives to help another person appeared spontaneous. There was no night of anguish spent searching one's soul to find the strength to do the right thing. Rescuers simply responded as they said any ordinary human being would respond to another's need.

IDENTITY CONSTRAINS CHOICE   A second interesting phenomenon is closely related to the previous one: In describing their activities, altruists claimed to have had no choice in their actions toward others. This lack of choice was increasingly evident as individuals moved toward pure altruism, with canonical expectations about what constituted normal behavior appearing to limit the range of choice options perceived available by the altruist. Rescuers of Jews, for example, typically looked at me with incredulity when I repeatedly asked why they risked their lives for strangers. "But what else could I do?" was their constant reply. "They were human beings like you and me." This lack of a cost-benefit calculus, indeed of *any* conscious calculus, was remarkable in individuals having to decide whether to risk not just their own lives but also those of their families. Yet, uniformly, rescuers insisted they never thought about it, never saw that there was a choice to make. "The hand of compassion was faster than the calculus of reason," one rescuer told me, articulating both the spontaneous and the nonreasoning aspects of altruism. To my surprise, my later research suggests that this same process, wherein identity trumps or at least severely constrains choice, also seems to work for bystanders and for Nazis (Monroe, 1994, 2001b).[7]

Different Trigger Mechanisms

I concluded that earlier explanations of altruism have failed to identify the critical explanatory variable associated with altruism but have instead accurately identified many of the different mechanisms that trigger this altruistic perspective.[8] These factors may serve as catalysts that precipitate or encourage the development and growth of the altruistic perspective. But the perspective itself constitutes the heart of altruism. What causes it in any particular altruist will vary. It may emanate in factors as innate as a kind of genetic predisposition toward altruism or as explicit as parental or religious exhortations to think about others.[9] But it is the perception of a shared humanity with the other that these external mechanisms trigger which remains critical, not the mechanisms themselves.

In sum, then, I suggest that it is the altruistic perspective that most successfully explains altruism. It is the only factor that consistently and systematically predicts altruism among all the individuals I interviewed. This altruistic perspective consists of a common perception of themselves as individuals strongly linked to others through a shared humanity. This perspective constitutes such a central core of their identities that it leaves them with no choice in their behavior toward others in regard to ethical issues. It is this perspective that best distinguishes altruists from traditional rational actors.

Future Work

What do my findings suggest about broader issues of concern to future analysts? Let me answer this by responding to the general questions posed by the editors of this volume.

1. To what extent do human individuals and societies manifest behavior that is motivationally or consequentially altruistic? The short answer is that altruism is relatively rare. Empirically, probably more behavior seems driven by self-interest than by love for others, but this widely held conclusion is intimately related to the conceptual and methodological problems already discussed. Human behavior is intricate and complex and does not lend itself readily to the often-artificial categories scholars must construct for analytical purposes. A fuller answer to this question, then, is much more complicated and probably unreliable, given our current knowledge. For one thing, in the world of social science that I inhabit intellectually, it is difficult ever to know the consequences of our own acts or to know with great reliability the motives underlying the actions of others. We can guess about the consequences and make inferences about others' intentions based on their actions. But this still leaves great room for error. Furthermore, the consequences of an act do not always correlate highly with the actor's intent or motivation.[10]

2. What are the evolutionary origins and neurological substrates for altruistic behavior? This question is addressed by other chapters in this volume, but my own limited empirical work suggests that we simply don't know much about the evolutionary origins of altruism. My own research found kin and group selection explanations unconvincing, and I suspect that this approach is limited by the paradigmatic wedding of contemporary social science to self-interest. Work seeking to identify the neurological origins of altruism or love is similarly in its infant stage, although it is among the most exciting of the scientific literatures on altruism. Indeed, work by Insel (Chapter 14, this volume) and by Preston and de Waal (Chapter 17, this volume) suggest that there is, in fact, a biological foundation that underpins philosophical theories such as moral sense theory, a theory that was promising when originally developed in the 1700s but has not advanced much since then.[11]

3. What personal developmental processes foster or hinder altruistic attitudes and behavior? There is some exciting work on child development (see Kagan, Chapter 3, this volume) that suggests that a moral sense may be universal and, therefore, presumably innate. When we move to discussions of adults and morality, work such as Kohlberg's (1976, 1984) suggests that we develop our moral sense much as we develop our innate linguistic capacities. This approach builds on Piaget's (1948) work in cognitive development of children and has much in common with moral sense theory à la Shaftesbury (1711/1714/1977) and Hume (1740/1978). Although I am prepared to accept as a working hypothesis the idea that we do carry an inborn sense of right and wrong, I find that the existing literature, which stresses a cognitive developmental approach, has limited value for the kind of moral issues that concern me. I would agree in principle that there is a minimal level of cognitive development that is necessary for moral action. (We would not expect a 1-year-old to think or act morally, for example.) But when we discuss moral action among adults, I doubt if the developmental model has great predictive power. I would guess that most of us tend to vacillate morally, although each of us may have a kind of median point on a conceptual moral continuum. But I question whether the moral life of most adults follows the linear progressive model posited by cognitive developmentalists such as Kohlberg or Blasi (1995). Furthermore, we cannot ignore the many studies by social psychologists that point to the importance of situational or contextual effects on moral choice (Milgram, 1974) or the importance of gender (Gilligan, 1977) on the patterns and development of moral reasoning.

Empirically, I found no evidence of the traditional kinds of moral developmental models at work for the altruists I interviewed. The wartime behaviors of Oskar Schindler and Pope Pius XII provide an apt comparison, useful in illustrating my point that it is difficult to predict, based on their past behavior, who will act altruistically under difficult circumstances. People who would be deemed "good" in everyday life or who score highly on psychological tests measuring moral development are not always those who perform altruistic deeds. And scoundrels can act altruistically. (One of the rescuers I interviewed articulated this paradox colorfully when he said that his morals were no higher than those of the average U.S. congressman.) These examples return us to the methodological caution with which I began. Are we interested in altruistic acts or in a general character? And at what point do the two diverge? Clearly, any one individual may have a general median behavior that means he usually acts with such concern for others that we would call him an altruist. Yet that same individual may demonstrate shocking instances of callous disregard for others. At what point does such behavior cause him to lose his designation as an altruist? The debate over Schindler and over Pope Pius XII illustrates this dilemma (see Deák, 2000, for a review).

Returning to the substantive issues, I should add that, although I did not find it dispositive in my own research, I would not write off socialization factors, such as exhortations to duty or religious training. In terms of future work, I would like to know more about the ability of such socialization factors to induce the altruistic perspective. I then would draw on developmental psychological and linguistic research on categorization that suggests that the prototypical-idealized type for a category has the strongest impact on learning (Lakoff, 1987; Rosch, 1978). In applying this research to altruism, I would build on the social psychological literature on social identity and self-categorization (cf. Tajfel, 1981, 1982; Turner, 1987). In terms of actually encouraging altruism, I suggest we stress socialization that emphasizes an identity based on common membership in a shared humanity rather than an identity that lauds our group differences. In policy terms, this would privilege humanistic socialization over multiculturalism. This scholarly conclusion troubles me greatly, given the current trends within American society toward increasing the political and social salience of group identity (Monroe, Hankin, & VanVechten, 2000).

4. What psychological, social, and cultural factors influence altruism and caring? My prior work suggests that the correlations between religion, education, size of family unit, gender, and so forth, and altruism exist but are weak and do not differ significantly from those that exist in control groups. It may be that our operationalization of these factors is simply too crude as we currently measure them to detect the subtleties in behavior that interest me. It may be that what I have called an altruistic worldview might also be called spirituality. Certainly, I found many altruists who were deeply religious or who had a rich spiritual life, and this spirituality or religion was, indeed, critical for these individuals. I did not consider it the dispositive factor, however, because I also found an equal number who did not evidence this religiosity and because many of the altruists I interviewed did not speak of spirituality and evidenced no spirituality when I raised the issue with them.

Again, I must raise a methodological caution. My friend and former colleague, Dan Batson (1991; Batson & Shaw, 1991), found empathy a significant influence on altruism. I did not find this the case for the altruists I studied, although something closely related to empathy was at work. But I interpreted empathy to mean putting oneself into another's place enough to understand another's feelings, the assumption being that most normal, psychologically well-adjusted people would then feel compassion for the other. The empirical context that existed for some of my participants—World War II and the Holocaust—alerted me to the possibility that this kind of empathic knowledge could also be used to do harm if the person possessing the knowledge was sadistic or psychologically twisted in some way. Indeed, it was such empathic knowledge that drove much of the Nazi policies toward Jews (Bettelheim, 1960). I conclude that it is what one does with empathic knowledge that is critical, not having the knowledge itself. The consideration of empathy as explanans underscores the complexity of analyzing altruism and suggests the great caution we must exert in our comparative discussions.

5. How do spiritual and religious experiences, beliefs, and practices influence altruistic attitudes and behavior? Traditional religious affiliation had little impact in my study, although a sense of connection to others and to a common whole—what most of us would recognize as a spiritual life—*did* seem to matter. One might argue that the particular worldview I have described as the altruistic perspective is simply another form of religion; I believe this stretches our analytical categories unduly. But before we conclude too hastily that a sense of spirituality is critical, I again offer a caution, based on my work on genocide and some recent interviewing designed to understand the cognitive frameworks of bystanders and Nazis. It is the *content* of the spiritual life that is critical, not merely having a spiritual life. As odd as it may seem, the Nazis I interviewed genuinely seemed to believe they were doing something fine for the world by engaging in genocide. They spoke with equal frequency of matters of the spirit, evoking the name of religion—sometimes Christian, sometimes the "old religion" of Germanic mythology—as the drive behind their acts. Because I have noted this phenomenon in other studies of the psychology of genocide (Monroe, 1995), I think we must take care when discussing the importance of religion as a cause of altruism. The content of the religion cannot be ignored, and it must place the ultimate value on human life before it will trigger the altruistic perspective that I found critical.

6. *How does the giving and receiving of altruistic love interact with personal well-being and health?* The relationship between altruism and a sense of efficacy is addressed in this volume by Samuel Oliner (Chapter 8) and by Lynn Underwood (Chapter 5). My own findings on this relationship were mixed. Some of the people I interviewed would rank high on traditional measures of efficacy, but others would not.

I would assume that receiving love *always* makes us feel better, and my colleague Nick Colby (private communication, 1991) argues that altruism has a positive influence on the altruist's health; but I, myself, have no direct evidence of this. If we make the analytical move, however, to psychic health, some of my altruists said they could not have lived with themselves had they not behaved altruistically. I would argue that self-image again enters the equation here. All the cognitive dissonance literature suggests that, if we see ourselves as one kind of person, yet behave differently, we will undergo psychic discomfort (Festinger, 1975). This returns us to considerations of the tension between individual acts and general character and to one's sense of self in relation to both.

Proposals for Future Work

I conclude with two suggestions of a more specific nature. The first deals with general theories of social science and the second with ethics. Both proposals would have analysts institute important conceptual changes as they analyze altruism within social science, and both would open new avenues and approaches in our explications of altruism.

Paradigm Shift

Attempts to smuggle self-interest into acts of altruism make clear how difficult it is for disciplines founded on the assumption of self-interest to comprehend and explain altruism. To remain true to their intellectual foundations, analysts working within the confines of self-interest-based paradigms strain to explain away altruism as merely a veiled form of self-interest or as a strategy to obtain deferred self-interest. This is as true in economics as it is in evolutionary biology. The same tendency exists to a slightly lesser degree in psychology.

One way to bring about a paradigm shift in social science is to replace what is currently the dominant paradigm—rational choice theory—with a theory that more accurately captures the full range of the human psychology. Rational choice theory originated in economics and does reasonably well at predicting economic behavior by assuming that people try to maximize their individual self-interest, given information and opportunity costs. But when the theory is applied to other forms of behavior—as it has been to phenomena as diverse as marriage and suicide or discrimination, voting, and altruism—the theory carries crippling limitations.[12] In particular, the rational actor paradigm is too ideologically wedded to a particular view of human nature, one in which normal behavior is assumed to be self-interested, goal directed, and utility maximizing (Monroe, 1991, 2001a). Although I am not arguing that analysts should ignore self-interest entirely, I am suggesting that an overemphasis on this one aspect of our complex human nature results in theoretical paradigms that limit our public policies, discourage altruism, and laud selfishness as the norm for human behavior. This is bad science.

I have argued elsewhere that a theory based on identity can reduce rational choice theory to a subtheory, best utilized for certain kinds of choice-theoretic situations, specific conceptualizations of the self, and particular research topics.[13] The question then becomes: What kinds of considerations should we focus on in constructing alternative paradigms? I would argue that we should draw heavily on twentieth-century advances in psychological research that provide us with more scientifically verifiable information about the human psyche, information that in turn provides more empirically grounded answers to questions about our psyche that have occupied philosophers since Plato. This kind of focus would offer a more empirically grounded understanding of human psychology. I note three important points that may prove useful in constructing such a new paradigm for social science.

RECONCEPTUALIZING THE SELF   Altruism does exist. But theories wedded to the traditional view of the self, which make self-interest the critical driving force behind our political theories, miss much that is crucial about it. In a similar fashion, such theories fail to detect much that is central in other aspects of political and social life. It will be a major advance for social science to construct new theories that embrace a richer conceptualization of the self. This one move will have profound repercussions for social scientific theories of human behavior and will greatly aid us in constructing models to decipher the causes not only of altruism but also of other important social phenomena. Human beings are highly complex organisms living in a multiplicity of cultures, and any theoretical models designed to predict our behavior must try to allow for this complexity.

In particular, we must broaden our conceptualization of the self, moving away from the concept of economic man that has dominated social science since Hobbes (Hirschman, 1977; Monroe, 1991, 1996; Myers, 1983). Self-interest clearly explains much of human behavior, and we should not discard it as part of our basic theories. But we need to recognize that individual self-interest is neither universally nor necessarily the dominant force behind human behavior. Self-interest can remain a basic part of our ethical theories and our empirical work on altruism, but it should be balanced in our theoretical structures by human needs for sociability, defined as a feeling of belonging to a group or collectivity.[14] In this regard, the work of Jerome Kagan (Chapter 3, this volume) has been particularly important in providing reliable evidence, based on years of experimental research on children, that there is an innate and universal concern for the welfare of others.[15] Work by de Waal (see Preston & de Waal, Chapter 17, this volume) suggests that analogous social drives exist in other animals.

SALIENCE AND CONTEXTUAL INFLUENCES ON BEHAVIOR   When and why do we pursue self-interested behavior, and when will we exhibit more public-spirited behavior? To answer this question we must understand the complex linkages between the attempts to further self-interest and perceptions of self in relation to others. Consider as our typical individual someone we shall call Bert. Why does Bert sometimes pursue his individual self-interest and at other times pursue the interests of one of the many groups of which he is a member? The answer may depend on which of Bert's identities is made most salient by external conditions.

One way to ascertain this is to emphasize framing and social contexts. Such an accentuation responds positively to both the cultural and the cognitive critiques of rational actor theory.[16] Work in social identity theory and self-categorization theory also may suggest when we shift between our self-interested and our other-directed identities and the manner in which our perceptions of ourselves in relation to others define the domain of relevant options.[17]

Consider one example. Traditional political economic explanations of collective action hold that individuals join groups because the group mediates resources for that individual or provides side benefits (Olson, 1965). A broader conceptualization of the self can remind us that other forces also determine group memberships, for example, parental-offspring bonds or socialization. The logic of social and political (as well as economic) competition is often mediated by a group, and the group to which our friend Bert gives allegiance at a particular moment may be determined by the problems Bert confronts at the time and the way Bert views himself in relation to others in the group.

Many of the existing discussions of altruism assume that groups are static and fixed. The kind of behavior and actors that interest me belong to far more than one group, and the actors shift around a great deal among these different group identities.[18] Parsing out the relevant part of the process by which actors such as Bert shift back and forth from individual to group identity necessarily involves our understanding the cognitive frameworks of different actors. This allows for both internal stability and for changing conditions. It also allows for cultural variations, especially in that most critical variable: the actor's view of the relationship between the individual and society.[19] Moving to a theory that allows more fully for the complex ties among individuals, groups, and society in general will be an important advance and will yield insight on the debate between liberals and communitarians in political theory.

There is no one magical methodological solution to this problem, but, as I have suggested elsewhere (Monroe, 1991, 1996, 2001a), the focus on identity perception seems the right route to pursue, not least because it will reduce the individualistic bias of rational actor theory and will allow us to focus on the polity's role in shaping both public and private identities. I thus would argue that we need to build a conceptualization of the self that allows not only for the times when the actor will respond as a self-interested individual but also for those times when the actor conceives of himself or herself as part of a collective or even as an altruist. Doing so will focus us on the individual, rather than on preferences, and will encourage analysts to seek to understand how external stimuli shift our perceptions of ourselves in relation to others.[20]

THE IMPORTANCE OF OTHERS   A third advance in our theories would be to allow more fully for the importance of others in influencing our behavior. Political science, in particular, is too wedded to the lone actor of social contract theory, an actor that dominates economic theory and, through rational choice theory, has gained significant followers in sociology, law, and anthropology. In developing alternative theories, our conceptual frameworks need to recognize that even the most individualistic of actors exists in a social world populated by others and that the behavior of those "others" has direct and profound consequences on the actor's behavior, including the actor's sense of self.[21] This broader conceptualization allows us to introduce both psychoanalytic and sociological influences, including culture. It draws on social psychological work that seeks to emphasize the affective aspect of the cognitive processes of individuals. It also suggests the important interactive effect of human behavior. Scholars critical of rational actor theory have noted this omission, and rational actor theorists have responded by trying—mostly unsuccessfully—to incorporate these interactive effects into the basic theory. But such effects clearly exist. They must be allowed for in a myriad of ways because the interactive effect occurs at the most intimate level of personal relationships—such as the trust we place in others because of their past behavior—as well as in politics at both the domestic and the international levels. We need to ask more about how the behavior of others affects us. Such interactive effects are critical parts of our own perceptions of ourselves in relation to others. They affect both how we interpret others' behavior and how we construct our own responses toward others.

There is yet a further important aspect of the intermingled relationship of self to others. How do our acts, designed to influence others, affect us in turn, even if such acts originally are designed only to deceive or manipulate others and thus can be said to be "false" to our sense of who we truly are? Our attempts to influence the behavior of others may end by changing us, as Kurt Vonnegut suggests in *Mother Night* or as is depicted in the movie *Donnie Brasco*. In both these fictional instances, the main character pretends to be something he is not. Vonnegut's Howard W. Campbell Jr. is an American spy, posing as a radio propagandist for the Nazis while secretly sending coded messages to the Allies. Donnie Brasco is an FBI agent working undercover with mobsters. In both instances, however, the character ends by becoming what he has pretended to be. Campbell becomes the Nazis' most valued propagandist, and Brasco ends by committing the horrendous deeds of the mobsters he has been sent to infiltrate. Just as our identities influence our actions, so our acts shape and change us. The complex relationship between action and character extends far beyond discussions of altruism.

Ethics Shift

I turn now to my second proposal for future work. In addition to analyzing altruism by utilizing philosophical and social scientific theories based on first principles, we need to turn things around and begin by asking how actual people operate when they interact in the real world. In this case, studying individuals like the rescuers of Jews, who constitute the core of work such as mine and that of the Oliners, is particularly important. It is such empirical work that will allow us to construct our ethical theories on empirically grounded real-life situations and not on first principles. Let me draw on my own research to illustrate how this might work.

My studies of altruism revealed what seems an anomaly for existing theories of moral action: the fact that rescuers claimed they had no choice in their altruism.[22] Instead of being guided by religion or reason, altruists seemed to act out of a sense of self. I tried to take this somewhat anomalous finding and utilize it to develop a theory in which moral action is driven not by ratiocination or religion but by identity, especially one's sense of self in relation to others. I do not argue that traditional moral theories are wrong, merely that such theories need to be supplemented with additional theories that allow for alternative forces that drive us toward moral action.

My own incipient theory thus builds on literatures in three areas not traditionally the domain of moral theory: (1) psychological work on the need for consistency and self-esteem, (2) linguistic and psychoanalytic arguments on categorization, and (3) empirical work on the cognitive frameworks of altruists and genocidalists.[23] These literatures suggest a critical moral psychology in which our perceptions of ourselves in relation to others define the range of options we perceive to be available, not just morally but empirically.

The basic argument is too long to be reproduced here in full, but I can summarize it in the following five statements: (1) The need for both consistency and self-esteem is universal and innate in human beings. (2) We desire to be treated decently by others. (3) Psychoanalytic categorization and linguistic communication causes us to recognize this desire in others as in ourselves. (4) We thus are led to extend universal rights of entitlement reciprocally, treating others as we would ourselves wish to be treated. (5) This ethical reciprocity is more basic than an intellectualized sense of duty or a religious dogma. It is a fundamental correlate of the human capacity for intersubjective communication and the need to distinguish boundaries via categorization.

The resulting theory rejects cultural relativism in favor of a universal morality. The impulse toward moral action, however, emanates not from a Supreme Being or from a rational calculus but rather from a sense of universal entitlement related to individual needs for self-esteem.[24] This theory is intended as a critical empirical treatment of a universal humanist morality. This morality is emergent and pragmatic rather than foundationalist, but it is still rooted in fundamental commonalities of human communication and psychological needs for categorization rather than in a particular cultural tradition. Epistemologically, the theory resembles Kant's philosophy,[25] although the centrality of duty-based ethics in Kant's moral philosophy is supplanted by a more general sense of reciprocal entitlements based on shared humanity.[26] By emphasizing the psyche's needs for self-esteem and linking these needs to respect for the rights of others because of the reciprocal and categorical qualities of language and the construction of boundaries, this work provides support for the idea of an innate moral sense, an idea not currently in vogue but for which there may be empirical evidence in the work of biological chemists such as Insel (Chapter 14, this volume), primatologists such as de Waal (Preston & de Waal, Chapter 17, this volume) and child psychologists such as Kagan (Chapter 3, this volume).

In other work (Monroe, 2001b), I discuss this more fully. The first part of that article discusses the psychological work on consistency, especially the role consistency plays in linking identity formation to acts that confirm our sense of self. In the second part I drew on psychological studies on self-conceptualization to argue that the narcissistic need for self-esteem works to establish boundaries between oneself and others. In the third part, I linked this psychological need for individuation, boundaries, and identity formation to Chomsky's (1966, 1988) arguments about language analysis and categorization. In the fourth part, I applied Chomsky's arguments regarding the nature of language and speech communities to Smiley's (1992) work on pragmatist moral theory to argue that the only coherent understanding of moral community that we can reasonably form in the modern world will be a universal one. Finally, I argued that basic syntactic structures, encoded in an innate human capacity for language learning, are central to the establishment of behavioral expectations in interpersonal interaction. People *do* categorize. Such categorizations are universal. Once an individual creates or adopts such categories, however, he or she must accord equal treatment to all individuals within these categories. This means that normal human beings, who wish to be treated well by others, must recognize and honor the humanity of others if they wish to claim it in themselves.

Much work remains to be done on this theory and on our general studies of altruism, empathy, and agape. The challenge is formidable but inspiring.

NOTES

1. In summarizing my prior work, I draw heavily on findings presented in my book *The Heart of Altruism*, published by Princeton University Press in 1996. I appreciate Princeton University Press's permission to allow me to reproduce them here, in modified form.

Parts of the last section of this chapter appear in Monroe (2001b). I am grateful to the *American Journal of Political Science* for allowing me to summarize it here.

2. My research deals only with humans in nonexperimental settings.

3. For further methodological details on the research, see Monroe (1996).

4. This may be a critical methodological distinction between the Oliners' (1988) work and my own. The Oliners' pathbreaking work on altruism is based on the most thorough analysis of rescuers ever conducted. They concluded that learned habits of behavior became so ingrained that they produced an altruistic personality. Although I also found this among some of my much smaller sample of rescuers, I also found social learning factors important for the nonaltruists I interviewed. (For *The Heart of Altruism*, I also interviewed five entrepreneurs as a control group typifying the self-interested rational actor, and I have interviewed bystanders and a few Nazis as a contrast with rescuers.) I thus argued that it is the content of the learning that is critical and that other factors also may produce what I found to be critical, the altruistic perspective. See Monroe (1996), Oliner and Oliner (1988), and Oliner, Chapter 8, this volume.

5. Virtue ethics is a notable exception to this tradition. See Nussbaum (1986), Kupperman (1983, 1991), or Williams (1981).

6. This idea, articulated in philosophy by Plato and Kant inter alia, also is evident in literary analysis.

7. I have argued elsewhere (Monroe, 1994) that we can use this anomaly to construct a more realistic theory of ethical political behavior using identity and perspective as our explanatory vehicles.

8. The Oliners' work (1988) is a notable exception here, and their altruistic personality and the altruistic perspective seem closely related aspects of one similar underlying phenomenon and also closely related to identity.

9. In this, altruism may resemble talent, genius, or creativity. We know these exist. We share some common sense of what they look like. But so far, no one has been able to successfully identify what causes talent (or genius or creativity) to emerge in one person as opposed to another.

10. For example, I introduce Jane to Bert, hoping that Jane will like Bert. Jane does, indeed, like Bert. But after a brief time, Bert decides he does not like Jane, and he dumps her. The result of my good intentions is that Jane ends up being more unhappy because of my well-intended act than she was in her original state. Does this lessen the altruistic aspect of my act? Probably not. My conclusion, then, would be that in defining altruism we focus more on intentions and less on consequences, even though we are still left with difficulties in inferring intentions from action.

11. Shaftesbury (1711/1714/1977).

12. Work by Nobel laureate Gary Becker (1976) provides both the most creative and the most egregious illustrations of these limitations.

13. See Monroe (2001a), in which these issues are discussed in more detail.

14. This idea reflects the Aristotelian concept of man as a social being.

15. Kagan (Chapter 3, this volume) suggests that babies become anxious when they hear another baby cry and that even young children will try to help others.

16. See work by Kahneman, Slovic, & Tversky (1982) on framing and work by Almond (1991) and Eckstein (1991) on cultural constraints.

17. See Tajfel (1981, 1982), Turner (1987), and Hogg and Abrams (1988), inter alia.

18. The chapter by Samuel Oliner (Chapter 8, this volume) underlines the importance of a group analysis.

19. Both traditional and bounded concepts of rationality reflect a post-Enlightenment framework that separates the individual from the collectivity. Interests are not identified this

way in many non-Western societies, however; and even in Western society, individuals have conceptualized their relationships with society quite differently in other historical eras. This strict differentiation of the individual from society or critical groups may explain why so many Western decision models, based on individualistic assumptions, often fail to predict behavior outside the Western market system (Kreidie, 2000; Monroe & Kreidie, 1997).

20. For example, in certain situations Bert may see himself as in conflict with Ernie and thus presumably will act as the simple self-interested actor. At other times, Bert may see that he and Ernie have collective interests. At still others, Bert may even act altruistically toward Ernie. Why? What external conditions alter Bert's basic view of himself in relation to Ernie? And how does that influence Bert's behavior toward Ernie? Such a conceptualization allows us to draw on the richness of personality psychology, which might in this example help us understand why Bert has an average position along a continuum of self-interested–altruistic behavior. But it also allows us to benefit from work in social psychology, which suggests how environmental factors help shift Bert along different points on this continuum, as one aspect of Bert's identity is selected as more salient than others.

21. This idea differs from the communitarian or the group approach, which frequently emphasizes the group over the individual.

22. Genocidalists seemed to suggest a similar lack of choice, but their actions entail us in a more complicated discussion of motive and justification and are not directly relevant to our concerns in this book. See Monroe (1995) for a review.

23. I am grateful to William Durham for his marvelous illustration of how categorization affects behavior among the Tupis, from his comments presented at the conference "Empathy, Altruism, and Agape: Perspectives on Love in Science and Religion," held in Cambridge, Mass., October 1–3, 1999.

24. I wish to construct a theory of morality that is empirically based, not one based on first principles. This means I must attempt to build on the universals in human behavior, the patterns of behavior that occur with enough frequency that we can speak of them as constituting a social science, however crudely developed it may be, much as economists speak of the law of supply and demand or biologists of the drive to survive.

25. Like Kant, I assume that individuals perceive the world, make categories from their observations, and then draw inferences about appropriate forms of behavior that are related to their categorizations.

26. In constructing this argument, I need to distinguish between two principles of universality: (1) categorical equivalency à la group membership (e.g., all humans, all Englishmen, all women) and (2) subject-object reciprocity in which the emphasis is on recognizing the consciousness of the other or a kind of phenomenological mirroring. It is important to note the relationship between the two and language and to remember that reciprocity does not equal categorization. Both of these principles will enter into my discussion of how language categorization leads to the development of ethics. This work was done with the research assistance of Matthew Levy.

REFERENCES

Almond, G. (1991). Rational choice theory and the social sciences. In K. R. Monroe (Ed.), *The economic approach to politics* (pp. 32–52). New York: HarperCollins.

Batson, C. D. (1991). *The altruism question: Toward a social psychological answer.* Hillsdale, NJ: Erlbaum.

Batson, C. D., & Shaw, L. (1991). Evidence for altruism: Toward a plurality of prosocial motives. *Psychological Inquiry, 2*(2), 107–122.

Becker, G. (1976). *The economic approach to human behavior.* Chicago: University of Chicago Press.

Bettelheim, B. (1960). *The informed heart: Autonomy in a mass age.* Glencoe, IL: Free Press.

Blasi, A. (1995). A moral understanding and the moral personality: The process of moral integration. In W. M. Kurtines & J. L. Gewirtz (Eds.), *Moral development: An introduction.* Boston: Allyn & Bacon.

Chomsky, N. (1966). *Cartesian linguistics: A chapter in the history of rationalist thought.* New York: Harper & Row.

Chomsky, N. (1988). *Language and problems of knowledge: The Managua lectures.* Cambridge: MIT Press.

Colby, B. N. (1991). A cultural theory. University of California at Irvine Social Science Report No. 91.

de Waal, F. (1996). *Good natured: The origins of right and wrong in humans and other animals.* Cambridge: Harvard University Press.

Deák, I. (2000, March 23). The Pope, the Nazis and the Jews. *New York Review of Books,* pp. 44–49.

Eckstein, H. (1991). Rationality and frustration in political behavior. In K. R. Monroe (Ed.), *The economic approach to politics* (pp. 74–93). New York: HarperCollins.

Festinger, L. (1957). *A theory of cognitive dissonance.* Stanford, CA: Stanford University Press.

Gilligan, C. (1977). *In a different voice: Psychological theory and women's development.* Cambridge: Harvard University Press.

Hirschman, A. (1977). *The passions and the interests.* Princeton, NJ: Princeton University Press.

Hogg, M., & Abrams, D. (1988). *Social identifications: A social psychology of intergroup relationships and group processes.* New York: Routledge.

Hume, D. (1978). *A treatise of human nature.* Oxford: Clarendon Press. (Original work published 1740)

Kahneman, D., Slovic, P., & Tversky, A. (1982). *Judgment under uncertainty: Heuristics and biases.* New York: Cambridge University Press.

Kant, I. (1969). *The foundations of the metaphysics of morals* (L. B. White, Trans.). Indianapolis: Bobbs-Merrill. (Original work published 1785)

Kohlberg, L. (1976). Moral stages and moralization: The cognitive-developmental approach. In T. Lickona (Ed.), *Moral development and behavior: Theory, research, and social issues* (pp. 31–51). New York: Holt, Rinehart & Winston.

Kohlberg, L. (1984). *Essays on moral development.* San Francisco: Harper & Row.

Kreidie, L. (2000). Deciphering the construals of fundamentalism. Unpublished doctoral dissertation, University of California, Irvine.

Kupperman, J. (1983). *The foundations of morality.* London: Allen & Unwin.

Kupperman, J. (1991). *Character.* New York: Oxford University Press.

Lakoff, G. (1987). *Women, fire, and dangerous things: What categories reveal about the mind.* Chicago: University of Chicago Press.

Milgram, S. (1974). *Obedience to authority: An experimental view.* New York: Harper & Row.

Monroe, K. R. (1991). *The economic approach to politics.* New York: HarperCollins.

Monroe, K. R. (1994). "But what else could I do?" A cognitive-perceptual theory of ethical political behavior. *Political Psychology, 16,* 1–22.

Monroe, K. R. (1995, February). The psychology of genocide: A review of the literature. *Ethics and International Affairs, 9,* 215–239.

Monroe, K. R. (1996). *The heart of altruism: Perceptions of a common humanity.* Princeton, NJ: Princeton University Press.

Monroe, K. R. (2001a). Paradigm shift: The case for replacing rational actor theory with a theory of perspective on self and others. *International Political Science Review* (July 2001), in press.

Monroe, K. R. (2001b). Morality and a sense of self. *American Journal of Political Science* (July 2001), in press.

Monroe, K. R. (2001c). An innate moral sense: New evidence for an old theory? Submitted for publication, April 2001.

Monroe, K. R., Hankin, J., & VanVechten, R. (2000). The psychological foundations of identity politics. In Nelson Polsby (Ed.), *Annual Review of Political Science* (vol. 3, pp. 419–447). Palo Alto, CA: Annual Reviews, Inc.

Monroe, K. R., & Kreidie, L. (1997). The perspectives of Islamic fundamentalists and the limits of rational choice theory. *Political Psychology, 9,* 215–239.

Myers, M. (1983). *The soul of economic man.* Chicago: University of Chicago Press.

Nussbaum, M. (1986). *The fragility of goodness: Luck and ethics in Greek tragedy and philosophy.* New York: Cambridge University Press.

Piaget, J. (1948). *The moral development of the child.* Glencoe, IL: Free Press.

Oliner, S., & Oliner, P. (1988). *The altruistic personality.* New York: The Free Press.

Olson, M. (1965). *The logic of collective action.* Cambridge: Harvard University Press.

Rosch, E. (1978). Principles of categorization. In E. Rosch & B. B. Lloyd (Eds.), *Cognition and categorization.* Hillsdale, NJ: Erlbaum.

Shaftesbury, Earl of [Anthony Ashley Cooper]. (1977). *An inquiry concerning virtue, or merit.* Manchester, England: University of Manchester Press. (Original work published 1711)

Smiley, M. (1992). *Moral responsibility and the boundaries of community: Power and accountability from a pragmatic point of view.* Chicago: University of Chicago Press.

Tajfel, H. (1981). *Human groups and social categories: Studies in social psychology.* New York: Cambridge University Press.

Tajfel, H. (1982). *Social identity and intergroup relations.* New York: Cambridge University Press.

Turner, J. (1987). *Rediscovering the social group: A self-categorization theory.* Oxford: Blackwell.

Williams, B. (1981). *Moral luck: Philosophical papers.* New York: Cambridge University Press.

8

Extraordinary Acts of Ordinary People

Faces of Heroism and Altruism

SAMUEL P. OLINER

> There's a light in this world: a healing spirit more powerful than any darkness we may encounter. We sometimes lose sight of this force when there is suffering, too much pain. Then suddenly, the spirit will emerge through the lives of ordinary people, who hear a call and answer in extraordinary ways.
>
> —Richard Attenborough, from the film *Mother Teresa*

> They did not ask any questions, and I did not think that they thought of themselves as doing anything heroic when they saved my life. They did it out of love.
>
> —A Jewish Holocaust Rescued Survivor

One of the Holocaust rescuers that I interviewed said, "Without love and care, what have you got? A world without a heart." What do we know about altruistic love and compassion? Under what conditions will individuals or groups regard others as true neighbors deserving of their concern, care, and love? What are the reasons that millions of people remain bystanders and witness others suffer or even perish? The great sociologist Pitirim Sorokin was concerned in the 1940s and 1950s with the crisis in Western civilization, in which he saw divisiveness and dehumanization. His antidote to a divided and troubled world was altruistic love or agape, which "can be manufactured" (i.e., can be instilled in millions of people if society as a whole and the various institutions in particular could model altruism and compassion).

We characterize behavior as altruistic when it (1) is directed toward helping another, (2) involves a high risk or sacrifice to the actor, (3) is accompanied by no external reward, and (4) is voluntary. In the following discussion, I regard altruism as a continuum. At one end is heroic altruism, involving greater risk to the helper, and at the other is conventional altruism, not normally life threatening to the helper. In this chapter I include: (1) *heroic Gentile rescuers of Jews* during the Holocaust, comparing them with nonrescuers; and (2) *hospice volunteers,* who fall at the conventional end of the continuum, comparing them with nonhospice volunteers and nonvolunteers in general.

The data were gathered over several years. The research on rescuers of Jews in Nazi-occupied Europe consisted of a sample of bona fide rescuers recognized by Yad Vashem who were compared with bystanders and rescued survivors.[1] Ninety-three hospice volunteers and 73 nonhospice volunteers were interviewed using both open- and closed-ended questions in order to learn the salient factors that motivated them.

In addition to asking questions about respondents' backgrounds, upbringings, and values, we were interested in the triggering mechanisms that moved these individuals to help. We identified three categories of rescuers/helpers. Those individuals who took part in rescue/helping activities and had internalized highly valued norms—the expectations of social groups, their moral community, or leadership of a highly regarded authority—we term *normocentric.* Rescuers/helpers who responded to external events that arouse a heightened sense of empathy were considered *empathic.* Rescuers/helpers who responded to their own overarching moral principles (mainly autonomously derived), who were moved to action by external events that they interpreted as violations of social justice and human rights principles, were deemed *autonomous/principled.*[2]

Looking closely at the two groups, one can discern common triggering mechanisms for acting on behalf of others. My discussion focuses on the common motivating factors of the two groups and draws conclusions about the implications.

Gentile Rescuers during the Holocaust

The study of rescuers was guided by the following three questions: (1) Was rescue or helping primarily a matter of opportunity, that is, external circumstances, or situational factors (recognizing that help was needed [awareness]; having hiding places, food, and so forth)? (2) Was rescue or helping primarily a matter of individual character, that is, personal attributes such as empathy, caring for others, and so forth, and if so, what were those traits and how were they acquired? (3) Was rescue or helping a matter of moral and ethical values?

The study, which was undertaken in the early 1980s, included Gentile rescuers residing in Poland, France, Germany, Italy, and Norway and rescuers who had immigrated to the United States and Canada after the war. It involved the use of scales for self-esteem, social responsibility, locus of control, and empathy and a commonality scale developed by Oliner and Oliner (1988) (see nn. 5, 6); also, importantly, in-depth taped interviews were conducted with more than 700 respondents. In addition, there was a comparison group of bystanders. A group of rescued survivors were also interviewed because it was felt that they might have insights into why the rescuers helped them during these trying times. The comparison of the rescuers and bystanders showed that both had *equal opportunity to rescue* and both were *equally aware of the tragedy and plight of Jews.* Whereas rescuers took action, bystanders refrained from helping. We can say with a degree of confidence that opportunity may have facilitated rescue somewhat but did not by any means determine it.

Of the several reasons expressed by the rescuers for their actions, at least one ethical or humanitarian reason or value was cited by an overwhelming majority (87%). The ethical reasons cited included justice and fairness, that Jewish victims were deserving of help, and that persecution of the innocent could not be justified. But the ethic that mattered most was the *ethic of care and compassion*. Most of the rescuers' helping was rooted in a need to assume personal responsibility to relieve suffering and pain. Some felt a particular affection toward Jews they knew; most felt an obligation *toward others in general*. Pity, compassion, concern, and affection made up 76% of the reasons rescuers gave for extending help to strangers. More than 90% said they had helped at least one stranger, as well as a friend. Typical expressions of rescuers were the following: "Our religion says we are our brother's keepers." "I sensed I had in front of me human beings who were hunted down like wild animals. This aroused a feeling of brotherhood with the desire to help." "I was always filled with love for everyone, for every creature, for things. I infuse life into every object. For me, everything is alive."

Caring compelled action. Rescuers assumed responsibility—not because others required them to but because failure to act would destroy innocent people: "I knew they were taking them and that they wouldn't come back. I didn't think I could live knowing that I could have done something."

Acquisition of Caring Values

Many values of caring and social responsibility were acquired directly from parents.[3] Although parents played an important role for both rescuers and nonrescuers, significantly more rescuers perceived them as benevolent figures who modeled moral and spiritual values conducive to forming close, caring attachments to other people. The values rescuers learned from their parents—and from other significant people in their lives—differed significantly from those learned by nonrescuers. One was related to ethics and ethical behavior. Significantly more rescuers said that they owed an obligation to *all people*. We term an orientation of caring for all living things *extensivity*.[4] The extensive-personality predisposition comprises emotionally healthy attachment to family and inclusion of diverse others as deserving of care: "They taught me to respect all human beings." "I have learned from my parents' generosity to be open, to help people. I learned to be good to one's neighbor . . . to be responsible, concerned, and considerate. To work—and to work hard. But also to help—to the point of leaving one's work to help one's neighbor." "He taught me to love my neighbor—to consider him my equal whatever his nationality or religion. He taught me especially to be tolerant." "She taught me to be responsible, honest, to respect older people, to respect all people—not to tease or criticize people of other religions. She taught me to be good."

Significantly more rescuers felt a sense of responsibility toward others—feeling an obligation to help even when nothing could be gained for themselves. In contrast, many nonrescuers felt exempt from such obligations. Nonrescuers often were unaffected by such suffering, more detached, and less receptive to other people's helplessness and pain. "I could not comprehend that innocent persons should be persecuted just because of race. We all come from the same God." "They believed in humanity and were incredulous that people were being killed simply because of their Jewishness." "They are very noble, very fine people. They felt that people should not be hurt for no reason at all. When they saw injustice, they felt they should do something. . . . Whether it was religion or their sense of justice—they didn't mind paying the price for this."

Modes of discipline were also important in inculcating ethical behavior. As children, rescuers were more likely to have been disciplined by reasoning and explanation of the consequences of their misbehavior rather than by verbal or physical punishment, as was common among nonrescuers.

Normocentric Motivation

For some rescuers, witnessing arrest or persecution of Jews triggered a response based on the norms of the social group with whom they strongly identified and to which they looked for moral guidance. Their motivations arose not from their connection with the victim but rather from feelings of obligation to their group or community, the implicit and explicit rules of which they felt obligated to obey. Thus, for *normocentric* rescuers, inaction was a violation of the community's religious and moral norms of behavior. For them, feelings of obligation or duty were frequently coupled with anticipation of guilt or shame should they fail to act. The norms of the community, its habits and culture, encouraged tolerance and helping. For certain Italian rescuers—military officials, religious leaders, and diplomats—such social norms legitimated and encouraged them to sabotage, thwart, slow down, and resist deportation of Jews. Approximately 52% of our respondents said they were motivated by obligations that fell into the *normocentric* category.

Such an internalized *normocentric* orientation characterized a Danish rescuer who began his rescuing activities in this way:

> In 1943, on the twenty-ninth of August, we heard that the Nazis were going to make a *razzia* and put Danish Jews into German concentration camps. Together with friends from the police department, we organized a refugee organization—it had no name. We ferried by taxi, and even by police cars, down to the commercial fishing harbor and arranged for people to go over to Sweden. The harbors were controlled partly by the German Navy but also by the Coast Police—a special department of the Danish police force. We had to be rather careful to do our "shipment" from places where controllers would not stop fishing boats and where we knew German Navy patrol boats would not be present. After a week's time, we managed to get all people of Jewish extraction out of the country—7,000 of them.

Empathic Motivation

Empathic motivation involves concern with the fate of another in distress, and compassion, sympathy, and pity are its characteristic expressions. Reactions may be emotional or cognitive and frequently contain elements of both. The following account demonstrates an instance in which empathy was the major motivator of rescuer behavior:

> In 1942, I was on my way home from town and was almost near home when M. came out of the bushes. I looked at him, in striped camp clothing, his head bare, shod in clogs. He might have been about thirty or thirty-two years old. And he begged me, his hands joined like for a prayer—that he had escaped from Majdanek and could I help him? He joined his hands in this way, knelt down in front of me, and said: "You are like the Virgin Mary." It still makes me cry. "If I get through and reach Warsaw, I will never forget you." Well, how could one not have helped such a man? (A Polish rescuer)

> Human compassion. When someone comes and says "I escaped from the camp," what is the alternative? One alternative is to push him out and close the door—the other is to pull him into the house and say, "Sit down, relax, wash up. You will be as hungry as we are because we have only this bread."

Empathic reactions create overpowering feelings that lead people to react spontaneously. Some rescuers could not stand by when seeing people in pain—could not withstand the agony and grief it caused them. The direct face-to-face encounter with a distressed person further heightened the impulse to act. Thirty-eight percent of rescuers said that they were moved empathically to their first helping act.

Principled Motivation

People with *principled* motivation, autonomously derived, interpreted persecution of Jews as a violation of their own moral precepts. Unlike normocentric motivation, which prescribed a certain group behavior, *principled* motivation involved acting on one's own. The main goal of such behavior was to reaffirm and apply the individual's personal moral principles, even when their actions on behalf of others might prove futile. An Italian rescuer, responding to the statement that what rescuers did was extraordinary (i.e., that rescuing a great number of people was a truly remarkable act), answered that it really was something simple. He did it without considering risk or thinking about being either lauded or maligned. He did it because it had to be done, and he didn't even weigh the danger. Persecution was unacceptable; justice had to be done.

> No, no. It was all something very simple. Nothing grandiose was done. It was done simply without considering risk, without thinking about whether it would be an occasion for recognition or to be maligned, it was in effect done out of innocence. I didn't think I was doing anything other than what should be done, or that I was in any special danger because of what I was doing. Justice had to be done. Persecution of the innocents was unacceptable.

Principle-motivated rescuers felt challenged in fundamental ways by the acts they were observing—they felt that allowing such acts was tantamount to condoning such behavior. Only a small minority of rescuers—approximately 11%—fell into this category.

The Religious Factor and Rescuers

Although no officially organized bodies in the top echelons of religious leadership advocated rescue of Jews, there are examples of religious institutions that were deeply involved. Ewa Kurek (1997) studied convents and orphanages in Poland, interviewing nuns in various orders and the children who survived because of them. The nuns had no central authority to coordinate common action and no communication between orders; they performed these heroic acts on their own. When asked what motivated them to rescue the children, they usually gave a dual response: (1) they rescued for missionary reasons—to convert them to Catholicism, and (2) for purely humanitarian reasons—dictated by Christian ethics. They asked Jesus for advice and always concluded that rescue was what He would have wanted. These nuns now look at their deeds with great pride; the Jewish children (now adults) express great appreciation for the nuns' heroism.

The Huguenot congregation in Le Chambon, France, under the strong leadership of Pastor Andre Trocme and his assistant Edouard Theis, were by sheer determination able to rescue 5,000 Jews in the Le Chambon area. This was a moral community; it knew its own history of suffering, had internalized well the parable of the Good Samaritan, and acted upon it (Sauvage, 1985–1986).

Father Ruffino Niccacci of Assisi, Italy, saved about 5,000 Jews. This Franciscan monk operated a refuge and underground escape route in Nazi-occupied Italy that began in the summer of 1943 when nine Jews appealed for sanctuary, and his bishop charged him with the task of saving Jews. Eventually, the Nazis suspected that Father Ruffino and other friars were hiding and transporting Jews, and they mounted sudden raids. Had they discovered the victims, they would probably have been executed along with the friars and innocent citizens. Father Ruffino eventually organized several hundred priests and half the townspeople: local porters, cleaning women, and even hangers-on at Nazi police headquarters coalesced into an efficient counterespionage service. When danger threatened, they gave the priests advance warning (Fischman, 1964).

Although we cannot say that religiosity determines rescue, there are religious individuals who internalized the value of compassion and helping from their parents. Douglas Huneke (1985–1986), examining the backgrounds of major righteous rescuers of Jews, showed that they were often motivated by religious beliefs. Herman (Fritz) Graebe, a German rescuer of many Jews in the Ukraine, was greatly influenced by his profoundly religious mother, who constantly preached the ethic of helping as one of the most important aspects of human behavior.

In the homes of some religiously oriented rescuers, there were discussions about Jews—that they were God's people—which simultaneously emphasized an ethic of care. I reached the conclusion that parental values and culture were importantly correlated with rescue behavior. Religion in this context was a lesser factor than other aspects of living and relating, but it was embedded in the whole of living, in which trust and mutuality, nurtured by parental caring, were reenacted in religious expressions.

Moral and Political Climate Conducive to Rescue

Yahil (1969), Zuccotti (1987), Ramati (1978), Carpi (1977), Chary (1972), Flender (1964), Friedman (1978), and Baron (1988) have addressed climates in which social, cultural, and political conditions were more conducive to rescue of Jews and in which anti-Semitism was less rampant. Partly because of such a climate, most of the Danish Jewish population was shipped to Sweden and rescued. In Italy, 85% of the Jewish population was rescued, which is attributed to a general lack of anti-Semitism and an absence of sharply drawn distinctions between Jewish-Italians and other Italians. Fleischner (1988), Kurek-Lesik (1992), and Huneke (1985) concluded that a major factor for rescue was compassion for Jewish victims. Others found that Christian charity and other religious factors help explain rescue. Among these are Baron (1992), Sauvage (1986), Huneke (1986), Fleischner (1988), Zeitoun (1988), and Oliner and Oliner (1988 and in their latest analysis of their data).

Hospice Volunteers

Volunteerism can be defined as a nonspontaneous helping behavior for which one receives no material compensation. It can be parochial, within one's own social group, or nonparochial. Nonparochial volunteerism is a form of conventional altruism in that it is directed at others beyond the parochial group and is accompanied by no external reward. It has been established in the literature that volunteers generally score high on measures of *empathy, social responsibility*, and *moral development* (Allen & Rushton, 1983). Piliavin (1990) states that individuals are more likely to volunteer if their parents did; the parents modeled volunteerism. The work of hospice volunteers can be said to be nonspontaneous, nonparochial prosocial behavior that fits the definition of conventional altruism.

In 1967 Dr. Cicely Saunders, a British physician, established St. Christopher's, a medical facility for the care of the terminally ill in London. The hospice model of care developed by Saunders and others was less an innovation in health care than it was a return to an earlier model. The name "hospice" comes from the Latin word *hospes*, meaning guest. Like other derivations of the root word, such as hospitality, host, hotel, and hospital, it connotes the ideas of kindness and generosity to strangers and travelers. Ancient and medieval hospices were sanctuaries for poor travelers, the sick and the dying, and religious pilgrims. In the medieval period hospices were generally run by religious orders who saw the care of the poor and sick as part of the Lord's work. For many centuries hospices and hospitals were one and the same. Life was thought of as a journey from this world to the next, and all travelers were in need of comfort, whether they were journeying from one land to another or from one life to the next.

During the past century the care of the sick and dying ceased being a private and religious function and became a public, governmental one (Buckingham, 1983, p. 12). Advances in medical science and technology resulted in a total transformation of medical science from a palliative model to an aggressively therapeutic one. However, in the post–World War II years, some health care professionals began to suggest that, although the system was well equipped to deal with acute life-threatening situations, it was ill equipped to meet the special needs of terminally ill patients. Indeed, the terminally ill patient was considered a sign of medical failure and frequently shunned by medical personnel, who were at a loss to deal with patients to whom they could not offer any hope of recovery. This medical avoidance of death was accompanied by an increasing aversion to death because it was no longer so visible. No longer was death a part of everyday life. Few people died at home, and many died all alone in hospitals, separated from their families.

St. Christopher's Hospice set out to address these problems by seeking to combine the old concept of hospitality with the medical skill and technology of the modern hospital (Buckingham, 1983, p. 13). Emphasis was placed on control of pain and other adverse symptoms. Families were incorporated into the care plans for each patient. After the death of the patient, staff continued bereavement care for the patients' families.

Both Saunders's writings and those of Dr. Elisabeth Kübler-Ross (1997) were well received in the United States; by 1974 the first hospice program was operating in this country in New Haven, Connecticut. Since that time, approximately 2,000 hospice programs have been established in the United States. Hospice programs in this country vary considerably in design, ranging from those that rely on volunteer care and charge nothing for their services to institutionalized programs with staff who are paid by third-party payers (Medicare, private carriers, state and local government). Although there are some in-patient hospices in this country, home care is the norm (Buckingham, 1983, p. 13).

That hospice programs have been able to provide a high level of personal care is due in no small part to the efforts of volunteers. Nearly every hospice program employs both laypersons and health professionals as volunteers in their programs. These volunteers are interviewed by hospice staff and, if accepted, undergo orientation and training before being assigned to patients and their families. Volunteers meet regularly with each other and with staff to discuss both patient care and the problems they themselves may be facing as part of their interaction with the terminally ill and their families.

My study had a twofold purpose: to identify the characteristics and motivations of hospice volunteers in comparison with nonvolunteers and to compare these findings with other research on volunteerism. The study was guided by two considerations: Was the decision to become a hospice volunteer a matter of *opportunity*, that is, a result of particular facilitating external circumstances, or was it the result of *character*, that is, a result of particular values and attitudes?

To answer this question, 93 hospice volunteers from Humboldt and Marin Counties in California and from the Boston area were interviewed by trained interviewers. These interviews were recorded and transcribed. Seventy-three nonhospice volunteers (who may have volunteered in other settings) and nonvolunteers were given an abbreviated version of the hospice volunteer questionnaire, which they completed by themselves. This group was categorized by level of volunteering. Forty-three respondents, who volunteered substantially more than 6 hours per week, were classified as high-level volunteers. The other 30 individuals either volunteered occasionally or not at all.

The questionnaire consisted of three sections, which included both open- and closed-ended questions. Section A dealt with the characteristics of the family milieu during the respondents' childhood and the relationship between family members. Section B explored the respondents' parental, educational, and occupational background, their political beliefs, religiosity, values, and the disciplinary techniques used on volunteers. Section C focused on such matters as the respondents' degree of closeness to parents and significant others, religious background and relative health of parents and significant others, whether parents or significant others volunteered, and how parents felt about their own volunteer experience. Also included in Section C were 42 personality items comprising four psychological scales:[5] (1) the Social Responsibility Scale, developed by Berkowitz and Luterman (1968); (2) the Internal/External Locus of Control Scale, developed by Rotter (1966) and modified by Gurin, Gurin, and Morrison (1978); (3) the Self-Esteem Scale, developed by Rosenberg (1965); and (4) the Empathy Scale, developed by Mehrabian and Epstein (1972) and modified by E. Midlarsky (1981). In addition, we included Oliner and Oliner's Diversity Scale, which measures identification with nonparochial groups.[6]

In addition to the categorization of nonhospice volunteers by amount of time spent in volunteer activities, this sample was also separated into two groups based on the nature of volunteer activity, that is, parochial and nonparochial volunteer behavior. Nonparochial volunteers were those who volunteered beyond their own social group, whereas parochial volunteers limited their volunteer activities to their children's schools or their churches, clubs, or political groups. The responses to closed-ended questions were analyzed by computer, and open-ended questions were assessed and coded into categories for comparison.[7] The nature of the sample did allow for simple correlations and percentages.

The hospice sample was 73% female, with 88% of the sample being 40 years old or older. It was overwhelmingly Caucasian (96.9%), and, although only 57% identified with a Judeo-Christian religious tradition, 85% described themselves as "very" or "somewhat" religious. Within the hospice sample, 97% had prior volunteer experience. Seventy-five percent reported that their mothers had volunteered, and 49% that their fathers had done so.

Within the high-level volunteer group, 63% were female, 58% were over 40, and 83% were Caucasian. Seventy-six percent identified themselves as Protestant, Catholic, or Jewish, and 83% described themselves as "very" or "somewhat" religious. Of the high-level volunteers, 58% reported that their mothers had volunteered, and 49% that their fathers were volunteers. Within the low-level and nonvolunteer group, which was 58% female, 36% were over 40 and 80% were Caucasian. Ninety-two percent were either Protestant or Catholic, and 76% described themselves as "very" or "somewhat" religious.

Comparisons of hospice volunteers and nonhospice volunteers demonstrated no significant difference with regard to self-esteem or internal/external locus of control. Hospice volunteers and high-level volunteers scored significantly higher on measures of empathy and social responsibility, and hospice volunteer scores were higher than those of high-level volunteers on these two measures. Hospice volunteers scored significantly higher on measures of intrinsic religiosity, that is, religiosity that is implicit in its nature and in the personal orientation by which one lives as opposed to an extrinsic religious orientation that is utilitarian, explicit, and self-justifying in nature.

In response to the question, "What is the most important thing you learned from your mother?", the most frequent response among hospice volunteers was religion, followed by kindness, compassion, and empathy. Religion was also found to be the most frequent response in the nonhospice group.

Hard work and honesty were the most frequent responses in both samples to the question, "What is the most important thing you learned from your father?"

There was little difference between the two groups when asked who they most admired, parents and spouses being the most frequent response of those who cited individuals known personally. The next most frequent response among hospice volunteers was hospice workers and administrators or hospice patients.

Another question which sought to illustrate the respondents' values and beliefs asked what advice they would give to young people about what things are important in life.[8] The most frequently cited advice by hospice volunteers was to be true to oneself and respect others, followed by advice to "follow your heart," to be aware of self and others, and to recognize one's connection to others. High-level volunteers' most frequent responses were similar, whereas low-level volunteers' and nonvolunteers' most frequent responses were to have faith in God, enjoy life, and be responsible.

The responses to this question were then classified as to extensivity, that is, whether they referred to the respondent's connection to others in terms of service, care, respect, and acceptance. Half of the hospice volunteers and high-level volunteers gave extensive responses, whereas among the low-level volunteers and nonvolunteers extensive responses were found in 25% or less of the responses. This tendency toward extensivity was also found to correlate with type of volunteering when the nonhospice volunteers were categorized on that dimension. Forty-five percent of nonparochial volunteers gave extensive responses, whereas only one third of the parochial volunteers mentioned connection to others and putting the welfare of others before their own.

By their responses to the diversity scale, hospice volunteers and high-level volunteers demonstrated that they felt they had more in common with diverse groups of people than did the low-level or nonvolunteer group. This included more favorable attitudes toward African Americans, Jewish Americans, homosexuals, and so forth.

That hospice volunteers appeared to value acceptance of others is also indicated by their response to a question regarding what groups they have strong negative feelings toward. Of the 52 hospice volunteers who admitted strong negative feelings toward a group, 95% identified groups such as the Ku Klux Klan, Aryan Nation, religious fundamentalists, bigots, or polarizing and intolerant groups.

Although there was no apparent difference in history of discipline as children among the groups, with over 95% in all groups responding that they were disciplined as children, there did appear to be a difference in the type of discipline reported. Thirty-nine percent of the hospice volunteers reported being physically disciplined, whereas 60% of the high-level volunteers and 78% of the low-level and nonvolunteers reported physical discipline.

Motivations for Volunteering

The responses to the question regarding motivations for volunteering were placed within four categories: (1) self-enhancement, (2) empathic, (3) normocentric, and (4) principled. No hospice volunteer gave only a single motive for volunteering, and many gave several.

Sixty-eight hospice volunteers gave responses that can be categorized as *self-enhancing*, including responses describing a need to confront or learn more about death, a desire to feel needed and useful, a need to develop a sense of connection to the community, and a desire for job-related experience: "I was probably trying to fill a personal need. I was looking for something meaningful to do." "I sought it out to become involved in something where I was needed."

Others wanted to feel better about themselves, fill up time, or feel less lonely. Eleven individuals described their motives as "selfish." "I had a purely selfish motive in that I thought it would be a good way to get into the community. . . . I needed to get away from the rather shallow, glitzy life I lived in New York."

Still others described how this motivation was transformed by the hospice experience: "When I first went in as a volunteer, I was trying to fill a lot of stuff in me, and now I feel like I'm more sure of who I am, and I'm able to be there as a true person, to really be there."

But the most frequent response concerned the need to confront death, either because of fear or simply lack of knowledge. Many of these individuals also remarked on how working with hospice had led to an acceptance of death: "I think that part of our message is that dying is part of our whole life journey. The media tells us that we never have to grow old if we use certain products, we are told we can live forever if we have enough money . . . whatever they do, it's just not accepting this wonderful right of passage that is ours. It's a gift. We've lost it." "I've lived most of my life, but I still have some time to go . . . but identifying what's around the corner feels good to me, seeing that death is really not such a terrible thing, that it's really the last stage in life."

A similar percentage of both high- and low-level nonhospice volunteers gave responses that could be categorized as self-enhancing. Most frequent were responses that referred to enjoyment, fulfillment, and reward, followed by references to a desire to feel helpful and needed.

Seventy percent of the hospice volunteers gave responses that could be characterized as *empathic*, that is, they reflected an identification with hospice patients and their needs. This figure compares with 12% for the high-level volunteers and 5.5% for the low-level volunteers.

The most frequent of all motivations given for becoming a hospice volunteer was the death of a parent, spouse, or close friend. Thirty-seven percent of the hospice volunteers included this as a motivation. Those respondents who indicated that the experience was a negative one and who wished to spare or mitigate that negative experience for others were categorized as empathic. One woman whose husband had died of cancer commented on how the painful experience led her to volunteer: "I felt I could do something for someone that I wished I could have had when my husband died. I wanted to offer what I would have liked to have had."

Three of the hospice volunteers were cancer patients themselves and related that they knew how it felt to suffer alone and wanted to spare others. Others had had bad experiences with cancer patients and wanted to prevent the same bad experiences from happening to others. One woman spoke of being in the hospital for her own cancer treatment and encountering a woman who was being forced to accept treatment against her will: "I felt so sorry for this woman. She seemed so alone. And I remembered going in there not knowing if I could do anything. . . . She was in a situation that nobody understood. Nobody even cared what she was feeling."

Another volunteer, a registered nurse, related an experience from her early nursing career: "I would see nurses virtually ignoring dying patients. Giving them their medication, changing their beds, but avoiding any real contact. I thought, what good are we if we can't give comfort to these people? Whenever I had a patient who was dying I would really try to spend whatever free time I had, giving them sips of water, back rubs . . . just holding their hand. But I always had to leave knowing the next shift would ignore them again."

Those who cited a personal experience with the death of a significant person in their lives were equally divided between the aforementioned categories, those who wished to spare others the difficulty they themselves had experienced and those whose experience had involved hospice and who volunteered out of a sense of gratitude and a desire to share that positive experience: "I felt I owed them an obligation to contribute whatever I could . . . I wanted to continue my association with those marvelous people who did so much for her and me too."

As previously stated, volunteering is a widely accepted social norm in the United States, perhaps more so than in any other Western country. Thus it can be said that many volunteer because of social expectations and pressure, that is, for *normocentric* reasons. Forty-four percent of the hospice volunteers gave responses that were considered to be normocentric. Only 7% of high-level volunteers gave normocentric responses, and none of the low-level volunteers gave responses that could be interpreted as normative.

Hospice volunteers often referred to the importance of volunteering, reflecting societal norms: "I think as you get older, you start thinking, what am I doing for my community, and you start feeling the need to just do something, to put something back." Still others stated that they were directly recruited: "Some people that I knew were volunteers, and they recruited me. They told me I would be good at it and they needed volunteers."

The fourth category, *principled* responses, were those that reflected underlying principles or beliefs and that were cited by 30% of the hospice volunteers as compared with 5% and 11% of the high- and low-level volunteers, respectively. The responses arise out of abstract, ethical principles, which hold that all humanity is deserving of justice, fairness, and equity and that caring and compassion should be available to all—friends and family, as well as other diverse groups. It is difficult to extract purely "principled" responses from normocentric or empathic forces, but generally they indicate a more autonomous or axiological nature than normocentric responses.

The most frequent response was a strong belief in the hospice concept, as seen in the following statements: "I had seen on several occasions how inadequate the health care system was in taking care of dying patients. I felt there had to be a better way. Hospice has a philosophy that I am very comfortable with, that is, that people have a right to live until the second they die . . . a right to live as well as we can possibly make it for them." "I guess I thought I could make a difference in the way people died and the way they went out of this lifetime, make it a little less difficult maybe . . . It's nice to have someone there when you need them. I'm strong, I can help." "I believe we all need a hand getting into life and we all need a hand getting out of life."

Other responses included in this category reflected a more generalized belief in the role of service that, in contrast to the normocentric responses, indicated an autonomous belief in the importance of service to others: "I think it is important for people to know they are part of a society. So many people think that what they do doesn't affect other people. There isn't anyone like that. You affect everyone, every person who touches you or the groups you touch."

Hoffman (1983) has said that the development of the caring, altruistic individual requires setting boundaries between right and wrong, moral and immoral, and deviant and normative behavior. In childhood, the hospice volunteers were more likely to have been disciplined by reasoning and less by physical means than the nonvolunteers, a finding that reflects our findings on rescuers and nonrescuers in Nazi-occupied Europe. In addition, there appears to be a cultural theme in America that we have an obligation, even a divine obligation, to contribute to the betterment of the community (Adams, 1990). Throughout U.S. history, the truest form of charity in volunteering is found in local, one-on-one relationships. Adams (1991) examined 159 articles from 19 popular magazines between 1980 and 1989 focusing on motivation for volunteering and charitable giving. He found that Americans give because they want to help other people, especially those with whom they share communities.

Summary and Implications

Based on the data on the two groups, there is no single motivating explanation that triggers people to behave compassionately for the welfare of others. Rather, there are a variety of factors that converge to motivate them to help. We found that Gentile rescuers risked their lives because they had learned *compassion, caring norms,* and *efficacy* and could assume *responsibility for diverse others.* This increased extensivity is demonstrated by higher acceptance of diverse groups and increased awareness of the connectedness with all humankind. They had also acquired a *moral code of justice* and fairness from parents, significant others, and institutions, which dictated to them that the innocent must not be persecuted. Religious factors are evident; and although religiosity per se did not determine rescue, those who had learned religious principles of love and responsibility in a caring home were among the rescuers.

In the hospice volunteer study, we discerned factors such as *empathy,* including the need for *affiliation, reciprocal helping, self-enhancement,* and an *internalized norm of care.* Although there exist no profound differences between hospice volunteers and other volunteers, the former group has been shown to be more extensive in its outlook. Hospice volunteers also exhibit a higher degree of intrinsic religiosity, despite a lower incidence of affiliation with mainstream religious traditions. These differences can partially be explained by the role models and discipline styles of the volunteers' backgrounds and, in the case of hospice volunteers, the experience of the loss of a significant individual prior to their decision to volunteer for hospice. It should be pointed out that the assessment of hospice volunteers' attitudes occurred after the decision to volunteer and after one or more experiences with hospice. It is difficult to separate previous beliefs and attitudes from those shaped by the hospice experience. In fact, some participants referred directly to the transformation of beliefs and attitudes as a result of their experience.

Motivations were found to be varied, with most hospice volunteers citing self-enhancement and empathic motives, whereas nonhospice volunteers overwhelmingly cited self-enhancement reasons. The findings of other motivational studies of volunteering were reinforced—individuals seek out volunteer experiences that meet their particular needs for self-esteem, education, and social responsibility. The hospice organization was found to be remarkably effective in retaining volunteers, and this success was felt to be the result of the organization's ability to provide support, affiliation, and self-actualization for its volunteers.

So what can we say from studying these two groups of individuals? First, acts of heroic or conventional altruism are not the exclusive province of larger-than-life figures. Rather, they are usually the *deeds of ordinary people* whose moral courage arises out of the routine of their daily lives; their characteristic ways of feeling; their perceptions of what authority should be obeyed; the rules and models of moral conduct they learned from parents, friends, schools, religion, political leaders, co-workers, and peer groups; and what kind of moral code is to be followed. What we see is that these two groups at various times of their lives were engaged in moral behavior in general.

As Iris Murdoch (1970/1985) has observed, the moral life is not something that emerges suddenly in the context of traumas. Rather, it arises piecemeal in the routine business of living. It begins with parents who emphasize broadly inclusive ethical values, including caring and social responsibility, which they teach in the context of loving family relationships. Thus assuming caring roles seems to require prerehearsed scripts and previously learned skills acquired in ordinary activities. If we are serious about cultivating these characteristics associated with helping others, then we cannot leave the job to parents alone. Other social institutions—religious, educational, and workplace—need to seriously reconsider their roles, their responsibilities, and their routine behaviors. Until social institutions accept responsibility to nurture inclusive ethical commitment in a context of caring environments, it is likely that no more than a fragment of the population can be counted on to engage in heroic and conventional altruism. It is my firm conviction that caring and social responsibility can be nurtured in individuals and groups and that kindness and helping is rewarding and empowering not only for those helped but also for those who help.

Albert Schweitzer said it best: "One thing I know: The only ones among you who will be truly happy are those who have sought and found how to serve."

NOTES

I especially want to acknowledge Kathleen M. Lee for her participation with me on the research on hospice volunteers. In addition, I wish to gratefully acknowledge Kia Ora Zeleny, a Humboldt State University sociology graduate student, for her assistance with this chapter.

1. For a detailed discussion of methodology, see Oliner and Oliner (1988). Yad Vashem is the Holocaust Martyrs and Heroes Remembrance Authority, established in 1953 by an act of the Israeli Knesset in order to commemorate the 6 million Jews murdered by the Nazis.

2. For further discussion of empathic, normocentric, and principled motivations, see Oliner and Oliner (1988) and Reykowski (1987).

3. By values, I mean an enduring organization of beliefs concerning preferable modes of conduct and/or states of existence, along with continued values of importance and a collective conception of what is considered good, desirable, and proper, or bad, undesirable, and improper in a culture. Schulman and Mekler (1985) define moral values as consisting of empathy, kindness, and responsibility.

4. For a detailed discussion on extensivity, see Oliner and Oliner (1988). For an excellent discussion on caring and compassion, see Wuthnow (1991).

5. The Social Responsibility Scale was developed by L. Berkowitz and K. Luterman (1968); see Oliner and Oliner (1988, p. 376). The Internal/External Locus of Control Scale was developed by J. B. Rotter (1966); I used an adaptation developed by G. Gurin, P. Gurin, and B. M. Morrison (1978). The Self-Esteem Scale I used was developed by M. Rosenberg (1965); see Oliner and Oliner (1988, p. 378). The Empathy Scale was developed by A. Mehrabian and N. A. Epstein (1972).

6. Oliner and Oliner (1988). Using a Likert scale, we asked respondents whether they have something in common with diverse other people. The question asked was: "Some people think that they have things in common with others. Please tell me if you have very much in common with the following groups, something in common, not very much in common, or nothing at all in common." This commonality scale was originally developed for the research on the rescuers of Jews in Nazi-occupied Europe, so the groups identified were rich people, poor people, Catholics, Protestants, Jews, Turks, Gypsies, and Nazis. For purposes of the hospice volunteer study, the list was amended to: rich people, poor people, Catholics, Protestants, Jews, Native Americans, Mexican Americans, Black Americans, and homosexuals.

7. For example, for question B19, which asked, "What was the most important thing you learned from your mother?" responses could be grouped under headings such as religion, compassion, kindness, independence, getting ahead, and so forth.

8. This was question C35: "If you had an opportunity to speak to a group of young people, what kinds of advice would you offer them? That is, what would you consider the most important thing about life?"

REFERENCES

Adams, D. S. (1990). Issues and ideas in the culture of American volunteerism. Paper presented at the American Sociological Association meeting, Washington, DC.

Adams, D. S. (1991). Why should Americans volunteer? A content analysis of popular magazines. Paper presented at the North Central Sociological Association meeting, Dearborn, MI.

Allen, N., & Rushton, J. P. (1983). Personality characteristics of community mental health volunteers: A review. *Journal of Voluntary Action Research, 12*(1), 36–49.

Baron, L. (1988). The historical context of rescue. In P. M. Oliner & S. P. Oliner (Eds.), *The altruistic personality: Rescuers of Jews in Nazi Europe* (pp. 13–48). New York: Free Press.

Baron, L. (1992). The Dutchness of Dutch rescuers: The national dimension of altruism. In P. M. Oliner, S. P. Oliner, L. Baron, L. A. Blum, D. L. Krebs, & M. Z. Smolenska (Eds.), *Embracing the other: Philosophical, psychological, and historical perspectives on altruism* (pp. 306–327). New York: New York University Press.

Berkowitz, L., & Luterman, K. (1968). The traditionally socially responsible personality. *Public Opinion Quarterly, 32*, 169–185.

Buckingham, R. (1983). *The complete hospice guide.* New York: Harper & Row.

Carpi, D. (1977). The rescue of Jews in the Italian zone of occupied Croatia. In Y. Gutman & E. Zuroff (Eds.), *Rescue attempts during the Holocaust: Proceedings of the Second Yad Vashem International Historical Conference, April 8–11, 1974* (pp. 465–525). Jerusalem: Yad Vashem.

Chary, F. B. (1972). *The Bulgarian Jews and the final solution, 1940–1944.* Pittsburgh: University of Pittsburgh Press.

Fischman, W. I. (1964, December 1). The friar who saved 5,000 Jews. *Look Magazine.*

Fleischner, E. (Ed.). (1988). Can the few become the many? Some Catholics in France who saved Jews during the Holocaust. In *Remembering for the future: Jews and Christians during and after the Holocaust* (Theme 1, International Scholars Conference, Oxford, England, July 10–13, 1988). Oxford: Pergamon.

Flender, H. (1964). *Rescue in Denmark.* New York: Manor Books.

Friedman, P. (1978). *Their brothers' keepers.* New York: Holocaust Library.

Gurin, G., Gurin, P., & Morrison, B. M. (1978). Personal and ideological aspects of internal and external control. *Social Psychology, 41*(4), 275–296.

Hoffman, M. L. (1983). Affective and cognitive processes in moral internalization: An information processing approach. In E. T. Higgins, D. Ruble, & W. Hartup (Eds.), *Social cognition and social development: A socio-cultural perspective* (pp. 236–274). New York: Cambridge University Press.

Huneke, D. K. (1985). *The Moses of Rovno: The stirring story of Fritz Graebe, a German Christian who risked his life to lead hundreds of Jews to safety during the Holocaust.* New York: Dodd, Mead.

Huneke, D. K. (1986). Lessons of Herman Graebe's life: The origins of a moral person. *Humboldt Journal of Social Relations, 13*(1&2), 320–332.

Kübler-Ross, E. (1997). *On death and dying.* New York: Simon & Schuster.

Kurek, E. (1997). *Your life is worth mine.* New York: Hippocrene Books.

Kurek-Lesik, E. (1992).The role of Polish nuns in the rescue of Jews, 1939–1945. In P. M. Oliner et al. (Eds.), *Embracing the other: Philosophical, psychological, and historical perspectives on altruism* (pp. 328–334). New York: New York University Press.

Mehrabian, A., & Epstein, N. A. (1972). A measure of emotional empathy. *Journal of Personality, 40*(4), 525–543.

Midlarsky, M. I. (1981). Helping during the Holocaust: The role of political, theological, and socioeconomic identifications. *Humboldt Journal of Social Relations, 13* (1&2), 285–305.

Murdoch, I. (1985). *The sovereignty of good.* London: Ark. (Original work published 1970)

Oliner, S. P., & Oliner, P. M. (1988). *The altruistic personality: Rescuers of Jews in Nazi Europe.* New York: Free Press.

Piliavin, J. A. (1990).Give the gift of life to unnamed strangers: A review of research on blood donors since Oswalt (1977). *Transfusion, 30,* 444–459.

Ramati, A. (1978). *The Assisi underground: The priests who rescued Jews.* New York: Stein & Day.

Reykowski, J. (1987). Dimensions of development in moral values: Two approaches to the development of morality. In N. Eisenberg, J. Reykowski, & E. Staub (Eds.), *Social and moral values: Individual and societal perspectives.* Hillsdale, NJ: Erlbaum.

Rosenberg, M. (1965). *Society and the adolescent self-image.* Princeton, NJ: Princeton University Press.

Rotter, J. B. (1966).Generalized expectancies for internal versus external control of reinforcement. *Psychological Monographs, 80,* 1.

Sauvage, P. (1986). Ten things I would like to know about righteous conduct in Le Chambon and elsewhere during the Holocaust. *Humboldt Journal of Social Relations, 13* (1&2), 252–259.

Schulman, M., & Mekler, E. (1985). *Bringing up a moral child: A new approach for teaching your child to be kind, just, and responsible.* Reading, MA: Addison-Wesley.

Wuthnow, R. (1991). *Acts of compassion: Caring for others and helping ourselves.* Princeton, NJ: Princeton University Press.

Yahil, L. (1969). *The rescue of Danish Jewry: Test of a democracy* (M. Gradel, Trans). Philadelphia: Jewish Publication Society.

Zeitoun, S. (1988). The role of Christian community in saving Jewish children in France during the Second World War. In E. Fleischner (Ed.), *Remembering for the Future: The impact of the Holocaust and genocide on Jews and Christians* (supplementary vol., International Scholars Conference, Oxford, England, July 10–13; pp. 505–525). Oxford: Pergamon.

Zuccotti, S. (1987). *The Italians and the Holocaust: Persecution, rescue, and survival.* New York: Basic Books.

Conclusion to Part II

LYNN G. UNDERWOOD

This section has provided us with four very different but largely consistent looks at the human phenomena of altruism and altruistic love, looks that, in various ways, draw on the social sciences. All four proceed from the hypothesis that truly altruistic motives and actions exist. Underwood explores the subjective or experiential aspects of compassionate love. She presents a model of the factors that encourage and constrain such choices, and she gives insight into the processes by which people can make choices involving compassionate love. Batson, the most traditionally social-scientific in his approach, summarizes a series of experiments that strongly support his empathy-altruism hypothesis against the (more cynical) claims of those who would reduce all behavior to egoism. Monroe and Oliner both study groups of people who have done significantly altruistic things, attempting to identify common qualities, backgrounds, or mind-sets. In addition, Monroe argues explicitly for developing new theoretical models (paradigms) for studying human behavior in ways that do not beg the question regarding the possibility of altruism.

The topics of altruism and altruistic love have not been a central theme in the social sciences, despite their aim of better understanding human motivations, actions, and behaviors. The rational choice model of human behavior, with its typical assumption of self-interested behavior, comes from economics. And economists have struggled with different ways of introducing other-regarding motives into the picture (Sen, 1987; Hausman & McPherson, 1993; Hausman, 1994). But work in other social sciences is limited. Thus there is an active field in the health sciences looking at the role of social support in mental and physical health (Cohen, Underwood, & Gottlieb, 2000), but the subject of altruistic love and altruism has not been studied in this context. In contrast, there has been targeted research funding in violence and aggression, which has resulted in scientific publications in those fields.

For understanding of altruism and altruistic love to advance, there needs to be significant dialogue between disciplines, informing work in the social sciences with work from the humanities, theology, neurosciences, and basic biology. Some of this work is presented in this volume. What kinds of further work need to be done?

Observational work in this area can proceed in a number of different ways. We can observe the behaviors of the person, such as whether he or she rescued a Holocaust victim, placing his or her own life at risk. By observing actions in naturally occurring settings, we can develop and test hypotheses, using quantitative methods, such as those used in epidemiology, or qualitative ones, as are frequently used in anthropology. Twin studies utilize natural observations, which control for underlying common features in genetics and take account of environmental variations. Observation of natural neurological defects is another way to do observational studies, by exploring the relationship between impairments of various parts of the brain and effects on altruistic behaviors. Economists have studied patterns of blood donors and the effects of economic and other incentives on patterns of donation.

As we do observational work, we see the possibilities for manipulating variables, which can lead to *experimental studies*. In this section, Batson's approach is an example of an experimental approach to human behavior, as is some of Damasio's work. We also depend on *self-reports* for much of the detail we obtain in social science research, and this dependence will be particularly high in our area of altruism and altruistic love. Methods for obtaining good questions that accurately elicit the features of interest are crucial. Methodologies that optimize agreement between our implicit understandings and our external verbalizations are of help. Techniques that tap accurate self-awareness can also be particularly helpful. Both qualitative and quantitative methods can help our understanding of the various processes involved in altruistic acts and compassionate motivation. And *biological measures* can help to verify or question the congruence of self-reports with physical and mental variables. Biological parameters that can be measured, both in observational and experimental work, include such things as heart rate variability, skin conductance, hormonal and neurochemical markers of stress, and neural imaging.

A crucial and practical question that science might help us to answer is what practices and what intellectual, social, and religious structures most encourage the expression of altruistic love or compassionate love. The work of the Oliners (see Samuel Oliner, Chapter 8, in the preceding section) indicates some suggestively significant differences between the altruistic actors (rescuers, volunteer) and others. The tools that I have been discussing could enable us to answer this question.

This would be an investigation worthy of financial and human resources, which could really make a difference in the state of our communities and our world.

REFERENCES

Cohen, S., Underwood, L., & Gottlieb, B. (Eds.). (2000). *Measuring social support and intervention development: A guide for health and social scientists.* New York: Oxford University Press.

Hausman, D. M. (Ed.). (1994). *The philosophy of economic: An anthology* (2nd ed.). Cambridge: Cambridge University Press.

Hausman, D. M., & McPherson, M. S. (1993, June). Taking ethics seriously: Economics and contemporary moral philosophy. *Journal of Economic Literature, 31*(2), 671–731.

Sen, A. (1987). *On ethics and economics.* Oxford: Blackwell.

Part III

EVOLUTIONARY BIOLOGY

Introduction to Part III

JEFFREY P. SCHLOSS

It is a regrettable irony that in modern intellectual life the topic of altruistic love—so undeniably central to our experience of being human—has nevertheless received comparatively little scholarly attention. And, when it has taken place, such discussion has often occurred within methodological enclaves that subvert rather than cultivate the cross-disciplinary dialogue that is both necessary for altruism's appreciative elucidation and reflective of the very focus of study—other-regarding exchange. Over the past several decades, evolutionary theory has wielded particularly significant influence, both stimulating and inhibitory, on the terms of interdisciplinary engagement over altruism and altruistic love. There may be three reasons for this, brief mention of which can help illuminate the significance of this section.

First, evolutionary theory is somewhat unique among the natural sciences in that it studies not just proximal causal mechanisms but ultimate historical origins and adaptive or functional "ends." The myriad details of body plans, regulatory mechanisms, life histories, and mating or social systems are teleonomically coalesced into adaptive strategies by evolutionary analysis. Thus Dobzhansky's famous quote, "Nothing in biology makes sense except in light of evolution," is not just about evolutionary intimations of where biological structures came from but interpretations of what they are "for." Evolution, then, deigns to adjudicate matters of natural "purpose." For example, in a voice controversially uncharacteristic of

145

the other natural sciences, E. O. Wilson claims, "Human behavior—like the deepest capacities for emotional response which derive and guide it—is the circuitous technique by which human genetic material has been and will be kept intact. Morality has no other demonstrable function" (Wilson, 1978, p. 167).

This perspective has provoked energetic and fruitful collaboration between evolutionary theorists and many scholars in the human behavioral sciences. However, especially when conjoined, in its initial formulations, with reductionistically triumphalist assertions that the "biologization of social sciences" will eventually do away not only with them but also with "epistemology and epistemologists themselves" (Wilson, 1975), it has understandably escalated rather than attenuated disciplinary rivalries. Even if the aforementioned, or another evolutionary account of unique human attributes, proves to be scientifically adequate, it will still be a matter for philosophy, theology, and the other humanities, not biology, to make human sense of the situation (Midgley, 1978, 1994; Schloss, 1996). One of the purposes of this section is to bring into engagement contrasting perspectives of what the "sense of it" entails.

Second, the issue of altruism is not just a fascinating though ancillary project for the tools of evolutionary analysis; it figures prominently—Wilson (1975) describes it as "the central theoretical issue"—in devising a theoretically complete evolutionary account of social behavior (Holcomb, 1993). The reason is that, by definition, natural selection tends to eliminate any trait in a population that decreases the reproductive success of its bearer while increasing that of another. Of course, genetically "selfish" reproductive consequences are not isomorphic with self-regarding motivational intentions, and human altruistic love clearly entails the matter of intentionality. However, evolutionary accounts of fitness outcomes still have two important implications for understanding motivational altruism. First, whatever one's profession or experience of personal motive, Darwinian evolution entails that actual social behaviors established by natural selection be restricted to those that result in reproductive self-enhancement, not detriment. Second, even if we question the claims of some sociobiologists that other-regarding intentions are not genuine, it remains the case that traditional Darwinian accounts posit the domain of other-regard as being largely constrained to genetically related kin or socially mediated reciprocation. Indeed, a good deal, perhaps the bolus, of evolutionary explanation developed over the past three decades has tended to view the existence of authentic, "out-group" altruism as irreconcilable with Darwinian orthodoxy: "If natural selection is both sufficient and true, it is impossible for a genuinely disinterested or 'altruistic' behavior pattern to evolve" (Ghiseln, 1973, 967). That this attitude is changing is reflected by the continuum of perspectives present in this section.

Third, although the current mixing rate between the watershed of evolutionary theory and other disciplinary streams appears to be quite high, as with any new terrain, the topographic relief of the contemporary explanatory landscape is unusually pronounced. At present, ideas are flowing in wildly divergent directions: There are a number of virulent and not insignificant debates within contemporary evolutionary biology, both the intensity and import of which are magnified when it comes to theories of altruism. One such debate, by no means endemic to evolutionary studies, is over genetic determinism. Although there are no theories of hard determinism, there is a broad continuum of theory from soft determinism positing biological constraint or a genetic leash on the character and extensivity of altruism (Wilson, 1978; Alexander, 1987; Konner, 1982; Ruse, 1994), through a variety of intermediate hypotheses (Durham, 1991; Ayala, 1995) to virtual libertarian yet fully Darwinian assertions that in human culture the leash can be effectively broken (Blackmore, 1999; Plotkin, 1993, 1997).

A second axis of controversy entails the adequacy of the adaptationist paradigm and the question of whether—to whatever extent behavior is genetically determined—natural selection is a sufficient mechanism for the origin of major biotic innovation and whether extant variants—including human cognitive functions—are (or were in their initial environments) necessarily optimized for reproduction (Ayala, 1995; Cosmides & Tooby, 1992; Dennett, 1995; Gould, 1997; Gould & Lewontin, 1979). Yet a third dimension of quite animated disagreement concerns the use of hierarchical explanations in evolutionary theory. One case of this is gene-centric versus multilevel selection theory (Sober & Wilson, 1998), the latter positing that selection acts at different levels of structural configuration (e.g., gene, individual, conspecific group, interspecies community). Another even more controversial issue (Dennett, 1995; de Waal, 1996; Plotkin, 1997) is whether human social behavior in general and altruism in particular are the results of interacting but altogether different selectional processes operating on distinct, functionally hierarchical entities (e.g., material units of information, genes; nonmaterial units of information, memes). Finally, of course, there are vastly contrasting judgments about the existence of and human capacity for both genuinely unselfish other-regard and its extension beyond near and dear. We are very fortunate in this volume to have, in this section and others, leading explorers of different positions in the theoretical landscape described here.

In Chapter 9, evolutionary philosopher Michael Ruse both outlines the gene-centric sociobiological perspective on altruism and reflects on its significance for understanding the moral basis of cooperative behavior. Ruse asserts that a Darwinian interpretation of social behavior and of the morality that underlies it requires that they be reproductively beneficial. However, he is careful to maintain that genetically "selfish" behavioral functions do not necessarily entail consciously selfish behavioral motives. In fact, he argues that a genetically conferred sense of moral reality enables, perhaps compels, us to cooperate because it is "right," rather than for intentional benefit. Yet this is precisely the kind of cooperation that results in our reproductive benefit. Thus the traditions of radical altruism, which give no preference to near and dear or which urge us to degrees of self-relinquishment that threaten reproductive success, are not only evolutionarily but also morally untenable. Finally, Ruse argues on the basis of Darwinian naturalism against a realist metaethics and also against a merely emotivist or wholly relativist perspective on moral obligation for human beings.

In Chapter 10, theologian Stephen Pope takes to task both the radical altruist or agapic pole of theology and the selfish-gene pole of evolutionary theory. Pope maintains that sociobiological analysis can contribute much to our understanding of altruism by illuminating the origin and character of human caring affiliations and by describing the natural limitations and impediments to them. However, he criticizes some sociobiological theory for giving primacy to genetic, as opposed to cultural, components of human identity and for positing ultimately selfish goals for ostensible acts of other-regard. On the other hand, Pope also criticizes theologies of agape which see it in dialectical opposition to other loves and therefore dismiss both the goodness and necessity of the caring relationships our biology equips us to embrace. He argues for a middle ground that affirms the goodness of both natural, self-enriching attachment and also sacrificially extensive other-regard. And he urges us to envision appropriate altruism as something that comes out of who we are rather than being a religious imposition that occurs contrary to our deepest native needs and desires. Interestingly, although Pope takes issue with Ruse, they are actually far closer in perspective than they were at earlier junctures (Pope, 1994; Ruse, 1994) through ongoing exchange in this field.

David Sloan Wilson and Elliott Sober, leading proponents of group selection, take discussion to the next "level" in Chapter 11, which both surveys and extends multilevel selection theory. After describing the linked oscillations of ascendance and demise for both altruism and group selection in evolutionary theory, Wilson and Sober argue that multilevel selection theory represents not an alternative to but a synthesis of kin selection and reciprocal altruism, which are both special cases of the group selection superset. Altruism, not just strictly reciprocal but genuinely sacrificial, can evolve whenever between-group selection is stronger than within-group selection. Furthermore, although group coercion or social control within groups has until now generally been seen as opposing the development of voluntary altruism, Wilson and Sober point out that by attenuating within-group phenotypic variability, it can reduce the penalty of within-group fitness differences and therefore promote intergroup selection for innately helpful dispositions. Wilson and Sober not only address an argument against mechanisms for the establishment of genuinely sacrificial behavior on behalf of other group members but also suggest a case of interaction between cultural evolution and genetic selection.

In a wide-ranging review of data from evolutionary biology, primatology, and anthropology, Melvin Konner (Chapter 12) describes the obstacles to altruism—not to discourage its pursuit but to avoid the risks of underestimating the difficulties of its attainment. Konner maintains that, rightly understood, evolutionary theory does not rule out altruistic motives toward those near to us, but it does make the most disinterested forms problematic. He then reviews literature on aggression in primates and humans, arguing on both empirical and theoretical grounds that, contrary to sociological optimism, infanticide, sexual violence, and warfare are deeply rooted in human biology. Konner further suggests that evolutionary theories of self-deception apply not only to the opacity of personal motive but also to widely embraced cognitive distortions—lies—about the dark side of human nature. Although religion has generally squarely faced the deep ambiguity of human impulses, it has had only mixed success in stimulating good and consistently poor success in limiting evil. On the other hand, the experiment of democratic governance that grew out of a scientific conception of human nature has succeeded well as a "device for limiting evil, not promoting good," by harnessing rather than denying self-interest and balancing rival quests for power. He notes that the challenge of making such a system responsive to the powerless when devised by and for a creature evolved to pursue genetic self-interest.

In Chapter 13, population biologist Jeffrey Schloss surveys the significant and controversial breadth in evolutionary approaches to human cooperative behavior, describing how adaptationist, nonadaptationist, and hierarchical accounts differ in depicting the nature of and challenges to altruism. Some see altruism as limited in scope but deeply rooted in natural cooperative affections; others see it as unrestrained in extent but culturally imposed on a recalcitrant genetic substrate. These poles in current evolutionary theory represent tensions that have animated theological discussion for centuries. Schloss argues that they are not mutually exclusive but reflect fundamental ambiguities in human nature. The good news is that virtually all current theory is consilient in its affirmation of the natural basis for genuine other-regard within kinship or social groups. The challenging news is that the counterpart of such affiliation is exclusionistic group boundaries. We do not yet have even a provisional biological understanding of how out-group sacrifice, "love your enemy" altruism, can come about. Schloss concludes by observing that biological systems tend to incorporate external means as internal ends or set points, suggesting that moral and religious norms for social cooperation and the very exercise of altruism itself may have been internalized as biological needs, which, when met, confer homeostatic benefits to the organism independent of reciprocation.

REFERENCES

Alexander, R. D. (1987). *The biology of moral systems.* Chicago: Aldine de Gruyter.

Ayala, F. J. (1995). The difference of being human: Ethical behavior as an evolutionary byproduct. In H. Rolston III (Ed.), *Biology, ethics, and the origins of life* (pp. 113–136). Boston: Jones & Bartlett.

Blackmore, S. (1999). *The meme machine.* Oxford: Oxford University Press.

Cosmides, L., & Tooby, J. (1992). Cognitive adaptations for social exchange. In J. Barkow, L. Cosmides, & J. Tooby (Eds.), *The adapted mind: Evolutionary psychology and the generation of culture* (pp. 163–228). New York: Oxford University Press.

de Waal, F. (1996). *Good natured: The origins of right and wrong in humans and other animals.* Cambridge: Harvard University Press.

Dennett, D. C. (1995). *Darwin's dangerous idea: Evolution and the meaning of life.* New York: Simon & Schuster.

Durham, W. (1991). *Coevolution: Genes, culture, and human diversity.* Stanford, CA: Stanford University Press.

Ghiselin, M. T. (1973). Darwin and evolutionary psychology. *Science, 179,* 964–968.

Ghiselin, M. T. (1974). *The economy of nature and the evolution of sex.* Berkeley: University of California Press.

Gould, S. J. (1997, June 12). Darwinian fundamentalism. *New York Review of Books.*

Gould, S. J., & Lewontin, R. C. (1979). The spandrels of San Marco and the Panglossian paradigm: A critique of the adaptationist programme. *Proceedings of the Royal Society of London, 205,* 581–598.

Holcomb, H. R. (1993). *Sociobiology, sex, and science.* Albany: State University of New York Press.

Konner, M. (1982). *The tangled wing: Biological constraints on the human spirit.* New York: Holt, Rinehart, & Winston.

Midgley, M. (1978). *Beast and man: The roots of human nature.* Ithaca, NY: Cornell University Press.

Midgley, M. (1994). *The ethical primate: Humans, freedom and morality.* London: Routledge.

Plotkin, H. (1993). *Darwin machines and the nature of knowledge.* Cambridge: Harvard University Press.

Plotkin, H. (1997). *Evolution in mind: An introduction to evolutionary psychology.* Cambridge: Harvard University Press.

Pope, S. J. (1994). *The evolution of altruism and the ordering of love.* Washington: Georgetown University Press.

Ruse, M. (1994). Evolutionary theory and Christian ethics: Are they in harmony? *Zygon, 29* (1), 5–24.

Schloss, J. P. (1996). Sociobiological explanations of altruistic ethics: Necessary, sufficient, or irrelevant? In J. P. Hurd (Ed.), *Investigating the biological foundations of human morality* (pp. 107–145). New York: Edwin Mellen Press.

Sober, E., & Wilson, D. S. (1998). *Unto others: The evolution and psychology of unselfish behavior.* Cambridge: Harvard University Press.

Wilson, E. O. (1975). *Sociobiology.* Cambridge: Harvard University Press.

Wilson, E. O. (1978). *On human nature.* Cambridge: Harvard University Press.

9

A Darwinian Naturalist's Perspective on Altruism

MICHAEL RUSE

"The blood of the martyrs is the seed of the church." With that chilling dictum the third-century theologian Tertullian confessed the fundamental flaw of human altruism, an intimation that the purpose of sacrifice is to raise one human group over another. Generosity without reciprocation is the rarest and most cherished of human behaviors, subtle and difficult to define, distributed in a highly selective pattern, surrounded by ritual and circumstance, and honored by medallions and emotional orations. We sanctify true altruism in order to reward it, and thus to make it less than true, and by that means to promote its occurrence in others. Human altruism, in short, is riddled to its foundations with the expected mammalian ambivalence (Wilson, 1978, p. 149).

Even before Charles Darwin published his *On the Origin of Species* in 1859, evolutionists—notably Herbert Spencer—were using their theory as a basis for ethics. They felt that in a modern age, in which one saw rapid urbanization, industrialization, the rise of an educated middle class living by its abilities rather than its heritage, the ethics of the past—particularly the ethics of Christianity—was no longer adequate. One had to replace it with a new, forward-looking scientific ethics appropriate for the age. Evolution was the key (see Ruse, 1994, 1996, 2000; Spencer, 1851, 1892).

As is well known, evolutionary ethics—or, as it came to be called, "social Darwinism"—was a powerful and wide-ranging doctrine or set of beliefs. As is equally well known, it was something criticized very severely from its very inception: not just by theologians and like thinkers, but also by secular philosophers. Notably, G. E. Moore in his *Principia Ethica* (1903) dealt very severely with Spencer's own ideas. I have myself on many occasions criticized social Darwinism, both the traditional form and the updated version (Ruse, 1985, 1998). I do not intend to return to that particular doctrine again here; although I will say in fairness that I think that there is much more to be said for it than is often allowed in the traditional critique. In this chapter, rather, focusing on the key notion of *altruism*— I discuss the meaning of the concept subsequently—I put forward an alternative evolutionary ethics, one which pays as much attention to evolutionism, particularly modern-day evolutionism, as does social Darwinism. Specifically, I offer an evolutionary ethics that uses that modern-day Darwinian evolutionism that deals with social behavior and that goes under the name "sociobiology." And I argue that this offers us a plausible position that should recommend itself to the most hard-line of ethical thinkers. I am not sure how original my thinking is. I suspect that there are at least hints of the position I take even in Darwin's own writings, specifically *The Descent of Man* (1871). But my concern here is less with origins and credit and more with exposition. I should say, however, that I think of my position as being one very much in the philosophical tradition of David Hume. If the critic objects that little I have to say is not to be found in the *Treatise of Human Nature*, I shall take it as praise rather than condemnation.

As always in philosophical discussions about ethics and morality, it is useful to make a twofold distinction: between "substantive" or "normative ethics" and "metaethics." By the former, I mean that domain that asks questions about what one ought to do: as in, "Love your neighbour as yourself," or "Treat others as ends rather than as means." By the latter, I mean that domain that asks questions about why one ought to do what one ought to do: as in, "Follow the Sermon on the Mount because that is God's will," or "Act only in ways which avoid social contradictions." I realize that there are those who question the substantive/metaethical distinction, but for the rather broad purposes I have in this chapter it will serve us well.

Modern Evolutionary Biology

Mine is very much a naturalized position. I should explain that by "naturalism" in this context I mean either using the methods of the empirical sciences or the conclusions of them in one's philosophical inquiries (Ruse 1994, 1999). I do distinguish "naturalism" from "scientism," meaning by the latter the belief that science can solve all problems. I am not sure that this is true. Certainly, socially I doubt very much whether it is true, but this is not my concern here. I am a philosophical naturalist and this chapter is an exercise in philosophical naturalism, because I am working in the mode of the scientist, using the conclusions of the scientist. Because in this chapter I put forward a modern version of evolutionary ethics, to that end I begin with a discussion of the scientific grounds on which I base my arguments. I do not argue for this scientific position: I and others have done this many times elsewhere (Ruse, 1982). I simply state it. Specifically, I state the basic claims of modern Darwinian evolutionary theory about social behavior, particularly as it pertains to our own species *Homo sapiens.*

I start with the fundamental claim that all organisms including ourselves are products of evolution, that is to say, a long, slow, natural (law-bound) process of development from, as Darwin said, "one or a few forms." I accept here that the main method of evolutionary change is that fueled by the causal process known as natural selection. Darwin himself drew attention to the fact that more organisms are born than can possibly survive and reproduce and that this leads to what Darwin (following Robert Malthus) called a "struggle for existence." Truly, as Darwin recognized, it is more importantly a struggle for *reproduction.* Organisms come in many different kinds, and there is a constant supply of new heritable variation. Success in the struggle is a function of this heritable variation, and those that do survive and reproduce tend to be different on average from those that do not. This is what Darwin called "natural selection": Given enough time it leads to full-blown evolution. Absolutely central for the Darwinian is the fact that evolution is not just a random process but rather that it promotes characteristics that aid their possessors in the battle to survive and reproduce. Evolution through natural selection produces things such as hands and eyes and teeth and noses and penises and vaginas: things known as "adaptations."

Darwin recognized that behavior is as important in the struggle as are physical characteristics. Therefore, animal behavior must itself be subject to natural selection. Darwin realized also that behavior, even in the struggle for existence, does not necessarily imply all-out combat. Often there can be very good reasons for cooperation, that is to say, for social behavior. Evolutionary biologists refer to this cooperation as "altruism," and it is important at once to clarify the sense in which this term is being used. Altruism when used in everyday language—as in "Mother Teresa's altruism toward the poor of Calcutta was truly saintlike"—means giving and caring without thought of reward, acting and thinking in a certain way simply because it is good and right. Although I doubt that any evolutionist wants to deny the meaningfulness and validity of this term (although one may question its use in a particular situation), this is not the sense of the term as it occurs in biology. Here the use is metaphorical: It means acting or giving toward another because it furthers one's own survival and/or reproductive ends. There is absolutely no implication of consciousness or intentionality, and often, of course, it is fully realized that the biological "altruist" is anything but a thinker or a free moral agent.

Because we have a metaphor here at work, when speaking literally of Mother Teresa–type altruism, I refer to it simply, without quotation marks, and when speaking of biological "altruism," I use quotation marks. I do this to keep the two notions separate, and in no sense do I imply (as some philosophers have claimed) that the biological sense is illegitimate or second-rate. We use metaphors all of the time in our thought and speech—we cannot function without metaphor—and in evolutionary biology particularly metaphor plays a big and crucial role. Think of natural selection, adaptive landscape, arms race, to take but three. I see "altruism" to be part of a complex net of metaphors of intentionality or design which are associated with the teleology or functionality of adaptation-producing natural selection—as in "the eye is designed for sight" or "the teeth exist in order to chew food" or "male baldness has no direct function." I have no problem with the notion of biological "altruism," just so long as it is understood to be what it is, no more and no less.

Parenthetically, and toward an aid to even further understanding, I must admit that, like most new metaphors, there is some ambiguity in the literature as to the precise meaning of biological "altruism." Many, such as Edward O. Wilson in his classic *Sociobiology: The New Synthesis* (1975), suggest that biological "altruism" means simply giving to others at the expense of one's own reproductive chances or abilities. As Wilson recognizes, the trouble with such an understanding as this is that such "altruism" could never exist—could never persist—in nature. It would be wiped out at once by selection. One must add that biological "altruism" rebounds to the benefit of the "altruist," as for instance in situations involving the aptly named "reciprocal altruism," in which I help you in return for your helping me. Because of the need for this addition, I find it easier simply to build into my understanding of biological "altruism" this expectation of reciprocation—this return of biological benefit—however caused and whatever form it takes, and it is thus in this extended sense that I use the term in this chapter.

Darwin and subsequent Darwinians argue strongly that social behavior— what is here being called "altruism" (in the extended sense just clarified and specified)—must be no less a function of evolution through natural selection than are teeth or eyes or hands or penises or vaginas. In the past 30 or 40 years, there have been major breakthroughs in our understanding of the evolution of social behavior considered within the Darwinian context. In particular, it is argued that animals—from the ants up to the apes—work socially together in order to promote their own biological well-being (Wilson, 1975). Translating this into the language of modern biology: Animals work in an "altruistic" fashion, thus ensuring that their units of heredity (the "genes") are passed in higher percentages to future generations than otherwise would be the case. I should say that contemporary Darwinism argues also that one never gets selection working for the group, or at least only very rarely. In this sense, selection promotes what Richard Dawkins (1976) has called the "selfish gene": Social behavior or "altruism" must, in some sense, be looked upon as enlightened self-interest. One is never going to get organisms simply working altruistically, in a disinterested way, for the group. Working socially must always have some payoff for the individual, whatever the costs might be.

As I said, I am not going to defend this position here. I am certainly going to sidestep claims that selection can work for the group rather than the individual, a perennially popular alternative with those unable emotionally to face the stark nature of the Darwinian process (the flavor of which even infuses the passage quoted at the beginning of this chapter—a passage that opens the chapter on altruism in E. O. Wilson's *On Human Nature*, 1978). I nevertheless stress that the position I accept is something that has been articulated theoretically in great detail in the past decades and that there is a huge amount of experimental evidence backing its claims. Much more controversial is the extension of Darwinism to humankind. Charles Darwin himself always intended that we humans should be part and parcel of the animal world. Indeed, the very first speculations that we have by Darwin (in private notebooks) of selection working are in the context of human intelligence. In *The Descent of Man* (1871), Darwin brought us firmly within the natural sphere, and this has been the ongoing position of evolutionists ever since. Today's students of social behavior from a Darwinian perspective, sociobiologists, argue strongly that *Homo sapiens* must be considered a product of natural selection.

Specifically, because it is recognized by all that humans are a highly social species, it is argued that human social behavior must be seen as a product of natural selection. We survive as a species because we work together. But remember that survival is not for the benefit of the species: We survive as individuals because by working cooperatively together we do better as individuals than we would otherwise. We humans are not particularly fast, we are not particularly strong, we are not particularly ferocious or any of these things, but because we work together we do very well. In other words, natural selection has made humans the masters of biological "altruism." (Of course, what a Darwinian evolutionist argues is that there has been a circular or feedback process in our evolution toward our "altruistic" nature. We have developed social adaptations, and, at the same time, things such as aggressive behavior have declined because these are incompatible with being social. But because we are so social, we no longer need the speed or aggressive behavior possessed by top rank predators like lions.)

Do not be deceived by claims that humans are really violent apes, with a blood lust toward conspecifics. Even if you take into account all of the killings of this century, we still come out very low on the murder scale. Compared with such animals as lions or lemmings, even ethnic cleansers come out as wimps. The question now becomes how it is that humans act together so well socially. Why are we such good biological "altruists," that is, how is it that natural selection has made our biological "altruism" such a successful phenomenon? I think there are at least three possible answers to this question and that in some respects we humans have taken all three.

The first way in which human "altruism" might have been produced and might function—the way in which humans might interact socially—is purely innately, that is to say, purely by instinct. I take it that this is the way that much if not most "altruistic" social behavior in the animal kingdom comes about. No one thinks, for instance, that the ants are thinking beings, and yet they cooperate in the most marvelous ways (Wilson, 1971). They do everything entirely by instinct. They are, to use a modern metaphor, hard-wired in their behavior. Fairly obviously, humans follow this pattern to a certain extent also. Parents and children often interact on an instinctive basis: The love that a mother feels for her child has nothing to do with reason or rationality in any way. It is something that comes about naturally, as it were. It is part of human nature, meaning that it is part of instinctive or biological human nature.

However, this is not the only way in which humans interact socially, and there is a very good reason why we humans must have taken a different evolutionary route from lower organisms such as the ants. Their instinct has both strengths and weaknesses. The strengths are that one can start action immediately. There is no need for training or education, so the ants can work with fairly simple brains and do not need any instructing as to what they ought to do. But there are major drawbacks to such "altruism." In particular, there is the big problem that if something goes wrong, instinctive behavior is (generally speaking) unable to respond and put things right immediately. If, for instance, a stream of ants is out foraging—doing all of this instinctively—and then it starts to rain, it is more than likely that many of these ants will fail to find their way back to the nest. To this point, they have been guided out and back by chemical (pheromone) trails. The rain washes these trails away, and consequently because of the disruption many of the nest members are lost.

A queen ant can afford to lose many offspring, because she is turning out literally millions. Humans do not have this luxury. We have evolved in such a way as to produce only a few offspring, and we simply cannot afford to lose them if something goes wrong. (The difference I am referring to is known technically as the distinction between r-selection and K-selection. With the former, you produce many offspring but do not put too much parental care into tending them. With the latter, you produce very few offspring but do put a lot of parental care into tending them. Humans are very much K-selected organisms; although, of course, again one has feedback, selective loops. As we have developed our social adaptations in the way that we have, we have become K-selected.)

My point is that instinct simply will not do as the exclusive cause of the social interactions—of the "altruism"—of organisms such as humans. What then would be a second option? The most obvious is to go completely the other way. Instead of being purely instinctive, we might be hardly, if at all, instinctive, forever calculating the payoff in social interactions (Axelrod, 1984). Two humans meet and (for some reason) the issue arises as to whether they should interact socially or not. Remembering now that in the modern biological context everything is done from the individual perspective, what these two individuals will do is reason together or apart, deciding whether cooperation is in their interests or not. If it is, then they will cooperate, and if it is not then they will not cooperate. (It is often thought that purely rational beings, that is to say, humans with super brains, would necessarily be really nasty beings, like Darth Vader before his reformation. In fact, this is not necessarily so. Because everybody is a super being, you will recognize that it is going to be impossible to be universally nasty, because everyone else is in the same condition. Hence you will have to cooperate. Note, however, that this kind of biological "altruism" does not imply literal altruism—the very opposite, in fact. Doing things in hope of gain is not necessarily immoral, but in itself is not a disinterestedly good thing.)

In some respects, as with the first option (instinct), humans have taken this causal path toward sociality, toward "altruism." Much of our dealings with our fellow humans is done in a purely reasonable or rational way. I go to buy a shirt from Mr. L. L. Bean. I give him money for the shirt; he gives me the shirt. I do this not because I like Mr. Bean, nor does he reciprocate because he likes me. Rather, it is in our own self-interest to interact socially together here. However, again there are limits to this mode of interaction. There are good biological reasons why we have not become just super-brained, rational calculators, even if this were biologically possible. The big drawback to being a super calculator is that it takes time, and in the evolutionary world time is money. Often, one simply does not have the temporal luxury available to make the perfect calculations. Suppose you and I are out on a savannah and a lion is coming at us. If I spend much time deciding whether or not it is in my interests to let you know that the lion is coming and that we should cooperate in escaping, before the decision is made we will both be in the lion's stomach. What we need therefore is some kind of quick and dirty solution in order to cooperate rapidly together, a method which will usually work quickly on a day-to-day basis, even though it is not fail safe.

The analogy that comes to mind here is that of a chess-playing machine. The early chess-playing machines calculated every move. They were like the super brains of the second option. But of course, as we all know, the early chess-playing machines were virtually useless. They took so long after two or three moves to make the next move that nothing could progress. What happened then was that the designers of such machines started to "build in" certain strategies: When a configuration of pieces came up on the board, the machine could run through its various options and come up with a quick solution. Initially, the early machines were not very good and could be beaten easily by human beings. But as we all know from the story of Deep Blue, before long the machines became so sophisticated that, although they could in fact be beaten, generally they were not. I think that humans have in fact taken this third option. We are hard-wired in some sense to act socially together, but we are not hard-wired in such a way that we never make mistakes. The point is that we use this hard-wiring to apply to particular situations on a day-by-day basis.

Less metaphorically, I suggest that we humans have built in innately, or instinctively if you like, a capacity for working together socially. And I suggest that this capacity manifests itself at the physical level as a moral sense—as genuine, Mother Teresa–type altruism! Hence I argue—on purely naturalistic, Darwinian grounds—that morality, or rather a moral sense—a recognition of the call of altruism and a propensity to obey—is something which is hard-wired into humans. It has been put there by natural selection in order to get us to work together socially or to cooperate. This is not to say that we do not have freedom in any sense. I am not saying that we never disregard our moral sense, but rather that we do have the moral sense and that we have the moral sense—the urge to altruism—not by choice or decision, but because we are human. (Of course, there are psychopaths without a moral sense, but in biology you know that there are exceptions for every rule.)

My claim, therefore, is that when humans find themselves in a position in which cooperation might pay, morality kicks into place. In order to make us good biological "altruists," nature has made us literal altruists. This is not to say that we always will cooperate or be moral. We may feel the tug of Mother Teresa altruism; few of us are Mother Teresas. We are influenced by many factors, including selfish and other sorts of desires. But morality is one of these factors, and overall we humans do generally work together. Sometimes the morality backfires. I might go to the aid of a drowning child and drown myself. This is hardly in my self-interest. But on balance it is in my interests to have the feeling that I ought to help people in distress, particularly children in distress. This is both because I myself was at some stage of my life a child and also because I myself will probably have or be having children. I want others to be prepared to take a risk on my behalf or on the behalf of my children.

Let me stress that the biological claim (I am not yet talking philosophically) is that humans have a genuine sense of morality. This really is true, 24-karat altruism. It is the kind of morality or altruism that someone like Immanuel Kant (1949) talks about. This is not a scientific position of pure ethical egoism, in the sense that we are all selfish people just simply calculating for our own ends. That is the second option given previously. We are, rather, people with a real moral sense, a feeling of right and wrong and obligation. Admittedly, at the causal level this is brought about by individual selection maximizing our own reproductive ends. But the point is that, although humans are produced by selfish genes, selfish genes do not necessarily produce selfish people. In fact, selfish people in the literal sense tend to get pushed out of the group or ostracized pretty quickly. They are simply not playing the game. In a way, therefore, we have a kind of social contract. But note that it is not a social contract brought about, in the long-distant past, by a group of gray-bearded old men sitting around a campfire. It is, rather, a social contract brought on by our biology, that is to say, by our genes as fashioned and selected by natural selection. (Strictly, using the style of this discussion, we should say that "selfish" genes do not necessarily produce selfish people; they produce altruistic people because "altruism" can be a good "selfish" strategy.)

This then is the Darwinian perspective on the evolution and current nature of morality, how it treats the central notion of altruism. Let us now see how this plays out in a naturalized way, seeking thereby to find how moral thinking and knowledge come out on such a biological background.

Substantive Ethics

I argue that humans cooperate for biological ends, namely that they are "altruists" for their own biological ends. I argue that human moral behavior, altruism that serves the end of "altruism," has to be such that it is going to serve the individual. That is not to say that it is going to serve the individual on every occasion, nor is it to say that one will be thinking about the personal gain every time one acts morally. As I have intimated already, in fact the whole point about morality is that one tends not to think in such a way. Perhaps by definition morality excludes such thinking. But it is to say that morality must be such that it will be of personal benefit. I spoke previously of a social contract, and although I deny a social contract in the traditional sense, it is clear that the kind of substantive ethics to which Darwinian biology leads is an ethics very much akin to what one would expect to find in a social contract.

More than this, I argue that this is the kind of ethics that we do have in real life. So, in that I offer a naturalized position (that is, one consciously based on the methods and results of the physical sciences), we have the kind of empirical justification (which is not to be confused with moral justification) that is demanded by the kind of position I propose and endorse. The altruism (or the urge to altruism) that we do experience phenomenologically, and that which moral philosophers seize on, is precisely that which would support (bring about) the biological "altruism" needed by such animals as we. Most particularly, I would say that the best-known contemporary exposition of the social contract theory, that offered by John Rawls in his 1971 book *A Theory of Justice,* yields just the kind of altruism that one would expect from a Darwinian perspective. It is incidentally interesting and significant that Rawls himself acknowledges this fact. He agrees that the social contract was hardly an actual event but was rather something that was brought on by the struggle for existence working on our innate biology. Let us explore this point.

As is well known, Rawls argues for a position that he calls "justice as fairness." He argues that in order to be just, one ought to be fair. For Rawls, being fair does not necessarily mean giving everybody absolutely equal shares of everything. Rather, he invites us to put ourselves behind what he calls a "veil of ignorance," not knowing what position we might find ourselves occupying in society: whether we will be male or female, rich or poor, black or white, healthy or sick, or any of these things. Then he asks what position self-interest dictates as the best kind of society to find oneself in, and Rawls's answer is that it is a society in which in some sense everybody does as well within the society as one might possibly expect, given our various talents. It may well be that we will be born male and rich and powerful and healthy and so forth. If we knew we were going to find ourselves in that position, then we would want maximally to reward people in that position. But of course we may be female and poor and helpless, in which case we would lose out. So there is a kind of initial presumption of equality. Yet this is overthrown as soon as one recognizes that something like the availability of good medical care is going to be of benefit to everybody. And if, in fact, the only way that you can get the most talented people to become doctors is by paying them more than twice what you pay university professors, then "justice as fairness" dictates the propriety of this kind of inequality. So what Rawls ends up with is a society with inequalities, but in some sense a society in which the inequalities benefit each and every individual in the group.

I suggest that this is very much the kind of society that one expects evolutionary biology to have produced. That is to say, a group of people who think that one ought to be just, meaning that one ought to be fair; a group that recognizes that there will be inequalities but also recognizes that these inequalities in some sense are of benefit to all. I do not suggest that every actual society has turned out like this, but that is not really the point. One recognizes that there are all sorts of ways in which biology will fail to catch up with individual circumstances. There may be inequalities brought about by particular circumstance or fortune or whatever. But the point is how we think a society ought to be, even if it is not necessarily always that way—that is to say, how we think *morally* that a society ought to be, even though it does not always work out that way.

Here I must dwell for a moment longer on this distinction between what one might think morally ought to be and what actually comes about. The way that things actually come about is due to individuals, but nobody ever says that people always act morally or follow the dictates of their consciences. Remember Wilson: "Human altruism, in short, is riddled to its foundations with the expected mammalian ambivalence." Morally, it is a question of how you ought to behave, not how you do behave. If, for instance, I find myself rich and powerful, then from a purely selfish point of view I might simply ignore the call of morality or suppress it or educate myself or my children to ignore our biology. I do not say, nor does any other Darwinian, that this sort of thing might never happen. At times of great social stress because of a natural disaster like a plague, one might well find the rich and powerful looking after themselves alone. This is not to deny that in the long run things such as education can have a lasting effect for good or ill or, conversely, to assert that biology can simply be brushed aside when we feel like it. The call of feminists to certain courses of action may, indeed, in this modern day and age of labor-saving devices and reduced childbearing be altogether admirable. Whether our biology, which was forged in the Pleistocene when things were very different, can necessarily follow quite as readily and rapidly is entirely another matter. (Please do not mistake my realism here for sarcasm or cynicism.)

There are many moral systems other than the social-contract, neo-Kantian view of John Rawls. Morever, I am much aware that the notion of justice does not really coincide with the notion of altruism. There is the question of mercy, for instance. One might speak truly of a judge being just but regret that he or she does not temper this with compassion or forgiveness. However, as a Darwinian I suggest that these alternative systems and needs to expand fully to capture the complete sense of altruism do not necessarily refute or repudiate what has just been said in favor of a social contract theory. The simple fact of the matter is that most moral systems agree on the basics—agree on what constitutes a fully and truly altruistic person—and tend to focus on only some aspects of the whole question, coming apart only on the kinds of esoteric, artificial examples that philosophers delight in. Everybody, whether a Kantian or a utilitarian or a Christian or other, thinks that one ought to be kind to small children and that gratuitous cruelty toward the aged is wrong and that there is something to be said for honesty and decency in business and relationships and so forth. Most morality in fact is a fairly commonsense morality, rather than a well-articulated system as produced by philosophers (Mackie, 1977). And this point is precisely on what the Darwinian would insist. Real human beings have a commonsense morality that guides them in their everyday life. Real human beings can spot real altruism. Leave philosophy to the philosophers.

There are certainly real cases in which it is less than obvious what one ought to do or in which one runs into contradictions as one tries to put things together. If one is in favor of abortion, does this mean that one ought to be in favor of capital punishment also? If one is in favor of free speech, does this mean that tobacco manufacturers ought to be allowed to advertise? Should anti-Semites be allowed to educate their own children in their beliefs? So in some ultimate sense, I do not deny the virtues of what philosophers do. I do say that most everyday morality, or what I call commonsense morality—something that is shared by all lasting moral systems—is backed by Darwinian biology. Real altruism is backed by biological "altruism," and in turn real altruism exists for the end of biological "altruism." Be kind to others. Don't let your friends down. Try to be as truthful as you can. Care about your kids.

(Incidentally, I must refute here one of the most popular counterarguments to the Darwinian at this point. Is not the soldier going over the top in the Battle of the Somme putting duty and country above self-interest? Is this not a case in which altruism fails to serve the end of "altruism"? Well, yes, but note what one account after another about World War I always stresses (Ferguson, 1998). What drove men forward was not God or country or glory. The real force was the desire not to let down your pals on either side of you. That and revenge for the Canadian sergeant who had been crucified by the Hun. Pure Darwin! Although this is not to say that the generals and the sky pilots did not put on their own spin. "We sanctify true altruism in order to reward it and thus to make it less than true, and by that means to promote its recurrence in others.")

Indeed, I press my defense of a Darwinian commonsense morality. I defend my notion of altruism against the somewhat idealized notion that one finds in some moral systems, for instance, various versions of Christianity. Some such systems at the substantive level—famously, Christian systems which hark back to the radical, Anabaptist strain of the Protestant Reformation—urge on you behavior that is surely counter to the selfish-gene perspective of sociobiology (Singer, 1981). For instance, one sometimes finds calls to give everything one has to the poor and to give up on any kind of self-regard or preferential favoritism for one's family or friends. This clearly and unquestionably goes against Darwinian biology. You are not going to promote "altruism" in this way. Such biology does not say that you should never care for the stranger, because apart from anything else you may well find yourself a stranger at some point. It does not say that one should never worry about international relations and the well-being of children in Africa. In this day and age particularly, we have what has been called the "Global Village." There are good reasons, therefore, from a biological perspective, for some kind of regard for even the most distant human. However, from a biological point of view, you are clearly going to do better for yourself if you look after your own children rather than other people's children and if you are nice to your own friends who might in turn be nice to you than if you care about people far distant. The fact is that the sociobiological approach at the substantive level puts the emphasis on the individual rather than the individual's close acquaintances and, in turn, on the individual's close acquaintances rather than the group. Radical altruism, if I may so call it, is no friend of biological "altruism."

I would say, however, that here is a point in favor of Darwinism rather than otherwise. It is one thing for people to say one ought to care about others. It is another to feel genuinely that one ought to care about others and act on it. As David Hume pointed out perceptively, our passions follow our relationships. "A man naturally loves his children better than his nephews, his nephews better than his cousins, his cousins better than strangers, where every thing else is equal. Hence arise our common measures of duty, in preferring one to the other. Our sense of duty always follows the common and natural course of our passions" (Hume, 1978, pp. 483–484).

Following the same line, Charles Dickens in his brilliant novel *Bleak House* savagely criticized Mrs. Jellyby because she spent all her time worrying about the benighted heathen in Borrioboola-Gha. She should have concerned herself with her own neglected family, then, after that, with people in her own social group, particularly people like poor Jo the crossing sweeper. Dickens is saying that charity begins at home, and this is the commonsense morality that we all have. If you learned that Michael Ruse was giving three-fourths of his salary to Oxfam, while at the same time his wife and children were having to shop at the Salvation Army and go to the food bank for food, you would have good reason to think that Michael Ruse was trying to buy his way into the Kingdom of Heaven at the expense of others. God will not buy this and neither should we. Darwinism is definitive here, and so it should be. We admire and venerate the soldier who throws himself on the grenade to save his buddies. The soldier who threw himself on the grenade to save the enemy would be looked on in surprise—contempt, probably.

Do not misinterpret my message. I am not saying that there is nothing to radical altruism. I am not saying that a preacher should never press radical altruism on his or her flock. Perhaps by pushing the extreme we can better effect the more limited. I am saying that one should not wave it triumphantly as an immediate refutation of the Darwinian naturalist.

Metaethics

We now come to the real core of the Darwinian approach to morality—the Darwinian approach to altruism—and it is here that we get the full epistemological force of the system. What kind of metaethical justification can one give for such claims as that one ought to be kind to children and that one ought to favor one's own family over those of others? I would argue, paradoxically but truthfully, that ultimately there is no justification that can be given. One can offer empirical support for the position but ultimately no moral foundation. That is to say, I argue that at some level one is driven to a kind of moral skepticism: a skepticism, please note, about foundations rather than about substantive dictates. What I am saying, therefore, is that, properly understood, the Darwinian approach to ethics leads one to a kind of moral nonrealism.

In this respect, the Darwinian ethics I put forward in this chapter differs very dramatically from traditional Darwinian ethics, social Darwinism. There are probably differences in the very understanding of altruism, although I doubt they are as great as popular lore would have. But now I speak of justifications. In the traditional case, the foundational appeal is to the very fact of evolution. People such as Herbert Spencer argue that one ought to do certain things because by so doing one is promoting the welfare of evolution itself. Specifically, one is promoting human beings as the apotheosis of the evolutionary process. Famously, this move is condemned by philosophers as a gross instance of the naturalistic fallacy (this was Moore's charge) or as a flagrant violation of Hume's law (which denies that one can move legitimately from the way that things are to the way that things ought to be). My kind of evolutionary ethics agrees with the philosopher that the naturalistic fallacy is a fallacy and so also is the violation of Hume's law. My kind of evolutionary ethics also agrees that social Darwinism is guilty as charged. But my kind of evolutionary ethics takes this failure as a springboard of strength to its own position. The Darwinian ethics of this chapter avoids fallacy, not so much by denying that fallacy is a fallacy but by doing an end run around it, as it were. There is no fallacious appeal to evolution as foundations because there are no foundations to appeal to! Altruism ultimately has no justificatory basis.

To be blunt, my Darwinian ethics says that substantive morality is a kind of illusion, put in place by our genes, in order to make us good social cooperators (Ruse & Wilson, 1985). Altruism is a film show to make us "altruists." I would add, incidentally, that the reason why the illusion is such a successful adaptation is that not only do we believe in substantive morality but we also believe that substantive morality does have an objective foundation. As with the prisoners in Plato's cave, we think that what we see is what there is. We think that altruism is more than just a personal whim. An important part of the phenomenological experience of substantive ethics is not just that we feel that we ought to do the right and proper thing but that we feel that we ought to do the right and proper thing because it truly is the right and proper thing. As John Mackie (1979) argued previously, an important part of the moral experience is that we objectify our substantive ethics. There are in fact no foundations, but we believe that there are in some sense foundations. Being altruistic is not an option. It is an obligation.

There is a good biological reason why we do as we do and feel as we feel. If, with the emotivists, we thought that morality was just simply a question of emotions without any sanction or justification behind them, then pretty quickly morality would collapse into futility. I might dislike you stealing my money, but ultimately why should you not do so? It is just a question of feelings. But in actual fact, the reason why I dislike you stealing my money is not simply that I do not like to see my money go but that I think that you have done wrong. You really and truly have done wrong in some objective sense. This gives me and others the authority to criticize you. Substantive morality stays in place as an effective illusion because we think that it is no illusion but the real thing. Thus, I argue that the epistemological foundation of evolutionary ethics is a kind of moral nonrealism but that it is an important part of evolutionary ethics that we think it is a kind of moral realism. Being altruistic is an obligation. It is not an obligation that exists beyond human nature. (And although it is activated by human nature, it is not justified by such nature.)

In a way, this section thus far has given just statements rather than proofs. What justification can I offer for my position? Why should one not say that there truly is a moral reality underlying what I have said about morality at the substantive level, and that our biology has led us to it? Why should altruism be left dangling thus? After all, we would surely want to say that we are aware of the speeding train bearing down on us because of our biology, but this in no sense denies the reality of the speeding train (Nozick, 1981). Why should we not say, in a like fashion, that we are aware of right and wrong because ultimately there is an objective right and wrong lying behind moral intuitions? Altruism truly does have more ontological status than simply that of serving the causal ends of "altruism."

However, things are rather different in the moral case from the speeding train case. A more insightful analogy can be drawn from spiritualism. In World War I, when so many young men were killed, the bereaved—the parents, the wives, the sweethearts, on both sides of the trenches—often went to spiritualists, hoping to get back in touch with the departed dead. And indeed they would get back in touch. They would hear the messages come through the Ouija boards or whatever assuring them of the happiness of the now deceased. Hence, the people who went to spiritualists would go away comforted. Now, how do we explain this sort of thing? Cases of fraud aside, we would say that people were not listening to the late departed but rather were hearing voices created by their own imaginations which were in some sense helping them to compensate for their loss. What we have here is some kind of individual illusion brought about by powerful social circumstances. No one would think that the late Private Higgins was really speaking to his mom and dad. Indeed, there are notorious cases in which people were reported killed and then found not to be dead. How embarrassing it would be to have heard the late departed assure you of his well-being, and then to find out that the late departed was in fact lying injured in a military field hospital.

In the spiritualism case, once we have the causal explanation as to why people hear as they do, we recognize that there is no further call for ultimate foundations. I would argue that the biological case is very similar. There are strong biological reasons for cooperation; naturally, we are going to be selfish people but as cooperators, as altruists, we need some way to break through this selfishness; and so our biology has given us morality in order to help us do it. Once again I stress that this is not to say that we are always going to be moral people: in fact, we are an ambivalent mixture of good and bad, as the Christian (and the Darwinian) well knows. It is to say that we do have genuine moral sentiments —urges to altruism—which we think are objective and that these were put in place by biology—to serve the end of "altruism." Once we recognize this, we see the sentiments as illusory (although, because we objectify, it is very difficult to recognize this fact).

But still, you might protest, that does not mean that there is no objective morality behind all of this: either an objective morality of a Platonic ilk which actually exists out there or an objective morality of the Kantian form which is a kind of necessary condition for rational beings getting along. One can surely thereby avoid the distasteful conclusion that Mother Teresa's altruism was no more than a biological flimflam show. However, first, no one is saying that altruism is brought on by a flimflam show—that is to trivialize it or to suggest that it has less than honorable origins, whereas the point is that it has no such origins of this kind at all. And second, the Darwinian can come back with a further argument. It is an absolutely essential part of modern Darwinism that evolution is not ultimately progressive (Ruse, 1993). There is no natural climb upward from the blob up to the human, from the monad to the man, as people used to say in the nineteenth century. Rather, evolution is a directionless process, going nowhere rather slowly. What this means in this particular context is that there is really no reason why humans might not have evolved in a very different sort of way, without the kind of moral sentiments that we have. From the Darwinian perspective, there is no ontological compulsion about moral thinking.

It is true that, as Kant stressed, it may possibly be that social animals may necessarily have to have certain formal rules of behavior. But it is not necessarily the case that these formal rules of behavior have to incorporate what we would understand as commonsense (substantive) morality. In particular, we might well have evolved as beings with what I like to call the "John Foster Dulles system of morality," so named after Eisenhower's secretary of state during the cold war in the 1950s. Dulles hated the Russians, and he knew that the Russians hated him. He felt he had a moral obligation to hate the Russians because if he did not everything would come tumbling down. But because there was this mutual dislike, of a real obligation-based kind, there was in fact a level of cooperation and harmony. The world did not break down into war and destruction. As a Darwinian, it is plausible to suggest that humans might have evolved with the John Foster Dulles kind of morality, by which the highest ethical calling would not be love your neighbor but hate your neighbor. But remember that your neighbor hates you, and so you had better not harm him or her because they are going to come straight back at you and do the same.

Now, at the very least, this means that we have the possibility not only of our own (substantive) morality but also of an alternative, very different kind of morality: a morality which may have the same formal structure but which certainly has a different content. We could have a morality serving the end of biological "altruism" but in which literal altruism was thought either irrelevant or ridiculous or positively harmful. The question now is, if there is an objective foundation to substantive morality, which of the two—an altruism-cherishing morality or an altruism-spurning morality—is right? At a minimum, we are left with the possibility that we humans now might be behaving in the way that we do but that in fact what is objective morality is something quite else from what we believe. We believe what we do because of our biology, and we believe because of our biology that our substantive morality is objectively justified. But the true objective morality is something other from what we have. Perhaps God has little time for altruism!

I am not sure that this possibility could absolutely never exist. The God of some Calvinists seems to regard anything more than strict justice (which is in turn a function of His unfathomable choice to favor only some with His grace) to be unwarranted sentimentality. But the possibility is surely a sheer contradiction to what most people mean by objective morality. What most people mean by objective morality incorporates the fact that it is going to be self-revealing to human beings. Not necessarily to all human beings but—like Descartes' clear and distinct ideas—certainly self-revealing to all decent human beings who work hard at it. We cannot be mistaken about the fact of self-existence, and no more can we all be mistaken about the existence and content of altruism and the urge to its performance. So, given Darwinism, we have a refutation of the existence of such a morality. Darwinian evolutionary biology is nonprogressive, pointing away from the possibility of our knowing objective morality. We might be completely deceived, and because objective morality could never allow this, it cannot exist. For this reason, I argue strongly that Darwinian evolutionary theory leads one to a moral skepticism, a kind of moral nonrealism.

(I admit that I am allowing a possibility of some kind of moral relativism. Perhaps there are today beings in the universe with the Dulles morality. There may be no altruists on Andromeda. But here on earth, I doubt the evolutionist gives much comfort to the relativist. We humans have all the same, recently shared origins. More important, there are some adaptations which, being social, cannot step too far out of line from the norm. Language is one. Genital size is another. I may speak perfect BBC English, but can you from the Canadian Maritimes follow a word of what I say? I may be endowed like a pre-Castro Cuban sex star, but will it play in Alberta? Likewise with morality. Unless we are all in the same game—unless we all appreciate altruism and recognize the urge toward it—it will not function for any of us. And do not incidentally think that my telling you all of this is going to give you the power to kick over the moral traces. Freud may have thought that the truth will set you free. The sociobiologist knows better.)

Conclusion

This then is the naturalized understanding of altruism to which modern-day Darwinism leads one. It is a system that believes that altruism is a function of "altruism." As I said at the beginning, in major respects I do see the Darwinian moral system of this chapter as being one very similar in spirit to that moral system that is expounded by David Hume in his *Treatise*. There is a genuine substantive morality, but ultimately there is no objective foundation. Therefore, if you say in conclusion that my position is one of David Hume brought up to date by Charles Darwin, I will agree with you heartily. I look upon this as the highest possible praise.

REFERENCES

Axelrod, R. (1984). *The evolution of cooperation*. New York: Basic Books.
Darwin, C. (1859). *On the origin of species*. London: Murray.
Darwin, C. (1871). *The descent of man*. London: Murray.
Dawkins, R. (1976). *The selfish gene*. Oxford: Oxford University Press.
Ferguson, N. (1998). *The pity of war*. London: Allen Lane.
Hume, D. (1978). *A treatise of human nature*. Oxford: Oxford University Press.
Kant, I. (1949). *Critique of practical reason* (L. W. Beck, Trans.). Chicago: University of
    Chicago Press.
Mackie, J. (1977). *Ethics*. Harmondsworth, England: Penguin.
Mackie, J. (1979). *Hume's moral theory*. London: Routledge & Kegan Paul.
Moore, G. E. (1903). *Principia ethica*. Cambridge: Cambridge University Press.
Nozick, R. (1981). *Philosophical explanations*. Cambridge: Harvard University Press.
Rawls, J. (1971). *A theory of justice*. Cambridge: Harvard University Press.
Ruse, M. (1982). *Darwinism defended: A guide to evolutionary controversies*. Reading, MA:
    Benjamin/Cummings.
Ruse, M. (1985). *Sociobiology: Sense or nonsense?* (2nd ed.) Dordrecht: Reidel.
Ruse, M. (1993). Evolution and progress. *Trends in Ecology and Evolution, 8*(2), 55–59.
Ruse, M. (1994). *Evolutionary naturalism: Selected essays*. London: Routledge.
Ruse, M. (1996). *Monad to man: The concept of progress in evolutionary biology*. Cam-
    bridge: Harvard University Press.
Ruse, M. (1998). *Taking Darwin seriously: A naturalistic approach to philosophy* (2nd ed.)
    Buffalo, NY: Prometheus.

Ruse, M. (1999). *Mystery of mysteries: Is evolution a social construction?* Cambridge: Harvard University Press.

Ruse, M. (2000). *Can a Darwinian be a Christian? One person's answer.* Cambridge: Cambridge University Press.

Ruse, M., & Wilson, E. O. (1985). The evolution of morality. *New Scientist, 1478,* 108–128.

Singer, P. (1981). *The expanding circle: Ethics and sociobiology.* New York: Farrar, Straus, & Giroux.

Spencer, H. (1851). *Social statics; or the conditions essential to human happiness specified and the first of them developed.* London: Chapman.

Spencer, H. (1892). *The principles of ethics.* London: Williams & Norgate.

Wilson, E. O. (1971). *The insect societies.* Cambridge: Harvard University Press.

Wilson, E. O. (1975). *Sociobiology: The new synthesis.* Cambridge: Harvard University Press.

Wilson, E. O. (1978). *On human nature.* Cambridge: Harvard University Press.

10

Relating Self, Others, and Sacrifice in the Ordering of Love

STEPHEN J. POPE

Christian theology, like ordinary discourse, uses the term *love* in a wide variety of ways. It can mean a powerful emotional attachment, an internal psychological state such as compassion or empathy, or an attitude such as respect or good will. In contemporary contexts, it is often equated with *altruism*, that is, with acting out of concern for the well-being of another person and not merely out of self-interested motives. The term *altruism* was created as a counterbalance to the emergence of the term *egoism* in modern philosophy, but in many ways its ambiguity limits its usefulness as a concept for understanding human conduct. Altruism, other-regarding action, can after all be quite immoral, as in the altruistic dedication of the fanatic who cares only about the well-being of his or her group. Altruism can also be destructive of self or others when it is seen in mindless and ineffectively self-denying behavior. One can argue, then, that altruism is good only when it is exercised in the context of the cardinal virtues of prudence, justice, temperance, and fortitude.

In the ordinary language of our culture, the term *love* typically connotes either a deep attraction or affection of one person for another or a deep affective bond between two friends or lovers. *Love* strikes a much deeper, more ancient, and more powerful affective cord than does the term *altruism*. If love is not to be identified purely and simply with altruism, it is also the case that genuine love issues in altruistic acts, that is, acts intended to enhance the well-being of the beloved or friend. Though it is often simplistically reduced to unilateral altruism, even agape, the radical love advocated in the New Testament, is based on a deep fellowship in faith and a religious bond of shared discipleship.

Love has many objects. To love in a way that respects differences in relationships and in kinds of moral responsibilities requires some kind of operative system of priorities. The old notion of the "order of love" might refer to priorities among any or all of these: preferences among objects of beneficence or caregiving, among our affections, among those for whom we feel compassion, among degrees of benevolence, or perhaps even among attitudes of greater or lesser respect for different individuals.

The essential question addressed by the "order of love" in the history of Christian theology concerned priorities. Are we ethically required (or, in some cases, even allowed) to feel greater affection for some people than others? Are we required to embrace enemies as our friends? Are we obliged to sacrifice the good of our family members to help hungry strangers? Are we supposed to give alms to the itinerant poor, as well as to the poor of our own community? Are we to be more generous to well-off intimates than to needy acquaintances? Are we allowed to care for ourselves, as well as, or even more than, others? These are the kinds of questions taken up in the magisterial discussions of the "order of love" found, among others, in the writings of St. Augustine, St. Thomas Aquinas, and Jonathan Edwards.

At least two perspectives regard these kinds of questions as objectionable or perhaps even as unintelligible. The pure moral egoist dismisses them as nonquestions posed only by the hopelessly naive; we *always* prefer ourselves and our own, and the real question is whether we ought to, or even can, be genuinely concerned about others. This kind of so-called "realism" demands an honest admission of the significant limits to human compassion and a rejection of ridiculously idealistic standards that can never be met even by advocates of altruism, let alone by most members of the human race.

From the opposite direction, the pure moral altruist condemns these questions as catering to human selfishness, narrow-mindedness, and tribalism and believes that the stingy concern of the "realist" constitutes a self-fulfilling prophecy. First we describe people as Machievellian, and then we look so intently for egoistic motives that we ignore the counterevidence. The moral point of view, the altruist declares, must demand ethical impartiality or even radical other-regard that decenters the self and its parochial attachments and makes it responsible for "the other." The model of pure moral altruism is Jesus, who taught unconditional love, exemplified uninhibited compassion, and died on the Cross out of love.

This simple dichotomy would have us choose between three pairs of terms: egoism versus altruism, unilateralism versus mutualism, and particularism versus universalism. It takes agape, for better or worse, to be unilateral, altruistic, and universal: Agape renounces self-gratifying ties of friendship, family, and community and embraces radical self-sacrifice as a way of life. This position has the benefit of clarity but the attending weakness of distorting oversimplification.

My thesis is that this stark dichotomy is mistaken and that the relation between these pairs of terms, if their meanings are properly construed, can be reconciled under the notion of the "ordering of love." Negatively, I believe the dichotomy rests on erroneous views about both agape and the implications of evolutionary accounts of human nature. Positively, I believe that the goods valued by both the moral egoists and the moral altruists can be assimilated and properly coordinated within a balanced interpretation of the ordering of love. Conversely, I also believe that failing to sustain a sense of the ordering of love can, ironically, lead to the abandonment of altruistic love and its replacement by a more modest but supposedly more "realistic" mitigated form of egoism.

Strong versus Weak Theories of Christian Love

The writings of philosopher Michael Ruse (1994, pp.16–17), who distinguishes between "strong" and "weak" interpretations of agape, provide a helpful starting point for our reflection on this issue. The "strong interpretation" requires love of neighbor as oneself and commands each Christian to count himself or herself as one and only one person among others. The "weak interpretation," on the other hand, allows for special love of self, family, and friends. According to Ruse, the latter position is consistent with and made possible by our evolved emotional predispositions and therefore is ethically legitimate, but the former runs so contrary to our nature that it is "unacceptable," "irresponsible," and even "morally perverse" (1994, pp.17, 19).

To give credit where credit is due, Ruse is obviously correct to point out that there are real limits to what we can expect ourselves or others to do. Kant observed that "ought" implies "can" (see Kant, 1956, p. 38; Sullivan, 1989); obviously any injunctions to altruism must lie within our capacities as moral agents. We are finite, we have only limited time, energy, and material resources, and therefore we cannot be expected to act as if we could take on unlimited responsibilities. As Franz de Waal puts it, "Altruism is bound by what we can afford. The circle of morality reaches out farther and farther only if the health and survival of the innermost circles are secure" (1996, p. 213). Instead of Singer's (1981) "expanding circle" (see also de Waal, 1996), de Waal suggests an image of a "floating pyramid" in which the "force lifting the pyramid out of the water—its buoyancy—is provided by the available resources. Its size above the surface reflects the extent of moral inclusion" (1996, p. 213).

Therefore, there is, or at least ought to be, no debate over whether we need moral priorities, only about how they ought to be arranged. Some pattern of ordering, either implicit or explicit, is unavoidable; the question is whether our ordering will be thoughtful, deliberate, and responsible or merely haphazard, unreflective, and unwise.

Ruse proposes that constraints on altruism come not only from sheer finitude but also from the distinctive structure of our evolved emotional capabilities. "Biologically," he explains, "our major concern has to be towards our own kin, then to those at least in some sort of relationship to us (not necessarily a blood relationship) and only finally to complete strangers" (Ruse, 1986, p. 106). Theories of kin selection, reciprocity, cooperation, parental investment, and sexual selection all shed light on the evolved options and inclinations for human caregiving. Sociobiology insists that we not confuse psychological altruism—acting for the benefit of another—with evolutionary or genetic altruism, which, as Ridley and Dawkins explain, is seen in any act that "has the effect of increasing the chance of survival (some would prefer to say 'reproductive success') of another organism at the expense of the altruist's" (Ridley & Dawkins, 1981, p. 19). Sociobiologists claim that we are willing to help others either when they will help us in return ("direct reciprocity" or Trivers' "reciprocal altruism"; Trivers, 1971) or when third parties will help in return (R. D. Alexander's "indirect reciprocity"; Alexander, 1987). Capacities to engage in this kind of conscious, moral assistance-giving have evolved because, over time, doing so has contributed to the inclusive fitness of our forebears.

Sociobiology, then, claims that we have evolved to be more likely to help reciprocators than nonreciprocators, kin than non-kin, trustworthy people than cheats, people like us than people unlike us, and in-group members than out-group members. These priorities point to patterns of behavior that more often than not contribute to the individual's inclusive fitness. In this view, the self manipulates, deceives, and coerces others in the relentless pursuit of genetic self-interest; indeed, in the most reductionistic versions (e.g., that of Dawkins), even the self is manipulated, deceived and coerced into doing what is most likely to promote the replication of its genes.

Physiologically "priming" me to become genuinely attached to my children is the best means my genes have for ensuring that I will raise my progeny to the age of reproductive viability. Because, conversely, I am not "wired" to develop the same kind of attachment to just any children I happen to encounter, then I cannot be expected to care for other children the way I care for my own. Herein lies the absurdity of the "strong view" of Christian love, holds Ruse, because that is exactly the kind of ethic it proposes.

Moral altruism, according to sociobiology, is based on evolutionary egoism: The emotional capacity to want to give to others is itself a trait that has more often than not been adaptive. According to the sociobiologists, this kind of behavior is "morally altruistic" because it intends to aid others—we really do want to help others, or at least we can be taught to want to help them. But these acts are also "genetically egoistic" because they tend to contribute to our inclusive fitness. The mother who stays up all night with a sick child is motivated to do so by maternal love, but this motivation inspires acts that protect her own "genetic investment" because they promote her child's health and thereby increase her child's future reproductive viability. When the same mother acts altruistically toward a neighbor, she may be motivated by friendship, but this motivation exists because we have evolved to desire reputational enhancement in our communities. People known to be trustworthy reciprocators and altruists elicit acts of assistance giving from others more readily than do their more stingy opposites.

Christian Ethics and the Ordering of Love: Dialectical versus Sacramental Theologies

Ruse, in effect, attacks a widespread view that agape admits of no ordering. Indeed, one has to acknowledge that within Christian theology, what can be called the "dialectical" position defines love as self-sacrifice and opposes it to all forms of self-love and relationships that provide some form of gratification to the self. In the rigorous and perfectionistic ethic of Jesus, Reinhold Niebuhr insisted, "self-love is never justified," and even "concern for physical existence is prohibited" (1979, pp. 33, 25). Christians must deny themselves, hate their family members, leave their friends and neighbors, and so forth—anything less is a half-hearted compromise. Better to trim the ethic down to manageable size, argues Ruse, so that it can sustain altruism within the small circle for which it has been adapted.

The "dialectical" Christian theology of love, for its part, repudiates Ruse's proposal as Darwinian propaganda oblivious to the true meaning of the Gospel and its demands. Agape is superior to and restraining of, if not ideally abolishing, other forms of love. This position is credited for striking a heroic chord, repudiating cheap accommodation, and calling for loyalty to a distinctive religious community against secular culture and merely natural ties. It holds a special appeal for people who are tired of attempts to domesticate the demands of the Gospel. Christians take instruction from the command of God, it holds, not from human conventions. Life is to be lived from within the biblical narrative, not the Darwinian epic of evolution. Christians affirm the saving power of Christ and the power of the Holy Spirit to make each disciple a "new creature" (2 Cor. 5:17). Disciples graced with the "mind of Christ," as St. Paul puts it, are not limited to what is possible for mere human nature, especially not fallen human nature. Those who trust in Christ strive to imitate his unconditional love, including his renunciation of violence and revenge, his special care for the outcast, his unlimited willingness to forgive, his call to leave family, his love of enemies, and, in short, his Cross.

The "dialectical" perspective seems to exemplify Ruse's "strong interpretation" of love, yet in fact many biblical texts concerned with love present more complex cases of interpretation. Consider, for example, the so-called Farewell Discourse of Jesus to the disciples in chapter 15 of the Gospel of John. Anticipating his passion and death, Jesus surrounds himself with his disciples, whom he calls "friends" rather than "servants." His command that they "love *one another*" (15:17; italics added) underscores mutual love within the community of faith, not unilateralism; sacrifice within friendship; self-denial within the context of communal love and affirmation. Yet Jesus also reminds his disciples to obey his commands, to adhere to his teachings despite pressure to the contrary, to stand firm in the face of persecution, and to remain steadfast in the danger of death.

There is here no dichotomy separating friendship from sacrifice. The rich complexity of biblical love often evades simple ethical categorization, either that of the "dialectical" reduction of agape to self-sacrifice or its sociobiological bifocal reduction into "weak" or "strong" versions. Biblical texts, and the rich theological tradition that interprets them, are complex and context specific in their meanings.[1]

It is important, then, not to make the mistake of reducing biblical injunctions to one abstract ethical command, rule, norm, or "preference rule" (Hallett, 1989), such as self-sacrifice, other-regard, self-subordination, and so forth. Attempts to do so ignore the specificity of biblical texts and inevitably reduce the multiplicity of biblical perspectives to one.

In contrast to the previous viewpoint, what can be called the "sacramental" view offers an interpretation of Christian love that acknowledges the legitimacy and the necessity of ordering love without at the same time domesticating it. The sacramental view regards all human relationships, like all people, as created good, potentially transformed by grace, and bearing a sacred meaning. It holds that creation, though sinful, is redeemed rather than obliterated by God. In the classic formulation of St. Thomas Aquinas, "grace does not destroy nature, but perfects it" (Aquinas, 1948, 7.I.1.8). Our awareness of the power of evil and sin underscores the serious and persistent obstacles to its actualization, but the counterbalancing sacramental affirmation of the goodness of the creation affirms its constructive possibilities.

Just as human relationships can be corrupted, so they can be healed and reordered by grace. The sacramental view therefore appreciates the crucial differences between legitimate and illegitimate self-love, wise and foolish love of others, and proper and improper love of God—it recognizes, in short, a proper ordering of love (see Pope, 1994). It gives a special place to marriage and family as religious and social developments of "the natural bases of human love" (Gustafson, 1984, p. 160) that in turn provide the emotional and cognitive resources for more extensive altruism. If the circle of altruism is to expand, it must do so on the basis of emotional, psychological, and moral resources developed in the intimate spheres of interpersonal life. The sacramental view does not identify all family ties with nepotism, all erotic desire with sin, all self-love with unbounded egocentrism, or all friendship with mercenary instrumentalism.

Biblical injunctions to "hate" one's family should not be interpreted as a reversal of the Fourth Commandment—"honor thy father and mother"—but simply as a stern warning against disordered "familialism" and a command not to "care more for" family than for Christ (see Mt 10:37–39; see also 1 Tm 5:8). The same is true of friendships. Indeed, if Rodney Stark is correct, family ties and other forms of interpersonal attachment, along with an extension of charity "beyond the bonds of family and tribe," played key roles in the rapid growth of early Christianity (Stark, 1996, p. 86).

Biblical literature approves of self-love; for example, among many references, consider Ps 1:1: "Happy are those who do not follow the counsel of the wicked . . ." and Jesus' promise to steadfast disciples: "your reward will be great in heaven" (Mt 5:12). It also approves of and recommends priorities among recipients of love. Jesus himself shifted the primary reference away from kin group to the Kingdom, but he too showed a special love for "his own" (Jn 13:1). Biblical texts do not give a universal order of love to be applied to the life of every Christian, the way, say, a house is built on the basis of an architect's blueprint. These are specific instructions offered to particular communities in light of their struggle in the midst of concrete difficulties. Instead of applying an all-purpose moral maxim or a homogeneous biblical ethical theory, Christians need to cultivate a capacity for discernment and to exercise the virtue of prudence.

There is no doubt that the general thrust of biblical teachings on love, especially in the New Testament, demands conversion away from selfishness and toward a way of life attentive to the needs of those who are marginalized, ignored, and oppressed. Scripture simply takes for granted our natural orientation to self-love and to family ties and concentrates instead on dismantling oppressive boundaries. The same might be said to apply to the stress on the "kenotic" self-emptying and openness to "alterity" in the hagiographic narratives interpreted by Edith Wyschogrod (1990).

Injunctions to engage in self-renunciation, to take up the Cross, to deny oneself, to hate oneself, and so forth have often been interpreted as laying down an absolute ban on all forms of self-love. These do indeed make problematic Christian appropriation of evolutionary theory. Yet a more adequate approach to these kinds of sayings recognizes in them a warning against corrupt and disordered self-love and a way of life that, as Augustine points out, "is better called self-hate" (1958, p. 20). We "commit sin to promote our own welfare," he writes, "and it results instead in our misfortune" (1984, p. 553). Our deeply ingrained tendency to prefer ourselves to others is corrected not by ceasing to love ourselves altogether but rather by loving ourselves properly and truly.

Søren Kierkegaard was as profoundly suspicious of any forms of self-preference as any religious thinker in the history of Christianity. Every person, he observed, "has in himself [or herself] the most dangerous traitor of all" (1962, p. 39). This treachery consists not only in the betrayal of others but also in the self-destruction that comes from not being willing to love oneself in the right way. But even the dialectical Kierkegaard, the arch-critic of selfishness, recognized the legitimacy of ordered self-love: "To love oneself in the right way and to love one's neighbor correspond perfectly to one another . . . The law is therefore: you shall love yourself in the same way as you love your neighbor when you love him as yourself" (1962, p. 39).

In the sacramental view, interpretations of Christian love are not positively evaluated according to the extent to which the self is denigrated or the neighbor elevated in value. Negation of self can be good or bad, depending on circumstances; an obedient Serbian commander, after all, might selflessly follow all orders to ethnically cleanse a village. The moral challenge is to move beyond sinful self-love, not to hate oneself or become oblivious of one's true good.

The absence of self-love is often regarded as a kind of litmus test for agape, yet what sense can we make of "love your neighbor as yourself" if self-love is forbidden? What feminists lament as the destructive effect of an unmitigated ethic of selflessness on women can apply, though with some differences, to all people. As Jonathan Edwards observed, "If Christianity did indeed tend to destroy man's love for himself, and to his own happiness, it would threaten to destroy the very spirit of humanity" (1978, p. 159).

In proper self-love, we still have primary responsibility for ourselves, know ourselves better than we know others, find our happiness in that of our friends, experience satisfaction in belonging to a good community, and act according to our convictions and sense of what is good and right—behavior only possible when one in fact has a strong sense of self-worth. Proper self-love inspires an extension of love for others, an intensification of friendship, and an expansion of the boundaries of the self.

Applied to neighbor love, similarly, the Gospel requires the virtuous love of neighbor, not self-sacrifice for its own sake. Scripture provides ample witness to the moral worth of true friendship, including that between Jesus and his disciples. Even the passion and death of Christ were for the sake of reconciliation between humanity and God.

Agape is thus manifested in the *quality* of love rather than simply in the kinds of objects to which it is directed. Everyone is to be loved, as St. Augustine put it, "in God" (1961, p. 82). Agape embraces everyone—far as well as near, unattractive as well as attractive, lost as well as found, outsider as well as insider. There is, pace Ruse, nothing particularly "weak" about love for family and friends. As we see in the challenge faced by parents caring for children with severe attention-deficit disorder or by adult children caring for elderly parents afflicted with severe Alzheimer's disease, the quality of love required by the Gospel in these spheres can be just as demanding, though in different ways, as love for strangers. Indeed, because of the emotional intensity and degrees of vulnerability it involves, love of intimates can be more painful, can require kinds of self-denial, and can call on emotional resources that do not characterize expectations generated from more distant relations.

Evolutionary Theory and the Ordering of Love: Simple versus Complex Anthropologies

Ruse credits the "weak" version of agape because it allows for a reasonable ordering of love and accords with what we know about human nature and its full range of moral possibilities. Ruse, however, might be accused of exaggerating what sociobiologists "know" about human nature. Sociobiology is particularly unhelpful when its calculations of "coefficients of relationship," reiterated prisoner's dilemmas, and the like are taken to *demonstrate* rather than to assert that human nature is almost locked into one set pattern of responses and one system of priorities beginning with self and ending with reciprocators.

Our evolved genetic substrate may include "elemental emotional preferences," but it is not all that we are by any means. Human nature includes a significant amount of plasticity and indeterminacy, and our "elemental preferences" do not unfold automatically into actions (see Rose, 1998). We may be "primed" to learn more readily to care for close relatives than for nonrelatives, but, as Kristen Renwick Monroe points out, heroic rescuers during the Third Reich neglected and even risked the lives of their family members to save perfect strangers (1996, pp. 165–166). We may have an underlying "elemental preference" to cooperate with "cooperators" and to mistrust "cheats," yet we hear of women who continue, against the pleas of people who love them, to return to men who beat them. There may be good evolutionary reasons for preferring in-group members to outsiders, but it is also possible to respond to a stranger as another "Thou." And of course, though we are naturally geared to self-love, we honor those people who, like

Maksymilian Kolbe, sacrifice their own legitimate claims, even the right to life itself, out of devotion to others.

We are not sure of the extent to which, or the ways in which, these elemental preferences influence human behavior. The existential question, however, concerns how we *ought* to allow them to influence us. Common sense acknowledges the powerful attraction of family life, the need we have for social bonds and friendships, and our desire to fit into networks of social relationships. These human goods, and others such as knowledge, morality, and aesthetics, are deeply rooted in human nature and play some role in good human lives.

Elemental preferences do not constitute a rigid, automatic, and universal system governing human conduct. Their manifestation is always influenced by culture and personality, and they are overridden often enough to indicate that they offer an "open program," something we are naturally prepared to learn but not inescapably "hard wired" to implement. We may be genetically prone to love our own more than we do others, but we can also learn to extend care for others who are nonreciprocators and non-kin.

It is particularly important, then, not to assume that elementary self-preference translates into an inflexible psychological egoism. We need to distinguish between a basic inclination to promote our own well-being and an inflexible preference in which self-interest always outweighs other-regard. We are, to be sure, constantly tempted to slide from proper self-love to improper egocentrism. Yet we also have an ability, in some circumstances, to prefer the common good to our own private good. Human nature, then, is essentially ambivalent, comprising a range of motivations that run from egoism to altruism. Human beings obviously have a strong tendency to be excessively self-concerned, but we are also capable of genuine friendship and other forms of self-transcending love. Darwin himself acknowledged our emotional capacity for sympathy, as well as for selfishness (Darwin, 1871/1979).

Acknowledgment of our moral ambivalence must be complemented by an awareness that we exert some degree of self-direction over our elementary proclivities. Our behavior is no doubt profoundly subject to external and internal influences, both cultural and organic. There are reasons to doubt that we have a specific faculty called "free will" hovering above other influences and making decisions in utter transcendental freedom (see Damasio, 1994). Yet there is a great deal of indeterminacy surrounding human action within which we make genuine choices. We have the capacity to exert some self-direction over which factors play the determinative role in our actions. People do adopt children, donate blood, give philanthropic gifts anonymously, and take solemn religious vows of poverty, chastity, and obedience—none of which seem to contribute to their inclusive fitness. The array of choices we make together have a cumulative effect of gradually shaping the specific pattern of priorities, including especially the ordering of love, that operates in our lives. This ordering is built on elemental proclivities, but at its best it directs and shapes their expression within the larger context of a higher vision of authentic human flourishing.

If there are elemental emotional preferences embedded in our organic nature, are we *morally* bound to conform to them? Thomas Aquinas believed that it is ethically legitimate to act in accord with the order of nature whereby we love those closest to us more than those who are farther away (Aquinas, 1948, 3, IIaIIae,q.26). He justified this claim with a variety of arguments, one of which is that this order is most "fitting" or "right" for human conduct. It is morally appropriate, for example, that, other things being equal, we honor our parents more than strangers, even if strangers are more admirable in other ways, and it is morally fitting that we care for the children we bring into this world more than for others. These, along with requirements such as promise keeping, helping someone in urgent need if possible, and following the Golden Rule, are part of the "natural law" that is known by all reasonable people.

This kind of argument has a certain intuitive appeal for all but the most uncompromising of voluntarists, who hold that there are no responsibilities other than those created by the agent's uncoerced agreements. Aquinas held that human flourishing is best obtained by living in accord with the natural order of love (see Pope, 1994). Communities thrive when parents care for their children, when the bonds of loyalty between friends are strong, when commitment between husbands and wives is honored. This kind of argument can indicate concretely and in detail how people flourish through certain patterns of ordering and how their well-being is diminished in other patterns of ordering.

From our perspective, Aquinas's flaw lay in taking the concrete ordering of his culture to be normative for all cultures everywhere, that is, to be human nature as such. An analogous kind of flaw permeates popular sociobiology, which even in its theory of "epigenetic rules" continues to give a strong primacy to genes and the organic substrate of human nature and thereby to downplay the significance of culture for human identity. Biological reductionism is inadequate. The analysis of biological levels of human action is a necessary but not sufficient condition for understanding human behavior.

It is clear, then, that what is "natural" is not necessarily what is good and that the elemental emotional preferences based in our genes are not by any means morally obligatory or even necessarily ethically justifiable in every case. Parents following a strict policy dictated by "parental investment" strategy might well cut their losses by abandoning a compromised newborn, males might apply a "mating strategy" of impregnating as many females as possible, and so forth. In some cases these elemental proclivities can contribute to human flourishing, but at other points they undermine it. We may have an elementary proclivity to seek revenge and punish defectors, but we can also forgive and renounce retaliation. The challenge of moral integrity charges each of us with the responsibility of selecting from among this range of ambiguous inclinations and of morally shaping, as much as possible, our emotional responses to and behavioral expression of them.

What is uniquely significant about the human experience is that, taking full advantage of the evolution of a highly complex biological and especially neurological substrate and of the advantages of cultural transmission, we have evolved to the point of being able to love and know something *for its own sake* and beyond what would be instrumental for fitness. This capacity is what in fact characterizes the genuine altruism of love in its full sense.

Science cannot explain how out-group altruism is possible on the basis of evolutionary principles. Yet this incapacity, rather than demonstrating the illusory nature of out-group altruism, can be taken to be an indication of the inability of evolutionary theory to "explain" everything that is possible for human beings. This shortcoming is only debilitating to those who believe that science, and science alone, provides the warrants for our moral standards and ideals.

In theological language, this capacity for "self-transcendence" marks our existence as created in the "image of God" (see Kerr, 1997). As creatures we must live within rather than outside some reasonable pattern of priorities that acknowledges the limits imposed on and capacities given by human nature. So, for example, there are real constraints on altruism; we cannot be expected to give constantly to all people all the time without counting the cost. One cannot always implement literally the words of Jesus, "Give to everyone who asks of you" (Lk 6:30). At the same time, we cannot expect to live a truly fulfilled life if our actions are constantly calibrated according to Machiavellian self-interest; societies would consist of only groups of reciprocators, not communities constituted by friendship. The challenge we face is one of scrutiny, assessment, and self-direction: We need to identify what patterns of elemental ordering are operative (always in and through culture, of course), to make moral judgments about whether those patterns are appropriate, and, when they are inappropriate, to decide how to live in accord with a wiser set of priorities.

This by no means suggests that elemental preferences be simply ignored or abandoned. The evolved order offers many positive capacities that we can enlist and build on—capacities for bonding, group loyalty, generosity, empathy, and so forth. Yet even these can be misused and misdirected, as in the bonding of criminals, the group loyalty of hate groups, the generosity of a Mafia don, empathy unbalanced with good judgment, and so forth. Conversely, what we normally assume are negative capacities, such as violence and deception, can serve positive functions under certain circumstances, for example, for the sake of self-protection in the face of unjust aggression. Elementary preferences can be enlisted to support good or bad lives. The key issue is how we learn to express them, what shape they take over the course of our personal and communal development.

The character of our moral habits, in other words, determines the shape that elemental proclivities take in our lives; they are appropriated through choice within each person's ordering of love. The virtuous person—the person who exercises the virtues of prudence, justice, temperance, and fortitude—incorporates the energies flowing from natural proclivities in constructive directions. Love must be guided by the virtue of prudence. It does not automatically lead to heroic altruism, which in some circumstances—especially for people with multiple and demanding responsibilities—might be fruitless, reckless, and harmful.[2]

Most of us, of course, are caught somewhere in the vast no-man's-land between perfect moral integrity and complete disorder. We acknowledge a commitment to fairness, for example, yet feel the tempting pull of nepotism. Though alert to the dangers of excessive group loyalty, we can be taken aback at the apparent ineradicability of our own chauvinism. Disgusted at the degradation and exploitation of sex by our consumer culture, we might be discouraged at the persisting impersonality of sexual desire in ourselves. This ambiguity underscores the fact that although elemental preferences might be fairly constant in the abstraction we call "human nature," our own character and selfhood will always be incomplete "works in progress."

Conclusion

The beginning of this chapter criticized the dichotomization of egoism versus altruism, unilateralism versus mutualism, particularism versus universalism. Ideally, the Christian ordering of love reconciles the values indicated by these terms without obliterating their distinctions. First, the ordering of love affirms the value of both proper self-love and proper neighbor love. Seen in their shared human nature, self and neighbor need not necessarily be related as competitors but rather can be understood as "linked to others through a common humanity" (Monroe, 1996, p. 91). Conflict can and does exist, obviously, but the presence of conflict underscores the need for self-scrutiny, dialogue, compromise, mutual affirmation, forgiveness, and reconciliation. The mere presence of conflict does not warrant a description of human nature as a relentless Hobbesian war of all against all, nor does it justify the perpetuation of the simplistic dualism of egoism versus altruism.

Second, the same is the case for the choice between unilateralism and mutualism. "Unilateralism" is the claim that the ethical core of agape flows in one direction: from the agent to the recipient. "Mutualism," on the other hand, holds that agape consists in bilateral fellowship, friendship, and "brotherly love." The ordering of love includes both an attitudinal readiness to serve the neighbor in need, as seen in the parable of the Good Samaritan, and the deep friendship expressed in the table fellowship of the Last Supper—indeed, the Last Supper encompasses both sacrifice and fellowship. The minimal core of agape is a benevolent and steady commitment to serve, but its true fruition is manifested in mutuality, by which radical "otherness" is ultimately overcome and replaced by genuine friendship. "Christian love," as Post puts it, "is participatory and mutual within the *koinonia* or fellowship of the faithful, although this circle is by no means 'hermetically sealed'" (Post, 1990, p. 13). In fact, it is precisely this fellowship that inspires and empowers outreach to the "other."

Third, and finally, some insist that, though it is the product of a particular community, agape calls for an unlimited concern for all human beings. This "universalist" view is countered by the "particularist" objection that the first task of disciples is to "be church" and to provide a witness to the truth of the Gospel. The "particularist" thus has a primarily inward focus, cultivating an evangelical way of life within the Christian community. The Christian ordering of love requires response to needy others beyond as well as inside the circle of family, friends, and fellow believers: "If you love only those who love you, what credit is that to you? Even sinners love those who love them" (Lk 6:33). Yet it also underscores the importance of the special commitment to build up what St. Paul called the "body of Christ" (1 Cor. 12:12–27) that is the Christian community.

Along with the prophetic call to serve all humanity, the Church also recognizes the need to sustain the special ties that bind those belonging to the Christian community itself. The theological doctrine that all are created in the "image of God" supports the ethical vision that we are, as Monroe puts it, "all part of a human family" (Monroe, 1996, p. 129). The notion of a closely bound in-group based on a common faith, in other words, can actually inspire, rather than undercut, a complementary sense of inclusive openness and generous love for all others with whom the members share a common humanity. Both commitments are essential to Christianity, but their unity and difference can be appreciated only within an acknowledgment of the moral significance of the ordering of love.

NOTES

1. Making his dichotomy even less attractive is the fact that Ruse never offers a clear explanation of what makes a position "strong" or "weak" in the first place. If "strength" depends on the person making the claim on the agent, we need to keep in mind that demands placed by family and friends are typically much "stronger" than those made by people who are remote. If "strength" turns on the extent to which the claim runs against the grain of human nature, then Ruse also needs to recognize that it can be much more difficult to attain reconciliation with a hurtful family member than it is to forgive offensive acquaintances.

2. But see Monroe (1996) on rescuers' heroism that ignored the well-being of their families (pp. 153–155, 164–166, 172). At what point does this type of heroism become unethical?

REFERENCES

Alexander, R. D. (1987). *The biology of moral systems.* New York: de Gruyter.

Aquinas, T. (1948). *Summa theologiae.* Rome: Marietti.

Augustine. (1958). *On Christian doctrine* (D. W. Robertson, Jr.,Trans.). Indianapolis: Bobbs-Merrill.

Augustine. (1961). *Confessions.* (R. S. Pine-Coffin, Trans.). New York: Penguin.

Augustine. (1984). *Concerning the city of God against the pagans* (H. Bettenson, Trans.). New York: Penguin.

Damasio, A. R. (1994). *Descartes' error: Emotion, reason, and the human brain.* New York: Avon Books.

Darwin, C. (1979). *The descent of man.* In P. Appleman (Ed.), *Darwin: A Norton critical edition* (2nd ed., pp. 196–208). New York: Norton. (Original work published 1871)

de Waal, F. (1996). *Good natured: The origins of right and wrong in humans and other animals.* Cambridge: Harvard University Press.

Edwards, J. (1978). *Charity and its fruits.* London: Banner of Truth Press. (Original work published 1852)

Gustafson, J. M. (1984). *Ethics from a theocentric perspective:* Vol. 2. *Ethics and theology.* Chicago: University of Chicago Press.

Hallett, G. L. (1989). *Christian neighbor-love: An assessment of six rival versions.* Washington: Georgetown University Press.

Kant, I. (1956). *Critique of practical reason* (L.W. Beck, Trans.). Indianapolis: Bobbs-Merrill.

Kerr, F. (1997). *Immortal longings: Versions of transcending humanity.* Notre Dame, IN.: University of Notre Dame Press.

Kierkegaard, S. (1962). *Works of love.* (H. & E. Hong, Trans.). San Francisco: Harper & Row.

Monroe, K. (1996). *The heart of altruism: Perceptions of a common humanity.* Princeton, NJ: Princeton University Press.

Niebuhr, R. (1979). *An interpretation of Christian ethics.* New York: Crossroad.

Pope, S. J. (1994). *The evolution of altruism and the ordering of love.* Washington: Georgetown University Press.

Post, S. G. (1990). *The theory of agape: On the meaning of Christian love.* Lewisburg, PA.: Bucknell University Press.

Ridley, M., & Dawkins, R. (1981). The natural selection of altruism. In J. P. Rushton & R. M. Sorrentino (Eds.), *Altruism and helping behavior: Social, personality, and developmental perspectives* (pp. 19–39). Hillsdale, NJ: Erlbaum.

Rose, S. (1998). *Lifelines: Biology beyond determinism.* New York: Oxford University Press.

Ruse, M. (1986). Evolutionary ethics: A phoenix arisen. *Zygon: Journal of Religion and Science, 21,* p. 106.

Ruse, M. (1994). Evolutionary theory and Christian ethics. *Zygon: Journal of Religion and Science, 29,* 16–17.

Singer, P. (1981). *The expanding circle: Ethics and sociobiology.* New York: New American Library.

Stark, R. (1996). *The rise of Christianity: A sociologist reconsiders history.* Princeton, NJ: Princeton University Press.

Sullivan, R. J. (1989). *Immanuel Kant's moral theory.* Cambridge: Cambridge University Press.

Trivers, R. L. (1971). The evolution of reciprocal altruism. *Quarterly Review of Biology, 46,* 35–57.

Wyschogrod, E. (1990). *Saints and postmodernism: Revisioning moral philosophy.* Chicago: University of Chicago Press.

11

The Fall and Rise and Fall and Rise and Fall and Rise of Altruism in Evolutionary Biology

DAVID SLOAN WILSON AND ELLIOTT SOBER

The concept of altruism has had a turbulent history in evolutionary biology, as the title of our chapter suggests. Darwin's theory was controversial in part because of its "nature red in tooth and claw" image that seemed to deny the possibility of other-oriented behaviors. This image is partially deserved; altruism *is* more difficult to explain than selfishness from an evolutionary perspective (the first fall). However, Darwin perceived a way for altruism to evolve. Even though altruists are less fit than selfish individuals within a given social group, groups of altruists are more fit than groups of selfish individuals. Natural selection at the group level can evolve other-oriented behaviors, despite their selective disadvantage within groups (the first rise). Today this fundamental insight is known as multilevel selection theory (Sober & Wilson, 1998).

During the 1960s, altruism was again rejected by most evolutionary biologists (the second fall), not because it is theoretically impossible but because group selection was thought to be invariably weak compared with individual selection (Williams, 1966). The enthusiasm that this conclusion generated at the time is puzzling in retrospect. It was treated as a great advance, similar to the rejection of Lamarckism, that allowed evolutionary biologists to close the door on one set of possibilities and concentrate their attention elsewhere. For the next few decades, all of nature was interpreted as a manifestation of self-interest.

The rejection of group selection as an important evolutionary force proved to be premature (see Sober & Wilson, 1998, for a detailed analysis). Robust theoretical models began to appear as early as the 1970s, and by now they have been amply confirmed in both natural populations and laboratory experiments (the second rise). Group selection was probably an especially strong force in human evolution. However, we do not mean to imply that altruism exists everywhere in nature and human nature. There is still a conflict between levels of selection, and selfishness often prevails, but it does not *invariably* prevail. The balance between levels of selection simply needs to be worked out on a case-by-case basis.

Our thumbnail history of the group selection controversy fails to convey the passion with which it was argued and the atmosphere of skepticism that still hangs over the subject. Kenneth Binmore (1998), an economist and game theorist interested in evolution, does a better job of describing the charged atmosphere in his review of our book *Unto Others: The Evolution and Psychology of Unselfish Behavior*.

> Sober and Wilson illustrate the mood that held sway until recently by quoting the following advice offered by a biological guru to a novice: "There are three ideas you do not invoke in biology—Lamarckism, phlogiston, and group selection." My own experience in lecturing from my recent *Just Playing: Game Theory and the Social Contract II* endorses their evaluation of this kneejerk hostility to group selection ideas. It soon became clear to me that no mainstream biologist was likely even to turn the pages of a book in which group selection was treated as a serious proposition. I, therefore, shamefacedly went through my text systematically altering the words *group selection* to *equilibrium selection*, lest I be thought the kind of social scientist who writes about evolution without having read any biology books.
>
> Although group selectionists have been unfairly vilified until comparatively recently, my impression is that the prejudice with which they have struggled in the past is rapidly evaporating and that the controversy will survive into the future only if old resentments are not laid to rest. (1998, p. 539)

Throughout its history, altruism and group selection have been treated as twin concepts joined at the hip. Altruism evolves by group selection and should be observed whenever group selection is stronger than individual selection. This relationship came under scrutiny as group selection began to be taken seriously again. Altruism is a two-dimensional concept; it involves helping others at a sacrifice to oneself. Imagine another behavior that helps others just as much but at no sacrifice to oneself. Both behaviors are favored equally by group selection, whereas only the first behavior is opposed by individual-level selection. The evolution of strongly altruistic traits, the self-sacrificing nature of which cries out for an explanation, requires not one but two conditions. First, group selection must be strong enough to oppose individual selection. Second, there must be no other way to benefit others at less individual expense.

An example from human life will make this idea clear. Suppose you lived in a group that relied upon voluntary giving to support all communal efforts. Each person can give according to his or her desire, but no social control of any kind, positive or negative, is used. This group would be highly vulnerable to freeloaders who benefit from their more altruistic neighbors without sharing the costs of communal efforts. For this kind of voluntary giving to evolve, group selection must be very strong to counter the very strong advantage of selfishness within groups. Now imagine a group that supports communal efforts with the full panoply of social control mechanisms known to exist in our species, including taxes enforced by law. These mechanisms appear far more effective than voluntary giving, but the character of altruism has been lost. A person who pays his taxes under the threat of punishment is a far cry from Mother Teresa!

Following this line of reasoning, multilevel selection models have separated the twin concepts of group selection and altruism. Groups are increasingly recognized as adaptive units that evolved by group selection, but the specific mechanisms look more like social control than voluntary altruism (Smuts, 1999). This is the third fall of altruism in evolutionary biology. It is very recent and different in character from the first two falls.

We think that the concept of altruism deserves to rise again, hopefully for the last time; its history is not fated to resemble a yo-yo forever! However, the final rise of altruism is subtle. We agree with the emphasis on social control in modern multilevel selection theory and have contributed to this literature ourselves. Nevertheless, in this chapter we show that social control promotes the evolution of altruism rather than replacing altruism. Their relationship is positive rather than negative.

Defining Altruism

So far we have been using the term *altruism* casually, as if it has a single well-established meaning. In fact it has many meanings, both in science and in common language, that we have discussed at length elsewhere (Sober, 1994, Chapter 1, this volume; Sober & Wilson, 1998; Wilson, 1992, 1995; Wilson & Dugatkin, 1992). For the purpose of this chapter we distinguish three definitions. *Evolutionary altruism* is defined entirely in terms of fitness effects without any reference to how the individual thinks or feels about its actions. If an individual increases the fitness of others while decreasing its own fitness, it is an evolutionary altruist. Even plants and so-called lower organisms such as parasites can be evolutionary altruists (see Sober & Wilson, 1998, for examples). In multilevel selection theory, "increase" and "decrease" are defined in relative terms. If an individual increases the fitness of its group, *relative to other groups*, while decreasing its own fitness, *relative to other individuals in the same group*, then it qualifies as an evolutionary altruist. The focus on relative fitness, although appropriate and consistent throughout the history of the subject, has been a source of much confusion even among evolutionary biologists. Consider a behavior that increases the fitness of the individual but that also increases the fitness of everyone else in its group even further. The behavior decreases relative fitness within the group and qualifies as altruistic in multilevel selection theory despite increasing the absolute fitness of the individual. Many social control mechanisms that appear self-interested in everyday terms actually qualify as weakly altruistic according to multilevel selection theory (Sober & Wilson, 1998).

Psychological altruism is defined entirely in terms of the thoughts and feelings that motivate behavior, regardless of their ultimate consequences. If I value the welfare of others as an end in itself, rather than as a means to the end of my own welfare, then I am a psychological altruist. This simple statement becomes complicated when we try to clarify the concepts of means, ends, and welfare. After a detailed analysis, Sober and Wilson (1998) concluded that psychological altruism is quite likely to have evolved by natural selection as a proximate mechanism for motivating helping behavior in humans and other species. However, it can be very difficult (although not impossible) to distinguish psychological altruism from other proximate mechanisms that also motivate helping behavior but that count as psychologically egoistic.

These two definitions of altruism leave a gap that needs to be filled by a third definition. Consider Barbara, the nicest person you could ever hope to meet. Whether through her genes or her upbringing, she always helps others without being asked. Larry is nice enough and would never dream of doing something like evading his taxes, but he does not help spontaneously the way that Barbara does. Beware of Lola, however, who does evade her taxes and exploits people at every opportunity. These three people illustrate a continuum of dispositions, from extreme helpfulness expressed in the absence of social control to extreme unhelpfulness except in the presence of strong social controls.[1] Most people would call Barbara altruistic and Lola selfish in everyday language, but even Barbara might fail to qualify as a psychological altruist if we knew enough about her internal wiring (e.g., she might be so helpful because it makes her feel good or to avoid feeling guilty).[2] There are good reasons for defining psychological altruism narrowly, but this definition excludes such a broad range of dispositions that we need a vocabulary to distinguish the Barbaras from the Larrys from the Lolas of the world. To avoid coining a third term that uses the word *altruism*, even though it would be fully appropriate and even closer to common usage than the other definitions, we propose the term *helpful nature*. Barbara has an extremely helpful nature, regardless of whether she counts as a psychological altruist, and Lola has an extremely unhelpful nature. A helpful nature is a disposition to behave, not an actual behavior. Lola might be induced to behave the same way as Barbara but only by the imposition of external social controls. Barbara's helpfulness comes from within, Lola's from without. Now that we have a precise vocabulary, we can return to our main question: What is the relationship between helpful natures and social control in multilevel selection theory?

Norms of Reaction for Helpful and Unhelpful Natures

Most organisms are phenotypically plastic; they exhibit different behaviors (and also nonbehavioral traits) in response to different environments. To characterize a phenotypically plastic organism, we must know its repertoire of responses. In evolutionary jargon this is called its "norm of reaction," and it is portrayed graphically by showing the different environments on the *x*-axis and the corresponding phenotypes on the y-axis. If we want to compare the fitness of two organisms, we can show the fitness associated with the phenotypes rather than the phenotypes themselves. The fitness of an organism is a weighted average of its fitness in each environment multiplied by the proportion of time spent in each environment.

In its simplest form, the norm of reaction is interpreted as the response of a given genotype (y-axis) to the different environments that it encounters (x-axis). However, the strict separation between genotype and environment needs to be modified, not only for humans but also for many other species. For example, sex determination is genetic in some species but environmental in others—for example, turtles become males or females depending on the temperature at which they develop (Shine, 1999). Imagine a norm of reaction with "temperature" on the x-axis and "sex" on the y-axis. For species with genetic sex determination, any individual is fated to be a male or a female regardless of the temperature and so will be depicted by a flat norm of reaction. For turtles, all individuals will become male at one temperature and female at another, resulting in a "step-function" norm of reaction. Now imagine that we want to study the behavior of adult males and females—say, their willingness to feed in the presence and absence of predators. We construct a norm of reaction with "presence of predators" on the x-axis and "willingness to feed" on the y-axis. This norm of reaction can be constructed for adult males and females regardless of whether sex determination was genetic or environmental. As long as an individual responds in a predictable way to the environments represented on the x-axis, a norm of reaction can be constructed regardless of the genetic and past environmental influences on its currently predictable behavior. This is an important point because we have already emphasized that helpful natures might be made rather than born. Even if people's natures are determined fundamentally by their upbringing (just as turtle sex is determined by temperature), we still can construct a norm of reaction for them in their current state and in the range of environments that interests us.

Possible norms of reaction for a helpful and an unhelpful nature are shown in Figure 11.1. By definition, the helpful nature helps regardless of the degree of social control, whereas the unhelpful nature requires social control to be helpful. If the phenotypic trait of "helpfulness" were on the y-axis, the norm of reaction would be flat for the helpful nature and positively sloped for the unhelpful nature. However, the y-axes in Figure 11.1 measure the fitness associated with the phenotype rather than the phenotype itself. The left graph assumes that the two natures are phenotypically indistinguishable in the presence of social control, and because everyone is helpful, the fitness of everyone is high. The two natures become phenotypically distinguishable in the absence of social control. The unhelpful natures increase their relative fitness by exploiting the helpful natures (the square is above the circle), but the fitness of everyone declines because less helpfulness is being expressed (fitness in absence of social controls is lower than in the presence of social controls).[3]

Even though helpful natures do not have the higher relative fitness in any environment (at best their fitness equals that of unhelpful natures in the presence of social controls), they can still have the higher relative fitness in the global population if they are concentrated in environments with social controls and unhelpful

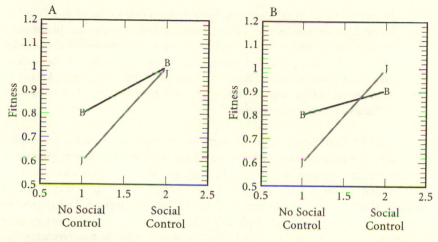

B = Unhelpful Nature
J = Helpful Nature

Figure 11.1. Two possible norms of reaction for a helpful nature (B) and an unhelpful nature (J). In the left-hand graph, unhelpful natures exploit helpful natures in the absence of social controls and have the higher relative fitness. Both types behave helpfully in the presence of social controls and therefore have the same relative fitness. In the right-hand graph, helpful natures are more fit in the presence of social controls (see text for details).

natures are concentrated in environments without social controls. We return to this point later, but first we argue that more realistic norms of reaction might look like the right-hand graph in Figure 11.1, in which helpful natures actually out-compete unhelpful natures in the presence of social controls. Their superiority might exist for at least three reasons.

1. The figure on the left assumes that individuals never make mistakes in assessing their social environment. An unhelpful nature that mistakenly assumes the absence of social controls has a probability of being punished, depending on the efficiency of the social control mechanisms. A helpful nature might make the same mistake but will not suffer the same consequences because it is not primed to behave selfishly in the absence of social controls.[4]

2. Unhelpful natures might need to cogitate longer and harder than helpful natures before deciding to help. Helpful natures do not need to constantly monitor their social environment to calibrate their degree of helpfulness. They just do it.

3. Social controls might include punishing unhelpful natures directly whenever they can be detected. "Social control" is not an environment that we experience like a desert or a rain forest. It is an environment that we create, and therefore it must itself be explained as a product of evolution (see

Sober & Wilson, 1998, chapter 4, for a detailed discussion of this topic). If punishment of unhelpful behaviors can evolve, then so also can preemptive punishment of those who are prone to behave unhelpfully—if they can be detected. For example, unhelpful natures might be detected on the basis of their occasional mistakes (Item 1) or because they must pause longer to think before acting helpfully (Item 2) or because they have been observed in the absence of social controls.[5]

If the right-hand figure accurately portrays the norms of reaction for helpful and unhelpful natures, then we have gone a long way toward achieving our goal. Far from making genuine helpfulness illusory, social control provides the environment that allows helpful natures to outcompete unhelpful natures. As we mentioned earlier, however, the fitness of an organism is a weighted average of its fitness in each environment multiplied by the proportion of time spent in each environment. To complete our model, we must specify how the two types are distributed in the two environments. The most favorable conditions for the evolution of helpful natures would be for individuals with helpful natures to seek (or build) environments with strong social controls from which individuals with unhelpful natures are largely excluded. This would create a strong positive correlation between the presence and absence of helping behavior and the presence and absence of social controls in the population, a correlation that also exists at the individual level for unhelpful natures but less so at the individual level for helpful natures.

To clarify this point, consider the following 2-by-2 table, which shows how the fitness of an individual depends on whether the individual has a helpful nature and on whether there are social controls:

	Social controls	
	Present	Absent
helpful nature	w1	w2
unhelpful nature	w3	w4

The left-hand figure corresponds to the assumption that w1 = w3 and that w2 < w4; the right-hand figure says that w1 > w3 and w2 < w4. Notice that, in both cases, helpful natures are less fit when social controls are absent but that this relationship is transformed when social controls are present. If helpful individuals tend to be found in environments with strong social controls and unhelpful natures tend to be found in environments that lack strong social controls, most individuals will be found in either the upper-left or lower-right cells. The result is that there will be a correlation between helping behavior and social controls, so that the evolutionary fate of the traits we are considering will depend mainly on whether w1 > w4. If helpful individuals living under strong social controls are fitter than unhelpful individuals living without strong social controls, helpful natures can evolve. Notice that helpful natures could evolve even if helpful and unhelpful individuals behaved identically in the presence of social controls; even if w1 = w3, it still is possible that w1 > w4. And if w1 > w3, it is even more likely that helpful natures will evolve.[6]

It might seem that the adaptive helpful natures predicted by our model depart from the ideal of helpfulness because they avoid exploitation and punish unhelpfulness in others (which itself can be a form of altruism; Sober & Wilson, 1998; Bowles & Gintis, 1998). We agree that our model cannot explain helpfulness that is unconditional in every way, especially when "social control" is understood as an environment that is built rather than provided. Nevertheless, people who do not exploit others, who avoid being exploited, and who punish exploiters still deserve to be called "genuinely helpful" compared with people who are quick to exploit others whenever the opportunity arises. Barbara might still be the nicest person we can ever hope to meet, even if she avoids Lola and does not shed a tear when Lola is punished for tax evasion.

Our model is simple and similar to models developed by Hirshleifer (1987) and Frank (1988) to explain the evolution of emotional commitment. Nevertheless, so many people seem to assume that strong social controls undermine the case for genuine helpfulness that clarification is needed. The reasoning we are criticizing can be thought of as saying that social controls suffice to explain helpful behavior so it is unparsimonious to hold that individuals who live in the presence of social controls in fact have helpful natures. Our model shows that there are reasons to doubt this argument; individuals who help can be expected to have two reasons for helping. They are affected by the expectation of rewards and punishments that social controls create; but they also help because they have helpful natures. We do not deny that the surest *test* of a person's nature is to observe their behavior in the absence of social controls, but if we want to *find* people with helpful natures, we are best advised to look in environments with strong social controls. After all, what reasonable person with a helpful nature would choose to remain any longer than necessary in an environment without social controls, in which they are fair game for all those people with unhelpful natures?

Our model is obviously a gross simplification of real individual natures, which vary along many dimensions and also continuously, rather than consisting of two discrete types. The distinction between "environment" (the x-axis) and "behavior" (the y-axis) is also artificial, as we have already emphasized. Nevertheless, adding complexity will not change the essentials of our argument as far as we can see. Social control mechanisms are more likely to promote genuine helpfulness than to make them illusory.

Our model is empirically testable. If the helpfulness of a person's nature and the degree of social control in his or her environment can be measured, we predict a positive correlation. We do not attempt a rigorous test here but leave the reader with one man's portrayal of what people in strongly cooperative communities actually think and feel, suggesting that a spirit of genuine helpfulness prevails and is at least as important as the presence of social controls for the success of the community (Shenker, 1986).

> We do not say "if the community does or achieves such and such, then I will stay, otherwise I won't," since this implies that there is an individual identity ontologically and

morally distinct from the community's. No true community could operate successfully or manifest its raison d'etre with such limiting conditions or separate identities.
Identity of fate also means that members relate to each other in an atmosphere of mutual trust, i.e., they consider their presence to stem from a common desire to express
their humanity and recognize that this can only be achieved through mutual effort.
Should one person claim that he has an inherent right to gain for himself at the expense of others, the entire fabric collapses. Life in the community presupposes that
each will work for the benefit of others as much as for himself, that no-one will be egoistic. The moment this assumption is undermined, mutual suspicion, jealousy and
mistrust arise. Not only will people probably consider themselves silly for being self-
righteous while others are feathering their nest, but operationally the community will
have a different character (primarily through use of coercion) and the entire moral nature of the community disappear. (1986, p. 93)

NOTES

1. There was a controversy in social psychology for many years concerning the relative
importance of the "person" versus the "situation" in explaining prosocial behavior. We concur with the view adopted by Schroeder, Penner, Dovidio, and Piliavin (1995, pp. 180 ff.)
that both matter. This "interactionist" viewpoint includes the idea that there are more or
less persistent traits of personality that affect the probabilities of helping in different situations. The psychological literature on Machiavellianism (Wilson, Near, & Miller, 1996,
1998) and sociopathy (Mealey, 1995) demonstrates individual differences in propensities to
help and exploit.

2. In Sober and Wilson (1998), we argue that psychological altruism is a more direct
and therefore a more reliable proximate mechanism for producing helping behavior than
various forms of psychological egoism. This suggests that one might expect helpful natures
to be psychologically altruistic. In principle, however, the proximate psychological mechanisms that lead to a helpful nature can include many forms of hedonism and egoism, in addition to altruism.

3. The fitness of helpful and unhelpful natures in environments without social control will depend on the relative frequency of the two types, which is hard to represent on the
norm of reaction graph. Unhelpful natures will always be more fit than helpful natures, but
their fitness will be higher if there many helpful natures to exploit than if there are few helpful natures to exploit. Figure 11.1 assumes that helpful natures are rare in environments
without social control, for reasons discussed later in the chapter.

4. Psychologically egoistic helpful natures might be more prone to make selfish mistakes than psychologically altruistic helpful natures, not because they mistakenly assume
the absence of social controls but because of other mistakes that occur in the circuitous
route from egoistic ultimate motive to other-oriented behavior (Sober & Wilson, 1998).
Nevertheless, an egoist with a helpful nature would be more likely to help (and thus avoid
the sanctions imposed by social controls on individuals who fail to help) than an egoist with
an unhelpful nature.

5. Christian belief systems such as Calvinism work hard to instill a "second nature" in
which helpfulness springs from the heart. Helpful acts based on insincere motives are as
sinful as unhelpful acts (Wilson, 2001).

6. This complex and counterintuitive relationship between individual-level properties and population-level properties is an example of Simpson's paradox, discussed in
Chapter 1 of Sober and Wilson (1998).

REFERENCES

Binmore, K. G. (1999). [Review of the book *Unto others: The evolution and psychology of unselfish behavior*]. *Management and Decision Economics, 19,* 539–540.

Bowles, S., & Gintis, H. (1998). Is equality passé? *Boston Review, 23,* 4–26.

Frank, R. H. (1988). *Passions within reason.* New York: Norton.

Hirshleifer, J. (1987). On the emotions as guarantors of threats and promises. In J. Dupre (Ed.), *The latest on the best: Essays on evolution and optimality* (pp. 307–326). Cambridge: MIT Press.

Mealey, L. (1995). The sociobiology of sociopathy. *Behavioral and Brain Sciences, 18,* 523–599.

Schroeder, D. A., Penner, L., Dovidio, J. F., & Piliavin, J. (1995). *The psychology of helping and altruism.* New York: McGraw-Hill.

Shenker, B. (1986). *Intentional communities: Ideology and alienation in communal societies.* London: Routledge.

Shine, R. (1999). Why is sex determined by nest temperature in many reptiles? *Trends in Ecology and Evolution, 14,* 186–189.

Smuts, B. (1999). Multilevel selection, cooperation and altruism. *Human Nature, 10,* 311–327.

Sober, E. (1994). *From a biological point of view: Essays in evolutionary philosophy.* New York: Cambridge University Press.

Sober, E., & Wilson, D. S. (1998). *Unto others: The evolution and psychology of unselfish behavior.* Cambridge: Harvard University Press.

Williams, G. C. (1966). *Adaptation and natural selection: A critique of some current evolutionary thought.* Princeton, NJ: Princeton University Press.

Wilson, D. S. (1992). On the relationship between psychological and evolutionary definitions of altruism and selfishness. *Biology and Philosophy, 7,* 61–68.

Wilson, D. S. (1995). Language as a community of interacting belief systems: A case study involving conduct toward self and others. *Biology and Philosophy, 10,* 77–97.

Wilson, D. S. (2001). *The religious organism.* Chicago: University of Chicago Press.

Wilson, D. S., & Dugatkin, L. A. (1992). Altruism. In E. F. Keller & E. A. Lloyd (Eds.), *Key words in evolutionary biology* (pp. 29–33). Cambridge: Harvard University Press.

Wilson, D. S., Near, D., & Miller, R. R. (1996). Machiavellianism: A synthesis of the evolutionary and psychological literatures. *Psychological Bulletin, 199,* 285–299.

Wilson, D. S., Near, D. C., & Miller, R. R. (1998). Individual differences in Machiavellianism as a mix of cooperative and exploitative strategies. *Evolution and Human Behavior, 19,* 203–212.

12

Some Obstacles to Altruism

MELVIN KONNER

Altruism (variously defined) is universally deemed both very desirable and insufficiently common, a tension that explains much about traditional religion and modern politics. This chapter considers obstacles to altruism arising from evolution by natural selection. I briefly review some essentials of Darwinian and neo-Darwinian theory, some evolutionary explanations for such altruism as does exist, some unique relevant features of higher primates, and some unique relevant features of human beings. I go on to consider two classic solutions to the problem of insufficient altruism, that of some traditional religions and that of American democracy. Both are based on more realistic appraisals of human nature than exist today among professional social scientists. American democracy has been more successful so far in limiting selfishness than traditional religion has because it is based on an invented device for harnessing selfishness and the energy of conflict in the paradoxical service of limiting both.

Darwinian Theory, Old and Neo-

Charles Darwin wrote in 1859, "When the views advanced by me in this work, and by Mr. Wallace, or when analogous views on the origin of species are generally admitted, we can dimly foresee that there will be a considerable revolution in natural history." The revolution began almost immediately, although some implications of it were not apparent in natural history until well over a century later. But as for human history, or for that matter human nature, the outcome has been far less clear. At first, easy inferences were made in an attempt to create what would be called social Darwinism. Unfortunately, this movement in its most extreme forms used Darwin's theory to support racism, sexism, colonialism, and the most severe and unforgiving interpretation of capitalism. As Darwin famously put it in the eloquent last passage of the *Origin*: "Thus, from the war of nature, from famine and death, the most exalted object which we are capable of conceiving, namely, the production of the higher animals, directly follows ... and that, whilst this planet has gone cycling on according to the fixed law of gravity, from so simple a beginning endless forms most beautiful and most wonderful have been, and are being, evolved." If this were true, then war, famine, and death did not seem so bad after all. They were merely nature's, or perhaps God's, way of creating forms most beautiful and wonderful, not to mention the most exalted object we are capable of conceiving. In any case, they could not be interfered with very conveniently, so why not stop whining and accept the war of nature as it is, especially if the end result justifies the means?

But in a much less public forum—a letter to botanist Joseph Hook in 1856—Darwin took a less exalted view: "What a book a Devil's Chaplain might write on the clumsy, wasteful, blundering low and horribly cruel works of nature!" The author of this letter was, presumably, the other Darwin, the one for whom evolution was a lifelong bellyache, apparently because he was ambivalent at best and anguished at worst about its possible moral implications. History showed that he was right to be worried, but this is mainly because of the improper logic used by some of his more benighted followers, who often failed to distinguish "ought" from "is." As I discuss, there is no "ought" in Darwin, unless it is this one: *We really ought to figure out what is going on.* Some of us still think that, whatever "ought" you have in mind, you will not be able to make any real headway with it unless you know something about the prevailing evolutionary winds. So what *do* we know?

Natural selection, as Darwin presented it, requires: (1) variation; (2) some heritability of the variation; and (3) some differential reproductive success tied to the variation. This is evolution by natural selection in its most elemental form (Ridley, 1997). Notice that it does not require "survival of the fittest" or any other differences in survival. It only requires differences in reproduction. Also, it does not require Malthusian crowding, although that idea did help inspire the theory. All it requires is that there be variation, that the variation be partly heritable, and that the partly heritable variation lead to differences in reproductive success.

Today we understand that there must also be an ultimate source of renewable variation, now understood as mutation. Ronald Fisher showed that selection reduces variation, so the latter must be renewed for evolution to be sustained (Fisher, 1958). It also must be based on particulate inheritance, or the blending of traits will quickly erase variation as well. Darwin did not understand these finer points, but that didn't stand in the way of his setting forth the theory, because he understood its three necessary and sufficient elements. Differential reproduction is the goal, differential mortality being just one way to realize it. Overproduction in the face of scarce resources accelerates the process but is not essential to it. Above all, Darwinian fitness means greater than average reproductive success and does not mean—except sometimes, incidentally—ethical, medical, or even physical fitness.

Because some people think (and Darwin sometimes implied) that evolution is necessarily directional or progressive, it is worth digressing to say that it is not. Evolution is noisy and formally chaotic. It ultimately depends on random variation and proceeds in a way that is sensitive to initial conditions, which makes prediction difficult to impossible. Replay the tape and you will get a different result. To be sure, increases in size, complexity, and information storage capacity are likely long-term trends wherever evolution occurs—which is to say, wherever there is life. For instance, on the third rock from the modest star known as the sun, massive asteroid impacts have, on an average of every 26 million years, decisively slapped down most of nature's best efforts (Conway Morris, 1998). This is a problem for the theory of progressive evolution but not for the theory of natural selection, which is quite comfortable having the slate wiped more or less clean from time to time, allowing it to resume its iterations with a vengeance.

Also, not all that glitters is adaptive. Evolution proceeds as a kind of bricolage, pasting up the next best thing from the last using whatever genes, spit, and chewing gum happen to be lying around. Organismic and developmental constraints, not to mention the laws of physics, make it tough to invent anything useful, much less anything perfect (Maynard Smith & Burian, 1985). What has been called Panglossian adaptationism—all for the best in this (Darwinian) best of all possible worlds—is clearly wrong as a model of what we see (Gould & Lewontin, 1979). As a research strategy, though, it is frequently very useful, as it sometimes generates falsifiable models.

In any case, the assumption that things may be adaptive even when they look as if they are not has produced many interesting notions, some of which seem to be true. In any case, it has tremendous heuristic value. That is, it has generated a grand web of hypotheses about which thousands of clever, hard-working naturalists have deployed their best resources. If Stephen Jay Gould—by far the most famous critic of neo-Darwinian theory—would simply read the other articles in each issue of *Natural History*, the magazine in which his column has appeared for decades, he would be dazzled, as most of us are, by the theory's great successes. Still, adaptation is admittedly and decidedly imperfect.

However, not all these facts are news. Darwin wrote in 1871 "that in the earlier editions of my 'Origin of Species' I probably attributed too much to the action of natural selection or the survival of the fittest. . . . I had not formerly sufficiently considered the existence of many structures which appear to be, as far as we can judge, neither beneficial nor injurious; and this I believe to be one of the greatest oversights as yet detected in my work" (Darwin, 1871/1981). What we now call "punctuated equilibrium" was recognized by Darwin as marked variation in rates of evolution and was set forth in some detail by G. G. Simpson, the great paleontologist of the modern evolutionary synthesis, in his 1944 book *Tempo and Mode in Evolution* (Simpson, 1944). It is nice to make new discoveries, and it is even nice to revive old neglected ones, although in that case it is considered polite to recognize one's antecedents.

In its most extreme form, the neo-Darwinian worldview is succinctly stated: *A person (or any organism) is only a gene's way of making another gene* (Dawkins, 1989). However, it is a clumsy way. Our intrepid gene must find its way among perhaps fifty thousand others and contend with the status quo decreed by a multi-million-year-old genetic establishment around it. It is like an enterprising brick in an ugly ancient building that an unseen designer is trying to find the time and money to renovate. Will our lovely and efficient new brick find a place in the new architectural order? Maybe. Meanwhile, life goes on in its dull, inelegant way. It does not optimize, it satisfies. It is not ideal or even excellent; it is just good enough. But good enough at or for what? Reproduction, or, to be more exact, reproduction that, at the margin, is just a tad better than that of the other bumbling gene machine next door. Lousy machines, organisms, but good enough.

The Problem of Altruism

Unfortunately, we are left with the following puzzle: If a creature is only a gene's way of making another gene, how can altruism have evolved? It is too consistent and common, especially in some kinds of organisms, to be explained as something missed by an inefficient satisficing selection. It is easily shown to be too costly. It would have been brutally and relentlessly culled.

A large part of neo-Darwinian theory has been devoted to a quite successful attack on this puzzle. The late William D. Hamilton (1964), who invented the algebra of kin selection back in the 1960s, did acknowledge his antecedents. One of them, the English geneticist J. B. S. Haldane, put the problem this way (Dawkins, 1989): Suppose my brother were drowning. How great a risk could I run in saving him before natural selection would work against me—or rather, work against the "altruistic gene" that made me save him? All else being equal, I could run a maximum 50% risk of death, because the chance that he carries the same gene by common descent is 50%. Over the long run of evolution, considering many such acts of heroism, the frequency of the gene for altruism would not decline at that risk. If the hapless drowner were my nephew, however, I could run only a 25% risk of death without reducing the frequency of the altruism gene. And if he were, alas, my first cousin, I could only take a 12.5% chance of dying to save him.

Hamilton applied this theory to ants and honeybees, which have special patterns of genetic relatedness and special patterns of altruism; witness the worker bee's rash self-evisceration in the act of stinging an intruder—say, us. Hamilton also generalized the Haldane model to cover all altruistic acts (Hamilton, 1964). They should be favored by selection if and only if the altruist loses less (in fitness or reproductive success) than is gained by the beneficiary (same units) *divided by his or her percentage of shared genes.* In other words, altruism is largely nepotism, occurring whenever $b_r > c_a/r$—when the benefit to the recipient exceeds the cost to the altruist divided by his or her coefficient of relatedness.

According to the second solution to the puzzle, altruism is largely a form of investment, occurring when memory and life span enable reciprocation. Reciprocal altruism, proposed by Robert Trivers in 1971, can evolve in animals that have the ability to recognize and remember whom they have helped and that are long-lived enough to be paid back (Trivers, 1971). Monkeys and apes are ideal in these respects. They evolved subtle abilities to distinguish and store memories of faces, as well as to recall both helping and being helped, and they live long enough to benefit from the payback. Altruism and repayment alike might come by way of aid in fights, and coalitions thus formed could easily trump a bully who never could be beaten one on one.

Unfortunately, it is difficult to make such a system resistant to the evolution of cheating. The third solution, the prisoners' dilemma model, whose evolutionary implications were most fully worked out by Robert Axelrod, accounts for this by making the reciprocity simultaneous—in effect, cooperation (Axelrod, 1984; Axelrod & Dion, 1988; Axelrod & Hamilton, 1981). In the game two prisoners must either cooperate or not cooperate (defect). The reward is greatest if you defect and the other fellow cooperates. However, if the game is repeated again and again, and the other fellow has some learning capacity, he will not continue to cooperate. When you both defect, which you will soon be doing repeatedly, you both gain less than you would have if you had both cooperated. It is not obvious what you should do in this situation, assuming that there will be many trials, but computer simulations show that the most successful strategy is tit for tat—doing what the other fellow did last time—rather than consistent defection. It may be to your advantage occasionally to test the negative pattern, to cooperate once and see if your partner is also playing tit for tat. A shift could make you much better off.

One can go a surprising distance with this type of theory in an effort to explain away every act of human or animal courage or generosity as based on nothing more than raising or lowering the future frequency of "the altruism gene." No such gene exists in complex animals, but it does not need to; all that is needed is for one or more genes to enhance altruism in some way or other, and this is highly likely. In fact, identical twins resemble each other in altruistic inclination more than do fraternal twins (Rushton & Fulker, 1986). Genes *affecting* altruism will eventually be identified and cloned; the flaw in the argument is not in the nonexistence of such genes.

But there is a problem here: The theory seems to tell us about mechanism when it really does not; that is, it obscures the fact that there are many possible paths to the goal of distributing generous acts as adaptation demands. For example, suppose a human hunter-gatherer were programmed by nature to save drowning people according to how well he loved them. The resulting distribution of risk across drowning victims might be a good approximation of what kin selection predicts. Yet the love guiding his efforts might come from none other than the usual processes of maturation and learning. And the same hunter-gatherer, having been thrust in the course of a few thousand years into a new kind of social world full of nonrelatives, would still learn to love. Many species have a specific chemical signal enabling them to recognize their kin by smell (Greenberg, 1979). But humans do it by association and emotion. Perhaps a simple signal exists in humans too, although it would probably be a seen rather than smelled signal. Indeed, this may be an adaptive function of our keen interest in faces: the "are you related to so-and-so" reaction. In a social world thoroughly sorted into kin groups, that ability may have been vital. And that same discrimination may have helped males detect cuckoldry in the faces of their alleged offspring. For better or worse, it may also figure in our strong sense of what constitutes facial attractiveness, and, negatively, in our penchant for bigotry.

This brings us to a fourth explanation for altruism, which is that it evolved in the service of group competition. Group selection remains an embattled addition to the theory, but most evolutionists now give it a minor role. A brief in its favor, widely criticized but still interesting, is Elliott Sober and David Sloan Wilson's *Unto Others: The Evolution and Psychology of Unselfish Behavior* (Sober & Wilson, 1998; see also Nunney, 1998; Smuts, 1999). Finally, many neo-Darwinians look at altruistic behavior through the lens of deception, on the theory that it is often either simply false or combined with other motives in an effort to pursue selfish gain. With the exception of group selection, these other attempts to explain altruism may be seen as explaining it away. That is, if we are pursuing selfish genetic goals by distributing altruism so specifically and carefully, why call it altruism? This, however, seems almost to revert to the college-dorm debater's claim that altruism must be selfish because it feels good to the altruist. It is more useful to retain our commonsense notion of altruism, which includes sacrifices for relatives, for nonrelatives who may return the favor, and for partners in cooperation and which also admits of the possibility of mixed motives. Nevertheless, it does seem that altruism has evolved in such a way as to make its purest, most ideal forms problematical.

The Problem of Aggression

Clearly one of the main obstacles to altruism would be a natural tendency toward aggression, if such a tendency exists. In the last decades of the twentieth century, there was a sea change in the natural history of aggression, a shift from classical ethology to a more Darwinian sociobiology. According to the old view, championed by Konrad Lorenz, the function of aggressive behavior is to distribute members of a group over a territory (Lorenz, 1970). The group as a whole benefits because individuals stay out of each other's way. Threats and other aggressive displays reduce actual violence by spacing individuals and arranging them in a hierarchy. Studies of wild animals seemed to support this view (Wynne-Edwards, 1962). Humans were said to be almost unique among animals in that we kill our own kind. One explanation for this distinction was that weapons such as projectiles give us a distance from our victims that weakens our natural tendency to limit the damage we do.

These claims are largely false. As E. O. Wilson pointed out many years ago, if a troop of baboons killed their own kind at the same rate as people in New York City do, you would have to watch the baboons for hundreds of years before you would be likely to see a killing (Wilson, 1975). Not surprisingly, as hundreds of person-years of field observations were logged by naturalists, killings were seen. Many species do kill their own kind. In other words, "natural" mechanisms for the limitation of violence do not work much better in nonhuman animals than they do in us. Animals, like humans, kill when they have more to gain than to lose by doing so (Popp & DeVore, 1979).

With the evolution of the higher primates, certain complexities are introduced into social behavior, and they appear to favor cooperation rather than aggression. Monkeys and apes are generally capable of far more varied facial expression than are other mammals, and their brains are adapted for interpreting these expressions. Along with these capacities goes an ability to recognize a large number of different individuals' faces and to adapt behavior in subtle ways in the context of enduring relationships. A rudimentary form of intersubjectivity—the ability to take the perspective of the other—emerges, further strengthening the potential for long-term relationships. Coalitions become important, even in the context of aggression, and perhaps especially so. Finally, well-documented rituals of peacemaking often bring opponents together immediately after fights, defusing anger and perhaps introducing a kind of forgiveness into the lives of our ancestors. However, none of these changes, nor all of them together, alter fundamentally the tendency to selfishness and violence. Peacemaking is real and important, but so is agonistic mimesis, the mirror-imaging of violence in confrontations. Violence is rare compared with friendship, but it makes little sense to criticize those who focus their research on violence because cooperation is more common. Volcanos are usually quiescent, but nobody criticizes geologists for their interest in eruptions.

Killing takes many forms, but the grimmest and most intriguing is competitive infanticide, first observed by Sarah Hrdy in langur monkeys (Hrdy, 1977, 1979). Langur troops consist of a hierarchy of female relatives with their young and a small number of males. From time to time new males appear and drive the old males out of the troop. Within a few days the new males kill all infants under 6 months of age and reimpregnate the infants' mothers soon thereafter. Similar patterns appear in lions, wild dogs, and many other species (Hausfater & Hrdy, 1984). Sociobiological theory, with its emphasis on individual selection and competition rather than on group selection, would have to predict something like competitive infanticide. Its discovery was a major setback for group selection. Here is a pattern that grotesquely disrupts the group while giving a strong advantage to a few individuals. Some proponents of group selection continue to defend it (Sober & Wilson, 1998), but most evolutionists remain skeptical (Nunney, 1998; Smuts, 1999). Most neo-Darwinians believe that each individual is in competition with every other in its environment (Williams, 1966), and that group selection is a minor factor (Williams, 1992).

So altruism and cooperation are adaptive but fragmentary and transient. At the other extreme, aggression evolved to serve the interests of individuals, and that is why some individuals use it more successfully than others (Popp & DeVore, 1979). It garners resources for the victor, and in the case of males, it means access to female reproductive capacity. As Irven DeVore showed in the 1960s, dominant male baboons have privileged access to females when they are ovulating (DeVore, 1965). Glenn Hausfater later confirmed this in baboons (Hausfater, 1975), and Kim Wallen found a similar pattern in rhesus monkeys (Wallen & Tannenbaum,

1997). It is likely that male predominance in all physical forms of aggression is mainly due to this evolutionary background of competition for fertile females. However, only a highly controlled form of aggression will succeed over time.

As for violence in human phylogeny, there is little directly relevant fossil evidence until the emergence of our species itself (Keeley, 1996). It was once thought that hunting had important implications for human aggression—the "killer ape" hypothesis (Ardrey, 1963). This is not likely because of the physiological and behavioral differences between predatory aggression and fighting one's own kind. All over the animal world are examples of vegetarian species whose members fight violently among themselves and who inflict great damage with such natural weapons as beaks, hoofs, and antlers. Even our close relatives the chimpanzees, for whom meat makes up only a small part of the diet (Teleki, 1973; Stanford, 1999), show intraspecies aggression of the severest sort. This aggression includes violence between groups at territorial boundaries, violent attacks on females by much larger males, and competitive infanticide committed by females against the infants of other females (Goodall, 1977; Goodall, 1979; Goodall, 1986; Manson & Wrangham, 1991; Wrangham & Peterson, 1996).

Jane Goodall, the great naturalist and observer of wild chimpanzees, chronicled this violence and eventually changed her earlier view of these animals as harmonious and peaceful in all their relationships. One mother-daughter pair made a habit of killing the infants of other females, and they were not the only perpetrators of infanticide. More important, Goodall and her colleagues observed systematic attacks on adult chimps by groups of males from adjacent communities. The victims were temporarily separated from their own communities and easily set on by a gang that beat, stamped, dragged, and bit them to death. Victims could be of either sex, but females of reproductive age were often spared and incorporated into the other group—an outcome that incidentally demonstrates why individual selection is a better theory even in this situation. In two cases whole groups were eliminated through a combination of one-by-one ambush killings and female transfer (Goodall, 1986). Interestingly, tribal warriors in New Guinea have nightmares about being separated from their comrades in combat, surrounded, and slaughtered by merciless enemies (Keeley, 1996).

Bonobos, equally close relatives of ours, are very different. Males have fights, but much less injurious ones, and they never attack or abuse females. The difference may be due to female power (Kano, 1992). Although females change groups at adolescence just as chimps do, bonobo females forge intense relationships and effective coalitions. These relationships are deepened by food sharing and face-to-face sex—rubbing together of their large clitorises to what appears to be orgasm (Kano, 1989; Wrangham, 1993). Males cannot dominate females as chimpanzee males do because females band together too effectively (Parish, 1996). Ethologist Frans de Waal believes that peaceful bonobos are a better model for what our ancestors were like than chimps are (de Waal, 1996). But, as Richard Wrangham and Dale Peterson argue in *Demonic Males*, male bonobos seem prepared to behave as badly as chimp males if the lid of female power were removed—which basically happened in human evolution (Wrangham & Peterson, 1996). And in any case, chimps have done far better than bonobos, which are very close to extinction.

But the best way to find out what humans are like is to study human behavior. Martin Daly and Margo Wilson (1988) use Darwinian theory to generate novel hypotheses. For example, deadly fights may occur between men in inner cities because of an imagined slur or even the wrong kind of eye contact. How could so much be risked for so little? Daly and Wilson show that it is not little at all; it is something that might be called honor or respect or merely status, and it is worth a great deal. Using computer simulations, they assigned various values to winning and losing in terms of reproductive success (in part a consequence of status), as well as to the risks of fighting (being killed, for instance). Within a wide range of reasonable assumptions, the tendency to have such fights "over nothing" are favored by simulated natural selection (Daly & Wilson, 1988).

More dramatically, using real crime statistics from the United States, Canada, and England, Daly and Wilson tested the hypothesis that children in a household with their mother and an unrelated male would be at greater risk for abuse than those living with their mother and genetic father. Not only was this hypothesis confirmed, but also the difference was vast (Daly & Wilson, 1985; Daly & Wilson, 1998; Wilson & Daly, 1995). A child living with a stepparent is about 100 times more likely to be killed than one living with genetic parents only. This exceptionally strong finding applies to all three countries and is independent of socioeconomic status. It is one of the most illuminating findings in the history of child abuse research, and it came directly from evolutionary psychology. In essence, it is the human version of competitive infanticide.

Regarding male violence against females, Barbara Smuts showed that it has a long and complex evolutionary history, often in the service of sexual coercion (Smuts, 1992; Smuts & Smuts, 1993). Far from justifying male violence, she prepares the groundwork for understanding human parallels. For example, Daly and Wilson also found that women are at highest risk for being killed by their husbands or boyfriends when they are trying to leave these men, but the reverse is not true (Daly & Wilson, 1998). The rationale seems to be, *If I can't have her, no one can*, and it is consistent with sociobiological claims about the proprietary nature of male sexual jealousy. The murder of Nicole Simpson appears to be in this category. Male jealousy is also a main pretext for homicide in a wide range of hunting and gathering societies, including the !Kung, Eskimo, Mbuti, Hadza, and others (Knauft, 1987; Lee, 1979).

What about the wider cross-cultural evidence? The easy way to suggest innate aggressive tendencies in humans is to describe the most violent of human societies (Bohannan & American Museum of Natural History, 1967; Otterbein, 1970): the Yanomamo of highland Venezuela, the Dani or Enga of highland New Guinea, the equestrian Plains Indians of the United States, the Aztec, the Mongols, the Zulu of southern Africa, the Germans of the Third Reich. Among the traditional Enga, studied by Mervyn Meggitt, 25% of adult male deaths were due to violence, and social life was largely organized around it (Meggitt, 1977). The Yanomamo, called "the fierce people" by Napoleon Chagnon, as well as by themselves, are comparably violent (Chagnon, 1968, 1992). Forty percent of men have killed at least one other man, and those who have killed have demonstrably higher reproductive success than those who have not (Chagnon, 1988).

Such descriptions of the most violent societies can be multiplied at length and easily give the impression that humans are a very bloody species, composed of dysfunctional or, in the words of Robert Edgerton, "sick societies" (Edgerton, 1992). Irenaus Eibl-Eibesfeldt, in *The Biology of Peace and War* (1979), reviewed many ethnographic accounts of warfare in primitive societies, including some allegedly nonviolent ones (Eibl-Eibesfeldt, 1979). Archeological evidence assembled by Lawrence Keeley has demolished "the myth of the peaceful savage" (Keeley, 1996). The tenacity of this myth is a subject in itself, as it required an astonishing degree of blindness to hard evidence, in accounts that Keeley has aptly called "interpretive pacifications" (Keeley, 1996, p. 20). The archeological record, sparse for prehuman species, leaves no doubt that homicidal violence was part of life from the dawn of our own (Keeley, 1996, p. 37). With the rise of agriculture, evidence of warfare becomes decisive. Indeed, the whole of human history since the hunting-gathering era can be best understood as a process of relentless, expansionist tribal warfare (Keegan, 1993; Schmookler, 1983).

The greater challenge to a hypothesis of innate aggression, however, is to look at the least violent societies. Differences in the degree of violence among cultures are real and large, and understanding those differences should help us reduce violence. But first consider the claim that there are truly nonviolent societies. The !Kung San of Botswana are used as a common example of the least violent end of the human cultural spectrum (Thomas, 1959). Like most hunter-gatherers, they do not have war or other organized group conflicts, at least not in recent times. Still, that is far from being equivalent to nonviolence—their homicide rate matches or exceeds that of American cities (Lee, 1979). Most !Kung are quite capable of violence, and there are many nonlethal acts of violence as well (Shostak, 1981, 2000). Moreover, their explicit contempt for non-San people, and even for !Kung in other villages who are not their relatives, makes it clear that if they had the technological opportunity and the ecological impetus to make war, they would be capable of the requisite emotions. Historical accounts show that they have made war in the past (Eibl-Eibesfeldt, 1979).

Among the Semai, slash-and-burn gardeners of Malaysia studied by anthropologist Robert Knox Dentan, violence is said to be virtually nonexistent and abhorrent. "Since a census of the Semai was first taken in 1956," Dentan wrote in 1968, "not one instance of murder, attempted murder, or maiming has come to the attention of either government or hospital authorities" (Dentan, 1968):

> People do not often hit their children and almost never administer the kind of beating that is routine in some sectors of Euro-American society. A person should never hit a child because, people say, "How would you feel if it died" . . . Similarly, one adult should never hit another because, they say, "Suppose he hit you back?" . . .
>
>   As long as they have been known to the outside world, they have consistently fled rather than fight, or even than run the risk of fighting. They had never participated in a war or raid until the Communist insurgency of the early 1950's, when the British raised troops among the Semai, mainly in the west . . . Many did not realize that soldiers kill people. When I suggested to one Semai recruit that killing was a soldier's job, he laughed at my ignorance. (Dentan, 1968, p. 58)

But when the British engaged the Semai in counterinsurgency against Communist rebels in the mid-1950s, they underwent a transformation:

> Communist terrorists had killed the kinsmen of some of the Semai counterinsurgency troops. Taken out of their nonviolent society and ordered to kill, they seem to have been swept up in a sort of insanity which they call "blood drunkenness." A typical veteran's story runs like this. "We killed, killed, killed. The Malays would stop and go through people's pockets and take their watches and money. We did not think of watches or money. We only thought of killing. Wah, truly we were drunk with blood." One man even told how he had drunk the blood of a man he had killed. (Dentan, 1968, pp. 58–59)

What followed was equally remarkable:

> The Semai seem, not displeased that they were such good soldiers, but unable to account for their behavior. It is almost as if they had shut the experience in a separate compartment . . . Back in Semai society they seem as gentle and afraid of violence as anyone else. To them their one burst of violence appears to be as remote as something that happened to someone else, in another country. The nonviolent image remains intact. (Dentan, 1968, p. 59)

Despite this reversal of a nonviolent tradition, cultural contexts can reduce violence. But whatever cultural conditioning we do, human beings conditioned to be nonviolent retain the capacity for violence. The tendency to do grievous harm is a part of our evolutionary legacy (Blanchard & Hebert, 1999). The continued pretence by some social scientists and philosophers that human beings are basically peaceable has so far prevented little of human violence.

Human Dimensions, Human Denial

Much as we hold in common with animals, and especially with higher primates, there are some transformations in human evolution that seem to hold out hope for transcending our evolutionary legacy. These include language, symbols, explicit social contracts, and legal and moral codes that formulate standards of behavior and institute collective punishments for violators. However, none of these actually has to change the fundamental adaptations. Language is often an instrument of deception, symbols routinely incite people to partisanship and violence, social contracts often disadvantage one party and may be imposed by the strong on the weak, and codes of behavior are frequently designed by a dominant group in society to control the behavior of others. The claim that these changes in human evolution negate the basic evolutionary legacy of selfishness is in itself a form of deception. As Marx—Groucho, not Karl—is said to have remarked, "The secret of success is honesty and fair dealing. If you can fake those, you've got it made."

Human deceptions reach the highest level of intellectual discourse and persist for millennia. As Robert Trivers has pointed out, deceptions work best on others if they are also self-deceptions, and the most enduring of our deceptions fill that bill (Trivers, 1991). Four of them, together with the evidence that should by now have refuted them, are as follows:

1. "All is rational." Humans are obviously capable of rational thought and action, but reason is an instrument of baser as well as nobler motives. It is a tool readily and frequently cast aside, but, more important, it is often a mask. Darwin and Freud have been rejected by most people because they remove the mask, and in Freud's view rationality is always suspect as rationalization. Robert Frank has shown that "irrational" behavior often serves adaptive interests (Frank, 1988), and Antonio Damasio has shown that rational decision making is impossible in the absence of emotion, suggesting that reason itself is hopelessly contaminated by motives and feelings (Damasio, 1994). All this does not mean that human reason is feeble or fake, but it shows that the common philosopher's or economist's notion that human action is dominated by processes akin to those of a good student of Euclid's geometry is false and deceptive.

2. "All is modifiable." Most twenty-first century Westerners are ameliorists and believe that human behavior is easily modifiable with exhortations, training, cultural influence, and the like. They have missed the behavioral science of the late twentieth century, which overturned dominant notions of extreme plasticity. Robert Plomin (Plomin & Owen, 1994), Jerome Kagan (Kagan, 1995; Kagan & Snidman, 1999), Sandra Scarr (Scarr, 1992; Scarr, 1993; Scarr & McCartney, 1983), and Thomas Bouchard (Bouchard & Segal, 1990) are among the many scientists who have established genetic influences on human behavior and temperament that are strong and enduring and that even help to shape environments in a self-reinforcing cycle. Their research does not mean that behavior is unmodifiable, only that it is difficult to modify, and that to say otherwise is deceptive.

3. "All is well intentioned." Unlike traditional religious thinkers, who have always believed in the reality of evil, many modern social scientists and philosophers have believed that human intentions are good but that errors of reasoning lead to bad outcomes. The Freudian movement of the twentieth century should have laid that idea to rest, but as Freud fell into disfavor in that century's closing decades, the neo-Darwinian revolution established more firmly than ever that human motives are fundamentally selfish and often base, if not necessarily evil. The preceding discussion of evolutionary theories of altruism and aggression provides decisive evidence that good intentions in human affairs are often deceptive. If the road to hell is paved with good intentions, it is partly because that is the road they generally start out on.

4. "All will work out in the end." As Lionel Tiger demonstrated decades ago, human thought and action are pervaded by a thoroughgoing and usually unwarranted optimism (Tiger, 1979). Although this tendency is surely adaptive in many personal circumstances, for example those of life-threatening illness (Taylor, 1989), it is likely to be the wrong adaptation for action on a global scale, which is what we now need. It is difficult to believe that a century such as the twentieth could lead to optimism at the dawn of the twenty-first, but that is the nature of human foresight, or the lack thereof. Thomas Malthus predicted disaster for the human species not merely because of elementary calculations about food and

mouths to feed but because of the features of human nature, which as a man of the cloth he knew all too well (Malthus, 1798/1985). In fact, human nature was what his book was largely about. He knew less about technology, so he could not foresee the ingenuity that would delay utter disaster. But in fact much of what he predicted has already come to pass in many parts of the world, and increasing population density has been implicated in many wars of the past two centuries. Foolish claims that the world will stabilize because of a bit of arithmetic—dividing the grain available by the peak number of mouths in 2050 or so—ignore the realities completely (Cohen, 1995). Twenty-first century wars will be fought over fresh water, pollution-degraded land, and (above all) rising aspirations that cannot be met under any reasonable projections (Kibben, 1997). History shows that altruism fares quite poorly in the face of such pressures.

Evil and Altruism at the Dawn of the Judeo-Christian Tradition

Early in the book of Genesis the snake, an appropriate symbol either in Freudian or Darwinian terms, introduces evil (read: rebellion) into a previously pristine pair of human hearts. Their lapse condemns the one to a life of hard labor scratching the dirt to eke out a living and the other to a different kind of labor, perhaps the most painful and threatening birth process in any animal. Many begats later, the sons and daughters of Adam and Eve are deemed so hopeless as to deserve complete destruction, except for one man and his family. But after the flood God more or less repents of his action, recognizing that the creature he has made is deeply flawed: "And the Lord said in his heart, I will not curse the ground any more for man's sake; for the imagination of man's heart is evil from his youth" (Genesis 8:21).

Thus the Judeo-Christian tradition, like that of most major religions, posits a tendency to evil as more or less inborn. This means there must be a struggle to achieve the good, and that involves moral guidelines and exhortations to be mindful of them. Among the guidelines are those that urge against revenge and in favor of love. For example, "Thou shalt not avenge, nor bear any grudge against the children of thy people, but thou shalt love thy neighbor as thyself" (Leviticus 19:18). This of course could be construed as urging group solidarity, potentially dangerous to outsiders. But we have already had the exhortation of Exodus 22:21, "Thou shalt neither vex a stranger, nor oppress him; for ye were strangers in the land of Egypt." In the prophetic books that bring the Jewish Bible to a close, the exhortations to altruism grow steadily stronger and culminate in the message of the Gospels, a universalist message of love and redemption, including a decisive rejection of revenge.

But Jesus famously said, "I came not to send peace, but a sword" (Matthew 10:34), and the book of Revelation spells out an imaginative revenge that remains close to the hearts of many believers. More important, it was the sword that guided Christians' behavior during their two millennia of dominance in Europe, just as it had guided the Hebrews during their own few hegemonic centuries. Judaism began in the Egyptian imperium, Christianity in the Roman, but both turned violent and hegemonic themselves at the first historical opportunity. This is a universal feature of major religions, which have all had periods of violent conquest and hegemony. There is no religion that has been immune to the disease of bigotry, and in most it has been florid, contagious, and at some times epidemic.

This was only a continuation of the process begun by the ancient civilizations as they arose, quite literally, from the mud of the Nile, Tigris, Euphrates, Indus, and Yellow Rivers, and in the New World from Lakes Texcoco and Titicaca, among other life-sustaining bodies of water. The mud made bricks, the bricks made houses and then towns, and the towns made almost relentless war against other towns as they depleted the resources around them. The winners of these vicious millennial contests were the groups we call the ancient civilizations. Marx (Karl, not Groucho) said that capitalism had emerged from the mud with blood oozing from every pore. This may not have been true of capitalism, but it is unquestionably true of "civilization," which is almost completely synonymous with violence, conquest, exploitation, slavery, and human sacrifice. Civilization emerged from the mud with blood baked into every brick. Judaism, Christianity, Buddhism, and other major extant religions certainly toned down the violence inherent in civilizations, but for much of their history "fine-tuned" might be a better euphemism than "toned-down."

Carved in stone above a famous New England law school are the words, Non sub homine sed sub Dei et lex—"Not under man but under God and law." A fine sentiment, but difficult to implement, as, from the moment they were conceived, God and law have sanctioned conquest, slavery, caste, purdah, genocide, mutilation, torture, human sacrifice, and almost unremitting war.

A Darwinian Social Machine

If exhortations and moral codes cannot be relied on to keep human selfishness under control, what can? Fortunately for the species, there appears to be at least a tentative answer to this question. Contrary to some claims, the implications of evolutionary theory are not inherently conservative, but they are inherently materialist and suggest that life is fraught with conflict. The revolutionaries of the nascent American republic, although they were not much interested in evolution, appear to have been comfortable with both these implications.

In *The Lost World of Thomas Jefferson*, Daniel Boorstin showed that Jefferson's circle—including Benjamin Rush, the physician and psychiatrist—had a definite model of human nature. Scientific materialists, they believed that all humans were descended from a single pair, giving universal features to the mind. What Rush called "the anatomy of the mind" was an attempt to put human behavior and psychology on a continuum with the physical sciences and even more so with the lives of animals, undermining human arrogance. As one of the group, Tom Paine, put it, "all the great laws of society are laws of nature" (Boorstin, 1981, p. 173), and order in human affairs stems from "the principles of society and the natural constitution of man" (1981, p. 172).

In this light, we could say that the 1789 monograph from the laboratory of Madison et al. (the one that begins "We the people . . .") described an epochal social science discovery. It presented a plan for an intricate, elegant device, a sociological invention for keeping human nature in check, while creating safety valves for the release of constantly seething conflict. In fact, you could say that the machine harnesses conflict itself to provide the energy that drives it. For unlike other machines, this one would be built out of people, so it would depend on some understanding of what those people were. Jefferson—an affiliate of the lab, but absent in Paris when the monograph appeared—had a dark view. "In questions of power," he would later write, "let no more be said of confidence in man, but bind him down from mischief by the chains of the constitution." Paine similarly saw the purpose of constitutions as "to restrain and regulate the wild impulse of power" (Boorstin, 1981, p. 190). These thinkers, social scientists all, were also engineers, and it was their great gift to take a Hobbesian view of life without applying a Hobbesian solution.

Their naturalistic view encompassed even political differences. Jefferson wrote that "the terms of whig and tory belong to natural as well as civil history. They denote the temper and constitution of mind of different individuals" (Boorstin, 1981, pp. 120–121). For Rush, there was "the same variety in the texture of minds, that there is in the bodies of men" (1981, p. 120). But if differences of opinion are really matters of temperament, ultimately reflecting brain differences, then what could be more hopeless than to pursue universal consensus? "I never saw an instance of one of two disputants convincing the other by argument," Jefferson facetiously remarked. "I have seen many, on their getting warm, becoming rude, and shooting one another" (1981, p. 121). No, consensus was a vain dream. Instead, the constitution would have to take the permanence of those differences as a given and create a government that would harness the energy of unremitting conflict.

Boorstin's history is extremely helpful, but we could just read the monograph itself and infer the underlying theory. Human nature is eminently corruptible. People seek power and abuse it, turning it to selfish ends, regardless of how collective and representative its roots. Nepotism, greed, self-aggrandizement, intractable conflict, and suppression of dissent naturally and relentlessly threaten human institutions. A democratic republic is inherently improbable and will tend to degenerate into hereditary dictatorship, oligarchy, or chaos, regardless of good intentions. As Publius—either Madison or Hamilton—asked famously in Federalist 51, "But what is government itself, but the greatest of all reflections upon human nature? If men were angels, no government would be needed."

The Madison lab assumed the worst about human nature, and under that assumption, they invented a device to bully it into decency—"a policy of supplying, by opposite and rival interests" (Federalist 51 again) "the defect of better motives." They analyzed human nature and built a machine, as tightly and intricately balanced as the cotton gin or a mill wheel, but far more complex, positioning mirror-image antagonisms in stable opposition and weighing selfish human nature down with a ballast of communal responsibility. At one end you could put in a collection of greedy, selfish, power-hungry humans locked in angry conflict, and at the other end something resembling order, peace, and fairness would somehow be turned out. Creaky, noisy, seemingly ready to break down at any time, the machine they built has more or less worked (with one very bloody interruption) for two centuries—a moment in evolutionary terms, but a beginning. Inexact working replicas are also cranking away in various places on the planet, proposing to make order out of human nature elsewhere, with different, always limited, degrees of success. For those who think that human nature is inherently good, unselfish, and cooperative, the result is a poor substitute for a functional, organically coherent, and truly fair society.

But for those of us who see human nature as the product of too many eons of individual selection, the machine makes an acceptable stew out of questionable meat. Or, to borrow Isaiah Berlin's metaphor, nothing straight was ever made from the crooked timber of humanity, yet with democratic devices we have built a livable dwelling. Many are shut out of it and clamor for shelter, but that probably means we should build on another wing, not tear the thing down and start over again. Given the grain of the lumber, we could end up with something a good deal worse.

Conclusion

So does this take us back to social Darwinism, to a grim, inhuman world of survival of the fittest? No. Democratic institutions are devices invented for limiting evil, not promoting good. Limiting evil is a hard enough task in itself, but in the long run it will not suffice, because inequalities can grow to a point at which stability is threatened. In the wake of the failure of Communism, virtually everyone in the world agrees that a furnace of greed must burn in the basement of the economic house. Given our nature, shaped by evolution, no other basic solution is possible. But the question remains, how high do we build the floor under the poor? Even Adam Smith, who saw the invisible hand, believed that the all-too-visible hand of government plays a role in preserving communal integrity by performing tasks that markets do not do well. Even the Madison lab, deeply suspicious of government, included the phrase "promote the general welfare" in the abstract of their monograph.

The old, the very young, the ill, the disabled, and those whose natural gifts do not permit them to compete no matter how hard they try—these people will always be at the mercy of the capable and strong, even in the most democratic social machines. Darwinian processes did not design human nature to look out for them automatically, so only programs and supports designed by a collective, humane political will—a will that also restrains the worst excesses of markets—can, after wide debate, create a decent community and set some limit on selfishness. But here the logic appears to break down. How can a creature designed by a blind, random, evolutionary process to pursue relentlessly whatever is best for its genes take action that is contrary to genetic interest?

There are two possible answers. First, in a global economy made irreversibly interdependent by an exponentially growing web of instantaneous communication, it is not so clear where our genetic interests lie. Cooperation and reciprocity have always been favored over nepotism in certain circumstances, and the next few generations may see an expansion of those advantages to a planetary scale. Second, evolutionary theory gives us an *is*, not an *ought*. That human nature is fraught with intractable tendencies would come as no surprise to the inventors of either the great religious or the great democratic traditions. Today we are discovering our own intractable tendencies in unprecedented detail, because we finally have the right theory for understanding them. But that does not make them any more desirable to human beings who, in the end, can make a collective decision to restrain or reject them.

Cultural evolution is to some extent an independent path and may yet lead us out of the morass of a world still controlled by a basically selfish human nature. Religions, for all their self-deceptions, eventually put an end to human sacrifice and slavery. Democracies have reduced the risk of tyranny and, according to some theories, may also be reducing the risk of war. It is our challenge to secure those gains and extend them to the billions of members of our species who cannot yet enjoy them. It is an unprecedented challenge, as much intellectual as moral, and it will certainly help to have the right theory of human nature and to have a political will that rivals that of the Founders. But perhaps what we need to do now must also echo the ancient exhortation of the Psalmist (10:18), "to right the fatherless and the oppressed, that man who is of the earth may be terrible no more."

REFERENCES

Ardrey, R. (1963). *African genesis: A personal investigation into the animal origins and nature of man.* New York: Dell.

Axelrod, R. (1984). *The evolution of cooperation.* New York: Basic Books.

Axelrod, R., & Dion, D. (1988, December 9). The further evolution of cooperation. *Science, 242,* 1385–1390.

Axelrod, R., & Hamilton, W. D. (1981). The evolution of cooperation. *Science, 211,* 1390–1396.

Blanchard, D. C., & Hebert, M. (1999). Continuity versus (political) correctness: Animal models and human aggression. In M. Haug & W. R. E. Washington (Eds.), *Animal models of human emotion and cognition* (pp. 297–316). Washington: American Psychological Association.

Bohannan, P., & American Museum of Natural History (1967). *Law and warfare: Studies in the anthropology of conflict.* Garden City, NY: Natural History Press.

Boorstin, D. J. (1981). *The lost world of Thomas Jefferson.* Chicago: University of Chicago Press.

Bouchard, T. J. J., & Segal, N. L. (1990). Genetic and environmental influences on special mental abilities in a sample of twins reared apart. *Acta Geneticae Medica Gemellologiae, 39,* 193–206.

Chagnon, N. A. (1968). *Yanomamo: The fierce people.* New York: Holt, Rinehart, & Winston.

Chagnon, N. A. (1988). Life histories, blood revenge, and warfare in a tribal population. *Science, 239,* 985–992.

Chagnon, N. A. (1992). *Yanomamo: The last days of Eden.* San Diego: Harcourt Brace.

Cohen, J. (1995). Population growth and the earth's human carrying capacity. *Science, 269,* 341–346.

Conway Morris, S. (1998). *The crucible of creation: The Burgess shale and the rise of animals.* Oxford: Oxford University Press.

Daly, M., & Wilson, M. (1985). Child abuse and other risks of not living with both parents. *Ethology and Sociobiology, 6*, 197–210.

Daly, M., & Wilson, M. (1988). *Homicide.* New York: Aldine de Gruyter.

Daly, M., & Wilson, M. (1998). The evolutionary social psychology of family violence. In C. Crawford & D. L. Krebs (Eds.), *Handbook of evolutionary psychology* (pp. 431–456). Mahwah, NJ: Erlbaum.

Damasio, A. (1994). *Descartes' error: Emotion, reason, and the human brain.* New York: Putnam.

Darwin, C. (1981). *The descent of man, and selection in relation to sex.* Princeton, NJ: Princeton University Press. (Original work published 1871)

Dawkins, R. (1989). *The selfish gene,* rev. ed. New York: Oxford University Press.

de Waal, F. (1996). *Good natured.* Cambridge: Harvard University Press.

Dentan, R. K. (1968). *The Semai: A nonviolent people of Malaysia.* New York, Holt, Rinehart, & Winston.

DeVore, I. (1965). Male dominance and mating behavior in baboons. In F. Beach (Ed.), *Sexual behavior* (pp. 82–99). New York: Wiley.

Edgerton, R. B. (1992). *Sick societies: Challenging the myth of primitive harmony.* New York: Free Press.

Eibl-Eibesfeldt, I. (1979). *The biology of peace and war: Men, animals, and aggression.* London: Thames and Hudson.

Fisher, R. A. (1958). *The genetical theory of natural selection.* New York: Dover.

Frank, R. H. (1988). *Passions within reason: The strategic role of the emotions.* New York: Norton.

Goodall, J. (1977). Infant killing and cannibalism in free-living chimpanzees. *Folia Primatologica, 28*, 259–282.

Goodall, J. (1986). *The chimpanzees of Gombe: Patterns of behavior.* Cambridge: Harvard University Press.

Goodall, J. V. L. (1979). Life and death at Gombe. *National Geographic, 155*, 592–621.

Gould, S. J., & Lewontin, R. C. (1979). The spandrels of San Marco and the Panglossian paradigm: A critique of the adaptationist programme. *Proceedings of the Royal Society of London, Ser. B, 205*: 581–598.

Greenberg, L. (1979). Genetic component of bee odor in kin recognition. *Science, 206*, 1095–1097.

Hamilton, W. D. (1964). The genetical evolution of social behavior (Parts 1 and 2). *Journal of Theoretical Biology, 12*, 1–52.

Hausfater, G. (1975). *Dominance and reproduction in baboons* (Papio cynocephalus). Basel, Switzerland: Kargar.

Hausfater, G., & Hrdy, S. B. (Eds.). (1984). *Infanticide: Comparative and evolutionary perspective.* New York: Aldine de Gruyter.

Hrdy, S. B. (1977). *The langurs of Abu: Female and male strategies of reproduction.* Cambridge: Harvard University Press.

Hrdy, S. B. (1979). Infanticide among animals: A review, classification, and examination of the implications for the reproductive strategies of females. *Ethology and Sociobiology, 1*: 13–40.

Kagan, J. (1995). *Galen's prophecy: Temperament and human nature.* New York: Basic Books.

Kagan, J., & Snidman, N. (1999). Infant temperament and anxious symptoms in school age children. *Development and Psychopathology, 11*(2), 209–224.

Kano, T. (1989). The sexual behavior of pygmy chimpanzees. In P. G. Heltne & L. A. Marquardt (Eds.), *Understanding chimpanzees* (pp. 176–183). Cambridge: Harvard University Press/Chicago Academy of Sciences.

Kano, T. (1992). *The last ape: Pygmy chimpanzee behavior and ecology.* Stanford, CA: Stanford University Press.

Keegan, J. (1993). *A history of warfare.* New York: Vintage Books.

Keeley, L. H. (1996). *War before civilization: The myth of the peaceful savage.* New York: Oxford University Press.

Knauft, B. (1987). Reconsidering violence in simple human societies: Homicide among the Gebusi of New Guinea. *Current Anthropology, 28,* 457–500.

Lee, R. B. (1979). *The !Kung San: Men, women and work in a foraging society.* Cambridge: Cambridge University Press.

Lorenz, K. (1970). What aggression is good for. In C. H. Southwisk (Ed.), *Animal aggression: Selected readings* (pp. 88–120). New York: Van Nostrand Reinhold.

Malthus, T. (1985). *An essay on the principle of population.* New York: Penguin. (Original work published 1798)

Manson, J. H., & Wrangham, R. W. (1991, August–October) Intergroup aggression in chimpanzees and humans. *Current Anthropology, 32*(4): 369–390.

Maynard Smith, J., & Burian, R. (1985). Developmental constraints and evolution. *Quarterly Review of Biology, 60*(3): 265–287.

Meggitt, M. J. (1977). *Blood is their argument: Warfare among the Mae Enga tribesmen of the New Guinea highlands.* Palo Alto, CA: Mayfield.

Nunney, L. (1998, September 11). Are we selfish, are we nice, or are we nice because we are selfish? *Science, 281,* 1619–1621.

Otterbein, K. F. (1970). *The evolution of war: A cross-cultural study.* N.p.: Human Relations Area Files Press.

Parish, A. R. (1996). Female relationships in bonobos (*Pan paniscus*): Evidence for bonding, cooperation, and female dominance in a male-philopatric species. *Human Nature, 7*(1), 61–96.

Plomin, R., & Owen, M. J. (1994). The genetic basis of complex human behaviors. *Science, 264,* 1733–1739.

Popp, J. L., & DeVore, I. (1979). Aggressive competition and social dominance theory: Synopsis. In D. A. Hamburg & E. McCown (Eds.), *The great apes.* Menlo Park, CA: Benjamin/Cummings.

Ridley, M. (Ed.). (1997). *Evolution.* Oxford: Oxford University Press.

Rushton, J. P., & Fulker, D. W. (1986). Altruism and aggression: The heritability of individual differences. *Journal of Personality and Social Psychology, 50,* 1192–1198.

Scarr, S. (1992). Developmental theories for the 1990s: Development and individual differences. *Child Development, 63,* 1–19.

Scarr, S. (1993). Biological and cultural diversity: The legacy of Darwin for development. *Child Development, 64,* 1333–1353.

Scarr, S., & McCartney, K. (1983). How people make their own environments: A theory of genotype-environment effects. *Child Development, 54,* 424–435.

Schmookler, A. B. (1983). *The parable of the tribes: The problem of power in social revolution.* Berkeley: University of California Press.

Shostak, M. (1981). *Nisa: The life and words of a !Kung woman.* Cambridge: Harvard University Press.

Shostak, M. (2000). *Return to Nisa.* Cambridge: Harvard University Press.

Simpson, G. G. (1944). *Tempo and mode in evolution.* New York: Columbia University Press.

Smuts, B. (1992). Male aggression against women: An evolutionary perspective. *Human Nature, 3*(1), 1–44.

Smuts, B. (1999). Multilevel selection, cooperation, and altruism: Reflections on *Unto others: The evolution and psychology of unselfish behavior. Human Nature, 10*(3): 311–327.

Smuts, B. B., & Smuts, R. W. (1993). Male-aggression and sexual coercion of females in nonhuman- primates and other mammals: Evidence and theoretical implications. *Advances in the Study of Behavior, 22,* 1–63.

Sober, E., & Wilson, D. S. (1998). *Unto others: The evolution and psychology of unselfish behavior.* Cambridge: Harvard University Press.

Stanford, C. B. (1999). *The hunting apes: Meat eating and the origins of human behavior.* Princeton, NJ: Princeton University Press.

Taylor, S. E. (1989). *Positive illusions: Creative self-deception and the healthy mind.* New York: Basic Books.

Teleki, G. (1973). *The predatory behavior of wild chimpanzees.* Lewisburg, PA: Bucknell University Press.

Tellegen, A., & Lykken, D. T. (1988). Personality similarity in twins reared apart and together. *Journal of Personality and Social Psychology, 54*(6), 1031–1039.

Thomas, E. M. (1959). *The harmless people.* New York: Vintage Books.

Tiger, L. (1979). *Optimism: The biology of hope.* New York: Simon & Schuster.

Trivers, R. (1991). Deceit and self-deception: The relationship between communication and consciousness. In M. H. Robinson & L. Tiger (Eds.), *Man and beast revisited.* (pp. 175–191). Washington: Smithsonian Institution Press.

Trivers, R. L. (1971). The evolution of reciprocal altruism. *Quarterly Review of Biology, 46,* 35–39.

Williams, G. C. (1966). *Adaptation and natural selection.* Princeton, NJ: Princeton University Press.

Williams, G. C. (1992). *Natural selection: Domains, levels, and challenges.* New York: Oxford University Press.

Wilson, E. O. (1975). *Sociobiology: The new synthesis.* Cambridge: Harvard University Press.

Wilson, M. I., & Daly, M. (1995). Familicide: The killing of spouse and children. *Aggressive Behavior, 21,* 231–361.

Wrangham, R. (1993). The evolution of sexuality in chimpanzees and bonobos. *Human Nature, 4,* 47.

Wrangham, R. W., & Peterson, D. (1996). *Demonic males: Apes and the origins of human violence.* Boston: Houghton Mifflin.

Wynne-Edwards, V. C. (1962). *Animal dispersion in relation to social behaviour.* New York: Hafner.

13

Emerging Accounts of Altruism

"Love Creation's Final Law"?

JEFFREY P. SCHLOSS

Over the past several decades, the field of evolutionary biology has been described as participating in two concomitant revolutions that have ushered in highly significant implications for our understanding of human altruism. The first revolution, an internal one (Holcomb, 1993), has involved the development of new theories of behavioral evolution that contribute much to resolving a long-standing theoretical quandary regarding sacrificial behavior. Noted by Darwin himself, the question has been how natural selection, which retains only those traits that confer reproductive success, can generate or even allow behaviors that entail assistance to another at apparent reproductive cost to the actor. So significant is this problem, and so tentative was our prior ability to rigorously address it, that Richard Alexander claims, "That certain opinions on these various topics . . . happened to be correct during previous periods of history (while others were not) gives us no leave to cite their authors as having either demonstrated or understood the essentials of evolution by natural selection . . . or as having employed such knowledge in reaching their conclusions" (Alexander, 1993, pp. 64–65).

The second revolution, an external one, involves the energetic (perhaps initially imperialistic) extension of these new theories to human behavioral analysis. When E. O. Wilson attempted to apply sociobiological ideas to human behavior in 1975, he broke what Mary Midgley has described as a "precarious truce," in which "social scientists agreed not to deny the reality of human evolution, so long as nobody attempted to make any intellectual use of it." (Midgley, 1982, p. xi). Whereas early articulations of sociobiology were justifiably criticized for being both naively reductionistic and triumphalistic, more varied and nuanced attempts to under-stand evolutionary influences on human behavior have been developed by and in-tegrated into a wide variety of human behavioral sciences (Barkow, Cosmides, & Tooby, 1992; Cronk, 1999; de Waal, 1996; Dugatin, 1999; Durham, 1991; R. Frank, 1988; S. Frank, 1998; Lopreato, 1984; Plotkin, 1993, 1997; Richerson & Boyd, 1999; Trivers, 1991). Quite arguably, evolutionary theory has wielded more expansive influence than any other discipline on our current understanding of the altruism question.

My goals in this chapter are threefold. First, I briefly characterize the so-called sociobiological "revolution," correct some common misunderstandings that persist in spite of its having been so widely discussed, and make some initial connections between sociobiological and theological perspectives on altruism. Second, I de-scribe aspects of human altruistic behavior that are still inadequately understood by expressly sociobiological or wider evolutionary theory and review a variety of contemporary, though highly contrasting, approaches to explaining it. Third, I propose an integrative model of human altruism, mention several questions in need of further biological research, and suggest areas of congruence and potentially fruitful interaction between scientific and religious perspectives on altruism.

From Darwin to Sociobiology

Darwin (1859/1967) suggested a mechanism for the origin of biological diversity that did not require divine agency or even imply intelligent design. But in addition to revolutionizing understandings of the *origins*, he also contributed profoundly to reforming perceptions of the *character* of living things. The Victorian view of nature shifted from that which romantically testified of a good creation to that which was "red in tooth and claw." In fact, this familiar phrase from Tennyson's *In Memoriam* is part of a stanza that is quite relevant to the theme of this volume:

> Man, her last work, who seem'd so fair
> Such splendid purpose in his eyes
> Who roll'd the psalm to wintry skies
> Who built him fanes of fruitless prayer,
> Who trusted God was love indeed
> And love Creation's final law—
> Tho' Nature, red in tooth and claw
> With ravine, shriek'd against his creed.

Over the past century and a half, there has been a deep and progressive loss of confidence that love is a central feature of creation's law or even that it plays any role at all. Although often laid at Darwin's feet, Tennyson's (and the general Victo-rian) initial disillusionment may have come more from geological evidence of ex-tinction and encounter with inhospitable tropical natural history, which are unsettling with or without Darwinian mechanism. In fact, Darwin himself did not wholly subscribe to the vilification of nature. Although he recognized the disturbing role of competition and death, he argued that their results were "the good of each individual species" (1859/1967) and, moreover, that death was usually swift and the lives of individual organisms were structured more by pleasure than pain. Thus, if anything, Darwinism contributed a theory by which the brutality of nature could be viewed as redemptively generating beneficial outcomes (Oates, 1988).

However, the preceding portrait misses one of the most profound implications of Darwin's theory of natural selection, which is not that the natural world contains manifold carnage and misery (that is surely evident without Darwin), but that what the natural world does not—indeed cannot—contain is genuinely sacrificial, self-disinterested goodness. If the struggle for existence is the engine of natural selection and survival of the fittest is the direction of travel, then those organisms that sacrifice their biological well-being for the good of another will be kicked off the train. Darwin observed that any characteristic that existed for the "good of another, would annihilate my theory, for such could not have been produced through natural selection" (1859/1967). Not only does love appear to fail as creation's final law, but it is legislated out of existence.

Theoretical expectations notwithstanding, it nevertheless appeared as though there were many examples of sacrificial traits in nature, such as sterile castes that care for the offspring of another in social insects, warning calls in mixed-species flocks of birds, interspecific parental care of young, and so forth. Although Darwin speculated on a variety of solutions to these puzzles, it was more than a century until they were definitively addressed by notions of inclusive fitness (Hamilton, 1964) and reciprocal altruism (Trivers, 1971).

Inclusive fitness theory affirms rather than denies the selective value of sacrificial cooperation, as long as the actual diminishment of an individual's reproductive success is less than the benefit to recipients times their index of genetic similarity. The significant aspect of inclusive fitness theory is that it not only makes sense of many previously puzzling behaviors (such as sterile castes in insects) but that it also reconceptualizes fitness to entail both progeny and kin, that is, direct offspring and nonprogeny who share a proportion of an individual's genes and therefore transmit them into the next generation. In his review of sociobiological theory, Holcomb (1993, p. 204) observes: "Even the toughest cases of altruistic social behavior suddenly became understandable using inclusive fitness. Facts about social behavior that had been counterexamples to the completeness of evolutionary theory were turned victoriously into shining examples of its successful application to social behavior." Of course many organisms sacrifice or endure risk of sacrifice for non-kin, and reciprocal altruism theory helped solve this puzzle by a cost-benefit logic similar to that of inclusive fitness. In the case of reciprocal altruism, selection should favor the establishment of costly cooperative behaviors as long as the average fitness penalty to the actor is less than the fitness benefit of receiving a compensatory act times the likelihood of its occurrence.

These theories and their extensions have been tremendously productive and have revolutionized—indeed virtually launched—studies of behavioral ecology and social evolution. Besides the fact that they successfully make sense of a broad range of proximally sacrificial behavior within the context of ultimate reproductive benefit, they have two implications that bear on the discussion of altruism. First, inclusive fitness theory is part of a significant reconceptualization not only of fitness but also of our understanding of organisms themselves. Although selection may act on individuals (or other units), what it filters is genetic information: Fitness therefore is a property of genes, and organisms can be viewed as the vehicles which carry them across generations. Wilson (1975) claims "the organism is only DNA's way of making more DNA," and Dawkins (1976) claims that organisms are "robot vehicles" that genes use to reproduce themselves.

Second, sacrificial behaviors are selectively constrained to the domain of reproductive self-interest, that is, that which realizes a net enhancement of fitness via kinship or reciprocation. Of course reproductively self-interested outcomes do not require intentionally selfish motives (or any motive at all). But the preceding two mechanisms entail differing though complementary implications for motive. With kin selection, it is not necessary to expect reciprocation, because the compensatory return is guaranteed by genetic relatedness. Wilson (1978) calls this "hard core" altruism and notes that it is free to be completely unselfish motivationally; however, it is the most exclusivistic form of cooperation, often aggressively so. Reciprocal altruism expands the domain of cooperation but at a cost of either consciously calculating benefit or autonomically adjusting set points for cooperation, calibrating them to the likelihood of return in the prevailing social ethos.

The picture of human nature that thus emerges is one wholly governed by "nepotism and favoritism" (Wilson, 1978). Indeed, the hallmark of sociobiology —controversial even among evolutionary biologists—is that kin selection and reciprocal altruism are taken to be sufficient explanations of and constraints on virtually all human cooperativeness. According to Alexander (1987, p. 195), "there do not seem to be any remaining reasons for regarding morality, as normally expressed, as necessarily self-sacrificing, or for invoking anything other than nepotism and reciprocity to account for human societal structure." Hence it is a case of choosing your poisons, and Wilson along with most sociobiologists sees the explicitly selfish though plastically interactive character of soft-core (or reciprocal) altruism as a means for extending cooperation and constraining the out-group hostility of hard-core altruism. Because we are "sufficiently selfish and calculating" to recognize the benefit of reciprocity, "true selfishness, if obedient to the other constraints of mammalian biology, is the key to a more nearly perfect social contract" (Wilson, 1978, p. 157).

In a sense, as Adam Smith argued (1776/1948), competitive self-interest could result in corporate betterment, and as Darwin's theory argued that the Malthusian "struggle for existence" could result in the goodness of "endless forms, most wondrous and diverse," so sociobiology suggests that the road to cooperation is paved by selfishness. However, the rub is that not only is the pavement concretely selfish but also the destination itself—the only terminus in the journey of life—is self-interest. Virtually all the primary architects of sociobiology are emphatic on this point. In his seminal text, David Barash claims, "evolutionary biology is quite clear that 'What's in it for me?' is an ancient refrain for all life" (Barash, 1977, p. 167). George Williams (1988, p. 399) paints "natural selection as a process for maximizing selfishness." Richard Dawkins declares, "Universal love and the welfare of the species as a whole are concepts which simply do not make evolutionary sense" (Dawkins, cited in Plotkin, 1997, p. 21). And in a passage that is often abstracted but infrequently cited in its rhetorically powerful entirety, Michael Ghiselin (1974, p. 247) professes, "given a full chance to act in his own interest, nothing but expediency will restrain him from brutalizing, from maiming, from murdering—his brother, his mate, his parent, or his child. Scratch an 'altruist,' and watch a 'hypocrite' bleed. No hint of genuine charity ameliorates our vision of society, once sentimentalism has been laid aside. What passes for cooperation turns out to be a mixture of opportunism and exploitation."

Critiques

Critics of such conclusions drawn from initial sociobiological applications of kin selection and reciprocal altruism theory have described it as a "slapdash egoism . . . a natural expression of people's lazy-minded vanity, an armchair game of cops and robbers which saves them the trouble of real inquiry and flatters their self-esteem" (Midgley, 1980, p. 132). And even recent supporters of the theory take issue with the fact that "the impression Wilson, Barash, Alexander, and others generate is that sociobiology functions as our intellectual savior and will tell us the most profound truths about who we are. Such bold claims are neither legitimate science nor legitimate philosophy, but so much entertainment and advertising" (Holcomb, 1993, p. 286). Nevertheless, repudiating the rhetorical vulgarity of popular hyperbole does nothing to distinguish hype from scientific substance, nor does it engage the intellectual significance of the underlying theory. Therefore, I want to briefly consider the strengths and limitations of several objections to sociobiological depictions of human selfishness, some advanced by contributors to this volume.

Motives versus Consequences

Perhaps the most crucial and least debatable response to sociobiological maxims of selfishness is that they provocatively conflate self-perpetuating reproductive outcomes with self-promoting behavioral motivations (Schloss, 1996; D. S. Wilson, 1992). This point is now so widely acknowledged that it needs no further elaboration. However, recognizing the important distinction between genetically selfish outcomes and interpersonally selfish intentions addresses the polemical form but not the scientific content of sociobiology's challenge to altruism. For it remains the case that traditional kin selection and reciprocal altruism theory suggest first that, regardless of motive, the *domain* of cooperative behavior must be restricted to kin or a reciprocating social matrix and second that exchanges with non-kin must be strictly self-benefiting. Motives notwithstanding, actual behaviors are held to be tightly constrained with respect to both the extensiveness and degree of sacrifice.

Determinism

A common chorus of criticism is that sociobiological theories of behavior are biologically deterministic (Gould, 1997; Gould & Lewontin, 1979; Pope, Chapter 10,
this volume; Rolston, 1999). It is true that early population genetic models
employed simplifying assumptions about the relationship between genes and
behaviors (Wilson & Sober, Chapter 11, this volume). However, even the most deterministic of sociobiological approaches views behavioral phenotypes as gene-
by-environment interactions. For example, E. O. Wilson believes that virtually all
of the extensive diversity in cultural behavior since the Pleistocene is unrelated to
genetic variability (1978, p. 34). Thus "the form and intensity of altruistic acts are
to a large extent culturally determined. Human social evolution is obviously more
cultural than genetic" (Wilson, 1978, p. 153). However, the range of possible
human behaviors is ultimately constrained on a "genetic leash." More recent and
nuanced extrapolations of sociobiological theory propose that culture has effectively broken the genetic leash: Although there may be biologically influenced central tendencies, there are no demonstrable, genetically determined constraints on
the range of sacrificial behavior (Blackmore, 1999; Plotkin, 1997).

Such theories posit biological influence but not hard determinism and merely
attempt to take seriously the notion that as organic beings, biology contributes to
our behavior in a way that has to be true of anything other than Gnostic libertar-
ianism. Mary Midgley, a staunch critic of sociobiology, nevertheless observes that
reflexive objections to deterministic accounts often reflect an ambivalence about
causal explanations of behavior in general and a reticence to responsibly confront
the limits of human freedom—the very nexus of morality. Whether it is alco-
holism, violence, or selfishness, biological explanations can surely be misused as
justification—or at least as rationalization—of destructive behaviors; yet causal
analysis is also central to any informed attempt to modify behavior. It may be the
case that the account of biological influence given by sociobiology overstates selfishness (indeed, I shall argue just that). But this could reflect a misconstrual of direction and not necessarily a degree of biological influence. Moreover, to whatever
extent sociobiological accounts are on target, it is vital to engage rather than to
dismiss their claims, for it would then be the case that "we need all the help we can
get in trying to overcome billions of years of selection for selfishness" (Williams,
1988, p. 210).

Reductionism

Yet if the sociobiological account is true, from where would we get such help? A
second objection to gene-centric evolutionary accounts of altruism is that they are
reductionistic. Indeed, E. O. Wilson's initial articulations of sociobiological theory
were imperialistically reductionistic in asserting that other disciplines could and
would be subsumed into sociobiology (1975, 1978), and they reflected what is traditionally referred to as both methodological and theory reductionism (Plotkin,
1998). Einstein's aphorism, "things should be made as simple as possible, and no
more," describes the unfortunate error of these early articulations. However, there

has been not only an ensuing flowering of collaborative work relating sociobio-logical principles to higher levels of disciplinary analysis (Holcomb, 1993) but also vigilant repudiation of Wilson's position and recognition that higher levels of analysis are crucial for comprehensive understanding (Barkow et al., 1992; Holcomb, 1993; Plotkin, 1993, 1998).

Still, gene-centric theory remains reductionistic in two ways. First, it is onto-logically reductionistic by virtue of its materialistic or physicalist view of nature, which holds that all phenomena are in principle understandable as interactions between matter and energy (yet which does not deny hierarchical ordering in levels of interaction; see Plotkin, 1998). This type of reductionism is understandably objectionable to metaphysical or anthropological dualists (Moreland & Rae, 2000; Swinburne, 1997). But such ontological reductionism is not unique to sociobiological theory and does not capture the character of sociobiological reductionism widely objected to even by materialists. Philip Kitcher quips, "Physicalism is true; no antireductionist should deny it" (Kitcher, cited in Plotkin, 1998, p. 90).

Going beyond the ontological reductionism of generic materialism, gene-centric theory is reductionistic in a virtually teleological sense, by virtue of the ultimate purpose it assigns genes. It is not just that genes influence, constrain, or even determine behavior. It is that genes are what behavior—indeed the organism and everything about it—are *for*. Wilson (1975) maintains that "the organism does not live for itself . . . it reproduces genes, and serves as their temporary carrier." Dawkins (1976) provocatively asserts that our genes "created us, body and mind; and their preservation is the ultimate rationale for our existence."

These statements function "clearly as a rhetorical tool . . . virtual parables of Darwinism that are used not merely factually but representatively: they are intended to present the inner truth of nature" (Oates, 1988). Pronouncements of the ultimate end, function, telos, rationale, or "for-ness" of life can only be viewed as a kind of teleological—Plotkin (1997) and Brown (1999) say metaphysical—reductionism. It is not that there are no other levels of causality operating or levels of analysis possible; it is just that the genic level is what ultimately matters. "All adaptations are for the preservation of DNA; DNA itself just is" (Dawkins, 1982). Assertions of genes as the ultimate reality for which all else exists go beyond materialist causal explanation and represent ontological reductionism gone to church. Plotkin (1997, p. 94) points out, "in the end, underlying all the biological and social sciences, the reason for it all, is the 'need' (how else to express it, perhaps 'drive' would be better) for genes to perpetuate themselves. This is a metaphysical claim, and the reductionism that it entails . . . is best labeled as metaphysical reductionism. Because it is metaphysical it is neither right nor wrong nor empirically testable. It is simply a statement of belief that genes count above all else."

Whether such metaphysical claims are neither false nor falsifiable is another issue altogether, but this metaphysical position has manifest implications for views of altruism and the morality that underlies it. For example, Wilson (1978, p. 167) immediately joins the empirical claim, "human behavior . . . is the circuitous technique by which human genetic material has been and will be kept intact," to the metaphysical conclusion "morality has no other demonstrable ultimate function." Richards (1993) points out that the traditional distinction between moral and empirical justification of ethics has been done away with and discussion reduced to the latter. (For an approach that explores the ethical implications of evolutionary ontological reductionism but that attempts to avoid the naturalistic fallacy in Wilson's teleological reductionism, see Richards, 1986, 1993, and Ruse, 1994, Chapter 9, this volume). Wilson explicitly acknowledges his exegetical agenda and promotes sociobiology as an ultimate, life-informing myth (1978), claiming that it is not only "the best myth we will ever have" but is also "the only mythology that can manufacture great goals from the sustained pursuit of pure knowledge" (1978, p. 207).

Positivism

Given the overtly metaphysical convictions attending many of the most reductionistic sociobiological portrayals of humanity as rampantly self-interested, it is ironic that a concomitant problem with them is the naively objectivist, indeed universally positivistic, account of their derivation. I was first impressed by this in the introduction of E. O. Wilson's *Sociobiology* (1975), in which he invites the reader to uncover the real truth to human behavior by being wholly objective—as if we were visitors on a spaceship from another planet. There is an uncanny parallel between Wilson's invitation to extraterrestrial objectivity and the one extended by Konrad Lorenz's earlier and equally negative depiction of human nature in his popularization of ethology (1966). Lorenz suggests that his explanation is what we would get by seeking to understand human behavior as if we were Martians viewing humanity through a telescope. It turns out that this posture of absolute, indeed extraterrestrially, inhuman objectivity is invoked in many popularized accounts of human altruism and moral evolution. We "imagine meeting intelligent extraterrestrials" (Bradie, 1994, p. 15), interpret the transmission of human behavioral phenotypes as "a Martian geneticist" visiting earth (Blackmore, 1999), entertain the discernments between ape and human behavior of "extraterrestrial observers" (de Waal, 1996, p. 10), note that "zoologists from outer space" would recognize no difference between human and beaver behavior (Diamond, 1992, p. 2), assert that our scientific theories are those which we would expect to be discovered "by aliens (if such there be), no matter what" their peculiarities or "peccadilloes" (Dennett, 1995, p. 495). In the most extended argument of this genre, Dawkins (1991, p. 24) asserts, "if we are visited by superior creatures from another star system . . . what common ground shall we find for discussion with them? . . . It seems unlikely that the star travelers will want to talk about . . . music, religion, or politics. . . . Mathematics and physics are another matter. . . . there will be common ground. We shall agree that certain questions about the universe are important, and we shall almost certainly agree on the answers to many of these questions."

Dawkins concludes that, given the idiosyncratic particularities of human existence, it is doubtful that Shakespeare will be viewed as important. But the version of Darwinism he advocates will not only be recognized as true—"universal and timeless"—but also, more important, it "really matters in the universe." This is not just an assertion of metaphysically reductionistic personal belief about what matters (as per Plotkin's previous point); it goes on to ground this assertion in a claim of universal, objective knowledge.

There are several obvious but profound problems with the way assertions of ultimate selfishness are anchored in such rhetoric. First, although objective observation is one important methodological goal for any scientific study of behavior, so is appropriate recognition of limits to objectivity. To claim that the theories we have arrived at are what any intelligent being any place in the universe would verify (especially when not even all earthly scientists agree on their truth or interpretation) is naively if not arrogantly positivistic. There is, here, not only a validation of method but also a rhetorical justification of conclusion based on an appeal to "higher" authority, or a kind of interplanetary *ad populum*—"ET believes it, so should you!"

Second, although it goes without saying that none of these writers has met or has the slightest clue about what other beings would find important, still anyone who holds to a modest notion of scientific realism would expect there to be areas of congruence between like rationalities. But there is the rub. The preceding inferences reflect an important misunderstanding not about alien, but about human, rationality. They view the subjective experience of human emotion and the aesthetic, ethical, and meaning-making enterprises as entailing issues either uninteresting or intractable to other intellects (indeed, to any generalized intelligence), whereas the conclusions of scientific rationality are taken to be universally comprehensible and significant. In so doing, there is a bifurcation of reason and affective or intersubjective experience that is inconsonant with emerging neuroscientific (and ancient sapient) understandings of rationality itself (Damasio, 1995, 1999). Ironically, although purporting to be physicalistic, this perspective reflects an epistemological and neuroscientific idealism which disembodies reason and uncouples conscious thought from the integrating affective and sensory matrix of organic being.

Contrary to the preceding accounts, it is quite possible, maybe even necessary, that if we encounter beings whose embodied existence gives rise to self-conscious, rational thought comparable to our own, they will also have commensurate subjective experiences of an aesthetic, moral, or religious nature. Thus it is not at all clear that Ruse (1994; Chapter 9, this volume) is justified in assuming that it is likely or even possible that a moral sense antithetical or hostile to a cooperative ethic could evolve in another part of the universe. In fact, Russell (1998) argues on biophysical grounds that intelligent beings should be expected to have cognate senses of moral reality, of the tension between this reality and the natural world, and even of personal moral failure. Just maybe, Tennyson really matters in the universe.

Who knows? My point is not to argue for a particular extraterrestrial personality profile but to argue against projecting a fractured portrait of human nature into outer space and then inventing aliens to beam it back to us as truth. This is precisely what Wilson does when he invites us to study humanity from the vantage point of alien beings and then concludes that only this perspective can bring about "the true humanization of altruism" (Wilson, 1978, p. 166).

The irony is that restricting study of human altruism (or any other behavior) to those notions accessible to an alien objectivity relinquishes the reservoir of important data on internal states available to us by firsthand experience and also dismisses the significance of cognition and personal agency in the same way extreme versions of behaviorism did. Indeed, once sentiment "has been laid aside," it is surely true that "no hint of genuine charity ameliorates our vision of society" (Ghiselin, 1974, p. 247). It could not be otherwise, for empathic sentiments are part of the perceptual apparatus with which we recognize care, and affective acumen is an indispensable component of our rational engagement with the world itself.

I should be careful to say that none of the preceding points argue against the truth of sweeping sociobiological imputations of selfishness. They only caution that such statements are not necessarily entailed by the scientific theory alone. Nor do they critique inclusive fitness and reciprocal altruism as wholly sufficient explanations of human social behavior. However, it turns out that there are widely accepted empirical grounds for seeking explanations of social behavior in terms more extensive than unelaborated "nepotism and favoritism." Human beings often manifest radically sacrificial, consequentially altruistic behavior that reduces reproductive success without compensatory reciprocation or kinship benefit. Behaviors such as voluntary poverty, celibate orders of benevolence, Holocaust rescuers, and religious asceticism or martyrdom are examples in humans that have provoked reconceptualization or substantial refinement of evolutionary approaches to human altruism. And even less extreme behaviors, such as adoption of non-kin, anonymous philanthropy, and costly investment in reproductively inert endeavors such as art (Diamond, 1992) or funeral caches (Campbell, 1991) have stimulated the extension or nuancing of initial sociobiological accounts.

Nonadaptive Approaches

One approach to explaining a variety of counterreproductive sacrificial behaviors in humans or nonhumans is to develop post hoc theories that acknowledge that the behaviors in question are maladaptive but that link them to an adaptive phenotype. For example, notions of genetic lag point out that because genetic change does not proceed as rapidly as environmental change, some genetically influenced behaviors that were adaptive in their originating environment are no longer reproductively beneficial. Although this is expected of all species, it is especially important in humans, because the rate of change in the cultural environment since the Pleistocene has been so dramatic, presumably unaccompanied by genetic change. Human adoption has been described as a vestigial behavior, formerly adaptive in establishing reciprocal alliances in tribal stages of cultural development (Diamond, 1992).

A similar but complementary concept is that of phenotypic plasticity, which posits not that we have unchanged (vestigial) behaviors that fail to keep up with environmental change but that environmental change induces change in behavioral phenotypes. Thus we can develop maladaptive traits that did not manifest in the environments in which our social behavior initially arose. Adoption has been described as a shift in behavioral phenotype induced by changes in culturally mediated attitudes toward the distress of childbirth. These first two approaches have been widely criticized as "just so stories" that entail the imaginative invention of prior adaptive scenarios without empirical demonstration (Gould & Lewontin, 1979). However, this does not make them false, only in need of further work. Moreover, post hoc scenario building is a standard way of dealing with ostensibly anomalous observations in science (Hull, 1978).

Yet a third explanation is manipulation. A common application of this concept is interspecific "adoption" in birds, which can be viewed as nest parasitism. By laying its eggs in nests of another species, the parasitic species manipulates the host species' parental care instincts. Human adoption has been viewed as manipulating the parental care instincts of adult non-kin by the neoteny, or juvenile "cuteness," of human infants (Alexander, 1987). Recall, however, that because biological altruism is a question not of motives but of consequences, "manipulation" does not make a behavior nonaltruistic. It just explains how natural selection could allow it to slip through. Moreover, because manipulated feelings may be entirely sincere, deceptively exploited sacrifice may also be entirely motivationally altruistic as well.

Finally, a somewhat more novel and nuanced approach entails pleiotropy, which involves a gene (or genes) causing incidental, interactive effects or multiple phenotypes. In such a case, a sacrificially counterreproductive behavior may be associated with or an incidental by-product of other phenotypes that are adaptive. For example, Ayala (1995) does not believe human morality is a biological adaptation put in place by natural selection at all but a pleiotropic consequence of reason and self-awareness, both of which are adaptations. Adoption can be viewed as being pleiotropically associated with genes for bonding with one's progeny. (In fact, nest parasitism can be viewed in the same way. It can also be viewed as genetic lag related to releasing mechanisms for parental care that evolved in an earlier, preparasitic environment. There is overlap in these approaches.) However, of all the aforementioned approaches, the pleiotropy hypothesis may have the most import for understanding human altruistic sacrifice. Recall that kin or "hard-core" altruism is least vigilant about requiring paybacks. Thus, several recent analyses have explored the role of pleiotropic modification of nurturance or familial bonding as a foundation for altruism (Boehm, 1999b; Eibl-Eibesfeldt, 1978, 1996).

Two things should be said about all of the preceding approaches. First, they are altruism affirming; that is, they acknowledge the existence of genuinely sacrificial behavior. How can this be, as it is a sociobiological maxim that "if natural selection is both sufficient and true, it is impossible for a genuinely disinterested or 'altruistic' behavior pattern to evolve" (Ghiselin, 1973, p. 967)? The truth of natural selection is not in dispute. But it turns out that natural selection is not sufficient to micromanagerially prevent all altruistic behavior from emerging. Because phenotypes are in long-term steady state rather than continual, instantaneous equilibrium with selection pressures, the snapshot of the world we get at any given time contains more altruism than we might have initially expected from the most stringent selectionist perspective.

However, the second point to note is that the preceding proposals all entail constraints on the stability and/or extent of such altruism. In cases of lag, plasticity, or manipulation, it is expected that selection will eliminate or modify the underlying genotypes. And with pleiotropy, the degree of sacrifice for non-kin cannot exceed the fitness benefits of parental nurture to one's own progeny, at least not without extinction. Moreover, the domain of sacrifice is unlikely to extend beyond those who in some way provoke familial nurturant responses (Boehm, 1999a; Rushton, 1989).

From the nonadaptive perspective, love may not be Creation's final law, but natural proscriptions against it have not eliminated its availability on the black market. How much illicit traffic in altruism actually exists? An unresolved, indeed—due in part to prevalent theoretical expectations—largely unaddressed, scientific question involves mapping the frequency and natural history of reproductive sacrifice. An interesting theological implication entails the possibility that love, although existentially crucial, is evolutionarily contingent and even marginal: "that which the builders rejected, has become the cornerstone." Like Synoptic accounts of the Nativity, it slips into the world through the back door so to speak, and, in both a Darwinian and a Bonhoefferian sense, may easily be squeezed out. To give altruism a more secure albeit narrower foothold on the scaffolding of organic life requires approaches that emphasize its adaptive function.

Adaptationist Approaches

Another approach to ostensible altruism, more affirming of selection's power to filter nonadaptive behavior and especially important when a behavior is a distinguishing and abiding characteristic, is to ask, "Is the behavior unusually likely to lead to reproduction via an unusual route?" (Alexander, 1979, p. 203). There has been a tremendous amount of innovative, nuanced, and fruitful work on human altruism from this perspective, especially in exploring implications of reciprocal altruism theory.

Self-Deception Theory

One of the most provocative and energetically explored approaches involves self-deception theory (Cronk, 1994; Lockard & Paulus, 1988; Trivers, 1991). A widely recognized problem in the origin and maintenance of reciprocal altruism is the existence of defectors or cheaters who receive but do not return cooperative benefits (Cosmides & Tooby, 1992; Sober, Chapter 1, Wilson & Sober, Chapter 11, this volume). One solution is to keep vigilant track of personal relationships and their exchange histories. But this constrains the benefits of cooperation to small group sizes in which relational history can be tracked; moreover, even in small groups there is a commitment barrier to first-time or very costly exchanges when one does not know the disposition of the other. Thus accessing the benefits of inclusion in a cooperative matrix can be facilitated by costly or hard-to-fake displays, which signal commitment to faithful reciprocation. Humans evidence a variety of nonverbal, largely autonomic signals of internal state (e.g., blushing, trembling, goose bumps, tearing). Though not particularly costly, they are hard for most to fake because of their involuntary character. In fact, several theories of the emergence of consciousness view it as a unique adaptation to reading the intentions of others, thereby equipping the bearer to detect cheaters and to flourish in a social environment based on reciprocity (Alexander, 1987, 1993; Trivers, 1991).

In such a social context, the very best way of not having cheating motives detected is to be self-deceived about one's own motives (Trivers, 1991) and thereby to avoid manifesting autonomic cues of deceitful intention. Self-deception theory explains professions of unconditional altruism—including and perhaps especially religious affirmations of the importance of giving without expectation of return—not as consciously hypocritical attempts to manipulate others by urging their submission to such maxims but as a sincere though self-deceived strategy for exploiting the cooperativity of others through displays of beneficence that is volitionally inert. Such sincere though inauthentic professions of good will we would normally call sentimentality, defined by Oscar Wilde as "the desire to enjoy the pleasure of an emotion, without the willingness to pay the price of it." It is precisely this sentimentalism, which Ghiselin may have had in mind and which, once seen through, deprives us of any illusion that altruism is present in society. Of course the question is whether all altruistic sentiment is sentiment*alistically* uncoupled from the genuine will to sacrifice.

There has been understandable and widespread objection to the cynical deconstruction of human altruism as a device to exploit others (de Waal, 1996; Midgley, 1979, 1980, 1982). However, there is abundant empirical evidence of human self-deception and self-bias (Barkow et al., 1992), and the theory is highly plausible in the context of what we understand about reciprocity in both humans and nonhumans. Moreover, both personal experience and the accumulated insights of wisdom and religious traditions confirm rather than dismiss our propensity to deceive ourselves, especially in matters of motivational goodness. The Hebrew prophetic tradition asserts, for example, that "the heart is deceitful and desperately wicked, who can know it" and "people draw near to me with their lips, but their hearts are far from me." In fact, one view of the intense criticism that self-deception theory has received is that it has met with the corporate rage frequently encountered by any prophetic challenge of culturally cherished illusions. I believe self-deception theory can be immensely helpful in stimulating true altruism by unmasking its pretentious counterfeits, by dereifying its widespread behavioral icons, and by reminding us not only that, but why, any altruistic profession or sentiment, no matter how sincerely or intensely felt, may be ingenuinely decoupled from commitment to sacrificial outcome.

There is, however, a significant difference between suggesting that any radically altruistic impulse or profession may be self-deceived and that all must be self-deceived. It is the latter claim, by virtue of both its nihilism and its aspirations to explanatory totipotency, that has rankled many, including evolutionary biologists and human behavioral scientists (de Waal, 1996; Kagan, 1998, Chapter 3, this volume; Sober & Wilson, 1998). De Waal laments, "How can these scientists make such claims? . . . A more cynical outlook is hard to come by" (De Waal, 1996, p. 17).

However, these issues do not need to be settled on the field of ideological battle, as the self-deception thesis is, at least in principle, empirically resolvable. By definition, self-deception entails profession of (sincerely believed) beneficent motivation, uncoupled from actual inclination to make a reproductively costly sacrifice. The question then becomes, In human society, do those who profess altruistic intentions evidence actual follow-through with behaviors that appear contrary to maximizing gain from "reciprocal" exchanges or ostensibly reduce fitness? The answer to both of these questions is widely agreed to be affirmative. The first class of behaviors has been addressed by approaches that are not based on strict reciprocity but that nevertheless are adaptationist in perspective.

Beyond Reciprocity

There are a couple of emotivist proposals that attempt to make adaptive sense of behaviors that do not conform to strict reciprocity or rational self-interest. Frank (1988) proposes that a suite of human emotions, contrary to the logic of self-interest, propels us to behaviors—and autonomic signals—that nevertheless can result in benefit to the actor in ways that are not straightforwardly apparent. For example, pursuing revenge at profound and mutually escalating personal cost, or even something as simple as tipping in an out-of-town restaurant at which there is no conceivable relational or reputational consequence, may each confer benefit to the actor even though neither is amenable to the calculus of rational self-interest.

In the first instance, knowing an individual will retaliate even if such retaliation will cost more than nonvengefully bearing the offense is a sort of reverse solution to the prisoner's dilemma. A rationally self-interested actor, assessing the implications of another's irrational commitment to costly retaliation, would view the consequences of betrayal as too great. Thus ostensibly counterreproductive emotions of extreme malice (formally defined in social ecology as injuring the fitness of another at the cost of greater injury to self) can serve as a deterrent to betrayal that may be fitness enhancing if averaged across the life history of many individuals. (This is, in fact, the nuclear "logic" of MAD, or mutually assured destruction. The problem is, such strategies manage the mean but not the range of outcomes: They usually tend to work only because the possibility that they will not work is real and therefore effectively deterrent.)

On the positive side, Frank argues via the second example that commitment to or participation in unreciprocated acts of benevolence—even in a setting in which indirect reciprocity cannot be furthered through reputational enhancement—can benefit the individual by cultivating autonomic signals of a reciprocating character. Unlike the self-deception thesis, such cues are rooted in personal authenticity. Like the self-deception thesis, however, the ultimate impact of such behaviors must, on average, be reproductively enhancing.

Finally, in an approach that is both innovative and elegant, Tooby and Cosmides (1996) propose a role for friendship in the evolution of adaptations designed to "deliver benefits to others" in ways that do not conform to strict reciprocity. They note that human friendships appear to reflect a logic contrary to tit-for-tat or reciprocal exchange and, "indeed, explicit linkage between favors or insistence by a recipient that she be allowed to immediately repay are generally taken as a lack of friendship" (1996, p. 130). Of course, self-deception, or even intentional other deception, is one way of explaining this, in which case magnanimous professions are viewed as manipulative social posturing. However, this misses both the essence of our interior experience of friendship and its unique significance as an effective adaptation to the "banker's paradox"—the dilemma that when we most need an extension of aid, we are least able to convey to others the likelihood that we will be able to repay. The crucial importance of cooperative assistance to human beings, across a long and often variable life history, make a potential solution to the banker's paradox highly beneficial. This is the proposed role of friendship, and the deeper the friendship, the greater willingness there is to deliver benefits that are highly costly to the benefactor and/or not immediately (or conceivably ever) repayable by the recipient.

However, although strict reciprocation is unnecessary and indeed contrary to friendship alliances, for friendship to be genuine and adaptive, commitment must be mutual. This generates the need to detect cheaters or "fair weather friends" who profess friendship when your reciprocation ability is high and defect when it is low. Because tit-for-tat relational history is precisely *not* how friends detect genuineness, Tooby and Cosmides suggest that we have developed a variety of means for both cultivating and detecting "deep engagement." Deep engagement entails occupying an irreplaceable role in the life of another, by virtue of our unique individuality. In a manner similar to romantic love, such deep engagement generates trust, overcoming commitment barriers erected by the threat of being cheated. As Tooby and Cosmides write:

> The dynamics of this kind of world are considerably different from what the cooperator-defector models, in isolation, suggest. . . . Losing a valued friend, being able to spend less time with the friend, becoming less valued by that friend, or at the extreme, social isolation, may be more costly than being cheated. . . . Instead of being cheated, the primary risk is experiencing a world increasingly devoid of deeply engaged social partners, or sufficiently beneficial social partners, or both. (1996, p. 22)

There are three highly significant implications of this proposal for an evolutionary understanding of altruism. First, unlike egoistic caricatures of theories in evolutionary psychology, this proposal affirms both the existence and the importance of genuine other-regard linked with costly investment in individuals who are not necessarily kin and who are not expected to keep closely balanced accounts of reciprocal exchange. Second, it is an adaptationist account, and both the behaviors and the underlying psychology of friendship are expected to be evolutionarily sustainable. Our desire to be liked and needed, the selection criteria for choosing friends from among competing possibilities, our means of monitoring friendships, and, most important, the fact that friendships are by definition exclusive alliances all reflect the ultimate self-interests (though not necessarily conscious selfishness) of the individual. Third, the notion of "deep engagement" represents a move toward internalizing the calculus of social adaptation: Relational connection is not just a means toward acquisition of external resources (though it is that) but is also itself a significant interior need. In fact, the solution to the banker's paradox entails another paradox: Friendship may be most reproductively beneficial precisely to the extent that it is pursued in a way that is insensitive to the computation of benefit. This may be why friendship has appeared to many classical and contemporary commentators as the most transcendent or ostensibly "least biological of human loves" (Lewis, 1960). (For an account that argues for a more direct biological cause and consequence of friendship altruism, see Rushton, 1989, who suggests that choices of close friends reflect genetic similarity and may be driven by kin selection.)

The adaptive role of deep engagement generates a potentially vexing trade-off in human psychological architecture, though. On the one hand, we have the adaptively necessary desire to avoid distress or—to use the metaphor of banker's paradox—situations in which we desperately need a loan. On the other hand, such situations constitute events that clarify the engagement of others in our lives and their commitment to our well-being. The stability of some modern cultural environments may therefore leave "people in genuine and uncharacteristically protracted doubt . . . whether anyone is deeply engaged in their welfare . . . an individual may have apparently warm social contacts, and yet feel lonely, uneasy, and hungry for the confident sensation of deep social connectedness" (Tooby & Cosmides, 1996, p. 18). This particular evolutionary perspective on human nature posits a legacy of ambivalence between individual autonomy and deep social embeddedness. Of course this observation is not novel, being frequently emphasized in sociological reflections on modernity (Bellah, Madsen, Sullivan, & Tipton, 1996; Durkheim, 1997; Putnam, 2000). What is significant, though, is making the point in the context of an evolutionary argument and, as I mentioned, viewing altruistic relationships not just as means of orchestrating external exchanges but as an internal need.

Although the preceding proposals differ significantly in their views of the genuineness of altruistic intention and the degrees of sacrificial behavior, they all have in common the conviction that the domain of altruism must be limited to those behaviors that ultimately have reproductive advantage at the individual level. In part because there are so very many behaviors in humans (and perhaps only in humans) that appear to be fitness attenuating if not annihilating, alternative theories have recently emerged that explore other forms or levels of selection more hospitable to the emergence of sacrificial behaviors.

Hierarchy Theory

Structural Hierarchy

A long-standing debate in evolutionary theory, distinct from though related to the altruism issue, concerns the levels at which selection operates (Sober & Wilson, 1998; Wilson & Sober, Chapter 11, this volume). There have been two fronts to this debate, both of which have significant implications for altruism. Evolution is a two-step process, involving the replication and selective transmission of information. The information that gets replicated is contained in genes, or "replicators." The differential selection of information occurs through environmental filtering of the structural assemblages that carry genes into the next generation, or "vehicles." The two debated aspects of hierarchy theory can be thought of as relating to these two steps.

Structural hierarchy theory posits that the vehicles that carry genes can be environmentally filtered at varying levels of structural organization—gene, genome, population, and so forth. Although selection at group or population levels was thought at one time to require differential extinction (just as it entails differential reproduction at the individual level), Sober and Wilson (1998) have argued that it is not group extinction per se that drives group selection but situations in which between-group fitness advantage more than compensates for within-group fitness disadvantage of a trait. In this way, viewing kin groups and reciprocal matrices as groups, both kin selection and reciprocal altruism can be seen as special cases of group selection. Indeed, the friendship proposal of Tooby and Cosmides (1996) is another such example.

The significance of the group selection hypothesis for altruism is that behaviors do not have to be strictly reciprocal and can in fact incur a fitness penalty relative to other group members, so long as the contribution to group function facilitates a compensatory increase in fitness relative to other groups. In principle, this logic works for any group of reproducing organisms, but more recently there have been elaborations of how human social structure can increase the likelihood of group selection.

Wilson and Sober (Chapter 11, this volume) argue that social controls, at one time thought to inhibit the evolution of voluntary altruism, can actually promote it. Boehm (1999a,b) pursues a similar vein of argument and suggests that a crucial step in the evolution of human altruism though group selection was the development of egalitarian social structure. Boehm argues that egalitarianism represented a fitness-enhancing rejection of status hierarchies by low-status individuals in the Paleolithic, which both gave rise to and was facilitated by the unique development of human moral communities. Once in place, egalitarian moral expectations attenuated phenotypic, though not necessarily genotypic, variance in cooperation and reduced the rewards of dominance. Recall that selection works on the phenotype or vehicle, not the gene, so with the reduction of in-group phenotypic variability, there is less within-group selection. Between-group fitness differentials became selectively important. Such socially facilitated group selection could even generate a causal cascade, with increased cooperativeness enabling group warfare rather than individual conflict and warfare itself increasing intergroup selection. Ultimately, this unique environment may have selected for the internalization of egalitarian impulses and desires. Boehm maintains as follows: "The capacity for genuine altruism in mammals has been denied on a widespread, often vehement basis. Eminent sociobiologists and evolutionary psychologists have taken the lead in so doing, but I suggest that our species (and our species alone) was given a unique chance to develop altruistic traits—precisely because social dominance hierarchies were definitively reversed for a long period of evolutionary time" (1999a, p. 12).

Therefore, multilevel selection (MLS) theory harbors three important implications for views of human altruism. First, it gives an account of the emergence of behaviors that are both motivationally unselfish and consequentially sacrificial, directed beyond kin and even beyond limited friendship alliances (although the latter may be seen as an instance of MLS). Second, those versions of MLS which posit that unique developments in the human social environment promoted selection of altruistic, genetic adaptations to that newly emerging environment leave us with ambivalent genetic heritages reflecting legacies of both social dominance and egalitarianism. This makes for "our well-known individual selfishness and nepotism, but also for a long-denied altruistic component that is strongly reflected in moral codes and helps to shape social life" (Boehm, 1999a, p. 15). Such theories do not represent a rejection of sociobiological theory but an addition to it. And like the theory of deep engagement (Tooby & Cosmides, 1996), they leave us, though for different reasons, with a culturally induced ambiguity in human nature.

Third, as with all the foregoing proposals, the cooperative domain is strongly constrained to group membership. In fact, it is out-group competition and exclusion that is the driving force behind the origin of altruism through MLS. This leaves us with the very significant challenge of explaining—or even accepting the existence of—radically altruistic behaviors that are either directed at out-group members or that sacrifice so much on behalf of group members that the within-group fitness reduction overrides between-group benefit. It is in part this problem that has generated the next form of hierarchy theory.

Functional Hierarchy

In its most straightforward version, multilevel selection involves a structural hierarchy of vehicles (analogous to soldier, squad, platoon) that carry the replicators or information. But at all levels of selection, the unit of information that is selectively transmitted (or differentially reproduced) is held to be the gene. Thus, in its simplest form, the structural hierarchy of MLS posits genes as the only unit of information that is replicated, selectively transmitted, and translated into traits. In contrast, with functional hierarchy, we have a proposal for a different kind of replicator or "higher level" unit of information altogether. It is not just the structural arrangement of vehicles but the functional relationship of replicators that is hierarchical: Rather than graded levels of organization, as in the distinction between soldier, squad, and platoon, there are nested levels of control, as in the distinction between private, sergeant, and lieutenant. The higher level replicators in such hierarchical proposals are taken to be culturally transmitted units of information, widely referred to as memes (Blackmore, 1999; Dawkins, 1976; Durham, 1991).

In positing functional hierarchy, theories of coevolution or gene-culture evolution are highly significant for two reasons. First, they are anthropologically (though not necessarily metaphysically) nonmaterialist: They propose that nongenetic, "ideational" units of information evolve over time and influence human behavior within time. Of course even nonhierarchical notions of evolution recognize that the environment, including the cultural environment, influences phenotypes. But the difference here is that culture is viewed not merely as influencing the developmental expression or as filtering the reproductive transmission of genes, as does the physical environment. The human cultural environment is held to entail its own replicators which both evolve and inform behavior. Thus humans, and, it is argued, only humans, have two modes of inherited information and two control inputs to behavior—one material, one ideational.

The second significant feature of this approach entails the relationship between the two modes of inheritance. Dual inheritance does not mean dualistically uncoupled, for the hierarchical or nested relationship of genetic and cultural information entails that the former confers capacities for the latter to emerge. However, and this is very significant, even in a specified physical environment, cultural information is not reducible to genetic information; otherwise it would not represent another level of control. Moreover, most current articulations suggest that cultural information is not even wholly constrained by genetic information.

Thus ideas or memes can emerge that influence behavior in ways that actually oppose the influence or reproductive interests of genes (Blackmore, 1999; Dawkins, 1976; Durham, 1991; Plotkin, 1993, 1997). This has obvious implications for altruism. In fact, it is the rather widespread existence of clearly counter-reproductive behaviors such as celibacy and martyrdom that generated the conclusion that "the only explanation is that culture entails causal mechanisms that are somehow decoupled, not necessarily completely, but some partial decoupling is necessary, from the causal mechanisms of our biological evolution. It certainly cannot be that culture is tightly held on some biological 'leash'" (Plotkin, 1997, p. 231). Interestingly, invoking the common extraterrestrial rhetoric (though this time to affirm rather than deny altruism), Plotkin argues that a variety of counterreproductive cultural innovations "would be final proof to an alien intelligence, that culture has this power over our biology."

Structural and functional evolutionary hierarchies are not mutually exclusive, and there is currently a wide variety of coevolutionary proposals for relating them. Although no simple taxonomy could do justice to their breadth, I want to comment on two dimensions of variability. First, there is a continuum of views on the degree to which memes are uncoupled from genes. Although no dual inheritance model suggests that cultural variability maps to genetic variability, some assert that the range of variability is constrained by a genetic leash (Lumsden & Wilson, 1983; E. O. Wilson, 1978). Others allow for greater plasticity while still understanding the central tendency of cultural behavior to be strongly influenced by the reproductive agenda of the genes (Cronk, 1999; Dugatin, 1999). In such cases a major means of memetic transmission may be their replication by enhancing genetic reproduction (the middle case described by Wilson & Sober, Chapter 11, this volume). Finally, memetic selection may occur largely independently of genetic selection, though interacting with it in a variety of ways that include opposition, either rarely (Durham, 1991; Plotkin, 1997) or more commonly (Blackmore, 1999).

The second area of very significant variability in coevolutionary theory entails the employment of reductionism as a primary interpretive perspective. It may seem contradictory to call a "hierarchical" proposal reductionistic. But some dual-inheritance proposals—notably the memetic models that have come from sociobiologists—are in fact teleologically reductionistic in the very same way in which gene-centric sociobiology is. Both perspectives see the ultimate telos or driving force of life in terms of the agenda of replicators, whether genetic or memetic. The vehicles—in the case of genes, organisms; in the case of memes, minds—are passive conduits of the replicators' quest for transmission. A mind is simply a meme's way of reproducing itself.

An upshot of memetic teleological reductionism is that it not only partially uncouples the evolution of genetic and cultural information (as do all dual-inheritance proposals) but it also subsumes the personal agenda of the individual mind to the reproductive interests of the meme. Thus individuals can do all sorts of things that serve a meme's reproductive agenda but that are neither genetically nor rationally self-interested. Ironically, this makes room for altruism. Like a pathogenic virus, memes can be infectiously transmitted to our mind. Referring to the radical relinquishment of what he calls ascetic altruism, Lopreato (1984, p. 234) argues thus: "Some conceptions of a cultural nature at times thwart the self-serving thrust of the gene. The soul, principal among them, may be thought of as the kernel of an internalized morality, reinforced by the will of fictitious forces, whereby some humans are in varying degrees led to subordinate their genetic fitness (and their self-interest in general) to the fitness and interests of others, even strangers who are in no position to reciprocate. Thus, the concept of the soul has to some extent modified the genetic action of natural selection."

Of course, the preceding statement entails a metaphysical position that assumes that souls, moral realism, and attendant "forces" are fictions. Without this metaphysical commitment, the preceding could easily have been written by a representative of any number of religious traditions believing that knowledge of God or the eternal is personally transformative. (And if one viewed the ultimate end of human existence in terms of self-giving love rather than fitness maximization, then a more apt metaphor for altruistic memes might be beneficial symbionts than pathogenic contagions.) However, what is significant to human altruism in the preceding statement is not so much the metaphysics but the anthropology. Here, and in other memetic approaches that have emerged out of sociobiology, the picture given of human biological nature is that it is intrinsically selfish and that somehow moral goodness entails an externally imposed call to "resist the tyranny of the selfish replicators" (Dawkins, 1976). Ignoring for a moment the logical problem entailed by the fact that the memes that supposedly help us resist such tyranny are themselves selfish replicators, there has been intense controversy over both the biological and ethical implications of such dualism. First, it is not clear how biology gives rise to something that resists or contravenes biology. Gunter Stent calls it a "biological absurdity" (1980, p. 12).

Second, such views not only imply an almost Cartesian meme-gene duality but are also virtually Gnostic in their location of altruism in an extramaterial domain—reminiscent of Huxley's assertion that morality lay not in imitating but in "combatting the cosmic process" (Huxley, 1894/1989). Critics argue that such views depict altruism (and goodness in general) as a "colonial imposition on human nature rather than a fulfillment of it" (Midgley, 1980). Indeed, in order to explain behaviors that appear biologically anomalous, they invoke nonmaterial entities held to be ontologically real, which have not been operationally defined, have no measurable mass or energy, enter and use human minds for their own agendas, and cause people to do things that may be contrary to biological or personal well-being. This description of the emerging discipline of memetics could apply equally well to the elaborate sixteenth-century discipline of demonology. Franz de Waal chides, "By thus locating morality outside nature, these scientists

have absolved themselves from trying to fit it into their evolutionary perspective.
. . . It must be rather unsatisfactory, to say the least, for gene-centric sociobiologists
to be obliged to exclude one domain from their Theory of Everything. And not a
trivial domain, but precisely the one many of us consider to be at the core of being
human" (1996, pp. 16–17).

Not all coevolutionary accounts, however, are thus dualistic or reductionistic.
Many entail nuanced but highly contrasting proposals for the nature of interactions between genetic information, cultural information, human organismal biology, cognitive function, and personal agency. For example, Cronk strongly advocates the need to go beyond memetics, maintaining that it "treats people as more
or less passive transmitters of culture, paying little more attention to it than they
pay to the burrs that stick to their socks" (1999, p. 91). He develops a proposal that
takes both cultural meanings and human intentionalities seriously. Yet it is very
much sociobiological in its emphasis on manipulating the terms of reciprocity for
the sake of personal advantage. In his view, it is not memes that use people but
people who use memes for their own ends. In fact, he argues that memes are not
so much like common viruses but "biological warfare viruses in that they are designed and used by people in their efforts to manipulate one another" (1999,
p. xii). Thus, although not memetically reductive, Cronk's coevolutionary account
does depict culture and human agency as quite tied to the biology of self-interest.

From the perspective of evolutionary psychology, Plotkin (1998) argues that
culture is a human adaptation to the "uncertain futures problem." As was mentioned earlier, genotypic adaptation cannot always keep up with environmental
change, resulting in genetic lag. Humans have the ability, through cultural evolution, to develop adaptations and transmit information more rapidly than could be
done with genetic replicators alone. In order to change independently of genetic
information, cultural information has to be irreducible to and at least partially uncoupled from genetic information. This means that through cultural evolution we
can not only change at a greater rate than we can through genetic evolution but
also that we can change in ways that may be contrary to genetic self-interest.

There is the possibly of good news and bad news here. The good news is that
behavioral plasticity may be amenable to learning genuinely sacrificial other-
regard. And the ability of humans to envision and expend themselves for that
which is viewed as more important than their own self-interest constitutes a potential solution to the tragedy of the commons. The bad news is that our ability to
generate cultural innovations independent of biological necessity opens the possibility of devising destructive practices—from cigarettes to greenhouse gases—
that amplify perturbation of the social or environmental commons. Such developments are not wholly unchecked, because cultural innovation is understood as
an adaptive heuristic that entails not just the tautology of successful memetic
transmission but both nested relationship to genomic information and corre-
spondent fit between memetic information and biologically relevant environmental patterns. (Durham, 1991, makes a similar observation.) This more nuanced
picture of hierarchical evolution takes human social and cognitive processes seriously and does not make the simplistic mistake of locating altruistic goodness
outside and selfishness within human biology. Our biology is viewed as contain-

ing both self-serving and other-regarding tendencies (Boehm, 1999a,b; de Waal, 1996; Dugatin, 1999). Culturally transmitted information may confirm, extend, or oppose biological defaults.

Integrative Approaches

The proposed explanatory pathways for altruism in all of the aforementioned categories tend to segregate along two axes. The first axis entails variation in how much "unselfishness" we can get out of human biology, that is, how tied to strict reciprocity the biological pole of behavior is. Traditional sociobiological and emerging self-deception models emphasize maximizing the exchange ratio in social interactions. Friendship and costly display approaches relinquish rational self-interest in lieu of deferred and/or indirect benefits, which accrue from deep engagement or reputation. But the net impact on resource exchange must be positive. Group selection may entail an actual sacrifice of resources (and fitness) relative to other group members. But the behavior is tightly constrained to group members; furthermore, it is limited to situations in which the benefit to the group in the face of between-group competition generates intergroup fitness enhancement that more than compensates for intragroup fitness reduction to the altruist. Finally, nonadaptationist approaches allow for genuinely counterreproductive behavior. But it is tentative and metastable.

The second axis regards the nature and significance of extrabiological or ideational modes of inheritance. As already mentioned, there is a continuum of proposals about how tightly embedded cultural evolution is in the biological matrix—from constrained on a leash to virtually disconnected. Although theories that acknowledge a greater degree of uncoupling allow more readily for radical or counterreproductive altruism, it is an altruism that would seem to have an ambivalent foothold in human natural desire.

I would like to suggest that these tensions or axes of disagreement do not merely reflect conflicting ideological allegiances or altogether differing scientific judgment (though both of these factors enter in) but that they represent fundamental ambiguities in the human experience itself. Similarly, Boehm observes, "the divergent scholarly views themselves reflect innately structured psychological ambivalences harbored by each of us . . . our own contradictory nature causes us to draw caricatures" (1999a, p. 228). As we shall see, these same tensions animate the history of theological reflection on altruism as well.

Such highly contrasting accounts may not be mutually exclusive, and polar ambiguity in human experience provokes rather than relieves us of the need to seek coherent, if not integrated, understanding of human nature. Ironically, one thing that is characteristic of almost all of the preceding proposals is that analysis is undertaken at levels nonintegral, or external, to human organismal functioning. In all of the sociobiological and derivative approaches, from reciprocal altruism to self-deception to emotional signaling and friendship proposals, the emphasis is on the ratio of goods and services received and given. It is assumed that individual behavior is pitched toward optimizing the symmetry of exchange, and, moreover, that this will translate into fitness. Multilevel selection models broaden the domain of analysis and make it possible for someone to be genuinely sacrificial, that is, to have a lower giving-receiving ratio than others in the group. But the analysis still focuses on cooperative symmetries. Of course, this is not true of memetic theory, but here there is another externality introduced, that of the abiological meme.

What we have not yet done is look at the internal costs and benefits of cooperating and not cooperating. If, in fact, humans are highly adapted to an intensively cooperative social environment, it may be that we have internalized benefits for cooperative engagement and detriments for defection or isolation. We already know this to be true of other relational dynamics. The need not only for maternal provisioning and nurturance but also for emotional intimacy is so internalized that deprivation results in irreversible cognitive dysfunction and even death. Social rejection is correlated with morbidity, and animal studies indicate a hormonally mediated causal connection (Ray & Sapolsky, 1992; Sapolsky & Ray, 1989; Virgin & Sapolsky, 1997). A variety of studies indicate that involvement in supportive personal relationships is negatively correlated with morbidity and mortality (see Kohn, 1990; Lewis, Amini, & Lannon, 2000). It is worth asking whether not only relational engagement but also the generous and other-regarding dispositions that facilitate them have internal physiological rewards, just as Kagan (1998, Chapter 3, this volume) maintains that it is pursuit of the internal psychological reward of goodness that distinguishes humans.

Such internal psychophysiological rewards, if they exist, could attenuate the necessity of maximizing the giving-receiving ratio in interpersonal exchange. Indeed, economic and ecophysiological models acknowledge that it is not just the input of resources but the efficiency of internal processing that determines profitability (Townsend & Calow, 1981). Fox-Keller (1991), Fox-Keller and Ewing (1993), and Schloss (1996) have suggested that more cooperative dispositions might entail lower internal costs or more efficient processing of resources.

There are several conceivable routes to such a situation, a number of which are consistent with several of the preceding theories. First, both Boehm (1999a,b) and Wilson and Sober (Chapter 11, this volume) posit the development of egalitarian social controls that influence the selectional environment. Internalization of initially external social standards could benefit the individual both by signaling group commitment or reliable character (a la Frank, 1988) and by streamlining the computation and attendant costs of investment decisions (Ruse, 1995). (Indeed, Holocaust rescuers frequently say they never did risk assessment or even ethical analysis and that there was no decision to make; Monroe, 1996.) Second, the pleiotropy hypothesis would entail conferring the sense of emotional well-being usually associated with familial nurturance to altruistic affiliation with non-kin. Because positive emotions not only reflect but also influence physiological well-being, what has been viewed as pleiotropic load or disbenefit could entail an evolutionarily stable, pleiotropic benefit. Third, Tooby and Cosmides (1996) are quite explicit about suggesting the existence and adaptive significance of an intensively felt need for deep engagement, the unfulfillment of which could be more detrimental than being unreciprocated. Although the ultimate origin of such a need may reflect the long-term probability of receiving external assistance, the proximal consequences of fulfilling or not fulfilling affiliative needs—that is, achieving relationship set-points—are internal and potentially fitness affecting.

Regardless of route, the possibility of internalized benefits from other-regard suggests a revision of the payoff structure in the prisoners' dilemma. Sober (Chapter 1, this volume) already makes the point that banished from formulations of the dilemma is the notion of utility—that is, how payoff computation should reflect the differing assessment values of rationally self-interested and benevolent actors. He suggests that caring about the other person can make his or her consequence as significant as your own. This changes the calculus of benefit and alters the outcome. (Imagine being in a prisoners' dilemma when the person in the other cell is a close friend or even a revered stranger.) I suggest, however, that the unit costs and benefits themselves may not be constant for cooperators and defectors. That is, 6 months in jail may be intrinsically less injurious for a cooperator and more injurious for a defector. This could be because a cooperative disposition facilitates social support or resource exchange that eases the trauma or, as I suggest here, it may entail relational engagement or purely internal states conducive to resilience. In fact, it is somewhat ironic that the issue of self-interest has been linked to the "prisoner's" dilemma, when many actual prisoners in the most horrific conditions testify to the paradox that personal survival can be aided by caring about more than personal survival. As Bruno Bettelheim notes:

> The prisoner, cramped into an unimaginably small space, could not so much as lie down without taking away the space of the prisoners who lay next to him; still they managed. Although they were starving, they did not fight each other for the slice of bread they so desperately needed; some even shared it . . . the true message of the concentration camp: . . . even under such conditions, or particularly under such conditions, one can discover a life of harmony. . . . Those who see survival as a mere staying alive wash their hands of the true survivor . . . [who] cannot help objecting—not to their being forgotten, not to the world's going on as usual, but to their being used to bear witness to the opposite of the truth. (Bettelheim, 1979, pp. 312–313)

Finally, I point out two things about the aforementioned internalist approaches. First, because they rightly expand the notion of organismal advantage beyond the maximization of resource acquisition to include benefits of internal efficiency or resilience, they provide a biological substrate for other-regard that is genuinely uncoupled from direct or even indirect reciprocity. In some natural, nontranscendent sense, it really may be "better to give than to receive."

Second, the calculus of biological benefit—internal or external—remains tied to fitness. Thus, although the preceding scenarios represent possible routes to nonreciprocal altruism, they do not yield reproductive altruism. In fact, there are no proposals for the evolution of biological dispositions to radical altruism or reproductive sacrifice. This is not so much an issue of theoretical incompleteness (as suggested by Holcomb, 1993) as of logical incompatibility: Differential reproduction of genotypes is not the mechanism to turn to for explaining the origin and maintenance of reproductively subversive phenotypes. In the last analysis, either we deny the existence or importance of the human propensity toward counterreproductive behavior or we invoke accounts of its origin that posit some measure of uncoupling from genomic evolution and concomitant transcendence of biological constraints. Integrative accounts do not relieve the need to attribute memes or beliefs or other ideational replicators with such counterreproductive potency. What they do accomplish is to avoid the dualistic incommensurability of some memetic approaches by suggesting why our cognitive and affective architecture may be conducive to memetic notions of nonreciprocity. Moreover, genes and memes may reinforce one another by the process of memetic drive (Blackmore, 1999; Durham, 1992), which entails the evolution of biological capacities to exploit niches created by cultural memes. Just as enlargement of the forebrain both facilitated and was facilitated by language development, so altruistic dispositions may have both given rise to and been extended by cultural values of altruism (Boehm, 1999a,b; Wilson & Sober, Chapter 11, this volume).

In this view, Midgley's criticism that altruism is viewed as a "colonial imposition on human nature rather than a fulfillment of it" is answered on two counts. First, culture is not imperialistically abiological: Altruism is not an alien colonizer of human biology but an extension of it. Second, human nature is not a static entity to fill up but a dynamic relationship between genes and labile culture. As suggested by the expanding domain of social cooperativeness across human history, which came to advocate "enemy love" in the relatively recent cosmopolitan religions, altruism may be less a fulfillment of fixed human nature than a progressive realization of it. Pascal's pensee is especially prescient: "I am afraid that nature is but a second culture, as culture is a second nature" (Pascal, 1958).

Theological Dialogue

Several of the theologians contributing to this volume distinguish two significant traditions in Christian thought (also common in other religions) about love. First, the agapeist or dialectical perspective (Pope, Chapter 10, this volume) views totally self-disinterested love as the chief moral obligation of human beings. This entails both the intensiveness of caring for others at great personal cost and the extensiveness of caring for those who are remote and even for those who are opposed to one's well-being. Extreme forms of this ethic give no preference to the natural embeddedness of personal relationship and in fact may claim that the natural loves are "carnal" or ultimately selfish.

There are, however, a wide variety of Christian traditions that embrace less extreme versions of the agape ethic, while still holding the central tenet that agape is the highest love and is not an extension of but a supernatural addition to or enhancement of natural loves. Some holiness traditions emphasize a second work of grace or "entire sanctification" as the portal to attaining wholly self-disinterested love of God and others. More modest versions simply emphasize a literal interpretation of the Sermon on the Mount as a prescription for right living, entailing the call to move beyond reciprocity to love of enemy. Those interpretations of the Calvinist principle of total depravity that have a low view of common grace understand natural loves as unregenerate and devoid of goodness in themselves. Of course, even moderate versions of the Anabaptist tradition have long-standing commitments to enemy love and affirm a crucial, even definitive, moral obligation in such practices as pacifism, eshewal of pursuing self-interest in courts or voting, and so forth. And across history a variety of Catholic monastic orders of benevolence have embraced poverty, celibacy, and charity as the path of discipleship. Augustine himself had a low view of relational attachment.

I do not say this to make an *ad populum* case for the agapeist view so much as to point out that it is not rare or aberrational but widely represented throughout history and culture. It seems to me that its existence represents, in the hermeneutic context of various times and cultures, the polar tensions in human nature that current scientific controversies also reflect. Although it is often claimed that the view of human nature it advocates is abiological and incommensurable with that of evolutionary theory (Pope, Chapter 10, this volume; Ruse, 1994), actually it is quite consistent with those versions of evolutionary theory that emphasize human selfishness. Many believe that human beings are by nature exactly what is entailed in the basest sociobiological portrayals but that humans can be supernaturally transformed through divine grace. The scientific contradiction such a view entails is not that it is inconsistent with evolutionary views of human nature but that it is incompatible with metaphysical naturalism, which suggests that there is nothing beyond human nature. Ironically, however, even the notion that naturally selfish affections must be opposed or transcended by extrabiological means is analogous to some versions of gene-centric sociobiology, which invoke memes to "resist the tyranny" of our native selfishness. The saga of intrinsic selfishness—extrinsic goodness is an ancient story. A benefit of this narrative is that it affirms high ideals while not glibly minimizing our inherent obstacles to pursuing them. A serious problem of memetic, but especially dialectical, theology is that it vilifies natural desire and leaves us with the quandary of how to fulfill longings for intimate, mutual, personal relationships while calling us to mortify or transcend them.

On the other hand, the "ordering of loves" tradition conceives of the biological affinities and affections of human beings as good gifts from God. Like all gifts, especially living ones, they must be tended, disciplined, and cared for. But the view of humanity here is that we are capable of both great selfishness and great other-regard. Fulfillment comes from cultivating the latter. Radically self-relinquishing love is not taken to be necessarily a higher moral obligation than giving or receiving care for near and dear. In fact, if radical altruism involves neglecting or betraying the trust and obligations of personal relationships, it may be immoral. Thus, "enemy love" is affirmed as consonant with and a gracious extension of the natural loves, rightly overseen and ordered. This tradition is congruent with those evolutionary accounts that attribute a greater native benevolence to human biological nature, though recognizing that we have conflicting impulses. And its emphasis on grace extended through the good gifts of nature is perhaps more consistent with those understandings that reject radical uncoupling between biological and cultural evolution (de Waal, 1996). It certainly is more amenable to a naturalistic worldview. In affirming both the goodness and extendibility of natural affections, it provides a picture of altruism as fulfilling our deepest desires. A problem, however, is that in making altruism more biological, it dismisses rather than engages the nexus of evolutionary thought on radical sacrifice. Diversity notwithstanding, virtually all evolutionary accounts view biological affinities as in-group delimited and resistant to extension outside group boundaries. Hoe the garden of evolved affections free of toxic weeds, and enemy love still does not spring up exuberantly.

Finally, there is a third or median tradition, not always specified (perhaps because both "sides" own it), that somewhat integrates the preceding two. In this view, the natural loves are good gifts from God, in that they both enrich life and contain hints of a love beyond themselves. They are in no way intrinsically selfish, though they are prone to selfish distortion and, as is all human sentiment, are intrinsically feeble. Therefore, they call us beyond themselves both by virtue of their goodness and by virtue of their need to be sustained by resources greater than the native affections they entail (Lewis, 1960). Anyone who has spouse, friends, or children knows that "love your enemy" can—and in a virtuous, committed relationship must—apply to the near and dear. Therefore, this third tradition recognizes that self-sacrificial altruism is not something that is extended only to the remote or extended to all without preference. Though it is a unique kind of other-regard, perhaps not at all an extrapolation of the nurturing or empathic affections, yet it is quite legitimately extended by personal preference, first to those who are nearest by nurture. In that way it both fulfills and enriches—maybe even rescues—our native longings for intimate and mutually other-regarding relationships. But it is not restricted to them, nor is it sustained by either intimacy or mutuality (though it may hope for each).

A scandalous claim of the New Testament is, "We comfort others with the comfort we receive from God." This middle position views the desire to extend agape—to friends or enemies or both in the same person—as not so much opposing or transcending but transforming natural affections through the cognitive and affective reorganization that attends a conviction and experience of God's love. Whether the experience of comfort "from God" entails a memetic self-deception, a divine grace made available through natural processes, or an actual encounter with transcendent presence is not something open to empirical investigation.

In the meantime, there are aspects of these issues about which we currently know very little and which are open to research. Important and largely unexamined questions involve (1) the psychological and neurological relationships between altruism and various forms of nurture and bonding, (2) the relationship of religious experience and conviction to altruism, and (3) the relationship of altruistic behavior and attitude to manifold aspects of physiological and psychological well-being. Given both the crucial importance and complexity of these issues, I suspect there will continue to be charged ambiguity and explanatory tensions in their study. In the context of our own present uncertainties, it would be good to extend a bit of altruism itself to those at countervailing ends of its explanatory axes.

REFERENCES

Alexander, R. D. (1987). *The biology of moral systems.* Chicago: Aldine de Gruyter.

Alexander, R. D. (1993). Biological considerations in the analysis of morality. In M. H. Nitecki & D. V. Nitecki (Eds.), *Evolutionary ethics* (pp. 163–196). Albany: State University of New York Press.

Ayala, F. J. (1995). The difference of being human: Ethical behavior as an evolutionary byproduct. In H. Rolston III (Ed.), *Biology, ethics, and the origins of life* (pp. 113–136). Boston: Jones & Bartlett.

Barash, D. P. (1977). *Sociobiology and behavior.* New York: Elsevier.

Barkow, J., Cosmides, L., & Tooby, J. (Eds.). (1992). *The adapted mind: Evolutionary psychology and the generation of culture.* New York: Oxford University Press.

Bellah, R., Madsen, R., Sullivan, W., & Tipton, S. (Eds.). (1996). *Habits of the heart: Individualism and commitment in American life.* Berkeley: University of California Press.

Bettelheim, B. (1979). *Surviving and other essays.* New York: Knopf.

Blackmore, S. (1999). *The meme machine.* Oxford: Oxford University Press.

Boehm, C. B. (1999a). *Hierarchy in the forest: The evolution of egalitarian behavior.* Cambridge: Harvard University Press.

Boehm, C. B. (1999b).The natural selection of altruistic traits. *Human Nature, 10*(3), 205–243.

Bradie, M. (1994). *The secret chain: Evolution and ethics.* Albany: State University of New York Press.

Brown, A. (1999). *The Darwin wars: The battle for the soul of man.* New York: Simon & Schuster.

Campbell, D. (1991). A naturalistic theory of archaic moral order. *Zygon, 26*(1): 91–114.

Cosmides, L., & Tooby, J. (1992). Cognitive adaptations for social exchange. In J. Barkow, L. Cosmides, & J. Tooby (Eds.), *The adapted mind: Evolutionary psychology and the generation of culture* (pp. 163–228). New York: Oxford University Press.

Cronk, L. (1994). Evolutionary theories of morality and the manipulative use of signals. *Zygon, 29*, 81–101.

Cronk, L. (1999). *That complex whole: Culture and the evolution of human behavior.* Boulder, CO: Westview Press.

Damasio, A. (1995). *Descartes' error: Emotion, reason, and the human brain.* New York: Avon Books.

Damasio, A. (1999). *The feeling of what happens: Body and emotion in the making of consciousness.* New York: Harcourt Brace.

Darwin, C. (1967). *On the origin of species by means of natural selection; or, the preservation of favored races in the struggle for life.* Cambridge: Harvard University Press. (Original work published 1859)

Dawkins, R. (1976). *The selfish gene.* Oxford: Oxford University Press.

Dawkins, R. (1991).Darwin triumphant: Darwinism as a universal truth. In M. H. Robinson & L. Tiger (Eds.), *Man and beast revisited* (pp. 23–40). Washington: Smithsonian Institution Press.

de Waal, F. (1996). *Good natured: The origins of right and wrong in humans and other animals.* Cambridge: Harvard University Press.

Dennett, D. C. (1995). *Darwin's dangerous idea: Evolution and the meaning of life.* New York: Simon & Schuster.

Diamond, J. (1992). *The third chimpanzee: The evolution and future of the human animal.* New York: HarperCollins.

Dugatin, L. (1999). *Cheating monkeys and citizen bees: The nature of cooperation in animals and humans.* Cambridge: Harvard University Press.

Durham, W. (1991). *Coevolution: Genes, culture, and human diversity.* Stanford, CA: Stanford University Press.

Durkheim, E. (1997). *The division of labor in society.* New York: Simon & Schuster.

Eibl-Eibesfeldt, I. (1978). *Love and hate: The natural history of behavior patterns.* New York: Holt, Rinehart, & Winston.

Eibl-Eibesfeldt, I. (1996). Reply to Christopher Boehm. *Current Anthropology, 37,* 779–780.

Fox-Keller, E. (1991). Language and ideology in evolutionary theory: Reading cultural norms into natural law. In J. J. Sheehan & M. Sosna (Eds.), *The boundaries of humanity: Humans, animals, machines* (pp. 85–102). Berkeley: University of California Press.

Fox-Keller, E., & Ewing, M. S. (1993).The kinds of "individuals" one finds in evolutionary biology. In M. H. Nitecki & D. V. Nitecki (Eds.), *Evolutionary ethics* (pp. 349–358). Albany: State University of New York Press.

Frank, R. H. (1988). *Passions within reason: The strategic role of the emotions.* New York: Norton.

Frank, S. A. (1998). *Foundations of social evolution.* Princeton, NJ: Princeton University Press.

Ghiselin, M. T. (1973). Darwin and evolutionary psychology. *Science, 179,* 964–968.

Ghiselin, M. T. (1974). *The economy of nature and the evolution of sex.* Berkeley: University of California Press.

Gould, S. J. (1997, June 12). Darwinian fundamentalism. *New York Review of Books,* pp. 34–37.

Gould, S. J., & Lewontin, R. C. (1979).The spandrels of San Marco and the Panglossian paradigm: A critique of the adaptationist programme. *Proceedings of the Royal Society of London, 205*: 581–598.

Hamilton, W. D. (1964). The genetical evolution of social behavior. *Journal of Theoretical Biology, 7,*1–16.

Holcomb, H. (1993). *Sociobiology, sex, and science.* Albany: State University of New York Press.

Hull, D. (1978). Scientific bandwagon or travelling medicine show? In M. S. Gregory, A. Silvers, & D. Sutch (Eds.), *Sociobiology and human nature* (pp. 136–163). San Francisco: Jossey-Bass.

Huxley, T. H. (1989). *Evolution and ethics.* Princeton, NJ: Princeton University Press. (Original work published 1894)

Kagan, J. (1998). *Three seductive ideas.* Cambridge: Harvard University Press.

Kohn, A. (1990). *The brighter side of human nature: Altruism and empathy in everyday life.* New York: Basic Books.

Lewis, C. S. (1960). *The four loves.* New York: Harcourt Brace.

Lewis, T., Amini, A., & Lannon, R. (2000). *A general theory of love.* New York: Random House.

Lockard, J. S., & Paulus, D. L. (Eds.). (1988). *Self-deception: An adaptive mechanism?* Englewood Cliffs, NJ: Prentice-Hall.

Lopreato, J. (1984). *Human nature and biocultural evolution.* Boston: Allen & Unwin.

Lorenz, K. (1966). *On aggression.* New York: Harcourt Brace Jovanovich.

Lumsden, C. J., & Wilson, E. O. (1983). *Promethean fire: Reflections on the origin of mind.* Cambridge: Harvard University Press.

Midgley, M. (1979). Gene-juggling. *Philosophy, 54*(210), 108–134.

Midgley, M. (1980). Rival fatalisms: The hollowness of the sociology debate. In A. Montague (Ed.), *Sociobiology examined* (pp. 15–38). New York: Oxford University Press.

Midgley, M. (1982). Foreword. In G. Breuer (Ed.), *Sociobiology and the human dimension* (pp. xi–xii). New York: Cambridge University Press.

Monroe, K. R. (1996). *The heart of altruism: Perceptions of a common humanity*. Princeton, NJ: Princeton University Press.

Moreland, J. P., & Rae, S. B. (2000). *Body and soul: Human nature and the crisis in ethics*. Downers Grove, IL: Intervarsity Press.

Oates, D. (1988). Social Darwinism and natural theodicy. *Zygon, 23*(4), 439–454.

Pascal, B. (1958). *Pensees* (T. S. Eliot, Commentator). New York: Dutton.

Plotkin, H. (1993). *Darwin machines and the nature of knowledge*. Cambridge: Harvard University Press.

Plotkin, H. (1997). *Evolution in mind: An introduction to evolutionary psychology*. Cambridge: Harvard University Press.

Putnam, R. D. (2000). *Bowling alone: The collapse and revival of American community*. New York: Simon & Schuster.

Ray, J. C., & Sapolsky, R. (1992). Styles of male social behavior and their endocrine correlates among high-ranking baboons. *American Journal of Primatology, 28*(4), 231–250.

Richards, R. J. (1986). *Darwin and the emergence of evolutionary theories of mind and behavior*. Chicago: University of Chicago Press.

Richards, R. J. (1993). Birth, death, and resurrection of evolutionary ethics. In M. H. Nitecki & D. V. Nitecki (Eds.), *Evolutionary ethics* (pp. 113–131). Albany: State University of New York Press.

Richerson, P., & Boyd, R. (1999). Complex societies: The evolutionary origins of a crude superorganism. *Human Nature, 10*(3), 253–290.

Rolston, H. (1999). *Genes, genesis, and God: Values and their origins in natural and human history*. Cambridge: Cambridge University Press.

Ruse, M. (1994). Evolutionary theory and Christian ethics: Are they in harmony? *Zygon, 29*(1), 5–24.

Ruse, M. (1995). Evolutionary ethics: A defense. In H. Roston III (Ed.), *Biology, ethics, and the origins of life* (pp. 89–112). Boston: Jones & Bartlett.

Rushton, J. P. (1989). Genetic similarity, human altruism, and group selection. *Behavioral and Brain Sciences, 12*, 503–559.

Russell, R. J. (1998). The theological consequences of the thermodynamics of a moral universe: An appreciative critique of the Murphy/Ellis project. *CTNS Bulletin, 18*(4), 19–24.

Sapolsky, R., & Ray, J. (1989). Styles of dominance and their physiological correlates among wild baboons. *American Journal of Primatology, 18*(1): 1–13.

Schloss, J. P. (1996). Sociobiological explanations of altruistic ethics: Necessary, sufficient, or irrelevant to the human moral quest? In J. Hurd (Ed.), *Investigating the biological foundations of human morality* (pp. 107–145). New York: Edwin Mellen Press.

Smith, A. (1998). *An inquiry into the nature and causes of wealth of nations*. Oxford: Oxford University Press. (Original work published 1776)

Sober, E., & Wilson, D. S. (1998). *Unto others: The evolution and psychology of unselfish behavior*. Cambridge: Harvard University Press.

Stent, G. S. (1980). *Morality as a biological phenomenon*. Los Angeles: University of California Press.

Swinburne, R. (1997). *The evolution of the soul*. New York: Oxford University Press.

Tooby, J., & Cosmides, L. (1996). Friendship and the banker's paradox: Other pathways to the evolution of adaptations for altruism. In W. G. Runciman, J. M. Smith, & R. I. Dunbar (Eds.), *Proceedings of the British Academy: Vol. 88. Evolution of social behavior patterns in primates and man* (pp. 119–143). Oxford: Oxford University Press.

Townsend, C. R., & Calow, P. (Eds.). (1981). *Physiological ecology: An evolutionary approach to resource use.* Sunderland, MA: Sinauer.

Trivers, R. (1991). Deceit and self-deception: The relationship between communication and consciousness. In M. H. Robinson & L. Tiger (Eds.), *Man and beast revisited* (pp. 175–191). Washington: Smithsonian Institution Press.

Trivers, R. L. (1971). The evolution of reciprocal altruism. *Quarterly Review of Biology, 46,* 35–39.

Virgin, C. E., & Sapolsky, R. (l997). Styles of male social behavior and their endocrine correlates among low-ranking baboons. *American Journal of Primatology, 42*(1): 25–39.

Williams, G. C. (1988). Huxley's evolution and ethics in sociobiological perspective. *Zygon, 23*(2), 383–407.

Wilson, D. S. (1992). On the relationship between evolutionary and psychological definitions of altruism and selfishness. *Biology and Philosophy, 7*(1), 61–68.

Wilson, E. O. (1975). *Sociobiology: The new synthesis.* Cambridge: Harvard University Press.

Wilson, E. O. (1978). *On human nature.* Cambridge: Harvard University Press.

Conclusion to Part III

JEFFREY P. SCHLOSS

I introduced this section by commenting on the extraordinary divergence that has characterized evolutionary thinking about altruism over the past two decades. Yet although contributors were chosen to represent contrasting perspectives, there is a notable convergence of thinking, which reflects growing congruence in the field at large. At present, it appears that consensus has emerged on certain fundamental propositions, setting the agenda for future research.

- Initial formulations of sociobiology were reductionistically and deterministically incautious, yet as evolutionary analysis of behavior has become more rigorous and nuanced, it has become more rather than less evident that human cognitive capacities and behavioral inclinations are not tabulae rasae with respect to the imprint of an evolved biology.
- Although human beings evidence kinds of sacrifice on behalf of one another that, by virtue of reproductive relinquishment, do not appear to be rigidly constrained by a "genetic leash," there is nevertheless a central tendency in human social behavior that comports well with a naturally selected behavioral repertoire.
- The central tendency in human altruism entails behaviors that can be understood to contribute to fitness via kin or sexual selection, direct and indirect reciprocity, and other modes or levels of selection; however, the effect

243

of these processes that emphasize positive reproductive outcomes is not necessarily to exclude, and may often promote, genuinely other-regarding motivations.

- There is growing openness to coevolutionary and/or hierarchical mechanisms that extend the domain of human cooperativeness beyond that of kin or strictly compensatory reciprocity. However, virtually all present proposals achieve more robust sacrifice via bounded cooperativeness, that is, exclusionary group or relational alliances. We still lack a coherent proposal for out-group sacrifice or "enemy love."

- It is likely that what we call altruistic behavior, and even more so altruistic love, actually represents a highly varied suite of affective and behavioral capacities resulting from multifactorial, layered, perhaps even ambivalent or conflicting causal pathways. Understanding them will require cooperation between the full spectrum of biological, social/psychological, and humanistic disciplines.

The aforementioned common ground deemphasizes personality or disciplinary skirmishes and brings into relief four important questions for future research, which are implied by overlap between or made explicit by proposals within the chapters in this section.

Both Michael Ruse and Stephen Pope make clear that the most radically self-relinquishing notions of altruistic moral obligation appear incommensurable with evolutionary theory. However, such notions—and attendant behaviors—persist. What we don't know much about is why they do. We do not have extensive demographic data on the actual extent to which human moral or religious systems are implicated in uncompensated, counterreproductive behaviors. Nor do we have comparative fitness or psychometric data on participants in these traditions.

A fascinating and, in our view, crucially important scientific question is generated by what was at one time a wholly theological dispute between what Stephen Pope describes as dialectical and sacramental views of love. Are the most radical extensions of other regard furtherances of capacities for bonding to and caring for near and dear (Boehm 1999; Tooby and Cosmides, 1996)? Or do they represent contrary impositions on or cultural reformulations of an otherwise hostile biological substrate (Blackmore, 1999; Dawkins, 1976)? As these views reflect poles on a continuum of options that are not mutually exclusive, they illustrate questions about mechanisms and character of out-group care, questions which may be amenable to neurological, psychological, and anthropological analysis. The scant data we have on these issues are provocative but ambiguous. Oliner and Oliner (1988) found that Holocaust rescuers took people in at significant, ongoing personal risk, without any substrate of interpersonal affiliation; yet releasers looked the other way at transitory risk when prisoners escaped, based on experiences of interpersonal exchange.

Wilson and Sober, in Chapter 11, present proposals for multilevel selection involving not only the operation of selection on vehicles at individual and group levels but also interaction between genetic and cultural level replicators or information. They describe how group level ideas could influence gene frequencies, entailing interactions between both phenotypic and genotypic altruism. The unanswered questions here are not so much evolutionary as developmental: We simply don't have a model for how ideational (cultural) information can emerge from genetic information in a manner that is faithful to the properties of the lower level yet is not only irreducible to it but also sufficiently autonomous to "oppose" it (Dawkins, 1976; Durham, 1991; Plotkin, 1997).

Schloss (Chapter 13) and Wilson and Sober (Chapter 11) make related though differing proposals for how religion might influence the origin and maintenance of altruism. Wilson and Sober argue that social controls can enhance group adaptiveness by reducing within-group fitness costs of cheaters. Schloss argues that biological needs to give and receive altruistically—perhaps in part due to internalization of social controls—also reduces within-group fitness differential to the point that group selection may not be necessary and altruism "is its own reward." However, we lack two crucial data sets for these issues and for altruism study in general. We need more empirical data on within- and between-group fitness differentials for egalitarian and hierarchical human communities. And we need morbidity, mortality, and psychometric data for individuals of varying altruistic dispositions.

REFERENCES

Blackmore, S. (1999). *The meme machine.* Oxford: Oxford University Press.
Boehm, C. (1999). The natural selection of altruistic traits. *Human Nature, 10*(3), 205–253.
Dawkins, R. (1976). *The selfish gene.* Oxford: Oxford University Press.
Durham, W. (1991). *Coevolution: Genes, culture, and human diversity.* Stanford, CA: Stanford University Press.
Oliner, S. P., & Oliner, P. M. (1988). *The altruistic personality: Rescuers of Jews in Nazi Europe.* New York: Free Press.
Plotkin, H. (1997). *Evolution in mind: An introduction to evolutionary psychology.* Cambridge: Harvard University Press.
Tooby, J., & Cosmides, L. (1996). Friendship and the banker's paradox: Other pathways to the evolution of adaptations for altruism. In W. G. Runciman, J. M. Smith, & R. I. Dunbar (Eds.), *Proceedings of the British Academy: Vol. 88. Evolution of social behavior patterns in primates and man* (pp. 119–143). Oxford: Oxford University Press.

Part IV

THE SCIENCE OF ALTRUISM

Introduction to Part IV

WILLIAM B. HURLBUT

Whereas Part III considered primarily the evolutionary process that gave rise to altruism, in this section we turn our focus to the fundamental biological capabilities and consequent social dynamics that enable altruism to exist. In doing so, we discuss the evolutionary advantages of particular anatomical, physiological, and psychological developments and consider how they provide the basis for the varied forms of altruism. Specifically, we look at how the most primary affiliative and affectional relations are grounded in biologically significant processes, including reproduction, nurturance, and social communication and coordination. We discuss the fundamental role of emotions in biological regulation and their extension in communication, empathy, and conscious moral awareness. Drawing on current scientific explanations and evidence, we also consider how discoveries in biochemistry, neurophysiology, and ethology may provide perspectives for further inquiry into the scientific basis of both the sentiments and active manifestations of genuine altruistic love.

In spite of being such a central and significant dimension of human life, the subject of love has received relatively little scientific attention. Part of the reason for this is historical. From the origins of the scientific method in Bacon, Galileo, and Descartes, the principles of inquiry had limited the scope of investigation. Certain questions, particularly those that involved human subjectivity, such as feelings and values, were not amenable to an analytic and reductive approach, and their realms somehow came to be considered less fundamental and less real. Furthermore, Descartes's metaphysical dualism had declared mind and body to be two distinct and independent substances. Animals and the human body were relegated to the realm of the physical, and the human mind, the source of intellect and intention (and love), was designated as pure immaterial soul. Regarding animals, Descartes wrote, "it is nature that acts in them according to the arrangements of their organs, just as we see how a clock, composed merely of wheels and springs can reckon the hours" (Sheehan & Sosna, 1991, p. 29). With the rise of logical positivism in the twentieth century, the idea of a soul became less compelling, and the mechanical model of animal behavior was extended to the study of human psychology.

For almost the whole of the twentieth century, studies in psychology avoided the realm of feelings, emotion, and consciousness. Descriptions in terms of input-output or stimulus-response reduced the living organism to an ineluctable series of atomized reactions (what William James labeled "domino psychology"). The image of a complex apparatus devoid of inwardness and experiential being replaced the notion of an intentional mind that is awake, aware, and passionately engaged in its life process. Consciousness became viewed as a mere epiphenomenon with no active executive function in the life of the organism. More recently, ideas of genetic determinism (including selfish genes) have replaced behaviorism, and images of life as pure information have reduced description below the level of matter in motion to pure mathematics. Such notions obscure and distort the very phenomena of life they seek to describe and erode the concepts of freedom, moral awareness, and rational thought that are essential to a meaningful understanding of love.

Beyond these historical and philosophical explanations, there are practical reasons for the neglect of love as a subject of scientific inquiry. Altruism and altruistic love span a vast territory of biological reality, ranging from the most primary affections and affiliations to the highest extremes of self-sacrifice. Within humanity the diverse cultural expressions of altruism make the very definition of love problematic. Even where there are universally recognizable manifestations, the nature of love makes it difficult to contain within a controlled and reproducible set of circumstances amenable to scientific study. In what terms do we measure love, quantifying and calibrating its dimensions and qualities, without reducing and destroying the very phenomenon we seek to understand?

Furthermore, for many people love is so sensitive a part of human life that the idea of scientific study seems a violation of its central significance and sacred source. A sense of danger is felt at even entering this "holy of holies." To seek an explanation of love in terms of a material and mechanical description seems to imply the disenchantment of love, an abnegation of the fullest expression of personal freedom and noble aspiration. Others fear the misuse of such scientific knowledge, the cold and calculated instrumental application of what has until now remained hidden and hedged in by the mystery of its source. They fear the manipulation of desire and the medicalization of its meaning, a disruption of the fragile balance of social and spiritual regulation of sexuality, sociality, and moral responsibility.

Notwithstanding these obstacles and objections to the study of love, few would oppose a concerted scientific inquiry into the nature of its disorders and distortions or into the causes of the absence of love. Loneliness and alienation, jealousy, infidelity, envy and exploitation, shame, humiliation and despair, hatred, violence, and war—there is an earnest and urgent imperative for the scientific study of love.

The powerful and pervasive nature of love, its passionate forms, and its compelling place within existence are evidence of its central significance in the biology and spirituality of human life. Charles Darwin recognized this and thought a great deal about the origins and implications of altruism. For most of his life he struggled with the religious meaning of his discoveries. Darwin's beloved wife Emma, a devout Christian, was deeply troubled by the corrosive effect of his theories on religious belief and wrote a letter in which she admonished him to reconsider his views on matters of faith. After his death the letter was found among his papers with these words penciled on the bottom: "When I am dead, know that many times, I have kissed and cryed over this" (Darwin, 1892/1958, p. 237). Notwithstanding his troubled agnosticism, Darwin believed there was a natural grounding for genuine altruism and had a strong negative response to explanations of human behavior that eroded its central core of freedom and nobility.

Darwin recognized that our capacity for altruism is built on fundamental anatomical, physiological, and psychological adaptations that trace their origins to the earliest forms of social species. He devoted much of his energy to thinking about the meaning of emotions in the development of life and their role in the expressive communication that culminates in the highest forms of human love. Though he spoke of the "indelible stamp of his lowly origins" which man carries in his body, he admitted that no animal had a self-consciousness comparable to that of man and he spoke of man's "noble qualities" and "god-like intellect."

Although Darwin is often characterized as instituting a pervasive materialism and mechanism into the interpretation of life, with mind as a fixed function of matter, this was a later transmutation of his ideas. Indeed, Darwin affirmed within human nature the reality of genuine altruism, that is, unselfish action directed toward the welfare of another. He decried theories, popular during his lifetime, that attributed all human actions to selfish motives. He maintained that pleasure was neither the usual motive nor the necessary end of moral acts. Rather, he suggested that the roots of human morality were to be seen in the social instincts of animals, by which cooperation led to what he called "the general good or welfare of the community" and which involved the rearing "of the greatest possible number of individuals . . . in full vigour and health" (Darwin, 1871/1981, p. 98).

Darwin was careful to affirm that only humans were truly moral, for only a human being "was capable of comparing his past and future actions or motive, and of approving or disapproving of them" (1871/1981, p. 88). Further, he added that human morality arose "either directly or indirectly much more through the effects of habit, the reasoning power, instruction, religion etc. than through natural selection" (1871/1981, p. 404). He seems to have envisioned within evolutionary process an automatic and inevitable assent to moral awareness. Describing evolution from animals to the high moral level of human beings, he asserted that "any animal whatever endowed with well-marked social instincts, the parental and filial affections being here included, would inevitably acquire a moral sense or conscience as soon as its intellectual powers had been as well, or nearly as well developed as in man" (1871/1981, p. 71).

In the chapters that follow, we renew the inquiry that Charles Darwin began into the natural foundations of altruism. In Chapter 14, the neuroscientist Thomas Insel discusses his work in the neurochemistry and neurophysiology of pair bonding and nurturant behaviors in certain rodent species. Grounded in these fundamental types of attachment behavior, and with an animal model that is (relative to humans) easy to study, he launches a trajectory of inquiry that may have far-reaching implications for the study of altruism. He points to direct genetic factors that underlie dramatic differences in complex behaviors between the sexes and between closely related species and suggests a molecular mechanism for these varied adaptive forms of gender difference and social organization. These findings point to the possibility that in human beings subtle genetic variation may underlie individual differences in the capacity and inclination for attachment and other forms of altruistic behavior. While acknowledging the current lack of direct evidence linking these findings with human behavior, he cites the evolutionarily ancient and pervasive conservation of these molecular mechanisms of basic sociosexual behavior across a great range of species. He concludes with a note of caution, affirming the more complex dynamics of human attachment, in which higher cortical processes may predominate.

In Chapter 15, neurologist Antonio Damasio discusses the evolutionary origins of emotions and feelings, their fundamental adaptive value, and their extensions in the empathic processes that allow human sociality and altruism. He characterizes emotions as specific collections of alterations in the brain and body organs that place the organism in a mode of readiness and response to particular stimuli or circumstances of biological significance. He distinguishes feelings from emotions as the brain's coordinated representations of all the changes that occur in the body and brain during an emotional state. In humans, feelings are represented as mental images, mappings that allow the individual a conscious awareness of an emotional state. The common biological basis of emotions and feelings accounts for their transcultural similarities, and their outwardly expressed manifestations provide grounds for empathy, our ability to sense the feelings and moods of others. In addition, Damasio makes the fascinating suggestion that the primary adaptive value of consciousness was in allowing organisms to "feel" their feelings of emotions. This capacity for awareness of the feeling of knowing that we have feelings then became the basis for making plans and organizing responses that were not already prescribed by our genes, including the states of sentiment and intentional actions that characterize genuine altruism.

In Chapter 16, neurologist Hanna Damasio documents and discusses case reports of patients with damage to portions of the brain that appear to be crucial in the foundational processes of altruism. She reports that patients with injury to localized sites in the prefrontal cortex, while maintaining normal functioning of other cognitive abilities, suffer impairment of specific social and emotional capabilities, including empathy. This clinical evidence, including interesting differences

between patients who suffer such brain damage early versus late in their development, points to the critical role of specific neural functions, as well as developmental learning, in certain social behaviors essential for empathy and altruism. In
accordance with the "somatic marker hypothesis," as explained by Antonio Damasio, she reports that decision making involves recall from memory of not only the
factual circumstances of prior decisions but also their associated emotional states.
Such findings concerning empathy and the deployment of emotional memories in
social decision making may shed light on the neurological basis of sociopathic behavior. This disorder is characterized by a notable lack of empathy and altruistic
concern and is a source of significant personal and social tragedy.

In Chapter 17, primatologists Stephanie Preston and Frans de Waal consider
a continuum of behaviors, based on emotional linkage between individuals, that
ranges from simple "emotional contagion" to the more complex "cognitive empathy," which involves a degree of understanding of the emotional state of the other.
They describe observations of various forms of such emotionally linked behavior
in a variety of species, suggesting phylogenetic continuity in the phenomena. Most
notably, they have observed what appears to be a degree of cognitive empathy
among the great apes. In addition, they suggest an explanatory model of empathy
based on neuroscientific evidence that perception and action share a common
manner of brain representation. This makes possible the communication and apprehension of emotional states that permit the kind of shared intersubjectivity
that is essential for the grounding of empathy.

In Chapter 18, I further elaborate on the biological basis of empathy and explore its role in the development of personal identity, language, and moral community. I discuss the evolutionary forces that have shaped the distinct psychophysical unity of mind and bodily form which bears the uniquely human
attributes of freedom, rationality, and self-awareness. I then reflect on the way the
material world, in its unity and multiplicity of forms, provides an intelligible "language" of being and the foundation for the remarkable extensions of personal and
social existence that allow the expression of genuine altruistic love.

These chapters, taken together, contribute new perspectives to the scientific
study of altruism. At the same time, they point to further lines of research that
may contribute valuable practical knowledge and greatly enrich human self-
understanding.

REFERENCES

Darwin, C. (1958). *The autobiography of Charles Darwin.* New York: Norton. (Original
    work published 1892)
Darwin, C. (1981). *The descent of man and selection in relation to sex.* Princeton, NJ:
    Princeton University Press. (Original work published 1871)
Sheehan, J. J., & Sosna, M. (Eds.). (1991). *The boundaries of humanity: Humans, animals,
    machines.* Berkeley: University of California Press.

14

Implications for the
Neurobiology of Love

THOMAS R. INSEL

The past decade has witnessed a revolution in our understanding of how the brain mediates sensory processing, motor function, and memory. We have learned the importance of a small family of developmental genes for specifying normal neural development. At the same time, we have discovered the remarkable plasticity of both the developing brain and the adult brain. Sadly, this revolution in neuroscience has taught us less about the neurobiology of emotion and has revealed very little about the neural basis of altruistic love.

Although neuroscientists recognize the importance of love as a complex emotion, few have wanted to address the challenge of studying where or how the brain mediates love. The problem is not simply that love is complex. There is an abundant literature on the neurobiology of aggression, which is equally complex. Many have studied the neural consequences of loss or separation, which may be considered equally complicated and perhaps the inverse of love or attachment. The problem is not that love (or attachment) is a positive state and less likely to be studied than emotions such as loss that can be tied to a disorder. We have nearly 50 years of research on the neuroendocrinology of sex, which is also a healthy, positive behavior.

The relative absence of neuroscience research on love can be attributed to two fairly obvious and related limitations. One is definitional. Love, whether considered as attachment, such as a pair bond, or viewed as a form of self-sacrificing altruism, is difficult to define operationally. How, for instance, do we distinguish love from infatuation, craving, or caring? A related problem for neuroscientists is that nothing remotely related to human love is observed in common laboratory animals, such as rats and mice. Yes, rat mothers will show intense devotion and defense of their young, but they are not selective in their maternal behavior, offering the same level of care to unrelated young placed in the nest.

The second major problem is one of measurement. Although most of us may recognize love as the most powerful psychological and biological experience of our lives, how do we quantify this experience? Are some forms of love greater than other forms? Can altruism be measured?

In the past few years, a series of studies have begun to address both of these limitations. By studying natural populations of monogamous rodents, we and others have investigated the neural correlates of pair-bonding behaviors that resemble, in certain features, what we call "love" between humans. In nonhuman monogamous species, pair bonding involves a lifelong selective attachment to one partner. It should be noted at the outset that the term *monogamy* as used by biologists refers to a pattern of social, not sexual, organization. About 3% of mammals are considered monogamous (Kleiman, 1977). Bonded pairs in these species share a territory and a nest, exhibit both maternal and paternal care, and usually are similar in size and appearance. But few if any of these species exhibit sexual exclusivity. That is, biological monogamy refers to how one lives, not how one mates (Dewsbury, 1988).

The availability of species that pair bond raises an option for addressing the second limitation of studying the neurobiology of love. Although we cannot directly ask rodents how they feel, we can measure the behaviors essential for pair bonding. In monogamous rodents, the formation of a preference for a specific partner, the time spent in physical contact, and the response to separation can be easily quantified and standardized. Using these sorts of measures, we can begin to ask which genes, neurotransmitters, and neural systems are critical for pair bonding.

Two peptide hormones, oxytocin and vasopressin, appear to be important for pair bonding in monogamous rodents. Molecular and cellular studies have provided new insights into the mechanisms by which these hormones act to influence attachment. As with all hormones, oxytocin and vasopressin act on specific cell surface receptors in the brain, as well as in other target organs, such as the kidneys. The location of these receptors provides a map of locations at which these hormones act, and, most likely, the regulatory regions of the genes for these receptors determine the locations of these receptors in the brain. The genes for oxytocin and vasopressin receptors are highly variable between species, providing a potential molecular mechanism for the evolution of monogamy. Variation in these same genomic regions within a species could account for individual differences in social attachment, or possibly, in human terms, altruistic love.

Voles as a Natural Model for the Study of Attachment

Monogamous mammals are found in many different taxa and in diverse environments. Among primates, gibbons, titi monkeys, and marmosets have been described as monogamous. Canids, the group that includes the domesticated dog, include several prototypically monogamous species (Kleiman, 1977). For neurobiological study, rodents are ideal; the microtine rodents or voles have proven especially informative (Carter, DeVries, & Getz, 1995). Prairie voles are highly social, biparental, and show long-term pair bonds. Indeed, in field studies, prairie voles are usually found in communal burrows with a single breeding pair. If the male or female breeder dies, 80% of the time the remaining prairie vole does not accept a new mate. Female prairie voles have an unusual pattern of reproductive development. They remain sexually immature while remaining in their natal group. Once exposed to an unrelated male, they ovulate for the first time, mate for 24 to 48 hours, and, apparently as a result of mating, develop a pair bond. Laboratory studies have demonstrated the importance of mating for the development of a partner preference (Williams, Catania, & Carter, 1992).

Part of what makes prairie voles so informative for study is the availability of closely related species that differ so markedly in their social behavior. For instance, montane voles are a nonmonogamous species, living in isolated burrows, and showing no evidence of paternal behavior. Montane voles do not pair bond in the field, and in laboratory studies they fail to develop partner preferences after mating (Shapiro, Austin, Ward, & Dewsbury, 1986).

Oxytocin and Vasopressin as Candidate Hormones for Attachment

Given the striking behavioral differences between these vole species, we and others have been attempting to define associated differences in brain anatomy or chemistry. Among the candidates for separating these two species are two neuropeptide hormones, oxytocin (OT) and vasopressin (AVP). These hormones are synthesized in the brain and have been previously shown to have important effects on social behavior in common laboratory animals, such as rats, mice, and even sheep (Insel, 1992). Both OT and AVP are found exclusively in mammals, but they belong to a family of structurally related neuropeptides implicated in sociosexual behaviors of reptiles, amphibia, and birds. In mammals, OT has been shown to be important for labor and lactation. In rats and sheep, OT working within specific neural circuits is critical for the onset of maternal behavior. This is perhaps the best example in the behavioral neuroscience literature of a single neuropeptide in-

Table 14.1. A Comparative Approach to Attachment

Behavior	Prairie Voles	Montane Voles
Shared nest	Yes	No
Affiliative contact	Yes	No
Pair bonds	Yes	No
Paternal care	Yes	No
Separation calls	Yes	No

fluencing attachment behavior in nonmonogamous mammals. In addition, OT is released during copulation and may influence female sexual behavior. AVP has been implicated in several aspects of male social behavior, including territorial displays, aggression, and social memory (Ferris, 1992).

Given the evidence linking OT and AVP to complex social behaviors, it is perhaps not surprising that these hormones should also influence pair-bond formation in the monogamous prairie vole. But there is an even better reason for investigating these two neuropeptides in pair-bond formation. As noted previously, in the normal life cycle of a prairie vole, mating is the critical event preceding pair bonding. Both OT and AVP are released with mating in other mammals, and presumably these hormones are released in the vole brain during copulation (Bamshad, Novak, & De Vries, 1994; Witt, 1995).

In female prairie voles, if OT is given during exposure to a male, a partner preference can be induced without mating (Insel & Hulihan, 1995). Conversely, females allowed to mate but treated with an antagonist or specific blocker of OT fail to form a partner preference (Insel & Hulihan, 1995). Thus, OT appears necessary and sufficient for partner preference formation in the female prairie vole. Surprisingly, OT is without effects in the male. For males, AVP is effective in the absence of mating, and an AVP antagonist blocks partner preference formation if given during mating (Winslow, Hastings, Carter, Harbough, & Insel, 1993). In addition, AVP facilitates and an AVP antagonist blocks paternal behavior.

These pharmacological studies provide two lessons for understanding the neurobiology of attachment. First, they suggest that neuropeptide release during mating leads to profound and enduring changes in prairie vole behavior. Does this mean that sex is essential for attachment? Perhaps in prairie voles, but that does not mean that other species, including our own, need to copulate to form a pair bond. Nevertheless, reproductive behavior may influence pair bonding, just as the release of oxytocin during nursing may facilitate the mother-infant bond in a variety of mammals, including humans. A second lesson from the pharmacological studies in voles is the importance of gender differences. Even when the social behaviors, such as partner preference, appear superficially similar, males and females may use different neural mechanisms.

Do the hormones induce monogamy in montane voles? Neither OT nor AVP, given in an identical fashion, influences social behavior in the nonmonogamous vole (Winslow, Shapiro, Carter, & Insel, 1993; Young, Winslow, Nilsen, &

Table 14.2. Central Effects of Oxytocin and Vasopressin

Oxytocin	Vasopressin
Facilitate maternal behavior	Facilitate paternal behavior
Female sex behavior	Induce territorial behaviors
Increase ingestion	Regulate osmoregulation
Increase grooming	Increase grooming
Improve memory (social)	Improve memory
Reduce isolation calls	Reduce isolation calls

Table 14.3.   OT and AVP Effects on Prairie Vole Partner Preference Formation

Treatment	Female	Male
Oxytocin	+	0
Oxytocin antagonist	−	0
Vasopressin	0	+
Vasopressin antagonist	0	−

Note: Oxytocin and vasopressin facilitate partner preference formation in the absence of mating; their respective antagonists block partner preference formation in mating animals.

Insel, 1997). Although these hormones can increase self-grooming or locomotor behavior, neither induces a partner preference or paternal care in montane voles. The different effects these peptides have appear to be due to species differences in the brain targets for both OT and AVP.

Oxytocin and Vasopressin Receptors: A Mechanism for Species Differences

All neurohormones act via specific receptors. After it is released from nerve endings, the hormone binds to receptors that initiate a series of intracellular events. It is important to understand that the location of the receptors in the brain determines what cells are activated. In other words, the behavioral effects of any hormone are defined not just by the amount of hormone but by the location of its receptors in the brain. Both prairie voles and montane voles make OT and AVP, but these species have markedly different patterns of receptor distribution (Insel & Shapiro, 1992; Insel, Wang, & Ferris, 1994). For example, OT receptors in the prairie vole brain are concentrated in reward pathways (nucleus accumbens and prelimbic cortex), targets that are likely to lead to conditioning (which we measure as a partner preference) following activation of these regions by OT release during copulation. In the montane vole, OT receptors are absent in these regions but are found in regions important for nonsocial behavior (e.g., lateral septum), and, therefore, OT release with copulation would not be expected to induce a partner preference. Differences in receptor location are found not only in prairie and montane voles but also in other monogamous (e.g., pine) and nonmonogamous (meadow) voles (Insel & Shapiro, 1992; Insel et al., 1994). Vole species do not differ in the brain distribution of several other hormone receptors that have been studied, suggesting that the differences in OT and AVP receptors are specific and potentially related to species differences in social organization (Insel & Shapiro, 1992).

It is important to emphasize that the difference between prairie voles and montane voles is not too much or too little OT (or AVP). The species have roughly equivalent amounts of both OT and AVP. The difference is where the receptors are.

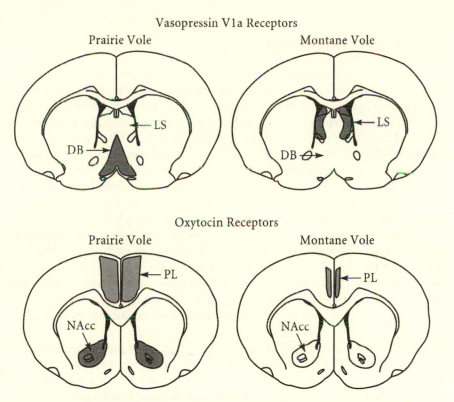

Figure 5.1. Autoradiograms of OT/AVP receptors: Prairie vs. montane voles. Prairie and montane voles have brain receptors for oxytocin and vasopressin, but these receptors are in different circuits. Pictures represent two levels of the brain from each species. Area in gray shows distribution of receptors. In the prairie vole, which forms attachments after mating, receptors are found in reward pathways, such as DB (diagonal band), PL (prelimbic cortex), and NAcc (nucleus accumbens). In the montane vole, which fails to form attachments, receptors are either absent or very sparse, except in the LS (lateral septum). These different patterns of receptor distribution provide a cellular mechanism by which oxytocin and vasopressin, released with mating or nursing, could have different behavioral effects in the two vole species.

Therefore, infusing micromolar quantities of either hormone into montane voles will not induce a pair bond. The receptors are in the wrong target areas of the montane vole brain for either hormone to influence social attachment. How do we know that receptor localization is important for attachment? In a recent study, we inserted the prairie vole vasopressin receptor gene into the mouse genome. As a result, this mouse responded to AVP with an increase in social interaction, such as investigation and grooming of an unfamiliar mouse (Young, Nilsen, Waymire, MacGregor, & Insel, 1999). Although these mice were not monogamous, these results demonstrated the importance of receptor localization for determining how hormones can influence complex social behavior.

The Molecular Basis of Monogamy

Thus far, we have demonstrated that (1) OT and AVP influence pair-bond formation in monogamous prairie voles (but not in nonmonogamous montane voles)
and (2) monogamous and nonmonogamous voles differ in the neuroanatomical
location of their receptors for OT and AVP. These observations suggest that the location of the receptors determines the capacity for OT or AVP to influence social
behavior. Why should such closely related species exhibit such striking differences
in receptor localization? The answer may reside in the molecular structure of their
OT and AVP receptor genes. Genes can be conceptualized as comprising two main
components: a coding sequence and a promoter sequence. The coding sequence
provides the DNA information for the formation of one specific RNA, which, in
turn, directs the formation of one unique protein. The coding sequence determines whether a gene will create a hormone, a receptor, an enzyme, or a structural
protein for the cell. The second part of the gene is the promoter sequence. This
area, which flanks the coding sequence, contains numerous response elements that
provide the stop or go signals for the gene. If the coding sequence provides the information to make a given protein, the promoter provides the information about
where and when this protein gets made.

There are few genomic differences between prairie and montane voles. When
comparing the coding sequences for OT and AVP receptors, these species appear
essentially identical. That is, they share the same OT and AVP receptors. Not surprisingly, given that these receptors are found in different brain regions, there are
differences in their promoter sequences. For OT receptors, prairie and montane
voles show only subtle differences, but these differences appear to be sufficient to
direct different patterns of expression in the brain (Young, Winslow, Wong, et al.,
1997). For AVP receptors, the species differences are more extreme. In both prairie
and pine voles (both monogamous), an unexpected sequence of about 460 nu-
cleotides, many of them repetitive, appears in the promoter region (Young, Nilsen,
et al., 1999). This repeat sequence, also known as a microsatellite, is lacking in
montane and meadow voles (both nonmonogamous).

The Evolution of Monogamy

If monogamy in voles is associated with DNA variability in the vasopressin receptor gene, where does this variability come from? We don't know the origin of these
microsatellite sequences, but they often occur in promoter regions of the genome,
"hot spots" which are prone to either recombination or expansion. These are likely
sites for mutation. The existing data are consistent with the hypothesis that mutational events in the promoter sequences for OT and AVP receptor genes lead to
different patterns of receptor expression, different functional effects of the hormones, and ultimately different patterns of social organization. Thus monogamy
may have resulted from a specific mutation and survived under specific socioecological conditions in which pair bonding and paternal behavior were adaptive. Of
course, it is also possible that monogamy was the ancestral condition and that

deletion of these microsatellites resulted in a polygamous or promiscuous social organization. Either way, it seems remarkable, given the gender dimorphism described previously, that separate mutational events must have facilitated pair bonding behaviors in males and females.

Of Human Bonding

We know very little about the neurobiology of human attachment. Humans have OT and AVP, and both hormones are released during copulation. Perhaps of greater importance, receptors for OT and AVP are found in the human brain, although the patterns are not quite like those of either the prairie vole or the montane vole (Loup, Tribollet, Dubois-Dauphin, Pizzolato, & Dreifuss, 1989; Loup, Tribollet, Dubois-Dauphin, & Dreifuss, 1991). We do not know if OT or AVP are involved in the formation of pair bonds in humans. Furthermore, we do not know if within a species, human or otherwise, there will be subtle differences in the number or location of receptors that account for individual variations within that species. However, the work on OT and AVP receptors in voles leads to several testable hypotheses in humans:

> *Hypothesis 1:* Areas of the genome that show marked species variation will also show marked within-species individual variation. This hypothesis can be tested by sequencing AVP and OT receptors in many individuals. A pilot study has revealed single nucleotide polymorphisms in the OT receptor and hypervariable regions within the vasopressin receptor promoter, but the functional importance of these findings has not been studied.

> *Hypothesis 2:* There will be marked differences in the neuroanatomical pattern of OT or AVP receptors across individuals. Although an initial study of OT and AVP receptors in the postmortem human brain failed to find significant variation (Loup et al., 1989; Loup et al., 1991), newer techniques will need to be applied to determine if there are subtle differences in receptor expression. In addition, the development of techniques for visualizing OT and AVP receptors in vivo with neuroimaging will be an important advance for investigating individual differences.

> *Hypothesis 3:* Individuals with a deficit in the ability to form attachments (e.g., autistic patients) will have a specific deficit in OT or AVP function. Although one recent study has reported that autistic children have about a 50% decrease in plasma OT, we know very little about brain pathways for OT in these children (Modahl et al., 1998). Clearly, this would be an important group for studies of both sequence variation and postmortem receptor distribution.

Conclusion

It has been said that the purpose of experimental models is to focus our questions, not to provide final answers. The use of nonhuman models to study attachment has provided a clear focus for beginning investigations into human attachment. Oxytocin and vasopressin are important candidate neural systems, and their receptor fields provide potential neuroanatomical nodes for processing the information necessary for attachment. We know that these receptor systems have substantial interspecies differences in regional expression based on hypervariable regions in their genes. It seems possible, although still unproven, that these same genomic regions will show intraspecies variability and may correlate with individual differences in the capacity for human attachment or for altruism.

Although we cannot say that attachment or altruism in humans involves oxytocin and vasopressin, the phylogenetic tradition is impressive. Throughout vertebrate evolution, these or related neuropeptides have been important for sociosexual behaviors. In a sense, it would be most remarkable if humans did not use these hormones to serve similar behavioral endpoints. The evidence is not yet in, but it seems likely that in humans, just as in several other mammals, the release of oxytocin during nursing contributes to the mother's affection for her infant. We do not know whether the release of oxytocin and vasopressin during copulation has a similar bonding effect between two adults, but this possibility would be consistent with the prairie vole results.

Finally, one must remember that in contrast to the brains of other mammals, the human brain is dominated by a massive cortex that governs the hypothalamus and other deep brain structures. Hormones from the hypothalamus, like oxytocin and vasopressin, may modify human behavior, but due to the dominance of the cortex, intellectual, spiritual, and cultural influences ultimately may determine human attachments independent of hormonal state.

REFERENCES

Bamshad, M., Novak, M., & De Vries, G. (1994). Cohabitation alters vasopressin innervation and paternal behavior in prairie voles (*Microtus ochrogaster*). *Physiology and Behavior, 56,* 751–758.

Carter, C. S., DeVries, A. C., & Getz, L. L. (1995). Physiological substrates of mammalian monogamy: The prairie vole model. *Neuroscience and Biobehavior Review, 19,* 303–314.

Dewsbury, D. A. (1988). The comparative psychology of monogamy. In D. W. Leger (Ed.), *Nebraska Symposium on Motivation: Vol. 2. American Zoology* (pp. 1–50). Lincoln: University of Nebraska Press.

Ferris, C. (1992). Role of vasopressin in aggressive and dominant/subordinate behaviors. In C. Pedersen, J. Caldwell, G. Jirikowski, & T. Insel (Eds.), *Oxytocin in maternal, sexual, and social behaviors* (652, pp. 212–227). New York: New York Academy of Sciences Press.

Insel, T. R. (1992). Oxytocin: A neuropeptide for affiliation: Evidence from behavioral, receptor autoradiographic, and comparative studies. *Psychoneuroendocrinology, 17,* 3–33.

Insel, T. R., & Hulihan, T. J. (1995). A gender specific mechanism for pair bonding: Oxytocin and partner preference formation in monogamous voles. *Behavioral Neuroscience, 109*(4): 782–789.

Insel, T. R., & Shapiro, L. E. (1992). Oxytocin receptor distribution reflects social organization in monogamous and polygamous voles. *Proceedings of the National Academy of Sciences USA, 89,* 5981–5985.

Insel, T. R., Wang, Z., & Ferris, C. F. (1994). Patterns of brain vasopressin receptor distribution associated with social organization in microtine rodents. *Journal of Neuroscience, 14*(9), 5381–5392.

Kleiman, D. G. (1977). Monogamy in mammals. *Quarterly Review of Biology, 52,* 39–69.

Loup, F., Tribollet, E., Dubois-Dauphin, M., & Dreifuss, J. J. (1991). Localization of high-affinity binding sites for oxytocin and vasopressin in the human brain: An autoradiographic study. *Brain Research, 555,* 220–232.

Loup, F., Tribollet, E., Dubois-Dauphin, M., Pizzolato, G., & Dreifuss, J. J. (1989). Localization of oxytocin binding sites in the human brainstem and upper spinal cord: An autoradiographic study. *Brain Research, 500,* 223–230.

Modahl, C., Green, L., Fein, D., Morris, M., Waterhouse, L., Feinstein, C., and Levin, H. (1998). Plasma oxytocin levels in autistic children. *Biological Psychiatry, 432*(4), 270–277.

Shapiro, L., Austin, D., Ward, S., & Dewsbury, D. (1986). Familiarity and female mate choice in two species of voles (*Microtus ochrogaster* and *Microtus montanus*). *Animal Behavior, 34,* 90–97.

Williams, J., Catania, K., & Carter, C. (1992). Development of partner preferences in female prairie voles (*Microtus ochrogaster*): The role of social and sexual experience. *Hormones and Behavior, 26,* 339–349.

Winslow, J. T., Hastings, N., Carter, C. S., Harbough, C. R., & Insel, T. R. (1993). A role for central vasopressin in pair bonding in monogamous prairie voles. *Nature, 365,* 545–548.

Winslow, J. T., Shapiro, L. E., Carter, C. S., & Insel, T. R. (1993). Oxytocin and complex social behaviors: Species comparisons. *Psychopharmacology Bulletin, 29,* 409–414.

Witt, D. M. (1995). Oxytocin and rodent sociosexual responses: From behavior to gene expression. *Neuroscience and Biobehavioral Reviews, 19,* 315–324.

Young, L. J., Nilsen, R., Waymire, K. G., MacGregor, G. R., & Insel, T. R. (1999). Increased affiliative response to vasopressin in mice expressing the V1a receptor from a monogamous vole. *Nature, 400,* 766–768.

Young, L. J., Winslow, J. T., Nilsen, R., & Insel, T. R. (1997). Species differences in V1a receptor gene expression in monogamous and nonmonogamous voles: Behavioral consequences. *Behavioral Neuroscience, 111*(3), 599–605.

Young, L. J., Winslow, J. T., Wang, Z., Gingrich, B., Guo, Q., Matzuk, M. M., & Insel, T. R. (1997). Gene targeting approaches to neuroendocrinology: Oxytocin, maternal behavior, and affiliation. *Hormones and Behavior, 31*(3), 221–231.

15

A Note on the Neurobiology
of Emotions

ANTONIO R. DAMASIO

The comprehensive understanding of love, from the forms of love best described as attachment to the forms of love known as altruistic, requires the elucidation of the biological underpinnings of emotion. Here I outline some of my views on the neurobiology of emotion and feeling in the hope that these views complement others coming from psychological, sociological, and philosophical scholarship.

Altruistic love is an emotion, a very complex emotion. Altruistic love is also a feeling, naturally a very complex feeling. This distinction between emotion and feeling is not trivial. By emotion I mean a collection of responses originated in some regions of the brain and aimed at other regions of the brain and myriad parts of the body. The prompt, the trigger or the inducer, if you will, that leads to the production of the particular collection of responses that I call an emotion is a certain class of object or situation. An object or situation becomes an inducer of emotion either because it is so specified in the genome of a given organism or because the organism *learns*, by association, to treat it as an inducer of emotion. It is perhaps fair to say that emotions can be triggered by either innate or learned inducers, depending on the complexity of the emotion and of the circumstances under which it is triggered, but that an emotion as complex as altruistic love is always triggered by a combination of inducers, some or most of which will have been learned.

When one has an emotion, altruistic love included, the organism deploys specific behaviors. Certain changes occur in the organism's internal milieu and in the viscera, and certain movements and actions are carried out in the physical and cultural environment surrounding the organism. Although not all responses of an emotion become external behaviors, many of them do. Those responses become public, observable by other organisms. Emotions, altruistic love included, are thus objective behaviors analyzable by third-party observers.

But the consequences of the emotions do not terminate with the accomplishment of certain public behaviors. Consequences of the emotions include the occurrence of feelings, the occurrence of feelings of emotions, that is. In humans the consequences of emotions also include the knowing of feelings of emotion; in other words, a *consciousness* of emotions mediated through feeling.

Feelings are, in short, the mental representation of all the changes that occur in the body and in the brain during an emotional state. Those representations occur in the form of neural patterns in the many brain structures that can map, in sensory form, events that occur internally in the organism. The neural patterns are then transformed into mental images, placed alongside other mental images in the ever-flowing stream of thoughts.

From a neurobiological perspective, then, the term *altruistic love* means one of two things: a complex emotion, that is, a collection of specific behaviors, some of which are publicly observable; or a feeling, that is, a set of internal, entirely private and nonobservable images of the organism transformations that occur in the emotional state.

Both parts of the emotion-feeling cycle are beginning to be understood in terms of biological structures and mechanisms responsible for their execution in both humans and animals (see Damasio, 1994, 1999, and Davidson & Irwin, 1999, for overall reviews of the field in humans; Panksepp, Nelson, & Bekkedal, 1997, for a review of the field in animals; and Adolphs, Tranel, & Damasio, 1994; Adolphs, Tranel, Damasio, & Damasio, 1995; Adolphs, Damasio, Tranel, & Damasio, 1996; and Adolphs & Damasio,1998, for reviews of emotion seen from the perspective of its recognition).

Defining Emotions

The term *emotion* usually brings to mind one of the so-called primary or universal emotions: fear, anger, happiness, sadness, disgust, and surprise. But the field of emotions is far broader. Embarrassment, pride, jealousy, or guilt are also emotions, usually termed secondary or social emotions; and the same is the case with calm or tension, well-being or malaise, all part of a large collection of emotions which I have termed *background* emotions. The constituents of emotions are variations on the states of pleasure and pain, along with complex behavioral programs known as drives and motivations. Pleasure and pain, drives and motivations, are the deep components of the complex phenomena we call emotions and feelings.

In the language of neurobiology, emotions are complicated collections of chemical and neural responses, initiated in the brain and forming a pattern. An example of a chemical response is the release into the bloodstream, under the brain's command, of a hormone such as cortisol. An example of a neural response is the brain's command to contract a muscle sent along nerve pathways that make contact with muscles (Damasio, 1994, 1999).

The brain devices which actually produce emotions are located in a small number of brain sites below the level of the cerebral cortex, mostly at the level of the brain stem, the hypothalamus, and the basal forebrain/ventral striatum. These devices are part of a set of brain regions that both help regulate the state of the body and, in good part, also represent that state. All of these brain devices, which I term *emotion effectors*, can be engaged automatically when an appropriate situation arises without the need for conscious deliberation. That engagement is controlled from a set of regions that I designate as *emotion induction sites* and that include the ventromedial prefrontal cortices, the cingulate cortex, and the amygdala.

In short, once the brain detects a stimulus capable of triggering an emotion, certain parts of the brain (the induction sites) send messages to other regions of the brain (the effector sites), which in turn send messages to yet other brain regions and to many parts of the body. These commands are sent via two avenues. One avenue is the bloodstream, in which the messages are sent in the form of chemical molecules that act on receptors in the cells that constitute body tissues. The other avenue consists of nerve pathways, in which the messages use electrochemical signals that act on muscular fibers or on hormone-secreting organs such as the adrenal gland.

The Double Theater of the Emotions: The Body and the Brain

The result of the chemical and neural messages just outlined is a global change in the state of the organism. For example, the muscles, whether they are smooth muscles in a blood vessel or striated muscles in the face, move as they are commanded to do. But the brain itself is also changed. The release of chemical substances such as monoamines and peptides from emotion effector regions of the brain stem alters the mode of processing of several brain circuits in the telencephalon—including the thalamus, the basal ganglia, and the cerebral cortex. But those chemicals also trigger certain specific behaviors, such as bonding, playing, and crying. Just as important, the release of chemical substances also modifies the manner in which the ongoing state of the body is multivariously represented in the brain. In other words, both the body proper and the brain are largely and profoundly affected by emotion-related messages, although the origin of those messages is circumscribed to a few small brain areas which are in the process of responding to a particular mental event.

In short, all emotions use the body as their theater. They use the body's chemistries, its viscera, and its muscles. But emotions also affect the mode of operation of numerous brain circuits, both the ones that represent and regulate the body and others that do not. Most emotions are responsible for profound changes in *both* the body and the brain. Moreover, note that emotions are not feelings. It is only when the brain manages to make a coordinated representation of all the emotional changes in the form of images that we come to *feel* an emotion. Note, finally, that it is only when we have consciousness that we come to *know* that we feel an emotion.

The Purpose of Emotions

All emotions play a regulatory role. All emotions participate in achieving, directly or indirectly, a biological correction of some kind. The correction leads to the creation of circumstances advantageous to the individual having the emotion. Emotions are *about* the life of an organism, and the role of emotions is to assist the organism in maintaining life.

So much for general purpose. The more particular biological function of emotions is twofold. One purpose is to produce a reaction to the object or situation that causes the emotion. A typical example: An animal confronted by a threatening stimulus may react by running or by becoming immobile or by attacking the source of threat, for example, a predator. An animal confronted by a potentially beneficial stimulus, such as the presence of food or of a possible mate, will react by engaging in approach behavior. This means that for certain kinds of dangerous or valuable stimuli, evolution has prepared an answer, in the form of emotion, that appropriately matches the stimulus. In humans the reactions are essentially the same, although they can be tempered by reason and wisdom, two functions that complement emotions and assist with the creation of altruistic behaviors.

Another biological purpose of emotion is to alter the internal state of the organism so as to make the organism ready to react in the appropriate manner. An example of such readiness is providing increased blood flow to the muscles in the legs so that they can receive the extra oxygen and glucose necessary for running.

The stimulus that triggers an emotion may be external to the organism, as, for example, when we see a familiar face or place. Or it may be internal to the organism, when it appears in the mind from within, conjured up from memory. An example is remembering the face of a friend or a place we enjoyed visiting.

Objects and events are consistently more linked to certain kinds of emotion than to others. It is apparent that the stimuli that cause happiness or fear or sadness tend to have consistent effects in the same person and in persons of similar cultural background. In spite of all the obvious individual variations in the expression of the emotions, there is a strong correspondence between the stimuli that cause emotions and the emotions that result. Humans have acquired the means to respond to stimuli that are potentially useful or potentially dangerous, with the neural "action-programs" called emotions. Some of those stimuli belong to classes of objects or situations that nature has prescribed, in the process of evolution, to cause emotional states. Other classes of stimuli are learned in the course of individual experience, but that learning occurs under the influence of emotions caused by the evolutionarily prescribed stimuli.

The Mechanisms of Emotion

Some emotional responses are easily observable—for example, the muscles in the face adopting the configurations of merriment, or the skin blushing in embarrassment, or the body postures that signify depression and discouragement. Other emotional responses are hidden from view—for example, the release into brain circuits of neuromodulators such as serotonin or dopamine. The typical consequences of releasing those neuromodulators include our sense that the processes of the mind speed up or slow down, but perhaps the main consequence is the sense of pleasantness or unpleasantness that suffuses mental experience. Noticing these mental changes is as much a part of the feeling of an emotion as is noticing what goes on in our heart or gut (Damasio, 1994, 1999).

The Experience of Emotion

The collection of organism changes that constitute emotions are subsequently represented in the form of images that constitute feelings. The images that constitute feelings thus arise from neural patterns that occur in structures capable of representing the ongoing body state and of representing certain aspects of the ongoing mental state. Among the structures that represent the body state are neural nuclei in the brainstem tegmentum and in the hypothalamus, as well as in regions of the cingulate cortex, and in the somatosensory cortices (the insular cortex, SII and SI). These regions can be acted upon by signals from the internal milieu, the viscera, and the musculoskeletal frame and can also be influenced by signals from emotional induction and effector sites. Among the regions involved in the metarepresentation of ongoing mental states I include some prefrontal cortices and some parietal association cortices.

Feelings and Their Functions

As I noted, in addition to having emotions, humans also have feelings of emotion, which are literally the mental mappings of all the emotional changes previously described. Feelings are images, and those images derive from the neural patterns that represent the entire range of changes associated with an emotion.

But what are feelings for? Someone might argue that emotions alone, without feelings, might be a sufficient mechanism to assist with the obvious main purpose of the exercise, that is the maintenance of life. But the argument is not valid. Having feelings is of great value in orchestrating the maintenance of life. Beyond the action programs of emotions, feelings *alert* the mind of an organism to the particular problem that an emotion is on the way to solving or has solved. The simple process of feeling provides the organism with an *incentive* to attend to the results of emoting.

Elsewhere, I have also argued that the availability of feeling is the basis for yet another biological process, *the feeling of knowing that we have feelings*, which in turn is the stepping stone for the ability to make plans and organize responses that were not necessarily prescribed by our genes (Damasio, 1999). In other words, the ability to "feel" feelings extends the reach of emotions by facilitating the creation of new forms of adaptive response.

Emotions in the History of Life

Emotions are biologically constructed processes and depend on brain devices available at birth. Yet it is apparent that learning and the cultural environment alter the expression of emotions and give emotions new meanings. The precise composition and dynamics of the emotional responses are shaped in each individual by a unique development and environment, but the evidence suggests that most emotional responses are the result of a long history of evolutionary fine-tuning. Emotions are part of the regulatory devices with which we are endowed by evolution. This is why emotions are so easily recognized anywhere in the world no matter what the culture is. The expressions vary, and the precise configuration of stimuli that can induce an emotion in different cultures and different individuals varies as well, but the similarity is more amazing than the difference. It is that similarity that makes cross-cultural relations possible, namely those that pertain to the arts and commerce. It is worth emphasizing that emotions cannot be taught, although their proper use *can* be taught, and that a civilized, humanly rich society probably depends on such teachings.

Emotion, Feeling, and Consciousness

As I noted at the beginning of the chapter, *feeling* is not *knowing feeling*. Knowing a feeling requires consciousness, that is, a knower subject. It is possible that the reason consciousness endured in evolution is that conscious organisms were able to "feel" their feelings. The mechanisms that permit consciousness may have prevailed because they allowed organisms to know of their emotions and because that knowledge became useful for their survival. Of course, although consciousness may have prevailed because it was useful to know emotions, consciousness went well beyond the "emotion-feeling function" and eventually allowed us to know any object or event that can be mentally represented (Damasio, 1999).

The Neural Basis for Empathy

Empathy is a critical element in altruistic love, and the elucidation of its neural basis has just begun. The brain regions in the metarepresentation of mental states are critical for the process of empathy, and they include, as noted previously, regions of parietal association cortex and of prefrontal cortex. A number of new findings is letting us know which regions precisely are involved in this process. For example, we know that damage to right somatosensory cortices impairs the ability of patients to imagine the feelings experienced by persons who exhibit certain emotional facial expressions. In other words, a patient with such lesions is unable to indicate that a person with the facial expression of sadness is probably feeling sad. The data presented in the study by Adolphs, Damasio, Tranel, Cooper, and

Damasio (2000) are especially compelling because the patients' task is visually based but the impairment is caused not by damage in the visual system but rather by damage in the right somatosensory system.

Damage to sectors of the prefrontal cortex, namely but not exclusively the ventromedial sector, alters the patients' ability to sense the feelings and moods of others (see H. Damasio, Chapter 16, this volume; Bechara, Damasio, & Damasio, 2000; Bechara, Damasio, Tranel, & Damasio, 1997; Bechara, Tranel, Damasio, & Damasio, 1996; Damasio, 1996). It is likely that in all of these situations there is an inability to create an internal simulation of the feeling state in someone else's mind, probably because the essential ingredients of such states—the representations of ongoing body and mental states—cannot be properly manipulated. The discovery of neurons in the frontal cortex of the monkey that fire when the animal observes certain movements of another animal adds detail to the neural mechanism which may subserve the simulation process.

Concluding Remarks

It is apparent that the process of emotion and feeling is beginning to be understood in terms of its cognitive and neural components. Emotion and feeling are not a mere remnant from prior evolutionary ages, although they are, to be sure, the consequence of long-standing evolutionary selections. Emotion and feeling are not a luxury. Most of the well-recognized emotions maintain their immediate adaptive value in humans, but, in addition, they participate in a broader set of processes whose consequences are felt beyond the immediate moment, in the longer term, and whose reach is thus larger. Such processes include the ability to sense not just states of the self but also states of the *other*. That sense is also known as empathy. The ability to reason and decide in a social realm and the ability to be intelligent and creative in a social realm depend, to a considerable part, on this combined knowledge of self *and* other.

In conclusion, many of the achievements that characterize humans at their best, such as the construction of an individual conscience, the elaboration of ethical rules, and the codification of the law, are based on the foundational processes of emotion and feeling coupled with an individual's ability to *know* of the existence of such emotions and feelings in the self and others (Damasio, 1999). Indeed, these evolutionarily grounded capacities are the foundation for one of the most extraordinary extensions in the phenomenon of life, the emergence of genuine altruism.

REFERENCES

Adolphs, R., & Damasio, A. R. (1998). The human amygdala in social judgement. *Nature, 393*, 470–474.
Adolphs, R., Damasio, H., Tranel, D., Cooper, G., & Damasio, A. R. (2000). A role for somatosensory cortices in the visual recognition of emotion as revealed by three-dimensional lesion mapping. *Journal of Neuroscience, 20*, 2683–2690.

Adolphs, R., Damasio, H., Tranel, D., & Damasio, A. R. (1996). Cortical systems for the recognition of emotion in facial expressions. *Journal of Neuroscience, 16,* 7678–7687.

Adolphs, R., Tranel, D., & Damasio, A. R. (1994). Impaired recognition of emotion in facial expressions following bilateral damage to the human amygdala. *Nature, 372,* 669–672.

Adolphs, R., Tranel, D., Damasio, H., & Damasio, A. R. (1995). Fear and the human amygdala. *Journal of Neuroscience, 15,* 5879–5891.

Bechara, A., Damasio, H., & Damasio, A. R. (2000). Emotion, decision-making, and the orbitofrontal cortex. *Cerebral Cortex, 10,* 295–307.

Bechara, A., Damasio, H., Tranel, D., & Damasio, A. R. (1997). Deciding advantageously before knowing the advantageous strategy. *Science, 275,* 1293–1294.

Bechara, A., Tranel, D., Damasio, H., & Damasio, A. R. (1996). Failure to respond autonomically to anticipated future outcomes following damage to prefrontal cortex. *Cerebral Cortex, 6,* 215–225.

Damasio, A. R. (1994). *Descartes' error: Emotion, reason, and the human brain.* New York: Putnam.

Damasio, A. R. (1996). The somatic marker hypothesis and the possible functions of the prefrontal cortex. *Transactions of the Royal Society (London), 351,*1413–1420.

Damasio, A. R. (1999). *The feeling of what happens: Body and emotion in the making of consciousness.* New York: Harcourt Brace.

Davidson, R. J., & Irwin, W. (1999). The functional neuroanatomy of emotion and affective style. *Trends in Cognitive Science, 3,* 11–21.

Panksepp, J., Nelson, E., & Bekkedal, M. (1997). Brain systems for the mediation of social separation-distress and social-reward. Evolutionary antecedents and neuropeptide intermediaries. In *The integrative neurobiology of affiliation: Proceedings of a conference. Annals of the New York Academy of Sciences, 807*: 78–100.

16

Impairment of Interpersonal Social Behavior Caused by Acquired Brain Damage

HANNA DAMASIO

In order for human beings to exhibit the sort of behaviors described under the rubric of altruistic love, a number of important conditions must be met. At the very least, the following conditions are required: (1) the neural devices necessary to produce the behavior must have been put in place effectively by the genome; (2) the current environment must be compatible with the behavior; (3) the current biological state of the individual's organism must be such that these neural devices are operational; and (4) the past environment must have allowed the individual to develop psychologically and biologically in such a way that the relation between the behavior and social situations can be properly adjusted.

In this chapter I consider a number of situations in which, as a result of brain damage, the neural devices necessary to exhibit empathy are destroyed or rendered dysfunctional. Considering these situations is important because empathy is a prerequisite for altruism and other socially adaptive behaviors. Studying these situations offers the possibility of investigating the biological underpinnings of such behaviors in individuals who do not have known disturbances at the genomic level and who lived in standard social and cultural environments prior to the time of brain damage.

To illustrate this idea, I use an example of one in a long series of patients studied in our laboratories:

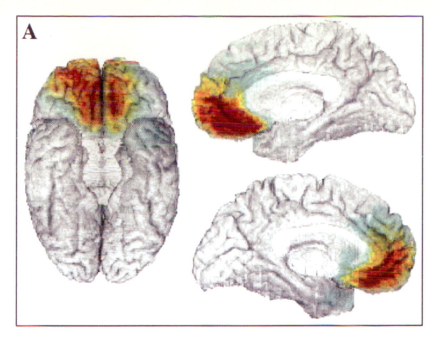

Color plate. (A) Map-3 of 13 patients with damage to prefrontal cortices. The image is obtained through the transfer of the individual lesion in each patient's brain onto a normal reference brain, using subprograms of Brainvox (Damasio & Frank, 1992). The number of overlapping lesions is color coded. The red-colored areas correspond to the brain regions with maximal overlapping lesions.

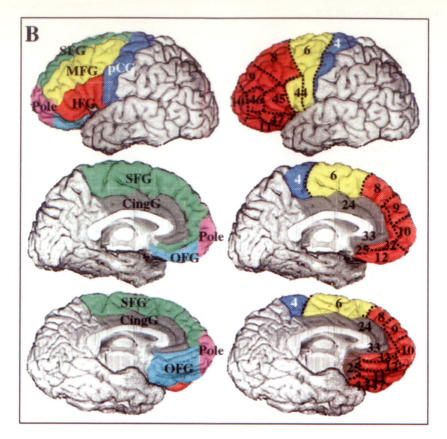

Color plate. (B) Three-dimensional reconstructed normal left hemisphere, seen in both columns in a lateral view (top), in a mesial view (middle), and a tilted mesial view (bottom) that allows the observation of the large inferior expansion of the orbital sector of the frontal lobe. The left column shows the typical subdivisions of the frontal lobe: precentral gyrus (pCG), inferior frontal gyrus (IFG), middle frontal gyrus (MFG), superior frontal gyrus (SFG), cingulated gyrus (cingG), orbitofrontal gyri (OFG), and the pole. The right column represents the functional divisions of the frontal lobe. The colors represent: red, the prefrontal region; yellow, the premotor region; and blue, the motor region. The numbers stand for the cytoarchitectonic nomenclature of Brodman.

Patient E. was an intelligent, hard-working, and successful man who performed a steady skilled job at which he was promoted due to his good performance. He was active in social affairs and was perceived as a leader and example by his siblings and by others in the community. At age 35 a frontal meningeoma was diagnosed, and the tumor was removed surgically. Due to the size and extension of the meningeoma, it was necessary to perform a bilateral removal of the ventromedial frontal cortices. After surgery, a completely changed person emerged. He remained skilled enough to hold his job, but he could not be counted on to report to work promptly or to execute all the tasks that were necessary for the job to be discharged effectively. He was fired and has never again been able to maintain a job. His ability to plan activities, both on a daily basis and into the short-term and long-term future, is severely impaired. The planning usually fails to include aspects that would be obviously required for the goal to be achieved and includes, instead, peripheral details that would be of no possible consequence. Often, on matters of relatively secondary import—for instance, what to wear, where to shop, what movie to go to—E. is plunged into an endless deliberation. He is unable to make a rapid choice and, instead, pursues a course of interminable comparisons and successive choices among many possible options that become more and more difficult to distinguish. His final response selection, if and when it ever comes, may end up being random.

Social behaviors constitute a particular area of difficulty, and among these financial planning is especially affected. It is not easy for E. to determine which persons are good and which are not, or which are trustworthy and which are not and to guide his future life course according to such determinations. He appears to lack a sense of what is socially appropriate, judging from his choices in real life, although it is obvious from his premorbid life and from his achievements that he used to have a keen sense of social appropriateness.

The spouses of these patients note a lack of empathy as one of the hallmark symptoms of the condition. For example, the wife of one of our patients noted how her husband, who, prior to his lesion, reacted with care and affection any time she was upset about some matter and cried, would now react with indifference in precisely the same circumstances. "If I am upset and start crying he will not say anything, he will not touch me, he may even leave the room." Patients who, prior to their lesions, were known to be concerned with social projects in their communities or who were known for their ability to counsel friends and relatives in difficulty no longer show any caring or any inclination to be involved in such projects. They are no longer sought by others for help. It is not just that in the lives of these patients there are no recorded episodes of altruistic love; they lack what is probably a precondition for altruistic love, which is empathy. (For details on patient E. and the many other such patients studied in our laboratory, see Damasio, 1994; Damasio, Tranel, & Damasio, 1991).

In general, the characteristics of patient E. and of the many comparable subjects studied so far in our laboratory fit the criteria for *sociopathy* as defined by the *Diagnostic and Statistical Manual of Mental Disorders* (DSM-IV; American Psychiatric Association, 1994): namely, "inability to sustain consistent work behavior," "lack of ability to function as a responsible parent," and "defective planning." There are, however, two key differences between E. (and patients like E.) and a typical sociopath: (1) in patients like E. the sociopathic manifestations appear in adulthood after brain damage to a specific site rather than during development; and (2) patients like E. tend to cause mostly difficulties for themselves rather than causing harm to others.

Many aspects of intellectual profile remain intact in these patients. In some cases, for instance in patient E., the abilities that remain intact are just as outstanding as those that become impaired. E. has verbal and performance IQs in the 97th and 99th percentiles, respectively. His memory quotient is also in the 99th percentile. His language, learning, and recall are normal. However, E. shows signs that the processing of emotions and feelings is abnormal.

It is not possible to account for these patients' acquired defects on the basis of a general impairment of intelligence or memory or language or perception. Furthermore, these patients also lack the subtle but characteristic signs of frontal lobe dysfunction. For instance, their ability to perform the Wisconsin Card Sorting Test, the Word Fluency Test, paradigms requiring cognitive estimation (Shallice & Evans, 1978), and judgment of recency and frequency (Milner & Petrides, 1984) are all intact.

What about laboratory tasks that require social knowledge? Performance on a number of those tasks reveals a normal performance as well. Examples of these tasks are as follows:

1. The Optional Thinking Task (Platt & Spivack, 1977) measures the ability to generate alternative solutions to hypothetical social dilemmas described in stories. Take a situation in which the protagonist of the story breaks a flower vase, and the participant is asked to generate alternative actions meant to avoid the anger of the spouse. There are a total of four stories, and the performance is scored on the basis of the number of alternative modes of action that are generated. The performance of E. is indistinguishable from those of normals (Saver & Damasio, 1991).

2. The Awareness of Consequences Test (Platt & Spivack, 1977) measures the amount of spontaneous consideration of consequences of actions. Again, four stories are presented in which hypothetical predicaments involving temptations to transgress ordinary rules of social conduct are depicted. For example, the participant cashes a check at a bank and, by mistake, is given too much money by the teller. What would the participant do? The performance of E. is indistinguishable from those of normals (Saver & Damasio, 1991).

3. The Means-Ends Problem-Solving Procedure (Platt & Spivack, 1975) measures the participant's ability to conceptualize step-by-step means to achieve a certain goal. Ten stories are presented in which a particular social need and a goal are set. The participant is asked to provide the means to achieve the goal. For example, a person who has recently moved to a new neighborhood desires to form new friendships and ends up having many new friends. The participant is asked to describe ways in which this end might have been achieved. Once again, E. performs exactly as normals do (Saver & Damasio, 1991).

4. The standard-issue moral judgment interview is more commonly known as the Kohlberg paradigm (Colby & Kohlberg, 1987). We use the Heinz dilemma. Here participants are asked to solve a social situation in which there are conflicts between moral inferences and to provide a detailed ethical justification for the response. For instance, the participant is presented with a story in which he has to decide if the character should or should not steal a drug to prevent his wife from dying. The response of E. is again equal to those of normals (Saver & Damasio, 1991).

In summary, in all these tasks participants like E. perform in a manner comparable to normals. It is interesting to note that even when presented with situations similar to those in which, in real life, participants have failed, they still perform normally when presented with the situations in verbal terms, in the laboratory setting.

Explaining the Condition

The cause of this collection of symptoms is brain damage in a specific site, most frequently in the mesial and orbital sectors of the prefrontal cortices (see color plate). Damage elsewhere in the brain does not cause this syndrome.

But how can we explain the neural mechanisms behind these symptoms? It becomes obvious that the symptoms shown by these patients in real life cannot be explained in terms of defects in pertinent knowledge, intellectual ability, language, basic working memory, or basic attention.

In order to account for the discrepancy between the real-life behavior of these patients, with its major problems, and the normalcy they show in the laboratory, as previously described, the *somatic marker hypothesis* was developed (Damasio et al., 1991; Damasio, 1994, 1996). This framework attempted to account for the condition and to develop new laboratory probes that might capture it more objectively.

The somatic marker hypothesis specifies that, throughout development and adult life, when we experience situations which call for responses that are either rewarded or punished, we are learning and categorizing critical sets of events: (1) a given situation; (2) related facts and options for action; and (3) a chosen option, which leads to consequences both immediate and long-term, both emotional and factual.

When we are confronted by new situations that somehow fit the categories we have formed for situations in our past experience, we can re-evoke not only many facts pertinent to such situations but also the emotional state that prevailed for those situations. The result of the re-evocation can be *overt*, that is, *explicit* or *conscious* (for example, in the form of a gut feeling); or it can be *covert*, that is, *implicit* or *nonconscious*, taking the form of a bias that modifies processing without our awareness (see Fig 16.1).

The evidence for covert emotion-related signals comes from experiments such as those described here using the Gambling Task (Bechara, Damasio, Damasio, &

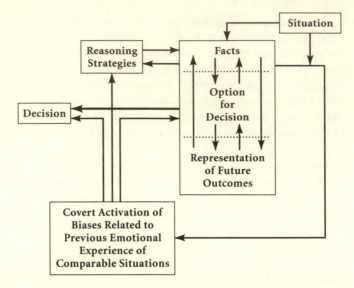

Figure 16.1.   Diagram of the proposed steps involved in decision making

Anderson, 1994; Bechara, Damasio, Tranel, & Damasio, 1997; Bechara, Tranel, Damasio, & Damasio, 1996).

The Gambling Task is an experimental procedure involving a game of cards. The purpose of the game is to keep as much as possible of an amount of money loaned to the participant by the examiner. The essence of the Gambling Task is as follows: There are four decks of cards—A, B, C, and D. The participants are given $2,000 in play money and are told to pick up one card at a time from any of the decks and that they will receive some money whenever they pick up a card. They are also told that, on occasion, they will not only get some money but will also lose some money. The aim of the game is to keep (or make) as much money as possible. What the participants are not told is the following: The game will last for 100 card turns. Decks A and B pay $100 each time, and decks C and D pay $50. The penalties are randomly dispersed within each deck, but they total $1,250 in every 10 cards in decks A and B and $250 in decks C and D. They occur rarely in A and C but are high each time they occur, and they occur more often and are smaller in B and D. In sum, if one picks cards from A and B, there will be a total loss in spite of the high upfront payment; but if one sticks to C and D, the low-paying decks, one will end up with a net profit. As in real life, the participant is given the bare basics of procedure and has to discover the rules of the game as he or she goes along.

While the task is being performed, we continually record the skin conductance responses (SCRs) of the participants, before and at the moment at which the participants pick up a card and after they do so.

There are several interesting results to report:

1. Both normal participants and patients start sampling across the decks.
2. After receiving the first few penalties, normal participants tend to veer toward decks C and D and avoid decks A and B.
3. Patients do not show such an early strategy.
4. As the task continues, normal participants completely shift their choices to decks C and D, whereas patients continue playing decks A and B, often exhausting those cards and going repeatedly "broke," needing to borrow more money.
5. Both normal participants and patients show an SCR following the delivery of a penalty.
6. Most interestingly, normal participants start showing anticipatory SCR whenever they ponder and choose a card from decks A and B. This anticipatory SCR starts relatively early and keeps increasing in magnitude for as long as cards from decks A and B are picked.
7. Patients never show anticipatory SCRs.
8. When normal participants are asked what they know about what is going on during the early stages of the game (when they already show anticipatory SCRs and some tendency to prefer decks C and D), they invariably respond that they do not know. A bit later they may say that they still do not know but that they feel decks C and D might be better. By the end of the game, most know and report that decks A and B are losers and that decks C and D are winners.
9. None of the patients ever report the early stages of "covert knowledge," in parallel with the lack of anticipatory SCRs. However, in spite of never changing their strategies, some report at the end that A and B are bad decks. Asked why they continued to play them, they say things such as, "They give more money to start with" and "I was waiting for you to change the rules."
10. If we retest normal participants some time later, they more rapidly play the good decks. But the retesting of patients produces exactly the same results as seen the first time around, even if the participant might have reached the stage of full explicit knowledge about which decks were winners and which decks were losers after their first experience with the task. (For more detail on these results, see Bechara et al., 1994; Bechara et al., 1996; and Bechara et al., 1997.)

I could summarize what I have just demonstrated by saying that previously normal adults who suffer damage to a specific brain sector are able to learn new factual knowledge but fail to use it in real time. They also preserve factual knowledge about what normal social behaviors ought to be like in general but fail to deploy those behaviors in real time. We have suggested that this failure is due to a breakdown of emotional-related memories that are either destroyed or not deployable (Damasio, 1994, 1996; Bechara et al., 1997; Bechara, Damasio, & Damasio, 2000).

Impairment of Social Behavior Caused by Damage During Early Development

The evidence that I present here completes the picture I have drawn and reveals another human condition in which adaptive interpersonal social behavior is profoundly compromised. The evidence comes from the study of individuals with very early onset of prefrontal lesions, as opposed to the adult-onset cases I have just described. The following are two examples studied in collaboration with my colleague Steven Anderson (Anderson, Bechara, Damasio, Tranel, & Damasio, 1999).

One patient shows a cystic lesion in the polar region of both frontal lobes. This cyst displaces and compresses prefrontal regions, particularly in the anterior orbital sector, and more so on the left. There is also damage to the mesial sector on the right. The other patient shows extensive damage to the right frontal lobe involving all three sectors—mesial, orbital, and dorsolateral (Figure 16.2).

The characteristics of these two patients are as follows:

1. Both patients come from middle-class homes with college-educated parents. The parents devoted time and resources to the upbringing of their children, and in both cases there are perfectly normal and socially well adapted siblings.
2. Both patients are in their early 20s. One, a woman, is 20; the other, a man, is 23.
3. Both patients suffered their injuries before 2 years of age (Patient A was run over by a truck at age 15 months, and Patient B suffered a tumor resection at age 3 months and had no tumor recurrence).
4. Both recovered well without any evidence of deficit from their injuries.
5. Both showed signs of deficient behavior control and poor peer interaction early in school.
6. Both were thought to be academically capable, but both showed poor working habits and needed tutoring and placement in special facilities during schooling years.
7. Both lacked friends and showed limited social interactions. One (Patient A) was confrontational with peers and adults; the other (Patient B) displayed mostly a neutral mood with occasional explosive outbursts of anger.
8. Both lacked any plans for their future and markedly deteriorated after graduation.
9. Both showed early and irresponsible sexual behavior. Patient A became pregnant at age 18 and never showed any interest in the child or its wellbeing, a fact noted by the nurses in the delivery room and immediately

Figure 16.2. (*opposite*) The brains of two patients with early-onset prefrontal damage, reconstructed in three dimensions from contiguous thin-cut MR slices, using Brainvox

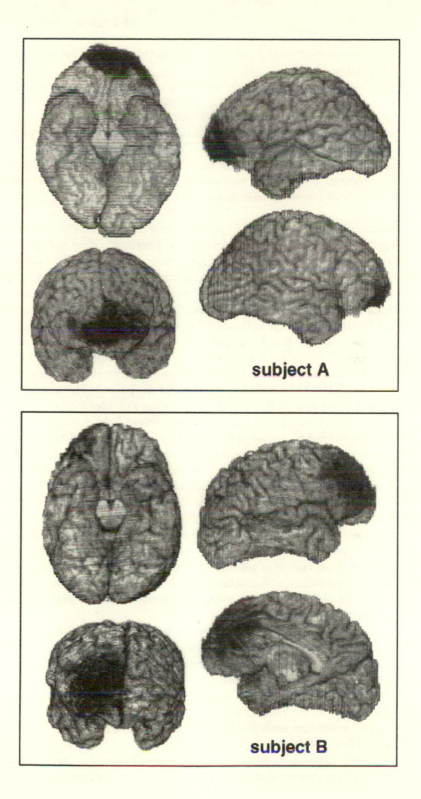

subject A

subject B

postpartum. Patient B fathered a child as a teenager and did not fulfill any paternal obligations.

10. Neither patient ever sought employment. Both were unable to keep any employment procured for them, not because of lack of ability to fulfill job requirements but because of lack of dependability.

11. Both were and are dependent on family for their financial support and guardianship.

12. Neither ever shows a sense of guilt or remorse. Patient A has been an inveterate liar since about age 5, used to steal from colleagues in school, and has been arrested several times.

Formal neuropsychological evaluation of these two patients shows them to be intelligent and with normal funds of knowledge. They have a good ability to repeat and reverse random sequences of digits, good mental arithmetic, good verbal reasoning, good nonverbal problem solving, normal verbal and visual anterograde memory, normal speech and language, normal visuoperceptive and visuomotor abilities, and normal academic achievement. In sum, their intellectual abilities are as much in the normal range as those of the participants in the adult-onset group.

The results on the Gambling Task also parallel those obtained in the adult brain-damaged participants. They fail to generate anticipatory SCR and to prefer the good decks C and D. In short, most of the test results for these last two patients are in no way different from those presented for the patients who acquired their prefrontal damage in adult life. However, their history profiles are remarkably different. These two patients are in fact indistinguishable from developmental psychopaths, as defined by DSM-IV. Besides, there is one group of tasks in which these early-damage patients perform differently from the late-onset patients described first. These are the tasks which address social and moral judgments. In those tasks, the behavior of these two young adults is completely different from the behavior displayed by the patients injured in adulthood, as shown by the following data.

In the Optional Thinking Task experiment, patients like E. who were chosen to match the two early-onset patients with respect to the site of damage are in no way different from a group of normal participants in the number of relevant responses they produce. On the other hand, both early-onset patients perform below the level of 2 standard deviations (SD) from the normal participants *and* from the matched frontal-lobe patients.

The same result can be seen with respect to the Awareness of Consequences Test, in which adult-onset frontal patients show frequencies of reference to consequences that are indistinguishable from those of normal controls and in which the early-onset patients are below 1.5 SD from normals.

In the Means-Ends Problem-Solving Procedure, the 23-year-old man is clearly abnormal in the number of relevant responses. The 20-year-old woman performs in a way comparable to both the normal controls and the group with adult-onset frontal-lobe damage.

In relation to the Heinz dilemma, it is interesting to note that one of the adult-onset frontal-lobe patients performed at Level 3, the postconventional level, which is achieved only by a minority of normal adults. The remaining 5 participant performed at Level 2, the conventional level, which is the level achieved by most normal adults. The two early-onset frontal-damage cases performed at the preconventional level, that is, the level characteristic of normal 9-year-old children.

Concluding Remarks

When we combine the results from patients with early-onset and adult-onset prefrontal lesions, it is reasonable to arrive at the following general conclusion: There is a system in certain sectors of the prefrontal cortex that is critical for the learning and maintenance of certain aspects of social behavior that pertain to interpersonal relationships. After damage to this system, empathy, as well as emotions such as embarrassment, guilt, pride, and altruism, are not evoked, and personal and social decisions become defective. In adults this failure is dramatic but partial, dissociating the factual aspects of a situation from the emotional aspects. On the other hand, in early-onset damage the failure is radical: Individuals develop without *both* the emotional *and* the factual basis for adaptive interpersonal social behavior.

The importance of learning in the acquisition of adequate social behavior should not lead to the conclusion that the brain begins as a clean slate. It is possible, and indeed likely, that some of the adaptive interpersonal behaviors that were lost in these patients are actually preset in neural systems that include prefrontal components. In other words, it is possible that the genome lays down those systems innately. Learning fine-tunes the connection between those preset behavioral repertoires and a number of specific stimuli and situations. In other words, the knowledge base that is lost in prefrontal damage is not just the knowledge that is acquired postbirth but also the knowledge acquired through evolution and transmitted genetically in the form of certain neural circuits. What is impressive, at any rate, is the specificity of these neural systems, regardless of the exact balance of evolutionary and postnatal knowledge that they support.

An important aspect of these systems is the fact that they are integral components of the brain devices that regulate the life process. In other words, the prefrontal structures whose damage impairs social interpersonal behaviors are closely interconnected with the structures in hypothalamus and brainstem that automatically regulate the chemical balance of the organism's internal milieu, what is known as homeostasis. As a whole, all of these structures regulate the life process in such a way that the organism can survive. Not surprisingly, when we look at these structures in this perspective, we realize that they are also involved in the process of attention, in the regulation of sleep and wakefulness, in the processes of emotion, in the processes of learning, and, as most recently demonstrated, in the process of consciousness (Damasio, 1999). The rationale for this functional overlap can be seen as the need to survive in progressively more complex and thus more demanding environments. In this light, adaptive interpersonal social behaviors are the latest addition to this list of biological arrangements aimed at better survival.

I certainly do not want to suggest that the prefrontal cortex contains a "center" for brotherly love or altruism. But it is true that, without certain sectors of the prefrontal cortex, empathy, along with other adaptive social behaviors, becomes impaired. It is thus possible that the many levels of behavior we can describe as altruistic *depend* on prefrontal cortex circuitry, although, of course, they do not depend *exclusively* on that circuitry, because any complex behavior requires the concerted participation of many different brain circuitries.

NOTE

The research for this chapter was supported in part by NINDS Grant PO1 NS19632 and by a grant from the Mathers Foundation.

REFERENCES

American Psychiatric Association. (1994). *Diagnostic and statistical manual of mental disorders* (4th ed.).Washington: American Psychiatric Association Press.

Anderson, S. W., Bechara, A., Damasio, H., Tranel, D., & Damasio, A. R. (1999). Impairment of social and moral behavior related to early damage in human prefrontal cortex. *Nature Neuroscience, 2,* 1032–1037.

Bechara, A., Damasio, A. R., Damasio, H., & Anderson, S. W. (1994). Insensitivity to future consequences following damage to human prefrontal cortex. *Cognition, 50,* 7–15.

Bechara, A., Damasio, H., & Damasio, A. (2000). Emotion, decision-making, and the orbitofrontal cortex. *Cerebral Cortex, 10,* 295–307.

Bechara, A., Damasio, H., Tranel, D., & Damasio, A. R. (1997). Deciding advantageously before knowing the advantageous strategy. *Science, 275,* 1293–1295.

Bechara, A., Tranel, D., Damasio, H., & Damasio, A. R. (1996). Failure to respond autonomically to anticipated future outcomes following damage to prefrontal cortex. *Cerebral Cortex, 6,* 215–225.

Brodman, K. (1999). *Localisation in the cerebral cortex* (L. J. Garey, Trans.). London: Imperial College Press. (Original work published 1909)

Colby, A., & Kohlberg, L. (1987). *The measurement of moral judgement.* New York: Cambridge University Press.

Damasio, A. R. (1994). *Descartes' error.* New York: Putnam.

Damasio, A. R. (1996). The somatic marker hypothesis and the possible functions of the prefrontal cortex. *Philosophical Transactions of the Royal Society of London,* 1413–1420.

Damasio, A. R. (1999). *The feeling of what happens.* New York: Harcourt Brace.

Damasio, A. R., Tranel, D., & Damasio, H. (1991). Somatic markers and the guidance of behavior: Theory and preliminary testing. In H. S. Levin, H. M. Eisenberg, & A. L. Benton (Eds.), *Frontal lobe function and dysfunction* (pp. 217–229). New York: Oxford University Press.

Damasio, H., & Frank, R. (1992). Three-dimensional in vivo mapping of brain lesions in humans. *Archives of Neurology, 49:* 137–143.

Milner, B., & Petrides, M. (1984). Behavioural effects of frontal-lobe lesions in man. *Trends in Neurosciences, 7,* 403–407.

Platt, J. J., & Spivack, G. (1975). *Manual for the Means-Ends Problem Solving Procedure.* Chester, PA: Widener University Institute for Graduate Psychology.

Platt, J. J., & Spivack, G. (1977). *Measures for interpersonal problem-solving for adults and adolescents.* Philadelphia: Hahnemann Medical College, Department of Mental Health Sciences.

Saver, J., & Damasio, A. R. (1991). Preserved access and processing of social knowledge in a patient with acquired sociopathy due to ventromedial frontal damage. *Neuropsychologia, 29*, 1241–1249.

Shallice, T., & Evans, M. E. (1978). The involvement of the frontal lobe in cognitive estimation. *Cortex, 14*, 294–303.

17

The Communication of Emotions and the Possibility of Empathy in Animals

STEPHANIE D. PRESTON & FRANS B. M. DE WAAL

The possibility of nonhuman animals having empathy and sympathy has thus far received little attention in behavioral biology. This is due in part to the portrayal of the natural world as a field of combat rather than as a place of social connectedness. Some prominent contemporary evolutionists, such as Williams (1989) and Dawkins (1976), still follow T. H. Huxley (1894/1989), seeing no room within the evolutionary realm for morality and kindness. According to Huxley, such tendencies could have come into being only secondarily, as a cultural innovation of the human species. According to many contemporary psychologists and neuroscientists, "true empathy" is a cognitive innovation akin to perspective taking (imagining yourself in the physical or mental place of another; e.g., Povinelli, Nelson, & Boysen, 1992; Povinelli, Parks, & Novak, 1992; Thompson, 1987; Ungerer, 1990). This characterization limits "true empathy" to those who can pass high-level cognitive tests, usually humans above a certain age.

Interestingly, Darwin (1871/1982) himself expressed in *The Descent of Man* a much more united view, partly inspired by moral philosophers such as Adam Smith and David Hume. Darwin saw morality, including one of its pillars—sympathy—as a natural tendency; a viewpoint that is now all but forgotten but one that is highly relevant to this discussion (Flack & de Waal, 2000). Empirical research on animals supports Darwin's view, revealing empathy to be a phylogenetically continuous phenomenon that exists to varying degrees in nonhuman species.

In experiments designed to elicit distress in children, the family dog often displays consolatory behaviors toward the human feigning distress (Zahn-Waxler, Hollenbeck, & Radke-Yarrow, 1984). Both rats and pigeons in the laboratory display a profound emotional response to the suffering of a conspecific and act to terminate the stress manipulation. Monkeys react similarly in experimental distress situations, even starving themselves to prevent a conspecific from being shocked in their presence. There are many striking examples of empathy in apes. Much research has empirically demonstrated the existence of consolation in chimpanzees, whereby one animal will act to soothe the distress of another.

To whet the appetite for the existence of empathy in apes, consider the following anecdotal example:

> Kidogo, a twenty-one-year-old bonobo [*Pan paniscus*] at the Milwaukee County Zoo suffers from a serious heart condition. He is feeble, lacking the normal stamina and self-confidence of a grown male. When first moved to Milwaukee Zoo, the keepers' shifting commands in the unfamiliar building thoroughly confused him. He failed to understand where to go when people urged him to move from one place to another.
>
> Other apes in the group would step in, however. They would approach Kidogo, take him by the hand, and lead him in the right direction. Care-taker and animal trainer Barbara Bell observed many instances of spontaneous assistance, and learned to call upon other bonobos to move Kidogo. If lost, Kidogo would utter distress calls, whereupon others would calm him down, or act as his guide. One of his main helpers was the highest-ranking male, Lody. These observations of bonobo males walking hand-in-hand dispel the notion that they are unsupportive of each other.
>
> Only one bonobo tried to take advantage of Kidogo's condition. Murph, a five-year-old male, often teased Kidogo, who lacked the assertiveness to stop the youngster. Lody, however, sometimes interfered by grabbing the juvenile by an ankle when he was about to start his annoying games, or by going over to Kidogo to put a protective arm around him. (de Waal 1997b, p. 157)

Macaque monkeys also show a high degree of tolerance and helping toward handicapped group members, attesting to a high degree of social attachment. Azalea, a rhesus macaque (*Macaca mulatta*) who lived in a socially housed group, had autosomal trisomy (de Waal, Uno, Luttrell, Meisner, & Jeanotte, 1996). As a result of her disorder, Azalea had motor defects and delays in developing social behavior. She had a high dependency on her mother and kin and poorly defined dominance relationships. Despite these physical and social defects in a group of highly structured, aggressive animals, Azalea was tolerated and accepted in the group. Up until her death at age 32 months, Azalea was not peripheralized from the group, and there were no signs of aggressive rejection by other group members. A wild female Japanese macaque (*M. fuscata*) named Mozu had congenitally deformed lower portions of her legs and arms. Despite her related difficulties with locomotion, foraging, and care of young, Mozu was an integrated member of her group and had five offspring who lived to reproduce (de Waal, 1996b).

Given that many animals are emotionally affected by the distress of another and sometimes show appropriate helping responses, we regard empathy as a general class of behavior that exists across species to different degrees of complexity.

As a general class, empathy relies on the fact that conspecifics are emotionally interlinked. The emotional state of one individual has the potential to elicit a similar state in nearby individuals. This emotional linkage has been present in primitive forms through much of the evolutionary history of chordates in the form of alarm and vicarious arousal. This basic linkage was then augmented by enhanced cognitive and emotional abilities through evolution and extended ontogeny (development of the individual), allowing individuals to experience empathy in the absence of releasing stimuli toward more distant individuals and without being overwhelmed by personal distress. These additions increase the likelihood of empathy and helping and allow for more and more complex forms of empathy, like those characteristic of the mother-infant bond and of highly cooperative animals, such as wolves, dolphins, and primates.

What Is Empathy?

Across and within disciplines, scientists use the term *empathy* differently (for reviews, see Eisenberg & Lennon 1983; Hornblow, 1980; Wispé, 1986). Some definitions hinge on psychophysiological aspects, some stress evolutionary emergence, and others developmental emergence. Usually, definitions are operationalized to support a specific research agenda rather than a broad theoretical perspective. For the purpose of clarity, working definitions are provided here for emotional contagion, empathy, and sympathy that are generally consistent with the definitions employed by current researchers (e.g., Eisenberg & Strayer, 1987; Hoffman, 1982; O'-Connell, 1995; Wispé, 1986).

Emotional contagion refers to an emotional state in an observer (hereafter, "the subject") as a direct result of perceiving the emotional state of another (hereafter, "the object"). The level of emotion in the subject is generally high and self-focused. Emotional contagion includes the spreading of all forms of emotion from one individual to another (e.g., the spreading of joy or distress through a crowd). For the purpose of this chapter, we focus on the contagion of distress, as most research in the field deals with this aspect. With respect to humans, the contagion of distress is also referred to as "personal distress" (e.g., Batson, Fultz, & Schoenrade, 1987; Eisenberg & Okun, 1996; Eisenberg, Wentzel, & Harris, 1998). The two terms are used interchangeably here. *Empathy* refers to situations in which the subject has a similar emotional state to an object as a result of the perception of the object's situation or predicament. In contrast to emotional contagion, the distinction between self and other is maintained, and the emotional state remains object-focused rather than self-focused. This may or may not result in succorant or prosocial actions to alleviate the distress of the object. Because empathy is a shared-state phenomenon, the definition usually implies some degree of "state matching." State matching is a broad term that implies some concordance between the subjective states of individuals, including physical, psychological, and cognitive components. However, because empathy is more a process than a result, an incidence can still qualify as empathy even if the subject's beliefs about the object are incorrect or if their states do not exactly match. *Cognitive empathy* refers to a shared state that is arrived at through cognitive means, as when the distress of the object is displaced spatially or temporally, when the situation of distress is unfamiliar, or when the object of distress is unfamiliar. *Sympathy* refers to a state in which the subject feels "sorry for" the object as a result of perceiving the distress of the object; this may or may not result in succorant or prosocial actions to alleviate the distress. Sympathy does not automatically imply an accurate representation of the other's state of mind or a matching emotional response, but it usually implies that any distress related to the perception of the other's situation is object-focused (as opposed to self-focused). Authors writing before the 1950s generally used the word "sympathy" for what we refer to here as "empathy," and some contemporary authors use "empathy" for what we call "sympathy."

The general class of empathy behavior includes any phenomenon whereby the subject comes to perceive or understand the state of the object through a shared-state mechanism. This includes emotional contagion, empathy, and cognitive empathy. Because we view empathy as a general class of behavior, one that exists across species to different degrees, the word is applied herein to cases that fall outside of more rigid definitions. For example, in many cases of animal empathy, the subject is agitated or distressed by the object's distress and acts to eliminate the stressor or soothe the object. Because of the subject's arousal, many people construe these as cases of emotional contagion and suggest that the subject's motivation to help is purely selfish. Such determinations are mistaken for multiple reasons. One cannot make a strict demarcation between emotional contagion and empathy, especially a demarcation that relegates the former to animals and the latter to humans. Because empathy evolved from emotional contagion, the two share much of their proximate mechanism and thus exist on a continuum. In each situation, the subject feels a unique degree of arousal, distinction from the object, and motivation to help. Moreover, empathy is by definition a shared-state phenomenon. As such, one cannot experience it without to some extent feeling the distress of another. In which case, any act that reduces the distress of the object can be seen as partially selfish. The selfish-versus-altruistic distinction is especially irrelevant if one takes an evolutionary perspective, because this larger context can construe any behavior that promotes reproductive success as partially selfish.

To illustrate these principles, consider a human adult who witnesses a terrible car accident. This subject may see the victims crying and injured, the cars shattered. This may elicit some shared emotional state of distress. The subject may elaborate further on the distress, thinking about what it would be like if their car was destroyed, if they or their children were injured, and so forth. All of this may lead to great distress in the subject. Despite the high level of distress, the subject may still have an awareness that he or she is not the one who was injured, and helping may occur *both* because it helps the object and because it soothes personal distress. Thus personal distress can coexist with an understanding of the subject-object distinction, and there is great difficulty separating selfish from altruistic motivations. This ambiguity is a result of the continuous nature of empathy; accordingly, the term is used flexibly in this chapter to connote any type of understanding that is arrived at by participating in the state of another organism or object.

The following sections elaborate on the evolution of empathy from the emotional linkage of individuals. They establish why it is adaptive for individuals to be emotionally linked, especially the role this linkage plays in group living, the mother-infant bond, and interactions between conspecifics. Experimental evidence for empathy in rodents, monkeys, and apes is provided. Following is a discussion of cognitive empathy and empathy disorders as they speak to the recent evolutionary changes in empathy and the proximate mechanism.

Group Living and Empathy

It is to the advantage of members of any cooperative social species to be emotionally affected by the distress of a conspecific. Emotional contagion is the most basic expression of this emotional linkage or "physiological linkage" (to use a term from Levenson & Reuf, 1992; see also Brothers, 1989; Plutchik, 1987). McDougall anticipated current evolutionary ideas of empathy when he stated that empathy must exist in all group-living animals, or those with the "gregariousness instinct," because these animals are innately affected by the emotions of others (McDougall, 1908/1923).

Early in individual development this emotional linkage is seen as the mere spreading of emotion, without any necessary facilitation of behavior. For example, in rhesus macaques, a severely distressed infant will often cause other infants to approach, embrace, mount, or even pile on top of the victim. These macaque scenes seem to result from the spread of distress to the other infants, who then seek contact to soothe their own emotional arousal (de Waal, 1989). Emotional contagion is also thought to be the first stage of empathic responding in humans, exemplified when infants in a nursery cry in response to other infants' cries (Sagi & Hoffman, 1976), and 1-year-old children seek comfort after witnessing the injury of another (Hoffman, 1990; Zahn-Waxler, Radke-Yarrow, Wagner, & Chapman, 1992).

Juvenile and adult members of all group-living species also show emotional contagion behaviors that facilitate group movements that are important for survival. For example, if one group member sees something dangerous, usually a predator, an alarm call is given, and in most cases the group collectively moves away from the source of danger. Thus the alarm of one individual alarms others. This phenomenon is well documented for many species, including ground squirrels (e.g., Sherman, 1977), birds (e.g., Powell, 1974) and monkeys (e.g., Cheney & Seyfarth, 1985). Given this mechanism, danger is more likely to be detected even though each individual spends less time on vigilance (Kenward, 1978; Powell, 1974). The "more eyes" phenomenon allows greater investment in activities that promote reproductive success, such as feeding and finding mates.

The vicariousness of positive emotions, such as excitement, is also representative of this innate emotional linkage between individuals. Wild dogs, for example, are described as nosing, licking, squeaking, and jumping at each other before the onset of a hunting expedition (van Lawick & Lawick-Goodall, 1971). Sled dogs similarly jump up and down, barking and whining, before the beginning of a mushing drive. In these situations, the energy is concentrated in time and intensity but reaches all individuals in the area, thereby maximizing the success of the effort.

The previous examples demonstrate the importance of the emotional linkage between group-living individuals in coordinating group movements. Such coordination is crucial for escape from predation, foraging, hunting, and mass migrations—all of which directly affect the reproductive success of the individual.

Mother-Offspring Empathy

Dyadic relationships are also characterized by an emotional or physiological linkage between individuals. The mother-offspring relationship offers the most basic example of this capacity (as noted by others, including Darwin, 1872/1988; McDougall, 1908/1923; and Plutchik, 1987).

Effects of the Mother on the Infant

Offspring are behaviorally and physiologically affected by the emotional state of their caregivers. For example, infant monkeys are aroused by the perception of fear in their mothers in the presence of a snake. These infants learn to fear snakes without the need for a more costly direct experience (Mineka & Cook, 1988; Mineka & Cook, 1993; Mineka, Davidson, Cook, & Keir, 1984). Similarly, normally developing human infants look to their mothers for social reference when approaching a visual cliff to determine whether or not to cross (Sorce, Emde, Campos, & Klinnert, 1985). Twenty-month-old infants with autism, who are impaired in empathic processes, do not attempt to engage the attention of an adult in response to an ambiguous object or situation (Charman et al., 1997). In the normal case, the emotion of the mother is perceived and adaptively incorporated into future decisions by the offspring without necessitating the same level of response by the subject (as in alarm) or previous experience by the subject (as required by conditioning models; e.g., Allport, 1924; Church, 1959).

Beyond these examples of learning, the infant's emotion regulation processes are regulated by continuous and coordinated emotional and physical contact between the mother and infant (e.g., Brazelton, Koslowski, & Main, 1974; Deboer & Boxer, 1979; Gable & Isabella, 1992; Levine, 1990; Stern, 1974, 1977). Infants and their caretakers are thought to use their emotional expressions to reinforce positive affect, transform negative affect, and allow for breaks when arousal is too high (Tronick, 1989). Such responsiveness by the caregiver is also thought to organize the child's behavior (Campos, Barrett, Lamb, Goldsmith, & Sternberg, 1983) and understanding of self, creating a sense of security and efficacy (e.g., Bell & Ainsworth, 1972).

A lack of coordinated activity between caregiver and infant is thought to contribute to behavioral problems associated with an inability to assess and control emotions, such as tantrums, poor impulse control, and risk taking (Tronick, 1989). Rhesus macaques raised without their mothers lack the normal adaptive relationship between behavior and neurochemistry in response to stress (Kraemer

& Clarke, 1996). They are also impaired in sending and receiving emotional expressions to normally developing conspecifics in an affect communication paradigm (described subsequently; Miller, Caul, & Mirsky, 1967). Human infants with autism may also be impaired with respect to the coordination of activity with their caregiver. They are less likely than normal children to smile in response to smiles from their mother and are less likely to combine eye contact with smiles (Dawson, Hill, Spencer, Galpert, & Watson, 1990; Kasari, Sigman, Mundy, & Yirmiya, 1990).

The ability to engage emotionally in the social environment while still regulating emotional arousal is crucial for appropriate empathetic responding throughout life (Eisenberg et al., 1998; Gurthrie et al., 1997; Ungerer, 1990). Data from animals and humans indicate that those who cannot regulate personal distress are less likely to be sympathetic or to help the object and more likely to direct helping toward themselves (Batson et al., 1987; Doherty, 1997; Eisenberg et al., 1994; Eisenberg et al., 1998; Eisenberg & Okun, 1996; Rice, 1964).

Effects of the Infant on the Mother

Eibl-Eibesfelt postulates that the evolution of parental care in birds and mammals created not only actions by the parent to care for the offspring but also concurrent actions by the offspring to request such care (1971/1974). Similarly, interactional views of development postulate that the infant directs the mother's behavior as much as the mother directs the infant's (Bell, 1968, 1971; Bell & Ainsworth, 1972; Brazelton et al., 1974; Osofsky, 1971; Wiesenfeld & Klorman, 1978; Yarrow, Waxler, & Scott, 1971). It is thought that infants modify the affective and behavioral responses of their caregivers through smiling and crying. Such behaviors can signal the infant's state and thus provide the impetus for attention and action by the caregiver (Acebo & Thoman, 1995; Bowlby, 1958). Illustrating the importance of this mechanism, a female chimpanzee at a zoo lost a succession of infants despite intense positive interest because she was deaf and did not correct positional problems (such as sitting on the infant or holding it the wrong way) in response to soft distress calls (de Waal, 1982).

Contagious distress from offspring to parent can also act as an unconditioned stimulus. This allows situational variables that precede the distress to act as conditioned stimuli, teaching parents to act before a stressful display erupts. This learning can result from direct experience with the offspring or can be indirectly applied from personal experience. For example, multiparous antelope cows, in agreement with data from many captive and wild ungulate species, anticipate the needs of their calves and approach them for nursing before the calves have emitted a response (Murdock, Stine, & Maple, 1983). The parents (indirectly, through inclusive fitness) and the offspring (directly) benefit because the offspring's needs are satisfied without the cost of a stressful display. Such predictive empathy can also eliminate the unwanted attention from group members and predators caused by a displaying infant.

Therefore, taking advantage of the physiological linkage between individuals is a successful and low-risk way to facilitate the mother-offspring bond. It simultaneously allows infants to develop emotional regulation abilities and to adaptively learn about the environment. It stimulates mothers to take action for the infant when appropriate and facilitates discrimination of the type of care needed. The emotional linkage between individuals thus fulfills many of the goals of extended caregiving simultaneously, proximately, and without the need for explicit instruction or a long history of conditioning.

Empathy outside the Parent-Offspring Relationship

Empathy may be phylogenetically and ontogenetically based in the emotional linkage between individuals, especially mothers and offspring. But empathy is thought to be more generally exercised across the life span in many mammals. How could empathy be extended outside of the mother-infant relationship? Empathy between parent and offspring is described as primarily the result of innate releasing stimuli. Such releasing effects, once in place, can also guide the extension of empathy toward non-offspring. A distressed chimpanzee, for example, who has just lost a major battle will "pout, whimper, yelp, beg with outstretched hand, or impatiently shake both hands" in order to solicit the consolatory contact of others (de Waal, 1996a). Eibl-Eibesfeldt argues that the infantile releasers of caregiving are used throughout adult human life, such as the use of a high-pitched voice or "baby names" between lovers (1971/1974). The following data from nonhuman animals attest to the fact that displays of distress by an object evoke distress in unrelated adult subjects.

Experimental Evidence for Empathy in Rodents

Church (1959) first established that rats were affected by the emotional state of conspecifics while testing to see if the pain reaction of a conspecific could be used as a conditioned stimulus for a subject. According to his conditioning model, if the distress of the object is followed by a painful stimulus to the subject, then the subject will be conditioned to fear the pain reaction of the object. This was thought to be a possible mechanism for altruism, as subjects would learn to help others in the absence of any obvious, immediate reward (Allport, 1924; Church, 1959). In the beginning of Church's experiment, all subjects decreased bar pressing when an adjacent rat was shocked even before having experienced any paired shock to themselves. Decreased bar pressing in these experiments is the dependent measure, thought to be a behavioral indication of fear (Estes & Skinner, 1941). The decreased pressing response rapidly adapted, with subjects returning to baseline levels after repeated trials. However, as predicted, when subjects were additionally pretrained with their own shock paired to that of the adjacent animal and then presented with a shock to the object only, their bar pressing greatly decreased for the entire 10-day duration of the experiment. Even subjects who had previously experienced shock without the conditioned pairing decreased bar pressing when the adjacent rat was shocked. This experiment was replicated with pigeons (Watanabe & Ono, 1986).

The effect from training the subject with shock paired to the object proves that an individual can be conditioned to fear distress in others. The source of distress in nature is often relevant to all of the animals in an area. Thus life experience may condition individuals to fear the distress of others in a similar way as achieved in the experiment. However, such conditioning is the result of the general design of the nervous system and need not be the only mechanism for empathy. The fact that animals showed distress without having a paired shock indicates that rats and pigeons are emotionally linked to their conspecifics. This is further supported by the following study, which investigated the potential for altruism in albino rats.

Rice and Gainer (1962) presented a rat with the sight of another rat being suspended just off the floor by a hoist. Bar pressing by the subject lowered the stimulus animal onto the floor and thus terminated its distress responses (wriggling of the body, distress vocalizations). Subjects in this experiment increased their bar pressing to the sight of the suspended animal, thus displaying what the authors referred to as an "altruistic response," operationally defined as a behavior that reduces the distress of another. The interpretation was bolstered by behavioral data as the subjects spent the duration of each trial in a location close to and oriented toward the suspended rat. Notice that the behavioral response of fear is traditionally represented by a *decrease* in bar pressing (Church, 1959; Estes & Skinner, 1941). Thus the subjects in this experiment were likely aroused by the sight of the object (in the form of emotional contagion) but were not pressing the bar out of fear.

Further discounting the role of fear in producing the "altruistic" response, in a subsequent experiment the rat subjects witnessed delivery of electric shocks to the object. Rather than pressing the bar to eliminate the shock of the object, the subjects "typically retreated to the corner of their box farthest from the distressed, squeaking, and dancing animal and crouched there, motionless, for the greater part of this condition" (Rice, 1964, p. 167). Noting the interference of fear with bar pressing in this study, Rice concluded that the increase in bar presses in the original "suspended distress" study was not the result of distress in the subject (as hypothesized by Lavery & Foley, 1963). The behavioral descriptions indicate that the subjects only in the later experiment were overly stressed by the sight of the stimulus animal receiving shocks and were thus unable to surpass their own distress to act altruistically. This is consistent with many findings in the human literature, which show that an overly distressed subject is less likely to respond with empathy or sympathy (Batson, Fultz, & Schoenrade, 1987; Doherty, 1997; Eisenberg et al., 1994; Eisenberg & Okun, 1996; Eisenberg, Wentzel, & Harris, 1998). It also provides further support for the idea that the development of emotion regulation abilities is important for empathic responding (above), even in rats.

Lavery and Foley (1963) tried to prove that the rat altruism findings were not altruistic but rather represented the fear of the subjects and the desire to eliminate the disturbing stimulus. They used recordings of rat squeaks as the stimulus, rather than a live conspecific, and compared the rate of bar pressing to the stimulus of white noise. The stimulus was extinguished if the subject pressed the bar. The animals pressed the bar more during the white noise than during the rat squeaks. The authors concluded that the white noise was more noxious, causing the increased bar pressing, and that the low response rate to actual rat squeaks indicated a low level of empathy. Although a recorded loop of squeaks may seem equivalent to live distress calls to a human researcher, it is unlikely to be perceived as a natural stimulus, especially after multiple iterations. It is equivalent to the recorded loop of screams one might hear coming from a haunted house, the response to which rapidly habituates. The experiment supports the idea that a single mode of affect does not have the same effect as the rich, multimodal cues of a live animal (e.g., Partan & Marler, 1999; Preston & Jacobs, forthcoming).

These data provide compelling nonprimate evidence for the physiological linkage between individuals and the expression of altruistic behavior. Faced with the mild distress of a live animal, with all of the relevant cues, albino rats and pigeons react as if the object emotionally affects them and take measures to eliminate the distress of the object. This is not to say that these reactions necessarily involve an intention to help the other: The reactions rely on state matching and are functionally altruistic, but the extent to which rats and pigeons understand the impact of their own behavior on others remains unknown. Also, learning in the form of past experience played a crucial role in the duration of the subjects' responses, illustrating that emotional contagion is not simply an innate response but is affected by experience in development. There exists vast support for the effect of previous experience with the distress situation or distressed individual (e.g., Batson, Duncan, Ackerman, Buckley, & Birch, 1981; Feshbach & Roe, 1968; Gruen & Mendelsohn, 1986).

Experimental Evidence for Empathy in Monkeys

Few experimental studies have been conducted on empathy in nonhuman primates, and most of those few occurred in the 1950s and 1960s. The most extensive inquiry comes from the Department of Clinical Science at the University of Pittsburgh. Murphy, Miller, and Mirsky (1955) were the first to show that a conspecific could act as the conditioned stimulus (CS) for rhesus monkeys. Interanimal conditioning provided a springboard for a long and successful investigation into the communication of affect between rhesus monkeys.

In one series of experiments, subjects were trained to avoid shock by pressing a bar in response to the sight of a conspecific. The subject and the stimulus animal were in different chambers. When a light went on in the adjacent chamber, the stimulus animal became visible, and the subject would have to press the bar to avoid or terminate shock to itself. After the response was extinguished to this paradigm, a series of trials delivered the shock instead to the stimulus animal (now the object) just after the lighting changed (Mirsky, Miller, & Murphy, 1958). Thus the sight of the object was now associated with shock to the object only, but the subject had exclusive access to the bar that terminated the shock. The subjects responded 71% of the time on the first day to the sight of the object in distress from the shock. The object quickly conditioned to the change in lighting as a conditioned stimulus (CS) that preceded the unconditioned stimulus (UCS). As a result, the object "began to leap and run around whenever its compartment was illuminated" (Mirsky et al., 1958, p. 437). Seventy-three percent of the bar presses by the subject occurred to this agitation in the object before the administration of the shock. In addition, the subject displayed "piloerection, urination, defecation and excited behavior" to the sight of the distressed object (1958, p. 437).

In manipulation checks, the conditioned monkeys did not respond to the sight of an albino rat being shocked or a monkey-like puppet thrashing around in the stimulus room. Avoidance learning in a subsequent study could be reinstated using pictures of monkeys, but the response was less strong and less clear than to the live stimulus animals (Miller, Murphy, & Mirsky, 1959a,b). The conditioned animals responded the strongest to pictures of familiar monkeys showing fear. The familiarity response is expected given that empathy and altruism are theoretically thought to be biased first toward kin and then toward familiar individuals (Trivers, 1971). There is also empirical support for this bias toward familiarity in the human literature from subjects of all ages, infants to undergraduates (e.g., Cialdini, Brown, Lewis, Luce, & Neuberg, 1997; Macdonald & Silverman, 1978; Stinson & Ickes, 1992; Zahn-Waxler & Radke-Yarrow, 1982).

Thus, similar to the findings with rats and pigeons, after learning the consequences of shock, these monkeys were aroused by the sight of a conspecific in distress and acted to eliminate the suffering of the stimulus animal, but they were less responsive to artificial or unfamiliar (but similar) stimuli.

A similar task tried to condition subjects to respond to the positive affect of objects by associating the affect with the delivery of food to the subjects. This version of the task was less successful in conditioning animals than the aversive version (Miller, Banks, & Kuwahara, 1966). This was due to a failure of reception by the conditioned animal and not to a lack of expressiveness by the stimulus animals. Importantly, heart rate data from the same experiment revealed that the responder and stimulus animals that were successful in communicating affect had matching heart rate data. These results confirm the proposed basis for empathy in emotional contagion and physiological linkage. They further attest to the fact that circumstances involving risk are more emotionally salient. Indeed, the emotion literature in general has been much more successful in finding the biological substrates for processing negative than positive emotions (e.g., Adolphs et al., 1994, 1995; Ekman, Levenson, & Friesen, 1983). The preponderance of circuits for processing negative emotions makes sense given that the failure to detect danger can have lethal consequences, dealing the most harmful blow to an individual's potential for reproductive success.

In a similar series of studies done at Northwestern University Medical School, monkeys were found to refrain from bar pressing to obtain a reward if it caused another monkey to receive a shock (Wechkin, Masserman, & Terris, 1964). In these experiments, the animals were first trained to pull one of two chains for the delivery of food, depending on the color of the conditioned light stimulus. Subsequently, one of the two chains was reprogrammed to also deliver a shock to the object in view of the subject. Thus the subject would have to witness the shock of the object in order to receive the conditioned food-reward for that chain. In the second set of experiments (Masserman, Wechkin, & Terris, 1964), 10 out of 15 subjects displayed a preference for the nonshock chain in testing, even though this resulted in half as many food rewards. Of the remaining 5 subjects, one stopped pulling the chains altogether for 5 days and another for 12 days after witnessing the shock of the object. These monkeys were literally starving themselves to keep a conspecific from being shocked. In agreement with the rat findings, starvation was induced more by visual than auditory communication, was more likely to appear in animals that had previously experienced shock themselves, and was enhanced by familiarity with the shocked individual (Masserman et al., 1964).

Familiarity effects are also seen in cognitive empathy experiments involving monkeys in role reversal tasks (Mason & Hollis, 1962). Although the monkeys in these experiments were unable to use perspective-taking information to switch roles with their partners, subjects who were housed together performed better than unfamiliar individuals, and familiar subjects increased food sharing with their partners after the experiment. In a later experiment, macaque pairs that were trained to cooperate for food similarly showed a dramatic increase in their conciliatory tendencies (Cords & Thurnheer, 1993). These data support the role of familiarity in facilitating communication and cooperation, further supporting theoretical models and empirical evidence for empathy and altruism (Cialdini et al., 1997; Macdonald & Silverman, 1978; Stinson & Ickes, 1992; Zahn-Waxler & Radke-Yarrow, 1982).

The aforementioned experiments suggest that nonhuman primates will act to avoid witnessing the distress of a conspecific. Beyond conditioning, subjects in some experiments accepted reductions in food, sometimes to the point of starvation, to avoid participating in or witnessing the distress of the object. Across experiments, familiarity with the stimulus animal affected the ability of animals to communicate affect and intention. Further, subject's responses were facilitated by their familiarity with the particular distress situation. Given that these monkey species are characterized by many as aggressive and of inferior intelligence, they showed remarkable empathic and altruistic responses to the distress of their conspecifics. These responses are especially notable given the unnatural laboratory conditions in which the studies were done and the lack of traditional social bonding opportunities for the animals in most cases.

Behavioral Data on Ape Empathy

In a content analysis of more than 2,000 anecdotal reports of nonhuman primate empathy, O'Connell (1995) counted the frequency of three types of empathy: emotional (understanding another's emotion—closest to the definition used here), concordance (understanding nonemotional states—similar to cognitive empathy), and extended (acts of helping tailored to the object's needs; O'Connell, 1995). Chimpanzees exhibited all three types of empathy. Understanding the excitement, grief, sadness, frustration, and fear of the subject were extremely common, with most outcomes resulting in the subject comforting the object of distress. Chimpanzees appeared to comprehend the emotions, attitude, and situation of another individual and even endangered their lives to save conspecifics in danger. In one case, an adult male chimpanzee died trying to rescue an infant who had fallen over the electric fence into a moat on the other side (Goodall, 1986, cited in O'Connell, 1995). Monkey displays of empathy, by contrast, were restricted to mediation of fights, adoption of orphans, and reactions to illness and wounding (as seen in the tolerance toward handicapped individuals mentioned previously).

Consolation is a primary example of empathy in chimpanzees (de Waal 1996b).[1] Consolation, as first defined by de Waal and van Roosmalen (1979), occurs when a bystander approaches a recipient of aggression shortly after a fight. De Waal describes how two adult female chimpanzees in the Arnhem Zoo colony used to console each other after fights: "Not only do they often act together against attackers, they also seek comfort and reassurance from each other. When one of them has been involved in a painful conflict, she goes to the other to be embraced. They then literally scream in each other's arms" (de Waal, 1982, p. 67).

Consolation involves contact initiation by a previously uninvolved bystander who is assumed to be less distressed and who directs consolatory efforts to the victim rather than to itself (de Waal, 1996a,b). Thus in consolation there is no direct benefit for the consoler. One can postulate that in consolation, the consoling individual has become distressed from the sight of the victim and seeks comfort for his or her own feelings. However, the consoler often does not show signs of distress, such as facial expressions or vocalizations, and may wait until after the most intense displays of distress have disappeared to initiate its approach (de Waal, 1996a,b).

The tendency to console seems to be unique to apes: It has not been found in any monkey species despite intensive efforts to find it (de Waal & Aureli, 1996; de Waal, 1996a,b). The reports on chimpanzees are far from anecdotal. De Waal and van Roosmalen (1979) based their conclusion on an analysis of hundreds of postconflict observations, and the recent study by de Waal and Aureli (1996) includes an even larger sample in which the authors sought to test two predictions regarding postconflict contact provided by third parties. They reasoned that if such contacts serve the alleviation of distress, they should occur more with recipients of aggression than with aggressors and more with recipients of intense than of mild aggression. Comparing third-party contact tendencies with baseline rates, they found statistical support for both predictions. An identical research design with macaques did not reveal these effects.

These data do not stand on their own, however. There is sporadic anecdotal evidence for what de Waal (1996b) calls cognitive empathy, that is, helping actions that seem to derive from an understanding of the other's predicament. Examples concern the way a bonobo male helped another male (see the example given at the beginning of this chapter), a case of a male chimpanzee who saw a female struggling with a technical problem and waited until she had left the scene to solve it and bring her the item that she was after (de Waal, 1996b), and, in perhaps the most remarkable case of cross-specific empathy, a bonobo female, Kuni, at the Twycross Zoo in England, tried to "help" a bird:

One day, Kuni captured a starling. Out of fear that she might molest the stunned bird, which appeared undamaged, the keeper urged the ape to let it go. Perhaps because of this encouragement, Kuni took the bird outside and gently set it onto its feet, the right way up, where it stayed looking petrified. When it didn't move, she threw it a little, but it just fluttered. Not satisfied, Kuni picked up the starling with one hand and climbed to the highest point of the highest tree where she wrapped her legs around the trunk so that she had both hands free to hold the bird. She then carefully unfolded its wings and spread them wide open, one wing in each hand, before throwing the bird as hard she could towards the barrier of the enclosure. Unfortunately, it fell short and landed onto the bank of the moat where Kuni guarded it for a long time against a curious juvenile. By the end of the day, the bird was gone without a trace or feather. It is assumed that, recovered from its shock, it had flown away. (de Waal, 1997b, p. 156)

Such anecdotes hint at underlying cognitive capacities rarely acknowledged in animals other than ourselves. Familiarity with their imaginative understanding and well-developed caring capacities explains why experts on apes reacted with little surprise to the most famous case of empathy, the rescue of a 3-year-old boy at the Brookfield Zoo in Chicago on August 16, 1996. The child, who had fallen 6 meters into the primate exhibit, was scooped up and carried to safety by Binti Jua, an 8-year-old female Western Lowland gorilla. The gorilla sat down on a log in a stream, cradling the boy in her lap, giving him a gentle pat on the back before she continued on her way. This act of sympathy touched many hearts, making Binti a celebrity overnight. Whereas some commentators have tried to explain Binti's behavior as the product of training or a confused maternal instinct (Davidson, 1996), her behavior fits entirely with everything else we know about apes, which is that they respond comfortingly to individuals in distress. The only significant difference was that in this case the behavior was directed at a member of a different species (de Waal, 1997a).

In sum, data currently exist for cases of subjects consoling the object but appearing distressed; this is traditionally referred to as emotional contagion. There are also cases in which the subject consoles the object but does not appear to share in the state of distress; this is traditionally referred to as sympathy. Therefore, behavioral data on consolation alone cannot prove the existence of what is called "true empathy" (e.g., Thompson 1987, Ungerer, 1990) or "cognitive empathy" (de Waal, 1996b). Anecdotes such as the preceding ones about Kidogo the bonobo or Kumi the chimpanzee point to the existence of cognitive empathy but also have a great weakness; they are unsuitable for comparing alternative hypotheses. Epistemological problems involved in proving the existence of an internal state pervade ethology and psychology, but these should not impede the development of theoretical ideas and empirical research. On the basis of systematic data on consolation, striking anecdotes of cognitive empathy (for other examples, see de Waal, 1996b), and data on cognitive perspective-taking abilities in other contexts, we venture to speculate that apes evaluate the emotions and situations of others with a greater understanding than is found in most other animals apart from ourselves. More research is needed, however, to determine the extent to which ape consolation is qualitatively similar to human consolation.

Cognitive Empathy

Only humans and the great apes, together classified as the Hominoids, have been cited as evincing cognitive empathy (de Waal, 1996b). The preceding reports on consolation behavior provide the only systematic data indicating a substantial, perhaps radical, difference between the way chimpanzees and some monkey species respond to distress in others caused by aggressive conflict. This difference seems to fit with the overall higher cognitive level and tendency to take another's perspective of apes relative to monkeys. In a cognitive empathy (i.e., perspective taking) task developed by Povinelli and colleagues, two animals cooperated to manipulate a lever device to obtain food from opposing sides of an apparatus. Each of the subjects had a different task requirement. Empathy was operationalized as the ability to transfer knowledge of the other subject's role when the roles were reversed. Chimpanzees but not monkeys successfully transferred knowledge in the task, further suggesting that apes can use perspective taking to transfer knowledge (Povinelli, Nelson, & Boysen, 1992a; Povinelli, Parks, & Novak, 1992b). In a similar experiment, monkeys were again unsuccessful in transferring roles with their partners in a communication paradigm (Mason & Hollis, 1962).

Empirical data from development and evolution speak to a correspondence between the emergence of cognitive empathy and the emergence of a whole suite of social-cognitive capabilities. Some suggest that cognitive empathy was made possible by the emergence of other higher cognitive abilities (like perspective taking). Others suggest that empathy is a prerequisite for the ability to attribute mental states to others (Premack & Woodruff, 1978). Short from solving this debate, we can assume that higher cognitive abilities aid social primates in understanding the relationships among individuals, attributing goals and needs to others, predicting others' reactions, and making appropriate decisions (see Byrne & Whiten, 1988). Higher cognitive abilities also facilitate optimization of the cost/benefit ratio of helping acts by keeping a record of giving and receiving. Many of these abilities can be accomplished with increases in working memory, long-term memory, behavioral inhibition, and general information processing capacities (Byrne & Whiten, 1988; Chance & Mead, 1988). All of these abilities are at least partially subserved by the prefrontal cortex (e.g., Fuster, 1997; Shiamamura, 1996; Thierry, Glowinsky, Goldman-Rakic, & Christen, 1994), an area in the neocortex, which is known to have expanded disproportionately in recent primate evolutionary history (Finlay & Darlington, 1995).

Dealing with empathy per se, increasing long-term and working memory increases the ability of the subject to imagine the state of the object. The subject has access to a larger base of knowledge of the object and its situation and has a larger capacity to hold the information to compare possible outcomes and decide on a course of action. The increase in inhibition associated with prefrontal development also decreases the amount of personal distress that results from thinking about distress situations. Taken together, an increase in prefrontal functions can increase the separation of subject from object and help determine the best course of action, increasing the overall effectiveness of empathy.

Empathy Disorders

There is neurological evidence to support the importance of the prefrontal cortex for empathy, as Hanna Damasio discusses in Chapter 16 in this volume. Empathy impairments in sociopathy (also called psychopathy) and autism are thought to be

partially due to a disruption in the prefrontal system because both involve defi-
ciencies on tasks requiring inhibition, planning, and attention (Campagna & Harter, 1975; Dawson, 1996; Gillberg, 1999). By definition, psychopathic individuals
are characterized by a lack of emotional responding to the distress of others. Physiological data supports the behavioral findings (e.g., Aniskiewicz, 1979; Blair,
Jones, Clark, & Smith, 1997; House & Milligan 1973, 1976). Children with autism
are less physiologically responsive to cues of threat than normally developing
peers, a condition that is thought to be an indication of their frontal damage
(Blair, 1999). They also show impaired attention and affect as early as 20 months
of age to the distress of an adult (Charman et al., 1997). Later in childhood, the effects remain on similar tasks (Dawson et al., 1990; Kasari et al., 1990; Loveland &
Tunali, 1991; Sigman, Kasari, Kwon, & Yirmiya, 1992). Children with autism also
do not report feeling the same emotion as a protagonist on a videotape (Yirmiya,
Sigman, Kasari, & Mundy, 1992).

Focal prefrontal cortex damage and closed-head injury in adults also result in
changes in empathy (reviewed by Eslinger, 1998). Patients with early-onset damage to the prefrontal cortex have a syndrome that resembles psychopathy (Anderson, Bechara, Damasio, Tranel, & Damasio, 1999). These subjects display little or
no empathy or remorse, lack lasting social relationships, and are significantly impaired on moral reasoning, although they perform normally on tasks of intellectual ability. They also fail to produce normal increases in skin conductance in response to the anticipation of losing money in a gambling task, in contrast to
subjects with autism. One of the two subjects with early prefrontal damage was a
mother marked by "dangerous insensitivity to the infant's needs" (Anderson et al.,
1999, p. 1032). The authors propose a mechanism for the disorder whereby brain
damage prevents patients from developing knowledge of the emotional aspects required for navigating and understanding social situations.

Psychopathy has recently been found to be a relevant dimension of chimpanzee personality, confirming the view that chimpanzees normally develop sympathetic attitudes. In a detailed study comparing both human subjective impressions of chimpanzee personalities and objective behavioral data, it was found that
psychopathy can explain part of the personality variation, as it does in people
(Lilienfeld, Gershon, Duke, Marino, & de Waal, 1999). This paper also reported
specific individuals described in the literature as being immune to punishment,
lacking in empathy, or prone to unusual deceptiveness and meanness.

It seems, then, that the quality of empathy (and lack thereof) has changed
along with other cognitive abilities in recent phylogenetic history, starting well before the appearance of our species. This change correlates with an increase in the
corresponding neural substrates. De Waal (1996b) speaks of "cognitive empathy"
to distinguish empathy that relies on perspective-taking from other forms. Yet this
does not in any way deny the continuity with more direct forms of state matching.
Cognitive empathy *encompasses* these more emotional processes. If scientists such
as Povinelli (1998) and Hauser (2000) deny the existence of empathy outside the
human species, this is because their focus is not on the emotional but on the cognitive aspects of the process (Povinelli, Nelson, & Boysen, 1992; Povinelli, Parks, &
Novak, 1992). Hence, what they deny in other animals is only cognitive empathy.

But even this position would seem premature given that we have thus far three empirical differences between apes and all other animals, which are: the possession of mirror self-recognition (e.g. Gallup, 1982), the occurrence of consolation (de Waal & Aureli, 1996), and the presence of special spindle cells in the brain (Nimchinsky et al., 1999). Whereas no one knows if and how these three unique features are related, their co-occurrence does warn at least against drawing a strict mental demarcation line between humans and apes. Indeed, the data reported here, across at least six species, warn against drawing demarcation lines between humans and other animals with respect to emotional aspects of empathy.

Toward a Proximate Model for Empathy

This chapter has described empathy from its roots in the basic emotional linkage between group members, which we may call attachment, to the more complex forms of empathy seen in apes and especially humans. The basis in emotional and social connectedness is crucial to an understanding of empathy and altruism because it creates the bridge between ultimate and proximate explanations and between phylogeny and ontogeny.

The lack of a proper proximate mechanism for empathy has allowed people to persist in thinking that empathy and altruism are phenomena restricted to humans. Thirty years ago, G. W. Allport said it best when he concluded, "the process of *empathy* remains a riddle in social psychology ... The nature of the mechanism is not yet understood" (Allport, 1968, cited in Wispé, 1987). Without a mechanism-level description, descriptions of empathy are derived from introspection and as a result may overestimate the cognitive component. For example, Mead (1934) paved the way for a cognitive theory of empathy by stressing the importance of role taking and putting oneself "in the place of" the object. Allport similarly defined empathy as the "imaginative transposing of oneself into the thinking, feeling and acting of another" (Allport, 1937, cited in Wispé, 1987). In current experimental paradigms, empathy is sometimes entirely cognitive, without any emotional component whatever (e.g., Povinelli, Nelson, & Boysen, 1992; Povinelli, Parks, & Novak, 1992). However, recent findings in neuroscience add empirical support to a lower-level mechanistic explanation of empathy that is at least a century old (Lipps, 1903; see F. Allport, 1924, Becker, 1931, and Scheler, 1928/1970, for opposing viewpoints). According to this theory (Preston & de Waal, under revision), the attended perception of another's state, especially an emotional state, involves to differing degrees not only the representation of the other's state in the brain but also a representation through the observer's own substrates of self-initiated behavior. Put more simply, in order to understand another, you must become the other, at least at the level of brain representation.

This "perception-action model" is grounded in the theoretical idea, adopted by many fields over time, that perception and action share a common code of representation in the brain (reviewed by A. Allport, 1987; Prinz, 1987, 1992, 1997; Rizzolatti & Arbib, 1998). This organization makes sense if, in general, perceptual systems evolved to provide accurate information about the environment in order to appropriately plan and guide movements (Prinz, 1992). These common codes are not necessarily restricted to physical movements but may include abstract, symbolic representations (Prinz, 1997). Thus, in the case of emotions, the representations need not just map body postures and facial expressions directly from actor to perceiver; they can also map the meanings or goals of the expressions.

The social world of primates is incredibly complex. Monkeys, apes, and humans participate in economies of exchange. They groom others in return for resources such as food, protection, or status (literally or metaphorically); they form alliances to protect themselves and to depose dominant individuals; they hide courtship and copulation and give deceptive calls to access food supplies (for a review, see Byrne & Whiten, 1988). This complexity requires the primate central nervous system to perceive the facial expressions, body postures, gestures, and voices of others accurately and quickly so that a response can be generated (Brothers, 1990). Parsimoniously, the same nervous system link between perception and action that helps us navigate the physical environment helps us navigate the social environment. Thus the perception-action link allows for facile motor skill acquisition, as well as facile social interaction, as external conditions are accurately perceived and incorporated into the current plan of action. It is hoped that once proximate explanations of empathy are developed further, it will be easier for science to conceive of empathy as a continuous phenomenon that relies on basic processes that evolved from and are shared with many other species.

Conclusions

With regard to altruistic love, the subject of this edited volume, reviewing the animal literature on empathy has borne out some important generalizations. Importantly, these generalizations are supported by the human literature. The basis of empathy in the caregiving bond supports the role of ontogeny in the proper development of the "innate" linkage between individuals. Specifically, continuous contact and coordinated activities are characteristic of a bond that develops a physiologically adaptive response to stress, accurate communication of affect with others, and the capacity for empathic responding.

There were also robust behavioral effects of familiarity with the object of distress and with the distress situation. Both types of familiarity can be subsumed under the general heading of "shared experience." The qualities of group living, under which empathy evolved, provided a shared experience between its members. Individuals were known to each other and were likely to experience many of the same stressors.

In today's era of e-mail, commuting, frequent moves, and bedroom communities, the scales are being increasingly tipped against the automatic and accurate perception of others' emotional states, without which empathy is impossible. Fortunately, adjustments can be made in the realms of urban planning, human interface, and the structuring of home and work environments to preserve the social connectedness of our world. Further, because explicit modeling, learning, and cognitive perspective taking can augment empathy, it can thrive despite this less fertile ground with the help of positive role models and education. All of this requires effort, but the benefits would be profound.

NOTE

1. This is equivalent to O'Connor's emotional category of "understanding grief/sadness/frustration" (1995).

REFERENCES

Acebo, C., & Thoman, E. B. (1995). Role of infant crying in the early mother-infant dialogue. *Physiology and Behavior, 57*(3), 541–547.

Adolphs, R., Tranel, D., Damasio, H., & Damasio, A. (1994). Impaired recognition of emotion in facial expressions following bilateral damage to the human amygdala. *Nature, 372*(6507), 669–672.

Adolphs, R., Tranel, D., Damasio, H., & Damasio, A. R. (1995). Fear and the human amygdala. *Journal of Neuroscience, 15*(9), 5879–5891.

Allport, A. (1987). Selection for action: Some behavioral and neurophysiological considerations of attention and action. In E. H. Heuer & A. F. Sanders (Eds.), *Perspectives on perception and action* (pp. 395–419). Hillsdale, NJ: Erlbaum.

Allport, F. H. (1924). *Social psychology.* Cambridge, MA: Riverside Press.

Anderson, S. W., Bechara, A., Damasio, H., Tranel, D., & Damasio, A. R. (1999). Impairment of social and moral behavior related to early damage in human prefrontal cortex. *Nature Neuroscience, 2*(11), 1032–1037.

Aniskiewicz, A. S. (1979). Autonomic components of vicarious conditioning and psychopathy. *Journal of Clinical Psychology, 35*(1), 60–67.

Batson, C. D., Duncan, B. D., Ackerman, P., Buckley, T., & Birch, K. (1981). Is empathic emotion a source of altruistic motivation? *Journal of Personality and Social Psychology, 40*(2), 290–302.

Batson, C. D., Fultz, J., & Schoenrade, P. A. (1987). Distress and empathy: Two qualitatively distinct vicarious emotions with different motivational consequences. *Journal of Personality, 55*(1), 19–39.

Becker, H. (1931). Some forms of sympathy: A phenomenological analysis. *Journal of Abnormal and Social Psychology, 26,* 58–68.

Bell, R. Q. (1968). A reinterpretation of direction of effects in socialization. *Psychological Review, 75,* 81–95.

Bell, R. Q. (1971). Stimulus control of parent or caretaker behavior by offspring. *Developmental Psychology, 4,* 63–72.

Bell, S. M., & Ainsworth, M. D. (1972). Infant crying and maternal responsiveness. *Child Development, 43*(4), 1171–1190.

Blair, R. J. R. (1999). Psychophysiological responsiveness to the distress of others in children with autism. *Personality and Individual Differences, 26*(3), 477–485.

Blair, R. J. R., Jones, L., Clark, F., & Smith, M. (1997). The psychopathic individual: A lack of responsiveness to distress cues? *Psychophysiology, 34*(2), 192–198.

Bowlby, J. (1958). The nature of the child's tie to his mother. *International Journal of Psycho-Analysis, 39,* 350–373.

Brazelton, T. B., Koslowski, B., & Main, M. (1974). The origins of reciprocity: The early mother-infant interaction. In M. Lewis & L. Rosenblum (Eds.), *The effect of the infant on its caregiver* (pp. 49–76). New York: Wiley.

Brothers, L. (1989). A biological perspective on empathy. *American Journal of Psychiatry,* *146*(1), 10–19.

Brothers, L. (1990). The neural basis of primate social communication. *Motivation and Emotion, 14*(2), 81–91.

Byrne, R. W., & Whiten, A. (Eds.). (1988). *Machiavellian intelligence: Social expertise and the evolution of intellect in monkeys, apes, and humans.* Oxford: Clarendon Press/Oxford University Press.

Campagna, A. F., & Harter, S. (1975). Moral judgement in sociopathic and normal children. *Journal of Personality and Social Psychology, 31*(2), 199–205.

Campos, J. B., Barrett, K., Lamb, M., Goldsmith, H., & Sternberg, C. (1983). Socioemotional development. In P. H. Mussen (Ed.), *Handbook of child psychology: Vol. 2. Infancy and developmental psychology* (pp. 783–915). New York: Wiley.

Chance, M. R. A., & Mead, A. P. (1988). Social behaviour and primate evolution. In R. W. Byrne & A. Whiten (Eds.), *Machiavellian intelligence: Social expertise and the evolution of intellect in monkeys, apes, and humans.* Oxford: Clarendon Press/Oxford University Press.

Charman, T., Swettenham, J., Baron-Cohen, S., Cox, A., Baird, G., & Drew, A. (1997). Infants with autism: An investigation of empathy, pretend play, joint attention, and imitation. *Developmental Psychology, 33*(5), 781–789.

Cheney, D. L., & Seyfarth, R. M. (1985). Vervet monkey alarm calls: Manipulation through shared information? *Behaviour, 94*(1–2), 150–166.

Church, R. M. (1959). Emotional reactions of rats to the pain of others. *Journal of Comparative and Physiological Psychology, 52,* 132–134.

Cialdini, R. B., Brown, S. L., Lewis, B. P., Luce, C., & Neuberg, S. L. (1997). Reinterpreting the empathy-altruism relationship: When one into one equals oneness. *Journal of Personality and Social Psychology, 73*(3), 481–494.

Cords, M., & Thurnheer, S. (1993). Reconciling with valuable partners by long-tailed macaques. *Ethology, 93.* 315–325.

Darwin, C. (1982). *The descent of man, and selection in relation to sex.* Princeton, NJ: Princeton University Press. (Original work published 1871)

Darwin, C. (1998). *The expression of the emotions in man and animals* (3rd ed.). New York: Oxford University Press. (Original work published 1872)

Davidson, K. (1996, August 28). Scientists debate animal motives. *San Francisco Examiner.*

Dawkins, R. (1976). *The selfish gene.* Oxford: Oxford University Press.

Dawson, G. (1996). Brief report: Neuropsychology of autism: A report on the state of the science. *Journal of Autism and Developmental Disorders, 26,* 179–184.

Dawson, G., Hill, D., Spencer, A., Galpert, L., & Watson, L. (1990). Affective exchanges between young autistic children and their mothers. *Journal of Abnormal Child Psychology, 18*(3), 335–345.

Deboer, M. M., & Boxer, A. M. (1979). Signal functions of infant facial expression and gaze direction during mother-infant face-to-face play. *Child Development, 50*(4), 1215–1218.

Doherty, R. W. (1997). The emotional contagion scale: A measure of individual differences. *Journal of Nonverbal Behavior, 21*(2). 131–154.

Eibl-Eibesfeldt, I. (1974). *Love and hate* (G. Strachan, Trans.). New York: Schocken Books. (Original work published 1971)

Eisenberg, N., & Lennon, R. (1983). Sex differences in empathy and related capacities. *Psychological Bulletin, 94*(1), 100–131.

Eisenberg, N., & Okun, M. A. (1996). The relations of dispositional regulation and emotionality to elders' empathy-related responding and affect while volunteering. *Journal of Personality, 64*(1), 157–183.

Eisenberg, N., & Strayer, J. (Eds.). (1987). *Empathy and its development*. New York: Cambridge University Press.

Eisenberg, N., Fabes, R. A., Murphy, B., Karbon, M., Maszk, P., Smith, M., O'Boyle, C., & Suh, K. (1994). The relations of emotionality and regulation to dispositional and situational empathy-related responding. *Journal of Personality and Social Psychology, 66*(4), 776–797.

Eisenberg, N., Wentzel, M., & Harris, J. D. (1998). The role of emotionality and regulation in empathy-related responding. *School Psychology Review, 27*(4), 506–521.

Ekman, P., Levenson, R. W., & Friesen, W. V. (1983). Autonomic nervous system activity distinguishes among emotions. *Science, 221*(4616), 1208–1210.

Eslinger, P. J. (1998). Neurological and neuropsychological bases of empathy. *European Neurology, 39*(4), 193–199.

Estes, W. K., & Skinner, B. F. (1941). Some quantitative properties of anxiety. *Journal of Experimental Psychology, 29*, 390–400.

Feshbach, N. D., & Roe, K. (1968). Empathy in six- and seven-year-olds. *Child Development, 39*(1), 133–145.

Finlay, B. L., & Darlington, R. B. (1995). Linked regularities in the development and evolution of mammalian brains. *Science, 268*(5217), 1578–1584.

Flack, J., & de Waal, F. B. M. (2000). 'Any Animal Whatever': Darwinian building blocks of morality in monkeys and apes. *Journal of Consciousness Studies, 7*(1–2), 1–29.

Fuster, J. M. (1997). *The prefrontal cortex: Anatomy, physiology, and neuropsychology of the frontal lobe* (3rd ed.). Philadelphia: Lippincott-Raven.

Gable, S., & Isabella, R. A. (1992). Maternal contributions to infant regulation of arousal. *Infant Behavior and Development, 15*(1), 95–107.

Gallup, G. G., Jr. (1982). Self-awareness and the emergence of mind in primates. *American Journal of Primatology, 2*, 237–248.

Gillberg, C. L. (1999). Neurodevelopmental processes and psychological functioning in autism. *Development and Psychopathology, 11*(3), 567–587.

Gruen, R. J., & Mendelsohn, G. (1986). Emotional responses to affective displays in others: The distinction between empathy and sympathy. *Journal of Personality and Social Psychology, 51*(3), 609–614.

Gurthrie, I. K., Eisenberg, N., Fabes, R. A., Murphy, B. C., Hdugren, R., Mazsk, P., & Suh, K. (1997). The relations of regulation and emotionality to children's situational empathy-related responding. *Motivation and Emotion, 21*(1), 87–108.

Hauser, M. D. (2000). *Wild minds: What animals really think*. New York: Henry Holt.

Hoffman, M. L. (1982). Affect and moral development. *New Directions for Child Development, 16*, 83–103.

Hoffman, M. L. (1990). Empathy and justice motivation. *Motivation and Emotion, 14*(2), 151–171.

Hornblow, A. R. (1980). The study of empathy. *New Zealand Psychologist, 9*(1), 19–28.

House, T. H., & Milligan, W. L. (1973). Heart rate and galvanic skin responses to modeled distress in prison psychopaths. *Newsletter for Research in Mental Health and Behavioral Sciences, 15*(3), 36–40.

House, T. H., & Milligan, W. L. (1976). Autonomic responses to modeled distress in prison psychopaths. *Journal of Personality and Social Psychology, 34*(4), 556–560.

Huxley, T. H. (1989). *Evolution and ethics*. Princeton, NJ: Princeton University Press. (Original work published 1894)

Kasari, C., Sigman, M., Mundy, P., & Yirmiya, N. (1990). Affective sharing in the context of joint attention interactions of normal, autistic, and mentally retarded children. *Journal of Autism and Developmental Disorders, 20*(1), 87–100.

Kenward, R. E. (1978). Hawks and doves: Factors affecting success and selection in goshawk attacks on wild pigeons. *Journal of Animal Ecology, 47,* 449–460.

Kraemer, G. W., & Clarke, A. S. (1996). Social attachment, brain function, and aggression. In C. F. Ferris & T. Grisso (Eds.), *Understanding aggressive behavior in children* (Vol. 794, pp. 121–135). New York: New York Academy of Sciences.

Lavery, J. J., & Foley, P. J. (1963). Altruism or arousal in the rat? *Science 140*(3563), 172–173.

Lawick, H. van, & Lawick-Goodall, J. (1971). *Innocent killers.* Boston: Houghton Mifflin.

Levenson, R. W., & Reuf, A. M. (1992). Empathy: A physiological substrate. *Journal of Personality and Social Psychology, 63*(2): 234–246.

Levine, S. (1990). The hormonal consequences of mother-infant contact. In K. Barnard & T. Brazelton (Eds.), *Touch: The foundation of experience: Full revised and expanded proceedings of Johnson & Johnson Pediatric Round Table X.* Madison, CT: International Universities Press.

Lilienfeld, S. O., Gershon, J., Duke, M., Marino, L., & de Waal, F. B. M. (1999). A preliminary investigation of the construct of psychopathic personality (psychopathy) in chimpanzees (*Pan troglodytes*). *Journal of Comparative Psychology, 113*(4), 365–375.

Lipps, T. (1903). Einfühlung, innere Nachahmung und Organempfindung (Empathy, inner imitation, and organ-experience). *Archiv für die gesamte Psychologie, 1,* 465–519.

Loveland, K. A., & Tunali, B. (1991). Social scripts for conversational interactions in autism and Down syndrome. *Journal of Autism and Developmental Disorders, 21*(2), 177–186.

Macdonald, N. E., & Silverman, I. W. (1978). Smiling and laughter in infants as a function of level of arousal and cognitive evaluation. *Developmental Psychology, 14*(3), 235–241.

McDougall, W. F. R. S. (1923). *An introduction to social psychology* (18th ed.). London: Methuen. (Original work published 1908)

Mason, W. A., & Hollis, J. H. (1962). Communication between young rhesus monkeys. *Animal Behavior, 10*(3–4), 211–221.

Masserman, J. H., Wechkin, S., & Terris, W. (1964). "Altruistic" behavior in rhesus monkeys. *American Journal of Psychiatry, 121*(6), 584–585.

Mead, G. H. (1934). *Mind, self, and society: From the standpoint of a social behaviorist.* Chicago: University of Chicago Press.

Miller, R. E., Banks, J. H., Jr., & Kuwahara, H. (1966). The communication of affects in monkeys: Cooperative reward conditioning. *Journal of Genetic Psychology, 108*(1), 121–134.

Miller, R. E., Caul, W. F., & Mirsky, I. A. (1967). Communication of affect between feral and socially isolated monkeys. *Journal of Personality and Social Psychology, 7,* 231–239.

Miller, R. E., Murphy, J. V., & Mirsky, I. A. (1959a). Nonverbal communication of affect. *Journal of Clinical Psychology, 15,* 155–158.

Miller, R. E., Murphy, J. V., & Mirsky, I. A. (1959b). Relevance of facial expression and posture as cues in communication of affect between monkeys. *Archives of General Psychiatry, 1,* 480–488.

Mineka, S., & Cook, M. (1988). Social learning and the acquisition of snake fear in monkeys. In T. Zentall & B. Galef (Eds.), *Social learning: Psychological and biological perspectives.* Hillsdale, NJ: Erlbaum.

Mineka, S., & Cook, M. (1993). Mechanisms involved in the observational conditioning of fear. *Journal of Experimental Psychology: General, 122*(1), 23–38.

Mineka, S., Davidson, M., Cook, M., & Keir, R. (1984). Observational conditioning of snake fear in rhesus monkeys. *Journal of Abnormal Psychology, 93*(4), 355–372.

Mirsky, I. A., Miller, R. E., & Murphy, J. V. (1958). The communication of affect in rhesus monkeys. *Journal of the American Psychoanalytic Association, 6*, 433–441.

Murdock, G. K., Stine, W. W., & Maple, T. L. (1983). Observations of maternal-infant interactions in a captive herd of sable antelope (*Hippotragus niger*). *Zoo Biology, 2*(3), 215–224.

Murphy, J. V., Miller, R. E., & Mirsky, I. A. (1955). Interanimal conditioning in the monkey. *Journal of Comparative and Physiological Psychology, 48*, 211–214.

Nimchinsky, E. A., Gilissen, E., Allman, J. M., Perl, D. P., Erwin, J. M., & Hof, P. R. (1999). A neuronal morphologic type unique to humans and great apes. *Proceedings of the National Academy of Sciences, 96*, 5268–5273.

O'Connell, S. M. (1995). Empathy in chimpanzees: Evidence for theory of mind? *Primates, 36*(3), 397–410.

Osofsky, J. D. (1971). Children's influences upon parental behavior: An attempt to define the relationship with the use of laboratory tasks. *Genetic Psychology Monographs, 83*, 147–169.

Partan, S., & Marler, P. (1999). Communication goes multimodal. *Science, 283*. 1272–1273.

Plutchik, R. (1987). Evolutionary bases of empathy. In N. Eisenberg & J. Straye (Eds.), *Empathy and its development* (pp. 38–46). New York: Cambridge University Press.

Povinelli, D. J. (1998). Animal self-awareness: A debate—Can animals empathize? Maybe not. *http://www.sciam.com/1998/1198intelligence/1198debate.html*. Posted and read November 1998.

Povinelli, D. J., Nelson, K. E., & Boysen, S. T. (1992). Comprehension of role reversal in chimpanzees: Evidence of empathy? *Animal Behaviour, 43*(4), 633–640.

Povinelli, D. J., Parks, K. A., & Novak, M. A. (1992). Role reversal by rhesus monkeys, but no evidence of empathy. *Animal Behaviour, 44*(2), 269–281.

Powell, G. V. N. (1974). Experimental analysis of the social value of flocking by starlings (*Sturnus vulgarus*) in relation to predation and foraging. *Animal Behaviour, 22*, 501–505.

Premack, D., & Woodruff, G. (1978). Does the chimpanzee have a theory of mind? *Behavioral and Brain Sciences, 1*, 515–526.

Preston, S. D., & Jacobs, L. F. (forthcoming). Conspecific pilferage but not presence affects Merriam's kangaroo rat cache strategy. *Behavioral Ecology*.

Preston, S. D., & de Waal, F. B. M.(under revision). Empathy: Its ultimate and proximate bases. *Behavioral and Brain Sciences*.

Prinz, W. (1987). Ideo-motor action. In H. Heuer & A. F. Sanders (Eds.), *Perspectives on perception and action* (pp. 47–76). Hillsdale, NJ: Erlbaum.

Prinz, W. (1992). Why don't we perceive our brain states? *European Journal of Cognitive Psychology, 4*(1), 1–20.

Prinz, W. (1997). Perception and action planning. *European Journal of Cognitive Psychology, 9*(2), 129–154.

Rice, G. E., Jr. (1964). Aiding behavior vs. fear in the albino rat. *Psychological Record, 14*(2), 165–170.

Rice, G. E., Jr., & Gainer, P. (1962). "Altruism" in the albino rat. *Journal of Comparative and Physiological Psychology, 55*(1), 123–125.

Rizzolatti, G., & Arbib, M. A. (1998). Language within our grasp. *Trends in Neurosciences, 21*(5), 188–194.

Sagi, A., & Hoffman, M. L. (1976). Empathic distress in the newborn. *Developmental Psychology, 12,* 175–176.

Scheler, M. (1970). *The nature of sympathy* (P. Heath, Trans.). London: Routledge & Kegan Paul. (Original work published 1928)

Sherman, P. W. (1977). Nepotism and the evolution of alarm calls. *Science, 197,* 1246–1253.

Shiamamura, A. P. (1996). The role of the prefrontal cortex in controlling and monitoring memory processes. In L. Reder (Ed.), *Metacognition and implicit memory* (pp. 259–274). Hillsdale, NJ: Erlbaum.

Sigman, M. D., Kasari, C., Kwon, J.-H., & Yirmiya, N. (1992). Responses to the negative emotions of others by autistic, mentally retarded, and normal children. *Child Development, 63*(4), 796–807.

Sorce, J. F., Emde, R. N., Campos, J. J., & Klinnert, M. D. (1985). Maternal emotional signaling: Its effect on the visual cliff behavior of 1-year-olds. *Developmental Psychology, 21*(1), 195–200.

Stern, D. (1974). The goal structure of mother-infant play. *Journal of the American Academy of Child Psychology, 13,* 402–421.

Stern, D. (1977). *The first relationship: Infant and mother.* Cambridge: Harvard University Press.

Stinson, L., & Ickes, W. (1992). Empathic accuracy in the interactions of male friends versus male strangers. *Journal of Personality and Social Psychology, 62*(5), 787–797.

Thierry, A.-M., Glowinsky, J., Goldman-Rakic, P. S., & Christen, Y. (1994). *Motor and cognitive functions of the prefrontal cortex.* Berlin: Springer-Verlag.

Thompson, R. A. (1987). Empathy and emotional understanding: The early development of empathy. In N. S. Eisenberg (Ed.), *Empathy and its development* (pp. 119–145). New York: Cambridge University Press.

Trivers, R. L. (1971). The evolution of reciprocal altruism. *Quarterly Review of Biology, 46,* 35–57.

Tronick, E. Z. (1989). Emotions and emotional communication in infants. *American Psychologist, 44*(2), 112–119.

Ungerer, J. A. (1990). The early development of empathy: Self-regulation and individual differences in the first year. *Motivation and Emotion, 14*(2), 93–106.

de Waal, F. B. M. (1982). *Chimpanzee politics: Power and sex among apes.* New York: Harper & Row.

de Waal, F. B. M. (1989). *Peacemaking among primates.* Cambridge: Harvard University Press.

de Waal, F. B. M. (1996a). Conflict as negotiation. In W. McGrew, L. Marchant, & T. Nishida (Eds.), *Great ape societies* (pp. 159–177). Cambridge: Cambridge University Press.

de Waal, F. B. M. (1996b). *Good natured: The origins of right and wrong in humans and other animals.* Cambridge: Harvard University Press.

de Waal, F. B. M. (1997a). Are we in anthropodenial? *Discover, 18*(7), 50–53.

de Waal, F. B. M. (1997b). *Bonobo: The forgotten ape.* Berkeley: University of California Press.

de Waal, F. B. M., & Aureli, F. (1996). *Consolation, reconciliation and a possible cognitive difference between macaqes and chimpanzees.* Cambridge: Cambridge University Press.

de Waal, F. B. M., Uno, H., Luttrell, L. M., Meisner, L. F., & Jeanotte, L. A. (1996). Behavioral retardation in a macaque with autosomal trisomy and aging mother. *American Journal on Mental Retardation, 100*(4), 378–390.

de Waal, F. B. M., & van Roosmalen, A. (1979). Reconciliation and consolation among chimpanzees. *Behavioral Ecology and Sociobiology, 5,* 55–66.

Watanabe, S., & Ono, K. (1986). An experimental analysis of "empathic" response: Effects of pain reactions of pigeon upon other pigeon's operant behavior. *Behavioural Processes, 13*(3), 269–277.

Wechkin, S., Masserman, J. H., & Terris, W., Jr. (1964). Shock to a conspecific as an aversive stimulus. *Psychonomic Science, 1*(2), 47–48.

Wiesenfeld, A. R., & Klorman, R. (1978). The mother's psychophysiological reactions to contrasting affective expressions by her own and an unfamiliar infant. *Developmental Psychology, 14*(3), 294–304.

Williams, G. C. (1989). A sociobiological expansion of "Evolution and ethics." In J. Paradis & G. Williams (Eds.), *Evolution and ethics: T. H. Huxley's* Evolution and ethics *with new essays on its Victorian and sociobiological context* (pp. 179–214). Princeton, NJ: Princeton University Press.

Wispé, L. (1986). The distinction between sympathy and empathy: To call forth a concept, a word is needed. *Journal of Personality and Social Psychology, 50*(2), 314–321.

Wispé, L. (1987). History of the concept of empathy. In N. Eisenberg & J. Strayer (Eds.), *Empathy and its development* (pp. 17–37). New York: Cambridge University Press.

Yarrow, M. R., Waxler, L. Z., & Scott, P. M. (1971). Children's effects on adult behavior. *Developmental Psychology, 5,* 300–311.

Yirmiya, N., Sigman, M. D., Kasari, C., & Mundy, P. (1992). Empathy and cognition in high-functioning children with autism. *Child Development, 63*(1), 150–160.

Zahn-Waxler, C., Hollenbeck, B., & Radke-Yarrow, M. (1984). The origins of empathy and altruism. In M. W. Fox & L. D. Mickley (Eds.), *Advances in animal welfare science* (pp. 21–39). Washington: Humane Society of the United States.

Zahn-Waxler, C., & Radke-Yarrow, M. (1982). The development of altruism: Alternative research strategies. In N. Eisenberg (Ed.), *The development of prosocial behavior* (pp. 133–162). New York: Academic Press.

Zahn-Waxler, C., Radke-Yarrow, M., Wagner, E., & Chapman, M. (1992). Development of concern for others. *Developmental Psychology, 28*(1), 126–136.

18

Empathy, Evolution, and Altruism

WILLIAM B. HURLBUT

In the middle of the twentieth century, paleontologists digging in an ancient human site found among the artifacts and remains two animal bones that appeared to have been intentionally inscribed. On close inspection, the markings were recognized as a kind of calendar, or chart, recording the phases of the moon in precise positions and groupings, and an accurate and artistically beautiful rendering of animals, depicting their biological changes with the cycle of the seasons.

It is stirring to reflect on the significance of this finding. There among the sediments of time and organic process were the markings of a being strangely distinct from the animal past from which it emerged. In these markings we recognize the signs of rationality, awareness of time, and symbolic representation. We sense a creature somehow different, detached from the flow of nature, able to stand apart and behold with aesthetic sensitivity, imaginative creativity, and a questing mind seeking order within the cosmos.

For almost the whole of recorded history there has been discussion of what revisions and refinements of our animal forebears distinguish the human species and our place within the order of the natural world. Suggestions include a broad range of specific innovations of form and function, but one capability seems to stand out above all others: our moral nature and its extraordinary manifestation as genuine altruistic love.

This chapter explores the particular human characteristics that give our species the capacity for altruistic love, both those that are extensions of capabilities prefigured in animal life and those that are wholly discontinuous and emergent within our species. I begin with an examination of the evolutionary forces that have shaped our distinct psychophysical unity of mind and body, culminating in the uniquely human attributes of freedom, rationality, and reflective self-awareness. In particular, I focus on the biological basis of human empathy and its contribution to the development of ethical awareness and altruism. To place empathy in its social and cultural context, I trace the processes of emerging consciousness and personal identity and the progressive development of empathy from awareness of self and others to fully enculturated moral awareness. Understanding the biological basis of empathy gives us an appreciation for the way our particular human form provides a common "language" of mental categories, emotional responses, and shared needs that serve as the basis for intelligible communication, moral community, and genuine altruistic love.

The Biology of Embodiment

If we reflect on the difficulty of formulating a scientific explanation of love, we are immediately struck by the incompatibility of the conceptual vocabularies of our different levels of description. It is counterintuitive that consciousness should emerge from chemicals, morality from molecules, and freedom from within a system of fixed laws. The Cartesian dualism of mind and body is an unsatisfactory sidestepping of the central issues; we recognize that the moral and the material are not entirely distinct realms of reality but are inextricably linked and comprehensible only within the terms of our physical embodiment.

Looking back on the evolutionary process that has formed us, we can see an emerging complexity that provides the fundamental conditions and capabilities of human existence. Across the scope of life the very qualities and contours of the world assured that certain configurations of form and function would be best able to navigate and utilize the resources of natural reality. Although chance may have generated the multitude of mutations and recombinations tossed up to the filter of natural selection, their preservation was not random or arbitrary. Vital powers of awareness, action, and appetite evolved, producing specific forms of embodiment with highly adaptive ways of being in the world. In human beings these adaptations of mind and body provide the biological basis of common comprehension, communication, and interpersonal concern—the essential foundations of altruism.

The beginnings of sociality are seen even in the most primordial configurations of living matter. Among the earliest life forms, organisms drew information from one another to pattern and coordinate such basic biological functions as reproduction and nourishment. With the increased complexity of multicellular creatures, new means of communication arose, making possible more flexible adaptation and sociability. Gradually the direct chemical coordination suitable for collectives or swarms gave way to richer and more individual communication between organisms of higher forms of differentiation. Throughout the phylogenetic process we see the development of increasingly complex external morphology with the concomitant refinement of internal neurological capacities. A major development in early evolution was the differentiation of the head region. This externally evident demarcation, with its organs of sensory perception and communication, was paralleled internally by cerebral structures capable of processing more complex impressions of the surrounding environment and of regulating the feelings and functions of the organism. The progressive integration of an organism's "inner life" with its external action and presentation of self was further extended in *Homo sapiens* with the radical cerebral reorganization that accompanied the transition to human upright posture. With upright posture came coordinated revisions of body form, increased range of motion, and the transformations of mind that made possible new relations with the world.

Our transformation to upright form is reflected in nearly every detail of our somatic and psychic structure. This unique psychophysical emergence opened new horizons of comprehending perspectives and transforming powers. During the transition to bipedalism, earlier primates underwent the retraction of the snout and the development of bilateral stereoscopic vision. Sight replaced smell as the prominent sense, allowing a significant increase in freedom. Whereas smell required direct chemical contact and sound gave formless information, sight gave a knowing and accurate encounter with the form and unity of wholes and allowed rapid perception of objects and actions at great distances. The detached beholding of sight allowed a deeper and more accurate apprehension of the reality of things; sight allowed insight. The cerebral processing and storage of visual images led to the detachability of object from image, symbolic representation, and the emergence of imagination and its creative powers. The extraordinary significance of this advancement and its implications for human comprehension and control was foreshadowed in the lunar calendar inscribed on the animal bones I mentioned at the beginning of this chapter. Furthermore, the development of sight as the prominent sense made possible a great increase in accuracy of communication. The emergence of complex social existence in primates appears to have been strongly correlated with a transition from an olfactory system of communication to a visual system. *Homo sapiens'* reliance on visual stimuli and the interpersonal relationships it makes possible allows the extension in awareness, appreciation, and receptivity that is best exemplified in our direct, face-to-face encounters with other human beings (Kass, 1985, pp. 285–289).

Facial expression and the perception of emotion play a vital role in our visual communication. With the thinning of primate facial fur, the face emerged as a canvas of self-presentation. Upward through mammalian evolution there was a progressive refinement of the structures of the face and improved neurological control of the facial muscles that facilitated active and increasingly subtle communication. During the transition toward visual sensory predominance, primates developed upper lips that were unattached to the gum, allowing a much wider range of expression. With more than 30 finely tuned muscles of facial expression and vocal control, human beings are capable of a wide array of communicative expressions of emotions and intentions.

We have an astonishing capacity to recognize and remember faces, an ability present at birth and developed throughout our maturation into adulthood. Neonates preferentially touch faces and within days discriminate their mother's face from that of a stranger. Within just 9 minutes of birth infants turn their head and eyes toward a normal image of a face but not toward a scrambled mix of facial features (Brothers, 1989, p. 13). Furthermore, we are uniquely sensitive to the dynamic changes and emotional expressions of faces. The lack of pigment in the human sclera, the white of the eye, highlights the iris and thereby enhances the detection of eye movements. Within 40 minutes of birth, human infants are able to discriminate some facial expressions and reflect them in the facial movements of their own brows, eyes, and mouth (Meltzoff & Moore, 1983). Studies on monkeys have shown that special ensembles of cells in the brain respond only to faces. Some cells are specialized to decipher the relationship between gaze and body posture, signaling direction of movement and inner intentions. Other cells selectively respond to the facial messages of inner feelings revealed in emotional expressions (Baylis, Rolls, & Leonard, 1985). This capacity to draw on visual cues to discern embodied states of intention and feeling, a crucial component in the communion of mind essential for coherent and compassionate community, relies on the ancient evolutionary development and universality of emotions. As Antonio Damasio explained in Chapter 15 of this volume, emotions have their evolutionary origins in the physiological processes of neurological regulation; the postural, visceral, and biochemical changes in emotional states place the organism in a condition of readiness for action or response. For example, the emotion of fear generates an increase in heart rate, preparing the individual for fight or flight. The subjective feelings of emotions are evolution's later additions in the service of the inner life of consciousness and purposeful desire. Emotions reflect survival strategies that have been highly refined by the physical and social parameters of our environment and are shared with other members of our species. Looking at more than a dozen cultures, including an isolated preliterate culture of New Guinea, Paul Ekman (1994) found a nearly universal language of facial expression of the emotions of anger, sadness, disgust, enjoyment, and surprise. In addition he noted correlative emotion-specific physiological changes in both the central nervous system (the voluntary nervous system that controls muscle movement) and the autonomic nervous system (the involuntary nervous system that controls functions such as blood pressure and heart rate; Ekman, 1994). This psychophysical unity of inwardly felt emotion and its outward expressions provides an essential element in the communicative process of empathy.

The shared quality of embodiment on which empathy depends, however, extends far deeper than emotion alone. Our common psychophysical nature goes to the very foundations of the mechanisms of our self-awareness and organized perception of the world. Lakoff and Johnson, in their book *Philosophy in the Flesh* (1999), maintain that "the mind is not merely embodied, but embodied in such a way that our conceptual systems draw largely upon the commonalities of our bodies and the environment we live in" (p. 6). They explore how some of our shared perceptual categories have developed from sense-based metaphors. Each sense supplies a particular relationship with reality and an experiential perspective that provides a shared language of common reference. For example, although many metaphors are visual, there are certain vague but emotionally substantial concepts that we find best conveyed by reference to odor or taste. There is evidence that suggests that in the cognitive processes of our moral evaluations we employ regions of our brain that are associated with sensations of taste. Certain words we use for moral description reflect such unconscious association, as when we speak of "distasteful" or "disgusting" behavior. Such representations are not merely useful analogies but are actual experienced realities that are effectively conceptualized and communicated with reference to common bodily experience.

The particular embodiment of the human mind may define not just our perceptual categories but the entirety of our conceptual processes. A growing body of evidence supports the idea that there is no such thing as raw sensory input or uninterpreted objective observation. Cognitive scientists speak of "hot" cognition, recognizing the inseparable role of emotions in the processes of perception, memory, and judgment. Drawing on observations from cases of neural injury, Antonio Damasio shows how the body, as represented in the brain, provides the indispensable frame of reference for a sense of self, consciousness, personal identity, and awareness of the world. He observes that "our very organism rather than some absolute external reality is used as the ground reference for the constructions we make of the world around us" (Damasio, 1994, p. xvi). And he goes on to say that "our minds would not be the way they are if it were not for the interplay of body and brain during evolution" (1994, p. xvi).

Similarly, Lakoff and Johnson (1999) argue that our reason is fundamentally metaphorical, not literal, and that the very structure of our concepts and categories of thought arise from the nature of our bodily experience in the world as we know it by living in it. Contrary to Enlightenment philosophers such as Descartes, they maintain that there is no mind separate from and independent of the body and no "pure reason" apart from bodily experience. Moral reasoning, they assert, is not developed through a radically autonomous self apprehending a transcendent source but is rooted in the very flesh and flow of our biological structures and dynamic biological life processes. They conclude, "what universal aspects of reason there are arise from the commonalities of our bodies and brains and the environment we inhabit . . . the result is that much of a person's conceptual system is either universal or widespread across languages and culture" (Lakoff & Johnson, 1999, p. 5).

The neurological embodiment that furnishes a basis for our perceptual and conceptual categories also provides a common biological ground for the desires and intentions from which we develop our shared systems of values. As the complexity of an organism increases, the primary evolutionary goals of survival and reproduction become served by pleasurable intermediate activities that become valued ends in themselves. Sexual pleasure is the most obvious example, in which the biological goal of reproduction may be unintended or even unrecognized; the same principle operates in many activities such as eating and play. Our evolutionary heritage and the characteristics of our embodied being that all humans share provide a common basis and capacity for social interaction and the context within which we develop the pervasive social milieu that defines us as persons. From these come both the possibility and personal significance of altruistic love.

Several conclusions relevant to the discussion of empathy and altruism emerge from this wealth of neurophysiological information. First, the information clarifies how much all human beings share in common, not only in our biological constraints but also in the desires and intentional actions that constitute our behavior and reveal our values. As the philosopher Henri Bergson noted early in the twentieth century, "for society to exist at all the individual must bring into it a whole group of inborn tendencies" (Bergson, cited in Degler, 1991, p. 270). Second, as we gain perspective on the evolutionary panorama, we see an emergence of genuine novelty that culminates in our species. What appears along the phylogenetic process is an overall increase in a generalized type of freedom of the organism relative to its environment. From the first development of primordial limbs that allowed movement in diverse terrain to the refined cerebral coordination of the "tool of tools," as Aristotle called the human hands, we see an ascent toward greater powers of comprehension and control. This broad trend of freedom represents a capacity within nature to transcend itself, to leap beyond that which exists and to express new possibilities and powers. In this sense we can see freedom as a fundamental characteristic of nature as a whole. In human nature the breadth of natural freedom is dramatically extended in the cultural consciousness and coherent community made possible by the extraordinary capacity for empathy.

The Origins of Empathy

The biological foundations of empathy are far more than a simple system of signs to be expressed and observed. Rather, as Preston and de Waal explain in Chapter 17 (this volume), empathy is a form of intersubjectivity in which the observer actually participates in the feelings of the other. This extraordinary capacity is built on a combination of evolutionarily ancient emotional responses and more recent anatomical and neurological innovations unique to primates and highly refined in human beings. Empathy is the extension and culmination of adaptations formed by the phylogenetic process and applied toward fuller and more effective social coordination and communication.

Simply defined, empathy is the ability to identify with and understand the situations, motives, and feelings of another. It is so natural to us that we rarely ponder the mystery of its mechanism. Although in popular discourse empathy has taken on the somewhat sentimental notion of sympathy, from a scientific perspective true empathy is a crucial ingredient in individual development, as well as in the full range of social interactions.

The first step in the empathic process of communication, the outward expression of the individual's inward state, depends on the fact that the human organism is a psycho-physiological unity. As mentioned earlier, Paul Ekman has noted that specific emotions correlate with certain facial and bodily expressions and lead to defined central and autonomic nervous system changes. Furthermore, Ekman writes that the very act of "voluntarily performing certain muscular actions [i.e., that normally accompany a specific emotion] generates involuntary changes in autonomic nervous system activity" (Ekman, 1992, p. 64, my interpolation). For example, just forming the muscle actions that express anger will cause an acceleration of the heart rate and a readiness for action. These studies suggest an innate, hard-wired connection between the subjective feelings, the motor and the visceral components of emotions, leading to an integrated psychophysiological state. The conclusion is that there are no subjective (psychological) states without visceral and postural correlates, and there are no body actions without psychological correlates. Thus emotions are simultaneously both inward and outward realities; they are intrinsically bodily based and have visible expressive manifestations which can be drawn on in the communication process.

In the second step of empathic communication, the interpretive task of the observing individual may be facilitated by specialized cells termed "mirror neurons." In monkeys, specific clusters of cerebral cells have been observed to fire not only when the animal made certain hand motions but also when it perceived others making the same motions (Brothers, 1989, p. 78). This finding suggests that similar neurons could be expected in humans, activated both by the perception and by the action of the same motion. Leslie Brothers writes, "based on preliminary data, it is likely that mirror neurons will also be found for other gestures, including facial movements" (1989, p. 78). It has been noted that while one is observing specific actions, a selective increase occurs in evoked potentials in the muscles that the observer would use in performing the observed actions. This suggests that we comprehend the motions of another by a kind of low-level imitation of the same action, thereby feeling both the action and something of its concomitant psychological context and intention. In other words, there is an innate ability to compare the sensory information of a visually perceived expression with the proprioceptive feedback of the movement involved in imitating the expression (Sagi & Hoffman, 1976). Observing a facial expression subtly activates in the subject the same muscular movements and autonomic responses which together constitute the physical grounding of an inwardly felt subjective state that would be represented by such a facial expression. We experience this, for example, when we see someone yawn or grimace in pain. With a neurologically based connection between seeing an action and performing it, an individual can interpret another's expression of emotion in terms of the experience of the action. Reflexively performing that same action on a smaller scale (so small that the body barely moves) would generate in the observer a state similar to that which he is perceiving. The emotional state experienced by one individual is manifest through the medium of facial expression. It is then translated into the same emotional state empathically felt by the other, the observing individual.

Studies of empathic mechanisms suggest that the shared neurological connections between the sensory, motor, and visceral components of emotions allow individuals to share a single psychophysiological state. Speaking of the neurological studies cited previously, Leslie Brothers writes, "findings such as these suggest that an archaic kind of sociality, one which does not distinguish self from other, is woven into the primate brain" (1989, p. 78). This primary sociality is most fundamentally experienced as emotional contagion, a kind of innate empathic resonance wherein communication of partial components of emotional states triggers in the observer the full psychophysiological expression of the perceived emotion.

This kind of emotional contagion has been noted not just in visually based systems in which actions are imitated but with auditory stimulation as well. One-day-old infants exhibit inborn empathic distress reactions at the cry of other newborns. They respond with vocalizations that have the same auditory marks of genuine distress (Sagi & Hoffman, 1976). Likewise, researchers have found that in adults, vocalizations of an emotional character can generate the concomitant emotion-specific autonomic nervous system changes. It is interesting to note that the "mirror neurons" are located in an area of the monkey brain that is the homologue of Broca's area in humans, a region associated with the generation of speech. These cells may play a crucial role in the emotionally grounded apprehension and imitation of the vocalizations essential to learning and expressing spoken language (Allman, 1999).

The adaptive value of emotional contagion is immediately obvious. The infant gains a rapid and fluid entrainment to the emotional states of those around him whose experience allows a disposition and reaction appropriate to a given situation. This may serve to coordinate readiness and response to circumstances, such as the presence of predators, which are of critical significance for survival. Furthermore, the foundational intersubjectivity of emotional contagion may serve as a platform for further extensions of coordinated sociality that combine primary emotional response with a more comprehending perspective. For such a shared state to become what Preston and de Waal (Chapter 17, this volume) called "cognitive empathy," it must be accompanied by a discernment of the other as distinct from self. Thus in human empathy, a higher order of cognitive process is needed in addition to the reflexive matching of emotional states. An understanding of human empathy must therefore include an investigation into the rise of reflective self-awareness. Individual self-awareness in turn is a vital component in the formation of a cohesive human community and the development of complex culture.

From Empathy to Culture

Human existence is by nature intrinsically social, located within the context of community and culture. The very process by which an infant enters the world engenders human cooperation. Human childbirth is painful, difficult, and medically risky due to the reconfiguration of the pelvic bone to allow upright posture and the proportionally large fetal cranium that must pass through the pelvic outlet. In some contemporary pretechnological societies, the maternal mortality rate associated with childbirth continues to be close to 20%. According to anthropologist Karen Rosenberg, "chimps hide at the time of birth; humans seek assistance" (Rosenberg, cited in Fischman, 1994, p. 1062). And after the difficult delivery, the long period of childhood dependency required by the infant's incomplete neurological formation ensures that the developing mind matures in the context of abundant social stimulation. It is this maturation in the social context that allows the complex cultural development of the human person.

From earliest infancy the interactive engagement between mother and child constitutes a uniting emotional bond. Even as newborns have innate perceptual discriminations and neurological dispositions that direct their attention toward the sights and sounds of human beings around them, so also adults have a repertoire of instinctive actions and responses that engage the baby. When talking to babies, adults in all cultures raise the pitch of their voice, slow the rhythm, and make the melody more pronounced and singsong. As Daniel Sterns writes, "Evolution has apparently shaped parental behavior to complement babies' auditory preferences" (1990, p. 69). Babies, in turn, shift their gaze to the region around the eyes while listening to speech. Sterns observes, "the distance between the eyes of a baby at the breast and the mother's eyes is about ten inches, exactly the distance for the sharpest focus and clearest vision for a young infant" (1990, p. 43).

As a further facet of interpersonal bonding, Paul MacLean (1985) cites the negative power of separation anxiety and the crucial role of the separation call. He points to the conservative evolutionary history of this essential mother-child communication. As the most primitive and basic mammalian vocalization, the separation call sustains contact and prevents dangerous distance between the helpless infant and the protective parent. A sense of anguished isolation is recognizable in the emotional tone of its slow, sad descending note. He suggests that the accompanying subjective state serves throughout life to motivate the maintenance of community and that this state may provide the negative affect of existential loneliness and unfulfilled longing (MacLean, 1985). MacLean goes on to note that opiates will extinguish the separation call in squirrel monkeys. This may suggest that a similar sense of loneliness and isolation is being "treated" by the drug addict (1985, p. 414).

By age 3½ months, the baby can control his gaze and initiate face-to-face encounters, thereby beginning to acquire a sense of himself as an agent or actor. In a process that psychiatrist Daniel Sterns has called "attunement," mother and infant engage in a kind of facial "duet," a reciprocity of small repeated exchanges in which the mother responds to her baby not with imitation but in a way that communicates that she has understood her baby's feelings. Psychologist Daniel Goleman writes, "Such small attunements give an infant the reassuring feeling of being emotionally connected, a message that Sterns finds mothers send about once a minute when they interact with their babies" (Goleman, 1995, p. 100). Such a jointly initiated mutual interaction, back and forth, is a kind of conversation of feelings, an unspoken communion of mind. Mutual gaze provides the ties of attachment, crucial lessons of pure social interaction and nonverbal foundations for the later development of language. Goleman goes on to say that "mutual gaze is, indeed, a world within a world. Looking into the eyes that are looking back into yours is like no other experience with another person. You seem to feel and follow vaguely the mental life of the other" (1995, p. 63). Such experience develops the foundations for the deepest engagements of love in later life. Indeed, there is evidence that our very concept of person, as a distinct living locus of subjectivity with its own hopes, fears, and intentions, is formed in a unique human extension of the neurological substrate in primates that processes facial and vocal expression (Brothers, 1989).

The basic congruency of feeling established between mother and infant is slowly extended into further dimensions of cognitive development, including language. MacLean (1985) speculates that the separation call, which in humans has the sound *aaah*, may provide the basic vowel for the vocalizations of human language. The other fundamental sound, the consonant *tsik*, may be provided by the sucking sound made from the lips of the infant suddenly breaking contact with the nipple. The same sound is made by the mother as an encouragement to the infant to resume nursing, whereas the infant emits the sound when searching for the nipple (MacLean, 1985). Later, in a process of "social referencing," the infant will point or gaze at an object to establish joint attention and then observe the mother's reaction. As the mother's spoken responses begin to carry specific semantic content in addition to the gestures, pauses, tonal prosody, and postural cues of emotional expression, a web of meaning is formed within this linguistic system. In a kind of "re-envoicement," the child begins to structure his understanding of the world and the very pattern of his thoughts by echoing the words of others. Slowly the child is enculturated to the society in which he is born and raised into a realm of beliefs and hopes inaccessible to an isolated individual.

In an orderly developmental progression, between the first and second year of life a child begins to crystallize a sense of self and other. He or she starts to differentiate between animate and inanimate beings and to discover the inner mental world of private beliefs and intentions. As conscious personal identity deepens, he or she develops an awareness of the identity of others as both distinct from and yet also similar in nature to himself or herself. As the child develops awareness of other selves like him- or herself, indiscriminate emotional contagion is superseded by cognitive empathy, a willed and knowing stepping into the role of the other. For instance, in one study on the development of empathetic concern, a 21-month-old child responded in stages to his mother's simulated sadness by (1) attending to his mother; (2) peering into her face to determine what was wrong (accompanied by verbal inquires); (3) trying to distract her with a puppet; (4) looking concerned; and (5) giving his mother a hug while making consoling sounds and sympathetic statements (Zahn-Waxler & Radke-Yarrow, 1990). This series of actions demonstrates the complex understanding of emotion fostered through empathetic interaction at a relatively young age.

In this context of empathically grounded sociality comes a growing sense of moral awareness. The child psychologist Jerome Kagan states that "a moral motive and its attendant emotions are as obvious a product of biological evolution as digestion and respiration" (1998, p. 155). Between the second and third year of life children develop an appreciation of the symbolic categories of good and bad and learn to apply these to their own actions, thoughts, and feelings. The child's sensitivity about the propriety of his or her behavior becomes related to a larger concern with the right order and relationship of things. Discrepancies such as broken toys and shirts missing buttons trouble the child, and he or she begins a lifelong search for a coherent and harmonious explanation of the larger order of the world. With a growing understanding of the relationship between present actions and future outcomes, a child begins to experience the conflict between acting on present desires and abstaining when he or she recognizes that action would have negative consequences on self and others.

Before the age of 5, children have difficulty restraining their desires, but by around 6 years the sense of self-control, and therefore accountability, allows them to feel shame or guilt in response to an action or consequence. The freedom of choice becomes, increasingly, the central moral axis and leads to the poignant and powerful drama of the individual self seeking a sense of moral worthiness. Kagan writes that "I am tempted to suggest that the continuous seeking of evidence to prove one's virtue is, like Darwin's notion of natural selection, the most potent condition sculpting each person's traits over their lifetime" (1998, p. 157). As a child matures, with greater cognitive empathy comes greater sensitivity to the needs of others and the associated moral imperatives.

Moral thinking is inherent in the development of human consciousness, for as the self becomes aware of other selves, the ethical issue inescapably arises as to how one person should treat another. The mind is irreducibly transactional, defined in a "conversation" that is grounded in empathy and experienced in community. The categories of thought based on our shared biology are placed in a web of meaning as our consciousness is constructed through the intercommunion of our minds. Our ideas of self, society, and the significance of life are all formed within the language of a shared cultural narrative. As Charles Taylor writes, "the genesis of the human mind is . . . not 'monological,' not something each accomplishes on his or her own, but dialogical" (1991, p. 33).

The Latin root of our word *conscience* means "joint or mutual knowledge"; and ethical norms are communal constructs. It is interesting that our modern word *consciousness* has the same root; its current meaning was originally included in the term *conscience*, meaning "consciousness of moral sense." Looked at in light of the neurophysiology and psychology of empathy, it is clear why consciousness and conscience must be related. For as our awareness of ourselves develops in relation to others, we empathically understand others' reactions to the way we treat them. Contrary to the Enlightenment's ethereal notion of pure reason, disengaged from messy embedding in our bodily constitution and human community, moral reasoning is intrinsically embodied, emotionally guided, and intersubjective by nature. Taylor writes, "reasoning in moral matters is always reasoning with somebody" (1991, p. 31). Asocial minds, like those of feral children raised by animals, are premoral minds. Our consciousness and conscience are thus inseparable, united in the communal nature of human life.

The Emergence of Moral Reality

Even as empathy contributes to human community and cooperation by sensitizing individuals to the emotions and needs of others, it also enables the perpetration of harmful or hurtful actions. Other human beings are both our companions and our competitors. The insight into the other person enabled by the capacity for empathy can be used for open communication or for calculated deception. Certain psychopathologies, such as the sociopathic personality, appear to involve disruptions of the basic empathic process. It is interesting that oxytocin is now being investigated as a possible therapeutic agent in these disorders. But beyond these obvious pathologies, the "natural" struggle of life may engage our empathic capacities for the purposes of intimidation, dominance, and exploitation. Thomas Hobbes in *Leviathan* wrote, "I put for a general inclination of all mankind, a perpetual and restless desire of power after power that ceaseth only in death" (Hobbes 1651/1968, p. 161). And from the perspective of sociobiology, ultimately all adaptations, including the empathic capacities of social life, must redound to the benefit of the individual through a selective advantage in the proliferation of his or her genes, or at least the genes of his group. There is little room in such genetic competition for altruism except in limited contexts to benefit one's group.

For human beings, where to act along the continuum between egoism and altruism becomes a moral choice, often experienced subjectively as an exercise of freedom. The philosopher R. E. Hobart wrote, "that we are free in willing is, broadly speaking, a fact of experience. That fact is more assured than any philosophical analysis" (1934, p. 3). Though the theoretical perspective of sociobiology would disagree with this statement, I side with the nearly universal human testimony that freedom is a compelling inner need and not illusory. It is central to how we understand both ourselves and our sense of significance within the world. Without freedom, there is no meaningful creativity, conscious choice, or morality in the common ordinary sense of such terms.

I commented earlier that the phylogenetic process appears to generate organisms with progressively greater freedom with respect to their environment. Our species now adapts to its environment not by intergenerational mutation but by a built-in individual freedom and flexibility of response. We have adapted for adaptability itself. Humans have evolved not for pure instinctive response but for comprehension and intentional, imaginative creativity. We are formed not for a particular ecological niche but for unpredicted possibility. We are the culmination of a proclivity, foreshadowed in the higher animals, for adventurous stretching forth into the world into exploration and discovery. We are the wandering, wondering creatures who imaginatively probe the world for possibilities and patterns, extending our freedom of thought and action outward in time and space and inward into a quest to understand the meaning of things. The evolution of progressively higher degrees of freedom thus reflects the freedom that is inherent in the very nature of nature. In particular, human freedom has evolved as a part of human nature in adaptation to a world in which such freedom is possible.

Freedom, however, is more than mere indeterminacy. The creative innovation that is part of the process of evolution operates within the context and in the service of survival. In human freedom we speak of the self as an agent, with individual intentions, free will, and personal aspirations. Yet without some form of guidance to channel and constrain our desires and free will, our freedom could lead to actions that are destructive to our individual and communal existence. There needs to be a balance between stability and innovation, continuity and change. Our novel human manner of being requires enlarging the imperative of basic biological survival to include a highly complex social flourishing. Likewise, the merely biological and environmental constraints on human innovation must be enlarged to include the more complex constraints of morality in order to serve such social flourishing.

Moral awareness, from the perspective of evolution, is an adaptation to govern and control choice in conditions too diverse or too complex for genetically based fixed action responses. By its very nature as a regulator of culture, morality cannot be simply encoded in the genes. In regulating our freedom of choice through the intricacies of social life, moral reason must be as profound as our capacity for innovation. It must be able to process the numerous inputs and complex analyses needed to preserve crucial and central life values across a wide array of novel and varied circumstances. It must channel free will into constructive, life-enhancing action without quenching the essential freedom that makes human life human and worth living. Guided by the deepest vision of life, moral action therefore consists in freely choosing to do that which promotes the flourishing and freedom of life. Like our freedom, the moral sense that is inextricably linked with it is at once a product of biological evolution and an agent in the creative extension of life. Morality allows both prudence on the level of individual actions and productive cooperation at the level of social reality.

Human Moral Community

One can gain some insight into how morals operate in human culture by looking at practices that are universal across cultures. In a search for evidence of the core qualities of human nature, the anthropologist George P. Murdock compiled what he called the "Human Relations Area Files" (cited in Brown, 1991, pp. 69–70). Drawing on the more than 400 ethnographic records available at the time (1945), he developed a list of 67 universals that included practices as diverse as hygiene, gift giving, property rights, and the concept of the soul. Such universals arise out of the basic human biological necessities and the cross-cultural challenges and rewards associated with communal life. Examined carefully, one can recognize in these universals themes that relate to the fundamental features of moral community.

The cultural universals seem to cluster around the two central issues of flourishing and freedom. Items in the first category relate, in our own peculiar human way, to the basic animal necessities of sustaining and reproducing the species, as with food preparation, medicine, and marriage. Items in the second category, however, are more uniquely human and highlight our distinctive qualities and capabilities as moral beings. In these items the central issues are freedom and self-control; and these practices are almost universally related via tradition-bearing narratives to some source of transcendent truth or spiritual power. In puberty rites, for example, a child leaves behind both complete dependence on others and the compulsion of infantile impulses and emerges into adult status characterized by freedom, self-control, and mastery over body, mind, and alien forces (or enemy spirits). The transition to adulthood is characterized by additional human universals related to freedom and its empowerment, including awareness of ethical truths and traditions and the mysteries of inviolate moral requirements. Rites, religious rituals, and initiations into the spiritual cosmology of the culture, often proclaimed by distinctive adult forms of body adornment, align the individual inwardly and outwardly with transcendent truths related to both life and death.

Such moral awareness both points beyond life to a deeper purpose or destiny and also sustains the flourishing of life by channeling the powers of individual freedom in a self-denial and self-sacrifice that sustains social community.

It is noteworthy that there is a universal honor accorded to self-sacrifice for the benefit of others. Proper restraint of our emotions, desires, and impulses by our moral sense need not be an impediment to life but can instead lead to a deeper community with others that reveals the richest currents of life. Inwardly, we feel the awareness of our conscious self and, through empathy, we recognize the same consciousness and sensitivity of others, with its implicit moral meaning. As Pope John Paul II has said, when we look into the eyes of another person we know we have encountered a limit to our self-will. Such awareness, together with our inwardly felt sense of significance, becomes the sense of a moral meaning within the cosmos that transcends a simple imperative of genetic propagation. As R. Shweder notes, "The most powerful motive of human life is a desire to gain a feeling of virtue, the desire to be 'good'—a desire unique among sentient animals" (1999, p. 798). Indeed, we are beings with an awareness of good and evil, of time and death. Who among us wants to have written on his tombstone "successful hedonist" or "prolific propagator of genes"?

I have discussed the utility of morality—and here I will speak of morality in its highest manifestation, as altruistic love—as protecting the essential values for life's flourishing while defending the freedom at the exploratory edges of our existence. Yet not only does love serve the flourishing of life, but there is also a sense in which love itself *is* the fullness of life. Love is at once both an external imperative and also an internal satisfaction and fulfillment of personal existence. That this is the case becomes evident if one considers love as a distillation of the good, the beautiful, and the true. As the philosopher Hans Jonas says, "it is one of the paradoxes of life that it employs means which modify the end and themselves become part of it" (1966, p. 106).

Such a conception of morality represents an ideal. That human beings would formulate ideals flows out of their very nature. Whereas most creatures live in a continuous immediacy of life, humans have the freedom to pull the past into the present through learning stored as memory and the freedom to pull the future into the present through the creative imagination. Together with the ceaseless drive to organize the unexplained, what has been called the "cognitive imperative," our capacities to calculate, extrapolate, and recombine are used to reconfigure that which *is* into the ideal of that which *could be*. Whereas most creatures are pushed by circumstances, we are pulled into the future by our dreams and images of fullest flourishing. We are not determined simply by our biology but by something previously unseen in the history of life: the freedom of coherent aspiration toward a moral ideal. As Leon Kass writes, "desire, not DNA is the deepest principle of life" (1994, p. 48).

It is a fact of life that many people violate their ideals, and this raises the question of how the desire for moral life is sustained. A clue is to be found among the items in the second category of Murdock's universals. What is especially interesting about them is not so much their universality, which is well accounted for within evolutionary psychology, but their focus on the transcendent. That morality should be linked to transcendent truths is understandable in our experience. To be effective without external coercion, moral norms must be believed; and to be believed they must be understood as true, as well as useful. As soon as moral obligations are not "real," they are irrelevant. Without a reference to truth, moral behavior rapidly loses its utility, pure relativism leads to anarchy, and rigid rules become tyranny. Pronouncements concerning the purely instrumental nature of morality are corrosive to human self-understanding and incompatible with the way morals operate within the community. It ironic that, according to some formulations of evolutionary psychology, the first creature requiring morality to govern its communal life should also be the one to "see through" morality and reject it as being without a grounding in anything more than social convention. As contemporary evolutionary theorist Randy Nesse laments, "Understanding this discovery can undermine commitment to morality . . . it seems silly to restrain oneself if moral behavior is just another strategy for advancing one's genes" (cited in Yancy, 1998, p. 29).

In review, I have covered the essential components of moral behavior: normative standards and the freedom and desire to act according to those standards. It is remarkable that these components are so deeply grounded in our biology. Our particular evolved form with its unique physiological and neurological structure provides us with a common biological basis for our emotional responses, mental categories, and psychological needs. Mediated by empathy, these in turn are the basis for intelligible communication and genuine social community and culture, all within the context of the sense of self and others. And out of such awareness of the other, in the shared experience of human life, arises the moral awareness and communal standards necessary to regulate social interaction. Despite local cultural variations, there is a substantial core of shared, cross-cultural moral sense that is based on our common biology and natural environment. The commonality of our biological needs and our personal freedoms ensures the similarity of the dynamic changes and challenges of our individual life journeys. And with our capacity for language and imagination, we weave similar interpretive stories, cultural narratives rich with ideals and aspirations that shape our shared desires.

Such a moral culture, rooted as it is in biological nature, can be seen as itself a phenomenon of nature. From the perspective of biological evolution, organisms adapt to fit their ecological niches and become congruent with the reality surrounding them. The nature of the organism thus reflects some aspect of environmental reality. It is therefore reasonable to ask if the development of moral awareness, and specifically the notion of transcendent moral truth, evolved in congruence with a corresponding moral characteristic of nature. In this sense the evolution of progressively higher degrees of freedom reflects a freedom that is embedded in the very nature of nature. In particular, human freedom has evolved in response to a type of world in which such freedom is possible. By the same argument, the emergence of moral culture could be regarded as reflecting a fundamental aspect of reality, in addition to its social utilitarian benefits, rather than being nothing more than a type of survival strategy serving a more primordial biological agenda.

Albert Einstein once said, "The most incomprehensible thing about the world is that it is comprehensible." Equally astonishing is the fact that the cosmos has produced a being capable of beginning to comprehend its order. That the human mind can discern fundamental principles of the material world is evident in our mathematical physics. But dare we extend our explanatory confidence to the realm of the moral, to attempt to discern a moral order in the world? Does not the moral, as Hans Jonas poses the dilemma, "originate in ourselves and merely come back to us from the putative scheme of things as our reflected voice?" (1966, p. 282). Even to ask such a question requires us to relax naturalistic presuppositions that exclude from initial consideration the category of moral truth. But we must provisionally undertake this disengagement in order to investigate what interpretation may most fully fit the available evidence.

The idea that the moral dimension of human life is in some sense a product of the universe, a part of the objective order of nature, is discordant with our prevailing scientific culture. Deterministic materialism and reductionistic mechanism dominate contemporary scientific thinking and theories and carry with them a skepticism concerning moral constructs and motivations. To assert an objective ethical order within nature would be to affirm teleology, the reality of human freedom, and the unique status of our species. Yet these are rejected from current scientific culture for reasons that are more ideological than evidential. For the stubborn evidentiary fact remains that, as Jerome Kagan expresses it, "although evolutionary biologists insist that the appearance of humans was due to a quirky roll of the genetic dice, our species refuses to act as if good and evil are arbitrary choices bereft of natural significance" (1998, p. 158).

Such a revision in the concept of nature may already be achieving a measure of general acceptance in regard to environmental concerns. Widespread moral awareness and a concomitant sense of obligation have been increasing with regard to environmental degradation and species extinction. We are beginning to realize the danger of continuing our environmentally destructive behavior and are now formulating moral convictions concerning preservation of the natural world. One might argue that such a change of attitude is instrumental utility and reflects only a fear of harmful consequences. But even as instrumental benefit is not incompatible with an ontologic basis of morals, so also pure instrumentalism is not true to the facts of the matter. Our environmental ethic goes beyond selfish concerns to include a genuine distress at the despoiling of the wilderness and the loss of species.

Conclusion

In this chapter I have traced the expanding logical and moral consequences of our evolved biological form of being, culminating in a perspective that suggests that empathically grounded human moral community represents an unfolding of deep characteristics of nature itself, with profound implicit meaning. I have suggested that such phenomena be understood in the context of a broader concept of nature, one in which genuine altruistic love is recognized as a reality in human existence.

It is appropriate to ask how such phenomena might be investigated further scientifically, with a view to benefiting from the resulting insights as we seek to preserve and enrich both the flourishing and freedom of human life. One possible approach to the difficult task of studying altruistic love might be to try to understand the neurophysiological and psychological dynamics of its relationship to empathy. Do certain attitudes or actions in life open or close channels of empathic resonance and sympathetic response? For example, might practices that promote inner peace, such as prayer or contemplative meditation, serve to regulate emotional response in a way that balances between apathy and overload and thereby allow the sensitivity of genuine sympathy? Do habits of humility or ascetic practices, such as fasting or solitude, biochemically down-regulate desires that impede the patience or perseverance necessary for love? And what of beliefs? Do certain ideas or expectations sustain self-denial, whereas others promote fears or the urgency of ambitions that preclude the very conditions of community? Is it possible, contrary to the assumptions of most formulations of evolutionary psychology, that human nature has been forged less by the struggles of scarcity than by the rivalry of prosperity and its concomitant of pride? It is interesting that our word *lust* comes from the same Latin root as the word *luxury*. It has been said that there is no cure for luxury, or again, that luxury is a disease that we have that kills other people. Something about success can at times break compassionate awareness, whereas it is everywhere evident that those who suffer are often drawn closer to the heart of love.

Indeed, for all the controversy concerning the possibility of genuine generosity and altruistic love, at the level of life, amid the sounds of the street and the strivings and struggles, there is everywhere, in small or greater ways, the evidence of love. Many people, perhaps most, in some way give the effort and energy of their lives from a belief in love and a desire to build a better world. If there is a natural sentiment and hope, it is that love is real. We sense that something of great significance is being played out in the drama of daily life. If, on guard against exploitation, we are cynical and sensitive to the lack of love, we are also alert for the signs of its grace and gratitude, generosity and joy. And the power of its presence leaves an echo that reorients and realigns our lives, not with obligation but with inspiration. Consider the story of Saint Francis. It is reported that Lenin once said, "If I had ten good men like Saint Francis, I could have changed the world." But what Francis did from a joyous faith in love he could never have done for the duty of an ethical ideology.

Francesco Bernardone was born 800 years ago in the tiny Italian city of Assisi. His father was a wealthy cloth merchant, and he lived a carefree and extravagant youth. But one day, as he rode out, he came to a poor man, a leper, begging by the side of the road. Francis got down and gave the man a coin. Then, in spite of his great fear of leprosy (which was common in Europe during the Middle Ages), he turned back and embraced the man. Later, he said that from that time a great joy flooded over him. He had overcome his deepest fears and was free—free to live in the fullness of love. He proceeded to give away all of his possessions and gave his whole life in humble service to the healing of the sick and the poor. Others joined him, and they called themselves the Friars Minor, the little brothers, forsaking all worldly power, pride, and prestige. And for nearly the whole of the millennium that has just ended, their spirit of humility and generous concern for others has echoed through our world.

What are we to make of such self-emptying, letting go of prerogatives and possessions and offering up of self for the good of others? Is this some kind of disproportion or extreme? (Could it be that he had some rare combination of genetic alleles or was homozygous for some recessive trait that is socially advantageous in heterozygous form?) Was he some kind of unbalanced idealist or exaggerated eccentric? The problem with saying he was eccentric is that he kept turning toward the center, to the heart of humanity, the central significance of being human.

What began as the earliest inscriptions of science, the cosmological chartings scratched on the bones of animals, has become in our era the comprehensive power of a global civilization. As we press forward with our modern biological technology, we will need to learn from examples such as Saint Francis more about the phenomenon of altruistic love. This is essential in a world in which an estimated 30,000 children die every day of starvation and diseases related to malnutrition. Indeed, last year we spent ten times more money on Rogaine to "cure" male pattern baldness than was spent in research on malaria, which affects 300 million people worldwide. And we will need the most profound understanding of our human nature to guide us as our technology begins to manipulate the fundamental biological parameters of our ancient evolutionary heritage. Without a wisdom informed by love, we may alter our basic biology and the social and cultural dynamics that flow from it in ways that prove irreversibly destructive.

Pascal noted that human existence is located between infinities, between the infinitely large and the infinitely small, the vast realms of cosmic space and the tiniest particles of matter. Brought into life by the fundamental forces of the cosmos, we are just the right size in form and function for genuine empathy, for sensitive awareness of other persons. We are cosmic matter come to community and moral consciousness. Indeed, the whole of the material world may be seen as an intelligible "language" of being and the foundation for the extraordinary extensions of personal and social existence that allow the expression of genuine altruistic love. Just as our body and mind have been formed and fashioned by the cosmos from which we have emerged, could it be that the manifestation of love further complements and completes that which is, revealing and reflecting both the fundamental nature of the universe and the full significance of human life?

REFERENCES

Allman, J. M. (1999). *Evolving brains.* New York: Scientific American Library.

Baylis, G. C., Rolls, E. T., & Leonard, C. M. (1985). Selectivity between faces in the response of a population of neurons in the cortex in the superior temporal sulcus of the monkey. *Brain Research, 342,* 91–103.

Brothers, L. (1989). A biological perspective on empathy. *American Journal of Psychiatry, 146*(1), 10–19.

Brown, D. E. (1991). *Human universals.* New York: McGraw-Hill.

Damasio, A. R. (1994). *Descartes' error.* New York: Grosset/Putnam.

Degler, C. N. (1991). *In search of human nature.* New York: Oxford University Press.

Ekman, P. (1992). Facial expressions of emotion: An old controversy and new findings. *Philosophical Transactions of the Royal Society of Scotland, 335,* 63–69.

Ekman, P. (1994). Are there basic emotions? In P. Ekman & R. J. Davidson (Eds.), *The nature of emotion: Fundamental questions* (pp. 15–19). New York: Oxford University Press.

Fischman, J. (1994). Putting a new spin on the birth of human birth. *Science, 264,* 1062–1063.

Goleman, D. (1995). *Emotional intelligence: Why it can matter more than IQ.* New York: Bantam Books.

Hobart, R. E. (1934). Free will. *Mind, 169,* 1–27.

Hobbes, T. (1968). *Leviathan* (C. B. MacPherson, Ed.). London: Penguin Books. (Original work published 1651)

Jonas, H. (1966). *The phenomenon of life: Toward a philosophical biology.* New York: Delta.

Kagan, J. (1998). *Three seductive ideas.* Cambridge: Harvard University Press.

Kass, L. R. (1985). *Toward a more natural science.* Chicago: University of Chicago Press.

Kass, L. R. (1994). *The hungry soul: Eating and the perfecting of our nature.* New York: Free Press.

Lakoff, G., & Johnson, M. (1999). *Philosophy in the flesh: The embodied mind and its challenge to Western thought.* New York: Basic Books.

MacLean, P. D. (1985). Brain evolution in relation to family, play, and the separation call. *Archives of General Psychiatry, 42,* 405–417.

Meltzoff, A., & Moore, M. K. (1983). Newborn infants imitate adult facial gestures. *Journal of Child Development, 54,* 702–709.

Sagi, A., & Hoffman, M. L. (1976). Empathic distress in the newborn. *Developmental Psychology, 12*(2), 175–176.

Shweder, R. (1999). Humans really are different. *Science, 283,* 798–799.

Sterns, D. N. (1990). *Diary of a baby.* New York: Basic Books.

Taylor, C. (1991). *The ethics of authenticity.* Cambridge: Harvard University Press.

Yancy, P. (1998, Fall). Evolutionary psychology and our mythical dark nature. *The Responsive Community, 8,* 24–35.

Zahn-Wexler, C., & Radke-Yarrow, M. (1990). The origins of empathic concern. *Motivation and Emotion, 14*(2), 107–130.

Conclusion to Part IV

WILLIAM B. HURLBUT

We have looked at altruism through the lens of science in an effort to see more clearly its origins, expressions, and possibilities. Taken together, these chapters give a new appreciation for the evolutionary process and the specific adaptations of form and function that make possible the varied manifestations of altruism and altruistic love. Descartes was indeed in error in separating body and mind. There is no pure self-verifying rationality, no human freedom or genuine love separated from what Charles Taylor has called our "messy embedding in our bodily constitution, our dialogical situation, our emotions and our traditional life forms" (Taylor, 1991, p. 102). The significance of this for the subject of our discussion, philosophically, theologically, and practically, can hardly be overstated. The meaning of love is grounded in the very purposes and processes of our bodily lives; love's context and content is framed and constituted in our apprehension of the good, the beautiful, and the true, known within the flourishing of life and its dynamic drama.

From the perspective of science, this embodiment means that altruism, in its varied forms, is a domain of life accessible to the principles of inquiry and tools of intervention that characterize our particular human relationship with the natural order. The work of Thomas Insel (Chapter 14) suggests that we can gain a measure of description and explanation of some biological dimensions of love. With a deeper understanding of the genetic, biochemical, and developmental factors that underlie human disorders of interpersonal relations such as autism or sociopathic personality, we may then be able to develop medical therapies. Likewise, we may better understand temperamental differences in inclinations and manifestations of affectional bonding and sociability. Suggestions have been made that one day oxytocin may be used in reconstituting disrupted bonding between mother and infant after the prolonged isolation of premature birth or medical intensive care. Others propose pharmacological interventions as part of marriage counseling (a sort of chemical equivalent of a renewal of vows!). The neuroscientist Walter Freeman has suggested that oxytocin and vasopressin, in their natural human functioning, may play a more generalized and pervasive role in social cohesion (Freeman, 1995). He cites the fundamental sexual atmospherics of rock concerts and religious rituals and suggests that these chemicals facilitate the dissolution and reconfiguration of patterns of basic ideological and social allegiance. The biology of affectional bonds, however, is multiply valenced: Bonding also creates borders; it promotes both union and exclusion. As seen in the case of rats, the neuropeptides of affection and alliance can also be the chemical agents of aggression.

The chapters by Antonio and Hanna Damasio (Chapters 15 and 16) give us a deeper appreciation for how the capacities for social reasoning and social relations involve an intricate integration of diverse dimensions of neurological functioning; there is no simple "love" module in the brain. Nevertheless, Hanna Damasio's studies of patients with neural deficits opens our understanding to a more sympathetic interpretation of the moral meaning of certain medical conditions. What seems like willful indigence or moral obstinacy may be genuine neurological malfunction. Such a perspective, however, becomes more difficult in the case of sociopathy, in which callous lack of conscience and a strong association with crime (50% of violent crimes and 20% of imprisoned criminals are linked with sociopathy; Calne, 1999) raises difficult questions about normal human variations and their implications for moral and legal responsibility. Will our investigation of the neuroscience of altruism one day lead us to the "medicalization" of all criminal behavior?

The findings that the same neurological damage incurred at different stages of development results in dramatically different levels of social functioning suggest that experience may play a crucial role not just in the attainment of moral balance and social skills but also in the development of the neurological dynamics that undergird them. This idea is consistent with Antonio Damasio's elucidation of the regulatory role of emotions (and their extension in conscious moral reasoning) and Stephanie Preston and Frans de Waal's (Chapter 17) reports of the importance of emotional regulation for the ability to show sympathy. It appears that certain critical dimensions of empathy and emotional balance, somewhere between apathy and overload, are essential for full and viable interpersonal relations. Do differences in experience during the formation of personal identity or the establishment of basic belief structures play a role in actual neurological patterns, priorities, and emotional balance? An affirmative answer would further underscore the importance of identifying the physical, psychological, and social factors that promote full personal and social integration and encourage the inner freedom and confidence to express altruistic behavior in a balanced and effective way.

These concerns lead us to an additional consideration related to our scientific understanding of altruism. How do our beliefs about love, its ultimate source and significance, affect our lives? Is it possible that certain ideas are of great importance in integrating and organizing both our psychological health and our bodily functioning? Do certain beliefs and the practices that accompany them facilitate a deepening of the process of empathic resonance and permit richer and more genuine social relationships? And how do our scientific findings in turn influence our beliefs about love?

Finally, we must recognize the limits of our scientific approach and acknowledge that its descriptions and explanations themselves rest on certain unproven assumptions about the nature of ultimate reality. It is that deeper mystery, of the source and significance of love, that is the focus of the concluding section of this volume.

REFERENCES

Calne, D. (1999). *Within reason: Rationality and human behavior.* New York: Pantheon.
Freeman, W. J. (1995). *Societies of brains: A study in the neuroscience of love and hate.* Hillsdale, NJ: Erlbaum.
Taylor, C. (1991). *The ethics of authenticity.* Cambridge: Harvard University Press.

Part V

RELIGION

Introduction to Part V

STEPHEN G. POST

The chapters in this section develop the ideal of religious thought that is deeply informed by current scientific developments. Our understanding of human nature and its capacities for altruism and altruistic love is much enhanced by attention to the sciences. On the other hand, religious rites of passage that encourage altruistic behavior suggest that culture can act to widen and deepen the scope of such behavior, pointing to a degree of plasticity and indeterminacy in human nature despite genetic and evolutionary constraints.

In this section, Don S. Browning, in Chapter 19, "Science and Religion on the Nature of Love," presents a sweeping overview of the ways in which the contemporary academic discussion of love (agape) within the Protestant tradition has been influenced by evolutionary biologists in a largely positive manner. This influence, with its emphasis on mutuality and kin altruism, has not been received uncritically, although it has generally moved theologians in a direction that Browning considers salutary. His chapter is noteworthy for its careful discussion of methodology in the dialogue between science and religion. He sees science as the study of those conditions that give rise to or correlate with love. With regard to language and definitions, Browning associates the Protestant agape with pure altruistic love, eros with pure egoism, and the Aristotelian-Catholic philia with the pluralistic view of human nature in which both altruistic (agape) and egoistic (eros) motivations and capacities exist in a constructive synthesis. Evolutionary biology, he argues, is moving religious thinkers toward the synthesis model. William Hamilton, George Williams, and Robert Trivers have affected the theological debates about love, as reflected in this volume (see Chapters 4, 10, and 19). Browning's masterful chapter could easily be construed as a conclusion to this entire volume.

Gregory L. Fricchione, a practicing psychiatrist, attempts in Chapter 20 to interpret the essential nature of human religious expression as an outgrowth of evolutionary developments centered around separation and attachment theory. More than any other author in this volume, Fricchione uncovers the evolutionary roots of the need for love, care, and solace in the need for attachment. The human brain evolved, he argues, with a need for altruistic love, and the fulfillment of this need is associated with successful healing. His chapter, "Separation, Attachment, and Altruistic Love: The Evolutionary Basis for Medical Caring," is unquestionably a bold one that pursues a full concilience between biological science, neurology, the health care profession, and religious concepts of love. Fricchione aptly draws on the equally broad approach of the philosopher C. S. Peirce, whose famous essay "Evolutionary Love" provides a creative baseline.

Ruben L. F. Habito, an eminent scholar of Southeast Asian religions, examines how religious traditions, and Buddhism in particular, encourage altruistic attitudes and behaviors. His powerful selection of classic Buddhist texts highlights the tension between the illusion of egoism and the reality of altruism. Enlightenment is not perceived in purely intellectual terms but primarily as a transformation of the self from egoism, separation, and greed, which constitute the source of all human evil and discord. The "enlightened" one overcomes the illusory wall of separation between self and other by becoming aware (see Wyschogrod, Chapter 2) of the other as truly an other, rather than as a means toward egoistic ends. Egoism is associated with false consciousness, and freedom with an emptiness of the self in its egoistic illusion in order to arrive at a truer ontological reality. All Buddhist ethics stems from this fundamental transformation, without which there simply can be no ethics.

19

Science and Religion on the Nature of Love

DON S. BROWNING

This chapter has two goals: (1) to outline a philosophical framework for productive collaboration between religion and science on discussions about love, and (2) to illustrate this approach by addressing some actual issues pertaining to the nature of love. A statement of the central question of this inquiry will help us stay on track. I believe it should go like this: In what ways can religion and science cooperate in defining the ideals and conditions of a theory of love needed to guide human development?

Two theses will organize my argument. First, a fruitful dialogue between science and religion should proceed within what Paul Ricoeur (1981, p. 59) called a "critical hermeneutical" perspective on both science and religion. Second, when this happens, science will have a clearer picture of some of the ideals of human love that it should clarify and serve but cannot itself invent or create. On the other hand, such a dialogue will provide religion with a more critical grasp of its own ideals and a clearer understanding of *some*, although not all, of the conditions needed to approximate these ideals.

Foundationalism versus Nonfoundationalism

The method governing such collaborative work needs to be clear from the beginning. A simple foundationalist approach to theoretical or moral knowledge will not prove adequate. Foundationalism, as philosopher Richard Bernstein defines it, sets aside the possible truths of all aspects of a culture's traditions—be they philosophical, religious, or linguistic—and assumes that all scientific and moral truth will be discovered and gradually assembled on the basis of sure and certain beginning points. These beginning points have been identified variously by scientists and philosophers as empirical observation, experimental procedure, phenomenological description, or logical deduction (Bernstein, 1983). Hans-Georg Gadamer, Paul Ricoeur, Richard Rorty, and Bernstein himself have exposed the potential cultural nihilism of a thoroughgoing foundationalism (Gadamer, 1982; Ricoeur, 1981; Rorty, 1979). It assumes that the wisdom of traditions would be delegitimized until science in some utopian future finally finishes rebuilding our edifices of cognitive and moral knowledge. Furthermore, it assumes that some day science finally will find a way to bridge the chasm between *is* and *ought* that most modern philosophers believe exists, at least in some fashion.

But I believe that much of continental philosophical hermeneutics and British ordinary language analysis goes too far toward a particular brand of nonfoundationalism. Because in these schools tradition provides the framework and background for all inquiry and all pursuits of truth, many critics believe that these antifoundationalist philosophical perspectives go too far toward uncritically crediting tradition with truth and authority. I argue that Paul Ricouer's critical hermeneutics is a better solution to understanding the proper relation between objectivity and historical conditionedness (1981). Ricoeur agrees with Gadamer: Traditions are storehouses of wisdom—moral, religious, and even cognitive. Scholarly inquiry cannot become oriented to any problematic moral or social issue—even the question of the nature of love—without starting with the history of the traditions that have formed our cultural thinking about that issue. This history is already in us; it is part of what Gadamer called our "effective history" (1982, p. 267). And this is so even if we are unaware of how the past shapes our present experience.

But critical hermeneutics—the version of hermeneutic theory that Ricoeur espouses and that guides this chapter—does not stay simply with history and tradition; it finds a place as well for the explanatory interests of science as a subordinate moment within the fuller process of inquiry. Ricoeur has a highly appreciative but nonfoundationalist view of science. He holds that science, especially the social or human sciences, can and should aspire only for various degrees of cognitive "distanciation" from the inherited traditions that form and shape all persons—even scientific inquirers (Ricoeur, 1981, p. 94). Total objectivity is both impossible and destructive to culture and human community; it alienates science and the cultures that it influences from the traditions to which they actually belong.

On the other hand, cognitive distanciation—in contrast to complete objectivity—is both possible and desirable. For Ricoeur, it makes possible the highly important submoment of "explanation" in the larger "understanding-explanation-understanding" model of wisdom that should guide the inquiries of the human sciences. This model of inquiry should be applicable, I think, to any discipline that identifies itself under the rubric of "evolutionary ethics." Such a discipline would have to be seen as an exercise in critical hermeneutics with a powerful subemphasis on distanciated description and explanation. To get oriented to the field of ethics, it first would have to survey the traditions that have carried our ethical discourse down through the ages; to get oriented to an evolutionary perspective on ethics, it would then, second, have to describe, compare, and explain the behavior of various species. Inevitably, the two moments—the retrieval of history and the submoment of evolutionary explanation—would overlap and interpenetrate, partially because the traditions themselves were often interested in giving accounts of patterns of nature as a dimension of their ethical interests. This is how we should conceive the dialectic of understanding-explanation-understanding within which cooperation between religion and science should proceed, especially on matters pertaining to practical wisdom and ethics.

Love and Traditions

I illustrate the meaning of this rather abstract discussion with the question of love—the central topic of this chapter. To assemble representatives of science and religion to inquire into the nature of love is, I take it, primarily an exercise in wisdom and understanding; we seek to understand love, possibly to achieve it more fully. But we also need in secondary ways to explain or account for *some* of the conditions that give rise to love or at least correlate with its appearance. Insofar as we are talking together, our discourse will be primarily philosophical—that is, a step or two removed from either the immediacy of religious confession or more focused exercises in scientific observation and experimentation. Furthermore, it should be clear from the beginning that we cannot become oriented to this discussion without starting first with the philosophical and religious traditions that have shaped our ideals and languages of love, hence the importance of the interpretive or hermeneutical beginning point.

A short history of our various languages of love is in order. I present one here not to be comprehensive but to illustrate the importance of beginning with our social inheritance—as Wittgenstein, his followers R. S. Peters and Peter Winch, and the continental hermeneutic philosophers would all urge us to do (Wittgenstein, 1953; Peters, 1958; Winch, 1958). We first learn that our various languages of love have been in conflict—a conflict, however, that the distanciated perspectives of science may help clarify, although probably not completely resolve.

Take the terms *agape, eros,* and *caritas.* They all can be translated in English as "love," but they have had historically quite different meanings. *Agape* is the Greek word for love as it was often used in the Christian scriptures, especially the letters of Paul. However, in the language of much of Protestant theology, as Anders Nygren has taught, this love has been defined as self-sacrificial activity on behalf of others with no thought for the good that might be returned to oneself (Nygren, 1953; Hallett, 1989). Such a strenuous love for the other was made possible by the wonderfully charitable love and grace of God that enables the faithful to love with a self-giving that clearly exceeds their natural capacities. This kind of love is understood, by Nygren, as totally disconnected with natural strivings for specific goods or anything that might be understood as *the good*—the *summum bonum.*

Nygren tells us that agape is "spontaneous and unmotivated," "indifferent" to the value of the object of love, yet "creative" in that it brings about "value" in the other. It was seen as initiated by God, that is, it flows first from God and then through the faithful and from there outward to others (Nygren, 1953, pp. 75–81). Even some influential secular models of love, such as the one associated with the moral philosophy of Immanuel Kant, reflect the values of this classic Protestant model (Green, 1992). They share the idea, at least, that love should not be predicated on the value of the loved or on some thought of return.

Nygren believes that eros and agape, however, are completely separate and disconnected. Eros reaches upward for the good and true; agape flows downward in generosity and superabundance to the lower and the more needy. Furthermore, eros has been seen generally as more egocentric; the lover is viewed as attempting to elevate or increase his good through the love of a higher or better being, be it God, a higher truth, or another person (Nygren, 1953).

Finally, *caritas*—the Latin translation of New Testament love rendered in Greek as *agape*—was interpreted in late medieval Roman Catholic circles as combining elements of both agape and eros. Nygren believed that love as caritas contains more elements of self-fulfillment (eros) and mutuality than do Protestant Reformation interpretations of Christian love.

Even this short historical review raises several questions. Which of these classic models should guide the direction or goals of human development? What conditions for love would scientific research uncover, depending on which of these three models guided the empirical investigation? Furthermore, what are the implications of recent scientific research into love—especially the newly clarified theories of kin and reciprocal altruism—for mediating between these conflicting classic views?

But the plot thickens when additional terms are introduced. Roman Catholic caritas models of love combined Aristotelian models of love as friendship (*philia*) with the love motifs of the New Testament. Aristotle discussed three kinds of friendship—friendships of pleasure, friendships of utility, and friendships of virtue. Aristotle valued each of these kinds of friendship but believed that one of them was more expressive of the uniqueness of human nature than others. For instance, he subordinated friendships of utility and pleasure to the higher good of friendships of virtue. Friendships of virtue were friendships in which intellectual and moral equals value one another for their intrinsic deliberative and moral qualities (Aristotle, 1941, bks. viii, iii). Thomas Aquinas, the great Roman Catholic Aristotelian, built his concept of Christian love significantly around Aristotle's model of friendships of virtue. This provided a stable place in Thomas's view of Christian love for elements of individual striving, fulfillment, and mutuality—features of love often absent, as I indicated previously, in classic Protestant models (Aquinas 1917, II,ii, Q. 26–27). The Catholic association of Christian love with mutual friendship seems justified. We must remember that the golden rule ("So whatever you wish that men would do to you, do so to them; for this is the law and the prophets"; Mt. 7:12) and neighbor love ("You shall love your neighbor as yourself"; Mt. 22:39) in some sense make self-regard and one's natural concern for one's own good a measure or guide to other-regard, thereby finding an equal place for both.

The Thomistic view, of course, does not eliminate the role of self-sacrifice in its view of Christian love; sacrificial love within Thomism, however, is not so much an end in itself as it is a matter of being, with the grace of God, steadfast and active in working to restore broken relationships to love as mutuality—or, as Gene Outka and Louis Janssens call it, love as equal-regard (Outka, 1972; Janssens, 1977). In its emphasis on steadfastness and the effort needed to renew and restore broken relationships, love as equal-regard has many of the features of the Hebrew scripture's covenantal view of love as *chesed.*

To speak of chesed requires us to introduce one final word for love—the idea of love as *storge,* or parental love. Steadfastness is a characteristic of both chesed and storge. But storge adds an element of deep and preferential investment by parents in their children, who are in some sense a part of themselves. It is noteworthy to observe how the metaphor of the parent-child relation has been used time and again—as Stephen Post and John Miller have reminded us—to symbolize the very heart of God (Post, 1994; Miller, 1998). When this happens, God is depicted not only as steadfast but also as moved by the misfortunes and delighted by the well-being of God's children.

From a psychological perspective, it could be suggested that Jewish, Islamic, and Christian views of God are attributions of the nature of kin altruism (as I define it below) into the very nature of God. In much of the Abrahamic tradition (the three faiths of Judaism, Christianity, and Islam that trace their origins to the biblical Abraham), there can be found the additional idea that not only is God like a good and invested parent but also that God is this kind of parent to all persons, making no fundamental ontological preferences between them. I argue in the following paragraphs that human parenthood when used analogically to characterize God also suggests that even divine love entails elements of investment, attachment, need, gratification, and joy of the kind that extreme agapic or self-sacrificial models find unacceptable as elements of ideal love.

Evolutionary Psychology and the Tensions between Traditional Models of Love

My excuse for presenting this entirely too brief history of different models of love in Christian ethics is to make the following point: *Various contemporary forces, including the insights of evolutionary psychology, are working to shift Christian models of love away from historic Protestant strong agapic models toward the synthesis of Aristotelianism and New Testament Christianity found in a variety of Roman Catholic formulations.* I make this report not as a Roman Catholic but as a liberal Protestant observer of the contemporary theological discussion. Hence love as mutuality or equal-regard, with self-sacrifice serving as a transitional ethic designed to restore love as equal-regard, is an emerging dominant model of love in contemporary theological ethics. It can be found in much of feminist theology (Gudorf, 1985), in some newer Protestant voices (Outka, 1972; Post, 1990), and in a variety of neo-Thomistic Catholic sources (Janssens, 1977). The pressure to reinterpret the tradition in this direction comes from several sources: new insights into the tradition itself (Furnish, 1982; Schottroff, 1978), new perspectives from the psychotherapeutic disciplines (Browning, 1987), changing gender roles in society, ideology critiques of extreme self-sacrificial models of love by feminists and minorities (Andolsen, 1981), and evolutionary psychology itself. I concentrate here on the contributions of evolutionary psychology.

The concepts of kin altruism, inclusive fitness, and reciprocal altruism are beginning to influence theological-ethical views of love. The breakthrough work of William Hamilton (1964), George Williams (1975), and Robert Trivers (1972) on these concepts has not gone unnoticed in theological debates about love. These concepts are defined at length in several chapters in this volume (see especially Schloss, Chapter 13; Wilson & Sober, Chapter 11; and Preston & de Waal, Chapter 17). In view of this, I will be brief. These theorists have advanced the idea that genetic parents work for the survival of their genes not only by preserving themselves but also by sacrificing their own welfare, under certain conditions, on behalf of offspring who carry their genes (kin altruism and inclusive fitness); that other family members, such as brothers and sisters, uncles and aunts, nephews and nieces, are more likely to sacrifice for one another than for non-kin (inclusive fitness); and that natural selection preserves the genes of caring parents and thereby passes them on to their offspring, making carers more likely to survive. In view of the predictive and clarifying power of the theories of kin altruism and inclusive fitness, some theological ethicists have researched the Western religious and philosophical tradition for similar insights assumed by, and sometimes embedded in, their respective concepts of love.

And such insights have been found. Pope and Browning (Pope, 1994; Browning et al., 1997) have found naturalistic observations in the thought of Aristotle and Thomas Aquinas that understood the role of kin preference in both mammalian behavior and human love. For instance, Aristotle used an implicit theory of kin altruism to refute Plato's proposal in *The Republic* that was designed to solve the divisive social effects of nepotism. Plato advanced a thought experiment that envisioned a society in which parents procreated but did not raise their own children. In fact, he proposed that parents would turn these children over to state nurses so that neither parents nor their children would know one another. This arrangement, Plato hoped, would undercut the development of the kind of clan and tribe favoritism that constantly threatened the cohesiveness of ancient societies (Bloom, 1968).

Aristotle thought that such a social arrangement would prove catastrophic. Aristotle argued that there was a general inclination among both animals and humans to have and care for their children. In his *Politics* he wrote, "In common with other animals and with plants, mankind has a natural desire to leave behind them an image of themselves" (Bk. I, ii). Aristotle thought that inhibiting the development of this parental tendency in the name of some abstract vision such as Plato's would undercut the foundations of human care and social solidarity. Aristotle believed Plato's proposal would lead to the general neglect of children. He wrote, "That which is common to the greatest number has the least care bestowed upon it" (Bk. II, iii). For Aristotle, parental care comes most profoundly from parental recognition that a particular child is his or her own and that the child is in some manner an embodiment of the parent. Because Plato failed to recognize this profound truth, Aristotle thought that in his envisioned state, "love will be watery. . . . Of the two qualities which chiefly inspire regard and affection—that a thing is your own and that it is your only one—neither can exist in such a state as this" (Bk. II, iv).

Thomas Aquinas, the great medieval Aristotelian and father of Roman Catholic theology, had his own theory of kin altruism and kin preference. Aquinas, more than any other thinker, is responsible for tilting the mass of Christian thinking toward accepting Aristotle's theory about the contribution of kin altruism to both parental and Christian love. For instance, Aquinas believed that something like what today's evolutionary psychologists call paternal recognition is a condition for a father's investment in his children. Aquinas knew that human females know with certainty that the infant they birth is theirs. He also knew that fathers never know with certainty that an infant is theirs. They make judgments that the child is theirs on the basis of trust, probability, and resemblance. Once paternal recognition is achieved, the dynamics of kin altruism lead to deeper parental investments by fathers in their children as a way of continuing themselves. Aquinas wrote, in his *Summas Contra Gentiles*, "Man naturally desires to be assured of his offspring, and this assurance would be altogether nullified in the case of promiscuous copulation" (1928, bk. III, ii, 115).

Aquinas used this insight to support his understanding of the naturalistic foundations of paternal investment. This concern to preserve one's children as a way of continuing the self is revealed when he also wrote in the *Summa Contra Gentiles*, "Since the natural life which cannot be preserved in the person of an undying father is preserved, by a kind of succession, in the person of the son, it is naturally befitting that the son succeed in things belonging to the father" (1928, bk. III, ii, 114). As androcentric as that passage sounds to today's sensibilities, it also shows that Aquinas, following Aristotle, had some implicit theory of kin altruism and saw it as the foundation of paternal investment.

These observations also show that Aquinas held that human biology contributed some, although certainly not all, of the reasons for monogamy. Monogamy occurs in those species, Aquinas taught, in which infants have a long period of dependency, thereby requiring assistance beyond the mother's contributions. The pressures of infant care stimulate a turn by the female to the male for help. When a male achieves some capacity to surmise that the infant born to his consort resembles him and therefore may be part of his "substance" (as Aquinas would say it), he may then stay with her and the child for a long period as an effort to extend his own life and to continue his access to his consort. For this reason, it behooves the male, Aquinas argued, to remain with his consort and invest in his offspring. This is a biological theory, but one much wider than the important view put forth by Thomas Insel (Chapter 14, this volume). Insel suggests that monogamy, as it is with some voles, may be a product of hormones such as oxytocin and vasopressin released during copulation. Aquinas's theory, instead, invokes the biology of human infant dependency and paternal recognition. Of course, Aquinas stabilized his quasi-biological theory of monogamy with his understanding of marriage as a supernatural and unbreakable sacrament. But we should be reminded that the sacrament does not itself, according to Aquinas, create the natural tendencies toward monogamy among humans; the sacrament simply makes these tendencies into a permanent institution and provides the energizing and reinforcing grace that makes permanence possible (1928, bk. III, ii, 115–116).

Aquinas had a pre-Darwinist theory of kin altruism (without, of course, the accompanying theory of genes). He had, as well, a theory of reciprocal altruism. He wrote in his *Summa Theologica* that one of the central purposes of marriage was "the mutual services which married persons render one another in household matters" (1917, III, Q. 41). Here Aquinas reminds us of contemporary anthropologists who show how this reciprocity works under various conditions. Take, for instance, the Aka pygmies. They show some of the highest levels of family cohesion and equality in the world. Aka husbands and wives stay together partly because they perform a great deal of mutual assistance in the daily pursuits of both parenting and fishing for a livelihood. I could say much more about the biological themes in both Aristotle and Aquinas, and I have done so with my colleagues in *From Culture Wars to Common Ground: Religion and the American Family Debate* (Browning et al., 1997), the summary book of the Religion, Culture, and Family Project that I have been heading for much of the past decade. But this is sufficient, I hope, to provide evidence that part of the Western religious tradition was interested in the naturalistic substrata of altruism, empathy, and love. Furthermore, Aquinas was aware, as was Aristotle before him, that love as kin preference could, under certain conditions, spread *analogically* to relationships outside the immediate family and maybe as far as the distant neighbor and stranger.

Stephen Pope, in his *The Evolution of Altruism and the Ordering of Love* (1994) and other writings, has done more than any other moral theologian to demonstrate how Aquinas's pre-Darwin observations on what we today call kin altruism were integrated into his view of Christian love. In short, these insights served to give rise to a theory of love that saw the developmental importance of kin preference, strong parental investment, and the dialectical relation between self-regard and other-regard and how these early formative influences, with the right communal and symbolic reinforcements, can be extended analogically to include non-kin neighbors, strangers, enemies, and God. Pope argues, and I concur, for a reconstruction and extension of Catholic naturalism in light of insights from evolutionary psychology.

Because self-regard and other-regard are related dialectically in both Christian Thomism and contemporary theories of kin and reciprocal altruism, new reconstructions of Christian love using these sources would give rise to a theory of love with the following features. It would place higher value on self-regard, would understand how early experiences of bonding and attachment prepare for adult capacities for sympathy, would give more emphasis to mutuality and equal-regard, and would interpret self-sacrificial love (and associated Christian symbols of the cross) as functioning to renew mutual love rather than constituting an end in itself. Something like this model of love is serving increasingly to guide theories of human development in certain contemporary Roman Catholic and Protestant circles.

The Metaphysics of Love

This emerging congruence between religious and evolutionary perspectives on love should not blind us to important remaining issues between the two perspectives. The naturalism that undergirds research guided by evolutionary theory is understandable and to be expected. However, when this naturalism hardens into a systematic worldview that functions to exclude or denigrate all visions of life that provide for some sense of transcendence, this is another matter. No matter how far Aristotelian-Thomistic models of Christian love go in acknowledging the more egocentric realities of kin and reciprocal altruism (and they do go far in this direction), love within this theological tradition finally grounds itself on the sacred status of human personhood, the belief that all good (and all specific goods) comes from God, and that the ultimate meaning and direction of all finite loves is the overarching love for and enjoyment of God. For instance, Aquinas wrote in the *Summa Theologica* that humans love their children for two mutually reinforcing reasons: (1) because they are extensions of their own substance, and (2) because they mirror the goodness of God (1917, II, Q. 26, a.3). The two worlds of biological functionality and divine transcendence coexisted in Aquinas's pre-Darwinist thought. Although these alternative worldviews are not easily reconciled, should evolutionary psychology and Christian ethics compete today with the idea that one or the other must eventually vanquish its alleged enemy?

Recent amendments to evolutionary psychology have softened the opposition between these alternative visions, but they have not dissolved the conflict altogether. For instance, there is the emphasis, summarized by James Q. Wilson, on natural selection as functioning to create a variety of secondary mechanisms, such as our positive response to the smile of an infant, even if it is not our own flesh and blood (Wilson, 1993). This insight suggests that rather than simply functioning to select the products of our own genes as such, natural selection has worked to create more generalizable responsive inclinations. This idea has loosened evolutionary psychology from what critics call the tyranny of the reproductive paradigm, thought by some to be a fault of early sociobiology. This advance makes it easier for theology to reconcile evolutionary models of love with more expansive theological models that do not center solely on reproductive love as such.

A second example comes from the work of Frans de Waal. His emphasis on the importance for reciprocal altruism of the cognitive mechanisms of remembrance and anticipation (and therefore the importance of what de Waal calls "cognitive empathy") helps us understand how an ethic of reciprocity can sometimes take the long-term rather than the short-term view of reward and satisfaction (de Waal, 1996). This makes reciprocal altruism sometimes resemble features of self-sacrificial love as theologians might define it.

But long-term reciprocal altruism and Christian sacrificial love are not quite the same. The moral theologian, even those influenced by Thomistic sensibilities, would finally ground the sacrificial element in love on the Christian's belief in the infinite value of the other and on the sense that some acts of self-sacrifice are both willed and *empowered* by God, even though self-sacrifice as such might not be seen as the central goal of Christian love. Furthermore, regard for the other person—when that person is viewed as both a rational creature deserving respect and as a reflection of the image of God—is always the central motivating factor in Christian understandings of love. This is true no matter how openly, in a subordinate way, a Christian perspective might also recognize the importance of the more egocentric elements of kin and reciprocal altruism. Hence Christian love as mutuality or equal-regard can never be reduced to a logic of reciprocity. This is true no matter how complicated and nuanced reciprocity theory becomes. It is also true no matter how important reciprocity is in a secondary way for parties who first treat each other as ends and never as means only, as must be the case for a Christian love ethic of equal-regard.

Evolutionary psychology can make immense contributions to understanding some of the conditions for the emergence of love as mutuality and equal-regard. The importance of kin altruism, the mechanisms of mutual adaptation and attachment in both parent and child, the rise of empathy as the capacity to feel and know the needs of the other in analogy to how the child comes to feel and know his or her own needs, the gradual extension of these dynamics to non-kin, and finally, the development of more abstract capacities of cognitive empathy for persons we do not even know—these are conditions that are essential for developing a love ethic of equal-regard and mutuality.

Stated in this way, such an evolutionarily informed equal-regard ethic would be continuous with Christian love but not identical to it. What makes love as mutuality and equal-regard uniquely Christian is the special way Christians ground their appreciation for the role of sacrificial love. This is grounded on the belief that both self and other are made in the image of God and that in renewing mutuality through sacrificial steadfastness, the Christian is somehow reliving the drama of Christ's own life—itself thought to be the final key to the nature of God. This narrative or story, when rightly presented, can absorb and recontextualize the more naturalistic view of the rise of mutuality.

The conflicting worldviews of evolutionary psychology and Christian theology should be relativized for the purposes of a more general public philosophy. Evolutionary psychology should realize that on the grounds of its discipline alone, it can neither confirm nor deny any particular worldview, even its own heuristic naturalism. Hence, at the margins of human thought, evolutionary psychology should be charitably agnostic on metaphysical issues. Something analogous should be the case with Christian ethics. It should rid itself of its phobia for naturalistic explanations and instead try to recontextualize the insights of naturalism into a broader view of reality that permits elements of transcendence. Both perspectives, evolutionary psychology and Christian ethics, should keep their focus on the *common ground between them,* with an eye toward developing a more rational and public ethic that can interrelate both secular and religious perspectives.

REFERENCES

Andolsen, B. (1981). *Agape* in feminist ethics. *Journal of Religious Ethics, 9,* 69–81.
Aristotle (1941). *Nichomachean ethics* (W. D. Ross, Trans.). New York: Random House.

Aquinas, T. (1917). *Summa theologica* (Fathers of the English Dominican Province, Trans.). London: Washbourne.

Aquinas, T. (1928). *Summa contra gentiles.* London: Oats & Washbourne.

Bernstein, R. (1983). *Beyond objectivism and relativism: Science, hermeneutics, and praxis.* Philadelphia: University of Pennsylvania Press.

Bloom, A. (1968). *The Republic of Plato.* New York: Basic Books.

Browning, D. (1987). *Religious thought and the modern psychologies.* Minneapolis: Fortress Press.

Browning, D., Miller-McLemore, B., Couture, P., Lyon, B., & Franklin, R. (1997). *From culture wars to common ground: Religion and the American family debate.* Louisville, KY: Westminster/John Knox.

Furnish, V. (1982). Neighbor love in the New Testament. *Journal of Religious Ethics, 10,* pp. 327–334.

Gadamer, H.-G. (1982). *Truth and method.* New York: Crossroad.

Green, R. (1992). Kant on Christian love. In E. D. Santurri & W. Werpehowski (Eds.), *The love commandments* (pp. 261–280). Washington: Georgetown University Press.

Gudorf, C. (1985). Parenting, mutual love, and sacrifice. In B. Andolsen, C. Gudorf, & M. Pellauer (Eds.), *Woman's consciousness and women's conscience: A reader in feminist ethics* (pp. 175–191). New York: Harper & Row.

Hallett, G. (1989). *Christian neighbor-love: An assessment of six rival versions.* Washington: Georgetown University Press.

Hamilton, W. D. (1964). The genetic evolution of social behavior (Pt. 2). *Journal of Theoretical Biology, 7,* 17–52.

Janssens, L. (1977). Norms and priorities of a love ethics. *Louvain Studies, 6,* 207–238.

Miller, J. (1998). *Biblical faith and fathering.* New York: Paulist Press.

Nygren, A. (1953). *Agape and eros.* Philadelphia: Westminster Press.

Outka, G. (1972). *Agape: An ethical analysis.* New Haven, CT: Yale University Press..

Peters, R. S. (1958). *The concept of motivation.* London: Routledge and Kegan Paul.

Pope, S. J. (1994). *The evolution of altruism and the ordering of love.* Washington: Georgetown University Press.

Post, S. G. (1990). *A theory of agape: On the meaning of Christian love.* Lewisburg, PA: Bucknell University Press.

Post, S. G. (1994). *Spheres of love: Toward a new ethics of the family.* Dallas: Southern Methodist University Press.

Ricoeur, P. (1981). *Hermeneutics and the human sciences.* Cambridge: Cambridge University Press.

Rorty, R. (1979). *Philosophy and the mirror of nature.* Princeton, NJ: Princeton University Press.

Schottroff, L. (1978). Non-violence and the love of one's enemies. In R. Fuller (Ed.), *Essays on the love commandment* (pp. 9–40). Philadelphia: Fortress Press.

Trivers, R. (1972). Parental investment and sexual selection. In B. Campbell (Ed.), *Sexual selection and the descent of man* (pp. 136–179). New York: Aldine de Gruyter.

de Waal, F. (1996). *Good natured: The origin of right and wrong in humans and other animals.* Cambridge: Harvard University Press.

Williams, G. (1975). *Sex and evolution.* Princeton, NJ: Princeton University Press.

Wilson, J. Q. (1993). *The moral sense.* New York: Free Press.

Winch, P. (1958). *The idea of a social science and its relation to philosophy.* London: Routledge and Kegan Paul.

Wittgenstein, L. (1953). *Philosophical investigations.* Oxford: Blackwell.

20

Separation, Attachment, and Altruistic Love

The Evolutionary Basis for Medical Caring

GREGORY L. FRICCHIONE

This book is dedicated to furthering the understanding of that other-regarding affirmative affection called altruistic love. I contend that medical caring as a vocation has traditionally relied on altruistic love as a guiding principle. Historically, more often than not, compassionate other-directed care was all the physician could offer to the suffering patient. Indeed, it may have been that empathic pain that physicians suffer in the presence of intractable illness that propelled them as scientists to discover treatments and cures. Unfortunately, scientific prowess has in some ways distanced doctors from their ability to truly care for their patients. As a result, physicians now run the risk of becoming time-constrained technologists. This dangerous trend ignores the fact that patients are not their diseases. They are persons with illness still deeply in need of human care. In fact, because of how we have evolved as human beings, the physician who provides other-directed care in an altruistic fashion may promote healing that otherwise would not always take place. Moreover, openness on the part of the physician to the spiritual sources of caring for their patients may foster true healing in the deepest sense of the word. As a medical psychiatrist, I have seen this human dynamic occur numerous times at the bedside, and supportive studies do exist (Fricchione, 2000).

Medical psychiatrists are often called on, along with their patients, to face what philosophers call the limit questions. Who am I? What is the meaning of my life? Where am I going? Will I be separated from my loved ones? These are the transitional limit questions uncovered in the midst of the crisis ignited by the severe physical illnesses we see. Horton (1981) has written eloquently about "transitional relatedness" as the wellspring of solace available in the relationship between the psychiatrist and his or her patient, basing the concept on the willingness and expertise to provide altruistic care by stepping into the "intermediate area" between separation and attachment that Winnicott described (Winnicott, 1953). Of course, such an opportunity to provide care to patients is not the exclusive province of the psychiatrist. Indeed, the origin of caring for all physicians can be traced to the separation-attachment experience of the person who is ill and the willingness of the physician to enter the patient's intermediate area between separation and attachment. In the process, the ill person derives the solace and confidence required to negotiate his or her illness-precipitated developmental challenge (Fricchione, 1993). The physician becomes a transitional object, a symbolic parental presence of protection and guidance, imbued with the power to transport the vulnerable individual faced with the specter of separation and the loss of attachment to a safe place, ideally within some higher, more mature level of attachment.

Transitional relatedness can easily become an add-on for physicians burdened by the pressures of managed competition. Nevertheless, it must be stressed that this transitional role is and always will be at the heart of every physician's calling. As Peabody said to medical students 70 years ago, "One of the essential qualities of the clinician is interest in humanity, for the secret of the care of the patient is in caring for the patient" (Peabody, 1927). Visitors to the Massachusetts General Hospital see these famous words etched in the lobby's marble wall. Alongside it is another famous quote, this time from Dr. Edward Churchill, speaking 50 years ago: "Charity in its broad spiritual sense, that is our desire to relieve suffering, is the most prized possession of medicine."

In this chapter I review the evidence establishing what might be called the separation-attachment dialectical process as a common referent in man's experience of illness; why this common referent resonates in the particular human brain that has evolved; and how it gives birth to man's spiritual imperative. It is this spiritual imperative that becomes the etiology of altruistic love and authentic healing.

The Separation-Attachment Dialectic and Evolution

A dialectic is a process involving the inseparable interconnectedness of two opposing forces, events, or thoughts. At the core of all dialectical thought, there are the basic concepts of separation and attachment. Therefore, if we take the primary thesis and antithesis to be attachment and separation respectively, then synthesis involves the inseparable interconnectedness of them both—in essence a higher synthesis of attachment. My hypothesis in this chapter is built on this: that the dialectical process of separation-attachment is a shared referent bestowing extensional identity to all levels of conceptual knowledge. This core dialectic offers an approach to the study of complexity and eventually to the study of altruistic love. Whatever level of the material universe we choose to examine, in the separation-attachment process we are offered a way to connect that level with subordinate levels before it and superordinate levels after it along the continuum of complexity.

The separation-attachment process can be used to understand prebiotic evolution. So when we talk about the physical universe, we find expression of what is really a more or less complex version of the separation-attachment process. For example, in the Big Bang, when presumably an infinite amount of matter was contained in an infinitely small space, quantum gravitational energy had to be counteracted by a gravitational separation of sufficient force for there to be a primeval explosion (Weinberg, 1992). We might say that we are dealing here with the quantum mechanical version of the separation-attachment process. The process is also crucial in our understanding of a universe that could develop to produce us. As Weinberg writes:

> There may in some sense or other be many different "universes," each with its own value for the cosmological constant . . . if the total cosmological constant were large and negative, the universe would run through its life cycle of expansion and contraction too rapidly for life to have time to appear. On the other hand, if the total cosmological constant were large and positive, the universe would expand forever, but the repulsive force produced by the cosmological constant would prevent the gravitational clumping together of matter to form galaxies and stars in the early universe and therefore give life no place to appear. (Weinberg, 1992, p. 226)

A cosmological constant therefore is somehow describing mathematically the ratio of repulsion-separation and attraction-attachment so as to allow this particular universe in which we could develop. This has been called the anthropic principle.

On the chemical level, when we talk about chemoattraction and chemorepulsion or reaction and diffusion, we are really talking about local versions of the separation-attachment dialectical process. When electrons are separated in oxidation, they must become attached in reduction, enabling a biosynthetic reaction to occur. If there is a simple chemical system composed of 3 molecules called A, B, and C that are capable of forward and reverse reactions, when energy is introduced, A goes to B goes to C and then back to A instead of separate $A \leftrightarrow B$, $B \leftrightarrow C$, $C \leftrightarrow A$ reactions. Free flux energy moves the open dissipative system around to reattachment, which opens up the possibility for enhanced attachment to other catalytic cycles, raising the level to that of a catalytic hypercycle. In their influential book *The Hypercycle: A Principle of Natural Self-Organization*, Manfred Eigen and Peter Schuster (1979) proposed that life is made possible because complex structures can be made persistent through the activity of an intertwined hierarchy of autocatalytic sets, a network of self-activating loops which Stuart Kauffman calls a collectively autocatalytic system (Kauffman, 1995). For Kauffman and others, it is the achievement of collective catalytic closure that is the secret of life. Life got its start here and later incorporated nucleic acids and genomes to improve reproduction and inheritance.

When we talk about these self-organizing systems in the chemical world, we are still talking about the separation-attachment process. Autocatalysis offers the possibility of spiraling in hypercycling fashion to ever-higher levels of attachment. Catalysis by enzymes, and perhaps initially by catalytic RNAs, represents an early key version of the selection mechanism based on the attachment complementarity of simple molecules (Chaisson, 1987; DeDuve, 1995; Laszlo, 1987; Mainzer, 1994).

This "attachment complementarity" led to the process of base pairing with adenine linked to uracil and guanine linked to cytosine. "The birth of this mechanism . . . signals the transition from the age of chemistry to the age of information," according to DeDuve (1995, p. 48). But it is essential to keep in mind that the separation-attachment dialectical process, through attachment complementarity expressed in the hydrogen bonding of base pairings overcoming the separation challenge of electrostatic repulsive forces, is necessary for and permits the development of evolutionary phenomena. The separation-attachment dialectical process can be traced from its cosmological origin in the Big Bang to the origin of the age of replicable information storable in nucleic acids.

If we focus on the history of brain evolution, we can again see this separation-attachment dialectical process at work. A living organism is a sensorimotor analyzer-effector. Any brain is really a complexified sensorimotor analyzer-effector organ for the organism fortunate enough to have one. By this we mean that an organ such as the brain will have the power to sense its environment, contribute a level of analysis to the sensory data perceived, and effect a motor response based on that analysis. Organisms thus have the capacity to form judgment policy. The initial and persistent decision any organism must make is between avoidance and approach. This began with the protocell, the earliest life form. It can be seen in examples from the world of bacteria, including E-coli, which move toward the gradient of food metabolites as their energy source. These prokaryotic cells therefore have a mechanism for chemo-attraction, as well as chemo-repulsion. Indeed, they may be said to possess "primitive intelligence," which may be described as optimization of behavior in light of incoming data. Cellular evolutionary history from single cell to multicell organisms can be understood in light of the separation-attachment dialectic (see Figure 20.1).

The evolution of life is intimately connected with the complexifying of the approach-avoidance task, and the key to this complexification is the increasing complexity of the evolved brain. Reviewing the evolution of the mammalian brain from that of the reptile serves to underscore this point. The brain is arranged in the form of circuits, which are called basal ganglia thalamo-cortical loops (Alexander, DeLong, & Strick, 1986). The basal ganglia provide a motor effector control system. The thalamus provides a sensory synchronizer and the cortex, both limbic and neocortex, provides an increasingly complex analysis system. All living organisms possess an attachment drive at the most primitive level toward food as a source of energy. Those organisms complexified enough to have developed sexual reproduction possess another level of attachment drive toward the sexual mate, for the purposes not only of self-preservation but also of species preservation and reproduction.

The reptile has a strategy based on these two levels of attachment drive. Overall, however, their social strategy is one of separation. A reptile mother will often cannibalize her young as a source of food attachment. Thus monitor lizard young

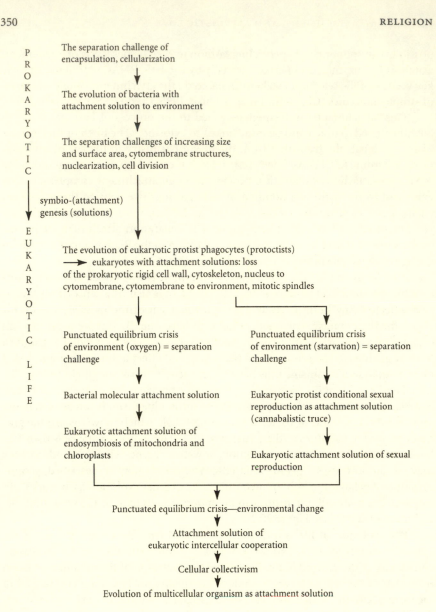

Figure 20.1.   Cellular evolutionary history. *Source:* Adapted from DeDuve, 1995, and Margulis, 1998.

roll in feces to discourage their mother's food attachment drive. In the mammal, however, the strategy is different. While maintaining the more primitive attachments to food and sexual mating, the mammal has evolved to a new level of attachment, that of the "mammalian behavioral triad." This includes maternal nurturance and caring, the separation cry, and mammalian play (MacLean, 1990). From the point of view of brain evolution this behavioral triad can be seen to foster parental attachments to offspring. It can be understood as a reflection of loop evolution from a primitive basal ganglia thalamo-amygdala-septum-piriform "cortex" equivalents to a more advanced loop consisting of connections to new cortical regions: namely, the anterior cingulate cortex and the medial orbital frontal cortex (see Figure 20.2).

Of course this was a very complicated process, involving genomic imprinting selection pressures in the mammalian line (Keverne, Fundele, Narashimha, Barton, & Surami, 1996). In man, after the development of the anterior cingulate/medial orbital frontal loop responsible for the mammalian behavioral triad and more complexified attachment, there is the further evolution of the dorsal lateral prefrontal cortical and the lateral orbital frontal cortical basal ganglia thalamo-cortical loops. Thus there is an increasing complexification in the sensory motor analyzer-effector function of the brain. With the development of prefrontal cortical loop structures, man develops the capacity to have a "memory of the future," as well as a "memory of the past" (Ingvar, 1985). This means not only that the human species has the ability to appraise the present situation in terms of past attachment experience but also that it has the ability to plan future attachments and to have them valenced with pleasure and pain mediated in the brain's reward circuitry. This reward circuitry consists of mesolimbic-mesocortical dopamine tracts modulated by dopamine, among other neurotransmitters and peptides, connecting the most ancient basal ganglia thalamo-cortical loops with the most advanced ones. Thus, although largely segregated, these loops are integrated via the reward circuitry and through corticocortical and corticostriatal tracts. This is how the brain meets Tononi and colleagues' criteria for neural complexity that is essentially a reflection of the separation-attachment dialectical process itself (Tononi, Sporns, & Edelman et al., 1994).

The human prefrontal cortex allows us to design and execute movement plans for future approaches to pleasurable attachments and avoidances of painful separations. This premotor templating is a miraculous evolutionary advance which is probably responsible for man's preeminence in the animal kingdom. However, it comes at a dreadful price. It is this: We are the only species capable of having a memory of our future separation. Thus, though we have eaten of the "tree of the knowledge of good and evil," gaining the wisdom of not only a memory of the past but also a memory of the future, we have also been thrown out of the Garden of Eden and into the hard cold world of separation dread.

Consciousness, Language, and Culture

And so it is, with the coming of human consciousness brought about in the more advanced basal ganglia thalamo-cortical loops in which reentry signaling can take place, there is a major improvement in the sensorimotor analyzer-effector functions of the brain optimizing approach-avoidance decision making (Edelman, 1992). Yet this source of our hope also leaves us in fear and trembling at the memory of our future separation. This, of course, is the psychological rendering of the basic core dialectical process of separation-attachment dialectic. What begins with

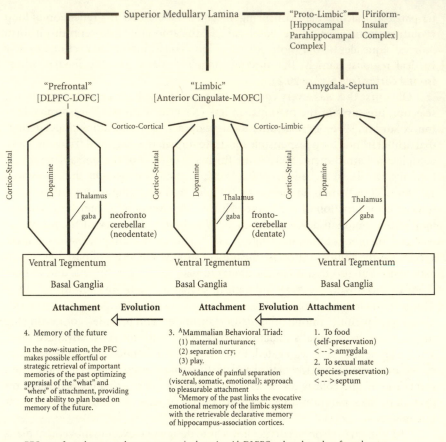

Figure 20.2. Brain loop evolution and attachment

the separation cry as the first human vowel sound as an expression of separation and isolation fear and a plea for attachment becomes extended into the emotional prosodic language that is right-hemisphere dominated and the propositional semantic language that is left-hemisphere dominated. An argument can be made that this complexification in expression and communication is the product of what Daniel Dennett calls "good tricks" which certain genotypically gifted early humans were capable of producing (Dennett, 1991). Such good tricks could also be learned by fellow humans close enough in genetic design space to learn the new behaviors. This rapid development in the evolutionary good trick of language could be understood in terms of what has come to be called "the Baldwin effect" (Dennett, 1995). Baldwin was a Darwinian in search of a pivotal role for "Mind" in evolution. Perhaps animals, through properties of mind, might help accelerate and orient evolution. Indeed, this is what he showed (Baldwin, 1896). We begin with a species marked by a continuum of genetic availability in brain hard wiring.

One genetic version of the wiring diagram may equip the organism for a good trick, which can be defined as a behavior that endows its possessor with a survival fitness advantage in its "adaptive" or "fitness landscape" (Wright, 1931). (Dennett fails to see that for the human mammal "the environment of evolutionary adaptiveness" is necessarily one of secure base attachment; Bowlby, 1969). In fact, all good tricks in the history of evolution may be contingent on the separation-attachment dialectic defined in terms of the benefit to attachment they can provide in increasingly complex ways.) However, what if, in addition to the individual genotypic variability, there is an added ability to customize the stock version by adjusting the wiring in response to the environment in a process called phenotypic plasticity? An individual's experience in an environment will produce a brain design different from what pure genetic endowment would predict. Those who are endowed with a genotype more proximal on the continuum to the good trick genotype and thus requiring fewer redesign measures through plasticity are more likely to recognize and maintain the good trick than are those more genotypically distant. Dennett the Darwinian acknowledges that in "the long run, natural selection-redesign at the genotype level—will tend to follow the lead of and confirm the directions taken by the individual organisms' successful explorations—redesign at the individual or phenotype level" (Dennett, 1995, p. 78). In order to disavow any heretical notion this might imply concerning a direction inherent in evolution perpetrated by a "mind-first" force or power, Dennett tries to stress that the Baldwin effect, which he correctly sees as responsible for the development of consciousness and language, requires only a mechanistic ability to learn through the feedback of random blind trial and error when a good trick has come along. There is little if any need for mind-stuff here. The Baldwin effect is a subprocess of the basic slow natural selection design process which permits the latter to be sped up in an explicable way. Phenotypic plasticity has the power to put to rest the need for a Lamarckian inheritance to explain the rapidity of design improvements in evolution. Baldwin, for Dennett, only discovered how the "blind" undirected process of natural selection could be aided "by a limited amount of 'look ahead' in the activities of individual organisms, which create fitness differences that natural selection can then act upon" (Dennett, 1995, p. 80). But, by saying "a limited amount of look ahead," Dennett opens the door to what a mind will become in evolution. What starts out as the good trick of a primitive "brain" reflexively using a simple neural network to mediate avoidance-approach becomes the good trick of a monumentally complexified neural network brain environmentally sculpted through the Baldwin effect to mediate separation-attachment and equipped with a true mind possessed of a memory of the past and a memory of the future self-consciousness so different from "a limited amount of look ahead" according to its level of complexity as to be qualitatively differentiated from the mechanistic mind Dennett presents. This is not to say that mind dropped down from above. It did indeed evolve from below. But we are talking here of the separation-attachment dialectical process as it spirals its way up in the evolution of the universe of life and of mind and of spirituality. Whereas Dennett retreats from Baldwin's scientific quest back toward the traditional conservative Darwinian stance, we proceed from Baldwin's position to where a scientific reading of the separation-attachment dialectical process seems to be leading us. R. J. Richards comments on Baldwin, "The mechanism conformed to ultra-Darwinian assumptions, but nonetheless allowed consciousness and intelligence a role in directing evolution. By philosophic disposition and conviction, Baldwin was a spiritualistic metaphysician. He felt the beat of consciousness in the universe; it pulsed through all the levels of organic life" (Richards, 1987, p. 480). As humans, as mammals, as living things, we all feel the beat of consciousness in the universe. It is the rhythm of the separation-attachment dialectical process as it has evolved in us and as it evolves through us. This most powerful "secret melody" evolutionarily demanded we keep humming it to ourselves, developing a memory of it in our past and our future, selecting for the good tricks of consciousness to reflect on these memories and language to comprehend and express them.

With this in mind, I argue that the impetus for the development of language is the evolutionary need to express and communicate approach/attachment and avoidance/separation behaviors. The key mammalian evolutionary survival strategy of parental attachment to offspring and social attachment would selectively bias for organisms capable of increasingly effective and sophisticated communication. And with the evolution of language there is the facilitation of "memes" (Dawkins, 1976). Reproducible information in the form of memes is passed from individual to individual, and communities sharing information are thus solidified. Memetic evolution begets cultural evolution, but cultural evolution can only be understood if we hearken back to the core dialectical issues that led to culture's development in the first place. Repulsion/avoidance/separation and attraction/approach/attachment are the key issues in cultural evolution. In his Pulitzer Prize–winning book *The Denial of Death*, Ernest Becker (1973) reviews for us how important the memory of future final separation is in the history of man and his culture. The theologian John Dunne (1965) looks at human myths and their cultural origins in relation to mortality and civilization in his book *The City of the Gods*. It is in human culture that we encounter the significance of altruistic love, but to truly understand it we must look for a process of evolution that is both broad enough and deep enough to encompass the biological, psychological, sociocultural, and spiritual concepts of altruism.

The Evolution of Altruistic Love

I would contend that the best candidate for an evolutionary theory of altruistic love is the separation-attachment dialectical process (see Figure 20.3). Separation-attachment is a common referent conferring extensional identity across different conceptual levels of complexity. It therefore has explanatory architectonic power in terms of physical-chemical prebiotic evolution, as well as in terms of biological evolution. Indeed, it is a hypothesis that offers a consilience of inductions drawing on a data pattern in a source of knowledge to illuminate a data pattern in a target of knowledge (Wilson, 1998). In the process new knowledge emerges. We can trace the origins of consciousness, memory, and language to this core process. The development of information and its dispersal required all of these. The purpose of consciousness, memory, language, and information is to facilitate and to optimize separation-attachment decision making. Separation-attachment decision making after all really represents the astonishing complexification of the chemo-attraction, chemo-repulsion "primitive intelligence" decision making of prokaryotic life.

The individual human being endowed with memory of the past and memory of the future information is attached by virtue of his mammalian heritage to social groups, as well as to parents and family. Other mammalian species form social group attachments and interactions without benefit of such sophisticated memory. This is likely secondary to the intricate interactions of primitive attachments to food, sexual mate, and the more advanced familial attachments that mammals possess. In overview, mammalian attachments to social groups can be interpreted as attachments in the service of meeting separation challenges which can emerge from environmental sources, including other social groups. This process fosters the evolution of cooperation, which has its distant antecedents in the symbiogenesis of bacteria in response to separation challenges. In man, this process eventuating in contract formation is obviously much more complexified.

As we have seen, the results of brain complexification include the development of memory of the past and memory of the future. Humans not only remember past, pleasurable attachments, allowing for the planning and execution of strategies to reattain such states, but we also possess the memory of the past, painful separations which enable us to predict our own future separations. Although this too allows us to plan and execute strategies to avoid such painful separations, the knowledge that in the end we and our fellow humans will lose our lives nevertheless is inescapable and dreadful. This most powerful realization greatly intensifies the separation-attachment dialectical process in the human species. Social group interactions become more powerfully valenced in empathic understanding of this dialectic. People develop the potential to be more deeply bonded even to the level of agape or selfless love.

Listening hard to those with illness may help us discover that in the predicament there is clarity as to what is most important in life and a hint as to the origins of altruistic love. When asked what the worst part of their illness experience is, most patients tell me, in so many words, that it is the fear of separation and loss of attachment. The medical psychiatrist Richard Berlin has written about the practical implications of this fear (Berlin, 1986). We psychiatrists may label this feeling as anxiety and depression, but it is perhaps more heuristically described as the separation-attachment process all humans share. I recently was asked to see a young woman with an infected ventricular-peritoneal shunt which had been placed for trauma-related hydrocephalus. She was having severe headaches, yet when I asked her what troubled her the most about her illness, she replied that she dearly missed her family and burst into tears. This was something neuropsychiatrists call emotional incontinence, yet it authentically expressed her fear of separation and her wish for restored attachment.

Man's spiritual imperative originates in what can be understood as a dialectic of separation and attachment. Spirituality emerges in our contemplation of the "pining emotion" we orphans feel, separated as we are from our Parent. As creatures experiencing the pain of separation, we seek healing in being bound back

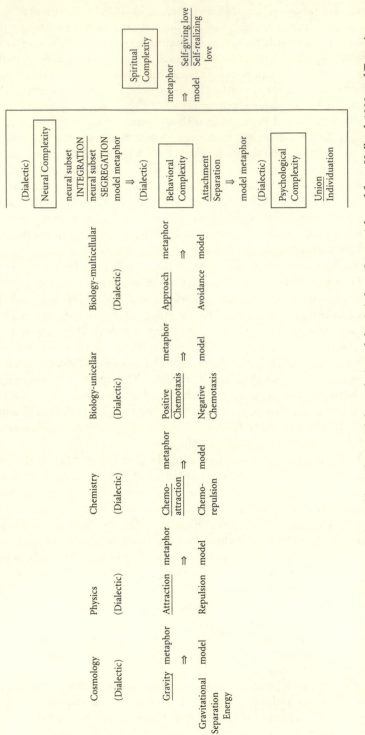

Figure 20.3. The separation-attachment dialectical hypothesis and the evolution of altruistic love. *Source:* Adapted from Holland, 1998, and Tononi, Sporns, & Edelman, 1994.

through authentic religion. The word *religio* itself means "to bind back." Fitchett, Burton, and Sivan (1997) recently published a study describing the religious and spiritual needs and resources of both psychiatric and medical-surgical patients.

Results showed that psychiatric patients (58%) and medical-surgical patients (50%) similarly reported religious needs during their hospitalizations. The most frequently reported needs were (1) expression of caring and support from another person; (2) knowledge of God's presence; (3) prayer; (4) purpose and meaning in life; and (5) a chaplain to visit and pray. We see here support for two major themes we have been underscoring. Illness uncovers our existential nakedness, clarifying for medical and psychiatric patients alike what the real limit questions are and that they are spiritual in nature. Thus, in the context of the need for purpose and meaning when ill, the solace of relationships with *caring* individuals (physicians, nurses, chaplains, as well as family members) and the *consoling* sense of God's presence become essential attachment resources in meeting the separation challenge of illness. Reception of altruistic caring and self-giving love would seem to endorse a sense of meaning resulting in healing of the minds and hearts of the severely ill.

Matthews and Larson (1995), in their review of 212 studies looking at the overall effects of religious resources and commitment on health care outcomes, found that 75%, or 160 studies, were positive, showing a better outcome; 7%, or 15 studies, were negative, showing poorer outcome; and 17%, or 37 studies, were neutral, showing either no effect or a mixed outcome. When a patient experiences altruistic love and the solace it provides, an attachment solution is found. This may result in mesocortical-mesolimbic brain changes that in turn may lead to salutary effects on stress response systems resulting in improved health (Fricchione, 2000).

Separation, Attachment, and Altruistic Love

Consciousness, memory, language, information, and memetic cultural evolutions allow for a myriad of social attachments that are achieved in response to separation pressure. Thus we have the bonds of sex, race, ethnicity, nationality, and religion strengthened by virtue of shared characteristics and information deemed necessary in the shared struggle for attachment security. In the human organism's decision to approach or avoid, such shared characteristics in information, that is, shared culture, will become essential sensory data associated with emotionally valenced memory. In such associations there will be a positive brain reward circuitry feedback via such neurotransmitters as dopamine and opioid neuropeptides.

As Ernst Mayr points out, although individual selection pressures gave rise to "inclusive fitness" and "reciprocal altruism," it was selection pressure on human cultural groups that gave rise to "genuine altruism" (Mayr, 1997). Enlarging the group in the face of separation challenge—an enhanced attachment strategy—was selected for. This required extending concern for well-being to nonrelatives. Cultural norms for behavior toward nonrelatives followed, counteracting the selfish tendencies of individuals in the group. Thus the constraints of altruism directly benefit the group as a whole. But for each individual human with the power of conscious reasoning, memory, language, and information, this genuine altruism requires separation-attachment decision making. Human altruistic behavior can thus involve the deliberate choice of ethical agape love over selfish behavior rather than relying on instinctual inclusive fitness. "The adaptive shift from an instinctive altruism based on inclusive fitness to a group ethics based on decision-making was perhaps the most important step in humanization" (Mayr, 1997). This is reflected in the Zulu concept of *ubuntu*. People are people through other people. One is deprived oneself when another is deprived (Carter, 2000). Altruism can be traced to the complexification of attachment solutions to separation challenges, with a lineage from parental care to hominid troop enlargement beyond the extended family to culture and traditions in societies.

Perhaps the most intensely felt human cultural attachment is that of religion. This may derive from the fact that religion and religion alone is powerful enough to do battle with the ultimate memory of future final separation that is responsible for man's existential pain. Even Freud, for whom religion represented a delusion, realized this. In Marx's epithet that religion is the opium of the people is hidden a sublime compliment when viewed in this context. Religious belief may indeed stimulate the brain's reward circuitry, resulting in a pleasurable emotional valence and an overriding attachment feeling. In terms of spirituality, this has been referred to as an oceanic feeling.

Religion becomes the repository for the memes that consecrate genuine altruism. Thus we hear the commandment, "love thy neighbor as thyself" and even "love thine enemies." But what is meant by "love"? Theologians will often distinguish between at least two forms of love in human experience. There is self-affirming love, or eros, in which a person seeks out a love object to satisfy his own being. Eros, of course, can be thought of as that attachment drive which, when fulfilled, leads to a culmination in the basic trust that one possesses self-worth and that life is nourishing. Then there is self-giving love, or agape, in which a person expends himself or herself in free and seemingly foolhardy love for the other person. There is a sacrifice in such a gift of one's self without concern for personal gain.

In his classic 1968 work, *The Spirit and the Forms of Love*, Daniel Day Williams argued that self-love, that is, self-affirming love, is nothing more than a desire to belong. Selfhood at a deep level is a desire to "feel at home in the world" and so to be in community; thus we have the paradox that selfhood (having our own being) is essentially an offer of communication (Fiddes, 1988). This realization suggests that love is in essence mutuality. Self-affirming love and self-giving love are harmonious. One individuates in community.

As Jungel (1983, p. 44) pointed out, agape is the "power which integrates eros." In the human being, brain loop evolution has supported more and more enhanced and refined attachment solutions in the context of separation selection pressures. Genuine altruism and agape love are the aspirational and achievable outcomes of this complexifying evolutionary process. We advance as human beings when we choose attachment solutions; even when those attachment solutions fail to provide us as individuals with survival advantage, they may benefit the group. Yet the individual human being with self-giving love still stands to benefit.

The altruistic benefactor does not seek survival advantage but rather surcease in the pain of separation felt in empathy with the benefacted person who receives the self-giving love. In such a way there is enhanced individuation in community.

Williams (1968) wrote, "I use the term agape to refer to the self-giving and forgiving love which God has decisively expressed in the world in his redemptive activity in Jesus. I mean by the human loves all our experiences of organic feeling and sympathetic attachment for things and persons in the world. This includes self-love" (p. 205). In self-love and self-assertion there is always "both the pole of autonomy, the affirmation of self-integrity and independence, and the pole of symbiosis which requires conformity and relatedness to the other. Both autonomy and symbiosis require communication and response. The autonomous self wants to be recognized as a self, and it seeks response in the other. Belonging involves communication and no self can exist without some fulfillment of this fundamental need" (Williams, 1968, p. 206).

And with this separation-attachment-based understanding:

> We now see human loves in a new light. Agape is not another love which is added to the others. Neither is it their contradiction. It is the love which underlies all others, leads them towards the discovery of their limits, and releases a new possibility in the self which is created for communion. God discloses himself as agape. We do not discover his love welling up within us. We discover it at the boundary of our existence, in the experience of crisis, and in the overwhelming goodness for which we give thanks, or at the abyss of despair toward which we plunge. Agape is the affirmation of life, the forgiveness of sin, the spirit in which the self can give itself away and yet be fulfilled. (Williams, 1968, p. 210)

For the separation crisis of life, we have an attachment solution which provides solace for our "memory of the future." Medical caring has its wellspring in this source of solace. The capacity for altruistic love should be nurtured in our future physicians. "Agape indeed bears an assurance for every future. It overcomes the fear of death and defeat. 'Nothing can separate us from the love of God.' Love never disappears. But what love may do and will do, what creative and redemptive work lies ahead, can only be known partially in the history of love until the 'end'" (Williams, 1968, p. 212).

C. S. Peirce sensed this over a hundred years ago when he wrote, "The movement of love is circular, at one and the same impulse projecting creations into independency and drawing them into harmony" (cited in Hauser & Kloesel, 1992, p. 353). Here we have encapsulated the spiritual project of humankind. It can be understood as the core dialectic of separation-attachment which, as both medium and message, led to the evolution of the capability of reflecting back on the separation-attachment dialectical process itself! Peirce may have been right when he argued for agapastic evolution based on the Golden Rule. In his 1893 essay, "Evolutionary Love," he wrote, "The philosophy we draw from John's gospel is that this is the way mind develops; and as for the cosmos, only so far as it is yet mind, and so has life, is it capable of further evolution. Love, recognizing germs of loveliness in the hateful, gradually warms it into life, and makes it lovely" (cited in Hauser &

Kloesel, 1992, p. 354). Theologians tell us that sin involves separation from God. If this is so, then our evolutionary and developmental salvation may lie in loving reattachment to our Parent as a response to this separation challenge.

And so agape or altruistic love can be seen as a completion of the separation-attachment dialectical process. It is the healthy synthesis of self-affirming/self-realizing love (that which separates us out as individuals) with self-giving love (that which attaches us in empathy to community). He who loses his life in self-giving love will find it in true self-realization.

REFERENCES

Alexander, G. E., DeLong, M. R., & Strick, P. L. (1986). Parallel organization of functionally segregated circuits linking basal ganglia and cortex. *Annual Review of Neuroscience, 9,* 357–381.

Baldwin, J. M. (1986). A new factor in evolution. *American Naturalist, 30,* 441–536.

Becker, E. (1973). *The denial of death.* New York: Free Press.

Berlin, R. M. (1986). Attachment behavior in hospitalized patients. *Journal of the American Medical Association, 255,* 3391–3393.

Bowlby, J. (1969). *Attachment and loss* (Vols. 1–2). New York: Basic Books.

Carter, J. (2000, January). Talk before the National Geographic Society Annual Meeting. Washington, DC.

Chaisson, E. (1987). *The life era: Cosmic selection and conscious evolution.* New York: Norton.

Dawkins, R. (1976). *The selfish gene.* Oxford: Oxford University Press.

DeDuve, C. (1995). *Vital dust. Life as a cosmic imperative.* New York: Basic Books.

Dennett, D. C. (1991). *Consciousness explained.* Boston: Little, Brown.

Dennett, D. C. (1995). *Darwin's dangerous idea: Evolution and the meanings of life.* New York: Simon & Schuster.

Dunne, J. (1965). *The city of the gods. A study of myth and mortality.* New York: Macmillan.

Edelman, G. M. (1992). *Bright air, brilliant fire: On the matter of the mind.* New York: Basic Books.

Eigen, M., & Schuster, P. (1979). *The hypercycle: A principle of natural self-organization.* New York: Springer.

Fiddes, P. (1988). *The creative suffering of God.* Oxford, England: Clarendon Press.

Fitchett, G., Burton, L. A., & Sivan, A. B. (1997). The religious needs and resources of psychiatric patients. *Journal of Nervous and Mental Disorders, 185,* 320–326.

Fricchione, G. L. (1993). Illness and the origin of caring. *Journal of Medical Humanities, 24,* 15–21.

Fricchione, G. L. (2000). Religious issues in the context of medical illness. In A. Stoudemire, B. S. Fogel, & D. Greenberg (Eds.), *Psychiatric care of the medical patient* (2nd ed., pp. 19–101). Oxford: Oxford University Press.

Hauser, N., & Kloesel, C. (1992). The essential Peirce. In N. Hauser & C. Kloesel (Eds.), *Selected philosophical writings, 1867–1893* (Vol. 1).) Bloomington: Indiana University Press.

Holland, J. H. (1998). *Emergence: From chaos to order.* Reading, MA: Helix Books/Addison-Wesley.

Horton, P.C. (1981). *Solace: The missing dimension in psychiatry.* Chicago: University of Chicago Press.

Ingvar, D. H. (1985). Memory of the future: An essay on the temporal organization of conscious awareness. *Human Neurobiology, 4,* 127–136.

Jungel, E. (1983). *God as the mystery of the world* (D. L. Guder, Trans.). Edinburgh: Clark.

Kauffman, S. (1995). *At home in the universe: The search for the laws of self-organization and complexity*. New York: Oxford University Press.

Keverne, E. B., Fundele, R., Narashimha, M., Barton, S. C., & Surami, M. A. (1996). Genomic imprinting and the differential roles of parental genomes in brain development. *Developmental Brain Research, 92*, 91–100.

Laszlo, E. (1987). *Evolution: The grand synthesis*. Boston: New Science Library.

MacLean, P. D. (1985). Brain evolution relating to family, play and the separation call. *Archives of General Psychiatry, 42*, 405–417.

MacLean, P. D. (1990). *The triune brain in evolution*. New York: Plenum Press.

Mainzer, K. (1994). *Thinking in complexity: The complex dynamics of matter, mind, and mankind*. Berlin: Springer-Verlag.

Margulis, L. (1998). *Symbiotic planet: A new view of evolution*. New York: Basic Books.

Matthews, D. A., & Larson, D. B. (1995). *The faith factor: An annotated bibliography of clinical research on spiritual subjects* (Vol. 3). Rockville, MD: National Institute for Health Care Research.

Mayr, E. (1997). *This is biology: The science of the living world*. Cambridge: Belknap Press of Harvard University Press.

Moore, T., & Haig, D. (1991). Genomic imprinting in mammalian development: A parental tug-of-war. *Trends in Genetics, 7*, 45–49.

Peabody, F. W. (1927). The care of the patient. *Journal of the American Medical Association, 88*, 877–882.

Peirce, C. S. (1992). Evolutionary love. In *The essential Peirce* (Vol. 1, pp. 352–371). Bloomington: Indiana University Press.

Richards, R. J. (1987). *Darwin and the emergence of evolutionary theories of mind and behavior*. Chicago: University of Chicago Press.

Tononi, G., Sporns, O., & Edelman, G. M. (1994). A measure for brain complexity: Relating functional segregation and integration in the nervous system. *Proceedings of the National Academy of Sciences, 91*, 5033–5037.

Weinberg, S. (1992). *Dreams of a final theory: The search for the fundamental laws of nature*. New York: Pantheon Books.

Williams, D. D. (1968). *The spirit and the forms of love*. New York: Harper & Row.

Wilson, E. O. (1998). *Consilience: The unity of knowledge*. New York: Knopf.

Winnicott, D. (1953). Transitional objects and transitional phenomena. *International Journal of Psychoanalysis, 34*, 89–97.

Wright, S. (1931). Evolution in Mendelian populations. *Genetics, 16*, 97–102.

21

Compassion out of Wisdom

*Buddhist Perspectives from the Past
toward the Human Future*

RUBEN L. F. HABITO

What brings about attitudes and behavior described as altruistic, loving, and compassionate? This is the key question addressed, in different ways, by the chapters in this volume, a cooperative venture involving scientists, philosophers, and religious scholars. A corollary question is this: How can we foster and nurture this kind of attitude and behavior on the individual and societal, as well as the ecological, levels of our being? This question becomes a crucial one in the face of a world situation marked by violence and conflict, by a woundedness of global proportions that now poses a threat to our very survival as Earth community.

In pursuing this theme, this chapter examines a religious tradition that has for two and a half millennia continued to shape many societies and cultures in the Eastern hemisphere and that since the last century has made significant inroads in the West as well.

Buddhism finds its origins in the enlightenment experience of Gautama Siddhartha (463–383 BCE), who by virtue of that experience came to be known as the Buddha ("Awakened One"). That pivotal experience is described in scriptures as one that enabled him to see "things as they truly are (*yathā-bhū-tam*)" and that transformed his whole being. The Awakened One also came to be known as "the Compassionate One" (*karunā-atmakā*), or as the one "whose being is compassion itself" (*karunā-ātmatā*). At the fount of Buddhism then is an affirmation of the inherent link between the religious experience that opens one to seeing "things as they truly are" and a mode of life and way of being whose basic mark is compassion.

In scriptures composed throughout different epochs in South and East Asia, we find attempts to express what this experience of awakening is all about, what it entails, in terms of views of reality and the concomitant mode of behavior or way of life stemming from those views. Here I examine a few selected texts in an attempt to shed light on Buddhist views of reality and the mode of living stemming from those views. I conclude with reflections on possible contributions from this tradition toward our task of forging a common viable future as Earth community.

Selected Texts from Buddhist Tradition

The Metta-Sutta (On Kindliness)

A collection of texts said to contain early strata of transmitted teachings of Gautama the Buddha, the *Sutta-Nipāta*, includes a passage titled "On Kindliness" (*Metta-sutta*) that describes the way of life and mode of being of one who traverses the path of peace (Pāli, *nibbāna*; Sanskrit, *nirvāna*; Andersen-H. Smith, 1913):

> One who knows the state of well-being, who seeks that place of peace, should live thus: able, upright, truly upright, of noble speech, gentle, humble.
>
> Knowing sufficiency, well-content, with few wants and simple tastes, With senses calmed, discreet, not arrogant, not attached to blood relations, Not pursuing the least thing for which one could be censured by the wise.
>
> May all beings be happy and safe, may they all be truly happy.
>
> Whether they be weak or strong, long or large, medium or short, without exception, Seen or unseen, dwelling far or near, born or yet unborn, May all beings be truly happy.
>
> Let no one deceive another, nor look down upon another anywhere, ever. Let no one wish harm on any other, in anger or ill will.
>
> As a mother would protect her only child with her whole life, let one cultivate such a boundless mind toward all beings.
>
> Let this kindly heart, this boundless mind, embrace the whole world. Above, below, across, unobstructed, free from hatred, free from ill will.
>
> Standing, walking, sitting, lying down, while awake, cultivate this mindfulness. This, it is said, is the sublime dwelling place.
>
> Not falling into wrong views, living virtuously, replete with insight, overcoming delusive desires, such a one will not enter the cycle of rebirth. (Andersen-H. Smith, 1913, nos. 143–152)

Noted for its simplicity and clarity in conveying the heart of early Buddhism, this passage is often excerpted in collections and anthologies. Let us note a few important elements conveyed. The opening lines refer to "one who is on the way to the place of peace." This "place of peace" is of course none other than the summit point of the Buddhist path, known also as *nirvāna* (Pāli, *nibbā-na*). In early Buddhist texts, *nirvāna* is understood not so much as a state in the afterlife, as it came to be held later on in popular usage, but as the state of being that was aspired to by followers of the Awakened One. These early followers sought to awaken themselves to the ultimate truth realized by the Buddha, understood as the arrival at that place of peace. A basic meaning of the term *nirvāna* derives from the verb "to extinguish." *Nirvāna* is a state of being wherein the flames of greed, hatred, and ignorant passions have been extinguished, and wherein one sees "things as they are" bereft of delusion. It is thus a term that came to denote ultimate reality in the Buddhist tradition (Stcherbatsky, 1975).

Another point to note involves a nuance of the translated phrase "should act thus." The Pāli term is *karanīyam*, meaning "that which is to be done." The passage can be read thus: "(the following ought) to be done by one . . . who seeks that place of peace." Thus it can be understood as a prescription for comporting oneself *in order to* attain that desired state of being called *nirvāna*. But there is another way of reading this term *karanīyam*: one who has arrived at that place of peace "should (naturally) act thus." The (compassionate, etc.) behavior described in the passage can be understood as stemming from the mode of being of one who is grounded in that place of peace. In other words, rather than as an ethical injunction or moral prescription given "in order to attain a desired end" (that is, the place of peace), the passage can be read as a descriptive one, delineating what "should" take place as that place of peace is attained. One who knows the state of well-being, that place of peace itself, should (naturally, inevitably) comport oneself and live thus: able, upright, with a boundless mind, and so forth.

In sum, the entire passage can be read in a twofold way. It is a *prescription* for a set of attitudes and actions conducive to attaining the most desirable state, that place of peace, as well as a *description* of the way of life, with its concomitant acts and attitudes that are but a natural outflow of that state. Attitudes and behavior flowing out of that sense of kinship (Pāli, *metta-*; Sanskrit, *maitri-*) with all beings, in other words, constitute the moral prerequisite or conditions for attaining the place of peace. Conversely, such attitudes and behavior are also but the natural outflow of the arrival at or realization of that place of peace. In short, the place of peace is both a point of arrival of a life characterized by kindliness and compassion, as well as a point of departure out of which such a life is fostered and nurtured.

The invocation "may all beings be happy" is a most direct expression of this mode of being, that is, of one desiring the happiness and well-being of all, without exception.

The familiar image of the mother's heart and mind toward her only child evokes deep resonance in all of us. This image is taken here to an entirely different level, beyond biological instinct: have this "mind toward *all beings* [italics added] whether they be weak or strong, long or large, medium or short, without exception, seen or unseen, dwelling far or near, born or yet unborn." Here we see a reinforcement of the earlier phrase "not attached to blood relations."

The maternal instinct is taken as the model of selflessness, calling attention to a dynamic power that breaks the wall of separation between an individual (the mother) and another (the child). But this (biological) maternal instinct in itself is restricted to "my" child and usually does not reach out to "other" children. It can even be a factor that brings about conflict, as when the well-being of "my" child is pitted against that of "others." The emphasis of the passage then is in this transposition of a biological reality, that is, the maternal instinct toward the protection of one's own child, into what can be described as a cosmological or ontological reality. This ontological reality is no other than the mode of being of one who lives in that place of peace; that is, one who has gone beyond attachment to blood relations and whose kindred heart and boundless mind embrace the whole world.

One who has abandoned all worldly attachments and has given one's life to the search for this place of peace as a follower of the Awakened One is also called "one who dwells in this (boundless mind and heart of) kinship" (*metta-vihā-rin*; *Dhammapada*, no. 368).

A further point calling our attention is the use of the term "sublime dwelling place" (*brahma–vihā-ra*) as a synonym for *nirvāna*, that place of peace. Needless to say, *Brahman* in Indian thought and religion refers to the supreme principle, the ground of the universe, that from which everything arises and on which everything depends. Incidentally, *brahmacarya*, which came to mean a life of purity or chastity, is another Hindu-based term also adapted in Buddhist usage. The notion of *brahma-vihā-ra*, which I consider in the following section, came to be a key feature describing the basic disposition of the follower of the Awakened One, in Theravada and also Mahāyāna Buddhism. One who is traversing the path of peace, imbued with a kindred heart and boundless mind that embraces the whole world, is regarded as residing in the "sublime dwelling place."

The Four Sublime Dwelling Places

The term *brahma-vihā-ra* refers to a tetrad of cardinal virtues, as follows: *maitri* (kindliness, kindred heart, friendliness), *karunā* (solidarity in sorrow = compassion), *muditā* (sympathetic joy), and *upeksā* (equanimity; Aronson, 1981). These are presented as a set of mutually related inner attitudes defining the way of life of one on the path of awakening, taken here from *The Large Sutra on Perfect Wisdom* (Conze, 1975):

> Furthermore, a Bodhisattva dwells with a thought connected with friendliness, a thought that is vast, extensive, nondual, unlimited, free from hostility, rivalry, hindrance, or injury to anyone, extends everywhere, and is well-cultivated; (a Bodhisattva) radiates friendliness in the ten directions of the world which has as its highest (development), the Dharma-element, and the space-element as its terminus. And so with compassion, sympathetic joy, and equanimity. (Conze, 1975, p. 133)

The term *maitri* is placed in the context of this tetrad, each also referred to as "immeasurable" (*aparima-nā*) or boundless. In the context of this fourfold set, later commentators have defined *maitri* as a mind that "seeks the well-being and happiness of (all) sentient beings," and *karunā* as the mind that "seeks to remove the unhappiness and suffering of (all) sentient beings" (Hajime, 1956, pp. 20, 26 n.8). Parallel to these two, the next two of the tetrad can be seen in symmetric co-ordination: sympathetic joy is the joy felt at seeing other beings happy, and equanimity is inner tranquility (a state of mind of not being adversely affected) in the face of the fact of suffering.

The fourth term of the tetrad provides a key to the understanding of the whole set. The Sanskrit word *upeksā* is a combination of the prefix *upa-* (toward, near) and the verb *īks*, to see (noun form: *īksa* = eyes). The underlying nuance of the term then is the clear vision of things "just as they are" (that is, devoid of one's clinging or attachment to one or another state of affairs). It is this clear eye that sees things as they are (*upeksā*) that grounds the other three virtues of the tetrad. It grounds the realization of that sense of kinship with all sentient beings, linked with the deep desire to see their happiness and to alleviate their suffering. It brings about inner joy at seeing them happy and joyful. In other words, the clear vision of things as they are is what ushers in this life of kindliness and compassion.

Saraha, Doha-kosa (Treasury of Couplets)

In the Wisdom sūtras and in Mahāyāna Buddhism in general, the key term used to describe this reality of "things as they are" is *śūnyatā*, "emptiness." In further historical development, the Vajrayāna ("Diamond Vehicle") develops the Mahāyāna notion of Emptiness and draws out its implications for a vision for compassionate living (Lopez, 1995).

Below is a passage ascribed to Saraha, written around the eleventh or twelfth century, in Apabhramsha (Snellgrove, 1954). It lays out the connection between the view of things as characterized by Emptiness and the life of compassion that it ushers:

> As Nirvana so is Samsara. Do not think there is any distinction. Yet it possesses no single nature, for I know it as quite pure.
>
> Do not sit at home, do not go to the forest. But recognize mind wherever you are. When one abides in complete and Perfect Enlightenment, where is Samsara, and where is Nirvana?
>
> Oh know this truth, that neither at home nor in the forest does enlightenment dwell. But free from prevarication, in the self-nature of immaculate thought.
>
> "This is my self, and this is another." Be free of this bond which encompasses you about, and your own self is thereby released.
>
> Do not err in this matter of self and other. Everything is Buddha without exception. Here is that immaculate and final stage, where thought is pure in its true nature.
>
> The fair tree of thought that knows no duality, spreads through the triple world. It bears the flower and the fruit of compassion, and its name is service to others.
>
> The fair tree of Emptiness abounds with flowers, acts of compassion of many kinds. And fruit for others appearing spontaneously, for this joy has no actual thought of another.
>
> So the fair tree of Emptiness also lacks compassion, without shoots or flowers or foliage. And whoever imagines them there, falls down, for branches there are none.

The two trees spring from one seed, and for that reason there is but one fruit. One who thinks of them thus indistinguishable, is released from Nirvana and Samsara.

If one in need approaches and goes away hopes unfulfilled, it is better to abandon that house. Than take the bowl that has been thrown from the door.

Not to be helpful to others, not to give to those in need, this is the fruit of Samsara. Better than this is to renounce the idea of a self.

One who clings to Emptiness, and neglects Compassion, does not reach the highest stage. But one who practices only Compassion, does not gain release from the toils of existence.

One, however, who is strong in the practice of both, remains neither in Samsara or in Nirvana. (Snellgrove, 1954, pp. 238–239)

This is a classic statement of a nondual view of reality (Loy, 1988). Let us note some significant points from the preceding passage. First, the statement "as is Nirvana, so is Samsara" is a cornerstone of Mahāyāna and also of Vajrayana Buddhism. It negates the opposition between what is regarded as the ultimate reality on the one hand and the everyday reality of this phenomenal world on the other. At the heart of this negation of the dualism between the ultimate and the mundane is the affirmation of Emptiness. From the standpoint of perfect enlightenment, by which all things (including *nirvāna* and *samsāra*) are seen as *empty*, "where is Samsara and where is Nirvana?"

Second, this realization of Emptiness thus frees one from the encumbrances and delusions that come from the (false) notion of "my self" as opposed to "another (self)." A person released from this delusive notion (of "my self" as distinct from "other selves") lives a life which abounds in acts of compassion, "appearing spontaneously, for this joy has no actual thought of another."

Third, however, if Emptiness is taken as merely another notion or idea (that is, as opposed to "Something-ness," for example, or to "being"), then it is a tree "without shoots or flowers or foliage," that is, a life without compassion.

Fourth, to cling to one pole (*nirvāna*) or the other (*samsāra*) is also to miss out on this life of compassion. Undue attachment to *nirvāna* as a notion connected with Emptiness leads one to thinking that "there is no suffering, nobody to save from suffering" and therefore to the abandonment of compassion. On the other hand, attachment to *samsāra*, to the notion of being, or to the idea that "there is something out there," that "there are suffering beings whom I need to save," weighs heavy on a person and itself becomes a source of attachment. "Better than this is to renounce the idea of self" (as well as the idea of "non-self") and be grounded in Emptiness that outflows into Compassion.

In short, the realization of the truth of Emptiness is the renunciation of the deluded notion of "my self" as opposed to "other selves." Such a realization is what enables the cultivation of the "fair tree . . . that abounds with flowers"—a life that bears fruits and abounds in acts of compassion. The realization of Emptiness, then, involves not only an epistemological apprehension but also, more significantly, a transformative realization with soteriological implications (Streng, 1965). To realize Emptiness is to *become* Emptiness, which is to overcome dualistic perceptions and thereby live a life that can identify with the pains and sufferings, as well as the joys, of all sentient beings as one's own.

Zhi-yi, the Great Calming of the Mind

The link between the ultimate reality of Emptiness and the mundane life, life in the phenomenal world, is a question that occupied Chinese Buddhist thinkers, notably the Tiantai Great Master Zhi-yi (538–597) and Huayan master Fa zang (643–712) and their followers. The theme of the link between Emptiness and compassion was addressed in the context of their grandiose metaphysical systems expounding a nondual view of reality. In their own distinctive ways, the Tiantai and the Huayan schools lay out a vision that can be described as "one-in-all, all-in-one." The former (Tiantai school) offers an image of "mutual interpenetration of the ten realms of existence," whereas the latter makes use of the imagery of Indra's net, wherein each eye of the net is a unique jewel that reflects all the others.

Of reference for us is a short passage from the *Mo ho zi guan* (*The Great Calming of the Mind*):

> Question: Why does the Bodhisattva, who has attained the realm of the Unborn, get born (again in this earthly realm)?
>
> Answer: Truly, it is because there is no ceasing of the cycle of birth of all sentient beings caught in defilements, and because of this, in the Bodhisattva there arises great compassion, and manifesting oneself as being born out of one's own free will, strives to deliver them from this cycle. (*Taishō*, Vol. 46, p. 60b, my translation)

The "realm of the unborn" is no other than the realm of Emptiness, the realization of which frees one from the cycle of birth and death, assuring entry into *nirvāna*. In this passage, the accomplished Seeker after Truth (the Bodhisattva) who has attained this realm of Emptiness is described as not attached to nor remaining in this realm. Rather, moved by great compassion, such a one chooses to be born again into this cycle of birth and death, in order to deliver sentient beings from it. In other words, the Bodhisattva is one who is born on this earth not out of "the desires of flesh and blood," but out of the power of great compassion, with a will toward the deliverance of sentient beings from their suffering.

One who has realized Emptiness, then, is not one who thereby escapes from this world nor one who ceases to be concerned with matters relating to the earthly realm. The realizer of Emptiness remains fully immersed in the world, not because of any attachment to its passing lures but out of great compassion, to show sentient beings the way to deliverance from their sufferings in this realm.

Shinran, Tannishō

The writings of thirteenth-century Japanese Buddhist masters, whose life and teaching continue to inspire countless individuals and groups in our day both in the Eastern and Western hemispheres, present various angles on compassion as outflow of wisdom.

Shinran (1171–1262), the founder of the Shin Pure Land school in Japan, taught utter reliance on the infinite compassion of Amida Buddha, given expression in the devoted recitation of Amida's name (*nembutsu*), as the way to enter into the Pure Land. The following passages (Unno, 1984) present his understanding of compassion, in consonance with his whole Buddhist teaching:

> There is a difference in compassion between the Path of Sages and the Path of Pure Land. The compassion in the Path of Sages is expressed through pity, sympathy, and care for all beings, but truly rare is it that one can help another as completely as one desires. The compassion in the Path of Pure Land is to quickly attain Buddhahood, saying the nembutsu, and with the true heart of compassion and love save all beings as we desire.
>
> In this life no matter how much pity and sympathy we may feel for others, it is impossible to help another as we truly wish; thus our compassion is inconsistent and limited. Only the saying of nembutsu manifests the complete and never-ending compassion which is true, real, and sincere. (Unno, 1984, No. 4)
>
> I, Shinran, have never even once uttered the nembutsu for the sake of my father and mother. The reason is that all beings have been fathers and mothers, brothers and sisters, in the timeless process of birth-and-death. When I attain Buddhahood in the next birth, each and everyone will be saved.
>
> If it were a good accomplished by my own powers, then I could transfer the accumulated merits of nembutsu to save my father and mother. But since this is not the case, when we become free from self-power and quickly attain the enlightenment of Pure Land, we will save those bound closest to us through transcendental powers, no matter how deeply they are immersed in karmic suffering of the six realms of existence and the four modes of birth. (Unno, 1984, no. 5, *Tannisho*)

For Shinran, genuine compassion does not consist in the feelings of pity or commiseration or sympathy that we frail humans can conjure for other sentient beings, nor in acts geared to alleviate the suffering of others. The dynamic power at the heart of all reality is no other than the infinite compassion of Amida, generated in the latter's all-embracing vow to save all sentient beings and now permeating the whole universe. We need only to surrender ourselves to this power, with total devotion and entrustment, expressed in the recitation of Amida's name, and let this be the operative force that governs our lives. As we abandon ourselves to this power, it will work in us and transform us into instruments of compassion, which will benefit all beings, beginning with the ones most proximate to us, our parents, brothers and sisters, and so on.

The significant point to note about this teaching is the emphasis on Amida's infinite compassion as the underlying power that pervades the universe. Shinran's teachings, expressed in his writings addressing learned Buddhists of his day, as well as the numerous followers from the lower strata of society, stem from this fundamental vision of reality, embodied concretely in Shinran's own life and career.

Dōgen, Shōbōgenzō

Dōgen (1200–1253) began his religious search early in life, spurred by the experience of the death of his parents. Led on to China to seek answers to basic questions of life and death with which he was struggling, he is said to have had a deep experience of enlightenment, under the guidance of and confirmed by the Chinese Chan Master Ru jing (1163–1228). Coming back to Japan, he established a center for Zen practice in the hinterlands toward the Japan sea, known as *Eihei-ji* (Temple of Everlasting Peace), and devoted his life to guiding seekers for truth and inner peace. His teachings are enshrined in a collection of his sermons, titled *Shōbōgenzō* (The Treasury of the Eye of True Dharma), originally addressed to practitioners who followed him in the monastic path in their search for their true Self.

> To study and learn the way of the Buddha is to study and learn your own self. To study and learn your own self is to forget yourself. To forget yourself is to be enlightened by the myriad things of the universe. To be enlightened by the myriad things of the universe is to let go of your own body and mind as well as the body and mind of others. The enlightenment attained thus comes to rest, and though it appears to have stopped it precisely continues on. (*Shôbôgenzô*, chapter on *Genjô Kôan* or "The Matter at Hand," my translation)
>
> I came to realize clearly, that mind is mountains, rivers, the great wide earth, the sun, the moon, the stars. (*Shôbôgenzô*, chapter on *Sokushin Zebutsu,* or "This Very Mind, the Buddha," my translation)

The passage just quoted gives us a glimpse into Dōgen's inner world, revealing to us his vision of what constitutes this true Self. In short, this true Self is manifested as one sees through the illusory barrier dividing "my" self from the rest of the universe. The term "myriad things of the universe," literally, "the ten thousand elements," refers to things immediately at hand, such as trees and rocks, rivers and mountains, animals, human beings, as well as those beyond the immediate sensation, as well as the sun, the moon, the stars, and all that there is. The character translated here as "enlightened" (by the myriad things of the universe) (*shô-ser-aruru*) can be also translated as "authenticated," "real-ized" (hyphen intended), "proved," or also, "awakened."

And this true Self comes to be awakened, as the passage suggests, as one lets go of that notion that divides, on one level, my "body" versus my "mind," and on a further level, "*my* body and mind" versus "*others*' body and mind." In other words, awakening, enlightenment, the manifestation of the true Self, involves an overcoming of this separation. This overcoming enables me to identify with my neighbor, with every sentient being as well, seeing in these the very manifestation of who I am.

This identification with every sentient being is what grounds a mode of being characterized by a deeply felt sense of kinship (*maitri-*) and compassion (*karunā*), identifying with the joys and sorrows of every sentient being, as I see them as they are, namely, as my own true Self.

Further, one is able to exclaim, as the second passage puts forth, that "mind is no other than mountains and rivers, the great Earth, the sun, the moon, the stars."

The term translated as "mind" here is *kokoro* in Japanese (Chinese, *hsin*) and refers not just to the intellect but to the core of my very being, a synonym thus for the true Self. A more direct translation would be "*I am* (no other than) the mountains and rivers, the sun, the moon, the stars." The awakening to who I am, my true identity, in other words, my sense of kinship, does not limit itself to the human level, nor to the level of the sentient, for that matter, but extends to *all* beings.

Such a realization would have tremendous implications, needless to say, for grounding a mode of being and way of life that could respond to the ecological crisis we face in our world today (Habito, 1997).

Nichiren, Selected Writings

Nichiren (1222–1282) is perhaps one of the most misunderstood, and for this reason maligned, figures in Buddhist history (Habito & Stone, 1999). This notwithstanding, this thirteenth-century religious thinker and activist has had a profound impact in the shaping of modern Japan, and the groups inspired by his person and thought have extended their sphere of activity into the world scene.

Nichiren caught the eye of the political authorities of his time with his submission of a treatise outlining his views on the deteriorating situation of the time, noting specific features of the plight of the people, indicating their causes, and offering prescriptions for their remedy. But instead of being given a hearing, he was exiled and subjected to repeated harassment and persecution, which in turn all the more strengthened him spiritually and confirmed him in his religious convictions (Yampolsky, 1990):

> In recent years, there are unusual disturbances in the heavens, strange occurrences on earth, famine and pestilence, all affecting every corner of the empire and spreading throughout the land. Oxen and horses lie dead in the streets, the bones of the stricken crowd the highways. Over half the population has already been carried off by death, and in every family someone grieves . . .
>
> Now I hope we may set forth about as quickly as possible taking measures to deal with these slanders against the Law (*Dharma*), and to bring peace to the world without delay, thus ensuring that we may live in safety in this life and enjoy good fortune in the life to come . . . (Yampolsky, 1990, p. 41)
>
> I, Nichiren, am the only person in all Japan who understands this. But if I utter so much as a word concerning it, then parents, brothers, and teachers will surely criticize me and the government authorities will take steps against me. On the other hand, I am fully aware that if I do not speak out, I will be lacking in compassion. . . . If I speak out, I am fully aware that I will have to contend with the three obstacles and the four devils . . .
>
> Nevertheless, I vowed to summon up a powerful and unconquerable desire for the salvation of all beings, and never to falter in my efforts . . .
>
> I, Nichiren, am sovereign, teacher, father, and mother to all the people of Japan . . . (Yampolsky, 1990, p. 146)

Nichiren's religious vision and teaching is based on his reading of the Lotus Sūtra (Chinese version, *Myoho renge kyo*, translated by Kumarajiva in the fifth century). A key teaching of the sūtra revolves around the continuing life of Sakyamuni as Eternal Buddha. Having himself gone beyond this world of turmoil and suffering, the Buddha comes to manifest himself in sundry times and places in this earthly realm, with acts of compassion to deliver all sentient beings from various situations of suffering.

In Nichiren's writings, the Eternal Buddha Sakyamuni is presented as the father of all sentient beings, and the latter as children who are foolish and who are rapt in their play, oblivious of the fact that their house is already being engulfed by flames. Nichiren is convinced of the truth of the teaching of the Lotus Sūtra above all other Buddhist scriptures and comes to understand himself as an emissary of the Eternal Buddha, called to propagate its message toward the deliverance of sentient beings from their sufferings. He also comes to assume on himself this heart and mind of the compassionate Eternal Buddha, seeing sentient beings, notably "all the people of Japan," as his own children whom he must save from their predicament.

Nichiren's compassion is grounded in a mystic experience of oneness with Sakyamuni Buddha, the Father of all sentient beings, who continues to act incessantly toward their deliverance from suffering. This mystic experience and the religious vision issuing from it empowers Nichiren to become a prophet of the Lotus, one who has given himself entirely to the propagation of its teaching. He is convinced that this acceptance of the Lotus Sūtra and its teaching will deliver people from their plight, part of which he describes in the opening lines of his treatise *Rissho ankoku ron* (Yampolsky, 1990). He spares no effort, at the risk of life and limb and in the face of exile and persecution, in carrying out this mission, challenging the political, as well as religious, leaders of his time, questioning the sociopolitical structures that he perceived were aggravating the causes of suffering.

Nichiren's life and teaching have inspired countless others after him to take up the message of the Lotus Sūtra and to be vehicles of its propagation. In the period of Japan's modernization, thinkers and activists adapted his thought in laying out their vision of the transformation of Japanese society. His teaching has also inspired the rise of several new religious movements that drew a large following from the masses seeking the betterment of their human condition amid a rapidly changing society.

Concluding Reflection

I have surveyed a variety of perspectives from the Buddhist tradition in search for clues to the question, What brings about compassionate behavior? This cursory glance at scriptural texts spanning a wide range of historical epochs and cultures reveals to us to a common theme underlying these passages.

The *Metta-Sutta*, a representative of early Buddhist teaching, presents the summit of the Buddhist path as a place of peace, the locus wherein the seeker of wisdom and truth attains ultimate reality. Described as a point of arrival for those who live cultivating a boundless mind embracing all beings, *nibbāna*, the place of peace, is also understood as a point of departure out of which flows a life of compassion.

The four cardinal virtues that constitute the sublime dwelling place, described in various texts, are further elaborations on the mode of life of those who traverse this path leading to and stemming from the place of peace. This is a life characterized by kindliness, compassion, sympathetic joy, and equanimity, brought about by an unimpeded view of "things as they are."

Śūnyatā, Emptiness, is the term in Mahāyāna and Vajrayāna scriptures referring to ultimate reality as manifested in the awakening experience. Emptiness is not construed in negative terms, such as in opposition to the notion of Being in Western philosophical discourse. Rather, it is elucidated on in the context of a transformative experience of soteriological import. This experience opens an individual to a realm wherein the wall of separation between "self" and "other" has crumbled. Emptiness is thus understood as the basis of a life that abounds in acts of compassion. Chinese Buddhist masters elaborated on this inherent link between the realization of Emptiness and a life of compassion in their metaphysical systems accentuating the interconnected nature of all reality.

Shinran, who gave a distinct thrust to the teachings of Pure Land Buddhism in Japan, experienced and understood ultimate reality as the all-pervasive action of the compassionate Amida Buddha. Human beings are called to open themselves to the workings of this Cosmic Compassion in an act of total entrustment (shinjin) and thereby themselves become embodiments of this cosmic compassion in their life in this phenomenal world, realizing kinship with all beings.

Dōgen, discoursing on the nature of Zen enlightenment, describes a world wherein the fissure between the self and the myriad things of the universe is overcome, and the individual human being (re)discovers his or her identity with the mountains and rivers and the great Earth. Such an identification with the myriad things of the universe opens out to a compassion that embraces not only animate beings but also the realm of inanimate life.

Nichiren's view of reality is centered on the figure of a transhistorical Sakyamuni Buddha who continues to act in history out of compassion. Propelled by his experience of mystical union with the Eternal Sakyamuni, Nichiren undertakes a lifelong mission to embody in his own historical being the work of compassion of the Buddha, in and through the propagation of the teaching of the Lotus Sūtra. This sense of mission is what empowers him to an engagement in the social and political, as well as religious, issues of his time.

The common theme that runs through these different Buddhist texts is this: The compassionate life is an outflow of the vision of reality, "the way things are," opened to a person in the pivotal experience of awakening. In various ways and using differing terminology, these texts present this experience as involving entry into a realm wherein the separation between "self" and "other" is overcome. The healing of this separation is what ushers in that place of peace and is at the same time what grounds and motivates a life of compassion, calling a person to active engagement in tasks geared toward the alleviation of the suffering of one's fellow sentient beings. Human beings tend to behave in ways that are selfish, violent, and destructive as long as they remain attached to the notion of "self," seen in opposition to or conflict with other selves, and to the myriad things of the universe. In other words, human beings act selfishly as they cling to this delusive notion of "self" viewed in an oppositional way. Such a situation is described from a Buddhist standpoint as a state of ignorance, understood in turn as the root of all evil and destructiveness.

Answering our initial question then from a Buddhist perspective, a compassionate life is but an outflow of the wisdom that truly sees "the way things are," the view of reality that overcomes the separation of self and other.

To the corollary question, as to what can foster and nurture a life of compassion, a basic Buddhist prescription can be summed up thus: Come and see (*ehi passiko*). In other words, the entire Buddhist tradition is an invitation for all to take a straight look at "what is." Its basic prescription for the human malady thus is to take a rigorous and disciplined look at "what is." The experiential realization of "what is" brings about genuine wisdom that will bring about fruits of compassion in one's life.

In a world such as ours, marked by so much conflict and violence between human individuals and groups, often aggravated by religious differences, we stand in dire need of finding some common ground that will in the very least enable discourse among disparate parties concerned. In his account of the Buddhist religious tradition, Huston Smith presents a summary of the Buddha's approach to reality, enumerating, among several items, its features as empirical, scientific, pragmatic, and therapeutic (Smith, 1997). More than its particular doctrines, beliefs, rituals, or practices, this tradition, with its fundamental approach to reality, may indeed offer a valuable contribution in forging our common future as Earth community. It offers us no less than a way to genuine wisdom that could unleash the power of compassion in our individual and communal lives.

REFERENCES

Andersen-H. Smith, D. (Ed. and Trans.). (1913). *Sutta Nipā-ta*. London: Pāli Text Society.
Aronson, H. (1981). *Love, compassion, sympathetic joy and equanimity in Theravada Buddhism*. Delhi, India: Motilal Banarsidass.
Conze, E. (Ed. and Trans.). (1975). *The large sutra on perfect wisdom*. Berkeley: University of California Press.
Habito, R. L. F. (1997). Zen and ecology: Mountains, rivers, the great earth. In M. E. Tucker & D. Williams (Eds.), *Buddhism and ecology* (pp. 165–175). Cambridge: Harvard University Press.
Habito, R. L. F., & Stone, J. (Eds.). (1999). Revisiting Nichiren [Special issue]. *Japanese Journal of Religious Studies, 26*(3/4).
Hajime, N. (1956). *Jihi (kindliness and compassion)*. Kyoto, Japan: Heirakuji Shoten.
Lopez, D. S. (Ed.). (1995). *Buddhism in practice*. Princeton, NJ: Princeton University Press.
Loy, D. (1988). *Nonduality: A study in comparative philosophy*. New Haven, CT: Yale University Press.
Smith, H. (1997). *The world's religions*. San Francisco: HarperCollins.
Snellgrove, D. S. (Trans.). (1954). *Saraha's Dohaakosa*. In E. Conze (Ed.), *Buddhist texts through ages* (pp. 238–239). New York: Harper & Row.

Stcherbatsky, T. (1975). *The conception of Buddhist nirvana.* (2nd ed.). Varanasi, India: Bharatiya Vidya Prakashan.

Streng, F. (1965). *Emptiness: A study in religious meaning.* Nashville: Abingdon Press.

Unno, T. (Trans.). (1984). *Tannisho: A Shin Buddhist classic.* Honolulu: Buddhist Study Center Press.

Yampolsky, P. (Ed. and Trans.) (1990). *Selected writings of Nichiren.* New York: Columbia University Press.

Conclusion to Part V

STEPHEN G. POST

As Don S. Browning argues, altruistic love requires the abrogation of selfishness, but it is a mistake to confuse the valid ideal of unselfishness with selflessness, its invalid exaggeration. Selflessness violates the reciprocal structures of most social existence and obscures the extent to which self-concern or care of the self is necessary for love of the other to be sustained in commitment. Moreover, selflessness is questionable because it invites exploitation of the moral agent and fails to correct the other's harmful behavior. Feminism, psychology, philosophy, and theology increasingly converge on this point. Analysis of intermediate norms between self-preference and radical self-denial, such as parity, other-preference, and self-subordination, is imperative. There are surely in every age tendencies toward solipsism, that is, extreme indulgence of and concern with self at the expense of social relationships that demand self-sacrifice. The chief value of selflessness might be strategic, as a counterpoint to solipsism.

Many partial descriptions of love can be combined to suggest that building on a foundation of solicitude love includes joy, compassion, commitment, and respect: Love rejoices in the existence, growth, and presence of the other; love responds supportively to suffering, although present in the absence of suffering; love is loyal and patient to a significant extent; love honors the other's freedom, integrity, and individuality. The solicitude of love can be grounded in bestowal, on appraisal of attractive qualities, or on the instincts of natural relationships and especially of parental love.

Love is not always distinguished from care, and the two words are often used interchangeably. I stated earlier that love is to person and care is to person in need. Greg Fricchione points out how much the being cared for is a part of the healing relationship between physician and patient. We can extrapolate from this professional context and generalize about a universal need for love that appears, if you will, "hard wired" into the human condition. Fricchione, like Browning, allows for considerable self-sacrifice in love, which may in some cases take a radical form. But he does not define love in terms of self-sacrifice. Instead, he uses the model of solicitude and attachment. His chapter substantiates our notion of love as "affective affirmation." Selfishness always vanishes in love, and unselfishness arises.

In religious traditions, there are no strangers, in the sense that we are all neighbors. The neighbor might be a distant acquaintance or an utterly unknown person encountered by chance. There are rare saints who seem to manifest an active love for everyone they encounter. This certainly is the Buddhist ideal of compassion, as Habito discusses it. William James describes saintly affectivity even for the enemy or those who are personally loathsome (1902/1961). Edith Wyschogrod suggests that the saintly dissolution of self-centeredness is critical for ethics in postmodernity (1990). Yet most of us live our lives and encounter our moral dilemmas in the familial sphere or in that of friendships built on reciprocity and are often unconcerned with the stranger (who is anything but a neighbor). We are saints only to those near and dear. An insular familialism does too little good for the stranger and therefore presents the problem of the order of love (see Pope, Chapter 10). Familialism ought never to provide an excuse for apathy to the fate of strangers.

In the final analysis, it would be difficult to find a better summary chapter for this book than that of Browning. It is perhaps surprising to scientists to see that theologians are taking concepts from evolutionary biology seriously and finding a connection between these concepts and other contemporary intellectual traditions. Yet the religious traditions, which exist under the sacred canopy of a presence in the universe, a pure Divine Love, will always at their best press us beyond the spheres of the near and dear toward the neediest. The moral balance between the nearest and the neediest is one that no easy formula can settle, although clearly the tradition of compassion and agape requires that the neediest, however unknown and unfamiliar and even unfriendly, be taken into account with an underlying equal regard.

Universal love for humanity is a tremendously important moral ideal but one that for most of us must be built up step by step from what is learned in committed special relations. Thus do the last lines of Alexander Pope's *Essay on Man* read:

God loves from the whole to the parts: but the human soul
Must rise from individual to the whole.
Self-love but serves the virtuous mind to wake,
As the small pebble stirs the peaceful lake;
The centre moved, a circle strait succeeds,
Another still, and still another spreads;
Friend, parent, neighbor, first it will embrace;
His country next; and next all human race.

Many readers will find Pope's hopeful movement of love from those near and dear to those far and unknown too naive, for there are many small circles in which the self limits itself in love and forgets the outsider. Yet it still seems that we learn about love in the special ties that both bind and instruct. Nevertheless, it is the background of universal impartial Divine Love that pressures the practitioner of agape and compassion toward the neediest and away from self-indulgence or the indulgence of the nearest and dearest.

REFERENCES

James, W. (1961). *The varieties of religious experience.* New York: Collier Books. (Original work published 1902)
Wyschogrod, E. (1990). *Saints and postmodernism.* Chicago: University of Chicago Press.

Concluding Summary

Future Research Needs on Altruism and Altruistic Love

STEPHEN G. POST AND LYNN G. UNDERWOOD

Just as human beings endeavor to understand and harness the power of the wind, the atom, and gravity, they might also endeavor to understand and facilitate the energies of altruism and love. To do so requires rigorous research in all disciplines, coupled with a willingness to conduct dialogues across disciplinary boundaries.

Agape is an ancient Greek word that describes an unlimited, unselfish, and accepting form of love. It is a word that was appropriated by early Christianity. This form of love is present in all the major world religions, from the Jewish notion of *chesed* (steadfast love) and the Buddhist ideal of *karunā* (compassion) to rough equivalents in Islam, Hinduism, Taoism, Confucianism, and Native American spirituality. Such love was the centerpiece of works of Carl Rogers, Rollo May, and Erich Fromm. Teilhard de Chardin commented that scientific understanding of the power of this love would be as significant in human history as the discovery of fire.

The Range of Disciplines

There is a wide range of questions to be studied. How can we better understand human altruistic motivations and actions, with a focus on all that these involve

379

evolutionarily, genetically, developmentally, neurologically, socially, emotionally, theologically, and conceptually? How might such motivations and actions be fostered?

Many of the questions that should be studied are so fascinating to professionals and to the lay public that such research will assuredly receive wide attention. To what extent is the so-called "selfish" gene compatible with unselfish motivations and behavior on the part of the individual beyond the sphere of reproductive interests? How does the "tit-for-tat" self-interested model of the evolution of cooperation relate to the phenomenon of human altruistic and agapic love? Is the human capacity for altruistic love really able to embrace all human beings in an unlimited and unconditional manner without the leaven of spiritual experience? How and why do people experience a sense of healing and restoration in even brief encounters with altruistic and compassionate love?

How can we move beyond in-group insularity? Can we learn to love our neighbor even when he or she is an enemy? Can love tame the problem of intergroup conflict? Can love tame the aggressive aspects of human nature already highlighted by presociobiological ethologists such as Konrad Lorenz? Can human beings turn their hate and aggression against disease, starvation, poverty, and other assaults on human well-being? If the inevitable correlate of altruism is aggression, is the capacity for empathy potent enough to overcome the in-group/out-group barrier, inhibiting aggressive tendencies? Can the symbols that live in us, and in which we live, contribute to the extension of love? Is empathy so thoroughly the product of in-group evolution that in-group insularity is ineradicable? Evolutionary debates over the very origin and significance of empathy are crucial, well-grounded, and as yet unresolved.

Empathy is not altruistic love, but it needs to be understood as one of love's evolved building blocks. How can we better understand those who behave nonaltruistically? What are the connections with neural wiring and brain chemistry? What is the link between empathy and frontal brain function?

The dominant theory of evolutionary biology looks at acts that increase the fitness (survival and reproduction) of others at the expense of the individual. In this biological sense, altruism does not imply any conscious benevolence. Many sociobiologists believe that such altruistic acts are a matter of either inclusive fitness, such that one's own genes are passed on through relatives who also possess them, or of reciprocal altruism, from which the self derives compensatory reproductive benefits. Robert Trivers, George Williams, and John Maynard Smith are all associated with this perspective. Sober and Wilson (Chapter 11), however, take a different view. They argue for a form of group altruism in which acts on behalf of other members of the group go beyond kin interests and reciprocity to the group as a whole. Forms of altruism that go beyond individual reproductive and survival interests would be evolutionarily plausible if they would help a group survive against competitors. Does group selection, if true, necessarily favor betweengroup insularity and conflict?

The preceding questions suggest general areas of potential inquiry that will require social scientific research into the quantitative and qualitative nature of altruism and love. Social scientists have devoted considerable attention to measures of motivational altruism in human experience. Some of this literature has focused on rescue behavior that places the agent at some risk, generating considerable disagreement as to the authenticity of ostensibly altruistic motives. But we must also be concerned with altruism and altruistic love on the parent-child axis. We must identify models of child development that are most likely to give rise to altruistic children who are attentive to all humanity.

All of the biological sciences are potentially relevant, including specialties such as evolutionary biology, neurology, cognitive science, and endocrinology. Although altruistic love seems to exist most obviously on the parent-child or kin selective axes, we do not really know much about the neurological and endocrinological aspects of this universal form of love and the extent to which it differs in males and females. Can we learn something about altruistic love on the parent-child axis that sheds light on the more extensive expressions of altruistic love? We can examine current scientific research in evolutionary biology and evolutionary psychology regarding the nature and limits of altruism as genetically grounded. The health sciences can contribute to our knowledge of whether and how compassionate and agape love enhances physical and emotional health.

The traditional methods of the humanities can help define the essential features of altruistic love. Human love cannot be reduced to emotion, as it involves the seeing of value in another, a use of the moral imagination, and a bestowal of worth that is very much a conceptual endeavor. Where do culture and symbols enter into the distinctly human capacity for universal altruistic love? How do religious and spiritual practices enhance love for all humanity? How is altruistic love associated with humility in the agent?

Specific Research Topics

The empirical study of altruistic love can be organized into *seven* major areas: spirituality/religion; ethics/philosophy; biology; psychology/human development; education; anthropology/sociology/political science/economics; and medical. There may be better ways to group these disciplines, and there may be additional disciplines worth listing.

Spirituality/Religion

On this axis, agape love is identified with Divinity. "God is love and he that dwells in love dwells in God and God in him," asserts the New Testament. The *Bhagavadgītā*, the *Dhammapada*, and the scriptures of virtually all the great world religions assert this as well in their different terms. God is believed to be absolute unlimited love, although this love need not exclude anger and judgment. This love is manifested in a way that does not ultimately discriminate against sinners. In many historical accounts, the inspired apostles of love—many great moral lights, founders of all genuine religions, and true sages, seers, and prophets—are also remembered as joyful. In spiritual and religious traditions, the life of altruistic and agape love has been understood to be a participation in divine love, replete with a sense of joy and universal extensiveness that goes beyond all intergroup conflict. This participation is shaped by the experience of prayer and meditation.

It would be good to encourage rigorous empirical studies into this phenomenon, as well as studies of the ways in which religious symbols, beliefs, stories, and rituals encourage agape love.

Some specific sample questions are:

- Do spiritual and religious experiences, beliefs, and practices influence behavior in the direction of altruistic, compassionate, and agape love? If so, when and how?
- What specific spiritual practices (e.g., types of prayer, meditation, silence, worship) might help to encourage altruistic love? How do these practices interact with the biological, social, and cultural substrate of the person?

Ethics/Philosophy

On the ethical plane, altruistic and agape love are associated with the unselfish affirmation, acceptance, and care of others for their own sake.

Study of this would include foci on the emergence and ascent of altruistic and agape love to constitute goodness itself in many significant moral traditions and on how altruism is analyzed in contemporary philosophy with regard to acceptable degrees of self-sacrifice, competing contractual theories of ethics, and moral psychology.

Some specific sample questions are:

- What is the place of altruism and altruistic love in philosophical traditions, and what empirical assumptions about human nature and the cosmos have been influential in this?
- How have religious concepts of altruistic, compassionate, and agape love shaped later secular conceptions of ethics and of other-regarding attitudes and behaviors?

Biology

Altruistic and agape love are not well understood biologically. Although this love is visible and palpable (e.g., like the tip of an iceberg), we understand very little of what lies under the water line. It is time to marshal the capacities of biology and all the life sciences to better understand the embodiment of agape love, as well as the evolution of these capacities and the emergence of such love.

Studies pertaining to the endocrinological, neurological, immunological, genetic, and all other biological aspects of altruistic or agapic love either as given or as received should be encouraged. Research on the evolutionary origins of altruistic behavior, on the relationship of received love to emotional memory, and on the impact of received love on child neurological development and thriving is important. A specific example would be the study of parental love, the "strong" form of altruism (according to evolutionary biology), which may serve as the biological underpinning of love for those who are not genetically related to the agent.

Some specific sample questions are:

- What are the evolutionary origins and neurological substrates of altruism and altruistic love?
- How might these interact with cultural, religious, and social factors?
- What are the physiological correlates of altruistic love both given and received?
- What role does attachment, bonding, or empathy play in the expression of altruistic love?

Psychology/Human Development

Altruistic and agape love are experienced psychologically by the recipient in life-transforming ways that are associated with peace and well-being. Individuals who have never experienced love or compassion may be extremely hostile and abusive in their responses to the world and may eventually reach a state of crisis. Yet after experiencing even a brief period of love, they may undergo a dramatic transformation in which they migrate from hatred to agape. We know very little about the transforming power of love or the inner reorientation of its recipient that turns him or her into its agent. Psychology and religion both speak of the experience of redemption through an accepting, unlimited, and unconditional form of love that does not discriminate against the recipient, no matter how sordid his or her past.

Studies on the redemptive features of altruistic and agape love should be encouraged. We need to understand how such love causes change in the recipient, how long the love must be sustained, how lasting this change is, and what the psychological health benefits of this transformation are with regard to sense of worth and self-esteem. We should encourage studies on how receiving such love unleashes the capacity to love, thereby producing a shift from egoism to altruism, and on how hatred, fear, anger, and resentment are reduced.

The psychological study of altruistic love also includes developmental psychology. Abuse and other forms of domestic violence sometimes rob the developing child of any opportunity to experience and learn altruistic love, care, and compassion. In the absence of such love, bonding cannot occur. The child may miss all the nonverbal expressions of love; for example, through caring touch, affective tone of voice, facial expression, and the like. A child who has suffered severe peer rejection during adolescence may also become hostile and even violent. Children and young people who have not experienced or seen love expressed are unlikely to manifest it themselves. Some individuals will not manifest altruistic love, if at all, until they face a severe life-threatening illness or even the imminence of death itself in old age.

Studies should be encouraged on the experiences of giving and receiving altruistic and agape love at all points in the human life cycle, including those aspects of each stage of the life cycle that seem to enhance or diminish growth in love.

Some specific sample questions are:

- What developmental processes foster or hinder altruistic attitudes and behavior in various stages of life, from early childhood onward? What role does emotional and social learning play in these processes?
- What can cognitive neuroscience and developmental psychology contribute to our understanding of altruistic, compassionate, and agape love? For example, how do narrative, symbol, and various views of reality influence our capacities to respond in love to various situations and to those who are neither kin nor friend but who are in genuine need?
- How do emotions and altruistic love interrelate? Which emotions support altruistic love and in what circumstances? Which emotions in what circumstances inhibit altruistic love?

Education

There is much debate about how and whether to teach a life of altruistic and agape love. Historically, this has been the province of spiritual and religious traditions, particularly in their presentation of the lives of the saints (i.e., hagiography). It is not clear that altruism can be taught in the absence of such images of human fulfillment, both secular and sacred. Research on education and altruism interacts with psychology and human development yet constitutes a unique set of concerns. Some specific sample questions are:

- What are the perennial roles of religious traditions in teaching altruistic and agapic love, as well as any other historical means by which such pedagogy has been implemented?
- Does love need to be seen and experienced before it can be learned?
- Does engaging young people in social benevolence efforts tap their altruistic capacities in ways that affect their entire lives?
- How deeply does a culture of violence and hostility adversely affect the emergence of altruistic behavior?
- What is the role of mentoring in altruistic love, and can the study of contemporary altruists—for example, Jean Vanier, Dame Cicely Saunders, and Millard Fuller—enhance the manifestation of altruistic love?

Anthropology/Sociology/Political Science/Economics

Social scientists have long tried to prove or disprove the very existence of motivational altruism through elaborate studies of human behavior in circumstances in which another person, often a perfect stranger, is in dire need of help. Anthropologists have compared more altruistic cultures with less altruistic ones. Economists have, since Adam Smith, attempted to analyze and balance the social sentiments and self-interested rational choice.

Studies should be encouraged on the extent to which human individuals and societies manifest behavior that is motivationally or consequentially altruistic; on what social and cultural factors influence the emergence of altruism or counteract it; on how much, if at all, altruists are limited by in-group tendencies that may give rise to hostility toward out-groups; on how altruistic love expressed in the spheres of family and friends can be expanded to include all humanity; on what can be learned from cultures in which a remarkable amount of altruistic and agape love is manifest; and on how can we better understand the link between love and its manifestation in compassion, care, and service.

Some specific sample questions are:

- In what ways might proper self-love and neighbor-love reinforce one another?
- How does altruistic love interact with prosocial motivations?
- What means are available to expand or extend altruism and altruistic love to those thought of as outside one's social group? How do we define the "outsider" and how does this influence our attitudes and actions?
- What role do the media play in encouraging or discouraging altruism and altruistic love?
- How do particular visions of reality and worldviews affect attitudes and expressions of altruism and altruistic love?
- What can economic research tell us about the nature and expression of altruism and altruistic love? How does such love affect our attitudes and behaviors toward money and the use of wealth? What is the basis of philanthropy, and can it be successfully encouraged?
- How might models of human action (e.g., utility maximization and profit maximization in economics, "game theory" in social science and biology), as well as cultural assumptions, affect the expression of altruism and altruistic love in human relations and social structures?

Medicine

Altruistic and agape love have long been associated with helping in recovery from various forms of physical and mental illness.

Studies should be encouraged on the physiological health impact of altruistic and agape love that is given or received.

Some specific sample questions are:

- How does the giving or receiving of altruistic, compassionate, and agape love affect mortality?
- How does such love affect persons with mental or physical illnesses, especially in severe cases?
- How does the receiving of such love affect persons with cognitive deficits, for example, persons with retardation or dementia or persons with serious mental disorders?

- To what extent are health care professionals motivated by altruistic love, and how does this motivation affect them and their patients?
- How do altruism and altruistic love enter into the context of organ donation, in which the donation of organs is viewed as a "gift of life" for the stranger in need?

ANNOTATED BIBLIOGRAPHY

Research on Personality and Individual Differences in Altruism

SHELLEY DEAN KILPATRICK AND
MICHAEL E. MCCULLOUGH

Spread love everywhere you go: first of all in your own house. Give love
to your children, to your wife or husband, to a next door neighbor. . . .
Let no one ever come to you without leaving better and happier. Be the
living expression of God's kindness; kindness in your face, kindness in
your eyes, kindness in your smile, kindness in your warm greeting.
—Mother Teresa

Kindness in words creates confidence
Kindness in thinking creates profoundness
Kindness in giving creates love.
—Lao-tzu

Altruism is a concept that is infused with goodness and positivity, yet great conflict exists
over its definition. Is altruism who you are, a set of personality traits and inborn characteristics, or is it simply a learned prosocial behavior pattern? Does altruism require sacrifice on
the part of the giver, or can giving from abundance also constitute altruism? Must the motivations of altruistic behavior be free from any expectation of benefit to the giver, or should
they only be free from the expectation of direct return for goods and services? The goal of
this annotated bibliography is to provide a broad overview of the literature concerning personality characteristics and individual differences associated with altruism—traditional
personality characteristics, gender, sociodemographics, and other individual differences are
all included. It does not seek to settle philosophical issues concerning the true nature of altruism. Furthermore, it does not settle the debate about whether the researchers in the studies presented use multiple operationalizations of altruism. Emergency helping, prosocial
behavior, positive societal behavior, and charity are all represented. Among the topics covered are the altruistic personality, altruistic behavior, empathy, empathic concern, helping
behavior, organizational behavior, religiosity, social responsibility, and volunteerism. A list
of articles by topic is provided at the end of this work. Methodologies are as diverse as the

operationalizations. Studies include experiments, quasi experiments, local surveys, national surveys, naturalistic observation, and combinations of these.

Although the goal of this bibliography is to be broad, representing approaches from sociology, social psychology, developmental psychology, education, and business, it is not designed to be comprehensive. An emphasis is placed on research from the 1980s and 1990s, along with the inclusion of a few "classics." Because social psychology has contributed much to empirical work on altruism, the articles represent more social psychological work than work in other areas. Also, only empirical research was chosen for the annotated bibliography. Review articles, books, and book chapters fall outside the scope of the annotated bibliography.

The most predominant theme that arose during preparation of this annotated bibliography is the clear evidence that altruistic behavior is multiply determined. Personality characteristics, such as inclination to be empathic toward others or general agreeableness, provide the building blocks on which altruism is based. These characteristics combine with differences in gender, culture, religion, and other sociodemographic variables that affect a *learned* general inclination to behave altruistically. In the midst of the situation, the type of appeal of the needy person or charity, the physical distance of the person from the potential giver, and a multitude of other factors affect whether an altruistically inclined person will actually enact the altruistic behavior. As is evident in the life and words of Mother Teresa and the words of Lao-Tzu, altruism involves kindness in thought, word, and deed that extends beyond the love of those who love you in return.

Preparation of this annotated bibliography was made possible by the generosity of the John Templeton Foundation in the hopes that it would encourage further research on altruism's unlimited love. We are grateful to the foundation's own altruism in making this project possible.

Archer, R. L., Diaz-Loving, R., Gollwitzer, P. M., Davis, M. H., & Foushee, H. C. (1981). The role of dispositional empathy and social evaluation in the empathic mediation of helping. *Journal of Personality and Social Psychology, 40*, 786–790.

OBJECTIVE   To determine the role that individual differences in empathy and situationally induced evaluation play in helping
DESIGN   Experiment
SETTING   University of Texas, Austin
PARTICIPANTS   Participants were 123 female students participating in partial fulfillment of course requirements. Participants were chosen who were above or below the median on a pretest measure of dispositional empathy.
ASSESSMENT OF PREDICTOR VARIABLES   Participants completed a measure of dispositional empathy (Mehrabian & Epstein, 1972) in a pretesting session. On arrival at the laboratory, participants were randomly assigned to one of four conditions. Two variables were manipulated: potential evaluation from others (demand) and false feedback indicating level of arousal (high or low). In the demand condition, participants were told that the experimenter would be aware of their level of autonomic arousal as measured by the Galvanic Skin Response meter attached to their fingers. In the low-demand condition, the participants were told that the machine recorded the information privately and that the experimenter would not know their level of autonomic arousal. All participants then watched two videotaped recordings. During the second videotape, concerning a graduate student who

needed volunteers for her experiment, half of the participants saw the Galvanic Skin Response meter needle increase to between +12 and +15 on a 30-point scale, indicating high arousal. The other half of the participants saw the needle range from −3 to +3 throughout the recording, indicating low arousal.

ASSESSMENT OF OUTCOME VARIABLES   All participants were given the opportunity to respond to the request for help from the graduate student by indicating how much time they would be willing to volunteer for her study in 30-minute increments. Reponses were placed in sealed envelopes so that the participant believed that the experimenter would be unaware of whether the participant volunteered. Participants also filled out a questionnaire addressing the amount of empathic concern they felt for the needy graduate student and the amount of personal distress they felt for themselves.

MAIN RESULTS   A multiple regression of demand, arousal, and dispositional empathy on *empathic concern* for the student revealed a three-way interaction, $F(1, 112) = 4.20, p < .05$. There was an interaction of arousal and demand for participants with high dispositional empathy, $F(1, 112) = 3.7, p < .056$, but not for participants with low dispositional empathy, $F < 1$, *ns*. For participants with high dispositional empathy, high arousal was related to higher reports of empathic concern for the graduate student for participants in the high-demand condition, $F(1, 112) = 5.90, p < .02$. There was no significant effect for participants in the low-demand condition on empathic concern. On self-reports of personal distress, there were main effects of dispositional empathy, $F(1, 112) = 5.2, p < .03$, and demand, $F(1, 112) = 4.17, p < .05$, such that participants with high empathy and high demand reported more personal distress than participants with low empathy and low demand.

A multiple regression of demand, arousal, and dispositional empathy on *number of hours volunteered* revealed a main effect for dispositional empathy, $F(1, 112) = 5.01, p < .03$. and a three-way interaction, $F(1, 112) = 6.25, p < .02$. Participants high in dispositional empathy helped more than participants low in dispositional empathy. There was an interaction of arousal and demand for participants with high dispositional empathy, $F(1, 112) = 4.13, p < .04$, but not for participants with low dispositional empathy, $F < 1$, *ns*. For participants with high dispositional empathy, high arousal was related to more helping for high-demand participants, $F(1, 112) = 10.26, p < .001$. There was no significant effect for low-demand participants on helping. For participants with low dispositional empathy, low arousal, or low demand, there was relatively little helping. In multiple regression analyses, empathic concern, $F(1, 116) = 23.28, p < .001$, and the interaction of empathic concern and personal distress, $F(1, 116) = 4.31, p < .04$, influenced willingness to help. For participants high in empathic concern, personal distress predicted helping.

CONCLUSION   "Empathy as a dispositional factor and social evaluation as a situational factor interacted with arousal feedback to predict helping." Confirming the authors' hypothesis, participants high in dispositional empathy, demand, and arousal helped more than those participants high in empathy and demand but low in arousal.

COMMENTARY   Archer et al.'s (1981) study is a typical example of how dispositional empathy acts in combination with a situational factor (public awareness) and perceived autonomic arousal to influence the person's willingness to respond altruistically. None of the factors alone was sufficient; and, with respect to empathic concern expressed and willingness to help, all three were necessary for altruism to be displayed. It is interesting that arousal was necessary for the display of altruism in this study, as arousal is one of the elements common in emergency situations in which prosocial behavior is required. The arousal may provide the physical energy necessary to carry out the altruistic act. Multiple determination of altruism is a theme that recurs throughout this bibliography.

CORRESPONDENCE   None available

Ashton, M. C., Paunonen, S. V., Helmes, E., & Jackson, D. N. (1998). Kin altruism, reciprocal altruism, and the Big Five personality factors. *Evolution
and Human Behavior, 19*(4), 243–255.

OBJECTIVE   To identify personality characteristics associated with kin altruism and recip-
rocal altruism and to relate those characteristics to the Big Five personality dimensions
DESIGN   Cross-sectional survey, questionnaire study with convenience sample
SETTING   Large Canadian university
PARTICIPANTS   One hundred eighteen introductory psychology students participated in
partial fulfillment of course requirements. The median age was 19 years old (range 17–30);
69 participants were women and 49 were men.
ASSESSMENT OF PREDICTOR VARIABLES   Kin altruism is defined as acting in a manner
that jeopardizes one's own well-being while protecting or promoting that of one's own kin.
In reciprocal altruism, actions are based on the notion that today's giver of supportive acts
will be tomorrow's receiver (Reber, 1995, p. 26). Kin altruism and reciprocal altruism personality measures were two sets of eight items—an empathy/attachment scale and a for-
giveness/nonretaliation scale. Empathy/attachment was presumed to measure kin altruism
(i.e., feeling sorry for one's relatives and close friends), whereas forgiveness/nonretaliation
was presumed to measure reciprocal altruism (i.e., the tendency to hesitate to forgive other
people).
ASSESSMENT OF OUTCOME VARIABLES   A self-report of overall altruistic behavior was
administered—the Responsibility subscale of the Jackson Personality Inventory, Revised
(Jackson, 1994). Kin and reciprocal altruism were measured with a money allocation task
(Kramer et al., 1986). Participants were to choose an amount of money to divide hypothet-
ically between themselves and another person. For example, a participant could choose between (1) $125 for self and $75 for other versus (2) $150 for self and $50 for other. The relationship of the participant to the hypothetical other (close friend or noncooperative
person) was varied in each allocation task. The Big Five personality factors were measured
in this study with the 40 adjectives of Saucier's (1994) Big Five Mini-Markers scale and 16
adjectives which represent the four quadrants of the Agreeableness and Emotional Stability
factor plane (i.e., patient, critical, sensitive, and unemotional).
MAIN RESULTS   Both the empathy/attachment scale and the forgiveness/nonretaliation
scale correlated positively with participants' scores on the Jackson Personality Inventory,
Revised. This suggests that each is related to altruistic behavior. The two scales are not, however, related to each other; $r = .04$, *ns*. In the money allocation task, 68% of participants were
altruistic in the close-friend condition but only 10% of participants were altruistic in the
noncooperator condition. When the altruistic money allocation involved a friend, the em-
pathy/attachment scale was positively correlated with money allocation, $r = .35$, $p < .01$,
whereas the forgiveness/nonretaliation scale was not, $r = .11$, *ns*. However, when the altruistic money allocation involved a noncooperator, the forgiveness/nonretaliation scale was
positively correlated with money allocation, $r = .26$, $p < .01$, but the empathy/attachment
scale was not, $r = $ <min>.06, *ns*.

Both the empathy/attachment scale and the forgiveness/nonretaliation scale were positively correlated with the personality factor Agreeableness, $rs = .41$ and .29, respectively; ps
< .01. However, they correlated in opposite directions with respect to the Emotional Stabil-
ity personality factor. The higher the participant's empathy/attachment score, the *lower* was
his or her Emotional Stability score, $r = -.19$, $p < .05$. The higher the participant's forgive-
ness/nonretaliation score, the *higher* his or her Emotional Stability score, $r = .21$, $p < .05$. The
16 adjectives that represent the four quadrants of the Agreeableness and Emotional Stability factor plane help present a consistent picture of the relationship between altruism and

personality. The high Agreeableness/low Emotional Stability quadrant is highly positively correlated with the empathy/attachment scale, $r = .50$, $p <.001$, and is not at all correlated with the forgiveness/nonretaliation scale, $r = -.02$, ns. In contrast, the high Agreeableness/high Emotional Stability quadrant is highly positively correlated with the forgiveness/nonretaliation scale, $r = .50$, $p <.001$, and not at all correlated with the empathy/attachment scale, $r = .17$, ns.

CONCLUSION   "The personality traits thought to facilitate altruism directed mainly toward kin are strongly related to high agreeableness and low emotional stability, whereas the personality traits thought to facilitate altruism directed mainly toward non-kin are strongly related to high agreeableness and high emotional stability." Also, altruism directed at kin is facilitated by personality traits of empathy and attachment, whereas altruism directed at non-kin is facilitated by personality traits of forgiveness and nonretaliation.

COMMENTARY   Ashton et al.'s (1998) study points out that prosocial behavior consists of at least two different sets. On one hand, we have prosocial behavior toward kin and close relationship partners. On the other hand, we have prosocial behavior toward non-kin or people in general. These two forms of prosocial behavior have some similar personality substrates (e.g., Agreeableness), but also have some different ones (e.g., Emotional Stability). These findings remind us that prosocial behavior (and its personality substrates) might very well differ across classes of prosocial behavior.

CORRESPONDENCE   None available

Axelrod, S. R., Widiger, T. A., Trull, T. J., & Corbitt, E. M. (1997). Relations of Five-Factor Model antagonism facets with personality disorder symptomatology. *Journal of Personality Assessment, 69*(2), 297–313.

OBJECTIVE   To assess the relationship between lower order facets of Agreeableness/Antagonism with personality disorder symptoms

DESIGN   Cross-sectional survey, questionnaire study including structured interview in a convenience sample

SETTING   A university

PARTICIPANTS   Participants were 81 undergraduate students enrolled in introductory psychology; 62% of the participants were female. The mean age was 20 years old (range 18–39).

ASSESSMENT OF PREDICTOR VARIABLES   The NEO-Personality Inventory, Revised (Costa & McCrae, 1992b), a self-report questionnaire, was used to measure the six facets of the Agreeableness versus Antagonism personality factor (trust, straightforwardness, altruism, compliance, modesty, and tender-mindedness). The Structured Interview of the Five Factor Model (Antagonism subscale) was also used to assess the degree to which the participant displayed each of the six facets of Agreeableness versus Antagonism. The scoring system ranges from 1 (prominent Antagonism) to 5 (prominent Agreeableness) on each of 48 items.

ASSESSMENT OF OUTCOME VARIABLES   Personality disorders were assessed with two self-report questionnaires: the Minnesota Multiphasic Personality Inventory, PD (Morey, Waugh, & Blashfield, 1985) and the Personality Diagnostic Questionnaire, Revised (Hyler & Rieder, 1987). The results of these two scales were combined to create composite measures of antisocial, borderline, narcissistic, paranoid, and passive-aggressive personality traits.

MAIN RESULTS   *Correlations of interview Agreeableness facet scores with personality disorder traits.* Correlations of the interview scores with the personality traits were generally supportive of hypotheses. Trust was negatively correlated with paranoid, passive-aggressive, antisocial, borderline, and narcissistic traits; $rs = -.62, -.41, -.29, -.26,$ and $-.27,$ respectively; $ps <.05.$ Straightforwardness was negatively correlated with antisocial, borderline, paranoid, passive-aggressive, and narcissistic traits; $rs = -.47, -.23, -.24, -.28,$ and $-.28,$ respectively; $ps <.05.$ Altruism was negatively correlated with antisocial and narcissistic traits; $rs = -.36, -.24,$ respectively; $ps <.05.$ Modesty was negatively correlated with narcissistic traits, $r = -.31, p <.05.$ Tender-mindedness was negatively correlated with antisocial and narcissistic traits, $rs = -.28, -.30,$ respectively; $ps <.05.$ Finally, compliance was negatively correlated with antisocial, borderline, and narcissistic traits; $rs = -.43, -.30, -.24,$ respectively; $ps <.05.$ *Correlations of questionnaire Agreeableness facet scores with personality disorder traits.* Trust was not significantly correlated with any of the personality disorder traits. Straightforwardness was negatively correlated with antisocial traits, $r = -.42, p <.05.$ Altruism was negatively correlated with antisocial traits, $r = -.24, p <.05.$ Modesty was negatively correlated with narcissistic traits, $r = -.31, p <.05.$ Finally, tender-mindedness and compliance were not significantly correlated with any traits.

CONCLUSION   The interview format for the assessment of facets of Agreeableness is successful in distinguishing characteristics of personality disorder traits.

COMMENTARY   As was shown in Ashton et al.'s (1998) research, the Big Five personality dimension of Agreeableness is quite relevant for conceptualizing the influence of personality traits on altruism and prosocial behavior. Indeed, one of the key facets of Agreeableness is itself called "altruism." People who score low on the altruistic personality facet are more likely than others to manifest antisocial and narcissistic personality traits—two clusters of personality traits that most people find highly undesirable in relationship partners. Thus Axelrod et al.'s (1997) study points to the fact that people with altruistic traits appear better suited to faring well in social relationships. Here a caveat must be made that once psychopathology is involved, generalization to the broader population becomes somewhat questionable.

CORRESPONDENCE   Seth R. Axelrod, River Valley Services, P.O. Box 351, Middletown, CT 06457

Batson, C. D., Bolen, M. H., Cross, J. A., & Neuringer-Benefiel, H. E. (1986). Where is the altruism in the altruistic personality? *Journal of Personality and Social Psychology, 50*(1), 212–220.

OBJECTIVE   To determine whether personality characteristics typically associated with altruism are more closely associated with an altruistic motivation to benefit another or an egoistic motivation to avoid shame and guilt for not helping

DESIGN   Experiment with a pretest survey

SETTING   University of Kansas

PARTICIPANTS   Sixty female students in introductory psychology classes fulfilling a course requirement

ASSESSMENT OF PREDICTOR VARIABLES   Prior to participation in the experimental portion of the study, participants filled out questionnaires addressing self-esteem (Rosenberg, 1965), social responsibility (Berkowitz & Lutterman, 1968), ascription of responsibility (Schwartz, 1968), empathy (Davis, 1983), and birth order. Participants were then randomly assigned to two experimental conditions, one involving easy escape from helping and the other involving difficult escape from helping.

ASSESSMENT OF OUTCOME VARIABLES   Participants were led to believe that they would watch as another person, in fact a confederate, received a number of electrical shocks. After the second shock trial, all participants were asked to rate their emotional response to the confederate's distress. Then participants were given an opportunity to help the person being shocked by taking her place for the remaining trials. In the easy-escape condition, participants were told that they would not need to watch any more of the shock trials if they did not choose to take her place. In the difficult-escape condition, participants were told that they would need to watch the remaining eight shock trials if they did not choose to take her place. Taking the confederate's place in the easy-escape condition would constitute genuine altruism, whereas taking the confederate's place in the difficult-escape condition could be construed as a way of avoiding the emotional distress of seeing another person hurt.

MAIN RESULTS   Participants who helped saw the shock victim as more similar to themselves than did participants who did not help; $t(58) = 2.24$, $p < .03$. The personality measure of perspective taking (a subscale of Empathy) was significantly correlated with the perception of the victim's need, $r = .32$, $p < .02$. Self-reported distress during the experiment was related to both perspective taking and empathic concern Empathy subscales; $rs = .31$ and .29, respectively; $ps < .05$. Self-reported empathy for the victim was related to ascription of responsibility, perspective taking, and empathic concern Empathy subscales; $rs = .29, .27,$ and .37, respectively; $ps < .05$.

When escape from helping was easy, 9 of 30 participants agreed to take the shocks; when escape from helping was difficult, 19 of 30 participants agreed to take the shocks ($z = 2.64$, $p < .005$, one-tailed). In the easy-escape-from-helping condition, there were no significant correlations between personality variables and helping. In the difficult-escape-from-helping condition, self-esteem, ascription of responsibility, and empathic concern were all significantly positively correlated with helping; $rs = .43, .32,$ and .41, respectively; $ps < .05$. The interaction between birth order and escape condition was significant, χ^2 (1, $n = 60$) $= 5.77$, $p < .02$, such that firstborns were more likely to help in the difficult-escape-from-helping condition and later borns were equally likely to help in both conditions. When the effects of the personality variables self-esteem, ascription of responsibility, empathic concern, and birth order are controlled for, self-reported empathy for the victim was related to helping in the easy-escape-from-helping condition, but not in the difficult-escape-from-helping condition; $r = .34$, $p < .05$ and $r = -.02$, ns, respectively. In the difficult-escape-from-helping condition, the association between self-reported empathy and helping is entirely due to the effects of the personality variables, but in the easy-escape-from-helping condition none of the association between empathy and helping is due to personality variables.

CONCLUSION   "Scales with which we measure three of the personality variables—self-esteem, ascription of responsibility, and empathic concern—did seem to be associated with prosocial motivation. But the pattern of correlations with helping across the escape manipulation suggested that for each of these three, the prosocial motivation was directed toward increasing the helper's own welfare rather than the welfare of the person in need."

COMMENTARY   Batson's program of research, of which this study is characteristic, has focused on isolating the social-psychological factors that promote altruism. Based on studies such as these, Batson has concluded that altruism is not so much the result of helpers' personalities as it is a result of their reactions, in real time, to the plight of another person. In particular, it is only when people have empathy for a distressed individual that they act in ways that are expressly designed to promote the distressed person's well-being. Personality might still be important, but it is empathy, in real time, that appears to promote true selflessness.

CORRESPONDENCE   C. Daniel Batson, Department of Psychology, University of Kansas, Lawrence, KS 66045

Batson, C. D., Duncan, B. D., Ackerman, P., Buckley, T., & Birch, K. (1981). Is empathic emotion a source of altruistic motivation? *Journal of Personality and Social Psychology, 40*, 290–302.

OBJECTIVE   To determine whether empathy leads to altruistic or egoistic motivation to help

DESIGN   Two experiments

SETTING   University of Kansas

PARTICIPANTS   *Study 1*: Participants were 44 female students in introductory psychology who participated in partial fulfillment of course requirements. *Study 2*: Participants were 48 female students in introductory psychology who participated in partial fulfillment of course requirements.

ASSESSMENT OF PREDICTOR VARIABLES   *Study 1*: Prior to participation in the experimental portion of the study, participants filled out questionnaires addressing personal values and interests. This bogus questionnaire contained items such as type of magazines liked. Participants were then randomly assigned to view the questionnaire of another participant, in fact a confederate, whose questionnaire was manipulated so as to show interests similar to or different from the participants' interests. Finally, participants were randomly assigned to two experimental conditions, one involving easy escape from helping and the other involving difficult escape from helping. *Study 2*: Participants were told that they were to be part of two experiments during the session. The first experiment allowed for a manipulation of empathic concern versus personal distress. Participants were randomly assigned to one of two placebo conditions. The participants were given a cornstarch placebo that they were told effected either a feeling of warmth and sensitivity "similar to what you might experience reading a particularly touching novel" (the empathic concern condition) or a feeling of uneasiness and discomfort "similar to that you might experience reading a particularly distressing novel" (personal distress condition). The participants were randomly assigned to easy- or difficult-escape conditions as in Study 1.

ASSESSMENT OF OUTCOME VARIABLES   *Study 1*: Participants were led to believe that they would watch as another person, in fact a confederate, received a number of electrical shocks. After the second shock trial, all participants were asked to rate the confederate's emotional response to distress. Then participants were given an opportunity to help the person being shocked by taking her place for the remaining trials. In the easy-escape condition participants were told that they would not need to watch any more of the shock trials if they did not choose to take her place. In the difficult-escape condition participants were told that they would need to watch the remaining eight shock trials if they did not choose to take her place. Taking the confederate's place in the easy-escape condition would constitute genuine altruism, whereas taking the confederate's place in the difficult-escape condition could be construed as a way of avoiding the emotional distress of seeing another person hurt. Whether the participant was willing to take the confederate's place and, if so, the number of trials the participant would be willing to take were the outcome variables. *Study 2*: The outcome variables were the same as in Study 1.

MAIN RESULTS   *Study 1*: The interaction between similarity and escape condition was significant, $\chi^2 (1) = 4.19$, $p < .04$, such that the proportion of participants willing to help was much lower in the dissimilar-victim/difficult-escape condition (18%) than in the other three conditions (average proportion helping = 79%). Furthermore, there was a main effect for similarity of the shock victim, $\chi^2 (1) = 11.69$, $p < .001$, such that participants were more willing to help the shock victims with similar interests than shock victims with dissimilar interests. A comparable pattern of results held for number of shock trials the participants volunteered to take for the victim. Specifically, participants in the easy-escape/similar-victim condition were willing to take more shock trials than participants in either of the difficult-escape conditions. *Study 2*: The interaction between emotion manipulation and escape condition was significant, χ^2 (1) = 6.10, $p < .02$, such that the proportion of participants willing to help was much lower in the personal-distress/easy-escape condition (33%) than in the personal-distress/difficult-escape condition (75%) or in the empathic-concern/easy-escape condition (83%).

CONCLUSION   "In the distress conditions, where motivation was assumed to be egoistic, the rate of helping was significantly lower under easy than under difficult escape. In the empathy conditions, where motivation was assumed to be at least in part altruistic, the rate of helping remained high, even when escape was easy. Results . . . support the hypothesis that empathy leads to altruistic rather than egoistic motivation to help."

COMMENTARY   Though this study does not come first in the alphabetically listed annotated bibliography, it does come first chronologically in Batson's line of research on the relationship between empathy and altruism. This classic study manipulated participant emotion instead of relying solely on self-report. Further, it set the scene for a whole series of studies in which researchers either allowed the participant to display altruism in the face of an easy out or forced the participant to act egoistically in a situation that may cause personal distress. The variants of manipulation and observation of empathy and the relation of empathy to altruism are annotated, in part, in this bibliography. Opposing points of view are also reviewed (Cialdini, Brown, Lewis, Luce, & Neurberg, 1997; Neuberg et al., 1997).

CORRESPONDENCE   C. Daniel Batson, Department of Psychology, University of Kansas, Lawrence, KS 66045

Batson, C. D., Klein, T. R., Highberger, L., & Shaw, L. L. (1995). Immorality from empathy-induced altruism: When compassion and justice conflict. *Journal of Personality and Social Psychology, 68*(6), 1042–1054.

OBJECTIVE   To examine whether empathy-induced altruism can lead one to act in a way that violates the moral principle of justice

DESIGN   Two laboratory experiments

SETTING   University of Kansas

PARTICIPANTS   *Study 1*: Participants were 60 females. *Study 2*: Participants were 30 males and 30 females. Participants in both studies were in introductory psychology classes participating to fulfill a course requirement.

ASSESSMENT OF PREDICTOR VARIABLES   *Study 1*: Participants were randomly assigned to one of three conditions: no communication, communication/low empathy, and communication/high empathy. In the communication conditions, participants received a fictitious account from one of two fictitious fellow participants. The communication addressed a recent relationship breakup. In the high-empathy condition, participants were instructed to "imagine how the student feels about what is described." In the low-empathy condition, participants were instructed to "try to take an objective opinion to what is described." *Study 2*: Participants were randomly assigned to two conditions: low empathy and high empathy. All participants were asked to listen to an audiotape of a fictitious radio commercial for a local charity. The radio commercial described how the charitable foundation provides funds to help increase the quality of life for children with a serious illness. It then describes a particular child who could benefit from an expensive drug treatment but has been placed on a waiting list due to unavailable funds. While listening to the tape, low-empathy participants were asked to "take an objective perspective to what is described." High-empathy participants were asked to "imagine how the child interviewed feels about what has happened and how it has affected this child's life."

ASSESSMENT OF OUTCOME VARIABLES   *Study 1*: The participant was asked to assign each of the fictitious fellow participants to tasks with either potential positive or potential negative consequences. One fellow participant was to be assigned to each outcome. Participants were then asked to rate whether they thought the task assignment was morally right, the degree to which they were concerned with fairness in making the decision, and the degree to which they were concerned with the welfare of the participant from whom they had received the sad communication. *Study 2*: The participant was asked to indicate whether the needy child should be moved up to the immediate-help group from her place on the waiting list at the expense of other children higher on that waiting list. Participants were then asked to what extent fairness and sympathy for the child each played a role in making their decision. Participants were further divided into two groups based on whether they rated fairness higher than sympathy (justice dominant) or sympathy higher than fairness (altruism dominant).

MAIN RESULTS   *Study 1*: Task assignment for the fellow participants to positive and negative consequences was even-handed in both the no-communication condition and the communication/low-empathy condition. In the high-empathy condition, participants more often assigned the fellow participant from whom they had received the sad communication to receive positive consequences; $z = 2.24$, $p < .02$, one-tailed. Participants in the no-communication and communication/low-empathy conditions rated fairness as more important, $Ms = 7.7$ and 8.2, than participants in the communication/high-empathy condition; $M = 6.4$, $ts = 1.89$ and 2.59, respectively; $ps < .04$, one-tailed. Mean concern for fellow participants' welfare was not significantly higher in the high-empathy condition than in the low-empathy condition; $Ms = 7.0$ and 5.9, $t = 1.34$, *ns*. No reliable differences were found between conditions on perceived morality of the decision. *Study 2*: Participants in the high-empathy condition were more likely to help the needy child than participants in the low-empathy condition; 73% versus 33%, $\chi^2 (1, n = 60) = 10.31$, $p < .01$. Participant gender did not affect this decision. Neither importance of fairness nor sympathy for the needy child differed by condition. The proportion of altruism-dominant participants was higher in the high-empathy condition than in the low-empathy condition, 67% versus 37%, $z = 2.36$, $p < .02$. Altruism-dominant participants were also more likely to help the needy child (95%) than justice-dominant participants, 30%; $z = 3.46$, $p < .01$.

A path model tested a three-step model from empathy manipulation to helping behavior. "The high empathy perspective should lead to increased empathic feelings (Step 1)," which should lead to increased dominance of altruistic over justice motivation (Step 2), which should lead to increased willingness to help the needy child (Step 3). The model fit well, CFI = .94, and the betas for the proposed paths were all significant, .405, .398, and .700, respectively; $ps < .001$, one-tailed.

CONCLUSION   "Empathy-induced altruism and justice are two independent prosocial motives, each with its own unique ultimate goal. In resource allocation situations in which these two motives conflict, empathy-induced altruism can become a source of immoral justice."

COMMENTARY   This study, conducted using similar methodology to those typically used by Batson in other studies of altruism, demonstrates that the desire to help a person in need (which is motivated by empathy) often conflicts with, and indeed overrides, other important moral principles, such as the principles of justice and fairness. These fascinating findings point out the limits to which we can consider altruism to be "truly moral."

CORRESPONDENCE   C. Daniel Batson, Department of Psychology, University of Kansas, Lawrence, KS 66045

Batson, C. D., Batson, J. G., Todd, R. M., Brummett, B. H., Shaw, L. L., & Aldeguer, C. M. R. (1995). Empathy and the collective good: Caring for one of the others in a social dilemma. *Journal of Personality and Social Psychology, 68*(4), 619–631.

OBJECTIVE   To determine whether feeling empathy for another member of a group would create a desire to benefit that person individually, reducing the benefit to other group members

DESIGN   Two studies, one experiment and one questionnaire study

SETTING   University of Kansas

PARTICIPANTS   *Study 1*: Participants were 120 introductory psychology students participating in partial fulfillment of a course requirement; 60 were males and 60 were females. *Study 2*: Participants were 45 introductory psychology students participating in partial fulfillment of a course requirement; 15 were males and 30 were females.

ASSESSMENT OF PREDICTOR VARIABLES   *Study 1*: Participants were randomly assigned to one of three conditions—no communication, communication/low empathy, and communication/high empathy. In the communication conditions, participants received a fictitious account of a recent relationship breakup from one of three fictitious fellow participants. In the high-empathy condition, participants were instructed to "imagine how the student feels about what is described." In the low-empathy condition, participants were instructed to "try to take an objective opinion to what is described." *Study 2*: Procedures were similar to those of the communication condition in Study 1. All participants read a sad story from a fictitious fellow participant, but participants were not induced to take a particular perspective while reading it. Self-reports of empathy for the other participant were completed. Participants were divided into low- and high-empathy groups based on a median split.

ASSESSMENT OF OUTCOME VARIABLES   *Study 1*: The participants were asked to allocate two sets of eight raffle tickets either to themselves, to the whole group, or to other (fictitious) participants in the group. Bonus tickets could be earned for generosity to the group on the part of the participant, but that could mean a cost to the self (a social dilemma). After the allocation task, participants were asked to what degree they wanted to maximize their own ticket outcomes, the other participants' individual outcomes, or outcomes for the whole group. *Study 2*: Outcome variables were the same as in Study 1.

MAIN RESULTS   *Study 1*: More participants in the communication/high-empathy condition (34%) allocated tickets to the sad fellow participant than did participants in the no-communication and communication/low-empathy conditions; 3%, combined; χ^2 (2, $N=119) = 26.92$, $p < .001$. Because bonus tickets could be earned by generosity to the group as a whole, conditions were compared on the total number of tickets allocated. Planned comparisons indicated fewer allocated tickets in the communication/high-empathy condition, $M = 18.90$, than in the other two conditions; $M = 20.60$, $ts < 2.20$, $ps < .03$. Therefore, when empathy was induced, the good for the group was decreased. In addition, there was a significant condition-by-target interaction on motives for allocation; $F (4, 234) = 8.16$, $p <.001$. Participants in the communication/high-empathy condition reported more desire to maximize tickets to the other participant than to the group as a whole. Among those participants who reported higher other-than-group interest, 37% of allocations actually were to the other participant (17% to the group and 47% to the self). So inducing empathy added a desire to maximize the benefits for the other. *Study 2*: More high-empathy participants than low-empathy participants allocated tickets to the other; 36% versus 4%; χ^2 $(1, N=45) = 7.20$, $p < .01$. Because bonus tickets could be earned by generosity to the group as a whole, conditions were compared on the total number of tickets allocated. Planned comparisons indicated marginally fewer allocated tickets by high-empathy participants, M

= 18.73, than by low-empathy participants; $M = 20.35$, $t(43) = 1.61$, $p < .06$. There was a significant empathy-by-target interaction on motives for allocation; $F(2, 86) = 4.83$, $p < .01$. Participants with high empathy reported more desire to maximize tickets to the other participant, $M = 5.95$, than to the group as a whole, $M = 5.27$. Again, inducing empathy added a desire to maximize the benefits for the other.

CONCLUSION   Participants who experience high empathy allocate more resources to the targets of the empathy, even when it reduces the overall good to the group.

COMMENTARY   Like the Batson, Klein, et al. (1995) study previously discussed, this study demonstrates the limits within which empathy-induced altruism can be considered moral. When people experience empathy-induced motivation to help a single person, they sometimes forgo consideration of group welfare, as well as principles of justice and fairness. The opposing forces of altruism and justice should be clearly articulated and better examined in future social science studies on altruism.

CORRESPONDENCE   C. Daniel Batson, Department of Psychology, University of Kansas, Lawrence, KS 66045

Batson, C. D., & Weeks, J. L. (1996). Mood effects of unsuccessful helping: Another test of the empathy-altruism hypothesis. *Personality and Social Psychology Bulletin, 22*(2), 148–157.

OBJECTIVE   To examine whether individuals induced to feel empathy will report lower mood after an unsuccessful attempt to help, even if the failure is justified

DESIGN   Two laboratory experiments

SETTING   University of Kansas

PARTICIPANTS   *Study 1*: Participants were 60 female introductory psychology students participating in partial fulfillment of a course requirement. *Study 2*: Participants were 30 female introductory psychology students participating in partial fulfillment of a course requirement.

ASSESSMENT OF PREDICTOR VARIABLES   *Study 1*: Participants were randomly assigned to one of four conditions in a 2×2 design. The conditions were based on low and high empathy induction and experiencing justified or unjustified failure. Participants listened to a fictitious account of a fellow participant who had just experienced a mild electric shock. In the high-empathy condition, participants were instructed to "imagine how the events described are affecting the speaker and how she feels as a result." In the low-empathy condition, participants were instructed to "just remain objective and detached." Participants were told that if they succeeded in their task, the other participant would have extra time to work on her task and perhaps avoid further shocks. All participants were informed that they had "failed" on the task. For some participants the task was described as "Moderately Easy," providing low justification for failure. For other participants the task was described as "Absolutely Impossible," providing high justification for the failure. *Study 2*: Participants were randomly assigned to two conditions: high empathy or low empathy. Participants read a note from a fictitious fellow participant who described the experience of receiving an electric shock either objectively (low-empathy condition) or with information about how the other participant felt (high-empathy condition).

ASSESSMENT OF OUTCOME VARIABLES   *Study 1*: Mood was measured by self-report of how positively or negatively the participant felt on seven 9-point bipolar scales (i.e., sad-happy). Mood was measured both at the beginning of the study and after participants learned that they had failed to help the other participant by succeeding on their own tasks. Mood change over time was the key outcome variable. *Study 2*: All participants were told that they had succeeded in their tasks but that their success did not help the other participant to avoid shock. Mood was measured in the same manner as in Study 1.

MAIN RESULTS   *Study 1*: Although all participants reported lower mood after failing to help the other participant avoid the shock, between-cell comparisons revealed that participants in the low-empathy conditions showed less negative mood than participants in each of the high-empathy conditions, $ts > 2.40$, $p < .01$. *Study 2*: Lower mood was reported in the high-empathy condition than in the low-empathy condition, $t(28) = 3.94$, $p < .01$. This effect remained even after removing the covariate effect of perception of the other's desire for help; $F(1, 27) = 11.81$, $p < .002$.

CONCLUSION   "Even when they could not be held responsible for the failure of their efforts to relieve the other participants' need, subjects induced to feel empathy for this person reported relatively strong negative mood change."

COMMENTARY   Batson's empathy-altruism theory predicts that, because the motive elicited by empathy is altruistic rather than egoistic, would-be altruists will experience affective distress when they cannot effectively help the target of their empathy. Batson and Weeks's study provides more evidence for the very interpersonal nature of empathy-induced altruistic motivation.

CORRESPONDENCE   C. Daniel Batson, Department of Psychology, University of Kansas, Lawrence, KS 66045

Ben-Artzi, E., & Mikulincer, M. (1996). Lay theories of emotion: IV. Reactions to negative and positive emotional episodes. *Imagination, Cognition and Personality, 16*(1), 89–113.

OBJECTIVE   To assess in what ways a person's appraisals of the emotional world contribute to that person's helping behavior when positive emotions are induced

DESIGN   Study 5 was a laboratory experiment.

SETTING   Bar-Ilan University, Ramat Gan, Israel

PARTICIPANTS   *Study 5*: Participants were 90 undergraduate social science students who participated in fulfillment of requirements for the first year of study. There were 59 females and 31 males ranging in age from 21 to 37 years old.

ASSESSMENT OF PREDICTOR VARIABLES   *Study 5*: In order to assess the individual's perception of an emotional situation, participants completed the Lay Theories of Emotion Scale. This scale addresses the perceived benefit of experiencing emotion (high or low) and the perceived threat of experiencing emotion (high or low). Participants were randomly assigned either to watch a videotape of a humorous skit by a popular comedy group or to watch a neutral videotape documenting the life of fish.

ASSESSMENT OF OUTCOME VARIABLES   *Study 5*: The outcome variable assessed was whether the participant attempted to help the experimenter who "accidentally" dropped a stack of papers.

MAIN RESULTS   *Study 5*: A three-way Analysis of Variance (ANOVA) for categorical data of benefit appraisal, threat appraisal, and video condition on helping behavior revealed a main effect for benefit appraisal, $\chi^2(1) = 7.04$, $p < .01$. There were more helpers among the high-benefit-appraisal participants than among the low-benefit-appraisal participants, 66% vs. 36%. There was also a significant interaction between benefit appraisal and video condition, $\chi^2(1) = 3.86$, $p < .05$. Following the comedy film, more participants in the high-benefit-appraisal group engaged in helping than in the low-benefit-appraisal group (80% vs. 35%). There was no effect of benefit appraisal on helping for the participants who watched the documentary (48% vs. 36%).

CONCLUSION   "The effect of positive affect on altruism was significant only for [partici-pants] who hold a benefit appraisal of emotion."

COMMENTARY   Ben-Artzi and Mikulincer (1996) uncovered an important individual dif-ference that appears to influence people's prosocial behavior. People who believe that expe-riencing emotions is beneficial tend to respond with greater prosocial behavior when put in a good mood than do people who do not hold such a beneficial view of emotions. Whether the helping behavior targeted in the present study was strictly altruistic was not assessed. However, it *was* prosocial, and it suggests how positive emotions might influence some peo-ple to help other people.

CORRESPONDENCE   Elisheva Ben-Artzi, Department of Psychology, Bar-Ilan University, Ramat Gan, Israel

Berkowitz, L., & Lutterman, K. G. (1968). The traditional socially responsible personality. *Public Opinion Quarterly, 32,* 169–185.

OBJECTIVE   To determine the relationship between dispositional social responsibility and measures of attitudes and behavior

DESIGN   Cross-sectional survey

SETTING   Wisconsin

PARTICIPANTS   Participants were 766 Wisconsin adults. They were selected from a statewide probability sample for interviews by the University of Wisconsin Survey Research Laboratory.

ASSESSMENT OF PREDICTOR VARIABLES   Social responsibility was assessed with eight items to which the participant could agree or disagree on a 5-point Likert-type scale (i.e., "Every person should give some of his time for the good of his town or country"). Partici-pants were classified as high, medium, or low on social responsibility based on their scores on this scale. Social class, age, and gender were also assessed.

ASSESSMENT OF OUTCOME VARIABLES   Several survey items assessed financial contribu-tions and activities associated with nonpolitical and political participation in the commu-nity. Several scores on the outcome variables were presented separately for middle- and working-class participants.

MAIN RESULTS   People who designated themselves as middle class had higher social re-sponsibility scores than people who designated themselves as working class. People with higher education levels and women were also more likely to have high social responsibility scores. Participants high in social responsibility more frequently contributed to educational institutions in the previous year than participants low in social responsibility (38% vs. 16% for the middle-class group, $\chi^2 = 16.94$, $p < .01$; 18% vs. 7% for the working-class group, $\chi^2 = 7.02$, $p < .05$). Similar results were found for volunteer activities and church member-ship. Participants high in social responsibility were more involved in volunteer activities than participants low in social responsibility (36% vs. 9% for the middle-class group, $\chi^2 = 17.70$, $p < .01$; 24% vs. 5% for the working-class group, $\chi^2 = 21.24$, $p < .01$). Participants high in social responsibility were more likely to be church members than participants low in social responsibility (93% vs. 79% for the middle-class group, $\chi^2 = 9.26$, $p < .01$; 92% vs. 73% for the working-class group, $\chi^2 = 16.07$, $p < .01$). The authors indicated that for par-ticipants high in social responsibility, church membership was more than simply a social activity. The participants also held conventional religious beliefs and tended to maintain that the church's most important function was to "save souls for God."

In the political arena, degree of interest in local and national politics, voting behavior, working for a party or candidate, and contributing money to politics were all engaged in more by high socially responsible participants than by low socially responsible participants. Participants high in social responsibility were more interested in national politics than participants low in social responsibility (23% vs. 3% for the middle-class group, $\chi^2 = 40.38$, $p < .01$; 15% vs. 6% for the working-class group, $\chi^2 = 32.60$, $p < .01$). Participants high in social responsibility were more interested in local politics than participants low in social responsibility (23% vs. 5% for the middle-class group, $\chi^2 = 26.58$, $p < .01$; 16% vs. 10% for the working-class group, $\chi^2 = 32.21$, $p < .01$). Participants high in social responsibility were more involved in voting than participants low in social responsibility (80% vs. 60% for the middle-class group, $\chi^2 = 15.66$, $p < .05$; 60% vs. 47% for the working-class group, $\chi^2 = 13.07$, $p < .05$). Participants high in social responsibility were more likely to work for a party or candidate than participants low in social responsibility (27% vs. 8% for the middle-class group, $\chi^2 = 9.32$, $p < .06$; 12% vs. 3% for the working-class group, $\chi^2 = 18.98$, $p < .01$). Participants high in social responsibility were more likely to contribute money to politics than participants low in social responsibility (23% vs. 5% for the middle-class group, $\chi^2 = 12.08$, $p < .01$; 15% vs. 6% for the working-class group, $\chi^2 = 5.71$, ns).

CONCLUSION   In this study, participants high in social responsibility were very involved in their communities through political and nonpolitical volunteer work, as well as through financial contributions. The authors further indicated that "'High responsibles' tend to be conservative people who embrace the traditional ideas of their society."

COMMENTARY   Berkowitz and Lutterman highlight the broad array of community and political involvement of people high in social responsibility. It is also likely tied to the ascription of responsibility to the self as evidenced in other studies in this bibliography (Carlo, Eisenberg, Troyer, Switzer, & Speer, 1991; Eisenberg et al., 1989). Berkowitz and Lutterman's scale for social responsibility and this early work became the basis of investigating social responsibility in the contexts of prosocial behavior (Romer, Bruder, & Lizzadro, 1986; Batson, Bolen, Cross, & Neuringer-Benefiel, 1986; Bierhoff, Klein, & Kramp, 1991). Social responsibility and the types of behavior it motivates could be considered a societal-level analogue of the ascription of responsibility that motivates altruism toward individuals.

CORRESPONDENCE   Leonard Berkowitz, Professor Emeritus of Psychology, University of Wisconsin, Peterson Office Building, A W 49, 750 University Avenue, Madison, WI 53706

Berndt, T. J., & Das, R. (1987). Effects of popularity and friendship on perceptions of the personality and social behavior of peers. *Journal of Early Adolescence, 7*(4), 429–439.

OBJECTIVE   To examine the relationships of popularity and friendship with perceptions of a classmate's personality and social behavior

DESIGN   Longitudinal study involving both questionnaires and individual interviews

SETTING   One elementary school and one junior high school in a predominantly white, middle-class, suburban community

PARTICIPANTS   Participants were 46 fourth-grade students (average age of 9 years 9 months) and 44 eighth-grade students (average age of 13 years 8 months). At each grade approximately half of the students were girls and half of the students were boys.

ASSESSMENT OF PREDICTOR VARIABLES   In the fall of the school year, all students completed questionnaires in which they indicated the names of their best friends and rated liking for every same-sex child in the same grade. From this researchers paired close and best friendship pairs based on mutual nomination and high liking ratings. Each child's sociometric status, indicating popularity among classmates, was computed from the average liking ratings of all fellow classmates. This assessment was repeated in the spring of the school year.

ASSESSMENT OF OUTCOME VARIABLES   Participants were interviewed in both the fall and the spring of the school year. Each participant was asked about the personality of the close friend, what was particularly good and bad about the friend, and how they could tell their partner was their friend. The total numbers of positive and negative comments were calculated. Each participant also answered a series of closed-ended questions about the friend's prosocial behavior ("How helpful is he/she?"), aggressive behavior ("How often does he/she get into fights or arguments with other kids?"), and academic ability ("How smart is he/she?").

MAIN RESULTS   A multivariate analysis of variance (MANOVA) on positive and negative interview comments revealed an interaction of Sex × Time, F $(2, 81) = 4.87$, $p < .01$. Boys made more positive comments about their friends in the fall than in the spring, Ms = .76 and .60. Girls made more negative comments in the spring than in the fall, $Ms = .59$ and .35. All participants viewed their friends more negatively in the spring than in the fall.

A MANOVA on the four aspects of personality and popularity revealed a three-way interaction of Sex × Friendship Status × Time on both prosocial behavior and aggression; F $(4, 79) = 2.65$, $p < .05$. On prosocial behavior, pair-wise comparisons revealed that girls with unstable friendships evinced a significant decrease in ratings of their friend's prosocial behavior. On ratings of aggressive behavior, boys with stable friendships and girls with unstable friendships reported an increase in the friend's aggressive behavior. Although the friend's sociometric status was related to perception of the friend's academic ability in fall and spring, $rs = .30$ and $.22$, $ps < .05$, sociometric status was not related to either perceptions of prosocial behavior or aggression, $rs = -.13$ to $.08$, ns.

CONCLUSION   Although perceptions of friends' personalities are affected by perceptions of both friendship status and popularity, popularity does not seem to affect perceptions of prosocial or aggressive behavior.

COMMENTARY   In this study, Berndt and Das portray a dynamic situation in which one member of a childhood or adolescent friendship rates the other member on several dimensions. Among those are perceptions of the friend's prosocial and aggressive behavior. For girls, a change in friendship status leads them to perceive their friends as less helpful and more aggressive. For boys, more aggression is perceived in steady friendships than unsteady friendships. At least among children and adolescents, perceptions of another's prosocial behavior, the concrete manifestation of altruism, is tempered by the relationship between the individuals and characteristics of the perceiver. Other measures of perception, such as self-reports, are often questionable when it comes to altruism. Altruism is embedded in a social context, as well as in situations (Leung & Foster, 1985) and the particular personalities of the actors (Farver & Branstetter, 1994).

CORRESPONDENCE   Thomas J. Berndt, Department of Psychological Sciences, Purdue University, West Lafayette, IN 47907-1364

Bierhoff, H. W., Klein, R., & Kramp, P. (1991). Evidence for the altruistic personality from data on accident research. *Journal of Personality, 59*(2), 263–280.

OBJECTIVE   To examine whether aspects of altruistic personality could be observed in persons giving help to victims of a traffic accident

DESIGN   Quasi-experimental design with questionnaires

SETTING   Medical University of Hanover, Germany

PARTICIPANTS   Participants were 34 people (26 males, 8 females) who had given aid at the scene of an accident as reported by an ambulance team and a control group of 36 respondents to a questionnaire who had witnessed an accident but had not helped (26 males, 10 females). The group of nonhelpers were matched to the group of helpers on age, sex, and social status. The mean age of helpers was 35.4 years old (range 13 to 65 years) and the mean age of nonhelpers was 30.5 years old.

ASSESSMENT OF PREDICTOR VARIABLES   The personality questionnaire consisted of a series of scales used in earlier research on personality and helpfulness. The questionnaire included measures of locus of control (Krampen, 1981), uncertainty (Ullrich de Muynck & Ullrich, 1978), empathy (Schmitt, 1982), belief in a just world (Dalbert, Montada, & Schmitt, 1987), a German version of the Social Responsibility Scale (Berkowitz & Daniels, 1964), sex-role orientation (Runge, Frey, Gollwitzer, Helmreich, & Spence, 1981), and self-concept (John & Keil, 1972). The self-concept scale had a subscale of empathy as it relates to self-concept.

ASSESSMENT OF OUTCOME VARIABLES   The outcome variable was whether participants had previously helped in a traffic accident.

MAIN RESULTS   Helpers saw themselves as more empathetic than nonhelpers. Helpers' scores on the self-concept/empathy subscale are considerably higher than scores for nonhelpers; $Ms = 5.52$ vs. 4.76; $F(1, 66) = 20.34$, $p < .001$. Helpers also scored higher on the Social Responsibility scale than nonhelpers; $Ms = 4.72$ vs. 4.28; $F(1, 66) = 11.47$, $p < .001$. Believing that they could influence events in their environments, helpers scored higher on internal locus of control than nonhelpers; $Ms = 4.82$ vs. 4.43; $F(1, 66) = 10.37$, $p < .002$. Helpers had a stronger belief in a just world than nonhelpers, $Ms = 3.13$ vs. 2.57; $F(1, 66) = 6.75$, $p < .012$, and showed lower negatively valued masculine instrumentality, $Ms = 1.86$ vs. 2.41; $F(1, 66) = 12.39$, $p < .001$. However, helpers and nonhelpers did not differ on feelings of competence, uncertainty, and empathy (Schmitt, 1982) nor on the self-concept subscale involving instrumentality.

CONCLUSION   "The results provide evidence consistent with an altruistic personality, which is characterized by a strong sense of internal control, a high belief in a just world, a pronounced sense of duty, and an empathy-oriented self-concept."

COMMENTARY   In this study Bierhoff, Klein, and Kramp utilized several standard measures of personality characteristics to investigate differences in helpers and nonhelpers at the scene of an accident. Prosocial behavior, such as helping in an emergency, cannot truly indicate the motives of the individual helper and thereby determine whether the individual behaved altruistically. However, it is concrete evidence for the possible existence of altruism when a choice not to help was available. In this study, seeing oneself as an empathetic, caring person promotes helping but not the general propensity to feel empathy. In Lerner's (1980, 1982) just-world hypothesis, individuals who believe people "get what they deserve and deserve what they get" find a victim of innocent suffering inconsistent with this view and are compelled to help by the discomfort this inconsistency produces. This study is consistent with Lerner's predictions. The moral obligation to help others in time of need, which is not necessarily a personality characteristic but rather a learned motivation, was also associated with helping. Finally, having the characteristic of internal locus of control, or believing oneself to be the master of one's own circumstances and outcomes, seemed to empower the participants to act on behalf of others.

CORRESPONDENCE   Hans W. Bierhoff, Department of Psychology, University of Marburg, Gutenbergst. 18, D-3550 Marburg, Germany

Burnstein, E., Crandall, C., & Kitayama, S. (1994). Some neo-Darwinian decision rules for altruism: Weighing cues for inclusive fitness as a function of the biological importance of the decision. *Journal of Personality and Social Psychology, 67,* 773–789.

OBJECTIVE   To investigate how individuals will use their resources to help others who vary in level of kinship, age, gender, and other characteristics

DESIGN   *Study 1:* Cross-sectional survey. *Studies 2, 3, 4, 5,* and *6:* Experiments utilizing scenarios

SETTING   University of Michigan and Shimane University in Japan

PARTICIPANTS   *Study 1:* Participants were 26 undergraduates at the University of Michigan. *Study 2:* Participants were 82 male and 4 female students at a university in Japan and 28 male and 44 female students at the University of Michigan. *Study 3:* Participants were 61 undergraduates. *Study 4:* Participants were 292 undergraduates at the University of Michigan. *Study 5:* Participants were 47 female and 32 male undergraduates at the University of Michigan. *Study 6:* Participants were 53 undergraduates.

ASSESSMENT OF PREDICTOR VARIABLES   *Study 1:* Participants were presented lists of 19 kin relationships with varying degrees of genetic relatedness (e.g., identical twin, relatedness (r) = 1.0; mother, r = .5; niece, r = .25; great grandfather, r = .125; stepbrother, r = 0). *Study 2:* Participants were randomly assigned to answer one of two forms of a questionnaire. One form presented an emergency helping situation in which they were to imagine helping people out of a burning house. The other form presented an everyday helping situation in which they were to imagine helping people by shopping for items in a store. The people in the scenarios varied by sex (male or female), age (3 days old, 10 years old, 18 years old, 45 years old, or 75 years old), and kin status (brother, nephew or uncle, cousin, acquaintance). Participant gender and country of origin were also taken into consideration. *Study 3:* Participants were presented with 20 paired descriptions of individuals who varied in age, as in Study 2. Half of the target pairs were male and half were female. All of the target pairs were moderately related kin (e.g., grandfather or nephew; relatedness = .25). Participants were asked to imagine living in a sub-Saharan country with high infant mortality and low life expectancy. *Study 4:* Participants were randomly assigned to fill out questionnaires in one of four conditions that differed on type of helping (emergency vs. everyday helping) and gender of target (male vs. female). Descriptions of pairs of target individuals differed on health (good health vs. poor health) and kinship status (relatedness = .5 vs. .25 vs. .125). *Study 5:* Procedures are the same as in Study 4, except that wealth of the target (rich vs. poor) was varied instead of health of the target. *Study 6:* Participants were given choices of groups to consider helping in either emergency or everyday situations. The groups varied on the three types of kin involved (brother, nephew, or cousin) and the summed relatedness value of the three kin in the group (relatedness = .5, 1.0, or 1.5).

ASSESSMENT OF OUTCOME VARIABLES   *Study 1:* Participants indicated the degree of relatedness they perceived with each type of kin relationship, from 0 ("completely unrelated") to 100 ("extremely closely related"). *Study 2:* In a series of descriptions of three individuals (triads) varying on age, sex, and gender, participants ranked which of the three people they would help either out of the burning building or by picking up items from the store. The person they were most likely to help got a score of 3, and the person they were least likely to help got a score of 1. *Study 3:* Participants were asked which member of the pairing they would rescue from a burning house and how likely they were to attempt a rescue, from 3 = "definitely" to 1 = "probably." *Study 4:* Participants were asked which member of the pairing they would help and how likely they were to help, from 3 = "definitely" to 1 = "probably."

Study 5: Same as in Study 4. *Study 6*: Participants chose between two target groups instead of two individuals and rated them as in Study 4.

MAIN RESULTS   *Study 1*: As actual relatedness decreased, perceived relatedness declined as well; $F (5, 100) = 216.9$, $p < .001$. Dunn's multiple comparisons revealed that the greatest drops in perceived relatedness occurred between very close kin and moderately close kin and, secondarily, between distant kin and acquaintances. *Study 2*: Participants' responses did not differ as a function of gender and nationality. Participants reported decreasing likelihood of helping with decreasing relatedness to target, $F (3, 430) = 108.60$, $p < .001$. Younger targets were more likely to receive help than older targets, $F (3, 450) = 17022$, $p < .001$. Both male and female participants were more likely to help female rather than male targets, $F (1, 150) = 27.71$, $p < .001$. The difference between the emergency helping and everyday helping scenarios was significant, $F (3, 450) = 5.86$, $p < .001$, such that close kinship led to greater helping in the emergency situation than in the everyday situation. The interaction of age and condition, $F (3, 450) = 2.88$, $p < .05$, fell in line with the recipient's fitness value. That is, in the emergency helping situation, when help was biologically significant, preference was shown to helping the young over helping the old. In the everyday helping situation, in which individuals could be more concerned with morality and civility, more help was given to the very old and the very young, with intermediate values for helping those aged 10–45 years. *Study 3*: The relationship between tendency to help and age of recipient had a curvilinear shape, $F (4, 240) = 28.73$, $p < .001$, such that participants were most likely to help 10- and 18-year-olds, somewhat less likely to help those less than 1 year old and those 45 years old, and very unlikely to help 75-year-olds. *Study 4*: A significant kin × helping situation × health status interaction, $F (2, 576) = 10.65$, $p < .001$, revealed that in emergency situations participants were more willing to help those in good health, whereas in everyday situations participants were more willing to help those in poor health. As in Study 2, participants were more willing to help close kin than less close kin, $F (2, 576) = 717.98$, $p < .001$, and the importance of kinship was greater in emergency situations than in everyday situations. *Study 5*: Participants reported being more willing to help close kin than less close kin, $F (2, 385) = 40.37$, $p < .001$. This was modified by the helping situation such that the importance of helping closely related kin was lower in everyday situations than in emergency situations, $F (2, 385) = 21.64$, $p < .001$. *Study 6*: Participants helped closer kin types more than less close kin types, $F (2, 102) = 50.4$, $p < .001$. They also helped more when the value of the relatedness of a group of targets was high than when the relatedness of the group of targets was low, $F (2, 102) = 65.6$, $p < .001$. Finally, the group's relatedness value was more important in helping decisions in emergency helping situations than in everyday helping situations, $F (2, 102) = 9.78$, $p < .001$.

CONCLUSION   "Following W. Hamilton's (1964) analysis of inclusive fitness . . . is that (a) natural selection favors those who are prone to help others as a function of the latter's relatedness, potential fecundity, or other features indicating a recipient's capacity to enhance the donor's inclusive fitness, and (b) this effect is especially strong when help is biologically significant (e.g., the recipient will not survive otherwise)."

COMMENTARY   Burnstein et al.'s (1994) article displays some of the traditional methods of exploring altruism from the perspective of sociobiology. Kin relationships are pitted against each other in hypothetical situations to show preferences for altruistic acts toward those with whom one shares greater genetic relatedness and toward those who display greater potential for reproduction of those genes (i.e., the young, healthy, female, etc.). One contribution of this series of studies is the clearly different effects displayed in emergency helping situations versus everyday helping situations. Clearly, different processes are activated in the different situations. It would be beneficial to see the sociobiological variables tested in models along with more proximal variables, such as empathic concern.

CORRESPONDENCE   Eugene Burnstein, Institute for Social Research, University of Michigan, Ann Arbor, MI 48106-1248

Bybee, J., Luthar, S., Zigler, E., & Merisca, R. (1997). The fantasy, ideal, and ought selves: Content, relationships to mental health, and functions. *Social Cognition*, *15*(1), 37–53.

OBJECTIVE   To differentiate (1) fantasy, (2) ideal, and (3) ought selves and then relate these self-conceptions to aspects of personality and behavior

DESIGN   Study 1 was a content analysis of self-descriptions. Study 2 was a questionnaire study involving self and peer reports describing the participant.

SETTING   A university

PARTICIPANTS   *Study 1*: Participants were 81 undergraduate students who participated in partial fulfillment of course requirements. There were 38 males and 43 females. *Study 2*: Participants were 74 undergraduates (43 females and 31 males) who participated in partial fulfillment of course requirements. Seventy-two peers also provided information on the participants but were not compensated for participation.

ASSESSMENT OF PREDICTOR VARIABLES   *Study 1*: Participants were asked to provide five descriptions of how they want to be in the future (ideal self), to describe what they would like to be like if anything were possible (fantasy self), and to describe how they thought they should be (ought self). *Study 2*: Participants indicated the extent to which each of several future self-descriptor words were important to them and the extent to which they thought about the self-descriptors. They also completed a comprehensive personality measure, the NEO-PI-R (Costa & McCrae, 1992a, b).

ASSESSMENT OF OUTCOME VARIABLES   *Study 1*: Self-descriptions were content analyzed based on 32 categories from previous research (Harter, 1982; Markus & Nurius, 1986; McGuire & Padawer-Singer, 1976; Singer & Switzer, 1980). *Study 2*: Participants rated the extent to which the self-descriptors caused them dejection or agitation. They also completed the Taylor Manifest Anxiety scale (Taylor, 1953). Peers rated the participants on assertive social skills, frustration tolerance, aggressiveness, and study skills (Hightower et al., 1986).

MAIN RESULTS   *Study 1*: The ideal self-descriptions contained the addition of new roles (e.g., occupational roles), physical attractiveness, cognitive abilities, and social competence—often described in egocentric ways. Ought self-descriptions contained conscience, role demands, and duties to others. Two-thirds of participants included desires to be caring and considerate in ought self-descriptions, whereas half of participants wanted to work harder in school. Fantasy self-descriptions contained wishes for wealth, power, perfection in all things, and achieving altruistic ends (i.e., discovering the cure for cancer). *Study 2*: Preoccupation with the ideal self-image was related to state anxiety, $r = .25$, self-consciousness, $r = .34$, and angry-hostility, $r = .25$, $ps < .05$. Surprisingly, ideal self-image was not related to academic achievement, positive social interactions, self-discipline, or peer-reported assertive social skills. Preoccupation with the ought self-image was related to altruism, $r = .36$, trusting, $r = .34$, straightforwardness, $r = .45$, and openness of feelings, $r = .28$, $ps < .05$. These individuals were also more warm, $r = .52$, gregarious, $r = .35$, and expressive of positive emotions, $r = .61$, $ps < .05$. They expressed higher achievement motivations, $r = .27$, $p < .05$.

Preoccupation with the fantasy self-image was related to several negative aspects of personality. Participants preoccupied with the fantasy self had higher state anxiety, more angry hostility, and lower scores on altruism, straightforwardness, compliance, and dutifulness (in order, $rs = .29, .45, -.33, -.43, -.47, -.38$; $ps < .05$). Their peers rated them with worse scores on study skills, assertive social skills, and frustration tolerance; $rs = -.35, -.25, -.39; ps < .05$.

CONCLUSION "The fantasy self-image shows numerous and maladaptive relationships with measures of personality and adjustment. Of the three future selves, it is the ought self-image that shows the most adaptive correlations with indicators of prosocial behavior, interpersonal competence, and goal-directed actions."

COMMENTARY When participants concentrated on the ought self, the self associated with conscience and duty, they evinced more prosocial self-descriptions. They also scored higher on altruism (one part of the Agreeableness personality dimension). This is consistent with studies by Ashton et al. (1998) and Axelrod (1997), in which the Big Five personality dimension of Agreeableness was important for conceptualizing the influence of personality traits on altruism. In Bybee et al.'s (1997) research we see the influence of both learned and personality characteristics that influence propensity for altruism. That is, the ought self was characterized by many participants as including prosocial behavior, a learned reaction to the needs of others. In addition, individuals who, as part of their personality, concentrated their efforts on the ought self above the ideal and fantasy selves also scored higher on propensity for altruism.

CORRESPONDENCE None available

Carlo, G., Eisenberg, N., Troyer, D., Switzer, G., & Speer, A. L. (1991). The altruistic personality: In what contexts is it apparent? *Journal of Personality and Social Psychology, 61*(3), 450–458.

OBJECTIVE To investigate the specific contexts in which the altruistic personality would be most apparent

DESIGN A laboratory experiment

SETTING Arizona State University

PARTICIPANTS Participants were 109 undergraduate psychology students who received course credit for participation. There were 47 males and 62 females ranging in age from 17 to 35 years old (mean age = 20.16).

ASSESSMENT OF PREDICTOR VARIABLES In the first session of the experiment, participants filled out questionnaires addressing ascription of responsibility (Schwartz, 1968), social responsibility (Berkowitz & Lutterman, 1968), social desirability (Crowne & Marlowe, 1964), affective intensity (Larsen & Diener, 1987), and three subscales from the Davis (1983) empathy measure (empathic concern, perspective taking, and personal distress). A varimax factor analysis of trait personality measures revealed a 2-factor solution: prosocial tendencies and emotionality. The first factor includes ascription of responsibility, perspective taking, social responsibility, and empathic concern and accounts for 42% of the factor variance. The second factor includes emotional intensity and personal distress and accounts for 22% of the factor variance. Because both gender and social desirability were related to scores on the personality indices (e.g., women scored higher on dispositional prosocial tendencies and emotionality), these variables were controlled for in further analyses.

In a second session, participants were randomly assigned to one of four conditions. The conditions varied on the level of emotion evoked in the participants (high or low) and in the ease of escape from the unpleasant situation (easy or difficult). In the condition that evoked high emotion, participants viewed a videotape of a fictitious other participant reading unpleasant scenarios concerning assault and answering questions about the scenarios. The fictitious participant was visibly emotional and choked back tears. In the low-emotional-evocation condition, the fictitious participant did not show signs of distress. In the easy-escape condition, participants were told that they would not have to watch the fictitious participant read any more scenarios and answer questions. In the difficult-escape condition, participants were told they would have to watch the fictitious participant read 13 more assault scenarios and answer questions.

ASSESSMENT OF OUTCOME VARIABLES   Participants were given the opportunity to take the place of the fictitious fellow participant who was experiencing distress and read some or all of the remaining scenarios. For all participants, helping required completing another session with no additional course credit, adding further cost for helping.

MAIN RESULTS   A planned comparison on helping in the high-evocative/difficult-escape condition versus the other three conditions combined revealed a main effect for condition, $F(1, 101) = 5.95$, $p < .05$. There was more helping in the high-evocative/difficult-escape condition than in the other three conditions combined; $Ms = .78$ versus .37, .34, and .49. Trait emotionality was positively related to helping in the low-evocative/easy-escape condition; partial $r = .44$, $p < .05$. Traits of prosocial tendencies were positively related to helping in the high-evocative/easy-escape condition; partial $r = .48$, $p < .01$. Gender differences revealed no effects of prosocial tendencies and condition on helping for men. However, for women, the effects of prosocial tendencies on helping are situationally dependent. It was positively related to helping in the high-evocative/easy-escape condition; partial $r = .69$, $p < .03$, but unrelated in the high-evocative/difficult-escape and low-evocative/easy-escape conditions; partial $r = -.01$, ns.

In order to test the hypothesis that the relationship between prosocial tendencies and helping would be strongest when effects due to the situation (vs. personality) were weak, a regression analysis compared the relation of helping scores with prosocial tendencies in the low-evocative/easy-escape condition compared with the high-evocative/difficult-escape condition. The tendency to be prosocial predicted helping; r^2 change = .12; $F(1, 99) = 6.82$, $p < .002$. However, there was no difference in the effect of prosocial tendencies by condition. Consistent with the hypothesis, trait emotionality was positively related to helping in the low-evocative/easy-escape condition; partial $r = .44$, $p < .05$, but it was not significantly related to helping in the high-evocative/difficult-escape condition; partial $r = .15$, ns.

CONCLUSION   "This pattern of findings supports the notion that there are altruistic individuals who assist primarily for other-oriented or moral reasons without regard to external rewards or punishments."

COMMENTARY   "The results of the present study provided some support for both predictions stemming from Batson's (1987) work on situational sympathy [empathy in Batson's nomenclature] and for Snyder and Ickes's (1985) distinction between weak and strong psychological situations. With regard to Batson's distinction between easy and difficult escape contexts, the finding that the prosocial composite scores were positively correlated with helping in the high-evocative, easy-escape condition (when both sex and social desirability were controlled for) is consistent with Batson's findings in regard to the relation of state sympathy to altruism (although the relation in this study held primarily for women)" (p. 456).

CORRESPONDENCE   Gustav Carlo or Nancy Eisenberg, Department of Psychology, Arizona State University, Tempe, AZ 85287

Carlson, M., Charlin, V., & Miller, N. (1988). Positive mood and helping behavior: A test of six hypotheses. *Journal of Personality and Social Psychology,* 55, 211–229.

OBJECTIVE   To summarize statistically 34 studies concerning the role of positive mood states in increasing helpfulness

DESIGN   Meta-analytic review

STUDIES   The review included 34 studies (with 61 comparisons of positive mood versus neutral mood) published in professional journals. All studies compared the level of helpfulness of participants in positive moods with the levels of helpfulness of participants in neutral moods, allowing for the calculation of the effect-size estimate of the level of helpfulness of the positive-mood group. The measure of helping occurred within 30 minutes of the positive-mood induction.

ASSESSMENT OF PREDICTOR VARIABLES   The following 16 variables were coded from each study: (1) participant and design characteristics (age, sex of participant, sex of helpee, year of study), (2) features associated with the positive-affect induction (amount of positive affect induced, amount of objective self-awareness induced, extent to which participant is the beneficiary of the positive event, amount of arousal of guilt or inequity in receiving positive-mood induction, extent to which induction would lead participant toward positive view of human nature, and amount of sociality of the positive event), and (3) variables related to the helping opportunity (pleasantness of the helping task, salience of the helping request, salience of prosocial values in the helping request, the extent to which participants feel responsibility to help, time delay between positive induction and helping, and whether helping entailed sustained and ongoing helping). Objective self-awareness is defined as being aware or conscious of oneself in a nonsubjective, honest appraisal of one's true personal nature (Reber, 1995, p. 701). A composite measure called "social outlook" was created by summing the positive view of human nature and sociality of the positive event measures and indicates whether social outlook was investigated in the course of the study.

ASSESSMENT OF OUTCOME VARIABLES   The effect size index used in the present study was d, the difference between the means of the positive-mood-induction group and the neutral group divided by the pooled estimate of standard deviation. All effect-size estimates were corrected for sample size. Predictor variables and effect sizes were also corrected for skewness where appropriate. Some effect-size estimates were calculated based on F, t, or r statistics using Glass, McGaw, and Smith's (1981) formulas.

MAIN RESULTS   Although the mean of the effect sizes was large and suggests that there is a relationship between positive mood and helping, $M = .54$, $t(60) = 5.27$, $p < .001$, the relatively large standard deviation of .8 suggests that these effects may be moderated by other variables. Studies with older participants, studies in which participants were asked to do pleasant helping tasks, studies in which participants' tasks led to pleasant views of human nature, and studies in which the participant was the direct recipient of the positive mood induction all had increased levels of helping; partial rs = .33, .34, .31, and .49, respectively; ps < .05. Studies involving participants with extremely high or low levels of happiness, studies with tasks that produced guilt, or studies with tasks that required the participant to engage in helping over a long period of time were associated with lower levels of helping; partial rs = −.38, −.44, and −.37, respectively; ps < .05.

Even after controlling for the effects of objective self-awareness of participants in the studies, studies in which positive events were directly experienced by the participant yielded higher levels of helping; partial $r = .49$, $p < .001$. This outcome was unaffected by the relationship between feelings of deserving the positive event and helpfulness; partial $r = −.09$, ns. In the studies analyzed, objective self-awareness and request salience are correlated with helping when other variables are partialed out; partial $r = .37$, $p < .01$. However, in studies in which social outlook and self as target of the positive event are removed, the relationship disappears, partial $r = .00$, suggesting that, in these studies, self-awareness may affect helping by enhancing the inclination to act on other factors that are activated by positive mood.

CONCLUSION   "The cognitive consequences of a positive mood may be either general (e.g., global priming effects) or help-specific (e.g., enhanced social outlook), and influence helpfulness by altering the perceived capacity of a given prosocial opportunity to provide self-reinforcement. In addition, perceptions of the inherent reward value of the helping task, as well as one's current degree of elation, influence whether or not one views engaging in the prosocial act as likely to maximize one's outcome."

COMMENTARY   Carlson, Charlin, and Miller's (1988) work on positive mood and helping behavior contributes to the understanding of the mechanism through which they are related. Positive mood changes the way that people view their whole world. Furthermore, people act in ways to maintain positive mood because it is rewarding. It is interesting that extremes of positive mood, whether slight positive mood or extreme elation, interfere with helpfulness. A potential caveat to this research is provided by Ben-Artzi and Mikulincer (1996), who found that the relationship of positive mood to helping is strongest for individuals who believe that experiencing emotion has positive benefits. Wegner, Vallacher, Kiersted, and Dizadji's (1986) work on how people understand the task they are engaged in also invokes social cognitive processes that make one more or less susceptible to continued helping behavior. In the present study, level of self-awareness also influences the degree to which people are responsive to other cues promoting positive mood and helpfulness. Work similar to the current research may be necessary to augment the understanding of effects of negative mood on helping (Batson & Weeks, 1996).

CORRESPONDENCE   Norman Miller, Department of Psychology, University of Southern California, Los Angeles, CA 90089-1061

Chau, L. L., Johnson, R. C., Bowers, J. K., Darvill, T. J., & Danko, G. P. (1990). Intrinsic and extrinsic religiosity as related to conscience, adjustment, and altruism. *Personality and Individual Differences, 11*(4), 397–400.

OBJECTIVE   To investigate the relationships between intrinsic religiosity, extrinsic religiosity, personality, and altruism

DESIGN   Cross-sectional survey

SETTING   University of Hawaii, Honolulu, and Northwest Missouri State University

PARTICIPANTS   Thirty-six male, 53 female, and 4 participants with no reported gender came from the University of Hawaii. Forty male and 64 females came from Northwest Missouri State University

ASSESSMENT OF PREDICTOR VARIABLES   Intrinsic and extrinsic religiosity were measured with the Allport and Ross (1967) I-E scale. Participants also completed the Dimensions of Conscience Questionnaire, a 30-item scale designed to measure guilt and shame. Finally, participants completed the revised Eysenck Personality Questionnaire (EPQ-R; Eysenck, Eysenck, & Barrett, 1985) to measure psychoticism, extraversion, neuroticism, and tendencies for dishonest responding.

ASSESSMENT OF OUTCOME VARIABLES   Participants completed 56 items measuring self-reported altruistic behavior (Johnson et al., 1989). For each item they described how often they had done the behavior, how often someone had done it for them, and how important the altruistic behavior was.

MAIN RESULTS   Correlations among measures were computed by sample and gender. Intrinsic and extrinsic religiosity were significantly positively correlated for Hawaii females and Missouri males, $rs = .50$ and $.40$, $ps < .05$. Intrinsic religiosity was significantly positively correlated with guilt for Hawaii females and Missouri males, $rs = .31$ and $.37$, $ps < .05$. However, it was not significantly correlated with shame for any of the groups; $rs = .10, .05, .08,$ and $.11$, ns. Positive correlations between intrinsic religiosity and the three measures of altruism—giving help, receiving help, and importance of helping—were found for Hawaii males, rs = .30, .42, and .30; ps < .05, as well as for Missouri males, rs = .38, .41, and .31; ps < .05. For females intrinsic religiosity was related only to receiving help for Hawaii females, r = .32; p < .05, and to giving help for Missouri females, r = .23; p < .05. Correlations among personality measures and religiosity were inconsistent, varying greatly by sample and gender.

CONCLUSION   Intrinsic religiosity is related to altruism for males and may also be related to guilt. Intrinsic religiosity appears unrelated to shame.

COMMENTARY   This interesting study is remarkable for its examination of the association of religious factors with measures of self-reported altruism. For males, intrinsic religious motivation was consistently associated with greater levels of help giving, help receiving, and beliefs about altruism. For females, the associations of intrinsic religious motivation with measures of altruism were considerably less robust. This finding suggests that religious involvement might promote the giving and receiving of altruistic help, but its effects may be particularly noteworthy for males. It is important to realize that what was measured in this study was not altruism per se but rather people's self-reports of their behavior and values. Studies that measure altruism through behavioral observations would be invaluable for confirming that the religion-altruism relationship observed in the present study was substantive rather than artifactual.

CORRESPONDENCE   None available

Cialdini, R. B., Brown, S. L., Lewis, B. P., Luce, C., & Neurberg, S. L. (1997). Reinterpreting the empathy-altruism relationship: When one into one equals oneness. *Journal of Personality and Social Psychology, 73*(3), 481–494.

OBJECTIVE   To examine the relationship between empathy and altruism when the participants feel a degree of self-other overlap

DESIGN   Three experimental scenario studies

SETTING   Arizona State University

PARTICIPANTS   *Study 1*: Participants were 44 males and 46 females in introductory psychology courses who received course credit for participation. *Study 2*: Participants were 36 males and 38 females in introductory psychology courses who received course credit for participation. *Study 3*: Participants were 82 males and 181 females in introductory psychology courses who received course credit for participation.

ASSESSMENT OF PREDICTOR VARIABLES   *Study 1*: Participants were randomly assigned to focus on one of four same-sex persons—a stranger, an acquaintance, a good friend, or a family member—as they read a scenario describing the eviction of that person from their apartment. Participants completed measures of empathy, personal distress, and sadness (Fultz, Schaller, & Cialdini, 1988). Finally, participants rated the degree of "oneness" felt with the described person using the Inclusion of Other in the Self (IOS) Scale (Aron, Aron, & Smollan, 1992). *Study 2*: The measures and procedure were the same as in Study 1. The scenario was changed to someone who died in an accident, leaving his or her two children without a home. *Study 3*: The measures and procedure were the same as in Studies 1 and 2, except that participants were also randomly assigned to read one of three different scenarios: the eviction from Study 1, the orphaned children from Study 2, and a new situation in which the target person needed help making a phone call.

ASSESSMENT OF OUTCOME VARIABLES   *Study 1*: Participants indicated the level of help they would offer the evicted person on a 7-point scale, from no help (1) to offering to let him or her come to live with them rent free (7). *Study 2*: Participants indicated the level of help they would offer the children on a 7-point scale, from no help (1) to taking in and raising the children as they would their own (7). *Study 3*: Again participants indicated the level of help they would offer on appropriate scales. The scale for the phone call ranged from no help (1) to cutting class on the day of the exam to drive the person to a phone (7). MAIN RESULTS   *Study 1*: Closer relationship type led to greater willingness to help, F $(3, 82) = 33.28$, $p < .001$. Closer relationship type also led to greater empathic concern, F $(3, 82) = 5.37$, $p < .01$, and feelings of oneness with the person in the scenario, F $(3, 82)$ $= 30.58$, $p < .001$. Both empathic concern and oneness were positively correlated with helping, $rs = .45$ and $.76$, $p < .01$. When entered as a last step in a hierarchical regression analysis, oneness predicted helping, $b = 1.10$, F $(1, 74) = 4.09$, $p < .001$, and made the effect of empathic concern nonsignificant; $b = .11$, F $(1, 74) < 1$, *ns*. *Study 2*: Closer relationship type led to greater willingness to help, F $(3, 70) = 17.43$, $p < .001$. Closer relationship type also led to greater empathic concern, F $(3, 70) = 6.73$, $p < .001$, and to feelings of oneness with the person in the scenario, F $(3, 64) = 27.75$, $p < .001$. Both empathic concern and oneness were positively correlated with helping, $rs = .33$ and $.53$, $p < .01$. When entered as a last step in a hierarchical regression analysis, oneness predicted helping, $b = .57$, F $(1, 57) = 10.39$, $p < .01$, and made the effect of empathic concern nonsignificant, $b = .37$, F $(1, 57) = 1.37$, *ns*. *Study 3*: A two-way analysis of variance (ANOVA) was performed for relationship type and severity of need on degree of helping. Closer relationship type led to greater willingness to help, F $(3, 243) = 62.35$, $p < .001$. There was a significant main effect for severity of need, F $(3, 243) = 217.62$, $p < .001$, such that as need increased, helping increased. The interaction of relationship type and severity of need was also significant, F $(6, 243) = 10.33$, $p < .001$. The impact of relationship closeness was more pronounced in the higher need situations. As in the previous two studies, for all three need situations feelings of oneness significantly predicted helping and rendered the effect of empathic concern on helping nonsignificant.

CONCLUSION   As relationship closeness and severity of need increased, so did helping, although the effects of relationship closeness were stronger in high-need situations. Even though empathic concern was consistently related to helping, it was reduced to nonsignificance when feelings of oneness with the person in need were taken into account.

COMMENTARY   This study is one of many in the ongoing debate regarding the existence of pure altruism. In this installment of the debate, Cialdini and colleagues address the possibility that the crux of the altruism debate is not an ethical one but an ontological one. Altruism occurs because we are actually helping someone that we cannot distinguish from our own identity. This paper produced interesting controversy in an exchange between Cialdini and Batson, and the replies and rejoinder (Batson et al., 1997) were published in volume 73 of the *Journal of Personality and Social Psychology*.

CORRESPONDENCE   Robert B. Cialdini, Department of Psychology, Arizona State University, Tempe, AZ 85287-1104

Clary, E. G., & Orenstein, L. (1991). The amount and effectiveness of help: The relationship of motives and abilities to helping behavior. *Personality and Social Psychology Bulletin, 17*(1), 58–64.

OBJECTIVE   To investigate the influence of helper's motives and abilities on the amount and effectiveness of a long-term altruistic activity

DESIGN   Longitudinal study

SETTING   Crisis Counseling Center in Minneapolis-St. Paul area

PARTICIPANTS   Participants were 125 female and 36 male volunteers at a telephone crisis counseling center. Participants were, on average, 28 years old (range = 18 to 63 years) and came from a variety of education levels (high school diploma to advanced college degrees).

ASSESSMENT OF PREDICTOR VARIABLES   At the end of the first volunteer training session, participants were given a survey that they returned at the second session. Altruistic motivation was measured by participant rankings of their top 5 reasons for volunteering from a list of 25 possible reasons. Altruistic motivation scores ranged from 0 (only egoistic reasons) to 15 (only altruistic reasons). Participants also completed the Davis (1983) Interpersonal Reactivity Index, which has four subscales: perspective taking, fantasy, empathic concern, and personal distress.

ASSESSMENT OF OUTCOME VARIABLES   Two outcome variables were examined: whether the volunteer was screened from the program by staff on the basis of skills and whether the volunteer completed 9 months or more of service working at least 4 hours a week. Three categories of volunteers were developed based on their behavior: screened volunteers, early-termination volunteers, and completed-service volunteers.

MAIN RESULTS   Early-terminating volunteers reported lower altruistic motivation, $M = 2.67$, than screened volunteers, $M = 4.44$, and completed service volunteers, $M = 4.06$; $t(156) = 2.99$, $p < .005$. A planned comparison between screened volunteers and the other two groups indicated that screened volunteers had lower perspective-taking skills than either early-termination or completed-service volunteers; $M = 19.26$ vs. 20.20 and 20.81; $t(159) = 1.73$, $p < .05$. The other measures of empathy—fantasy, personal distress, and empathic concern—did not distinguish among the three volunteer groups; $Fs < 1.40$. Altruistic motivation was related to empathic concern, $r = .22$, $p < .005$, but not to perspective-taking ability, $r = .00$, ns.

CONCLUSION   "These results argue for considering not only whether a potential helper will *try* to help, but also whether he or she *can* help" [italics in original]. Both willingness to help, that is, altruistic motivation, and skills necessary to the task, in this case perspective-taking ability, were important in determining which participants were qualified and would complete the term of service.

COMMENTARY   This study by Clary and Orenstein reveals three important points: (1) Without altruistic motivation, people drop out and do not carry out their altruistic behavior; (2) without perspective-taking skills people are judged as inadequately skilled for this type of service; and (3) people with altruistic motivation also had higher empathic concern. The specific skills to carry out the helping behavior are as important as the underlying motivation to help. Also, empathic concern may be a precursor to altruistic motivation.

CORRESPONDENCE   E. Gil Clary, Department of Psychology, College of St. Catherine, St. Paul, MN 55105.

Darley, J. M., & Batson, C. D. (1973). "From Jerusalem to Jericho": A study of situational and dispositional variables in helping behavior. *Journal of Personality and Social Psychology, 27,* 100–108.

OBJECTIVE   To examine the influence of situational and personality variables on helping in a setting inspired by the parable of the Good Samaritan

DESIGN   Experiment with questionnaires and field study

SETTING   Princeton Theological Seminary

PARTICIPANTS   Participants were 40 students at Princeton Theological Seminary who were paid $1 for the questionnaire session and $1.50 for the experimental session.

ASSESSMENT OF PREDICTOR VARIABLES   In a questionnaire session, participants were administered several religiosity scales. The Glock and Stark (1966) Doctrinal Orthodoxy Scale measured the extent to which participants agreed with classic doctrines of Protestant theology. Allport and Ross's (1967) intrinsic-extrinsic scales measured the extent to which participants believe that religion is an end in itself or an ends to a means, usually for some reward. Batson's (1971) Religious Life Inventory had three subscales: extrinsic external, extrinsic internal, and intrinsic. The extrinsic external subscale measured the degree to which religion was influenced by significant others and situations. The extrinsic internal subscale measured the "drivenness" in one's religiosity. Finally, the intrinsic subscale measured the degree to which one's religiosity involves questioning of the meaning of life. A principal components analysis of these scales revealed a three-component structure consisting of religion as a means to an end, religion as an end in itself, and religion as a search for meaning (also known as quest religiosity).

Participants returned for a second session in which they were randomly assigned to one of four conditions differing on two variables: (1) helping relevance of the message that the participant reads; and (2) amount of time pressure imposed on the participant. In the task-relevant message condition, participants were asked to prepare a 3- to 5-minute speech on possible occupations for seminary graduates. In the helping-relevant message condition, participants were asked to prepare a 3- to 5-minute speech on the parable of the Good Samaritan (a story about helping from the New Testament). Participants were instructed that they would not be allowed to make notes but would have to speak extemporaneously in an adjacent building in which recording equipment was set up. Participants were given a map to the office in which they were to give their talk. The second variable, time pressure, was manipulated by telling the participants either that they were running late and should hurry to the office, that they were just on time, or that they had plenty of time and might have to wait briefly at the office.

ASSESSMENT OF OUTCOME VARIABLES   On the path indicated by the map, a person, actually a confederate, was slumped in a doorway, head down. As the participant passed, the victim coughed twice. The outcome variable was the amount of help offered the victim, from 0 (failed to notice victim in need) to 5 (refused to leave the victim and insisted on offering help).

MAIN RESULTS   The extent to which participants were hurried was significantly related to helping, $F(2, 34) = 3.56$, $p < .05$. Of the participants in the unhurried condition, 63% offered help; of the participants in the intermediate hurried condition, 45% offered help; and of the participants in the hurried condition, only 10% offered help. The type of speech the participant was primed to deliver had no effect on helping, $F(2, 34) = 2.63$, ns. When participants who were high on quest religiosity stopped to offer help, they were more likely to offer small types of help which were also tentative in nature, unlike participants not high on quest religiosity; $r_{point\ biserial} = -.53$, $p < .05$. At the other extreme, participants high in religious orthodoxy were more likely to offer help that was rigid and did not allow information from the victim to change the plan than were participants low in religious orthodoxy, $r = .63$, $p < .01$.

CONCLUSION   "A person not in a hurry may stop and offer help to a person in distress. A person in a hurry is likely to keep going. Ironically, he is likely to keep going even if he is hurrying to speak on the parable of the Good Samaritan, thus inadvertently confirming the point of the parable."

COMMENTARY   Darley and Batson's (1973) study of situational and personality influences on helping is a true classic, cited in many textbook treatments of altruism. Perhaps the reason this study is so well known is that it clearly highlights the foibles of the human condition. This is a case in which the power of the situation (i.e., being hurried) had a stronger impact on the behavior of the participants than personality or even cognitive priming for helping behavior. Although personality affected what type of help was offered, the overriding influence of time pressure was strong. The authors suggest two competing explanations for this effect: first, that "ethics becomes a luxury as the speed of our daily lives increases"; second, that the participants experienced some conflict over two helping situations, one of helping the victim and another of helping the experimenter who depended on them to get to a place quickly.

CORRESPONDENCE   John Darley, Department of Psychology, Princeton University, Princeton, NJ 08540

Davis, M. H., Luce, C., & Kraus, S. J. (1994). The heritability of characteristics associated with dispositional empathy. *Journal of Personality, 62,* 369–391.

OBJECTIVE   To explore whether empathic concern, personal distress, and perspective taking are inherited traits

DESIGN   Survey of monozygotic and dizygotic twins

SETTING   National survey

PARTICIPANTS   Participants were 839 twin pairs consisting of 509 monozygotic pairs (MZ = identical twins; 216 male, 293 female) and 330 dizygotic pairs (DZ = fraternal twins; 135 male, 195 female). Participants were part of a large sample of twins recruited from the 1962 National Merit Scholarship Test (see Loehlin & Nichols, 1976).

ASSESSMENT OF PREDICTOR VARIABLES   Participants indicated on a checklist which of 28 adjectives applied to them. Items measured perspective taking (i.e., cooperative, critical of others), empathic concern (i.e., obliging, sensitive), and personal distress (i.e., emotional, excitable).

ASSESSMENT OF OUTCOME VARIABLES   Heritability was determined by the difference in the intraclass correlations of twin pairs for each trait and by Falconer's (1960) h^2 heritability estimate.

MAIN RESULTS   Of the adjectives for empathic concern and personal distress, 75% showed a significant MZ/DZ difference, with MZ scores higher. That is, MZ twins were more similar in empathic concern and personal distress than were DZ twins. For perspective taking, only 42% of the comparisons show this pattern; the others were not significantly different. The heritability estimates were 28% for empathic concern, 32% for personal distress, and 20% for perspective taking.

CONCLUSION   "Variation in characteristics associated with affective empathy seems to have a considerable genetic component. Variation in perspective taking, in contrast, displays evidence of noticeably weaker genetic contribution. We believe that this difference results from differential association with temperamental emotionality."

COMMENTARY   Many studies in this annotated bibliography investigate the relationship of dispositional empathy to some measure of altruism or helping (Archer et al., 1981; Carlo et al., 1991; Penner & Finkelstein, 1998; and others). It is because of this close relationship between dispositional empathy and altruism that this background article is included. The current work (Davis et al., 1994) suggests that this very basic personality construct, dispositional empathy, has a considerable degree of heritability. Of course this does not preclude the possible influence of nurture or learning on development of dispositional empathy, in particular, perspective-taking skills. It simply means that some people may be more predisposed to feel and act out of dispositional empathy than others.

CORRESPONDENCE   Mark H. Davis, Department of Behavioral Science, Eckerd College, St. Petersburg, FL 33733

Den Ouden, M. D., & Russell, G. W. (1997). Sympathy and altruism in response to disasters: A Dutch and Canadian comparison. *Social Behavior and
Personality, 25*(3) 241–248.

OBJECTIVE   To investigate cross-culturally the role of age, sympathy, and gender in
altruism

DESIGN   Cross-sectional survey with scenarios

SETTING   Utrecht University, The Netherlands, and University of Lethbridge, Canada

PARTICIPANTS   Participants were first- and second-year students at Utrecht University,
The Netherlands, and at the University of Lethbridge, Canada. From Utrecht there were 110
females and 53 males, with an average age of 20.71 years. From Lethbridge there were 113
females and 67 males, with an average age of 21.04 years.

ASSESSMENT OF PREDICTOR VARIABLES   All participants read 10 scenarios describing
worldwide disasters, with special care to avoid describing countries of special interest to
Holland or Canada. Participants were asked to rate how much sympathy they felt for those
involved in each disaster on a 7-point scale.

ASSESSMENT OF OUTCOME VARIABLES   Participants were asked to imagine that they had
just won $100 (or guilders) in a lottery. They were then asked how much of the money they
would donate to assist families and survivors of each of the 10 disasters.

MAIN RESULTS   To examine the effects of nationality, gender, and the disaster stories on
sympathy and altruism, two $2 \times 2 \times 10$ repeated-measure ANOVAs were performed. Canadian participants expressed greater sympathy, $M = 5.10$, than Dutch participants, $M =
4.76$; $F (1, 339) = 56.02$, $p < .001$. Females expressed greater sympathy, $M = 5.21$, than
males, $M = 4.44$; $F (1, 339) = 14.79$, $p < .001$. There was also a main effect for disaster scenario, $F (9, 3051) = 248.12$, $p < .001$, and an interaction between nationality and disaster
scenario, $F (9, 3051) = 4.48$, $p < .001$, on expressed sympathy. Canadian participants donated more money, $M = 116.47$, than Dutch participants, $M = 84.69$; $F (1, 339) = 5.13$,
$p < .03$. There was no main effect of gender on money donated, $F (1, 339) = 1.25$, ns. There
was also a main effect for disaster scenario, $F (9, 3051) = 67.70$, $p < .001$, and an interaction
between nationality and disaster scenario, $F (9, 3051) = 16.47$, $p < .001$, on money donated.
The relationships of age with sympathy and altruism were significant only for males. Older
Dutch men were less sympathetic than younger men, $r = -.29$, $p < .025$. Older Canadian
men were less willing to donate money than younger men, $r = -.23$, $p < .05$. For the two na-
tionality-by-disaster scenario interactions, the authors suggest that some particular types
of disaster were more personally relevant to each national group (i.e., floods to the Dutch
and landslides to the Canadians), evoking greater sympathy and altruism as personal relevance increased.

CONCLUSION   "Overall, it would appear that the relationship between sympathy for international disaster victims and the level of assistance people will extend is weak. The strength
of the affect-action postulated by Weiner (1980) appears to change as a function of sex and
culture."

COMMENTARY   Consistent with other research (Eisenberg, et al., 1989), Den Ouden and
Russell found that females expressed greater sympathy than males. It is interesting that the
greater sympathy expressed by females did not translate to greater donation of money to assist victims. This study also displays the role of culture in emotional and behavioral response to need in others. More cross-cultural research is needed to aid in determining what
personality and individual difference correlates of altruism are human qualities and what
are qualities that are tied to culture.

CORRESPONDENCE   None available

Eagly, A. H., & Crowley, M. (1986). Gender and helping behavior: A meta-analytic review of the social psychological literature. *Psychological Bulletin, 100*, 282–308.

OBJECTIVE To summarize statistically the results of 172 studies concerning gender and helping behavior

DESIGN Meta-analytic review

STUDIES Studies included were 172 studies (with 182 effect sizes) derived from literature in psychology, education, and the social sciences on altruism, prosocial behavior, helping behavior, assistance, and aid. All studies included a measure of helping behavior or commitment to help; the results allowed calculation of sex-of-subject effect size. The participants in the studies were male and female adults and adolescents over 14 years old from the United States or Canada.

ASSESSMENT OF PREDICTOR VARIABLES The following variables were coded from each study: (1) date of publication, (2) source of publication, (3) percentage of male authors, (4) sex of first author, (5) sample size, (6) setting (laboratory, campus, off-campus), (7) existence of surveillance of helping, (8) availability of other potential helpers, (9) type of appeal for help (direct appeal or presentation of need), (10) whether the victim and requester were the same person, (11) identity of victim or requester.

ASSESSMENT OF OUTCOME VARIABLES The effect size index used in the present study was d, the difference between the means of two groups, divided by the pooled (within-sex) standard deviation. An effect size was calculated for 99 helping behaviors. Where possible, effect size calculations were performed for differences in sex of victim or requester; statistical significance and/or direction of differences was recorded. Similarly, effect size calculations were performed separately for male and female participants on sex of victim or requester.

MAIN RESULTS The studies had moderate numbers of participants ($Mdn = 119.94$) and predominately male authors ($Mean = 75.88\%$). More of the studies were conducted in field settings than in laboratory settings ($N = 162$ vs. 41), and use of surveillance was more likely to be nonexistent or unclear than clear ($N = 156$ vs. 25). Studies were evenly distributed with respect to availability of other helpers and type of appeal. *Giving Help*: Effect size analyses reveal that men helped more than women (mean effect size = .07, 95% CI = .02 to .13, total N of participants = 48,945). Although men helped more than women across situations, the effect size was larger in studies conducted in off-campus settings than in campus settings; $\chi^2 (2) = 421.68$, $p < .001$; $\beta = .34$. The effect size was larger, with women helping more, in studies conducted in laboratory settings than in nonlaboratory settings; $\chi^2 (2) = 7.90$, $p < .025$; $\beta = -.16$. The effect size was larger, with the gender difference indicating men helping more than women, in studies in which there was surveillance than in studies in which there was no surveillance; $\chi^2 (2) = 66.59$, $p < .001$; $\beta = -.16$. Furthermore, male-female differences were larger in studies in which the appeal was in terms of an expressed need instead of a direct appeal; $\beta = .24$, $p < .001$. Examining the continuous variables affecting gender differences in helping, males (1) rated themselves more competent to help, $\beta = .58$, $p < .001$; (2) rated themselves as more comfortable in helping, $\beta = .27$, $p < .001$; (3) estimated that they faced less danger from helping, $\beta = .72$, $p < .001$; and (4) judged themselves more likely to help than the average woman, $\beta = .49$, $p < .001$. Interactions of competence and perceived danger with availability of other helpers revealed that in studies in which other helpers were present, men were more likely than women to help to the extent that they perceived themselves to be more competent to help, $\beta = .54$, $p < .001$, or in less danger from helping, $\beta = .55$, $p < .001$. In total these effect size moderators accounted for

69% of the variability in observed effect size. *Receiving Help*: Effect size analyses reveal that women were helped more than men (mean effect size = −.23, 95% CI = −.38 to −08, total N of participants = 22,357). Although women were helped more than men across situations, the effect size was larger in the off-campus settings than the campus settings, including the laboratory, Q_B = 200.03, $p < .001$; β = −.25. Effect sizes were larger, with women being helped more, in studies in which there was surveillance than when there was unclear surveillance; χ^2 (2) = 221.18, $p < .001$; β = −.62. Conversely, the effect sizes were larger, with men being helped more, in studies in which there was unclear surveillance than in studies in which there was no surveillance; χ^2 (2) = 39.28, $p < .001$; β = .32. Women were helped more than men in studies in which others were available to help than in studies in which availability of help was unclear or help was unavailable, β = .20, $p < .001$. Furthermore, women were helped more than men in studies in which the appeal was in terms of an expressed need instead of a direct appeal, β = .19, $p < .001$. Examining the continuous variables affecting gender differences in receiving help, females were helped more than males to the extent that males (1) rated themselves more competent to help, β = −.34, $p < .001$; (2) rated themselves as more comfortable in helping, β = −.22, $p < .001$; (3) estimated that they faced less danger from helping, β = −.22, $p < .001$; and (4) judged themselves more likely to help than the average woman, β = −.42, $p < .001$. In total, these effect size moderators and their interactions accounted for 61% of the variability in effect size.

CONCLUSION   "Results from our meta-analytic review of sex differences in helping behavior indicate that in general men helped more than women and women received more help than men."

COMMENTARY   Meta-analytic studies, such as this work by Eagly and Crowley, are invaluable in summarizing a large literature by averaging over the smaller inconsistencies between individual studies. Although other studies in this bibliography suggest that women may be more sympathetic than men (den Ouden & Russell, 1997; Eisenberg et al., 1989), this study suggests that actual helping behavior is more often enacted by men than by women. However, even though the effect size is of statistical significance, it is not large enough to be of much value in real-world terms. Eagly and Crowley also found that women are more likely to be the recipients of help than men. This effect size is quite large and represents a large effect in both statistical and real-world terms. The person-situation interaction appears to extend to gender. That is, the individual's gender (person effect) and the gender of the requester of help (situation effect) combine to create the complete picture of the helping situation. This includes variables related to the setting (i.e., whether there are other helpers available) and variables related to the individual's personality (i.e., perceived danger to self of helping) affecting likelihood of both helping and being helped. It should be noted that most social psychological studies focus on chivalrous acts toward strangers—the domain of male gender role behavior—and not on the kinds of social support women enact in the helping of friends and family. As further evidence of this bias in the literature, women rated the perceived helping in these studies as more dangerous than did men, felt less competent to help than did men, and were inhibited by the presence of an audience to witness the helping act.

CORRESPONDENCE   Alice H. Eagly, Northwestern University, 2029 Sheridan Rd #102, Evanston, IL 60208-2710

Eisenberg, N., Fabes, R. A., Schaller, M., Miller, P., Carlo, G., Poulin, R., Shea, C., & Shell, R. (1991). Personality and socialization correlates of vicarious emotional responding. *Journal of Personality and Social Psychology*, 61, 459–470.

OBJECTIVE   To examine the relationship between personality and family characteristics of a precursor to altruism: vicarious emotional responding

DESIGN   Laboratory experiment and survey

SETTING   Arizona State University

PARTICIPANTS   Participants were 44 male and 50 female undergraduates participating for partial course credit in introductory psychology. Average age of participants was 19 years old.

ASSESSMENT OF PREDICTOR VARIABLES   In the first session of the experiment, participants completed a questionnaire containing the following scales: (1) Marlowe-Crowne Social Desirability Scale (Crowne & Marlowe, 1964), (2) Davis's (1983) Interpersonal Reactivity Index, which has four subscales (empathic concern, perspective taking, fantasy empathy, and personal distress), (3) Larsen's (Larsen, Diener, & Cropanzano, 1987) Affect Intensity Measure, (4) the Family Cohesiveness subscale of Moos and Moos's (1981) Family Environment Scale, and (5) Halberstadt's (1986) Family Expressiveness Scale.

In the second session of the experiment, participants viewed two films. One was designed to elicit sympathy by showing an interview with a child who had spina bifida and displayed difficulty walking. The other film was designed to illicit personal distress and showed a young man picking up a hitchhiker who eventually threatened to do bodily harm to the young man. Participants were randomly assigned to either objective or perspective-taking conditions. Participants were told to view the videotape either imagining themselves in the place of the protagonist or objectively observing the protagonist's behavior.

ASSESSMENT OF OUTCOME VARIABLES   All participants were connected to equipment which measured skin conductance and heart rate via electrodes placed on the participant's body. Participants completed mood measures following each film, rating 15 emotion-related adjectives on a 7-point scale.

MAIN RESULTS   Women exhibited more skin conductance while viewing the sympathy and distress films than did men, $ps < .05$. They also reported higher levels of sympathy in response to both films and distress in response to the distress film than did men, $ps < .05$. Fantasy empathy, which measures the tendency to react emotionally to movies, books, and imagination, was related to vicarious emotional responding, assessed by skin conductance in both films; partial $r (75) = .27$ and $.34$, respectively; $ps < .02$. For participants in the perspective-taking instruction set, the measure of dispositional perspective taking was positively related to sadness, sympathy, and distress in reaction to the sympathy film; partial $r (75) = .47$, $.25$, and $.47$, respectively; $ps < .10$, and dispositional personal distress was negatively related to sympathy in the sympathy films; partial $r (75) = -.33$, $ps < .05$.

Family cohesiveness was significantly related to sympathy and sadness for the sympathy films; partial $r (88) = .23$ and $.21$, respectively; $ps < .03$. The significance of the measures of family expressivity on sadness, sympathy, distress, and physical response were driven, primarily, by the reactions of the women. For women, self-reports of sadness and sympathy were related to expression of positive emotion in the home for both films; partial $r (75) = .46$ and $.35$, respectively, for the sympathy film; partial $r (75) = .54$ and $.34$, respectively, for the distress film; $ps < .05$. Expression of emotion was related to distress in reaction to the sympathy film; partial $r (75) = .39$, $p < .01$. Heart rate was related only to positive emotional expression in the home for women during the distress film; partial $r (75) = .39$, $p < .01$.

CONCLUSION   "The results of the present study support the claim that personal variables, including dispositional characteristics of the individual and one's socialization history, are related to the degree to which adults react vicariously to sympathy-evoking and distressing stimuli. However, the relations vary as a function of the type of stimulus and the type of assessment of vicarious responding."

COMMENTARY   This work is a continuation of a line of research in which Eisenberg and colleagues investigate the roles of personality and empathy in producing prosocial behavior (Eisenberg et al., 1989). It has been argued that vicarious emotional responding is a precursor to altruistic or prosocial behavior. In the present study Eisenberg et al. examine the more distal relationships of vicarious emotional responding to personality and socialization variables. Although some of the variables examined are dispositional in nature, others are simply individual differences in history of socialization concerning emotion. The dispositional measures are related to spontaneous emotional responding for both men and women, but the individual differences in socialization of emotions was related to vicarious emotional responding only for women. The amount of sympathy and personal distress was appropriately tied to the situational setting of the film. Disposition, socialization, and situation interact to produce appropriate vicarious emotional responding which might, in turn, lead to situationally appropriate helping behaviors.

CORRESPONDENCE   Nancy Eisenberg, Department of Psychology, Arizona State University, Tempe, AZ 85287

Eisenberg, N., Miller, P. A., Schaller, M., Fabes, R. A., Fultz, J., Shell, R., & Shea, C. L. (1989). The role of sympathy and altruistic personality traits in helping: A reexamination. *Journal of Personality, 57*(1), 41–67.

OBJECTIVE   To examine the role of social evaluation in sympathy and helping and to examine whether altruistic personality traits and emotional responses affect intention to help

DESIGN   Experiment involving both questionnaire and laboratory sessions

SETTING   Arizona State University

PARTICIPANTS   Participants were 78 students, 37 females and 41 males, participating for partial class credit.

ASSESSMENT OF PREDICTOR VARIABLES   In a questionnaire session, participants completed the Ascription of Responsibility Scale (Schwartz, 1968), the Social Responsibility Scale (Berkowitz & Lutterman, 1968), the Marlowe-Crowne Social Desirability Scale (Crowne & Marlowe, 1964), the Fear of Negative Evaluation Scale (Leary, 1983), the Self-Monitoring Scale (Snyder, 1986), and a measure of emotional empathy (Mehrabian & Epstein, 1972). Approximately 1 week later, the participants returned for the experimental session. They were randomly assigned to an experimental or a control group. Although both groups were fitted with electrodes to measure heart rate, the experimental group was led to believe that the technician could detect truthful answers on questionnaires with the physiological measure. At the experimental session, participants also filled out a questionnaire, including the Davis Interpersonal Reactivity Index (1983), and measures of current emotional state, personal distress, sympathetic concern, and sad reactions (Fultz, Schaller, & Cialdini, 1988). The Davis Interpersonal Reactivity Index and its subscales of empathic concern, perspective taking, personal distress, and fantasy empathy are measures of dispositional empathy. Measures of current emotional state, sympathetic concern, and sad reactions are measures of situationally induced empathy.

ASSESSMENT OF OUTCOME VARIABLES   All participants saw a fictitious "human interest" news report about a single mother struggling to help her two children, who were in the hospital as a result of an auto accident. Participants were given the opportunity to help the mother by volunteering their time to run errands, do yard work, and so forth. Possible responses ranged from 0 hours to 18 hours, in 3-hour increments.

MAIN RESULTS   Participants who scored high on measures of emotional empathy, fantasy empathy, and perspective taking saw the mother's need as greater than did participants who scored lower on these measures; partial $rs = .27, .29$, and $.27$, respectively; $ps < .03$. In a 2×2 multivariate analysis of variance (MANOVA) on the four subscales of the Davis Interpersonal Reactivity Index, there was a main effect for gender, $F(4, 69) = 5.57, p < .01$, and an interaction between gender and experimental condition, $F(4, 69) = 2.74, p < .05$. Females scored higher on all dispositional empathy measures—empathic concern, perspective taking, fantasy empathy, and personal distress—than did males. Furthermore, females in the control condition scored significantly higher than males on fantasy empathy, as they did not think the experimenter could detect their real responses; $Ms = 25.84$ for females and 21.42 for males. Both empathic concern and perspective taking were positively correlated with helping the mother, $rs = .33$ and $.28$, respectively; $ps < .02$. Self-reports of situationally induced sympathy were also positively related to helping, $r = .27, p < .02$. Three measures of altruistic personality, Davis's Empathic Concern, Ascription of Responsibility, and the Mehrabian and Epstein Empathy Scale, were also related to helping, $rs = .33, .31$, and $.29$, respectively; $ps < .05$.

Situational sympathy and fear of negative evaluation were examined as potential moderators of the relationship between personality characteristics and helping behavior. Dispositional empathic concern was moderated by fear of negative evaluation; r^2 change $= .05, F(1, 71) = 4.05, p < .05$. A path model containing both the direct effects of dispositional empathic concern and situational sympathy on helping and the indirect effect of dispositional empathic concern through situational sympathy revealed significant paths for both direct and indirect effects, $W(1) = 4.06$ and 21.36, $ps < .05$. Similar patterns were revealed for dispositional perspective taking and situational sympathy, $W(1) = 3.83$ and 4.86, $ps < .055$, as well as for ascription of responsibility and situational sympathy, $W(1) = 4.61$ and 5.23, $ps < .05$. The three models each accounted for 13%, 13%, and 14% of the total variance in helping.

CONCLUSION   "There is indeed an altruistic personality, and the effects of an altruistic disposition on the intention to assist a needy other are partially mediated through individuals' sympathetic reactions to needy others in the given context."

COMMENTARY   This study, like other studies by Batson and colleagues (e.g., Batson, Duncan, Ackerman, Buckley, & Birch, 1981; Batson, O'Quin, Fultz, Vanderplas, & Isen, 1983) examined the extent to which personality traits such as empathy and social responsibility predict behavioral expressions of willingness to help. Eisenberg and colleagues found evidence that situational empathy did mediate, in part, the associations between personality variables and offered help. However, unlike Batson, Eisenberg and colleagues did not find that situational empathy *completely* mediated the association of personality and helping. Thus additional variables might be at work. Unlike Batson's studies, this experiment did not vary the "ease of escape." Instead, the whole study simulates the "easy escape" condition in which nonaltruistic motivation should not be activated. Nevertheless, this study shows quite clearly that personality does play a role in some forms of helping (even if the motivations of such forms of helping are not made completely clear).

CORRESPONDENCE   Nancy Eisenberg, Department of Psychology, Arizona State University, Tempe, AZ 85287

Fabes, R. A., Eisenberg, N., & Miller, P. A. (1990). Maternal correlates of children's vicarious emotional responsiveness. *Developmental Psychology, 26*, 639–648.

OBJECTIVE   To explore the relationship between mothers' sympathetic dispositions and their children's vicarious emotional responses and prosocial behavior

DESIGN   Direct observation and questionnaires

SETTING   Arizona State University

PARTICIPANTS   Participants were 59 second graders (25 females, 33 males), 58 fifth graders (25 females, 33 males), and their mothers. Nineteen children were dropped from analyses because of incomplete data or because they did not like recess at school (recess was related to the helping variable).

ASSESSMENT OF PREDICTOR VARIABLES   Mothers completed demographic information and three subscales of the Davis Interpersonal Reactivity Index (1983): perspective taking, empathic concern, and personal distress.

ASSESSMENT OF OUTCOME VARIABLES   Children were invited into a laboratory room to rate bogus TV broadcasts. The child was fitted with two electrocardiograph electrodes, which provided heart rate measures during a baseline period (when the newscaster was introducing the study) and during a critical segment (an emotion-provoking interview). The emotion-provoking interview was with a mother who described a bad auto accident her children had been in, the injuries and adjustment difficulties of the children, and the children's fears of getting behind in school. The mother in the interview was visibly upset. Facial expressions displayed by the children while watching the emotion-provoking video were recorded on videotape and rated by two judges. The ratings ranged from 0 for no sign of emotion to 5 for exceptionally strong facial display. Each of the following emotions were rated in facial expressions: happiness, sadness, distress, and sympathy. The child's general level of expressiveness as displayed when watching a neutral videotape was taken into account in analyses.

Following each videotape the children verbally rated the extent to which they felt each of 11 emotions on a 7-point scale, from "not at all" to "very much." The emotion words reflected personal distress (i.e., worried), sympathy (i.e., feeling sorry for someone), and general affect states (i.e., happy, sad). Finally, the experimenter gave the child an opportunity to help the injured children from the videotape by giving up their recess time to gather homework materials from the injured children's teachers. The children were to mark on a calendar which, if any, of 10 school days they were willing to give up their recess to help.

MAIN RESULTS   There were sex and age differences in children's vicarious emotional responses. After watching the film, boys reported less distress than girls, $F(1, 113) = 3.72$, $p < .05$. Girls were more willing to help than boys, $F(1, 114) = 3.90$, $p < .05$. Second graders showed less happiness and more sympathy, facially, than did fifth graders; $Ms = .06$ vs. $.15$ and $.69$ vs. $.44$, respectively; $Fs(1, 115) = 4.95$ and 3.62, $ps < .05$. Looking at overall linear trends in heart rate for helping between those who helped very little (1 or fewer days) and those who helped more, heart rate decelerated for children in the high-help group but not for those in the low-help group; $F(1, 111) = 3.61$, $p < .06$. Interrelations among measures of children's vicarious emotional responsiveness, helping, and measures of maternal empathy are presented separately for girls and boys.

For girls, verbal reports of negative affect were positively related to verbal reports of sympathy, distress, and facial sadness; $rs = .68, .50,$ and $.25$, respectively. Verbal reports of sympathy were also related to verbal reports of distress, $r = .38$, and facial sadness was inversely related to facial distress, $r = -.39$. Oddly, mothers' scores on empathic concern and perspective taking were positively related to girls' reports of negative affect, $rs = .38$ and $.29$, respectively, and mothers' reports of personal distress were related to daughters' reports of positive affect, sympathy, distress, and negative affect, $rs = .25, -.29, -.24,$ and $-.30$, respectively. Girls who reported more negative and less positive affect were most willing to help; $rs = .33$ and $-.28$, respectively.

For boys, verbal reports of negative affect were positively correlated with verbal reports of sympathy and distress and with heart rate deceleration; $rs = .62, .57,$ and $-.23$, respectively. Verbal reports of sympathy were positively related to verbal distress and heart rate deceleration; $rs = .63$ and $-.28$, respectively. Boys' facial sadness was positively related to facial sympathy, $r = .61$. Mothers' scores on perspective taking were negatively related to boys' reports of negative affect, $r = -.24$. Mothers' scores on personal distress were positively correlated with boys' reports of positive affect, $r = .21$. Mothers' scores on perspective taking and empathic concern were positively related to boys' helpfulness, $rs = .23$ and $.25$, respectively. Boys' reports of sympathy and distress were related to willingness to help, $rs = .22$ and $.23$, respectively. Also, boys' willingness to help was related to facial expressions of sadness and sympathy, $rs = .22$ and $.24$, respectively.

CONCLUSION "Mothers who were more sympathetic and better perspective takers had girls who reported feeling more sympathy and negative affect and less happiness after exposure to needy others. Fewer relations between mothers' sympathy and vicarious emotional response were found for boys; however, there were more relations between boys' emotional responses and their helpfulness."

COMMENTARY Fabes, Eisenberg, and Miller (1990) show three important links in this study: (1) the link between emotional responses, facial expressions, and physiological responses in children; (2) the link between those responses and willingness to help; and (3) the link between mothers' dispositional empathy and children's emotional responses. The link between mothers' empathy and children's emotional responses may show a passing of traits over generations, though it is impossible to tell what portion of these results may be due to heredity and what part to children observing and mimicking the mother's response or direct teaching of empathic reactions (cf. Davis et al., 1994). The link between verbal reports of emotion, independently judged facial expressions, and heart rate provides convergent validity for measures of dispositional empathy. Furthermore, this study of children joins the longer list of research linking dispositional empathy to helping behavior in adults.

CORRESPONDENCE Richard A. Fabes, Department of Family Resources and Human Development, Arizona State University, Tempe, AZ 85287-2502

Farver, J. A. M., & Branstetter, W. H. (1994). Preschoolers' prosocial responses to their peers' distress. *Developmental Psychology, 30*(3), 334–341.

OBJECTIVE To observe individual differences in children's responses to crying by other children

DESIGN Naturalistic observation study

SETTING University child development laboratory

PARTICIPANTS Fifty-two preschoolers in three child-care programs with a mean age of 49.4 months (range 36–56 months) participated; 26 participants were female and 26 were male.

ASSESSMENT OF PREDICTOR VARIABLES Each child's social interaction with peers was coded throughout a free-play period for positive social interactions, negative social interactions, shared positive emotion, social play, and orienting toward an adult. Assessments of friendship status were made by sociometric analysis, behavioral observation, and teacher nomination. Teachers rated each child's social competence on three scales: difficult child, hesitant child, and sociable child (Howes, 1988). Parents completed the Behavioral Style Questionnaire (McDevitt & Carey, 1978), which researchers used to classify children into three temperament categories: easy, slow-to-warm-up, and difficult. Easy children are happy and adapt easily to their environment. Slow-to-warm-up children are shy and slow to adapt to their environment. Difficult children are characteristically unhappy and do not easily adapt to their environment.

ASSESSMENT OF OUTCOME VARIABLES   Each child's behavior to the naturally occurring crying of a fellow preschooler was coded for the following categories: ignoring the incident, teasing the crying child, watching, commenting on why child is crying, mediating the conflict either physically or verbally, or comforting the crying child. Prosocial peer response was the summed proportions of approaching, commenting, comforting, and mediating. Ignoring the incident was considered a non-prosocial response, and no child teased the crying child.

MAIN RESULTS   Children rated as having an easy temperament behaved more prosocially to the crying child, $M = .91$, than children rated as having slow-to-warm-up, $M = .86$, and difficult temperaments $M = .67$, $F (2, 51) = 6.93$; $p < .01$. The proportion of time a child spent crying was related to proportion of prosocial responses when other children cried, $r (50) = .48$, $p < .01$. Positive social interaction was also positively correlated with prosocial responses, $r (50) = .40$, $p < .01$. There were no significant correlations for shared positive affect, social play, adult orientation, age, or gender. Children with at least one reciprocal friendship had more prosocial responses to peer crying, $M = .92$, than children without reciprocal friendships, $M = .51$, $F (2, 49) = 5.90$; $p < .01$.

CONCLUSION   "The results suggest that socioemotional functioning with peers and individual characteristics affect children's responses to a peer's distress."

COMMENTARY   Although many psychosocial processes function somewhat differently in young children than they do in adults, by examining young children we may see the underlying simpler processes and even the developmental issues related to altruism. One difference between this study and studies of adults is that there seems to be no gender differences in altruistic behavior or altruistic personality characteristics among the children. In studies of adults, females are consistently more empathic in temperament than males (Carlo et al., 1991; Chau et al., 1990; Eisenberg et al., 1989), and males perform more overt helping behaviors than females (Eagly & Crowley, 1986). Perhaps the most interesting finding in this study is that children who cry a lot themselves are more likely to act prosocially toward another child who is crying. Two explanations for this finding come to mind, either of which strengthens the argument for personality differences in altruistic behavior. The first is that the crying child is more sensitive, empathetic, or simply "soft-hearted" in general and therefore is more likely to respond to the needs of another. A second explanation is that we are witnessing rudimentary perspective taking. The child who cries at some level understands the distress of the other and is more likely to help the other to relieve that distress. As we have seen in other studies, personality variations function in the context of the social environment. Easy temperament, positive social interaction, and reciprocal friendships speak to the interactive nature of altruism in this study.

CORRESPONDENCE   Jo Ann M. Farver, Department of Psychology, University of Southern California, Los Angeles, CA 90089-1061

Gergen, K. J., Gergen, M. M., & Meter, K. (1972). Individual orientations to prosocial behavior. *Journal of Social Issues, 8,* 105–130.

OBJECTIVE   To examine the relationship between 10 personality measures and prosocial behavior

DESIGN   Cross-sectional survey

SETTING   Swarthmore College

PARTICIPANTS   Participants were 72 upper-level students enrolled in a personality theory course. There were 37 males and 35 females.

ASSESSMENT OF PREDICTOR VARIABLES   During the first class session, students completed several personality questionnaires, including seven subscales of the Edwards Personal Preference Schedule (Edwards, 1954): abasement, autonomy, change, deference, nurturance, order, and succorance. Abasement is the need to surrender one's self or will to another. Autonomy is the tendency to act independently of others. Change is the tendency to seek out new experiences and enjoy different activities. Deference is the need to admire and defer to a leader or superior. Nurturance is the tendency to protect, support, and encourage others. Order is the desire to have one's environment methodically and harmoniously arranged. Finally, succorance is the need to receive aid, assistance, and guidance from others. Participants also completed Zuckerman's test of sensation seeking (i.e., the degree to which individuals search out and enjoy activities with a high level of physical or social sensation; Zuckerman, Kolin, Price, & Zoob, 1964) and a self-esteem measure (i.e., the degree to which the participant values himself or herself; deCharms & Rosenbaum, 1960).

ASSESSMENT OF OUTCOME VARIABLES   At the end of the following class session, students were asked whether they would be willing to help the psychology department by volunteering to help with one or more of the following services: (1) help in counseling male high school students with personal problems, (2) help in counseling female high school students with personal problems, (3) aid a faculty research project on deductive thinking, (4) aid in research on unusual states of consciousness, and (5) help collate and assemble materials for the class.

MAIN RESULTS   Because 10 separate personality variables were investigated independently for males and females, the findings of this study were quite complex. Therefore, results for males and females are presented separately. For males, participants high in nurturance were more likely to volunteer to help counsel high school males, $r = .41$, $p < .05$. However, nurturance was not significantly correlated with any other measure of helping for males. For males, abasement was negatively correlated with willingness to counsel males, counsel females, and help with the deductive thinking experiment, $rs = -.30, -.31, -.33$, $ps < .05$, but not with willingness to help with the unusual-states experiment or collate class materials, $ps < .05$. Some of the correlations between helping and personality characteristics differed by situation. For example, for males, autonomy was negatively correlated with willingness to counsel females, $r = -.30$, $p < .05$, but positively correlated with willingness to collate class materials, $r = .29$, $p < .05$. Conversely, order was positively correlated with willingness to counsel females, $r = .35$, $p < .05$, and negatively correlated with willingness to collate class materials, $r = -.28$, $p < .05$. Males also showed significant correlations for willingness to help with unusual-states experiments and change, self-consistency, and sensation seeking, $rs = .40, -.40, .45$, $ps < .05$. Change and sensation seeking were related to each other, $r = .34$, $p < .05$. However, when sensation seeking was held constant, change failed to correlate significantly with willingness to help.

Females showed a similar, but not entirely consistent, pattern of correlations between dispositional variables and helping situations. For females, participants higher in deference, nurturance, and order were more willing to help counsel high school females, $rs = .32, .34, .40$, $ps < .05$. However, there were no significant correlations between these three variables and female participants' willingness to counsel high school males. Furthermore, deference was negatively correlated with willingness to collate class materials, $r = -.33$, $p < .05$. Willingness to counsel high school males was related to abasement, self-consistency, and sensation seeking for these female participants, $rs = -.39, -.33, .29$, $ps < .05$. In contrast to the males, for whom self-esteem had no significant correlations with helping, females showed positive correlations between self-esteem and willingness to help with the unusual-states experiment and collating class materials, $rs = .50, .42$, $ps < .05$. The unusual-states experiment was correlated with several dispositional variables for the females: autonomy, change, self-esteem, sensation seeking, and succorance; $rs = .36, .32, .50, .56, -.31$, $ps < .05$. Self-esteem and autonomy were positively correlated with each other, $r = .34$, $p < .05$, and with willingness to help collate materials. However, when self-esteem was held constant, autonomy fails to predict helping.

CONCLUSION   "Rather than finding trait-dimensions that generally predict prosocial activities, we find that all ten traits utilized in the study can be related to prosocial behavior. However, whether a relationship exists and the nature of this relationship *depends on the type of situation in question* [emphasis in the original]. There is widespread evidence of interaction among predictor variables. In particular, identical personality traits do not generally operate in similar ways for males and females." Furthermore, intercorrelations between dispositional variables may be evidence of some spurious associations.

COMMENTARY   Gergen, Gergen, and Meter's (1972) article is more than just a study of dispositional traits and helping behavior. They go to great lengths to discuss the pitfalls of simple correlations between dispositional traits and helping. Four areas are discussed: (1) the inconsistency of prediction of personality variables across situations, (2) interactions among dispositional variables and other individual differences (i.e., gender differences), (3) the need to isolate independent effects of predictors separate from their correlations with other predictors, and (4) that the inconsistency of personality variables over time may lower the magnitude of correlations. We need to use caution when interpreting correlations between personality traits and helping behavior. The context of the helping behavior and the intercorrelations with other traits should be considered at the very least. This article is considered a classic in this area of study. Much progress has been made in addressing these issues since its publication.

CORRESPONDENCE   Kenneth J. Gergen, Swarthmore College, Department of Psychology, 500 College Ave, Swarthmore, PA, 19081

Hendrick, S. S., & Hendrick, C. (1987). Love and sex attitudes and religious beliefs. *Journal of Social and Clinical Psychology, 5*(3), 391–398.

OBJECTIVE   To explore the relations between love and religious belief

DESIGN   Cross-sectional questionnaire study

SETTING   *Study 1:* University of Miami. *Study 2:* Texas Tech University

PARTICIPANTS   *Study 1:* Participants were 807 college students. *Study 2:* Participants were 567 college students.

ASSESSMENT OF PREDICTOR VARIABLES   Participants completed a self-rating of religiousness, from "very religious" to "very antireligious." Participants also completed a 51-item sexual attitudes inventory.

ASSESSMENT OF OUTCOME VARIABLES   Participants completed a 42-item love styles scale. The scale addressed each of the six theoretical types of love: eros (romantic, passionate love), ludus (game-playing love), storge (compassionate love), mania (possessive, dependent love), pragma (logical, practical love), and agape (selfless, religious love). Greater endorsement of items was indicated by marking lower numbers on the scale.

MAIN RESULTS   In both studies participants who rated themselves as "very religious" also rated themselves as having more storge, pragma, and agape love styles than nonreligious participants ($Ms = 2.3$ vs. 2.8 on storge, 2.6 vs. 3.0 for pragma, and 2.2 vs. 2.6 for agape; $Fs < 3.3$, $ps < .05$). Very religious participants rated themselves as having less ludus than nonreligious participants ($Ms = 2.3$ vs. 2.8 on ludus; $F = 4.6$, $p < .05$).

CONCLUSION   "Subjects who were more religious endorsed the more 'dependable' love styles of storge (compassionate), pragma (practical), and agape (selfless), while they relatively rejected ludus (game-playing)."

COMMENTARY   Lee (1977) defines the agape love style as altruistic and loving without concern for receiving anything in return. The dictionary of the *Information Please Almanac* defines agape as "unselfish love of one person for another without sexual implications; brotherly love." It is clear that the concept of agape love is related to altruism and, in the case of Lee (1977), is defined in terms of altruism. According to the findings of Hendrick and Hendrick's work (1987), religiousness is related to selfless, altruistic intentions in the form of the expression of agape love style. It would be easy to believe that these religious participants, who also evinced higher levels of practical and compassionate love styles, would be better prepared to behave altruistically. What this study cannot answer is whether the religiousness affects expression of agape altruism through individual personality differences or whether religious teaching leads to greater acceptance of altruistic love. Furthermore, there is no investigation of the direct link between the agape love style, religiousness, and prosocial behavior.

CORRESPONDENCE   Susan S. Hendrick, Department of Psychology, Box 42051, Texas Tech University, Lubbock, TX 79409-2051

Jackson, L. M., & Esses, V. M. (1997). Of scripture and ascription: The relation between religious fundamentalism and intergroup helping. *Personality and Social Psychology Bulletin, 23*(8) 893–906.

OBJECTIVE   To investigate the relationships between religious fundamentalism, threat to group values, and degree of helping for an outgroup

DESIGN   Experiment with questionnaires

SETTING   A university in eastern Canada

PARTICIPANTS   *Study 1:* Participants were 116 students (48 males and 68 females) from the University of Western Ontario, who participated in exchange for course credit. Participants indicated their primary religious affiliation as Protestant (29), Catholic (33), Jewish (16), "personal religion" (10), agnostic (13), atheist (4), or other, including Muslim and Hindu (10). *Study 2:* Participants were 92 individuals (46 males and 46 females) who participated either in exchange for course credit or $5.00. Participants indicated their primary religious affiliation as Protestant (24), Catholic (25), Jewish (7), "personal religion" (7), agnostic (11), atheist (4), or other, including Muslim and Hindu (12).

ASSESSMENT OF PREDICTOR VARIABLES   *Study 1:* Participants were randomly assigned to review materials concerning one of two target groups: homosexuals or Native Canadians. All participants then completed an open-ended measure of symbolic beliefs (Esses, Haddock, & Zanna, 1993). This measure asked participants to list values, customs, and traditions that were important to them and that they believed were either threatened or promoted by the target group. Participants gave ratings of threat or promotion to each of the values on a scale of −3 to +3. Next, participants read a short statement explaining that their assigned target group had disproportionally high unemployment. Then participants were asked to rate the extent that the target group members were responsible for the problem and to what extent the target group members were responsible for the solution to the problem on a 7-point Likert-type scale. Religious fundamentalism was assessed with the short form of the Religious Fundamentalism scale (Altemeyer & Hunsberger, 1992). *Study 2:* Study materials were identical to those of Study 1, except that the target groups were changed to never-married mothers and students.

ASSESSMENT OF OUTCOME VARIABLES   *Study 1:* Participants were asked to what extent they would endorse each of three helping styles: personal change, direct assistance, and empowerment. The personal change style is characterized by the belief that the solution to the problem is to change the person or the group with the problem. The direct assistance style is characterized by the belief that the solution to the problem is to deal directly with the problem at hand (i.e., "The government should provide funding for the creation of jobs"). The empowerment style is characterized by the belief that the solution to the problem is for individuals to accept that they caused the problem and to seek a solution through a recognized authority. *Study 2*: Study materials were identical to Study 1.

MAIN RESULTS   *Study 1*: For participants with the homosexual target group, religious fundamentalism was significantly negatively correlated with the belief that the target group promoted their values, $r = -.47$, $p < .001$. That is, participants high in religious fundamentalism espoused beliefs that were more threatening than promoting. This same relationship did not hold for participants with the Native Canadian target group. For participants with the homosexual target group, religious fundamentalism was significantly positively correlated with attributions of responsibility, $r = .33$, $p < .001$. That is, participants high in religious fundamentalism attributed more of the responsibility for unemployment to the group members than did participants low in religious fundamentalism. This same relationship did not hold for participants with the Native Canadian target group. Because the effect of religious fundamentalism was reduced to nonsignificance when placed in the model with symbolic beliefs, there is some support for the idea that the relationship between high levels of religious fundamentalism and attribution of responsibility is due to the perception that homosexuals threaten values. For both the homosexual target group and the Native Canadian target group, high attributions of responsibility were associated with high endorsement of personal change, low endorsement of direct assistance, and low endorsement of empowerment; $rs = .72$, $-.52$, and $-.69$ for the homosexual target group, $rs = .52$, $-.37$, and $-.44$ for the Native Canadian target group; $ps < .001$. *Study 2*: For participants with the single-mothers target group, religious fundamentalism was significantly negatively correlated with the belief that the target group promoted their values, $r = -.48$, $p < .001$. That is, participants high in religious fundamentalism espoused beliefs that were more threatening than promoting. This same relationship did not hold for participants with the student target group. For participants with the single-mothers target group, religious fundamentalism was significantly positively correlated with attributions of responsibility, $r = .32$, $p < .001$. That is, participants high in religious fundamentalism attributed more of the responsibility for unemployment to the group members than did participants low in religious fundamentalism. This same relationship did not hold for participants with the student target group. Because the effect of religious fundamentalism was reduced to nonsignificance when placed in the model with symbolic beliefs, there is some support for the idea that the relationship between high levels of religious fundamentalism and attribution of responsibility is due to the perception that single mothers threaten values. For the single-mothers target group, high attributions of responsibility were associated with high endorsement of personal change, low endorsement of direct assistance, and low endorsement of empowerment; $rs = .39$, $-.42$, and $-.45$; $ps < .001$. For the students target group, high attributions of responsibility were associated with high endorsement of personal change and low endorsement of empowerment; $rs = .73$, and $-.40$; $ps < .001$. There was not a significant correlation between attributions of responsibility and endorsement of direct assistance.

CONCLUSION   "Attributions of responsibility for the problem predicted endorsement of personal change and rejection of empowerment. Religious fundamentalism is related to endorsement of personal change, at least in part, through value threat and attributions of responsibility for problems."

COMMENTARY   These studies by Jackson and Esses suggest a model for intergroup helping that involves characteristics of the individual (religious fundamentalism), cognitive processes (attributions made under threat to values), and three types of helping (personal change, direct assistance, and empowerment). The model helps to explain why individuals choose to help out-group members in particular ways and in what ways the helper may feel threatened by out-group members. If the helper chooses to help the threatening out-group, he or she is more likely to do so through promoting or enabling the out-group member to make a personal change. The authors correctly suggest that this model is not necessarily generalizable to helping individuals who may or may not be out-group members. Furthermore, they suggest that future research might ask "how different religious value systems influence the way in which people define problems and their solutions."

CORRESPONDENCE   Lynne Jackson, Department of Psychology, Wilfrid Laurier University, Waterloo, Ontario, Canada N2L 3C5

Johnson, R. C., Danko, G. P., Davill, T. J., Bochner, S., Bowers, J. K., Huang, Y.-H., Park, J. Y., Pecjak, V., Rahim, A. R. A., & Pennington, D. (1989). Cross-cultural assessment of altruism and its correlates. *Personality and Individual Differences, 10,* 855–868.

OBJECTIVE   To investigate the personality correlates of giving help, receiving help, and importance of helping in six countries

DESIGN   Cross-sectional survey

SETTING   Universities in Australia, Egypt, Korea, the Republic of China (Taiwan), the United States (Hawaii and Missouri), and Yugoslavia.

PARTICIPANTS   Participants were recruited from universities in Australia (82 participants), Egypt (181 participants), Korea (403 participants), the Republic of China (Taiwan; 224 participants), the United States (Hawaii and Missouri; 216 and 104 participants, respectively), and Yugoslavia (243 participants). The Egyptian participants were from a small city of about 100,000 population, and the Missouri participants were from a town of about 10,000. All other participants were from large urban areas.

ASSESSMENT OF PREDICTOR VARIABLES   Participants completed the Eysenck Personality Questionnaire (EPQ-R; Eysenck, Eysenck, & Barrett, 1985) with subscales for psychoticism, extraversion, neuroticism, and dishonest responding. United States participants completed the Intrinsic-Extrinsic Religiosity Scale (IER; Feagin, 1974; Allport & Ross, 1967). Finally, participants filled out the Dimensions of Conscience Questionnaire designed to assess guilt (failure to fulfill norms of role reciprocity) and shame (status incongruity/embarrassment). Fifteen items for each of shame and guilt were assessed on a 7-point scale, ranging from feeling "not at all badly" to feeling "as bad as I could possibly feel."

ASSESSMENT OF OUTCOME VARIABLES   Participants completed a 56-item scale addressing altruism in the form of helping behaviors (i.e., "holding the elevator for someone"). Participants rated how often they had performed each behavior, how often they had been the recipient of each behavior, and how important each behavior was. The scale included 20 items from the Rushton, Chrisjohn, and Fekken (1981) altruism scale.

MAIN RESULTS   Main effects for sample country and gender were revealed on giving help; $Fs = 24.93$ and 45.68, respectively; $ps < .001$. Similarly, main effects for sample country and gender were revealed on receiving help; $Fs = 20.72$ and 15.68, respectively; $ps < .001$. Only a main effect of sample country was revealed for importance of help, $F = 26.77$, $p < .001$. Interactions between sample country and gender were found for both giving and receiving help, $Fs = 5.62$ and 6.25, respectively; $ps < .001$, but they were caused simply by a low level of giving and receiving help for both males and females in the Taiwan sample. Males report giving more help than females in Australia, Egypt, Korea, and Hawaii, $ts = 2.00$, 5.86, 5.29, and 3.07, respectively; $ps < .05$, but males and females reported giving the same amount of help in Taiwan, Missouri, and Yugoslavia. Males report receiving more help than females in Egypt and Korea, $ts = 5.42$, and 3.42, respectively; $ps < .05$, whereas females reported receiving more help than males in Taiwan, $t = 2.33$, $p < .05$. However, males and females reported receiving the same amount of help in Australia, Hawaii, Missouri, and Yugoslavia.

Correlations of personality variables with the three measures of altruism reveal significant findings for guilt, shame, extraversion, and intrinsic religiosity. Guilt is significantly positively related to giving ($rs = .09$ and .22, females and males respectively; $ps < .05$) and to receiving help ($rs = .19$ and .30, females and males respectively; $ps < .001$). As shame increased, propensity to give help ($rs = -.19$ and $-.14$, females and males respectively; $ps < .001$) and to receive help ($rs = -.21$ and $-.23$, females and males respectively; $ps < .001$) decreased while importance of help increased for males ($r = .17$, $p < .001$). The higher in extraversion a participant was, the more likely he or she was to report giving help ($rs = .30$ and .42, females and males respectively; $ps < .001$) and receiving help ($rs = .28$ and .36, females and males respectively; $ps < .001$). The higher in intrinsic religiosity a participant was, the more likely he or she was to report giving help ($rs = .22$ and .40, females and males respectively; $ps < .001$) and receiving help (for males; $r = .35$, $p < .001$), and the higher they rated the importance of help ($rs = .23$ and .30, females and males respectively; $ps < .001$).

CONCLUSION   "Sex differences are present for the altruism scale as a whole, with almost all of the differences showing males to be more altruistic. Guilt is positively correlated with importance of help and tends to be positively correlated with both giving and receiving help, while shame tends to be negatively correlated with both giving and receiving help. Psychoticism, neuroticism, and lie scale scores are generally unrelated to altruism, while extraversion is consistently, positively correlated with both giving and receiving help."

COMMENTARY   Johnson et al.'s expansive cross-cultural study is to be commended for its breadth and replication of previous findings in six countries. The authors note that, like the work of Eagly and Crowley (1986), this work deals primarily with altruistic acts toward strangers or acquaintances, situations in which males are found to report being more helpful, whereas females are typically more helpful toward close relationship partners. Johnson et al. found that guilt, possibly stirred by some sense of social responsibility (Berkowitz & Lutterman, 1968; Bierhoff et al., 1991), was related to both giving and receiving help. Conversely, shame seems to inhibit giving and receiving of help. Individuals who exhibit high levels of shame most likely fear the social repercussions of mistakenly trying to help someone who does not need help or of displaying weakness in asking help for oneself. The positive social effects of guilt and the negative social effects of shame are now well replicated and appear to be quite robust.

CORRESPONDENCE   Ronald C. Johnson, Professor Emeritus, Department of Psychology, College of Social Sciences, University of Hawaii at Manoa, 2430 Campus Road, Honolulu, HI 96822

Kerber, K. W. (1984). The perception of non-emergency helping situations: Cost, rewards, and the altruistic personality. *Journal of Personality 52*, 177–187.

OBJECTIVE   To evaluate individual differences in the perception of nonemergency helping situations

DESIGN   Experiments with questionnaires

SETTING   College of the Holy Cross, Worcester, Massachusetts

PARTICIPANTS   Participants were 132 undergraduates (58 males, 74 females) who participated in return for $2.00.

ASSESSMENT OF PREDICTOR VARIABLES   Participants completed three scales from the Omnibus Personality Inventory: complexity, social extroversion, and altruism (Heist & Yonge, 1968). They also completed the Marlowe-Crowne Social Desirability Scale (Crowne & Marlowe, 1964).

ASSESSMENT OF OUTCOME VARIABLES   Participants were randomly assigned to one of four conditions in which they read scenarios that were either high or low in costs and high or low in rewards. Costs were varied by manipulating the amount of time or money lost. Rewards were varied by manipulating the amount of appreciation, information, or money gained. Participants rated the amount of help they were willing to provide, the perceived costs of helping, and the perceived rewards of helping.

MAIN RESULTS   To examine whether rewards, costs, and altruism affected willingness to help, a $2 \times 2 \times 3$ (Reward $\times$ Cost $\times$ Altruism) analysis of covariance was performed on willingness to help, with social desirability as the covariate. High rewards led to more helping, $M = 5.52$, than did low rewards; $M = 3.83$, $F(1, 119) = 130.48$, $p < .001$. High costs led to less helping, $M = 4.02$, than did low costs; $M = 5.34$, $F(1, 119) = 78.92$, $p < .001$. High altruism led to more helping, $M = 5.01$, than did moderate altruism, $M = 4.92$, and low altruism, $M = 4.10$, $F(2, 119) = 14.02$, $p < .001$. The same analysis of covariance was performed on ratings of perceived rewards and perceived costs. Persons high in altruism perceived higher rewards, $M = 4.79$, than did people with moderate altruism, $M = 3.97$, and low altruism; $M = 3.79$, $F(2, 119) = 9.39$, $p < .01$. Conversely, persons high in altruism perceived fewer costs, $M = 3.31$, than did people with moderate altruism, $M = 3.57$, and low altruism; $M = 3.99$, $F(2, 119) = 5.25$, $p < .01$.

Path analyses revealed significant relationships between rewards and helping; $\beta = .44$; $t(126) = 5.81$, $p < .01$; between costs and helping; $\beta = -.42$; $t(126) = 5.54$, $p < .01$; between altruism and rewards; $\beta = .41$; $t(128) = 3.55$, $p < .01$; between altruism and costs; $\beta = -.37$; $t(128) = 3.42$, $p < .01$; between sex and altruism; $\beta = .21$; $t(129) = 2.69$, $p < .01$; and between social desirability and altruism; $\beta = .37$; $t(129) = 4.64$, $p < .01$.

CONCLUSION   "Altruism influences willingness to help indirectly through its effects on the perception of rewards and costs, while approval motivation and the sex of the subject have their primary effects on responses to the altruism scale."

COMMENTARY   Kerber's study shows an important link between dispositional altruism and helping through the cognitive interpretation of the situation. Persons high in dispositional altruism view help-giving situations as more rewarding and less costly than persons lower in altruism This is an important clue to the mechanisms by which dispositional altruism may lead to increased helping. Furthermore, this study shows clearly the relatively more distant link of gender and social desirability to dispositional altruism.

CORRESPONDENCE   None available

Korsgaard, M. A., Meglino, B. M., & Lester, S. W. (1996). The effect of other-oriented values on decision making: A test of propositions of a theory of concern for others in organizations. *Organizational Behavior & Human Decision Processes, 68*(3), 234–245.

OBJECTIVE   To examine the relationship between other-oriented values, value placed on personal outcome, and engaging cognition about costs and benefits

DESIGN   Two experiments with repeated-measures mixed design

SETTING   University of South Carolina

PARTICIPANTS   *Study 1:* Participants were 70 undergraduate business students enrolled in an introductory management class. They received course credit for their participation.

Study 2: Participants were 161 undergraduate business students enrolled in an introductory management class. They received course credit for their participation.

ASSESSMENT OF PREDICTOR VARIABLES   *Study 1:* Concern for others was measured with the Concern for Others subscale of the Comparative Emphasis Scale (Ravlin & Meglino, 1987a, b). Concern for others is the extent to which an individual places emphasis on being helpful to others and cooperative. It is related to dispositional empathy (Davis, 1980). *Study 2:* As in Study 1, participants completed the Concern for Others subscale. Participants were then randomly assigned to view a videotape designed to induce positive arousal or relaxation.

ASSESSMENT OF OUTCOME VARIABLES   *Studies 1 and 2:* Participants responded to several questions assessing their decision-making processes. Two variables assessed level of payoff and level of risk. Each question was of the format, "What is the most you would be willing to pay for a lottery ticket with a ____ chance of winning $____?" The three probabilities of winning presented were 10%, 50%, and 90%. The three levels of payoff were $10, $100, and $300. The attractiveness of each choice was measured by the amount of money the participant was willing to spend for each of the fictitious lottery tickets.

MAIN RESULTS   *Study 1:* Participants low in concern for others were willing to pay more for the lottery tickets, $M = 24.91$, than were participants high in concern for others, $M = 16.84$; $F = 4.44$, $p < .05$. There was an interaction between concern for others and level of payoff, $F = 22.82$, $p < .01$, such that in comparison to participants with high concern for others, participants with low concern for others were willing to risk more money as the level of payoff increased. Furthermore, there was an interaction between concern for others and level of risk, $F = 3.40$, $p < .05$, such that in comparison to participants with high concern for others, participants with low concern for others were willing to risk more money as the probability of winning increased. *Study 2:* The impact of concern for others on attractiveness of the gamble was moderated by positive affect arousal, $F = 4.46$, $p < .05$. The impact of concern for others was significant only in the positive arousal condition. In the positive arousal condition, participants low in concern for others were willing to risk more money, $M = 24.30$, than participants high in concern for others, $M = 14.60$. In the nonaroused condition, there was little difference between participants with high and low concern for others on amount of money risked. Parallel results were found in a significant three-way interaction between concern for others, level of payoff, and positive affect arousal, $F = 3.49$, $p < .05$. The interaction of concern for others and payoff was significant only in the positive arousal condition (positive arousal: $F = 3.39$, $p < .05$; nonarousal: $F = 1.24$, *ns*). In the positive arousal condition, the payoff had a stronger impact on willingness to spend money for participants with low concern for others than for participants with high concern for others.

CONCLUSION   "Persons who were high in the value of concern for others placed less importance on personal outcomes and were less disposed to engage in deliberate rational computations."

COMMENTARY   Korsgaard et al. (1996) investigated two variables related to altruism in opposite ways—concern for others and importance of personal outcomes. Presumably an altruistic person would be high on concern for others and low on importance of personal outcomes, as indicated by this study and by others (Batson et al., 1986; Carlo et al., 1991; Cialdini et al., 1997). Concern for others is conceptually related to Davis's (1980) Empathic Concern, but whereas empathic concern is a trait measured in absolute amounts, concern for others is measured as relative to other values and traits in the person's life (fairness, achievement, etc.). The importance of this study lies in the differences in cognitive processing utilized by the participants who are high and low in concern for others. These individuals did not just act differently in their decision making; they got to the behavior by different means. This leads one to wonder whether the individual differences between altruistic and nonaltruistic individuals is based on differences in cognitive processes and what role those cognitive processes play in combination with personality and environment to produce altruistic behavior.

CORRESPONDENCE M. Audrey Korsgaard, The Darla Moore School of Business, University of South Carolina, Columbia, SC 29208

Korsgaard, M. A., Meglino, B. M., & Lester, S. W. (1997). Beyond helping: Do other-oriented values have broader implications in organizations? *Journal of Applied Psychology, 82*(1), 160–177.

OBJECTIVE To determine whether the value of concern for others is related to sensitivity to social information and helping others

DESIGN *Study 1*: Cross-sectional survey. *Studies 2 and 3*: Experiments

SETTING University of South Carolina

PARTICIPANTS *Study 1*: Participants were 64 first-year students in a Masters of Business Administration program. The average age of participants was 25 years old; 70% were male and 30% were female. *Study 2*: Participants were 106 undergraduate business students from management classes. Participants were matched on scores on the Concern for Others subscale, then randomly assigned to conditions. *Study 3*: Participants were 55 undergraduate business students from management classes who volunteered to participate.

ASSESSMENT OF PREDICTOR VARIABLES *Study 1*: All participants received naturally occurring feedback on a classroom presentation. The professor's evaluation of each participant on each of 25 items (i.e., content, delivery style, etc.) represents the favorableness of feedback variable. Scores ranged from 77 to 98 with a mean of 88.6. Five to ten days following receipt of feedback, participants completed a questionnaire addressing Concern for Others, a subscale of the Comparative Emphasis Scale (Ravlin & Meglino, 1987a, b). *Study 2*: Participants completed a proofreading task at the beginning of a class session. At the end of the class session participants were randomly assigned to receive high- or low-specificity feedback: "You should be more sensitive to wrong word errors" or "You performed very well." They then completed the Concern for Others subscale and a second proofreading task. *Study 3*: Participants first completed the Concern for Others subscale. Then they were instructed to make a series of 10 daily decisions as if they were managers in a company. Next, participants were randomly assigned to receive feedback indicating that they had made either good management decisions ("above average") or poor management decisions ("below average").

ASSESSMENT OF OUTCOME VARIABLES *Study 1*: The postfeedback questionnaire also contained items addressing satisfaction with feedback (Giles & Mossholder, 1990) and acceptance of feedback (Ilgen, Fisher, & Taylor, 1979). Acceptance of feedback contains items addressing agreement with feedback and incorporation of feedback into self-view. *Study 2*: Number of lines proofread and number of errors detected were the outcome variables. *Study 3*: As in Study 1, the postfeedback questionnaire also contained items addressing satisfaction with feedback (Giles & Mossholder, 1990) and acceptance of feedback (Ilgen et al., 1979). Acceptance of feedback contains items addressing agreement with feedback and incorporation of feedback into self-view. Finally, participants completed a second set of 10 management decisions.

MAIN RESULTS *Study 1*: For participants high in concern for others, satisfaction was not related to favorableness of feedback, $r = .03$, *ns*, whereas for participants low in concern for others, self-ratings of satisfaction were directly related to the favorableness of feedback, $r = .48$, $p < .05$. For participants high in concern for others, self-ratings were not related to favorableness of feedback, $r = -.04$, ns, whereas for participants low in concern for others, self-ratings were directly related to the favorableness of feedback, $r = .62$, $p < .05$. Specifically, participants with low concern for others rated themselves higher if they received favorable feedback, $M = 3.26$, than if they received unfavorable feedback, $M = 2.91$. *Study 2:* There was an interaction between concern for others and specificity of feedback on both number of lines proofread, $\beta = -2.80$; $t = -.04$, $p < .05$, and number of errors identified, $\beta = -3.43$; $t = -2.30$, $p < .05$. For participants high in concern for others, specific feedback led to fewer lines proofread and fewer errors identified. For participants low in concern for others, specific feedback led to more lines proofread and no difference in number of errors identified. *Study 3:* The three-way interaction of concern for others, valence of feedback, and time, $F(1, 50) = 4.07$, $p < .05$. Examining the effects of concern for others and trial within each level of feedback revealed that the two-way interaction of concern for others and trial was stronger in the favorable feedback condition, $F(1, 25) = 3.30$, $p < .05$, than in the unfavorable feedback condition, $F(1, 25) = 1.10$, ns. That is, concern for others was more likely to be associated with changes in participants' management decisions when the participants received favorable feedback (low concern for others mean change $= .30$, high concern for others mean change $= .07$). The opposite pattern held when participants received unfavorable feedback (low concern for others mean change $= .14$, high concern for others mean change $= .29$).

CONCLUSION   "We found that individual's endorsement of this value [concern for others] was related to predictable differences in their affective reaction, acceptance, and behavioral response to social information in the form of feedback on their performance."

COMMENTARY   Building on previous work surrounding concern for others (Korsgaard et al., 1996), Korsgaard et al.(1997) continued to investigate the relationship between concern for others as a principal moral value and affective reaction, acceptance, and behavioral response. Participants high in concern for others were not swayed by favorable or unfavorable feedback to change their satisfaction or self-rating. Their reactions to situations were not contingent on whatever costs or benefits they might accrue in the situation. Like true altruism, this individual difference of placing concern for others as a high value directs behavior away from the self to the demands of the situation. As in the previous study, the difference in cognitive processes of participants with high and low concern for others is highlighted.

CORRESPONDENCE   M. Audrey Korsgaard, The Darla Moore School of Business, University of South Carolina, Columbia, SC 29208

> Leak, G. K. (1993). Relationship between religious orientation and love styles, sexual attitudes, and sexual behaviors. *Journal of Psychology and Theology, 21*(4), 315–318.

OBJECTIVE   To investigate the relationships among love styles, religious orientation, sexual attitudes, and sexual behaviors

DESIGN   Cross-sectional survey

SETTING   Creighton University

PARTICIPANTS   Participants were 84 students from introductory and upper-division psychology classes. Fifty-six were female and 28 were male. The mean age was 19.6 years. Seventy-five percent of the participants were Catholic, and the remaining participants came from various Protestant denominations.

ASSESSMENT OF PREDICTOR VARIABLES   Religious orientation was measured by the Allport and Ross (1967) Intrinsic and Extrinsic Religious Orientation Scales, as well as the Quest Scale (Batson & Schoenrade, 1991). Sexual behavior was measured with the 16-item version of the Sexual Experiences Questionnaire (Gerrard & Gibbons, 1982). Sexual attitudes were measured by the Sexual Attitudes Questionnaire (Hendrick, Hendrick, Slapion-Foote, & Foote, 1985).

ASSESSMENT OF OUTCOME VARIABLES   Participants completed a 42-item love styles scale. The scale addressed each of the six theoretical types of love: eros (romantic, passionate love), ludus (game-playing love), storge (compassionate love), mania (possessive, dependent love), pragma (logical, practical love), and agape (selfless, religious love). Greater endorsement of items was indicated by marking lower numbers on the scale.

MAIN RESULTS   Participants high in extrinsic religiosity were more likely to endorse sexually permissive and instrumental attitudes; $rs = .39$ and $.41$, respectively; $ps < .01$. On the other hand, participants high in intrinsic religiosity were less likely to endorse sexually permissive attitudes and more likely to address sexually conventional attitudes; $rs = -.35$ and $.25$, respectively; $ps < .05$. The love styles of mania and pragma were associated with extrinsic religiosity; $rs = .40$ and $.37$, respectively; $ps < .01$. The storge love style was associated with intrinsic religiosity, $r = .33$, $p < .01$. The agape love style was not related to any of the measures in this study.

CONCLUSION   Intrinsic religiousness, extrinsic religiousness, and sexuality are unrelated to the agape love style.

COMMENTARY   Unlike the Hendrick and Hendrick (1987) study, this study showed no relationship between religiousness and agape love style. This inconsistency in the literature would indicate that more research is needed to clarify the relationship between religiosity and altruism as represented by the agape love style. This is of interest to altruism research, because agape is typically defined in terms of altruism.

CORRESPONDENCE   Gary K. Leak, Ph.D., Department of Psychology, Creighton University, 2400 California Plaza, Omaha, NE 68178

Lefcourt, H. M., & Shepherd, R. S. (1995). Organ donation, authoritarianism, and perspective taking humor. *Journal of Research in Personality, 29*(1), 121–138.

OBJECTIVE   To investigate the effect of the personality variables authoritarianism and perspective-taking humor on the altruistic behavior of organ donation

DESIGN   Two cross-sectional surveys

SETTING   University of Waterloo

PARTICIPANTS   *Study 1*: Participants were 60 undergraduate university students. They volunteered, but the study also served as a laboratory for their course in personality; 45 participants were female and 15 were male. *Study 2*: Participants were 277 undergraduate university students from introductory and personality psychology courses; 155 participants were female and 122 were male.

ASSESSMENT OF PREDICTOR VARIABLES   *Study 1*: Thoughts, feelings, and behaviors related to death were measured with the Death Anxiety Scale (Temper, 1970). Participants also answered questions concerning the avoidance of activities that cause anxiety about death (Avoidance of Ontological Confrontation with Death Scale; Thauberger, Cleland, & Thauberger, 1979). Participants described how they felt when thinking about their own deaths on the Death Affect Checklist (McNair, Lorr, & Droppleman, 1971). Finally, participants completed the Situational Humor Response Questionnaire (Martin & Lefcourt, 1984) to assess humor or amusability. This last measure was used because it is thought that persons who use humor to help cope with negative events are less likely to suffer negative emotions when thinking about their own mortality. *Study 2*: Participants completed self-report measures of right-wing authoritarianism (Altemeyer, 1981, 1988) and humor

(Situational Humor Response Questionnaire) in mass testing situations. In a later laboratory session participants rated several of Gary Larson's "Far Side" cartoons on funniness (Cartoon Measure of Appreciation) and were then asked to describe what made the cartoon funny. Responses were coded for understanding of the humor (Cartoon Measure of Comprehension) on a scale of 1 (no or little understanding) to 3 (understanding of the human behavior being lampooned). The product of appreciation and comprehension was calculated to form the scale measure called the Cartoon Measure of Perspective Taking Humor.

ASSESSMENT OF OUTCOME VARIABLES   *Study 1*: Participants completed the Death Behavior Questionnaire (Shepherd, 1989) to assess readiness to confront death-related situations or tasks, such as organ and body donation. *Study 2*: Organ donor status was assessed by recording information from participants' drivers' licenses as a part of the laboratory portion of the study.

MAIN RESULTS   *Study 1*: The single item assessing organ donation was not significantly related to any of the other measures. However, overall scores on the Death Behavior Questionnaire were related to less avoidance of death, $r = .57$, $p < .001$, more humor and amusability, $r = .26$, $p < .05$, and fewer negative feelings about death (Death Affect Checklist $r = -.35$, Death Anxiety Scale $r = -.31$; $ps < .05$). *Study 2*: Approximately 30% of the participants in this study had signed the portion of the drivers' license indicating willingness to be an organ donor. Right-wing authoritarianism was negatively correlated with each of the humor measures; $r = -.17$ for Situational Humor Response; $r = -.30$ for Cartoon Measure of Perspective Taking Humor, $ps < .01$. All of the humor measures were also associated with having signed for organ donation; $r = -.20$ for Situational Humor Response; $r = -.18$ for Cartoon Measure of Perspective Taking Humor, $ps < .01$. However, the relationship with the Cartoon Measure of Appreciation is particularly small; $r = -.12$, $p < .10$. In a hierarchical regression analysis on organ donation, authoritarianism was entered first, followed by the Cartoon Measure of Perspective Taking Humor and the Situational Humor Response Questionnaire and the associated interactions. Authoritarianism accounted for 6.7% of the variance, $F = 19.84$, $p < .001$, and situational humor accounted for 2.2% of the variance, $F = 6.48$, $p < .025$, in organ donation. Analyses also revealed a significant interaction between authoritarianism and the Cartoon Measure of Perspective Taking Humor, $F = 4.34$, $p < .05$, such that for participants high in authoritarianism, more participants with high humor scores had signed for organ donation (33%) than participants with low humor scores (11%).

CONCLUSION   "Our data support the connotation that for some people, volunteering as an organ donor can arouse negative feelings associated with mortality, which in turn leave them refractory to appeals for organ donation and likely to avoid simple acts like signing the organ donation form attached to their driver's license. [Participants] who were high in authoritarianism and low in perspective taking humor were the least likely to have signed their organ donation forms."

COMMENTARY   Lefcourt and Shepherd's (1995) study reveals that elements of this particular kind of altruist behavior, organ donation, were related to situation-specific elements (i.e., willingness to think about death). Also, a combination of personality variables—authoritarianism and perspective-taking humor—contributed to an interaction on altruistic behavior beyond their main effects. For those participants high in authoritarianism, the ability to engage in perspective-taking humor may have helped them to see beyond the grim situation and engage in altruistic behavior. One wonders whether such highly specific interactions of personality variables, such as authoritarianism and perspective-taking humor, are specific to the organ donation situation or whether they would apply in other contexts, particularly those in which the altruistic behavior involves engaging in extremely unpleasant cognition.

CORRESPONDENCE   Professor Emeritus Herbert M. Lefcourt, Department of Psychology, 200 University Ave. W., University of Waterloo, Waterloo, Ontario, Canada N2L 3G1

Leung, J. J., & Foster, S. F. (1985). Helping the elderly: A study on altruism in children. *Child Study Journal, 15*(4), 293–309.

OBJECTIVE   To examine the effects of preaching, recipient deservingness, personality attractiveness, and participant gender on children's altruism toward the elderly

DESIGN   Experimental scenario study

SETTING   Five Roman Catholic schools in a western Canadian city

PARTICIPANTS   One hundred ninety-five fifth- and sixth-grade students participated in the study. In fifth grade, 52 students were male and 52 were female. In the sixth grade, 39 students were male and 53 were female.

ASSESSMENT OF PREDICTOR VARIABLES   Participants were randomly assigned to one of eight experimental conditions. In manipulation of the "preaching" variable, the children were either exhorted to help the elderly, who were described as less fortunate, or given a lesson addressing why the elderly may not need help. Children then read a story about a senior citizen (Mr. Brown) that manipulated two variables, deservingness and personality. Deservingness was manipulated by describing Mr. Brown either as having a refrigerator that he had saved for which then accidentally burned out or as having a refrigerator that he had received as a gift which burned out due to Mr. Brown's carelessness. Personality attractiveness was manipulated by describing Mr. Brown as a nice man who treated children kindly or as a mean man who was unsympathetic and threatening to children.

ASSESSMENT OF OUTCOME VARIABLES   The children were each given 50¢ in nickels, which they were allowed to either keep for themselves or donate to help the elderly Mr. Brown. The amount each child pledged and then subsequently donated were measures of helping. Participants were also asked how many half-page stories they would write to cheer the older man.

MAIN RESULTS   On all three outcome variables, girls were more generous than boys for pledged stories, $F(1, 179) = 7.31$, $p < .01$, pledged donations, $F(1, 179) = 5.79$, $p < .02$, and actual donations, $F(1, 179) = 4.45$, $p < .04$. Although questions about the stories indicated that the children understood the stories and that the manipulations were effective, preaching, deservingness, and personality attractiveness did not affect pledged or actual helping. Means on each of dependent variables were high regardless of condition. On average, 1.93 stories were pledged, 22.51¢ was pledged, and 20.98¢ was actually donated.

CONCLUSION   The children were uniformly generous to a needy older adult regardless of experimental condition. Girls were more generous than boys in both pledged and actual behavior.

COMMENTARY   Leung and Foster's (1985) study investigated whether situational variables, the personality of others, and exhortation would affect the way children responded to a needy person. They demonstrated only that children understand the norm of social responsibility. That is, they understand the benefit of helping those who need help, regardless of circumstances. Though the manipulation was effective, it could have been stronger—perhaps by presenting a video or audio appeal. Gender differences have been found in other studies in which it was investigated (Penner & Finkelstein, 1998; Carlo et al., 1991), with females showing greater altruism or the effects of gender on altruism being situationally dependent. Attempting to explain the gender differences in altruistic behavior in this study would be an exercise in attempting to unconfound the roles of socialization and biological drives. Whether the actions of the girls and boys in Leung and Foster's (1985) study were driven by nature or nurture is impossible to determine without more formal investigation of gender differences in altruism.

CORRESPONDENCE   None available

Litvack-Miller, W., McDougall, D., & Romney, D. M. (1997). The structure of empathy during middle childhood and its relationship to prosocial behavior. *Genetic, Social, and General Psychology Monographs, 123*(3), 303–324.

OBJECTIVE   To investigate the structure and development of dispositional empathy in children and its relationship to altruism

DESIGN   Experiment with questionnaires

SETTING   Five religious schools in Calgary, Alberta, Canada

PARTICIPANTS   Participants were 478 students from five schools in a Canadian city. Of the participants from the second grade, 119 were male and 98 were female. Of the participants from the fourth grade, 57 participants were male and 79 were female. Of the participants from the sixth grade, 60 participants were male and 65 were female.

ASSESSMENT OF PREDICTOR VARIABLES   Dispositional empathy was measured with a child-adapted version of the Davis (1980) Interpersonal Reactivity Index, which has four subscales: perspective taking, fantasy, empathic concern, and personal distress. Researchers cued situational empathy in half of the classes of children by asking them to "Watch this film not only with your eyes and ears, but also with your hearts and imaginations" and to imagine themselves in the sad situation of the foster children. The other half of the children were only told that they would be watching a film about foster families and that they would later be asked about the film. All children watched the same film.

ASSESSMENT OF OUTCOME VARIABLES   Altruism was measured in four ways. First, it was measured by the children's self-reports of how they would respond to each of six vignettes describing another person needing help. Second, teachers rated the children's tendencies to spontaneously comfort, help, share, and cooperate with peers. Following the film, the children were given an opportunity to pledge time and donate money to help the children. The children were each given 50¢ in nickels, which they were allowed to either keep for themselves or donate to help foster children. The amount of money each child subsequently donated was the third measure of helping. The children were also asked how much time they would be willing to volunteer to help with fund-raising for the foster children, a fourth measure of helping.

MAIN RESULTS   A multivariate analysis of variance (MANOVA) of age and gender on the four empathy subscales revealed main effects for grade, $F(10, 934) = 2.95, p < .001$, and gender, $F(5, 466) = 6.16, p < .001$. Sixth-grade students reported more empathic concern than did second- and fourth-grade students. Grade had no effect on the other empathy measures. Girls consistently scored higher than boys on perspective taking, $M = 3.34$ vs. 3.13, empathic concern, $M = 4.17$ vs. 3.91, and personal distress, $M = 3.20$ vs. 3.00, but there was no difference on fantasy.

To investigate the relationship between the dispositional empathy measures and the altruism measures, stepwise regression analyses were performed. Fantasy and personal distress did not significantly predict any of the altruism measures. Perspective taking predicted a significant portion of the variance in teacher ratings of comforting others, $\beta = .186; t = 2.66, p < .01$, monetary donations, $\beta = .193; t = 4.24, p < .01$, and scores on self-reported altruism vignettes, $\beta = .253$; $t = 3.04$, $p < .01$. Empathic concern predicted a significant portion of the variance in teacher ratings of comforting others, $\beta = .238$; $t = 3.39$, $p < .01$, helping, $\beta = .218$; $t = 3.04$, $p < .01$, sharing, $\beta = .254$; $t = 3.58$, $p < .01$, cooperation, $\beta = .218$; $t = 3.04$, $p < .01$, monetary donations, $\beta = .204$; $t = 4.50$, $p < .01$, and scores on self-reported altruism vignettes, $\beta = .134$; $t = 3.04$, $p < .01$. There were no significant effects of empathy instructions before the film on measures of altruism.

CONCLUSION   "Girls were more empathic than boys, and older children showed more empathic concern than younger children. Only empathic concern and perspective taking were significant predictors of prosocial behavior."

COMMENTARY   A relationship between dispositional empathy and prosocial behavior has been found in adults (Eisenberg, Fabes, et al., 1991; Eisenberg, Miller, et al., 1989). This study is important for its investigation of the developmental roots of the empathy-altruism link in children. It seems that the empathic concern and perspective-taking aspects of dispositional empathy are related to prosocial behavior but the personal distress and fantasy aspects of dispositional empathy are not. The expression of empathic distress is one of the first vicarious emotional experiences a child has, as early as the first year of life (Hoffman, 1975, 1977). Yet this type of empathy appears unrelated to prosocial behavior in these children. Also, in contrast to Batson's studies annotated previously (Batson, Batson, et al., 1995; Batson, Klein, et al., 1995; Batson & Weeks, 1996), the instruction to take the perspective of the needy other was not sufficient to influence the empathy or altruistic behavior in these children. However, it is important to note that Batson's manipulations of empathy were administered individually to participants and probably had a stronger impact. Litvack-Miller and colleagues did find that the capacity for empathic concern increases with age. The strength of the relationship between empathy and altruism may increase with age to the type of relationship we see in adults.

CORRESPONDENCE   Daniel McDougall, Department of Educational Psychology, The University of Calgary, Alberta T2N 1N4, Canada

Magee, M., & Hojat, M. (1998). Personality profiles of male and female positive role models in medicine. *Psychological Reports, 82*(2), 547–559.

OBJECTIVE   To examine the personality profiles of physicians nominated as positive role models

DESIGN   Cross-sectional survey

SETTING   Nationwide

PARTICIPANTS   Participants were 188 physicians nominated by the chief executive officers of their affiliated institutions nationwide as positive role models; 164 participants were male and 24 were female. The mean age was 50 years (range 31–86 years). Response rate was 80%.

ASSESSMENT OF PREDICTOR VARIABLES   Participants completed the 240-item revised NEO Personality Inventory (Costa & McCrae, 1992). The NEO can be used to distinguish five core personality characteristics, known as the Big Five: Agreeableness, Conscientiousness, Extraversion, Openness to Experience, and Neuroticism. Thirty personality characteristics, including altruism, can also be distinguished from scores on the NEO.

ASSESSMENT OF OUTCOME VARIABLES   Subscales of the NEO measure altruism.

MAIN RESULTS   When compared with national norms for males and females, several differences are found on the Big Five personality factors and the altruism personality trait. To control for chance findings when conducting multiple comparisons, alpha was set at .01 for the Big Five personality characteristics and .001 for each of the 30 personality traits. Both the male and female positive role models scored above the general population on Conscientiousness. Male role models scored higher than the average male on Agreeableness. Female role models scored higher than the average female on Openness to Experience and Extraversion, but lower than the average female on Neuroticism. Both male and female role models scored higher than the general population on the personality trait of altruism.

CONCLUSION   Physicians nominated by their CEOs as positive role models displayed higher levels of altruism than the general population.

COMMENTARY   The nomination as a "positive role model" may indicate some behavioral altruism that coincides with higher male agreeableness in general and higher male and female altruism in particular. That is, positive role models are not only knowledgeable but also of high character and helpful to their coworkers. It is interesting that these positive role models were high on traits that are generally considered favorable: conscientiousness, and for females, openness, extraversion, and emotional stability. The work of Magee and Hojat (1998) provides a parallel to the work of Ashton et al. (1998), who found that altruism directed toward non-kin, reciprocal altruism, is strongly related to high agreeableness and high emotional stability. The findings from this study must be presented with the caveat that the participants in the study differed from established national norms on the NEO. This deviation could be accounted for by the fact that the participants were all physicians; the difference is not necessarily related to their role-model status.

CORRESPONDENCE   Mike Magee, M.D., Senior Medical Advisor, Pfizer Inc., 235 East 42nd Street, New York, NY 10017-5755, or e-mail (mmagee@pfizer.com)

Mallandain, I., & Davies, M. F. (1994). The colours of love: Personality correlates of love styles. *Personality and Individual Differences, 17*(4), 557–560.

OBJECTIVE   To determine which personality characteristics are associated with love styles

DESIGN   Cross-sectional survey

SETTING   Birkbeck College and Goldsmiths College of the University of London

PARTICIPANTS   Participants were 120 undergraduate and graduate students at Birkbeck College and Goldsmiths College. There were an equal number of male and female participants. The mean age was 30.67 years (range 18–56 years). Sixty-two percent of the participants were currently in a relationship, and 23% were married.

ASSESSMENT OF PREDICTOR VARIABLES   Self-esteem was measured by the Cheek and Buss (1981) self-esteem scale. Emotionality was measured by the Buss and Plomin (1984) emotionality scale. Impulsivity was measured by the Buss and Plomin (1975) impulsivity scale.

ASSESSMENT OF OUTCOME VARIABLES   Participants completed a 42-item love styles scale. The scale addressed each of the six theoretical types of love: eros (romantic, passionate love), ludus (game-playing love), storge (compassionate love), mania (possessive, dependent love), pragma (logical, practical love), and agape (selfless, religious love). Greater endorsement of items was indicated by marking lower numbers on the scale.

MAIN RESULTS   Females scored higher than males on the storge love style, $Ms = 25.32$ vs. 22.38; $F(1, 101) = 6.03$, $p < .02$, but lower than males on agape love style, $Ms = 20.88$ vs. 23.38; $F(1, 101) = 6.00$, $p < .02$. Self-esteem was significantly negatively correlated with mania, $r = -.38$, storge, $r = -.26$, and agape, $r = -.18$. Self-esteem was positively correlated with eros, $r = .19$. Neither emotionality nor impulsivity was significantly correlated with storge or agape.

CONCLUSION "The results of the study provide some support for the hypothesis that love styles have trait-like characteristics. On the other hand, certain discrepancies between predictions and findings suggest that state rather than trait factors need to be taken into account when considering individual differences in styles of loving."

COMMENTARY Whereas Hendrick and Hendrick's (1987) and Leak's (1993) studies investigate the relationship of love styles, including agape, to religiosity, Mallandain and Davies (1994) investigate personality correlates of the love styles. Caution should be used in interpreting the small, though significant, negative correlation between agape love style and self-esteem. There is no theoretical or logical reason why selfless, loving people should have lower self-esteem. More research is needed on a diverse participant population to clarify and establish these results. In fact, it contradicts the authors' own findings concerning emotional stability and Ashton et al.'s (1998) work on altruism and the Big Five personality traits.

CORRESPONDENCE Martin F. Davies, Department of Psychology, Goldsmiths College, University of London, New Cross, London SE14 6NW, England

McAdams, D. P., Hoffman, B. J., Mansfield, E. D., & Day, R. (1996). Themes of agency and communion in significant autobiographical scenes. *Journal of Personality, 64*(2), 339–377.

OBJECTIVE To investigate themes of agency and communion in autobiographical memories as they relate to personality, social motives, and daily goals

DESIGN *Studies 1 and 3*: Cross-sectional survey. *Study 2*: Interviews

SETTING *Study 1*: Loyola University. *Studies 2 and 3*: A midwestern city

PARTICIPANTS *Study 1*: Participants were 130 undergraduate students enrolled in introductory psychology classes in a midwestern university. They received course credit for their participation. Of the participants, 67 were female and 63 were male. *Study 2*: Participants consisted of 86 adults. They were recruited through newspaper advertisements, school contacts, and community organizations and paid $50 for their participation. Of the participants, 50 were female and 36 were male. The mean age was 43.89 years (range 22–72 years). *Study 3*: Participants were 152 adults living in a small midwestern city. Of the participants, 80 were female and 72 were male. The sample was divided into distinct age groups. The "young" adults' age range was 22 to 27 years. The "midlife" adults' age range was 37 to 42 years. The "older" adults' age range was 67 to 72 years

ASSESSMENT OF PREDICTOR VARIABLES *Study 1*: The Thematic Apperception Test (TAT; Atkinson, 1958) was administered to participants in the standard group administration format. In the TAT, participants were given 5 minutes to write an imaginative story about each of six pictures of people (i.e., two people sitting on a park bench). Each participant's stories were scored for power, achievement, and intimacy motivation. *Study 2*: In the first session of the study, the participants were administered the TAT as in Study 1. *Study 3*: Participants generated a list of personal strivings, or goals and objectives they were trying to accomplish. The lists were coded for achievement, power, and intimacy motivation. They also completed the Personality Research Form (PRF; Jackson, 1984), a measure of the personality needs of achievement, dominance, affiliation, and nurturance.

ASSESSMENT OF OUTCOME VARIABLES *Study 1*: Participants were asked to write a description of their earliest memory and a life-story high point, or peak experience. These descriptions were coded by researchers for presence or absence (0 or 1) of themes of agency and communion. Each of four elements was coded for each theme, with a score range of 0 to 4 for each theme. Agency themes were self-mastery, status, achievement/responsibility, and empowerment. Communion themes were love/friendship, dialogue, care/help, and community. The themes of agency and communion come from work by Wiggins and Broughton (1985). *Study 2*: In a second session, participants were interviewed using the McAdams (1985, 1993) life-story interview. Each participant described his or her life as if it were a story or book with chapters, setting, scenes, and characters. In the interview, participants were asked to describe (1) a peak experience, (2) their earliest recollection, (3) an event in which they experienced a life transition, (4) a memorable event from childhood, (5) a memorable event from adolescence, (6) a memorable event from adulthood, and (7) one other "significant scene" from any point in their lives. Two coders scored transcriptions of the interviews for themes of agency and communion. *Study 3*: Participants were asked to write a description of their earliest memory, a life-story high point, or peak experience, and an event in which they experienced a life transition. These descriptions were coded by researchers for themes of agency and communion.

MAIN RESULTS   *Study 1*: Total agency summed across themes and memories was positively correlated with achievement motivation and power motivation, $rs = .40$ and .27, respectively; $ps < .01$. Power and achievement motives were uncorrelated with the communal themes, except that love/friendship showed a positive correlation with power, $r = .24$, $p < .05$. Total communion summed across themes and memories was positively correlated with intimacy motivation, $r = .47$, $p < .01$. *Study 2*: Total agency summed across themes and memories was positively correlated with achievement motivation and power motivation, $rs = .39$ and .29, respectively; $ps < .01$. These total correlations were driven by correlations of empowerment with power and achievement motives, $rs = .28$ and .29, respectively; $ps < .01$, and the correlation of self-mastery with achievement motivation, $r = .32$, $p < .01$. None of the other agency themes were significantly correlated with achievement or power motivations. Total communion summed across themes and memories was positively correlated with intimacy motivation, $r = 53$, $p < .01$. *Study 3*: Total agency summed across themes and memories was positively correlated with achievement motivation, power motivation, PRF Achievement, and PRF Dominance; $rs = .49$, .20, .17, and .29, respectively; $ps < .05$. Total communion summed across themes and memories was positively correlated with intimacy motivation, PRF Affiliation, and PRF nurturance; $rs = .39$, .21, and .27, respectively; $ps < .05$.

CONCLUSION   "The three studies provide empirical support for a thematic coherence in personality across the arenas of autobiographical memories, social motives, and daily goals."
COMMENTARY   McAdams and colleagues (1996) demonstrate individual differences in autobiographical memories based on two themes: a self-oriented agency approach and an other-oriented communal approach. These themes parallel the social motives of achievement motivation and intimacy motivation, respectively. In Study 3, communion is also related to affiliation and nurturance from self-report questionnaires. The communal approach seems to have some general quality that is consistent with Agreeableness from other studies (Ashton et al., 1998; Axelrod et al., 1997). Furthermore, the data could be reinterpreted to address aspects of participant descriptions of the ideal self (agency approach) and the ought self (communal approach; Bybee et al., 1997). Further research linking agency and communal orientations to other well-known psychosocial constructs seems important.
CORRESPONDENCE   Dan P. McAdams, Program in Human Development and Social Policy, Northwestern University, 2115 North Campus Drive, Evanston, IL 60208-2610

McNeely, B. L., & Meglino, B. M. (1994). The role of dispositional and situational antecedents in prosocial behavior: An examination of the intended beneficiaries of prosocial behavior. *Journal of Applied Psychology, 79,* 836–844.

OBJECTIVE   To distinguish between the antecedents of altruism toward an individual versus altruism toward an organization

DESIGN   Cross-sectional survey and ratings by multiple acquaintances of participants

SETTING   A southeastern university

PARTICIPANTS   Participants were 100 female departmental and administrative secretaries at a university. Secretaries' average age was 41 years old, and their average tenure with the university was 8.9 years. All participants were included in a raffle for free dinners for two as incentive for participation.

ASSESSMENT OF PREDICTOR VARIABLES   Job satisfaction was measured with a single item rated on a 7-point scale, from 1 ("strongly disagree") to 7 ("strongly agree"): "Considering all aspects of my job, I would say that I am very satisfied with my job." Perceived reward equity was measured with a single item rated on a 7-point scale, from 1 ("strongly disagree") to 7 ("strongly agree"): "I feel that job rewards, salary increases, and such are equitably and fairly distributed among employees in this organization." Perceived recognition for desirable behavior was measured with six items rated on a 5-point scale, from 1 ("strongly disagree") to 5 ("strongly agree"). Two items represented each of the three types of prosocial behavior: institutional, individual, and role prescribed (i.e., "If I am seen doing helpful things for others which are not part of the job requirements, it is likely that I will receive a pay increase"). Placing value on concern for others was measured with the Comparative Emphasis Scale (Ravlin & Meglino, 1987b). Empathic concern was assessed with the empathic concern subscale of the Davis (1980) Interpersonal Reactivity Index.

ASSESSMENT OF OUTCOME VARIABLES   The prosocial behavior of each participant was rated by her supervisor and at least one other person in her department who was familiar with her behavior. The response rate for the raters was 80%. Twenty percent of the raters were immediate supervisors, 32% were faculty, 30% were coworkers, and 18% were administrators, graduate students, and others. Three types of prosocial behaviors were rated: prosocial institutional behavior (i.e., "Offers ideas to improve the functioning of the department"), role-prescribed prosocial behavior (i.e., "Completes work requested as soon as possible"), and prosocial individual behavior (i.e., "Collects money for flowers for sick coworkers or funerals"). All items were rated on a 5-point scale, from 1 ("never does this") to 5 ("always does this"). Items were summed to form single measures of each type of prosocial behavior for each rater. Then ratings for each of the prosocial behaviors were averaged across raters to form the measures of prosocial behavior for each secretary.

MAIN RESULTS   Job satisfaction was significantly positively correlated with both prosocial behavior to the organization, $r = .25$, $p < .01$, and prosocial behavior to the individual, $r = .26$, $p < .01$. The more satisfied the secretaries were with their jobs, the more prosocially they behaved. Empathic concern and valuing concern for others were both significantly positively correlated with prosocial behavior to the individual, $rs = .21$ and .18, respectively; $p < .05$. Perceived reward equity and perceived recognition for desirable behavior were both significantly positively correlated with prosocial behavior to the organization, $rs = .20$ and .30, respectively; $p < .05$. Role-prescribed prosocial behavior was not related to job satisfaction, reward equity, recognition for desirable behavior, or the value of concern for others. However, it was negatively correlated with empathic concern, $r = -.19$, $p < .05$. In regression analyses, both job satisfaction and concern for others/empathic concern made independent contributions to explaining the variance in prosocial behavior to individuals; $R^2s = .07$ and .07, respectively; $ps < .05$. In regression analyses, only reward equity/

recognition for desirable behavior made independent contributions to explaining the variance in prosocial behavior to organizations, $R^2 = .10$, $p < .05$. Job satisfaction did not make a unique contribution to prosocial behavior to organizations.

CONCLUSION   "The relationship between empathy and prosocial individual behavior in this study is comparable to relationships involving empathy and various types of prosocial behavior outside of work." Concerning prosocial behavior toward organizations, "Employees probably viewed reward equity and recognition for desirable behavior as benefits provided by the organization. Thus, it is not surprising that they would direct their reciprocation efforts to the organization rather than to specific individuals."

COMMENTARY   McNeely and Meglino (1994) highlight the disparity in individual differences related to prosocial behavior directed toward individuals and prosocial behavior directed toward organizations. When the focus is individuals, the dispositions of empathic concern and the value of concern for others are key to prosocial behavior. This is consistent with much of the other research in this bibliography on dispositional empathic concern (e.g., Romer et al., 1986), including Neuberg et al.'s (1997) suggestion that empathic concern may serve an orienting function with respect to altruism. McNeely and Meglino (1994) interpret the role of job satisfaction in individual prosocial behavior as an indicator of a mood effect, an idea which should be investigated further. For prosocial behavior toward organizations, the perceptions that one's organization is fair and that recognition is made for positive behavior invokes the norm of reciprocity—facilitating organizational prosocial behavior. This equity/exchange approach to the situation is far from the communal orientation of the individual prosocial behavior. Therefore, the factors necessary to encourage prosocial behavior in business contexts might be surprisingly different from those necessary for prosocial behavior in personal contexts.

CORRESPONDENCE   Bruce M. Meglino, The Darla Moore School of Business, University of South Carolina, Columbia, SC 29208

Mohan, J., & Bhatia, S. (1987). Altruistic behaviour of engineers and teachers in relation to their personality. *Indian Journal of Applied Psychology, 24*(2), 87–90.

OBJECTIVE   To measure the relationship between altruism and personality of male engineers and teachers

DESIGN   Cross-sectional survey

SETTING   Chandigarh, India

PARTICIPANTS   Participants were 50 adults randomly selected from institutions in Chandigarh. Twenty-five were engineers and 25 were teachers. The mean age was 35 years.

ASSESSMENT OF PREDICTOR VARIABLES   Personality was measured with the Eysenck Personality Questionnaire (Eysenck & Eysenck, 1978), consisting of subscales for extraversion, neuroticism, and psychoticism. Psychoticism in this measure consists primarily of low conscientiousness and low agreeableness items.

ASSESSMENT OF OUTCOME VARIABLES   Participants completed the 20-item self-report altruism scale (Rushton, Chrisjohn, & Fekken, 1981). This is a self-report scale that asks participants about their history of helpful behaviors.

MAIN RESULTS   Teachers scored higher than engineers on extraversion, $M = 14.40$ vs. 11.56; $t = 2.37$, $p < .05$, and neuroticism, $M = 10.88$ vs. 7.44; $t = 2.62$, $p < .05$, but teachers scored lower than engineers on psychoticism, $M = 3.16$ vs. 6.80; $t = 6.38$, $p < .01$. There were no differences between the two groups on altruism, $M = 29.28$ vs. 27.64; $t = .67$, ns. Altruism was significantly negatively correlated with psychoticism for engineers, $r = -.56$, $p < .01$, but not for teachers, $r = -.15$, *ns*. No other correlations between personality variables and altruism were significant.

CONCLUSION   "The differences in personality of the two professional groups do not have any bearing on altruistic behavior."

COMMENTARY   As Mohan and Bhatia (1987) show, sometimes *not* finding relationships between variables is important. This study brings to question stereotypes concerning personality characteristics of particular professions—in this case, the stereotypes of teachers as being more helpful than engineers. More surprising, however, are the null findings for the relationship between personality and altruism. Of course, with only 25 in each group, power was extremely low, and it would be difficult to observe significant results even where they exist. In a somewhat more recent study of personality and altruism, using the same measures, Rushton, Fulker, Neale, Nias, & Eysenck (1989) found that altruism was positively related to extraversion and negatively related to neuroticism. In this study, altruism was related to lower psychoticism for engineers but not for teachers. Altruism in this case reflects higher levels of conscientiousness and agreeableness for the engineers. What part of the disparity in results is due to cross-cultural differences and what is due to the true nature of the relationships among the variables is unclear at this time.

CORRESPONDENCE   Jitendra Mohan and Sangeeta Bhatia, Department of Psychology, Panjab University, Sector 14, 160 014, Chandigarh, India

Neuberg, S. L., Cialdini, R. B., Brown, S. L., Luce, C., Sagarin, B. J., & Lewis, B. P. (1997). Does empathy lead to anything more than superficial helping? Comment on Batson et al. (1997). *Journal of Personality and Social Psychology, 73*(3), 510–516.

OBJECTIVE   To comment on and present evidence concerning the relationship between empathy, self-other overlap, and helping

DESIGN   Experiment

SETTING   Arizona State University

PARTICIPANTS   Participants were 79 students in introductory psychology courses who received course credit for participation.

ASSESSMENT OF PREDICTOR VARIABLES   Participants were randomly assigned to focus on one of four same-sex persons—a stranger, an acquaintance, a good friend, or a family member—as they read a scenario describing the eviction of that person from their apartment. Participants completed measures of empathy (Batson et al., 1997), personal distress, and sadness (Fultz et al., 1988). Finally, participants rated the degree of "oneness" felt with the described person using the Inclusion of Other in the Self (IOS) Scale (Aron et al., 1992). The order of presentation of the measures was modified from previous studies, such that ratings of empathy and oneness preceded helping decisions.

ASSESSMENT OF OUTCOME VARIABLES   Participants indicated the level of help they would offer the evicted person on a 7-point scale, from no help to offering to let him or her come to live with them rent free.

MAIN RESULTS   The closer the relationships, the more willing the participants were to help; $F(3, 76) = 61.51$, $p = .0001$. The closer the relationships, the more empathic concern the participants reported, $F(3, 76) = 10.82$, $p = .0001$, and the more oneness they felt with the described person; $F(3, 76) = 56.14$, $p < .0001$. Helping was positively correlated with both empathic concern and oneness, $rs = .62$ and $.80$. Once the effects of nonaltruistic variables (i.e., participant gender, sadness, and distress) were accounted for, empathic concern could not predict the amount of help participants were willing to give, $\beta = .068$, $F(1, 64) =$

.73, *ns.* However, oneness remained a unique predictor of helping, $\beta = .94$, $F(1, 64) = 44.74$, $p < .0001$.

CONCLUSION   The authors propose that "the function of empathic concern may be essentially preparatory, serving to orient people to opportunities for helping and acting to spur relatively superficial assistance."

COMMENTARY   This study is yet another installation in the debate concerning the existence of pure altruism, or true selflessness. In response to the criticisms of Batson and colleagues (1997), Neuberg et al. (1997) conducted an experiment to investigate the role of self-other merging and to pit it against empathic concern. Although helping was strongly related to empathic concern, this effect disappears as other variables, including feelings of closeness, are taken into consideration. The question remains whether there is conceptual overlap in feelings of oneness with another person and the participant's empathic concern for that person.

CORRESPONDENCE   Steven Neuberg or Robert B. Cialdini, Department of Psychology, Arizona State University, Tempe, AZ 85287-1104

Noonan, A. E., Tennstedt, S. L., & Rebelsky, F. G. (1996). Making the best of it: Themes of meaning among informal caregivers to the elderly. *Journal of Aging Studies, 10*(4), 313–327.

OBJECTIVE   To explore the reasons caregivers give for continuing in stressful caregiving situations

DESIGN   Cross-sectional interview

SETTING   Massachusetts Elder Health Project

PARTICIPANTS   Participants were 65 caregivers who were already participating in the Massachusetts Elder Health Project. The mean age was 63.4 years, and 87.7% of the participants were female.

ASSESSMENT OF PREDICTOR VARIABLES   Participants were interviewed by an investigator for approximately 1 hour and asked about their caregiving situations. Participants' responses were audiotaped and transcribed.

ASSESSMENT OF OUTCOME VARIABLES   The transcriptions were coded for amount of burden, relationship of caregiver to elder, disability of elder, and 16 possible caregiver meaning themes.

MAIN RESULTS   Caregivers focused on the following issues in their descriptions of why they care for the elderly: gratification and satisfaction with caregiving (i.e., "I'm glad I'm able to do it"), family responsibility/reciprocity (i.e., "You are supposed to take care of your family whether you love them or not"), friendship and company (i.e., emotional support and companionship), doing what needs to be done (i.e., "I do what I have to do and make the best of it"). Participants also mentioned personal growth for the caregiver, improved relationships between the elder and caregiver, and simply having a caring personality.

CONCLUSION   Caregivers report carrying out their duties to an elder because of situational factors such as social roles, emotional factors such as positive emotions, and having a caring nature. Caregivers perceive their behavior as multidetermined.

COMMENTARY   Noonan, Tennstedt, and Rebelsky do something few other researchers have done—they have asked the person carrying out consistent helping behavior why they do it. Although self-report and introspection can be suspect as sole methods of inquiry, they often give us insight into the motivations of the participant and are quite useful in the context of the broader body of research. Furthermore, these methods provide a rich picture, not stripped bare by the necessities of controlled laboratory research. In this case, the stated motives of the caregivers match much of what we know from other studies. That is, not all prosocial behavior is motivated by pure altruism; there are many paths to prosocial behavior, some of which are situationally determined; and factors of both the caregiver and the recipient are involved.

CORRESPONDENCE   Anne E. Noonan, New England Research Institutes, 9 Galen St., Watertown, MA 02472

Omoto, A. M. & Snyder, M. (1995). Sustained helping without obligation: Motivation, longevity of service, and perceived attitude change among AIDS volunteers. *Journal of Personality and Social Psychology, 68,* 671–686.

OBJECTIVE   To explore how helping dispositions, motivations, and experiences affect long-term volunteerism

DESIGN   Cross-sectional surveys

SETTING   An AIDS service organization

PARTICIPANTS   Participants were 116 active volunteers at an AIDS service organization (63% males, 36% females). Participants had been involved with the organization for 2 to 42 months and volunteered, on average, 4.8 hours a week.

ASSESSMENT OF PREDICTOR VARIABLES   The helping personality variable was operationalized by a 7-item measure of empathic concern (Davis, 1980), an 8-item measure of social responsibility (Berkowitz & Lutterman, 1968), and 10 nurturance items from the Personality Research Form (Jackson, 1974). Motivations for volunteering were measured with a specially created 25-item scale measuring five factors of volunteer motivation (values, understanding, personal development, community concern, and esteem enhancement). Social support was measured with several items tapping social network size and perceived availability of support. Fourteen items measured satisfaction with volunteering and six items tapped organizational integration (i.e., acceptance of goals of organization, number of meetings attended, and number of friends in organization). Nine items measured change in attitudes toward several objects: people with AIDS, volunteer work and agencies, people who do AIDS volunteer work, homosexuals, the gay community, themselves, and their outlook on life.

ASSESSMENT OF OUTCOME VARIABLES   The outcome variable was the duration of service at the AIDS service organization.

MAIN RESULTS   Fifty-four percent of the volunteers were still active 1 year later; only 16% were still active 2½ years later. Researchers specified a structural equation model with satisfaction, volunteer motivations, and social support variables each predicting duration of volunteering directly (path coefficients = .24, .31, and −.31, respectively). Helping personality predicts duration indirectly through satisfaction (path coefficient = .42). Organizational integration was affected by helping personality (path coefficient = .39) and was uncorrelated with satisfaction, $r = .16$, but it did not directly influence duration. Helping personality, volunteer motivations, and social support were allowed to intercorrelate. Although the model's χ^2 estimate did not indicate a good fit, $\chi^2(96) = 147.01$, other statistics better used to assess the goodness of fit of the structural model indicated that, indeed, the hypothesized model fit well, $GFI = .86$, $\chi^2/df = 1.53$, $RMR = .10$. In a similar model, perceived attitude change replaced duration of helping in model analyses. Satisfaction, volunteer motivations, and social support variables each predict attitude change directly (path coefficients = .26, .44, and .27, respectively). Helping personality predicted attitude change indirectly through satisfaction (path coefficient = .44). Organizational integration was affected by helping personality (path coefficient = .40) and was uncorrelated with satisfaction, $r = .17$, but it did not directly influence attitude change. Helping personality, volunteer motivations, and social support were allowed to intercorrelate. Although the model's χ^2 estimate did not indicate a good fit, $\chi^2(126) = 187.11$, other statistics better used to assess the goodness of fit of the structural model indicated that, indeed, the hypothesized model fit well, $GFI = .84$, $\chi^2/df= 1.49$, $RMR = .10$.

CONCLUSION   "Structural equation analyses indicate that dispositional helping influences satisfaction and integration but not duration of service, whereas greater motivation and less social support predict long active volunteer service. The model is generalized to the prediction of perceived attitude change." In an attempt to explain the unexpected relationship between social support and volunteering, the authors suggest, "Those who lack social support may be seeking to acquire it through volunteer service, and those with social support may be taking refuge from the stresses of volunteering by seeking the support they possess elsewhere."

COMMENTARY   Unlike Unger & Thumuluri's (1997) study, which found important relationships between trait empathy and continuous volunteering, Omoto and Snyder's study (1995) suggests that the influence of dispositional variables is indirect, through satisfaction with volunteering and integration in the organization. Clary and Orenstein (1991) examined the relationship of perspective taking and empathic concern with motivation and ability in volunteer work. Similarly, Penner and Finkelstein (1998) found that length of service and time spent volunteering were correlated with other-oriented empathy and helpfulness. The research in this area may be equivocal, but Omoto and Snyder did the field a service by putting variables reflecting a wider range of personal and situational processes involved in volunteering in a single model.

CORRESPONDENCE   Allen M. Omoto, Department of Psychology, 426 Fraser Hall, University of Kansas, Lawrence, KS 66045

Organ, D. W., & Ryan, K. (1995). A meta-analytic review of attitudinal and dispositional predictors of organizational citizenship behavior. *Personnel Psychology, 48,* 775–802.

OBJECTIVE   To examine the literature and determine whether job attitudes and dispositional variables influence individual contributions in the workplace above the call of duty

DESIGN   Meta-analytic review

SETTING   Indiana University

STUDIES   The meta-analysis included 55 articles, papers, conference presentations, and dissertations. Papers were specifically selected for inclusion if they had a general measure of organizational citizenship behavior (OCB) and an aggregate measure of an attitude or personality trait. Mean effect sizes were only calculated if data were available from at least four independent studies.

ASSESSMENT OF PREDICTOR VARIABLES   Measures of organizational citizenship behavior (OCB) included measures of altruism or aid to coworkers, good work behavior (good attendance, use of company property, etc.), courtesy, willingness to forbear personal inconvenience (sportsmanship), and constructive involvement in the governance of the organization (civic virtue). Satisfaction consisted of global job satisfaction scores. Fairness was computed from reported distributive and procedural fairness using combined correlations of the measures (Hunter & Schmidt, 1990). Other variables derived from study reports were organizational commitment, leader supportiveness, conscientiousness, agreeableness, positive and negative affectivity, tenure, and gender.

ASSESSMENT OF OUTCOME VARIABLES   Using procedures developed by Hunter and Schmidt (1990), correlations in the meta-analysis were corrected for sample sizes of the studies and unreliability of the measures. A coefficient of variation in OCB measures allowed for comparisons of high variability and low variability participant groups. The Q statistic was computed to examine whether the observed variability in the corrected correlations was greater than that due to sampling error alone as a precursor to examining potential moderators of effect size.

MAIN RESULTS   There was a modest effect size estimate for the relationship between altruism and satisfaction ($M = .28$). This relationship was moderated by method of measurement of altruism (self vs. other-rating) such that self-ratings of altruism produced higher correlations between satisfaction and altruism than did other-ratings of altruism and satisfaction; .39 vs. .26, $z = 4.08$, $p < .01$; $Q = 40.4$, $p < .01$. Perception of leader supportiveness and altruism had a moderately strong association ($M = .32$), although there was some evidence that this relationship was moderated by the number of studies conducted solely on males, $Q = 50.9$, $p < .01$. Fairness in the workplace, conscientiousness, agreeableness, negative affectivity, and positive affectivity had lower mean correlations with altruism ($M = .24$, .22, .13, $-.06$, and .15, respectively).

There was a modest effect size estimate for the relationship between compliance and satisfaction ($M = .28$). This relationship was moderated by method of measurement of compliance (self- vs. other-rating) such that self-ratings of compliance produced higher correlations between satisfaction and compliance than did other-ratings of compliance and satisfaction, .50 vs. .24, $z = 5.93$, $p < .01$. The relationship of compliance with conscientiousness ($M = .30$) was also moderated by method of measurement of compliance (self- vs. other-rating) such that self-ratings of compliance produced higher correlations between conscientiousness and compliance than did other-ratings of compliance and conscientiousness, .47 vs. .23, $z = 3.73$, $p < .01$. Perception of leader supportiveness and fairness in the workplace was moderately correlated with compliance, whereas agreeableness, negative affectivity, and positive affectivity were correlated with compliance at lower levels ($M\pi = .35$, .27, .11, $-.12$, and .07, respectively). The authors note that the moderating effects of self- versus other-ratings of constructs suggests a spurious inflation of the correlations due to common method variance.

CONCLUSION   Satisfaction, perceived fairness, organizational commitment, and leader supportiveness correlate with measures of organizational citizenship behavior. Dispositional measures do not correlate as well with measures of OCB. Although conscientiousness correlates with compliance measures of OCB, it does not correlate well with measures of altruism.

COMMENTARY   Organ & Ryan's (1995) work highlights a key distinction that should be made in the work on organizational citizenship behavior: that altruistic behavior enacted toward individuals is not the same as compliance to company norms. Compliance is not altruism, though it may be an important part of being a good worker or member of the company. McNeely and Meglino (1994) also note the differences between concern for individuals in the company and concern for the organization itself. Although job satisfaction in both studies is related to the more altruistic construct, fairness and good leadership invoke norms of reciprocity toward the organization. However, McNeely and Meglino (1994) suggest that job satisfaction may be a mood effect. In this more inclusive review of the literature, Organ and Ryan suggest that the effects of job satisfaction are not a mood effect and that more research is needed on these constructs.

CORRESPONDENCE   Dennis W. Organ, School of Business, Indiana University, Bloomington, IN 47405

Penner, L. A., & Finkelstein, M. A. (1998). Dispositional and structural determinants of volunteerism. *Journal of Personality and Social Psychology, 74*(2), 525–537.

OBJECTIVE   To examine the personality and situational correlates of volunteer behavior
DESIGN   Cross-sectional survey
SETTING   Southeastern United States
PARTICIPANTS   Participants were 146 unpaid volunteers from the mailing list of a large organization that serves people who are "infected and affected by HIV" in the southeastern United States. Of the participants, 56% were female and 44% were male. The participants' mean age was 35.9 years old.
ASSESSMENT OF PREDICTOR VARIABLES   Participants completed three sets of questionnaires, each separated by 4 to 5 months. Participants indicated to what extent each of five motives influenced their decisions to volunteer: community concern, esteem enhancement, understanding AIDS, personal development, and values. The personality variables of other-oriented empathy and helpfulness were derived from answers to the Prosocial Personality Battery (Penner, Fritzsche, Craiger, & Freifield, 1995).
ASSESSMENT OF OUTCOME VARIABLES   Participants completed questions regarding volunteer status (active vs. not active), length of service as a volunteer, how much time was spent volunteering, and how many volunteer meetings were attended. Other questions assessed feelings about, satisfaction with, and commitment to volunteering.
MAIN RESULTS   Length of service was significantly positively correlated with organizational satisfaction, other-oriented empathy, helpfulness, and the values motive for volunteering, $rs = .20, .21, .21$, and $.23$, respectively. For the first set of questionnaires, gender differences emerged on other-oriented empathy and helpfulness. Although there was a significant positive correlation of other-oriented empathy and amount of time spent volunteering for men, $r = .29$, the same relationship did not hold for women; $r = -.08$; $t(141) = 2.21, p < .05$. In contrast, for women helpfulness correlated with the number of meetings attended, $r = .27$, but the same relationship did not hold for men; $r = -.07$; $t(141) = 2.07, p < .05$. For the second set of questionnaires, other-oriented empathy was positively correlated with time spent volunteering, $r = .23$, for both men and women. The correlations between contact with persons with AIDS/HIV and other-oriented empathy was significant and positive for men, $r = .36$, but not for women; $r = -.08$; $t(72) = 1.86, p < .10$. Similarly, for the third questionnaire, the correlations between contact with persons with AIDS/HIV and other-oriented empathy was significant and positive for men, $r = .40$, but not for women; $r = -.10$; $t(51) = 1.84, p < .10$.

Correlations were computed between other-oriented empathy and helpfulness and each of the motives for volunteering. At the first questionnaire, both are correlated with the value of volunteering (i.e., "I enjoy helping other people"); $rs = .44$ and $.17$, respectively; $ps < .05$. For the second questionnaire, other-oriented empathy was positively correlated with satisfaction with volunteering, positive feelings toward volunteering, and the value of volunteering; $rs = .24, .26$, and $.43$, respectively; $ps < .05$. No other correlations at Questionnaires 1, 2, or 3 were statistically significant.
CONCLUSION   "Helping behaviors among people who score high on the helpfulness factor and among people who score high on other-oriented empathy are probably motivated by different needs and goals. Specifically, we believe that the motive of high scorers on other-oriented empathy are those that one would typically associate with prosocial actions: concern for the welfare of others, satisfaction derived from being helpful, and feelings of responsibility for others' welfare. In contrast, people who score high on the helpfulness factor may help primarily because it serves to reinforce their feelings of being efficacious and competent people."

COMMENTARY   Volunteerism is a type of prosocial behavior that goes beyond simple, single helping acts demonstrated in many of the studies of this bibliography. In volunteering, we see patterns of personality and behavior demonstrated over a period of time. For example, Penner and Finkelstein distinguish between patterns of motivation for the person whose primary desire is the welfare of others and the person whose primary desire is self-esteem. The latter pattern seems related to Berkowitz and Lutterman's (1968) depiction of the socially responsible person who is highly involved in the community. An interesting extension of this work would combine the present study with the work of Clary and Orenstein (1991) to investigate the motives of persons selected and not selected for volunteering.
CORRESPONDENCE   Louis A. Penner, Department of Psychology, University of South Florida, 4202 East Fowler Avenue, BEH 339, Tampa, FL 33620-8200 or e-mail to penner@chuma.cas.usf.edu

Ribal, J. E. (1963). Character and meanings of selfishness and altruism. *Sociology and Social Research, 47,* 311–321.

OBJECTIVE   To investigate the differences between personality types with varying needs for nurturance and succorance and the relationship of those personality types to other personality variables
DESIGN   Cross-sectional survey
SETTING   A university in California
PARTICIPANTS   Participants were 572 students (325 men and 247 women) from a university in California.
ASSESSMENT OF PREDICTOR VARIABLES   Participants completed the Edwards Personal Preference Schedule (Edwards, 1954), a questionnaire designed to address each of 15 personality needs (i.e., achievement, endurance, exhibition, affiliation, aggression, order). Participants also wrote autobiographical descriptions that included information on involvement in primary and secondary groups and patterns of socialization related to formation of personality needs. Taped interviews asking in-depth questions concerning socialization were also conducted.
ASSESSMENT OF OUTCOME VARIABLES   Participants scoring in the upper and lower quartiles on succorance and nurturance were chosen to fit each of the four social character types as follows. The altruistic personality type was high on nurturance but low on succorance. The receptive-giver was high on both nurturance and succorance. The selfish person was low on nurturance but high on succorance, and the inner-sustaining person was low on both nurturance and succorance. One hundred ninety-four participants (98 males and 96 female) represented each of the four possible social character types on the two dimensions of succorance and nurturance. Nurturance is defined as the need to give to others, and succorance is defined as the need to receive from others. Scores on this social character types questionnaire were then compared with measures of personality presumed to be related to altruism.
MAIN RESULTS   The results of this study are most clearly presented as descriptions of each of the social character types and the personality and individual difference variables related to each. First, the altruistic social character type is defined by high nurturance and low succorance levels. Altruistic males were higher than other males on endurance. Altruistic women were higher than other women on affiliation needs but lower on achievement and dominance needs. Altruists tended to passively await opportunities to be nurturing, did not seek and even rejected aid themselves, and were often attracted to selfish types. Family characteristics of altruists included coming from large families, being an only child, receiving

firm discipline with rewards for internalizing adult roles, being independent and self-reliant, and giving out of religious belief.

Second, the selfish social character type is characterized by low nurturance and high succorance. Selfish men and women tended to be higher in exhibition and lower in affiliation than other men and women. Selfish women tended to also be higher in aggression than other women. Selfish people had high dependency on others for gratification of their needs, were unmotivated to help others, and found relationships with altruists very satisfying. Family characteristics of selfish people included parental indulgence, frustration that intensified their needs, and few demands and little encouragement given to induce giving.

Third, the receptive-giving social character type is characterized by high nurturance and high succorance. Receptive-giving men and women tended to be lower in endurance than other men and women. Receptive-giving women tended to also be lower in dominance than other women. Receptive-giving men tended to be higher in affiliation but lower in autonomy than other men. Receptive-giving people preferred close relationships that were both dependent and supportive and found relationships with others like themselves most gratifying; giving was contingent on receiving in most cases. Family characteristics of receptive-givers included a model of learning that gratification depends on giving to others, the family being a "warm" providing unit, and parents being nurturing models.

Fourth, the inner-sustaining social character type is characterized by low nurturance and low succorance. Inner-sustaining men and women tended to be higher in autonomy, endurance, and aggression but lower in affiliation than other men and women. Inner-sustaining women tended to also be higher in achievement and exhibition than other women. Inner-sustaining people preferred detachment to involvement with others, were very autonomous so as to be very productive, and avoided both dependency and interdependency. Family characteristics of inner-sustainers included blocked learning of nurturing motives, early self-sufficiency, and overt rebellion in adolescence.

CONCLUSION   "The use of a social character typology formulated on the basis of personality needs for nurturance and succorance has been demonstrated with the possible outcome that some new insights and understandings about the structure of personality, the nature of human relations, and the process of socialization have resulted."

COMMENTARY   Like the more recent studies by Romer, Gruder, & Lizzadro (1986), Ribal utilizes a typology to fully describe personality and socialization characteristics associated with altruism. Note that both altruists and receptive-givers would be likely to perform prosocial behaviors. Further investigation might address the relationship between the altruist and the selfish person, which in this research approximates the relationship between a martyr and someone who manipulates the martyr for selfish gain. Also, the development of these giving-receiving personality types might be compared with more recent research on attachment styles in childhood and adulthood.

CORRESPONDENCE   None available

Romer, D., Gruder, C. L., & Lizzadro, T. (1986). A person-situation approach to altruistic behavior. *Journal of Personality and Social Psychology, 51*(5), 1001–1012.

OBJECTIVE   To determine the influence of nurturance, succorance, and situation on helping behavior

DESIGN   *Study 1*: Cross-sectional survey. *Study 2*: Laboratory experiment

SETTING   University of Illinois, Chicago

PARTICIPANTS   *Study 1*: Participants consisted of 94 undergraduate students who participated to complete a requirement for an introductory psychology course. *Study 2*: Participants consisted of 125 undergraduate students who participated to complete a requirement for an introductory psychology course.

ASSESSMENT OF PREDICTOR VARIABLES   *Study 1*: Study 1 was primarily a scale development and validation study. A measure of helping orientation was designed to distinguish four possible personality types on the two dimensions of succorance and nurturance. The altruistic personality type would be high on nurturance but low on succorance. The receptive-giver would be high on both nurturance and succorance. The selfish person would be low on nurturance but high on succorance, and the inner-sustaining person would be low on both nurturance and succorance. Scores on the Helping-Orientation Questionnaire were then compared with measures of personality presumed to be related to altruism. *Study 2*: Of the 125 original participants screened, 65 participants were chosen to represent three categories on the Helping-Orientation Questionnaire: 27 altruists, 20 receptive-givers, and 18 selfish persons. Half of the participants were assigned to a compensation condition and half to a noncompensation condition. Participants in the compensation condition were offered partial course credit for participation, whereas participants in the no-compensation condition were told that they could not receive partial course credit for participation.

ASSESSMENT OF OUTCOME VARIABLES   *Study 1*: Participants completed the nurturance and succorance subscales of the Jackson Personality Research Form (1967) to assess construct validity of the novel measures of helping orientation. For concurrent validity, participants completed the Social Responsibility Scale (Berkowitz & Lutterman, 1968) and the Interpersonal Reactivity Index (Davis, 1980). The latter contains subscales measuring personal distress, perspective taking, empathic concern, and fantasy. *Study 2*: Participants were telephoned and asked to participate in an experiment that needed to be completed by the end of the semester. If participants agreed to participate, they were asked how much time they were willing to spend at the experiment.

MAIN RESULTS   *Study 1*: Consistent with expectations, altruists and receptive-givers were more nurturant on the Jackson Personality Research Form than the other two types, $Ms =$ 11.31 and 11.00 vs. 9.78 and 9.00; $F(1, 90) = 8.23$, $p < .05$. Furthermore, the receptive-giving and selfish types were more succorant on the Jackson Personality Research Form than the other two types; $Ms = 9.64$ and 8.05 vs. 7.72 and 6.94; $F(1, 90) = 4.49$, $p < .05$. Empathic concern was expressed more by altruists and receptive-givers than by selfish and inner-sustaining participants; $Ms = 4.36$ and 4.05 vs. 3.67 and 3.63; $F(1, 89) = 20.62$, $p < .05$. Nurturant-type participants (altruists and receptive-givers) were also more likely to engage in perspective taking than nonnurturant-type participants (selfish and inner-sustaining; $Ms =$ 3.80 and 3.48 vs. 3.42 and 3.31; $F(1, 89) = 4.14$, $p < .05$. Nurturant types were more likely than nonnurturant types to engage in empathic concern and fantasy empathy; $Ms = 2.73$ and 2.89 vs. 2.67 and 2.69; $F(1, 88) = 4.47$, $p < .05$. *Study 2*: An interaction between personality type and compensation condition emerged, such that altruists who had not been offered compensation and receptive-givers who had been offered compensation were more likely to help the experimenter and to agree to participate in the study than were the other participants; 82% vs. 48%, $\chi^2 (1, n = 47) = 5.80$, $p < .05$. When no compensation was offered, altruists tended to give help more often than receptive-givers; 77% vs. 45%, $\chi^2 (1, n = 24) = 2.54$, $p < .15$. When there was compensation, receptive-givers tended to give help more often than altruists; 89% vs. 50%, $\chi^2 (1, n = 23) = 3.65$, $p < .07$. Selfish participants were equally likely to help in compensation and no-compensation conditions (33%).

Results for number of hours volunteered to help follow a similar pattern as agreement to help. An interaction between personality type and compensation condition emerged such that altruists who had not been offered compensation and receptive-givers who had been offered compensation volunteered more hours than did the other participants, t (59) = 2.47, $p < .02$. When no compensation was offered, altruists volunteered more hours than receptive-givers, .92 hrs vs. .45 hrs, t (59) = 1.71, $p < .08$. When there was compensation, receptive-givers volunteered more hours than altruists, 1.33 hrs vs. .79 hrs, t (59) = 1.78, $p < .08$. Selfish participants volunteered similarly low numbers of hours in compensation and no-compensation conditions, $M = .22$ hrs.

CONCLUSION   Both personality and situational variables are important in determining when helping will occur. "Receptive-givers appear to be strongly motivated by both nurturance and succorance and, hence, prefer to help in situations in which reciprocation or social rewards are forthcoming. Altruists, however, are just as motivated by nurturance, but they also prefer social independence (nonsuccorance) and, hence, prefer to help in situations in which social rewards are not forthcoming."

COMMENTARY   Like the early work of Ribal (1963), previously cited, that of Romer, Gruder, and Lizzadro explores the relationship of personality variables and helping behavior to social character types. Again, note that both altruists and receptive-givers would be likely to perform prosocial behaviors but that this time the motives for performing the behaviors and the conditions under which the behaviors are likely to occur are made more clear. Perhaps selfish people were less likely to help in all conditions because the incentives were too low, or perhaps their needs for nurturance so outstripped their needs for succorance that they felt unable to help.

CORRESPONDENCE   None available

Rushton, J. P., Fulker, D. W., Neale, M. C., Nias, D. K. B., & Eysenck, H. J. (1986). Altruism and aggression: The heritability of individual differences. *Journal of Personality and Social Psychology, 50,* 1192–1198.

OBJECTIVE   To estimate the heritability of altruism and aggression

DESIGN   Twin study with questionnaires

SETTING   England

PARTICIPANTS   Participants were 573 monozygotic (MZ = identical twins) and dizygotic (DZ = fraternal twins) twin pairs from the University of London Institute of Psychiatry Volunteer Twin Register. There were 206 MZ female, 90 MZ male, 133 DZ female, 46 DZ male, and 98 DZ mixed-sex twin pairs. Twins ranged in age from 19 to 60 years old.

ASSESSMENT OF PREDICTOR VARIABLES   Participants completed five questionnaires mailed to them on altruism (Self-Report Altruism Scale; Rushton, Chrisjohn, & Fekken, 1981), emotional empathy (Mehrabian & Epstein, 1972), nurturance (subscale of the Personality Research Form; Jackson, 1974), aggressive behavior, and assertive behavior (23 and 24 items, respectively from the Interpersonal Behavior Survey; Mauger & Adkinson, 1980).

ASSESSMENT OF OUTCOME VARIABLES   Correlations between twins' scores were computed separately by type of twin pairing (MZ vs. DZ), and Falconer's (1981) heritabilities were calculated in percentages. Analyses were also conducted separately by gender and age of participant. In twin correlations and heritability analyses, gender and age were covaried out.

MAIN RESULTS   In correlational analyses, altruism, empathy, nurturance, and assertiveness increased with age, $rs = .48, .43, .41$, and .23, respectively; $ps < .001$, whereas aggressiveness decreased with age, $r = -.40, p < .001$. As expected, women had higher mean scores than men on empathy and nurturance, and men had higher scores than women on aggression and assertiveness; $ts = 14.54, 13.98, 9.88$, and 6.27, respectively; $ps < .001$. Overall, the MZ twins showed greater correlations on each of the measures than did DZ twins: (1) self-report altruism .53 vs. .25, heritability = 56%; (2) empathy .54 vs. .20, heritability = 68%; (3)

nurturance .49 vs. .14, heritability = 70%; (4) aggressiveness .40 vs. .04, heritability = 72%; and (5) assertiveness .52 vs. .20, heritability = 64%. The heritability scores can be partitioned into variance due to genetic effects V(G), variance due to common environment shared by twins V(CE), and variance that is due to the uniqueness of each twin V(SE). Using a maximum-likelihood estimation procedure for self-reported altruism, V(G) = 51%, V(CE) = 2%, and V(SE) = 47%. Very similar results were revealed for empathy, nurturance, aggressiveness, and assertiveness, such that approximately half of the variance was due to genetics, half to individual differences, and none of the variance was due to common environment.

CONCLUSION "Altruism increased over the age span from 19 to 60. Women had higher scores than men on altruism and lower scores on aggression." Heritability estimates of 56%, 68%, and 70% were obtained for measures of altruism, empathy, and nurturance.

COMMENTARY Rushton et al.'s (1986) work suggests a strong heritable component to altruism and its dispositional correlates, empathy and nurturance. Davis et al. (1994) also explored heritability of another approach to empathy and found lower, but still important, genetic components. One of the important sections of this work is the partitioning of the variance into genetics, common environment, and unique personality components of heritability. It is clear that although genetics plays a substantial role, heredity is not destiny (nor is common environment). Individual differences, personality, and unique experiences that the individual brings to the situation also influence level of altruism, empathy, and nurturance. These differences are the focus of much of the other work in this bibliography.

CORRESPONDENCE J. Philippe Rushton, Department of Psychology, University of Western Ontario, London, Ontario, Canada N6A 5C2

Rushton, J. P., Fulker, D. W., Neale, M. C., Nias, D. K., & Eysenck, H. J. (1989). Ageing and the relation of aggression, altruism, and assertiveness scales to the Eysenck Personality Questionnaire. *Personality and Individual Differences, 10*(2), 261–263.

OBJECTIVE To examine the relationships between age, aggression, altruism, assertiveness, and scores on the Eysenck Personality Questionnaire

DESIGN Cross-sectional survey

SETTING Most geographic areas of the United Kingdom

PARTICIPANTS Participants consisted of 573 twin pairs from the University of London Institute of Psychiatry Twin Register. The mean age was 30 years (range 19 to over 60 years). Seventy percent of the sample was female.

ASSESSMENT OF PREDICTOR VARIABLES Participants completed the Eysenck Personality Questionnaire (Eysenck & Eysenck, 1975). Emotional empathy was measured with a 33-item self-report measure (Mehrabian & Epstein, 1972). Nurturance (Nurturance Scale; Jackson, 1974), aggressiveness (Mauger & Adkinson, 1980), and assertiveness (Interpersonal Behavior Survey) were also measured.

ASSESSMENT OF OUTCOME VARIABLES Altruism was measured with the 20-item Self-Report Altruism Scale (Rushton, Chrisjohn, & Fekken, 1981).

MAIN RESULTS Altruism was positively related to assertiveness, $r = .30$, $p < .001$, to nurturance, $r = .43$, $p < .001$, to empathy, $r = .15$, $p < .001$, and to extraversion, $r = .21$, $p < .001$. Altruism was negatively related to aggressiveness, $r = -.23$, $p < .001$, and to neuroticism, $r = -.15$, $p < .001$.

CONCLUSION Altruism has positive relationships with several personality variables and negative relationships with others. Perhaps the most surprising relationships are those of altruism and assertiveness and extraversion. The more outgoing a person was, the more altruistic he or she was.

COMMENTARY   In investigating a personality variable in relation to other traits, it is important to include all phases of the life span. Children (as in Berndt & Das, 1987; Farver & Branstetter, 1994; Leung & Foster, 1985; Litvack-Miller et al., 1997) and college students are much more common study participants than the adults investigated in this study. What we find in the results of Rushton et al.'s (1989) study is that the positive relationship between altruism and nurturance and empathy that we find in other studies carries through adulthood (for nurturance, see Ribal, 1963; Gergen et al., 1972; Romer et al., 1986; for empathy, see Archer et al., 1981; Batson et al., 1986). Of particular interest is the relationship between altruism and assertiveness and extraversion that conceptually replicates the findings of Schenk & Heinisch (1986). This strengthens the link between altruism and the ability to carry out altruistic acts, which is facilitated by instrumental traits such as gregariousness, comfort in social situations, and being able to put one's own (albeit prosocial) needs and desires forward.

CORRESPONDENCE   J. Philippe Rushton, Department of Psychology, University of Western Ontario, London, Ontario N6A 5C2, Canada

Rushton, J. P., Chrisjohn, R. D., & Fekken, G. C. (1981) The altruistic personality and the Self-Report Altruism Scale. *Personality and Individual Differences, 2,* 293–302.

OBJECTIVE   To examine the stability of individual differences in altruism across situations and to examine the properties of a self-report altruism scale

DESIGN   Cross-sectional survey and peer reports

SETTING   University of Western Ontario

PARTICIPANTS   *Study 1*: Participants were 118 undergraduate students (39 males and 79 females) at the University of Western Ontario and 416 friends/peers who answered questions concerning the students. The students completed the questionnaires during class time. *Study 2*: Participants were 146 undergraduate students (64 males and 82 females). *Study 3*: Participants were 200 university students.

ASSESSMENT OF PREDICTOR VARIABLES   *Study 1*: Participants completed the Self-Report Altruism Scale (SRA-scale), a 20-item scale that asks participants to rate how often they engaged in altruistic behaviors on a 5-point scale, from 1 ("never") to 5 ("very often"; i.e., "I have given directions to a stranger"). *Study 2*: Participants completed the SRA-scale to measure altruism. *Study 3*: Participants completed the SRA-scale to measure altruism.

ASSESSMENT OF OUTCOME VARIABLES   *Study 1*: Each participant was asked to give a questionnaire to eight people who knew them well. Each questionnaire was accompanied by a stamped, addressed envelope. The questionnaire contained the SRA-scale to be filled out in relation to the participant and four global ratings of the target person's altruism. Peers rated how caring, how helpful, how considerate of other's feelings, and how willing to make a sacrifice the participant was on a 7-point scale. Response rate for the peer ratings was 45%; 75% of the participants ($n = 88$) had one or more raters. Eighty participants had two or more raters. Peer ratings on the SRA-scale were summed across the 20 items and then averaged across all peers who rated a particular participant. A similar peer score was created for the global altruism items by summing the four items and averaging across the peer raters. *Study 2*: Over three testing sessions, eight "altruistic" responses were measured: (1) volunteering to read to blind persons in response to a telephone solicitation, (2) volunteering to participate in experiments for a needy experimenter, (3) whether participants had ever taken a first aid course, (4) whether participants had completed the organ donor card on their driver's licenses, (5) "sensitive attitudes" as measured by a questionnaire (Derman, French, & Harman, 1978), (6) the nurturance subscale of the Personality Research Form (Jackson, 1974), (7) paper and pencil measures of helping in emergency scenarios, and (8) having helping interests on the Jackson Vocational Interest Survey (Jackson, 1977). *Study 3*: Participants completed the Social Responsibility Scale (Berkowitz & Daniels, 1964), the Emotional Empathy Scale (Mehrabian & Epstein, 1972), the Social Interest Scale (Crandall, 1975), the Fantasy-Empathy Scale (Stotland, Matthews, Sherman, Hansson, & Richardson, 1978), the Machieavellianism Scale (Christie & Geis, 1968), the Rokeach Value Survey (Form C; Rokeach, 1973), the nurturance scale of the Personality Research Form (Jackson, 1974), and the Defining Issues Test (Rest, 1976).

MAIN RESULTS   *Study 1*: Split-half reliabilities for the peer ratings of the 80 participants who had two or more raters was significant for both the SRA-scale scores and the global altruism scores; $rs(78) = .51$ and $.39$, respectively; $ps < .01$. The internal consistency reliability of the peer rating form was high, $\alpha = .89$, $n = 416$. There was, as expected, a positive correlation between the peer-rated SRA-scale scores and the global altruism ratings, $r(86) = .54$, $p < .001$. Using Spearman's correction formula for attenuation due to unreliability, similarly strong relationships were found between participant SRA-scale scores and peer-rated SRA-scale scores and global altruism scores; $rs(78) = .56$ and $.33$, respectively; $ps < .01$. *Study 2*: The SRA-scale scores were significantly positively correlated with filling out an organ donation card, with the paper-and-pencil measure of "sensitive attitudes," with the nurturance scale, and with the responses to the emergency helping scenarios, $rs = .25, .33, .28,$ and $.33$, respectively; $ps < .01$, after social desirability was partialed out. The SRA-scale scores also predicted a linear combination of the eight measures; $r = .59$, $p < .01$, after correcting for measure unreliability. *Study 3*: The SRA-scale scores were significantly positively correlated with measures of social responsibility, with empathy, with nurturance, with having personal values of equality and helpfulness, and with having "high" levels of moral reasoning; $rs = .15, .17, .20, .28, .14,$ and $.16$, respectively; $ps < .05$. The SRA-scale scores were significantly negatively correlated with Machiavellianism, $r = -.13$, $p < .05$. The SRA-scale scores also predicted a linear combination of the eight measures; $r = .44$, $p < .001$, after controlling for measure unreliability.

CONCLUSION   "Findings from Study 1 support the idea of consistent individual differences in two ways. First, there was some agreement among peers' ratings of an individual's altruistic behavior. Second, better than chance agreement was also found between an individual's own report of his or her altruistic behavior and his or her peer's reports. [Study 2] found that an individual's self-reported altruism was related to a variety of altruistic criteria, and that when these criteria were combined a somewhat stronger relationship obtained. [Study 3] found significant positive relations among a variety of questionnaire measures of prosocial orientation. Self-reported altruism was related to all of these, and particularly so to an aggregated composite."

COMMENTARY   Rushton, Chrisjohn, and Fekken's (1981) work has become the basis of other research on self-reported altruism (Mohan & Bhatia, 1987; Rushton et al., 1989). The current study provides convergent validity for the scale. It also provides some evidence of the stability of individual differences in altruism with the use of the multiple other reports on the SRA-scale. Furthermore, the findings from Studies 2 and 3 are similar to findings from other studies concerning the relationship of altruism to empathy, nurturance, social responsibility, and other qualities.

CORRESPONDENCE   J. Philippe Rushton, Department of Psychology, University of Western Ontario, London, Ontario, Canada N6A 5C2

Sawyer, J. (1966). The altruism scale: A measure of cooperative, individualistic, and competitive interpersonal orientation. *American Journal of Sociology, 71,* 407–416.

OBJECTIVE   To investigate the properties of a scale to measure altruism

DESIGN   Cross-sectional survey with scenarios

SETTING   University of Chicago and George Williams College

PARTICIPANTS   Participants were 122 students from three groups. The first group consisted of social science students recruited from a class at the University of Chicago ($n = 28$). Most of these students were graduate students. The second group consisted of graduate business students from the University's Graduate School of Business ($n = 32$). The third group consisted of students from George Williams College, which at the time trained students for the YMCA and other social service positions ($n = 62$).

ASSESSMENT OF PREDICTOR VARIABLES   The independent variable in this study was college setting (i.e., the students from the three different schools were hypothesized to have differing levels of altruism). Participants completed the F scale to measure authoritarianism (Adorno, Frenkel-Brunswick, Levinson, & Sanford, 1950).

ASSESSMENT OF OUTCOME VARIABLES   Participants were asked to use a grid with three rows and three columns representing the participant's grade (A, B, or C) and another person's grade in a fictitious course. On the grid the participants were asked to rank their preference (from 1 to 9) for each of the nine possible outcomes. If participants had no preference between two or more outcomes, they were to give each of the outcomes in question the same rank. "To produce a measure of relative altruism, the discrimination between C's and A's for the other is divided by the discrimination between C's and A's for the self."

Relative altruism = (*Summed ranks for C to other*) − (*summed ranks for A to other*) / (Summed ranks for C to self) − (summed ranks for A to self)

Scores ranged from +1.0 to −1.0, with +1.0 = strictly cooperative, 0 = strictly individualistic, and −1.0 = strictly competitive. Participants ranked grades for self and each of three "others": a friend, a stranger, and an antagonist.

Then participants rated the amount of interest they had in the other person's grades on a scale of −1.0 to +1.0 in increments of tenths. The scale was anchored by descriptions such that +1.0 was "I am equally interested in how good his grade is and in how good my grade is," 0 was "I am only interested in how good my grade is," and −1.0 was "I am only interested in how much better my grade is than his; I do not care how good my grade is per se." Similar rankings of salaries ($6,000, $8,000, and $10,000) and amount of interest in own and others' salaries were also measured for a friend, a stranger, and an antagonist.

MAIN RESULTS   Across all groups altruism toward the friend was greater than altruism toward the stranger and the antagonist, *M*s = .45, .12, and −.18, respectively. The students training for the YMCA were more altruistic than the social science and business students, *M*s = .21, .02, and .07, respectively. The responses of business students were balanced around zero, having scores of .33 for friend and −.29 for antagonist, a spread of about .6. The social science students discriminated more, with a spread of about .8 between friend and antagonist.

Examining individual characteristics, authoritarianism as measured by the F scale was unrelated to altruism, $r = -.03$, but was related in predictable ways to group membership. Business students were the most authoritarian, followed by the YMCA students, and finally the social science students. Gender differences occurred on altruism for YMCA students and social science students. For all targets, female YMCA students were more altruistic than

male YMCA students. Female social science students were less punitive toward the antagonist than male social science students, $Ms = -.22$ vs. $-.42$, in that they did not necessarily
choose lower grades for the other than for the self.

CONCLUSION   "Grossly, the tendencies differentiating the three groups may be put as
follows: YMCA students help everyone, business students help themselves, and social science students help those who help them. Altruism toward a friend is substantially greater
than that toward a stranger, which in turn is substantially greater than that toward an
antagonist."

COMMENTARY   Sawyer's (1966) measure of altruism is a contrast to Rushton et al.'s (1981)
self-report measure and to other self-report or behavioral measures frequently used in research. Sawyer's measure hits behavioral tendencies at the microlevel of dyads, whereas
Rushton et al. measure self-reports of common altruistic behaviors. What we cannot know
is whether the group differences that occurred in the present study were because persons of
a given set of altruistic characteristics migrated toward those fields or whether the fields
themselves shaped the individual's understanding of interpersonal processes (or both).
Again, we see a bias in the participants, with altruistic behavior toward friends being greater
than altruistic behavior toward strangers or antagonists (cf. Ashton et al., 1998).

CORRESPONDENCE   None available

> Schenk, J., & Heinisch, R. (1986). Self-descriptions by means of sex-role
> scales and personality scales: A critical evaluation of recent masculinity and
> femininity scales. *Personality and Individual Differences, 7*(2), 161–168.

OBJECTIVE   To examine the relationship between instrumentality, expressiveness, and
various personality scales

DESIGN   Cross-sectional survey

SETTING   Germany

PARTICIPANTS   Participants consisted of 100 adults who attended various adult education
courses. There were equal numbers of male and female participants. The mean age for participants was 29 years for males and 27 years for females.

ASSESSMENT OF PREDICTOR VARIABLES   Instrumentality and expressiveness were measured using 40 items derived from the Bem Sex Role Inventory (1974) and the Personal Attributes Questionnaire (Spence & Helmreich, 1978). Instrumentality is the propensity to
engage in behavior that is goal directed or a means to some end. Expressiveness refers to the
degree to which a person exhibits stereotypically feminine traits, such as nurturing behavior, personal warmth, and higher emotionality.

ASSESSMENT OF OUTCOME VARIABLES   Altruism and helpfulness were measured by 13
items on self-report Likert-type scales. Altruism here is defined as "the willingness to sink
one's own needs and welfare in favor of someone else," and helpfulness was defined as "offering help to others who are in trouble, even if one's own interests are neglected by this."

MAIN RESULTS   Both altruism and helpfulness were strongly positively correlated with expressiveness, $rs = .59$ and $.43$, respectively, but were not strongly correlated with instrumentality, $rs = .13$ and $.15$, respectively. These findings correspond, roughly, to greater expressed
altruism in women than men, $M = 25.3$ vs. 23.5, $p < .06$, and greater expressed helpfulness
in women than men, $M = 22.2$ vs. 20.8, $p < .04$. It is interesting, in light of these results, that
participants' ratings of dealing with others' problems with empathy is significantly positively correlated for both males and females with self-confidence, $rs = .53$ and $.34$, assertiveness, $rs = .48$ and $.47$, leadership abilities, $rs = .64$ and $.63$, competency, $rs = .60$ and $.60$, am-
bition, $rs = .14$ and $.50$, and competitive orientation, $rs = .25$ and $.14$.

CONCLUSION   Altruism and helpfulness were more closely related to expressiveness than instrumentality. Women reported being more altruistic and helpful than men did. However, altruistic behavior—dealing with other's problems with empathy—was associated with instrumental qualities.

COMMENTARY   Schenk and Heinisch (1986) demonstrated the duality that we have seen in other studies in which self-reports of altruistic intentions or feelings are pitted against altruistic behavior (Rushton et al., 1989). Altruistic intentions and feelings are associated with the more feminine traits of empathy and expressiveness, but enacting altruistic behavior may require some instrumentality in conjunction with that expressiveness.

CORRESPONDENCE   J. Schenk and R. Heinisch, Psychologisches Institut, Belfortstrasses 18, 7800 Freiburg i.Br., F.R.G.

Schütz, A., & Tice, D. M. (1997). Associative and competitive indirect self-enhancement in close relationships moderated by trait self-esteem. *European Journal of Social Psychology, 27*(3), 257–273.

OBJECTIVE   To examine the ways in which people describe themselves and their romantic partners, especially in relation to self-esteem and publicness of description

DESIGN   Laboratory experiment with questionnaires

SETTING   A university

PARTICIPANTS   Participants consisted of 40 female undergraduates currently involved in a romantic relationship. They received course credit for their participation. The mean age was 19 years (range 17–22).

ASSESSMENT OF PREDICTOR VARIABLES   Participants completed a series of personality questionnaires, including a masculinity-femininity scale (Personal Attributes Questionnaire; Spence & Helmreich, 1978) and a self-esteem scale (modified Feelings of Inadequacy Scale; Fleming & Courtney, 1984). Participants were randomly assigned to public or private conditions. Then they were asked to write descriptions of their relationships and partners. In the public condition, participants expected to read their descriptions to other members of the group. In the private condition, participants were asked to put their descriptions in a box where they would not be seen by others.

ASSESSMENT OF OUTCOME VARIABLES   Participants' responses were coded for personality variables such as likeability, altruism, competence, sensitivity, and assertiveness/threat. Descriptions were also coded for self-presentational concerns of ingratiation, exemplification, self-promotion, supplication, and intimidation (Jones & Pittman, 1982). That is, researchers looked for evidence of participants presenting themselves in such a way as to establish themselves in the good graces of others, using themselves as an example of some trait, and putting themselves forward for some reward, asking for help, or trying to awe others or to overstate themselves by a display of wealth, talent, and so forth.

MAIN RESULTS   Participants made fewer comments about their own competence, F (1, 36) = 6.44, $p < .05$, altruism, F (1, 36) = 3.16, $p < .08$, and sensitivity, F (1, 36) = 4.62, $p < .05$, in public than in private. Furthermore, low self-esteem participants said they were proud of their altruistic nature more frequently, $M = 1.23$, than high self-esteem participants; $M = .53$; F (1, 36) = 4.93, $p < .05$.

CONCLUSION   "Low self-esteem [participants] may simply not be convinced that they possess abilities that are good enough to justify assertive self-presentation. To make favorable impressions, they may rely on areas where no specific abilities are necessary but where merely possessing a trait (such as altruism) increases one's likeability."

COMMENTARY Schütz & Tice (1997) find that reporting that one behaves altruistically in close relationships, whether the participants actually are altruistic or not, can be motivated by self-presentational concerns. If it is important for the person to be liked, they may present their altruistic behavior publicly to increase self-esteem. This behavior also avoids the appearance of bragging associated with talking about abilities. Management of self-esteem through altruism has been found in other studies. Work by Penner and Finkelstein (1998) suggests that those participants high in helpfulness were motivated by feeling efficacious, thereby raising self-esteem. Gergen et al. (1972) found that self-esteem in females was related to some types of helping but not to others. Therefore, the implications of self-esteem level for altruistic *behavior* is less straightforward than the implications of the motivation to present oneself as being altruistic.

CORRESPONDENCE Astrid Schütz, Department of Psychology, University of Bamberg, Postfach 1549, D-96045, Bamberg, Germany, fax: +49 951 1869; tel +49 951 1867; e-mail to astrid.schuetz@ppp.uni-bamberg.de

Schwartz, S. H. (1970). Elicitation of moral obligation and self-sacrificing behavior. *Journal of Personality and Social Psychology, 15*, 283–293.

OBJECTIVE To investigate the relationship between self-sacrificing behavior, feelings of personal responsibility, and costs related to the behavior

DESIGN Field experiment

SETTING Red Cross donation center

PARTICIPANTS Participants were 144 persons who had just donated blood at a Red Cross donation center. There were 109 males and 35 females, 78% of the sample was married, 32% of the sample was between 18 and 29 years old, 28% of the sample was between 30 and 39 years old, and 40% of the sample was 40 years old or older.

ASSESSMENT OF PREDICTOR VARIABLES Three variables were manipulated in a discussion of bone marrow donation with the participants who had recently donated blood: salience of the consequences of donation for the recipient, the odds that the volunteer would be called on to donate, and the salience of the personal responsibility of the participant to help. After a general description of bone marrow transplantation for leukemia, participants heard a description of the person needing the bone marrow which varied by severity of the consequences: low, "30-year-old female with no matching donor in her family"; moderate, "Young mother with no matching donor in her family"; or high, "Young mother with no matching donor in her family, survival is unlikely without transplant, and her death would be a tragedy for her kids." Next participants heard a description of the odds that they personally would be needed to serve as a bone marrow donor: low, "1 in every 1,000"; or high, "1 in every 25." Finally they heard a description of how donors were being solicited, an appeal with either low personal responsibility—"running ads for potential donors in newspapers across the state"—or high personal responsibility—"turning to people who are giving blood today, because your blood is already available to start the testing."

ASSESSMENT OF OUTCOME VARIABLES Participants' level of willingness to help with the bone marrow donation process was assessed on a 4-point scale created by summing the answers to several questions about the donation process. The four levels of commitment were 0 (not willing to have blood tested for compatibility), 1 (willing to have blood tested, but less than 50/50 chance would actually donate), 2 (at least 50/50 chance would actually donate, but not willing to be on call for future transplants), and 3 (at least 50/50 chance would actually donate and willing to be on call for future transplants).

MAIN RESULTS   Participants volunteered to help with bone marrow donation at high levels. Fifty-nine percent of the participants reached the highest level of commitment, another 24% said there would be at least a 50/50 chance that they would donate, and only
17% failed to commit at a low level. Because of the skewed nature of the distribution, a
squared transformation was performed to produce a more normal distribution. In an
analysis of variance for volunteering with two levels of responsibility, three levels of consequences, and two levels of odds of being called to volunteer, main effects emerged for
salience of responsibility, F (1, 132) = 6.70, $p < .02$, and salience of consequences, F (1,
132) = 3.18, $p < .05$. Participants were more committed to volunteering under conditions
of high responsibility than under conditions of low responsibility, Ms = 7.08 vs. 5.72. Participants were most committed to volunteering under moderate consequences for the
person needing a donation, slightly less committed under high consequences, and least
committed under low consequences; Ms = 7.23, 6.38, and 5.60, respectively. This main effect is qualified by an interaction of the consequences variable with the odds variable,
F (2, 132) = 4.88, $p < .01$. On examination of the means, it became evident that in the condition in which there were low odds of being called to actually donate there was a linearly
increasing effect of consequences for the donee on commitment to volunteer. However, in
the condition in which there were high odds of being called to participate, there was a
curvilinear relationship between the consequences for the donee and commitment to volunteer. The moderate-consequences condition produced the highest commitments to
volunteer, whereas the low- and high-consequences conditions produced equally low levels of commitment. A single post hoc comparison of these patterns was significant, F (4,
132) = 3.82, $p < .01$. Approximately 7% of the variance in volunteering was accounted for
by this comparison.

CONCLUSION   "The strikingly high rate of volunteering is traced to the momentum of
compliance. The chances of finding a compatible donor under 1/25 odds were good. The
intensity of pressure may therefore have been experienced as less legitimate, and reactance
may have been expressed more freely as refusal. [In the odds of 1/1000 condition] results
support the view that the more fully the consequences of action or inaction for the welfare of others are spelled out in the decision situation, the more difficult it is to neutralize
norms and hence to violate them. Based on the assumption that norms giving rise to a
sense of moral obligation were activated, the significant relationship between volunteering and salience of personal responsibility in the appeal may be interpreted as evidence
that this situational variable influenced the ease with which the moral norms could be
neutralized."

COMMENTARY   Two important points come from this research by Schwartz (1970). First,
willingness to act prosocially can be affected by the kinds of appeals made. Research in attitudes and in advertising has shown that it is possible to change opinions on political issues and to get people to buy products and services and even to volunteer or give money
to charities. The special message of this study is that increasing the persuasiveness of an
appeal on several variables at once can produce reactance and even lead to decreased
prosocial behavior. The second important point in this article is that people who engage
in prosocial behavior, particularly when enacting that behavior, act in accordance with
principles of consistency. Therefore, at the time they are behaving prosocially, they are
particularly susceptible to appeals for similar prosocial behavior. The work of Schwartz
here and elsewhere on individual differences in altruism is considered classic. This early
representative piece is supplemented by an extended list of references to his work in the
reference list at the end of this document.

CORRESPONDENCE   None available

Senneker, P., & Hendrick, C. (1983). Androgyny and helping behavior. *Journal of Personality and Social Psychology, 45*, 916–925.

OBJECTIVE   To investigate the relationship between masculinity, femininity, and androgyny and helping behavior

DESIGN   Laboratory experiment

SETTING   University of Miami

PARTICIPANTS   Participants were 78 male and 82 female students in introductory psychology classes who received partial course credit for participation. All of the participants had taken the Bem Sex Role Inventory (Bem, 1974) at an earlier point in the semester. Androgyny is defined as having approximately equally high levels of both masculine (instrumental) and feminine (expressive) traits. Sex-typed refers to having high levels of traits associated with one's gender and low levels of trait associated with the other gender. Sex-typed females have high levels of femininity and low levels of masculinity, whereas sex-typed males have high levels of masculinity and low levels of femininity. In this study there were 76 androgynous and 84 sex-typed participants approximately equally distributed among experimental conditions.

ASSESSMENT OF PREDICTOR VARIABLES   Participants were randomly assigned to one of three conditions that manipulated the number of bystanders: (1) participant was alone with the victim, (2) participant and victim were grouped with four confederates of the same sex as the participant, or (3) participant and victim were grouped with two male and two female confederates. All participants were ostensibly in a study of college living in which they would interact with another anonymous student via microphone and headphones. In reality, the anonymous student was a confederate who, in the course of the discussion, choked on some food, struggled for breath, cried out for help, and then went silent.

ASSESSMENT OF OUTCOME VARIABLES   Two outcome variables were measured: the amount of time it took participants to leave their cubicle and go for help (participants who did not leave were assigned a maximum response time of 3 minutes) and whether the participant engaged in direct help by going for the door labeled for the anonymous student or engaged in indirect help by going for the door labeled for the experimenter.

MAIN RESULTS   For *response time analyses*, there were three significant main effects and no significant interaction effects. Participants in six-person groups responded more slowly than participants alone with the victim; $Ms = 94.1$ seconds vs. 65.9 seconds; $F(2, 148) = 4.1$, $p < .05$. Females responded more slowly than males; $Ms = 95.0$ seconds vs. 74.3 seconds; $F(1, 148) = 4.3$, $p < .05$. Sex-typed participants responded more slowly than androgynous participants; $Ms = 94.2$ seconds vs. 74.6 seconds; $F(1, 148) = 4.4$, $p < .05$. When examining *helping behavior*, the data show that 69% of the participants offered some form of help and that, of those helping, 61% attempted to help the victim directly. There is a marginal difference between the number of male participants who attempted to help either directly or indirectly and the number of female participants that attempted to help; 74% vs. 63%; $z = 1.55$, $p < .07$. More male than female participants offered direct help; 71% vs. 50%; $z = 2.28$, $p < .02$. There was no difference between androgynous and sex-typed participants on number of participants offering help or type of help offered. More participants who thought they were alone with the victim offered help than participants who thought there were four other bystanders, 81% vs. 63%; $p < .01$. For sex-typed participants, more males offered direct help, and more females offered indirect help or no help at all, $\chi^2(2) = 7.2$, $p < .05$. The same pattern did not hold for androgynous participants; $\chi^2(2) = 3.16$, $p < .05$.

CONCLUSION   "Speed of helping and/or proportion of subjects helping showed: (a) more help by males than by females, (b) more help in subject alone conditions than in larger group conditions, and (c) more help by androgynous than sex-typed males and females but not between androgynous males and females. Results further suggested that such competence is due to masculinity rather than sex *per se*."

COMMENTARY   Like Eagly and Crowley (1986) and Johnson et al. (1989), Senneker and Hendrick (1983) found that males were more helpful than females. Furthermore, as Schenk and Heinisch (1986) and Rushton et al. (1989) found, enacting altruistic behavior may require some instrumentality in conjunction with expressiveness. The best demonstration of that in the current study is the higher levels of helping by males who have a naturally high level of masculine instrumentality and higher levels of helping by androgynous than by sex-typed females.

CORRESPONDENCE   Clyde Hendrick, Department of Psychology, Texas Tech University, Box 42051, Lubbock, TX 79409-2051

Sharma, V., & Rosha, J. (1992). Altruism as a function of self-actualization and locus of control of benefactor. *Psychological Studies, 37*(1), 26–30.

OBJECTIVE   To examine the relationship between altruism, self-actualization, and locus of control

DESIGN   Cross-sectional survey

SETTING   Punjabi University, Patiala, India

PARTICIPANTS   Participants consisted of 48 female students of Part I and II of Punjabi University, Patiala. The mean age was 21.9 years.

ASSESSMENT OF PREDICTOR VARIABLES   Participants completed a series of questionnaires measuring locus of control (Rotter, 1966) and self-actualization (Personality Orientation Inventory; Shostrom, 1964). Participants were statistically divided into four groups based on level of self-actualization (high or low) and typical locus of control (internal or external). Locus of control is defined as "the perceived source of control over one's behavior. It is measured along a dimension running from high internal to high external, with internal persons being those who take responsibility for their own actions and view themselves as having control over their own destinies, and externals being those who tend to see control as residing elsewhere and tend to attribute success or failure to outside forces" (Reber, 1995, p. 423). Self-actualization is the fulfillment of the full personal potential once all lower levels of basic needs are fulfilled. Qualities of the self-actualized person include: "independence, autonomy, a tendency to form a few deep friendships, a 'philosophical' sense of humor, a tendency to resist outside pressures, and a general transcendence of the environment rather than a simple 'coping' with it" (Reber, 1995, p. 700).

ASSESSMENT OF OUTCOME VARIABLES   Participants completed a self-report altruism inventory (Rushton, Chrisjohn, & Fekken, 1981).

MAIN RESULTS   High self-actualized participants scored higher on altruism, $M = 54.76$, than low self-actualized participants, $M = 46.67$; $F = 12.57$, $p < .01$. Participants with an internal locus of control scored higher on altruism, $M = 55.37$, than participants with an external locus of control, $M = 45.96$; $F = 17.41$, $p < .01$. An interaction effect of self-actualization and locus of control on altruism was significant. Participants who both scored high on self-actualization and had an internal locus of control were more altruistic than participants in any of the other three groups. The other three groups do not differ from each other on altruism scores.

CONCLUSION   Both high self-actualization and internal locus of control are personality characteristics associated with higher altruism scores in this sample.

COMMENTARY   In Sharma and Rosha's (1992) study of Indian students, a positive relationship between internal locus of control and altruism was found. This mimics the relationship between instrumentality and altruism (Schenk & Heinisch, 1986; Rushton et al., 1989) in that some internal motivation and action may be necessary for altruism to take place. The positive relationship between self-actualization and altruism suggests that altruists may be more psychologically healthy and mature than persons scoring lower on altruism. This idea is in agreement with other research in the current bibliography that has found a relationship between positive mental health and altruism (Mohan & Bhatia, 1987; Rushton et al., 1989). Johnson et al. (1989), however, found no relationship between neuroticism and altruism.

CORRESPONDENCE   Vandana Sharma, Lecturer, Department of Psychology, Punjabi University, Patiala-147 002, India

Sibicky, M. E., Schroeder, D. A., & Dovidio, J. F. (1995). Empathy and helping: Considering the consequences of intervention. *Basic & Applied Social Psychology,* 16(4), 435–453.

OBJECTIVE   To investigate whether people high in empathic concern would be sensitive to the long-term consequences of their altruistic behavior

DESIGN   Laboratory experiment

SETTING   A university

PARTICIPANTS   Participants consisted of 84 female introductory psychology students. They received course credit for their participation.

ASSESSMENT OF PREDICTOR VARIABLES   Participants were randomly assigned to one of four conditions. The conditions varied on whether the participants were instructed to imagine the feelings of a person who needed help on a puzzle or to objectively observe the actions of a person who needed help on a puzzle. The conditions also varied on the effect of the participant's potential intervention. Participants were allowed to give hints to the other person to help them solve the puzzle. They were told either that "each hint they provided would make it easier for the person to solve the puzzle and avoid the possibility of shock" or that "giving too many hints during the session could penalize the person in the future." Participants indicated their feelings for the other person on the Emotional Response Questionnaire (Toi & Batson, 1982). This questionnaire includes subscales for personal distress, empathic concern, and sadness.

ASSESSMENT OF OUTCOME VARIABLES   Participants flipped switches that they believed gave the person completing the puzzle hints. The experimenter recorded the number of hints the participant gave.

MAIN RESULTS   Participants who were asked to imagine the feelings of the other person reported greater empathic concern, $M = 4.42$, than did participants who were asked to objectively observe the other person; $M = 3.60$; $F(1, 80) = 10.17, p < .003$. There were no differences between the conditions on personal distress or sadness. Across all conditions, participants who were higher on empathic concern reported thinking more about the consequences of their hints for the person doing the puzzle, $r = .32, p < .001$. Participants who both imagined the feelings of the other and were warned of potential detriments for giving hints gave significantly fewer hints to the other person, $M = 1.86$, than participants in the other three conditions averaged; $M = 2.90$; $t(80) = 4.20, p < .001$. Furthermore, the relationship between empathic concern and number of hints given was positive when participants believed there was benefit for the other person, $r = .21$, $p < .20$, but there was a significant negative relationship between empathic concern and number of hints given when participants believed there was a detriment for the other person, $r = -.37$, $p < .02$.

CONCLUSION "As expected, an empathic orientation and greater empathic concern related to greater concern for the consequences of intervention. This greater concern was manifested in different levels of intervention, depending on whether [participants] were or were not aware that intervention had potential detrimental effects. As predicted, more empathic [participants] intervened *less* when they believed that such action might ultimately be harmful to the person requesting hints."

COMMENTARY Sibicky et al. (1995) demonstrate that altruism is not all one-sided. That is, the altruistic person does not act only to ease his or her own empathic concern but takes into consideration the outcome of his or her actions for the person needing help. Altruistic people are interested in helping and not harming those toward whom their behavior is directed. Consistent with other studies in this bibliography (Archer et al., 1981; Clary & Orenstein, 1991; Eisenberg et al., 1989), when there is no potential harm to the needy person, empathic concern leads to increased prosocial behavior. However, other studies in this bibliography found that empathic concern was associated with altruism under specific conditions (Batson et al., 1986) or that the relationship between empathic concern and altruism was mediated by feelings of oneness with the needy person (Carlo et al., 1991).

CORRESPONDENCE Mark Sibicky, Department of Psychology, Marietta College, Marietta, OH 45750

Smith, B. M. M., & Nelson, L. D. (1975). Personality correlates of helping behavior. *Psychological Reports, 37,* 307–316.

OBJECTIVE To differentiate between the personality variables associated with volunteers and nonvolunteers

DESIGN Quasi-experiment with survey

SETTING Community residents in Virginia

PARTICIPANTS Participants were 571 male rescue squad members and members of Big Brothers organizations in Virginia. Questionnaires were distributed to the volunteer participants by the directors of their organizations. Nonvolunteer participants were 566 males drawn from a statewide probability sample that excluded anyone who indicated membership in a helping organization.

ASSESSMENT OF PREDICTOR VARIABLES All participants completed Cattell's Personality Factor Questionnaire (also called the 16 PF because it evaluates 16 separate personality traits; Cattell, 1956).

ASSESSMENT OF OUTCOME VARIABLES The dependent variable in this study was whether the participant was a member of a volunteer group or not.

MAIN RESULTS Compared with nonvolunteers, volunteers were more outgoing, $Ms = 48.17$ vs. 51.83; $t = 6.13$, $p < .001$, happy-go-lucky, $Ms = 48.23$ vs. 51.77; $t = 5.93$, $p < .001$, venturesome, $Ms = 48.17$ vs. 51.83; $t = 6.13$, $p < .001$, and tender-minded, $Ms = 48.66$ vs. 51.36; $t = 4.52$, $p < .001$, and had higher superego strength; $Ms = 49.12$ vs. 50.89; $t = 6.13$, $p < .01$. Compared with nonvolunteers, volunteers were less shrewd, $Ms = 50.83$ vs. 49.16; $t = 2.79$, $p < .01$, less liberal, $Ms = 50.94$ vs. 49.05; $t = 3.17$, $p < .01$, and less self-sufficient, $Ms = 52.05$ vs. 47.96; $t = 6.87$, $p < .001$.

CONCLUSION "Members of volunteer groups and nonvolunteers scored significantly differently on Cattell's 16PF scale, volunteers being extroverted (out-going, happy-go-lucky, venturesome, and tenderminded), and scoring lower on shrewd, liberal, and self-sufficient."

COMMENTARY   Smith and Nelson's (1975) study is a nice addition to the group of studies that shows that extraversion and masculine/instrumental traits are related to prosocial behavior (Rushton et al., 1989; Schenk & Heinisch, 1986). It seems that for volunteering and other prosocial behavior to take place, there has to be a willingness to be among people and to engage in goal-oriented behavior. For extraverts, being among people in order to help is rewarding; for introverts, being among people is a cost. Note, however, that tender-mindedness is a construct that is more correctly associated with agreeableness than with extraversion and that high superego strength is more correctly associated with conscientiousness than with extraversion. Furthermore, whether work in this genre shows a relation between instrumentality and helping may depend on the type of prosocial behaviors that are examined (see the annotation of Eagly & Crowley, 1986).

CORRESPONDENCE   None available

Smith, K. D., Keating, J. P., & Stotland, E. (1989). Altruism reconsidered: The effect of denying feedback on a victim's status to empathic witness. *Journal of Personality and Social Psychology, 57,* 641–650.

OBJECTIVE   To explore the role of empathy in helping for the sake of seeing the other express joy

DESIGN   Laboratory experiment

SETTING   University of Washington

PARTICIPANTS   Participants were 64 undergraduates at the University of Washington who were recruited by phone for two 1-hour sessions.

ASSESSMENT OF PREDICTOR VARIABLES   Participants watched a videotape of a female freshman who was experiencing feelings of stress and isolation. Participants were randomly assigned to one of four conditions differing on two levels of empathy and two levels of expected feedback. For the low-empathy condition, participants were instructed to watch the videotape attending to body movement, trying to be as objective as possible, remembering exactly what the person does. In the high-empathy condition, participants were instructed to imagine how the person being interviewed feels, paying attention to tone of voice and facial expressions. Then participants were asked whether they would like to provide advice to the participant on dealing with college life. In the feedback condition, the participants were told that the woman would read the advice on her next trip to the lab, where she would videotape a response the participant could view later. In the no-feedback condition, participants were told that they would have no further contact with the woman, whether they decided to give advice or not.

ASSESSMENT OF OUTCOME VARIABLES   Whether the participant chose to write advice to the woman and the number of words the participant wrote were the outcome variables. Participants were also asked the extent to which they experienced eight emotions indicative of empathic concern (i.e., compassionate, touched) and eight emotions indicative of personal distress (i.e., alarmed, upset). Scores on personal distress were subtracted from scores on empathic concern to create a measure of *relative empathic concern*—that is, a measure of empathic concern unconfounded with personal distress.

MAIN RESULTS   A median split on relative empathic concern allowed for analysis of a 2×2 factorial design with two levels of relative empathic concern (low and high) and two levels of feedback (feedback and no feedback). The four conditions were high relative empathic concern/feedback, low relative empathic concern/feedback, high relative empathic concern/no feedback, and low relative empathic concern/no feedback. Planned comparisons revealed that more helping occurred in the high-relative-empathic-concern/feedback condition than in the other three conditions averaged (93% of respondents helping vs. 56% of respondents helping; Fisher's exact test, $p < .007$). Participants in the four conditions also wrote messages of considerably different length; ts (52) $\leq$ 2.95, $ps < .005$. In a 2 × 2 analysis of variance of empathy instruction × feedback condition on helping, main effects were revealed for feedback condition and empathy instruction, $Fs < 4.18$, $ps < .05$. Participants helped more when instructed to imagine the person's feelings than to observe her actions (77% vs. 54%) and helped more when told they would receive feedback than when told they would not receive feedback (81% vs. 50%). There was no interaction between the variables.

CONCLUSION   "The effect of empathic concern on motivation to help in this situation appears limited to conditions in which the witness expects renewed exposure to the help recipient. Moreover, the favorable effect of feedback is specific to persons high in empathy. We attribute the special responsiveness of empathic (participants) to the feedback manipulation to an enhanced sensitivity to empathic joy."

COMMENTARY   Smith, Keating, and Stotland (1989) challenge both the empathy-altruism hypothesis (Batson et al., 1981) and the negative state relief model (Cialdini et al., 1987) with a proposal that altruistic acts may be motivated by a "sensitivity to the vicarious joy at the resolution of the victim's need." They suggest that feedback in the presence of either dispositional or situationally induced empathy instead of simply empathic concern or personal distress drives the relationship between the variables. This relationship held for willingness to help, but no interaction was significant for the length-of-message dependent variable, indicating amount of helping. Sibicky et al. (1995) also found that altruistic people do not simply act to ease their own empathic concern but take into consideration the outcome of their actions for the person needing help. Although feedback may be desirable and even important in people's willingness to help, this study fails to acknowledge adequately the role of egoistic motives and does not firmly establish the role of joy in the influence of feedback.

CORRESPONDENCE   None available

Staub, E. (1974). Helping a distressed person: Social, personality, and stimulus determinants. In L. Berkowitz (Ed.), *Advances in experimental social psychology* (Vol. 7, 203–341). New York: Academic Press.

OBJECTIVE   To examine the social and situational determinants of helping behavior

DESIGN   *Studies 1, 2,* and *3*: Field experiment. *Study 4*: Ratings of film clips

SETTING   Cambridge, Massachusetts

PARTICIPANTS   *Study 1*: Participants were 60 passersby on a street in lower-middle-class residential areas in Cambridge, Massachusetts. During the experiment, there was no other person within 50 feet of the participant or confederate. *Study 2*: Participants were 58 passersby on a street in lower-middle-class residential areas in Cambridge, Massachusetts. *Study 3*: Participants were 40 passersby on a street in lower-middle-class residential areas in Cambridge, Massachusetts. *Study 4*: Participants were 82 undergraduates.

ASSESSMENT OF PREDICTOR VARIABLES   *Study 1*: In this naturalistic field experiment, naive participants walking down a sidewalk alone encountered a confederate who either (1) lay down on the sidewalk about 40 feet from the corner (no-information condition), (2) approached the same spot and grabbed his knee before collapsing (bad-knee condition), or (3) approached the same spot and grabbed his heart before collapsing (bad-heart condition). Following the collapse, the confederate either struggled to his feet and leaned against a wall (mild-distress condition) or struggled to get up but remained sitting on the ground (severe-distress condition). *Study 2*: In a similar manner to Study 1, participants encountered a confederate victim displaying either the severe-distress-with-bad-knee or severe-distress-with-bad-heart behavior. The difference in Study 2 was the addition of an easy-escape versus difficult-escape manipulation. In the difficult-escape condition, the confederate victim was on the same side of the street as the participant. In the easy-escape condition, the confederate victim was on the opposite side of the street. *Study 3*: The confederate in Study 3 followed the exact same procedures as in Study 1 (same part of the same street) with the severe-bad-knee and severe-bad-heart conditions. Study 4: Participants watched two film clips of each of two confederates enacting the severe-bad-heart condition.

ASSESSMENT OF OUTCOME VARIABLES *Study 1*: Two concealed experimenters confirmed that the participant noticed the confederate victim and then noted whether the participant approached the victim and made a call to a roommate as requested by the victim. *Study 2*: Outcome variables were the same as in Study 1. *Study 3*: Outcome variables were the same as in Study 1. *Study 4*: Participants rated the degree and nature of distress of the victim and then rated the personal characteristics of each victim.

MAIN RESULTS *Study 1*: Fifteen of the 60 participants approached the victim, but none of these participants were in the "bad heart" condition. Though there was no difference in the no-information and bad-knee conditions, approach was significantly lower in the bad-heart condition than the other two conditions; χ^2 (1, $n = 60$) = 8.10, $p < .01$. More participants made the requested telephone call when the confederate was in severe distress than in mild distress; χ^2 (1, $n = 60$) = 4.10, $p < .05$. *Study 2*: More participants approached the victim in the difficult-escape condition than in the easy-escape condition; 71.8% vs. 26.9%; χ^2 (1, $n = 58$) = 18.5, $p < .001$. In addition, more participants made the telephone call for the victim in the difficult-escape condition than in the easy-escape condition; 50% vs. 7.6%; χ^2 (1, $n = 58$) = 5.41, $p < .02$. In both escape conditions, more participants approached the victim in the bad-heart condition than in the bad-knee condition; 67.8% vs. 36.6%; χ^2 (1, $n = 58$) = 4.46, $p < .05$. *Study 3*: Six of ten participants in the bad-heart condition and four of ten participants in the bad-knee condition approached the confederate, but the difference was not significant. The frequency of help in the bad-knee condition was similar to that in Study 1, but the frequency of help in the bad-heart condition was greater (Fisher exact $p < .01$). *Study 4*: Participants described the confederate of Study 1 as slightly healthier, F (1, 76) = 3.20, $p < .07$, and more attractive than the confederate of Study 2, F (1, 76) = 26.23, $p < .001$. Participant ratings did not differ in trustworthiness, dangerousness, or credibility of performance. Participants described the Study 2 confederate's behavior as indicating a heart problem more often than the Study 1 confederate's behavior; χ^2 (1, $n = 82$) = 6.40, $p < .02$. Participants tended to describe the Study 2 confederate's behavior as due to something else.

CONCLUSION "A clear result was that when the victim was not in the path of a would-be helper he was helped less, perhaps because the social and personal costs of not helping were smaller. However, if involvement is forced on them by circumstances, psychological and social processes may be activated that will lead to helping behavior possibly even to a true concern for another's welfare and a desire to help him. [Study 4 results suggest that] a discrepancy between a person's general characteristics and his condition of need may create ambiguity, possibly suspicion, and as a consequence might reduce helping behavior."

COMMENTARY Staub's (1974) experiments are in line with the typical emergency helping experiments. Staub varied situational components, such as proximity of emergency to participant, and victim characteristics, such as degree and type of victim distress. The researchers experimentally manipulated the costs of helping, thereby manipulating the willingness to help. This is similar to Kerber's study (1984), in which willingness to help in a nonemergency setting was affected by manipulation of scenarios involving rewards and costs. The author's addition of Study 4 to explain the differences in helping the "bad heart" confederate in Studies 1 and 2 improves the interpretation of the results. In particular, the author's suggestion that the attractiveness and apparent health of the Study 1 confederate led to confusion of participants and confounded their reactions introduces another situational variable which explains willingness to help in an emergency situation—congruence of the current emergency with stereotypes of emergency situations.

CORRESPONDENCE   Ervin Staub, Department of Psychology, Tobin Hall Box 37710, University of Massachusetts, Amherst, MA 01003-7710

Switzer, G. E., Dew, M. A., Butterworth, V. A., Simmons, R. G., & Schimmel, M. (1997). Understanding donor's motivations: A study of unrelated bone marrow donors. *Social Science and Medicine*, *45*(1), 137–147.

OBJECTIVE   To investigate the reported motivations of bone marrow donation

DESIGN   Cross-sectional survey

SETTING   Nationwide

PARTICIPANTS   Participants were 343 individuals who donated bone marrow through the National Marrow Donors Program between December 1987 and December 1991. All participants were unrelated to recipients of the donations. Participants were contacted three times: predonation, 1 to 2 weeks postdonation, and 1 year postdonation. Sixty-six percent of the donors were men, 65% were currently married and had at least one child, 99% were high school graduates, 52% had completed some college, 43% were Protestant, 35% were Catholic, 3% were Jewish, and 19% did not consider themselves affiliated with any of these religions. Age ranged from 22 to 55 years old, with a mean of 38 years old.

ASSESSMENT OF PREDICTOR VARIABLES   Predonation participants completed the several questions about background characteristics: gender, age, religion, marital status, whether the donor had any children, and educational level. Then participants answered the open-ended question, "In your own words, what do you feel your reasons are for donating?" Up to four responses were categorized for each participant into six categories. Exchange-related motives were related to consideration of the rewards of donating and the costs of donating. Idealized motives concerned responses that were made automatically without any consideration of potential costs or even their own motivations. Normative motives concerned social obligation or duty. Positive feeling motives concerned the good feeling it gave to perform the helping act. Empathy-related motives concerned feelings toward the recipient. Experienced-based motives concerned other experiences of donating blood, volunteerism, or personal experiences that made the person aware of the need for bone marrow.

ASSESSMENT OF OUTCOME VARIABLES   At each of the three time periods, sets of questionnaires were administrated. Predonation participants were asked about feelings of ambivalence toward donation (i.e., "I sometimes feel unsure about donating"; Simmons, Schimmel, & Butterworth, 1977). Scale scores ranged from 0 to 7, with 0 representing no ambivalence and 7 representing complete ambivalence. One to two weeks after donation, participants were asked several questions about physical difficulties associated with donation (0 = no difficulties to 10 = high physical difficulty). Psychological reactions to donation were measured shortly after donation and again 1 year after donation (i.e., happiness with donation, worries about own health; 0 = no difficulties, 4 = high difficulties). Also at 1 year participants completed measures of self-esteem (Rosenberg & Simmons, 1972), measuring their feelings of being a better person as a result of the donation, and of concern about the recipient.

MAIN RESULTS   The types of motives the participants reported were as follows: exchange-related motives (45%), idealized helping motives (37%), normative motives (26%), positive feeling motives (25%), empathy-related motives (18%), experience-based motives (8%), and uncategorizable motives (9%). Because relatively few of the motives mentioned were experience-based or uncategorizable, these categories were dropped from further analysis. Female donors reported more empathy, 23% vs. 13%; χ^2 (1, $n = 342$) = 5.02, $p < .05$, and positive feeling, 31% vs. 21%; χ^2 (1, $n = 342$) = 3.83, $p < .05$, than male donors. Younger donors were more likely to report exchange-related, 48% vs. 38%; χ^2 (1, $n = 343$) = 3.66, $p = .056$, and idealized motives, 41% vs. 31%; χ^2 (1, $n = 343$) = 3.67, $p < .055$, than older donors. Protestants were more likely to report normative motives than other religious groups; 30% vs. 22%; χ^2 (1, $n = 343$) = 2.91, $p < .088$.

A series of hierarchical multiple-regression analyses were conducted with background characteristics entered in the first block, donor motives entered in the second block, and each of the donation reactions (i.e., ambivalence, physical difficulties) entered individually as dependent variables. After controlling for background characteristics, donors who expressed exchange-related and positive feeling motives reported more ambivalence predonation, βs = .13 and −.18, respectively; ps < .05, than those who did not express these motives. After controlling for background characteristics, donors who expressed idealized motives reported more psychological difficulty shortly after donation than those who did not report idealized motives; β = .18, $p < .01$. Similarly, after controlling for background characteristics, donors who expressed idealized motives reported more psychological difficulty 1 year after donation than those who did not report idealized motives; β = .14, $p < .05$. After controlling for background characteristics, donors who expressed empathy-related and positive feeling motives were more likely to report feeling like better people, βs = .12 and .14, respectively; ps < .05, than those who did not express these motives. Finally, after controlling for background characteristics, donors who expressed empathy-related motives reported more concern for the recipient 1 year after donation than those who did not report empathy-related motives, β = .22, $p < .001$.

CONCLUSION   Among the background characteristics, gender had the greatest effect on motives reported. Female donors reported more expected positive feelings, more empathy-related motives, and the desire to help someone than did males. In addition, "Donors who reported exchange motives (weighing costs and benefits) and donors who reported simple (or idealized) helping motives experienced the donation as less positive in terms of higher pre-donation ambivalence and negative post-donation psychological reactions than did remaining donors. Donors who reported positive feeling and empathy motives had the most positive donation reactions in terms of lower ambivalence and feeling like better persons post-donation."

COMMENTARY   Switzer et al. (1991) investigated the underlying motivations of prosocial behavior. Two of these motivations can be interpreted as predecessors of altruism—empathy-related motives and positive feeling motives—identified in other studies (Batson et al., 1989; Ben-Artzi & Mikulincer, 1996). Though these two motives were unrelated to physical and psychological effects for the donors, both led donors to feel like better people for their sacrifice. Donating bone marrow out of some abstract ideal without considering the consequences, however, led to more psychological difficulty postdonation. Unlike Schwartz (1970), who found that activating social norms related to prosocial behavior led to increased helping, Switzer et al. found that normative motives were unrelated to either the rewards or costs associated with helping. More research is needed in this area to clarify the relationship between normative pressures toward prosocial behavior and the consequences of those pressures.

CORRESPONDENCE   Galen E. Switzer, 3811 O'Hara Street, Pittsburgh, PA 15213

Unger, L. S., & Thumuluri, L. K. (1997). Trait empathy and continuous help-ing: The case of voluntarism. *Journal of Social Behavior and Personality,* *12*(3), 785–800.

OBJECTIVE   To examine the relationship between trait empathy and volunteering

DESIGN   Cross-sectional survey

SETTING   Eight midwestern cities

PARTICIPANTS   Participants were 372 adults in eight midwestern cities. The sample was similar to the U.S. population, though males and blacks were somewhat underrepresented. Questionnaires were distributed by undergraduate college students to their friends and rel-atives. All of the students were given age and gender quotas.

ASSESSMENT OF PREDICTOR VARIABLES   Participants completed the Davis (1983) Inter-personal Reactivity Index, which has four subscales: Perspective Taking, Fantasy, Empathic Concern, and Personal Distress.

ASSESSMENT OF OUTCOME VARIABLES   Participants were asked if they had "done volun-teer work in the past year without pay for a nonprofit organization." They were then asked to indicate how many hours per month and the types of organizations with which they vol-unteered. "Participants were categorized as continuous volunteers if they (a) answered yes to the first question, (b) averaged at least one hour per month of volunteering, and (c) in-dicated that they had worked for certain types of nonprofit organizations." The main de-pendent variable is a dichotomous variable of whether or not the participant was a contin-uous volunteer.

MAIN RESULTS   Sixty percent of the respondents reported that they had done volunteer work in the past year. Structural equation modeling was used to estimate the relationship between the four subscales of the Davis empathy measure (Perspective Taking, Empathic Concern, Personal Distress, and Fantasy) and status as a continuous volunteer. All subscales of the Davis empathy measure were allowed to intercorrelate. Although the model's χ^2 esti-mate did not indicate a good fit ($\chi^2(371) = 742.56$), other statistics better used to assess the goodness of fit of the structural model indicated that, indeed, the hypothesized model fit well; *GFI* = .92, *AGFI* = .90, *RMSR* = .08. Perspective Taking was directly related to volun-teerism, $\gamma_1 = .16$, $t = 1.91$. Empathic Concern was directly related to volunteerism, $\gamma_1 = .17$, $t = 1.92$. Personal Distress was directly related to volunteerism, $\gamma_1 = .11$, $t = 2.13$. However, Fantasy was not significantly related to volunteerism, $\gamma_1 = -.06$, $t = -1.10$.

CONCLUSION   "The results indicate that the Perspective Taking, Empathic Concern, and Personal Distress dimensions of trait empathy positively influence volunteerism. These find-ings extend the prosocial literature, where the investigation of empathy and altruistic behav-ior has focused primarily on one-time helping rather than ongoing prosocial behavior."

COMMENTARY   Unger and Thumuluri's (1997) study found important relationships be-tween trait empathy and continuous volunteering. Other research in this bibliography that addresses empathy and volunteering has found equivocal results. Clary and Orenstein (1991) examined both motives and abilities associated with volunteering. They found that volunteers who were not accepted to remain as volunteers had lower levels of perspective taking. They also found that empathic concern was related to altruistic motivation for seek-ing volunteer work. Penner and Finkelstein (1998) found that length of service and time spent volunteering were correlated with other-oriented empathy and helpfulness. To extend this line of research, it would be good to investigate the interplay of trait empathy with nor-mative pressures such as social responsibility (Berkowitz & Lutterman, 1968) and instru-mentality and expressiveness (Smith & Nelson, 1975).

CORRESPONDENCE   Lynnette Unger or Lakshmi Thumuluri, Department of Marketing, Miami University, Oxford, OH 45056

Wegner, D. M., Vallacher, R. R., Kiersted, G. W., & Dizadji, D. (1986). Action identification in the emergence of social behavior. *Social Cognition, 4*(1), 18–38.

OBJECTIVE To explore the relationship between the level of ambiguity at which people describe their actions and the consistency of future actions

DESIGN Laboratory experiment

SETTING Trinity University

PARTICIPANTS *Study 1*: Participants consisted of 39 undergraduate students at Trinity University. They received course credit in introductory psychology in exchange for their participation. There were 27 females and 12 males.

ASSESSMENT OF PREDICTOR VARIABLES *Study 1*: Participants were first engaged in a filler task designed to keep their attention for a period of time. Then participants were asked to complete a questionnaire describing their activities. Participants who described their activity at a low level (i.e., "completing a questionnaire") or in terms of the details of the task were designated as low-level-identification participants. Participants who described their activity at a higher level (i.e., "participating in an experiment") or in terms of the overall nature of the task were designated as absence-of-low-level-identification participants. Next, participants were given questionnaires with items concerning either helping with the experiment (the altruism condition) or gaining extra credit for participation (the egoistic condition). This was a situational manipulation to focus participants on either altruistic or egoistic explanations for their behavior.

ASSESSMENT OF OUTCOME VARIABLES *Study 1*: A representative from the psychology department then asked the participants to fill out a questionnaire, supposedly for administrative purposes separate from the experiment. The participants ranked 10 psychology activities (i.e., "learning about psychology books in the library," "helping by participating in a study," and "participate in a project for extra credit") on their preference for the activities. The ranking of the altruistic (i.e., "helping by participating in a study") and egoistic choices (i.e., "participate in a project for extra credit") were the outcome variables.

MAIN RESULTS *Study 1*: Although all participants demonstrated a preference for getting extra credit among the ranked psychology activities, participants who had been primed to think about altruism and identified their participation at a low level ranked helping higher, $M = 5.45$, than getting extra credit; $M = 3.80$; $F(1, 34) = 5.00, p < .05$. In a complementary fashion, participants who had been primed to think egotistically and identified their participation at a low level ranked getting extra credit higher, $M = 7.10$, than helping; $M = 5.36$; $F(1, 34) = 5.56, p < .05$. All effects for higher level (low-level absent) participants were nonsignificant; all Fs < 1.0.

CONCLUSION In this experiment, making an altruistic or egoistic choice was dependent on the participant's understanding of what they had just been doing. Participants who had a very general, low-level conception of what they were doing were susceptible to suggestion that the activity was either altruistic or egoistic. "They adopted the new identification of their action, and then went on to choose subsequent action consistent with that identification."

COMMENTARY As in the Schwartz (1970) study, participants' understanding of their actions as altruistic in the current study (Wegner et al., 1986) led to increased willingness to act prosocially. The difference in the two studies is not just a difference in the methods of influencing attitudes and behavior; the current study found that some participants were more susceptible to influence because they had not engaged in complex cognitions about their actions. This has implications for the ability to influence or encourage altruistic behavior. Individuals with low-level, detail-oriented understanding of their tasks can be influenced to think that they have behaved altruistically. They are thereby encouraged to continue behaving altruistically because they wish to maintain consistency of behavior. Individuals who understand their behavior at higher levels are not so easily influenced. It would be interesting to see if this concept of action identification is related to intelligence, cognitive complexity, or level of boredom with the experiment—all of which may be confounding factors.

CORRESPONDENCE   Daniel M. Wegner, Department of Psychology, University of Virginia, Gilmer Hall, Room 104E, Charlottesville, VA 22903

REFERENCES

❖ Article included in Annotated Bibliography

Adorno, T. W., Frenkel-Brunswick, E., Levinson, D. J., & Sanford, R. N. (1950). *The authoritarian personality.* New York: Harper.

Allport, G., & Ross, J. M. (1967). Personal religious orientation and prejudice. *Journal of Personality and Social Psychology, 5,* 432–433.

Altemeyer, B. (1981). *Right-wing authoritarianism.* Winnipeg: University of Manitoba Press.

Altemeyer, B. (1988). *Enemies of freedom.* San Francisco: Jossey-Bass.

Altemeyer, R. A., & Hunsberger, B. (1992). Authoritarianism, religious fundamentalism, quest and prejudice. *International Journal for the Psychology of Religion, 2,* 113–133.

❖ Archer, R. L., Diaz-Loving, R., Gollwitzer, P. M., Davis, M. H., & Foushee, H. C. (1981). The role of dispositional empathy and social evaluation in the empathic mediation of helping. *Journal of Personality and Social Psychology, 40,* 786–790.

Aron, A., Aron, E. N., & Smollan, D. (1992). Inclusion of Other in the Self Scale and the structure of interpersonal closeness. *Journal of Personality and Social Psychology, 60,* 241–253.

❖ Ashton, M. C., Paunonen, S. V., Helmes, E., & Jackson, D. N. (1998). Kin altruism, reciprocal altruism, and the Big Five personality factors. *Evolution and Human Behavior, 19*(4), 243–255.

Atkinson, J. W. (1958). (Ed.). *Motives in fantasy, action, and society.* Princeton, NJ: Van Nostrand.

❖ Axelrod, S. R., Widiger, T. A., Trull, T. J., & Corbitt, E. M. (1997). Relations of Five-Factor Model antagonism facets with personality disorder symptomatology. *Journal of Personality Assessment, 69*(2), 297–313.

Batson, C. D. (1997). Self-other merging and the empathy-altruism hypothesis: Reply to Neuberg et al. (1997). *Journal of Personality and Social Psychology, 73,* 517–522.

❖ Batson, C. D., Batson, J. G., Todd, R. M., Brummett, B. H., Shaw, L. L., & Aldeguer, C. M. R. (1995). Empathy and the collective good: Caring for one of the others in a social dilemma. *Journal of Personality and Social Psychology, 68*(4), 619–631.

❖ Batson, C. D., Bolen, M. H., Cross, J. A., & Neuringer-Benefiel, H. E. (1986). Where is the altruism in the altruistic personality? *Journal of Personality and Social Psychology, 50*(1), 212–220.

❖ Batson, C. D., Duncan, B. D., Ackerman, P., Buckley, T., & Birch, K. (1981). Is empathic emotion a source of altruistic motivation? *Journal of Personality and Social Psychology, 40,* 290–302.

❖ Batson, C. D., Klein, T. R., Highberger, L., & Shaw, L. L. (1995). Immorality from empathy-induced altruism: When compassion and justice conflict. *Journal of Personality and Social Psychology, 68*(6), 1042–1054.

Batson, C. D., O'Quin, K., Fultz, J., Vanderplas, M., & Isen, A. (1983). Influence of self-reported distress and empathy on egoistic versus altruistic motivation to help. *Journal of Personality and Social Psychology, 45,* 706–718.

Batson, C. D., Sager, K., Garst, E., Kang, M., Rubchinsky, K., & Dawson, K. (1997). Is empathy-induced helping due to self-other merging? *Journal of Personality and Social Psychology, 73,* 495–509.

Batson, C. D., & Schoenrade, P. (1991). Measuring religion as quest: Validity concerns. *Journal for the Scientific Study of Religion, 30,* 416–429.

Batson, C. D., & Shaw, L. L. (1991). Evidence for altruism: Toward a pluralism of prosocial motives. *Psychology Inquiry, 2,* 107–122.

❖ Batson, C. D., & Weeks, J. L. (1996). Mood effects of unsuccessful helping: Another test of the empathy-altruism hypothesis. *Personality and Social Psychology Bulletin, 22*(2), 148–157.

Bem, S. L. (1974). The measurement of psychological androgyny. *Journal of Consulting and Clinical Psychology, 42,* 155–162.

❖ Ben-Artzi, E., & Mikulincer, M. (1996). Lay theories of emotion: IV. Reactions to negative and positive emotional episodes. *Imagination, Cognition and Personality, 16*(1), 89–113.

Berkowitz, L., & Daniels, L. R. (1964). Affecting the salience of the social responsibility norm: Effects of past help on the response to dependency relationships. *Journal of Abnormal and Social Psychology, 68,* 275–281.

❖ Berkowitz, L., & Lutterman, K. G. (1968). The traditional socially responsible personality. *Public Opinion Quarterly, 32,* 169–185.

❖ Berndt, T. J., & Das, R. (1987). Effects of popularity and friendship on perceptions of the personality and social behavior of peers. *Journal of Early Adolescence, 7*(4), 429–439.

❖ Bierhoff, H. W., Klein, R., & Kramp, P. (1991). Evidence for the altruistic personality from data on accident research. *Journal of Personality, 59*(2), 263–280.

Brändstatter, H. (1988). Sechzehn Persönlichkeits-Adjektivskalen (16 PA) als Forschungsinstrument anstelle des 16 PF. *Zeitschrift für Experimentelle und Angewandte Psychologie, 35,* 370–391.

❖ Burnstein, E., Crandall, C., & Kitayama, S. (1994). Some neo-Darwinian decision rules for altruism: Weighing cues for inclusive fitness as a function of the biological importance of the decision. *Journal of Personality and Social Psychology, 67,* 773–789.

Buss, A. H., & Plomin, R. (1975). *A temperament theory of personality development.* New York: Wiley.

Buss, A. H., & Plomin, R. (1984). *Temperament: Early developing personality traits.* Hillsdale, NJ: Erlbaum.

❖ Bybee, J., Luthar, S., Zigler, E., & Merisca, R. (1997). The fantasy, ideal, and ought selves: Content, relationships to mental health, and functions. *Social Cognition, 15*(1), 37–53.

❖ Carlo, G., Eisenberg, N., Troyer, D., Switzer, G., & Speer, A. L. (1991). The altruistic personality: In what contexts is it apparent? *Journal of Personality and Social Psychology, 61*(3), 450–458.

❖ Carlson, M., Charlin, V., & Miller, N. (1988). Positive mood and helping behavior: A test of six hypotheses. *Journal of Personality and Social Psychology, 55*, 211–229.

Cattell, R. B. (1956). A shortened "Basic English" version (Form C) of the 16 PF Questionnaire. *Journal of Social Psychology, 44*, 257–278.

❖ Chau, L. L., Johnson, R. C., Bowers, J. K., Darvill, T. J., & Danko, G. P. (1990). Intrinsic and extrinsic religiosity as related to conscience, adjustment, and altruism. *Personality and Individual Differences, 11*(4), 397–400.

Cheek, J. M., & Buss, A. H. (1981). Shyness and sociability. *Journal of Personality & Social Psychology, 41*, 330–339.

Christie, R., & Geis, G. (Eds.). (1968). *Studies in Machiavellianism*. New York: Academic Press.

❖ Cialdini, R. B., Brown, S. L., Lewis, B. P., Luce, C., & Neurberg, S. L. (1997). Reinterpreting the empathy-altruism relationship: When one into one equals oneness. *Journal of Personality and Social Psychology, 73*(3), 481–494.

Cialdini, R. B., Schaller, M., Houlihan, D., Arps, K., Fultz, J., & Beaman, A. L. (1987). Empathy-based helping: Is it selflessly or selfishly motivated? *Journal of Personality and Social Psychology, 52*, 749–758.

❖ Clary, E. G., & Orenstein, L. (1991). The amount and effectiveness of help: The relationship of motives and abilities to helping behavior. *Personality and Social Psychology Bulletin, 17*(1), 58–64.

Costa, P. T., Jr., & McCrae, R. R. (1992a). *NEO-PI-R professional manual*. Odessa, FL: Psychological Assessment Resources.

Costa, P. T., Jr., & McCrae, R. R. (1992b). *Revised NEO Personality Inventory (NEO PI-R) and NEO Five-Factor Inventory (NEO-FFI): Professional manual*. Odessa, FL: Psychological Assessment Resources.

Crowne, D. P., & Marlowe, D. (1960). A new scale of social desirability independent of psychopathology. *Journal of Consulting Psychology, 24*, 349–354.

Crowne, D. P., & Marlowe, D. (1964). *The approval motive*. New York: Wiley.

Dalbert, C., Montada, L., & Schmitt, M. (1987). Glaube an eine gerechte Welt als Motiv: Validierungskorrelate zweier Skalen (Belief in a just world as motive: Validity correlates of two scales). *Psychologische Beiträge, 29*, 596–615.

❖ Darley, J. M., & Batson, C. D. (1973). "From Jerusalem to Jericho": A study of situational and dispositional variables in helping behavior. *Journal of Personality and Social Psychology, 27*, 100–108.

Davis, M. H. (1980). A multidimensional approach to individual differences in empathy. *JSAJ Catalog of Selected Documents in Psychology, 10*(4), 85.

Davis, M. H. (1983). Measuring individual differences in empathy: Evidence for a multidimensional approach. *Journal of Personality and Social Psychology, 44*, 113–126.

Davis, M. H., Luce, C., & Kraus, S. J. (1994). The heritability of characteristics associated with dispositional empathy. *Journal of Personality, 62*, 369–391.

deCharms, R., & Rosenbaum, M. E. (1960). Status variables and matching behavior. *Journal of Personality, 4*, 492–502.

❖ Den Ouden, M. D., & Russell, G. W. (1997). Sympathy and altruism in response to disasters: A Dutch and Canadian comparison. *Social Behavior and Personality, 25*(3), 241–248.

Derman, D., French, J. W., & Harman, H. H. (1978). *Guide to Factor Reference Temperament Scales 1978*. Princeton, NJ: Educational Testing Service.

❖ Eagly, A. H., & Crowley, M. (1986). Gender and helping behavior: A meta-analytic review of the social psychological literature. *Psychological Bulletin, 100*, 282–308.

Edwards, A. L. (1954). *Edwards Personal Preference Schedule.* New York: Psychological Corporation.

❖ Eisenberg, N., Fabes, R. A., Schaller, M., Miller, P., Carlo, G., Poulin, R., Shea, C., & Shell, R. (1991). Personality and socialization correlates of vicarious emotional responding. *Journal of Personality and Social Psychology, 61,* 459–470.

❖ Eisenberg, N., Miller, P. A., Schaller, M., Fabes, R. A., Fultz, J., Shell, R., & Shea, C. L. (1989). The role of sympathy and altruistic personality traits in helping: A reexamination. *Journal of Personality, 57*(1), 41–67.

Esses, V. M., Haddock, G., & Zanna, M. P. (1993). Values, stereotypes, and emotions as determinants of intergroup attitudes. In D. M. Mackie & D. L. Hamilton (Eds.), *Affect, cognition, and stereotyping: Interactive processes in group perception* (pp. 137–166). San Diego, CA: Academic Press.

Eysenck, H. J., & Eysenck, S. B. G. (1975). *Manual for the Eysenck Personality Questionnaire.* San Diego, CA: Educational and Industrial Testing Service.

Eysenck, H. J., & Eysenck, S. B. G. (1978). *Manual of Eysenck Personality Questionnaire.* London: Hodder and Stoughton.

Eysenck, S. B. G., Eysenck, H. J., & Barrett, P. (1985). A revised version of the Psychoticism Scale. *Personality and Individual Differences, 6,* 21–29.

❖ Fabes, R. A., Eisenberg, N., & Miller, P. (1990). Maternal correlates of children's vicarious emotional responsiveness. *Developmental Psychology, 26,* 639–648.

❖ Farver, J. A. M., & Branstetter, W. H. (1994). Preschoolers' prosocial responses to their peers' distress. *Developmental Psychology, 30*(3), 334–341.

Feagin, J. (1964). Prejudice and religious types: A focused study of southern fundamentalists. *Journal for the Scientific Study of Religion, 4,* 3–13.

Fleming, J. S., & Courtney, B. E. (1984). The dimensionality of self-esteem: II. Hierarchical facet model for revised measurement scales. *Journal of Personality and Social Psychology, 46,* 404–421.

Francis, L. J. (1989). Measuring attitude toward Christianity during childhood and adolescence. *Personality and Individual Differences, 10,* 695–698.

Fultz, J., Schaller, M., & Cialdini, R. B. (1988). Empathy, sadness, and distress: Three related but distinct vicarious affective responses to another's suffering. *Personality and Social Psychology Bulletin, 14,* 312–325.

❖ Gergen, K. J., Gergen, M. M., & Meter, K. (1972). Individual orientations to prosocial behavior. *Journal of Social Issues, 8,* 105–130.

Gerrard, M., & Gibbons, F. X. (1982). Sexual experience, sex guilt, and sexual moral reasoning. *Journal of Personality, 50,* 345–359.

Giles, W. F., & Mossholder, K. W. (1990). Employee reactions to contextual and session components of performance appraisal. *Journal of Applied Psychology, 75,* 371–377.

Glass, G. V., McGaw, B., & Smith, M. L. (1981). *Meta-analysis in social research.* Beverly Hills, CA: Sage.

Halberstadt, A. G. (1986). Family socialization of emotional expression and nonverbal communication styles and skills. *Journal of Personality and Social Psychology, 51,* 827–836.

Hamilton, W. D. (1964). The genetical evolution of social behavior (Pts. 1 & 2). *Journal of Theoretical Biology, 7,* 1–52.

Harter, S. (1982). The perceived competence scale for children. *Child Development, 53,* 87–97.

Heist, P., & Yonge, G. (1968). *Omnibus Personality Inventory Manual.* New York: Psychological Corporation.

Hendrick, S., Hendrick, C., Slapion-Foote, M. J., & Foote, F. H. (1985). Gender differences in sexual attitudes. *Journal of Personality and Social Psychology, 48,* 1630–1642.

❖ Hendrick, S. S., & Hendrick, C. (1987). Love and sex attitudes and religious beliefs. *Journal of Social & Clinical Psychology, 5*(3), 391–398.

Hightower, A. D., Work, W. C., Cowen, E. L., Lotyczewski, B. S., Spinell, A. P., Guare, J. C., & Rohrbeck, C. A. (1986). The Teacher-Child Rating Scale: A brief objective measure of elementary children's school problem behaviors and competencies. *School Psychology Review, 15,* 393–409.

Hoffman, M. L. (1975). Developmental synthesis of affect and cognition and its implications for altruistic motivation. *Developmental Psychology, 11,* 607–622.

Hoffman, M. L. (1977). Empathy, its development and prosocial motivations. In H. E. Howe (Ed.), *Nebraska Symposium on Motivation* (pp. 169–217). Lincoln: University of Nebraska Press.

Howes, C. (1988). Peer interaction of young children. *Monographs for the Society of Research in Child Development, 53*(1, Serial No. 217).

Hyler, S. E., & Reider, R. O. (1987). *PDQ-R: Personality Diagnostic Questionnaire—Revised.* New York: New York State Psychiatric Institute.

Ilgen, D. R., Fisher, C. D., & Taylor, M. S. (1979). Consequences of individual feedback on behavior in organizations. *Journal of Applied Psychology, 64,* 349–371.

Jackson, D. (1967). *Personality Research Form Manual.* Goshen, NY: Research Psychologists Press.

Jackson, D. N. (1974). *Personality Research Form Manual* (2nd ed.). Port Huron, MI: Research Psychologists Press.

Jackson, D. N. (1977). *Jackson Vocational Interest Survey Manual.* London: Research Psychologists Press.

Jackson, D. N. (1984). *Personality Research Form Manual* (3rd ed.). Port Huron, MI: Research Psychologists Press.

Jackson, D. N. (1994). *Jackson Personality Inventory—Revised Manual.* Port Huron, MI: Sigma Assessment Systems.

❖ Jackson, L. M., & Esses, V. M. (1997). Of scripture and ascription: The relation between religious fundamentalism and intergroup helping. *Personality and Social Psychology Bulletin, 23*(8), 893–906.

John, D., & Keil, W. (1972). Selbsteinschätzung und Verhaltensbeurteilung (Self-assessment and behavior assessment). *Psychologische Rundschau, 23,* 10–29.

❖ Johnson, R. C., Danko, G. P., Davill, T. J., Bochner, S., Bowers, J. K., Huang, Y.-H., Park, J. Y., Pecjak, V., Rahim, A. R. A., & Pennington, D. (1989). Cross-cultural assessment of altruism and its correlates. *Personality and Individual Differences, 10,* 855–868.

Jones, E. E., & Pittman, T. S. (1982). Toward a general theory of strategic self-presentation. In J. Suls (Ed.), *Psychological perspectives on the self* (pp. 231–263). Hillsdale, NJ: Erlbaum.

❖ Kerber, K. W. (1984). The perception of non-emergency helping situations: Cost, rewards, and the altruistic personality. *Journal of Personality, 52,* 177–187.

Khanna, R., Singh, P., & Rushton, J. P. (1993). Development of the Hindi version of a self-report altruism scale. *Personality and Individual Differences, 14,* 267–270.

❖ Korsgaard, M. A., Meglino, B. M., & Lester, S. W. (1996). The effect of other-oriented values on decision making: A test of propositions of a theory of concern for others in organizations. *Organizational Behavior and Human Decision Processes, 68*(3), 234–245.

❖ Korsgaard, M. A., Meglino, B. M., & Lester, S. W. (1997). Beyond helping: Do other-oriented values have broader implications in organizations? *Journal of Applied Psychology, 82*(1), 160–177.

Kramer, R. M., McClintock, C. G., & Messick, D. M. (1986). Social values and cooperative response to a simulated resource conservation crisis. *Journal of Personality, 54,* 576–592.

Krampen, G. (1981). *IPC-Fragebogen zu Kontrollüberzeugungen* (IPC-questionnaire for measuring locus of control). Göttingen, Germany: Hogrefe.

Larsen, R. J., & Diener, E. (1987). Affect intensity as an individual difference characteristic: A review. *Journal of Research in Personality, 21,* 1–39.

Larsen, R. J., Diener, E., & Cropanzano, R. S. (1987). Cognitive operations associated with individual differences in affect intensity. *Journal of Personality and Social Psychology, 53,* 767–774.

❖ Leak, G. K. (1993). Relationship between religious orientation and love styles, sexual attitudes, and sexual behaviors. *Journal of Psychology and Theology, 21*(4), 315–318.

Leary, M. R., (1983). A brief version of the Fear of Negative Evaluation Scale. *Personality and Social Psychology Bulletin, 9,* 371–375.

Lee, J. A. (1977). A typology of styles of loving. *Personality and Social Psychology Bulletin, 3,* 173–182.

❖ Lefcourt, H. M., & Shepherd, R. S. (1995). Organ donation, authoritarianism, and perspective taking humor. *Journal of Research in Personality, 29*(1), 121–138.

Lerner, M. J. (1980). *The belief in a just world: A fundamental delusion.* New York: Plenum.

❖ Leung, J. J., & Foster, S. F. (1985). Helping the elderly: A study on altruism in children. *Child Study Journal, 15*(4), 293–309.

Levenson, H. M. (1972). Distinctions within the concept of internal-external control: Development of a new scale. *Proceedings of the Eighteenth Annual Convention of the American Psychological Association.*

Litvack-Miller, W., McDougall, D., & Romney, D. M. (1997). The structure of empathy during middle childhood and its relationship to prosocial behavior. *Genetic, Social, and General Psychology Monographs, 123*(3), 303–324.

Loehlin, J. C., & Nichols, R. C. (1976). *Heredity, environment, and personality: A study of 850 sets of twins.* Austin: University of Texas Press.

❖ Magee, M., & Hojat, M. (1998). Personality profiles of male and female positive role models in medicine. *Psychological Reports, 82*(2), 547–559.

❖ Mallandain, I., & Davies, M. F. (1994). The colours of love: Personality correlates of love styles. *Personality and Individual Differences, 17*(4), 557–560.

Markus, H., & Nurius, P. (1986). Possible selves. *American Psychologist, 41,* 954–969.

Martin, R. A., & Lefcourt, H. M. (1984). The Situational Humor Response Questionnaire: A quantitative measure of the sense of humor. *Journal of Personality and Social Psychology, 47,* 145–155.

Mauger, P. A., & Adkinson, D. R. (1980). *Interpersonal Behavior Survey (IBS) Manual.* Los Angeles: Western Psychological Services.

McAdams, D. P. (1985). *Power, intimacy, and the life story: Personological identity.* New York: Guilford.

McAdams, D. P. (1993). *The stories we live by: Personal myths and the making of the self.* New York: Morrow.

❖ McAdams, D. P., Hoffman, B. J., Mansfield, E. D., & Day, R. (1996). Themes of agency and communion in significant autobiographical scenes. *Journal of Personality, 64*(2), 339–377.

McDevitt, S. C., & Carey, W. B. (1978). The measurement of temperament in 3–7-year-old children. *Journal of Child Psychology and Psychiatry, 19,* 245–253.

McGuire, W. J., & Padawer-Singer, A. (1976). Trait salience in the spontaneous self-concept. *Journal of Personality and Social Psychology, 33,* 743–754.

McNair, D. M., Lorr, M., & Droppleman, L. F. (1971). *Profile of mood states.* San Diego, CA: Educational and Industrial Testing Service.

❖ McNeely, B. L., & Meglino, B. M. (1994). The role of dispositional and situational antecedents in prosocial behavior: An examination of the intended beneficiaries of prosocial behavior. *Journal of Applied Psychology, 79*, 836–844.

Mehrabian, A. & Epstein, N. (1972). A measure of emotional empathy. *Journal of Personality, 40*, 525–543.

❖ Miller, P. A., & Jansen op de Haar, M. A. (1997). Emotional, cognitive, behavioral, and temperament characteristics of high-empathy children. *Motivation and Emotion, 21*(1), 109–125.

❖ Mohan, J., & Bhatia, S. (1987). Altruistic behaviour of engineers and teachers in relation to their personality. *Indian Journal of Applied Psychology, 24*(2), 87–90.

Moos, R. H., & Moos, B. S. (1981). *Family Environment Scale Manual.* Palo Alto, CA: Consulting Psychology Press.

Morey, L. C., Waugh, M. H., & Blashfield, K. B. (1985). MMPI scales for *DSM-III* personality disorders: Their derivation and correlates. *Journal of Personality Assessment, 49*, 245–251.

❖ Neuberg, S. L., Cialdini, R. B., Brown, S. L., Luce, C., Sagarin, B. J., & Lewis, B. P. (1997). Does empathy lead to anything more than superficial helping? Comment on Batson et al. (1997). *Journal of Personality and Social Psychology, 73*(3), 510–516.

❖ Noonan, A. E., Tennstedt, S. L., & Rebelsky, F. G. (1996). Making the best of it: Themes of meaning among informal caregivers to the elderly. *Journal of Aging Studies, 10*(4), 313–327.

❖ Omoto, A. M., & Snyder, M. (1995). Sustained helping without obligation: Motivation, longevity of service, and perceived attitude change among AIDS volunteers. *Journal of Personality and Social Psychology, 68*, 671–687.

❖ Organ, D. W., & Ryan, K. (1995). A meta-analytic review of attitudinal and dispositional predictors of organizational citizenship behavior. *Personnel Psychology, 48*, 775–802.

❖ Penner, L. A., & Finkelstein, M. A. (1998). Dispositional and structural determinants of volunteerism. *Journal of Personality and Social Psychology, 74*(2), 525–537.

Penner, L. A., Fritzsche, B. A., Craiger, J. P., & Freifield, T. R. (1995). Measuring the prosocial personality. In J. Butcher & C. D. Spielberger (Eds.), *Advances in personality assessment* (Vol. 10, pp. 147–163). Hillsdale, NJ: Erlbaum.

Ravlin, E. C., & Meglino, B. M. (1987a). Effect of values on perception and decision making: A study of alternative work values measures. *Journal of Applied Psychology, 72*, 666–673.

Ravlin, E. C., & Meglino, B. M. (1987b). Issues in work values measurement. In W. C. Federick (Ed.), *Research in corporate social performance and policy* (Vol. 9, pp. 158–183). Greenwich, CT: JAI Press.

Reber, A. S. (1995). *The Penguin Dictionary of Psychology* (2nd ed.). London: Penguin Group.

Rest, J. R. (1979). *Development in judging moral issues.* Minneapolis: University of Minnesota Press.

❖ Ribal, J. E. (1963). Character and meanings of selfishness and altruism. *Sociology and Social Research, 47*, 311–321.

Rokeach, M. (1973). *The nature of human values.* New York: Free Press.

❖ Romer, D., Gruder, C. L., & Lizzadro, T. (1986). A person-situation approach to altruistic behavior. *Journal of Personality and Social Psychology, 51*(5), 1001–1012.

Rosenberg, M. (1965). *Society and the adolescent self-image.* Princeton, NJ: Princeton University Press.

Rosenberg, M., & Simmons, R. G. (1972). *Black and white self-esteem: The urban school child.* Washington: American Sociological Association.

Rotter, J. B. (1966). Generalized expectancies for internal versus external control of reinforcement. *Psychological Monographs, 80*(1, Whole No. 9).

Rotter, J. B., Seeman, M., & Liverant, S. (1962). Internal versus external control of reinforcement: A major variable in behavior theory. In N. F. Washburne (Ed.), *Decisions,
values and groups* (Vol. 2). London: Pergamon Press.

Runge, T. E., Frey, D., Gollwitzer, P. M., Helmreich, R. L., & Spence, J. T. (1981). Masculine
(instrumental) and feminine (expressive) traits. *Journal of Cross-Cultural Psychology,
12*, 142–162.

❖ Rushton, J. P. (1984). The altruistic personality: Evidence from laboratory, naturalistic,
and self-report perspectives. In E. Staub, D. Bar-Tal, J. Karylowski, & J. Reykowski
(Eds.), *Development and maintenance of prosocial behavior* (pp. 271–290). New York:
Plenum.

❖ Rushton, J. P., Chrisjohn, R. D., & Fekken, G. C. (1981). The altruistic personality and the
Self-Report Altruism Scale. *Personality and Individual Differences, 2*, 293–302.

❖ Rushton, J. P., Fulker, D. W., Neale, M. C., Nias, D. K., & Eysenck, H. J. (1989). Ageing and
the relation of aggression, altruism and assertiveness scales to the Eysenck Personality
Questionnaire. *Personality and Individual Differences, 10*(2), 261–263.

❖ Rushton, J. P., Fulker, D. W., Neale, M. C., Nias, D. K. B., & Eysenk, H. J. (1986). Altruism
and aggression: The heritability of individual differences. *Journal of Personality and
Social Psychology, 50*, 1192–1198.

Saucier, G. (1994). Mini-Markers: A brief version of Goldberg's unipolar Big-Five personality factors. *Journal of Personality Assessment, 63*, 506–516.

❖ Sawyer, J. (1966). The altruism scale: A measure of cooperative, individualistic, and
competitive interpersonal orientation. *American Journal of Sociology, 71*, 407–416.

❖ Schenk, J., & Heinisch, R. (1986). Self-descriptions by means of sex-role scales and personality scales: A critical evaluation of recent masculinity and femininity scales. *Personality and Individual Differences, 7*(2), 161–168.

Schmitt, M. (1982). *Empathie. Kinzepte, Entwicklung, Quantifizierung* (Empathy. Concepts,
development, quantification). (Technical Report No. 9). Trier, Germany: University of
Trier.

Schmölders, G. (1966). *Psychologie des Geldes.* Reinbeck bei Hamburg: Rowohlt.

❖ Schütz, A., & Tice, D. M. (1997). Associative and competitive indirect self-enhancement
in close relationships moderated by trait self-esteem. *European Journal of Social Psychology, 27*(3), 257–273.

Schwartz, S. H. (1968). Words, deeds, and the perception of consequences and responsibility in action situations. *Journal of Personality and Social Psychology, 10*, 232–242.

❖ Schwartz, S. H. (1970). Elicitation of moral obligation and self-sacrificing behavior.
Journal of Personality and Social Psychology, 15, 283–293.

Schwartz, S. H. (1973). Normative explanations of helping behavior: A critique, proposal,
and empirical test. *Journal of Experimental Social Psychology, 9*, 349–364.

Schwartz, S. H. (1974). Awareness of interpersonal consequences, responsibility denial, and
volunteering. *Journal of Personality and Social Psychology, 30*, 57–63.

Schwartz, S. H. (1975). The justice of need and the activation of humanitarian norms. *Journal of Social Issues, 31*, 111–136.

Schwartz, S. H., & Ames, R. E. (1977). Positive and negative referent others as sources of influence: A case of helping. *Sociometry, 40*, 12–21.

Schwartz, S. H., & Bilsky, W. (1987). Toward a universal psychological structure of human
values. *Journal of Personality & Social Psychology, 53*, 550–562.

Schwartz, S. H., & Clausen, G. T. (1970). Responsibility, norms, and helping in an emergency. *Journal of Personality and Social Psychology, 16*, 299–310.

Schwartz, S. H., & David, A. B. (1976). Responsibility and helping in an emergency: Effects of blame, ability and denial of responsibility. *Sociometry, 39,* 406–415.

Schwartz, S. H., & Fleishman, J. A. (1978). Personal norms and the mediation of legitimacy effects on helping. *Social Psychology, 41,* 306–315.

Schwartz, S. H., & Fleishman, J. A. (1982). Effects of negative personal norms on helping behavior. *Personality and Social Psychology Bulletin, 8,* 81–86.

Schwartz, S. H., & Gottlieb, A. (1980a). Bystander anonymity and reactions to emergencies. *Journal of Personality and Social Psychology, 39,* 418–430.

Schwartz, S. H., & Gottlieb, A. (1980b). Participation in a bystander intervention experiment and subsequent everyday helping: Ethical considerations. *Journal of Experimental Social Psychology, 16,* 161–171.

Schwartz, S. H., & Howard, J. A. (1980). Explanations of the moderating effect of responsibility denial on the personal norm behavior relationship. *Social Psychology Quarterly, 43,* 441–446.

❖ Senneker, P., & Hendrick, C. (1983). Androgyny and helping behavior. *Journal of Personality and Social Psychology, 45,* 916–925.

❖ Sharma, V., & Rosha, J. (1992). Altruism as a function of self-actualization and locus of control. *Psychological Studies, 37*(1), 26–30.

Shepherd, R. S. (1989). What's so funny about death? Sense of humor, mood disturbance and beliefs as predictors of willingness to confront mortality. Unpublished doctoral dissertation, University of Waterloo.

Shostrom, E. (1964). *Personal Orientation Inventory (POI): A test of self-actualization.* San Diego, CA: Educational and Industrial Testing Service.

❖ Sibicky, M. E., Schroeder, D. A., & Dovidio, J. F. (1995). Empathy and helping: Considering the consequences of intervention. *Basic and Applied Social Psychology, 16*(4), 435–453.

Simmons, R. G., Schimmel, M., & Butterworth, V. A. (1993). The self-image of unrelated bone marrow donors. *Journal of Health and Social Behavior, 34,* 285–301.

Singer, J. L., & Switzer, E. (1980). *Mindplay: The creative uses of daydreaming.* Englewood Cliffs, NJ: Prentice-Hall.

❖ Smith, B. M. M., & Nelson, L. D. (1975). Personality correlates of helping behavior. *Psychological Reports, 37,* 307–316.

❖ Smith, K. D., Keating, J. P., & Stotland, E. (1989). Altruism revisited: The effect of denying feedback on a victim's status to empathic witness. *Journal of Personality and Social Psychology, 57,* 641–650.

Spence, J. T., & Helmreich, R. L. (1978). *Masculinity and femininity.* Austin: University of Texas Press.

❖ Staub, E. (1974). Helping a distressed person: Social, personality, and stimulus determinants. In L. Berkowitz (Ed.), *Advances in experimental social psychology* (Vol. 7, pp. 203–341). New York: Academic Press.

❖ Stevick, R. A., & Addleman, J. A. (1995). Effects of short-term volunteer experience on self-perceptions and prosocial behavior. *Journal of Social Psychology, 135*(5), 663–665.

Stotland, E., Matthews, K., Sherman, S. E., Hansson, R. O., & Richardson, B. Z. (1978). *Empathy, fantasy and helping.* Beverly Hills, CA: Sage.

❖ Strahilevitz, M., & Myers, J. G. (1998). Donations to charity as purchase incentives: How well they work may depend on what you are trying to sell. *Journal of Consumer Research, 24*(4), 434–446.

❖ Switzer, G. E., Dew, M. A., Butterworth, V. A., Simmons, R. G., & Schimmel, M. (1997). Understanding donor's motivations: A study of unrelated bone marrow donors. *Social Science and Medicine, 45*(1), 137–147.

Taylor, J. A. (1953). A personality scale of manifest anxiety. *Journal of Abnormal and Social Psychology, 48,* 285–290.

Temper, D. I. (1970). The construction and validation of a death anxiety scale. *Journal of General Psychology, 82,* 165–177.

Thauberger, P. C., Cleland, J. F., & Thauberger, E. M. (1979). The avoidance of ontological confrontation of death: A psychometric research scale. *Essence, 3*(1), 9–12.

Toi, M., & Batson, C. D. (1982). More evidence that empathy is a source of altruistic motivation. *Journal of Personality and Social Psychology, 43,* 281–292.

Ullrich de Muynck, R., & Ullrich, R. (1978). *Soziale Kompetenz: Meßmittel und Grundlagen* (Social competence: Measurement instruments and foundations). Munich, Germany: Pfeiffer.

❖ Unger, L. S., & Thumuluri, L. K. (1997). Trait empathy and continuous helping: The case of volunteerism. *Journal of Social Behavior and Personality, 12*(3), 785–800.

❖ Watson, P. J., Morris, R. J., & Hood, R. W. (1989). Intrinsicness, religious self-love, and narcissism. *Journal of Psychology and Christianity, 8*(1), 31–37.

❖ Wegner, D. M., Vallacher, R. R., Kiersted, G. W., & Dizadji, D. (1986). Action identification in the emergence of social behavior. *Social Cognition, 4*(1), 18–38.

Weiner, B. (1980). A cognitive (attribution)-emotion-action model of motivated behavior: An analysis of judgments of help-giving. *Journal of Personality and Social Psychology, 39,* 186–200.

Wiggins, J. S., & Broughton, R. (1985). The interpersonal circle: A structural model for the integration of personality research. In R. Hogan & W. H. Jones (Eds.), *Perspectives in personality* (Vol. 1, pp. 1–47). Greenwich, CT: JAI Press.

Wilson, G. D., & Patterson, J. R. (1968). A new measure of conservatism. *British Journal of Social and Clinical Psychology, 7,* 264–269.

Zuckerman, M., Kolin, E., Price, L., & Zoob, D. (1964). Development of a sensation-seeking scale. *Journal of Consulting Psychology, 28,* 477–482.

LIST OF ARTICLES BY SUBJECT

Agape

Hendrick, S. S., & Hendrick, C. (1987)
Leak, G. K. (1993)
Mallandain, I., & Davies, M. F. (1994)

Altruistic Motivation

Clary, E. G., & Orenstein, L. (1991)
Kerber, K. W. (1984)
Noonan, A. E., Tennstedt, S. L., & Rebelsky, F. G. (1996)
Omoto, A. M., & Snyder, M. (1995)
Penner, L. A., & Finkelstein, M. A. (1998)
Schütz, A., & Tice, D. M. (1997)
Switzer, G. E., Dew, M. A., Butterworth, V. A., Simmons, R. G., & Schimmel, M. (1997)

Behavioral Dependent Variables (i.e., Helping/Emergency Helping/Prosocial Behavior)

Archer, R. L., Diaz-Loving, R., Gollwitzer, P. M., Davis, M. H., & Foushee, H. C. (1981)
Bierhoff, H. W., Klein, R., & Kramp, P. (1991)
Burnstein, E., Crandall, C., & Kitayama, S. (1994)
Carlson, M., Charlin, V., & Miller, N. (1988)
Darley, J. M., & Batson, C. D. (1973)
Eagly, A. H., & Crowley, M. (1986)
Eisenberg, N., Miller, P. A., Schaller, M., Fabes, R. A., Fultz, J., Shell, R., & Shea, C. L. (1989)
Farver, J. A. M., & Branstetter, W. H. (1994)
Gergen, K. J., Gergen, M. M., & Meter, K. (1972)
Jackson, L. M., & Esses, V. M. (1997)
Kerber, K. W. (1984)

Senneker, P., & Hendrick, C. (1983)
Staub, E. (1974)

Caregivers

Noonan, A. E., Tennstedt, S. L., & Rebelsky, F. G. (1996)

Cross-Cultural

Burnstein, E., Crandall, C., & Kitayama, S. (1994)
Den Ouden, M. D., & Russell, G. W. (1997)
Johnson, R. C., Danko, G. P., Davill, T. J., Bochner, S., Bowers, J. K., Huang, Y.-H., Park, J. Y.,
      Pecjak, V., Rahim, A. R. A., & Pennington, D. (1989)
Mohan, J., & Bhatia, S. (1987)
Sharma, V., & Rosha, J. (1992)

Developmental Issues

Berndt, T. J., & Das, R. (1987)
Fabes, R. A., Eisenberg, N., & Miller, P. (1990)
Farver, J. A. M., & Branstetter, W. H. (1994)
Leung, J. J., & Foster, S. F. (1985)
Litvack-Miller, W., McDougall, D., & Romney, D. M. (1997)

Dispositional Empathy

Archer, R. L., Diaz-Loving, R., Gollwitzer, P. M., Davis, M. H., & Foushee, H. C. (1981)
Batson, C. D., Bolen, M. H., Cross, J. A., & Neuringer-Benefiel, H. E. (1986)
Carlo, G., Eisenberg, N., Troyer, D., Switzer, G., & Speer, A. L. (1991)
Clary, E. G., & Orenstein, L. (1991)
Davis, M. H., Luce, C., & Kraus, S. J. (1994)
Eisenberg, N., Fabes, R. A., Schaller, M., Miller, P., Carlo, G., Poulin, R., Shea, C., & Shell, R.
      (1991)
Eisenberg, N., Miller, P. A., Schaller, M., Fabes, R. A., Fultz, J., Shell, R., & Shea, C. L. (1989)
Fabes, R. A., Eisenberg, N., & Miller, P. (1990)
Litvack-Miller, W., McDougall, D., & Romney, D. M. (1997)
McNeely, B. L., & Meglino, B. M. (1994)
Penner, L. A., & Finkelstein, M. A. (1998)
Romer, D., Gruder, C. L., & Lizzadro, T. (1986)
Rushton, J. P., Fulker, D. W., Neale, M. C., Nias, D. K. B., & Eysenck, H. J. (1986)
Sibicky, M. E., Schroeder, D. A., & Dovidio, J. F. (1995)
Switzer, G. E., Dew, M. A., Butterworth, V. A., Simmons, R. G., & Schimmel, M. (1997)
Unger, L. S., & Thumuluri, L. K. (1997)

Empathy-Altruism Debate

Batson, C. D., Batson, J. G., Todd, R. M., Brummett, B. H., Shaw, L. L., & Aldeguer, C. M. R.
      (1995)
Batson, C. D., Duncan, B. D., Ackerman, P., Buckley, T., & Birch, K. (1981)
Batson, C. D., Klein, T. R., Highberger, L., & Shaw, L. L. (1995)

Gender

Kin/Reciprocal Altruism and Sociobiology

Measurement of Altruism

Monetary Allocations

Mood and Emotion

Moral Behavior

Batson, C. D., Batson, J. G., Todd, R. M., Brummett, B. H., Shaw, L. L., & Aldeguer, C. M. R. (1995)
Batson, C. D., Klein, T. R., Highberger, L., & Shaw, L. L. (1995)
Schwartz, S. H. (1970)

Organ Donation

Lefcourt, H. M., & Shepherd, R. S. (1995)
Schwartz, S. H. (1970)
Switzer, G. E., Dew, M. A., Butterworth, V. A., Simmons, R. G., & Schimmel, M. (1997)

Organizational Behavior

Korsgaard, M. A., Meglino, B. M., & Lester, S. W. (1996)
Korsgaard, M. A., Meglino, B. M., & Lester, S. W. (1997)
McNeely, B. L., & Meglino, B. M. (1994)
Organ, D. W., & Ryan, K. (1995)

Personality Measures: The Big Five

Axelrod, S. R., Widiger, T. A., Trull, T. J., & Corbitt, E. M. (1997)
Ashton, M. C., Paunonen, S. V., Helmes, E., & Jackson, D. N. (1998)
Bybee, J., Luthar, S., Zigler, E., & Merisca, R. (1997)
Magee, M., & Hojat, M. (1998)
Organ, D. W., & Ryan, K. (1995)

Personality Measures: Eysenck

Chau, L. L., Johnson, R. C., Bowers, J. K., Darvill, T. J., & Danko, G. P. (1990)
Johnson, R. C., Danko, G. P., Davill, T. J., Bochner, S., Bowers, J. K., Huang, Y.-H., Park, J. Y., Pecjak, V., Rahim, A. R. A., & Pennington, D. (1989)
Mohan, J., & Bhatia, S. (1987)
Rushton, J. P., Fulker, D. W., Neale, M. C., Nias, D. K., & Eysenck, H. J. (1989)

Personality Measures: Other

Bierhoff, H. W., Klein, R., & Kramp, P. (1991)
Magee, M., & Hojat, M. (1998)
McAdams, D. P., Hoffman, B. J., Mansfield, E. D., & Day, R. (1996)
Ribal, J. E. (1963)
Romer, D., Gruder, C. L., & Lizzadro, T. (1986)
Sharma, V., & Rosha, J. (1992)
Smith, B. M. M., & Nelson, L. D. (1975)

Perspective Taking

Davis, M. H., Luce, C., & Kraus, S. J. (1994)

Eisenberg, N., Fabes, R. A., Schaller, M., Miller, P., Carlo, G., Poulin, R., Shea, C., & Shell, R. (1991)

Lefcourt, H. M., & Shepherd, R. S. (1995)

Religiosity

Chau, L. L., Johnson, R. C., Bowers, J. K., Darvill, T. J., & Danko, G. P. (1990)

Darley, J. M., & Batson, C. D. (1973)

Hendrick, S. S., & Hendrick, C. (1987)

Jackson, L. M., & Esses, V. M. (1997)

Johnson, R. C., Danko, G. P., Davill, T. J., Bochner, S., Bowers, J. K., Huang, Y.-H., Park, J. Y., Pecjak, V., Rahim, A. R. A., & Pennington, D. (1989)

Leak, G. K. (1993)

Situational Factors

Archer, R. L., Diaz-Loving, R., Gollwitzer, P. M., Davis, M. H., & Foushee, H. C. (1981)

Burnstein, E., Crandall, C., & Kitayama, S. (1994)

Carlo, G., Eisenberg, N., Troyer, D., Switzer, G., & Speer, A. L. (1991)

Gergen, K. J., Gergen, M. M., & Meter, K. (1972)

McNeely, B. L., & Meglino, B. M. (1994)

Romer, D., Gruder, C. L., & Lizzadro, T. (1986)

Staub, E. (1974)

Social Cognition

Bybee, J., Luthar, S., Zigler, E., & Merisca, R. (1997)

Carlson, M., Charlin, V., & Miller, N. (1988)

Korsgaard, M. A., Meglino, B. M., & Lester, S. W. (1996)

Wegner, D. M., Vallacher, R. R., Kiersted, G. W., & Dizadji, D. (1986)

Social Responsibility

Batson, C. D., Bolen, M. H., Cross, J. A., & Neuringer-Benefiel, H. E. (1986)

Berkowitz, L., & Lutterman, K. G. (1968)

Bierhoff, H. W., Klein, R., & Kramp, P. (1991)

Eisenberg, N., Miller, P. A., Schaller, M., Fabes, R. A., Fultz, J., Shell, R., & Shea, C. L. (1989)

Omoto, A. M., & Snyder, M. (1995)

Penner, L. A., & Finkelstein, M. A. (1998)

Schwartz, S. H. (1970)

Socialization

Eisenberg, N., Fabes, R. A., Schaller, M., Miller, P., Carlo, G., Poulin, R., Shea, C., & Shell, R. (1991)

Sympathy

Den Ouden, M. D., & Russell, G. W. (1997)

Eisenberg, N., Fabes, R. A., Schaller, M., Miller, P., Carlo, G., Poulin, R., Shea, C., & Shell, R. (1991)
Eisenberg, N., Miller, P. A., Schaller, M., Fabes, R. A., Fultz, J., Shell, R., & Shea, C. L. (1989)

Volunteerism

Clary, E. G., & Orenstein, L. (1991)
Omoto, A. M., & Snyder, M. (1995)
Penner, L. A., & Finkelstein, M. A. (1998)
Schwartz, S. H. (1970)
Smith, B. M. M., & Nelson, L. D. (1975)
Unger, L. S., & Thumuluri, L. K. (1997)

INDEX